The Hiltons

The Hiltons

THE TRUE STORY OF AN AMERICAN DYNASTY

by J. RANDY TARABORRELLI

GRAND CENTRAL
PUBLISHING

New York   Boston

Grand Central Publishing
Hachette Book Group
237 Park Avenue
New York, NY 10017

www.HachetteBookGroup.com

Printed in the United States of America

RRD-C

First Edition: April 2014
10 9 8 7 6 5 4 3 2 1

Grand Central Publishing is a division of Hachette Book Group, Inc.
The Grand Central Publishing name and logo is a trademark of Hachette Book Group, Inc.

The Hachette Speakers Bureau provides a wide range of authors for speaking events. To find out more, go to www.hachettespeakersbureau.com or call (866) 376-6591.

The publisher is not responsible for websites (or their content) that are not owned by the publisher.

Library of Congress Cataloging-in-Publication Data
Taraborrelli, J. Randy.
   The Hiltons : the true story of an American dynasty / by J. Randy Taraborrelli. — First edition.
      pages cm
   Includes bibliographical references and index.
   ISBN 978-1-4555-1669-8 (hardcover) — ISBN 978-1-4789-2764-8 (audiobook) — ISBN
978-1-4789-2765-5 (audio download)   1. Hilton, Conrad N. (Conrad Nicholson), 1887–1979.
2. Hilton, Conrad N. (Conrad Nicholson), 1887–1979—Family.   3. Hotelkeepers—United States—
Biography.   4. Businessmen—United States—Biography.   5. Philanthropists—United States—
Biography.   6. Celebrities—United States—Biography.   I. Title.
   TX910.5.H5T37 2014
   647.94092—dc23
   [B]
                                        2013024369

For my family

CONTENTS

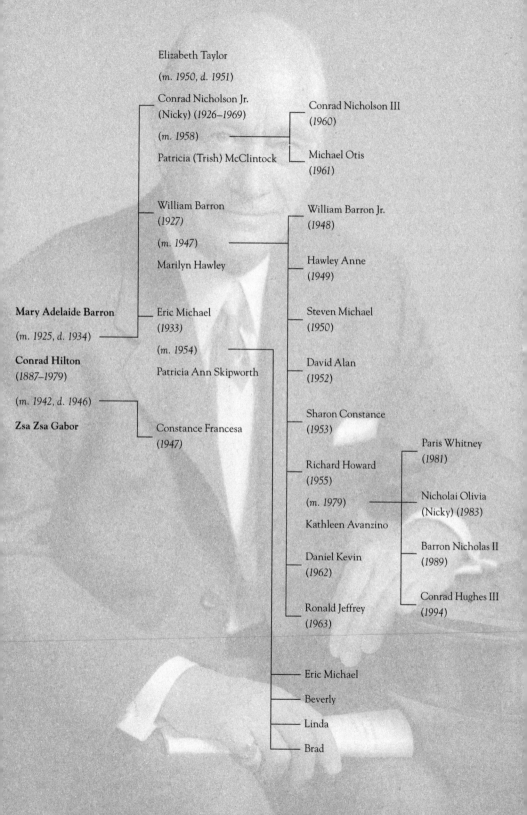

Elizabeth Taylor
(m. 1950, d. 1951)

Conrad Nicholson Jr.
(Nicky) (1926–1969)

(m. 1958)

Patricia (Trish) McClintock

Conrad Nicholson III
(1960)

Michael Otis
(1961)

William Barron
(1927)

(m. 1947)

Marilyn Hawley

William Barron Jr.
(1948)

Hawley Anne
(1949)

Mary Adelaide Barron

(m. 1925, d. 1934)

Conrad Hilton
(1887–1979)

(m. 1942, d. 1946)

Zsa Zsa Gabor

Eric Michael
(1933)

(m. 1954)

Patricia Ann Skipworth

Constance Francesa
(1947)

Steven Michael
(1950)

David Alan
(1952)

Sharon Constance
(1953)

Richard Howard
(1955)

(m. 1979)

Kathleen Avanzino

Daniel Kevin
(1962)

Ronald Jeffrey
(1963)

Paris Whitney
(1981)

Nicholai Olivia
(Nicky) (1983)

Barron Nicholas II
(1989)

Conrad Hughes III
(1994)

Eric Michael

Beverly

Linda

Brad

PROLOGUE

It was Monday morning, June 11, 1979. "Conrad Hilton is rolling over in his grave right now," Zsa Zsa Gabor was saying to the attorney Myron Harpole. The two were on the telephone, discussing the details of a sworn deposition Zsa Zsa was to give later that week about her relationship with her late husband, the international business pioneer and hotel magnate. "Oh, how he would love to be able to control what I say about him," she observed wryly.

"I don't know if that's true," Myron said carefully. He had been Conrad's attorney for more than thirty years, and even now, six months after his client's death, was still protective of him.

"Oh, Myron," she said, laughing. "You know that if Conrad could be there, sitting right behind me and whispering in my ear, he'd love it."

It was true that throughout his lifetime Conrad Hilton had been a man used to being in complete control—of himself and, some might argue, everyone around him. As one of the most successful businessmen in the world, he had made hundreds of millions of dollars, with hotels around the world bearing his name. He certainly didn't carve out such a niche by allowing others to impose their will upon him. Generally speaking, though, he was well liked and had a stellar reputation among his colleagues. He was a good man, known as much for his philanthropy as for his hotel empire. Privately, though, he did have his eccentricities, not the least of which was his stringent attitude about his wealth and the manner in which it should be distributed to immediate family members.

It had long been Conrad's belief that merely being related to him should not guarantee his heirs a carefree, privileged life. He had made his money in what he called "the good, old-fashioned way," meaning he had earned it. A product of the Great Depression, he wanted his relatives to inherit his work ethic, not his money. A loan might be given from time to time to one of his four children, but failure to pay it back would result in a breach of trust not easily remedied.

Now that Conrad was gone, some of his family members had serious reservations regarding his last will and testament. With hundreds of millions of dollars on the line, the stakes were high. There were hurt feelings, many questions. A legal effort to redress some of these grievances was the reason Zsa Zsa was now being compelled to share her private memories of Conrad with a battery of attorneys.

"Tell me, Myron, will you be at the interview?" Zsa Zsa asked.

"We'll see," Myron answered. "And, by the way, it's a *deposition*, my dear," he reminded her. "Not an interview."

"Well, when people ask me questions," Zsa Zsa said, "I give them answers. For me, that's an interview." Indeed, for the last three decades, she had been a staple on television talk shows, flamboyantly chatting it up with Merv Griffin and Jack Paar, Steve Allen and Johnny Carson about her life and times, often embellishing the truth for the sake of a good laugh. Zsa Zsa was flippant, irreverent, and entertaining, her thick Hungarian accent and uncommon beauty distinguishing her almost as much as her rapier wit.

"But, remember, you will be under oath this time," Myron said.

"Myron, please! You know me," she responded. "I always tell the truth!"

Three days later, at noon on Thursday, June 14, Zsa Zsa Gabor walked briskly past the front desk of the Beverly Hills Hotel, her head held high. Wearing a billowing red-and-gold-striped caftan and matching spiked heels, she tried to act oblivious to the stares of everyone she passed. She would have to admit that she loved the attention, though, and she didn't have to work hard to generate it. At sixty-two, she was still quite beautiful. Her skin was flawless, full of health and vitality, her teased hair a light ash blonde. Her steely and determined blue eyes were hidden behind oversized celebrity sunglasses. As she walked, her gait was one of real purpose, as if nothing could ever get in her way. Of course, this had always been her story.

Since arriving on the SS *President Grant*, overcrowded with refugees such as herself from Hungary, almost forty years earlier, Zsa Zsa had always known exactly what she wanted out of life: success, happiness, wealth...the so-called American dream, in all of its red-white-and-blue splendor. She would do a lot to get it, too, as she would prove many times along the way, even if that meant marrying for prosperity—which she did more than a few times. Including Conrad Hilton, seven times, to be exact. So far.

Zsa Zsa's footsteps echoed sharply as she marched across the marble foyer of the Beverly Hills Hotel. She nodded at the concierge; he touched his cap in recognition. She then walked quickly down the red-carpeted hallway, past the famous Polo Lounge restaurant, out a pair of French doors, and then through a lovely flower garden in the direction of a nearby bungalow. As she entered the bungalow where her deposition was to be conducted, she immediately switched on her stage persona and played to the audience at hand. "My God! Just look at all of these *gorgeous men!*" she marveled as she swept grandly into the room. Four attorneys and a male court reporter stood before her with big smiles. "I *love* being surrounded by gorgeous men," she enthused. "Everyone knows that about me by now."

"Zsa Zsa, how wonderful to see you," said Myron Harpole as he emerged from the group to greet her. A solid Harvard Law School graduate in a fastidiously neat dark suit, he extended his hand to shake hers, but she brushed it aside and embraced him. "Myron, can you believe that we are here?" she asked, looking around. "Why, my Connie used to *own* this hotel!" A tangle of gold bracelets on each wrist made clinking noises every time she used her hands to express herself, which was often.

"No, my dear, actually he didn't," corrected the lawyer. "He owned the Beverly *Hilton* Hotel, not the Beverly *Hills* Hotel."

She looked at him with a quizzical expression. "No, I think he owned this one, too," she insisted.

The lawyer smiled patiently and, with a small smile, shook his head no.

"Well, I can't blame you for not knowing," she said with a dismissive wave. "He owned so *many* hotels, who could keep track?" It was true. Zsa Zsa's ex-husband had either owned or managed luxury hotels all over the world, most of them—such as the famed Waldorf-Astoria in New York City, which he considered the favorite among his legion—were extraordinary when it came not only to ambiance but also to service. Hilton wanted his guests to be pampered and treated with the utmost respect. For him, it was as much a personal endeavor as it was professional. Therefore, a Hilton hotel would always be a cut above the competition, at least as long as Conrad Hilton had anything to say about it.

Just as Zsa Zsa and Myron Harpole finished their conversation, another lawyer representing the Hilton estate, Ralph Nutter, entered the bungalow. He would be the one asking most of the questions on this day. He greeted Zsa Zsa and quickly took his seat. After Zsa Zsa was sworn in, the deposition began.

The first subject raised had to do with the birth of Zsa Zsa's only daughter, Constance Francesca—known to all as Francesca. In preparation for what she suspected was coming, Zsa Zsa rummaged through a large leather handbag and extracted from it a copy of Francesca's birth certificate of March 10, 1947, in New York City. "As you can see, she was named after her father," she explained as the court reporter took down every word. "That's where the Constance came from. Conrad." She then took from her purse a copy of the baptismal certificate: "And she was baptized in her father's favorite church," she continued. "St. Patrick's Cathedral, on May 4, 1947."

"So, Mrs. O'Hara, is it your testimony today that Constance Francesca Hilton is Conrad Hilton's biological daughter?" Ralph Nutter asked, addressing Zsa Zsa by her present married name.

"Yes, of course," Zsa Zsa answered quickly. Now she was serious, displaying a no-nonsense demeanor. This was not a frivolous matter, and she knew it.

"Did Mr. Hilton have reason to doubt that this was true?"

She paused. A wistful look crossed her face, but then it hardened. "Exactly what is it you are trying to say to me?" she asked with an arched eyebrow.

"I'll rephrase," offered Ralph Nutter. "Mrs. O'Hara, did you have any reason to believe that Mr. Conrad Hilton felt that Francesca Hilton was not his biological daughter?"

"Well, Mr. Hilton was a complicated man," Zsa Zsa answered, clearly hedging.

"That does not answer the question," Ralph Nutter observed.

She fixed him with an icy glare. "That is not an easy question to answer," she remarked, glancing at the court reporter. That her responses were being memorialized seemed to unnerve her.

Taking a deep breath, Ralph Nutter paused to gather his thoughts. "Okay, Mrs. O'Hara," he said, beginning anew, "is it your testimony, then, that Conrad Hilton believed Constance Francesca Hilton to be his biological child?"

"I can only tell you," Zsa Zsa began, "that never once to my face did Conrad Hilton ever question the paternity of our daughter."

"Are you certain of that?"

"Yes."

"Why, Mrs. O'Hara? Why are you so certain?"

She looked him in the eye. "Because if he had, I would have killed him," she answered.

The attorney searched her face as if trying to discern if she was joking. He then looked at Myron Harpole for a reaction. Harpole just chuckled to himself.

"How, then, would you describe your relationship with Mr. Hilton?" Ralph Nutter asked.

Resurrecting her smile, Zsa Zsa took a deep breath and exhaled slowly. "It's harder for me to talk about this than I thought it would be," she answered. "Conrad Hilton was not an easy man to understand. So religious. Always with the nuns, the church. Every day going to the church or praying on his knees in the bedroom to a shrine. In some ways, I think it's the reason why we are here today," she said, motioning to their surroundings. "He would rather the nuns have his money than his own family. I don't think he would disagree with my saying it, either."

"Mrs. O'Hara, what were your first impressions of Mr. Hilton?"

"My first impression was that I was meeting someone completely different from other men," Zsa Zsa Gabor answered. "He was...he was just"—she paused as if reaching for the right word—"I guess you could say he was the most *interesting* man I had ever met." Now she seemed to relax into her chair, appearing eager to tell her story. "I had known European royalty before him, do not forget, but this man was special," she continued. "In some ways, he reminded me of my father—the same strong features, the same color of his eyes, the close-cropped gray mustache. The way he carried himself was big and strong, self-confident and powerful. He was a take-charge kind of man. Someone you sensed would always take care of you. He was so solid...so...*American*. He seemed to me everything that was American. So, yes," she decided, "I knew as soon as I met him that never would I be able to forget him. Of all men, I knew that Conrad Hilton would be the one I would remember..."

"...for the rest of your life?" the attorney asked, finishing her sentence with a smile. Now even he seemed swept away by Zsa Zsa's memories of the one man who had both enchanted and vexed her for the better part of her days.

"Yes," she answered, smiling back at him and nodding. "For the rest of my life."

PART ONE

Conrad

Curse of the Ambitious

On a brisk December morning in Los Angeles in 1941, Conrad Hilton stood on the outdoor patio of the master bedroom of his Spanish-style mansion on Bellagio Road in Beverly Hills. As was his morning routine, he gazed out into the distance at the lush landscape of the Bel-Air Country Club and took it all in. It had just stopped raining, the cloud cover having dispersed to reveal a vast, unblemished blue sky over a pristine eighteen-hole golf course. The air smelled fresh and clean. Gently sloping green hills for as far as the eye could see gave way to the skyscrapers of nearby Westwood, standing like sentinels against the horizon. A magnificent three-hundred-foot white suspension bridge that crossed the canyon between the tee and the green glistened in the golden glow of a new morning sun. Such a panoramic view could actually take a person's breath away, or at the very least pull him into reverie.

Conrad was a raconteur of the first order, and one of his favorite stories had to do with the time, back in October 1936, that billionaire Howard Hughes landed his airplane on the eighth fairway in order to impress Katharine Hepburn. "Kate was learning to golf right out there with an instructor," Conrad would say, pointing into the distance. "And sure enough, old Howard just landed his two-seater plane—a Sikorsky amphibian—right on the fairway. Then, as if this was the most normal thing in the world, he jumped from his plane with clubs in hand and walked up to Kate and her instructor and said, 'Mind a third?' Doggone if he didn't join her golf game right then and there for the back nine! How about that?" Conrad would ask, slapping his knee and laughing hard. "Now *that's* how you impress a lady!"

Conrad Hilton was also quite impressive. A lanky New Mexican who spoke with a languid southwestern drawl, he stood over six feet tall, his receding hairline now gray at the temples. With chiseled features, penetrating blue eyes that sometimes appeared green, and a close-cropped gray mustache, he took great pride in the fact that he had managed to retain his good looks even as he approached his fifty-fifth birthday, just weeks away.

Standing in his maroon velvet robe and matching slippers with insignias, Conrad faced the limestone courtyard to his left and watched as members of his dutiful gardening staff hosed it down. Meanwhile, other household employees descended upon the outdoor furniture with towels, drying off the tables and chairs in case anyone might want to later enjoy the comfort of the patio. Off his right side, he could hear the shouts of his young sons as they played a rowdy game of football with their school chums. The constant ringing of telephones could also be heard from another wing in the house. Since a great deal of Conrad's growing West Coast business was temporarily being conducted from his home while his new Beverly Hills office was being renovated, the lines of communication usually started ringing early and continued for most of the day. His office staff would arrive at around ten. Until then, there was no one to answer the phones. No matter the cacophony, it was always very formal in the Hilton manse, in a manner that might be considered Old World traditional. On this morning it appeared to be business as usual.

"Breakfast is served, sir," announced a voice behind Conrad as his personal maid, Maria, rolled a metal cart into the room. Her full name was Maria Elena Espinoza de Amaté. She and her husband, Juan, had migrated from Spain two years earlier. Maria began working for Conrad shortly after arriving in Los Angeles, supervising the other six maids who took care of the property. Her husband was also employed by Conrad as one of the property's many groundskeepers. There was something special about Maria's relationship with Conrad, though. She wasn't just an employee; he thought of her as a friend. Still, it was always with the proper "Mr. Hilton" or "sir" that she addressed him.

"Would you like to be served on the patio, sir?" Maria asked. "It's such a lovely day." When Conrad agreed that her suggestion was a good one, Maria quickly set a table for one on the patio, starting with the unfurling of a fresh white organdy tablecloth. Many years later, her daughter, Connie, would recall, "My mother often told me that it was the same thing every day: One plate. One set of utensils. One cup for coffee. One glass for juice. She would put a single rose in a crystal bud vase as a centerpiece. As she would serve his meal, usually something simple like scrambled eggs or pancakes, Mr. Hilton would watch with a grim expression. 'It's just you and me, again, Maria,' he would say to my mom. 'It's just you and me.' They had that kind of relationship."

Conrad had been married, back in 1925, to Mary Adelaide Barron
in a union that had produced three children: Conrad Jr.—known as
Nicky—Barron, and Eric. He and Mary divorced in 1934, almost a year
after Eric was born. The marriage ended so badly that some felt Conrad
never really got over it. Because he was a devout Roman Catholic, the
divorce left him perpetually unsettled, with deep unresolved conflicts of
faith. Since then, he had dated a few women, but would always lose interest quickly. No woman ever seemed to have a permanent hold on his
heart—not since Mary Barron, anyway.

To say that Conrad Hilton was a good catch would be an understatement; he was already becoming known as "the Innkeeper to the World."
With a dozen hotels bearing his name having already opened in Texas,
California, and New Mexico, he next had his sights set on New York and
then...the world.

Conrad was a new breed of businessman for his times—optimistic
when there seemed little reason to be, especially during the war and the
Depression. He had faith in America and in her ability to rise once again,
to be a nation greater than ever before and to prosper if just given a bit of
time to do so. But more than anything, he wanted to be at the forefront
of this national renaissance. He was also a firm believer that the even-
tual expansion of his hotel empire to Europe would stimulate the tourist industry there, and by extension, the travel industry as well, bringing
much-needed American dollars to the strife-torn continent.

Instead of sitting down at the table on the patio to enjoy his breakfast,
Conrad walked back into his elegantly appointed bedroom. Decorated
with expensive antiques and fine oil paintings, this room, with its deep
blue domed ceiling and expansive floor-to-ceiling windows, had long
been a place of repose where the busy mogul could retreat after a hectic
day. Maria de Amaté was the only one of his maids ever allowed entry
into this sanctuary. She had made it her mission to keep the room alive
with vibrant colors by filling it with fresh-cut flower arrangements on a
daily basis. They permeated the room with the sweet fragrance of the
outside gardens.

Against one wall of the bedroom there was an old-fashioned hand-
made Spanish wooden bed, so austere in its design that it looked as if
it belonged in a monastery. Next to it was a carefully constructed bed-

side shrine with religious statues, candles, prayer books, and a shiny gold crucifix before which Conrad would kneel and pray every night on a small Persian rug. When he was just a boy of about ten, his first confessor, Father Jules Derasches, had told him that if he said the Hail Mary and then "Saint Joseph, pray for us" three times in rapid succession, God would always take care of him. Therefore, every single day for the last forty-some years, he had made sure to start each prayer session with his God with those specific prayers, in that exact order.

His religion was always a source of comfort for him. Still, he often wondered how it was that a man so accomplished could also be so lonely. "I guess you could say it's the curse of the ambitious," he observed to a close friend when describing his life. "Perhaps I am a walking cliché," he would admit. "I have everything. Yet it sometimes feels as if I have little." He'd been alone for so long, it had gotten to the point where his greatest passions seemed to take the form of inanimate objects; he now referred to his hotels as his women. "She's a great dame, that one," he would say of one of his Texas holdings, the Abilene Hilton. "No woman can match her," he would opine of his Dallas Hilton. "Luckily for me, she could not find a better suitor," he observed of the Sir Francis Drake in San Francisco. Besides his religion, the only thing that truly mattered to him—that gave him the most pleasure—was his work. Might that one day change? He was open to the idea, but not particularly hopeful.

Despite reservations about any lack of romance, Conrad Hilton knew he had a good life. He deserved his success; he had worked hard for it. But still...something was missing. However, it wouldn't be long before Conrad would once again do what he had often done whenever he felt a lack of something in his personal life: He would go about the business of filling the void. And even though he would one day look back on this time and admit that he probably should have just left well enough alone—some of the choices he was about to make would haunt him for the rest of his life—he wasn't the kind of man to play it safe. He was shrewd; he liked to take chances. He wanted to live his life for all it was worth, damn the consequences!

Humble Beginnings

$\mathcal{T}$o fully understand Conrad Nicholson Hilton's remarkable journey from humble beginnings to the very pinnacle of fame and success, one must hark back to his father, August Halvorsen Hilton—known as Gus and born in Norway on August 21, 1854—a robust, imposing Norwegian immigrant, and to his mother, Mary Genevieve Laufersweiler—born in Iowa on December 3, 1861—a small, soft-spoken, deeply devout Catholic of German heritage. They were married on Lincoln's birthday in 1885 in Fort Dodge. Gus passed along to his son his determined work ethic and driving ambition; Mary provided his moral compass and spiritual path.

Though devoted and utterly committed to each other, the Hiltons were actually polar opposites—in appearance, temperament, personality, and demeanor. Gus was a big man, over six feet and handsome as a matinee idol with his deeply set dark eyes and well-groomed handlebar mustache. Mary wore her chestnut hair parted in the middle and pulled into a severe bun; a couple of years after marrying, she would go gray though still a young woman. She had luminescent brown eyes, a strong nose, and a full mouth against a round face. He was loud and opinionated; she was quiet and respectful. Both were devoted to the rigid tenets of the Catholic Church. This was the solid foundation upon which they would build their long life together.

Following the birth of his sister Felice almost two years earlier, Conrad was born on a snowy Christmas Day 1887. Named for his maternal grandfather—Conrad Laufersweiler—and the Fort Dodge doctor—Nicholson—who delivered him, he was the second of nine children (four daughters and five sons), all within an eleven-year period. He would be known by all as simply "Connie." Most of the children were born in the adobe dwelling that also housed Gus's general store, A. H. Hilton, in San Antonio, Territory of New Mexico, located in the midst of vast high deserts and stark mountains, halfway between Albuquerque and El Paso, Texas, near the Rio Grande.

Conrad looked like a force to be reckoned with, even as a youngster. Photographs of the time show a sturdy boy with big ears, carefully groomed brown hair, intense eyes, and a downward-sloping smile. While others in family portraits are seen grinning, Conrad appears serious and focused. Because he was the family's firstborn son, he was expected to take his place in the general store while still quite young. Thus it was at his father's elbow that he began his apprenticeship into the world of business, mastering the laws of supply and demand and honing the entrepreneurial skills that would serve him so well for the rest of his life. An adventurous, high-spirited lad, he also undertook on his own such productive ventures as going into the produce business, first by cultivating a piece of his father's land and then by planting and later selling vegetables door-to-door. Though he could barely peer over the counter at Gus's store, he was there almost every day after school; this was where he would first learn the value of hard work and tough negotiation.

It was during this time that the Hiltons suffered their first real sorrow, the death of two-year-old Julian, their fifth child and third son. After the loss, the family was inconsolable; for the first time, there were no baby noises in the home. However, joy returned in 1898 when baby Rosemary arrived. With the cradle once again filled, the house now felt like a home. Two more children would be added to the brood when Gus Jr.—called "Boy"—was born in 1901 and Helen, their fourth daughter, in 1906. As the family expanded, so did their home, with Gus adding a room onto the original structure for each of his eight children upon their arrival. There would be no sharing of rooms for his kids; each would have his or her own space, which was practically unheard of during the pioneering days of the expanding frontier. That's not to say, however, that the accommodations were lavish. Pictures of the homestead show a dilapidated structure that looked as if it might collapse at any moment. "We're talking cowboy country here," observed one of Hilton's relatives from the family's third generation. "Cowboy hats, horses, stagecoaches, dirt roads, moonshine, saloons... the works."

Conrad seemed content attending the one-room schoolhouse to which he rode to and from on his little pony, Chiquita. Though he excelled in English and learned Spanish from his Native American and Mexican friends, Mary came to believe that Conrad was, by about the age of twelve, receiving a substandard education. Therefore she packed him off to Goss Military Institute in Roswell (later renamed the New Mexico Military Institute), which was quite a blow for the home-loving youngster. He didn't want to go, but he also didn't have much choice. There he would continue his education and be required to wear the uncomfortable gray flannel, black braid–trimmed uniform of a cadet. Beyond arithmetic, he was not a good student, repeatedly being caught off school property after hours, often at music halls in which youngsters were not allowed— just one of the many ways he rebelled against the rigid strictures of military school. When the school burned to the ground, his celebration of a certain return to his home in San Antonio was short-lived; Colonel Goss simply rented another building and continued operating the institute. However, this time fearful that the school was not providing her son with the proper attention to nonsecular matters, Mary pulled the boy out of it and enrolled him at St. Michael's in Santa Fe, a parochial institution that suited her on two counts: It was Catholic and it was strict.

Conrad's summer vacations were spent back in San Antonio, working for five dollars a month at A. H. Hilton, an ever-growing business that now housed the post office, the telegraph office, the Studebaker dealership, a livery stable, and a lumber/building materials operation. Gus Hilton was nothing if not entrepreneurial. Not only was he managing the store, but he also bartered with prospectors, giving them provisions, clothing, food, and money in return for a percentage of their profits. On some days he would take off into the wilderness to sell tobacco and food to beaver trappers, sometimes trading his goods for theirs. Gus was busy all of the time, tough and unyielding not only in business but at home as well; he expected a lot of his children, but mostly from Conrad. Actually, he saw something of himself in Connie, and wanted nothing more than to see the boy make something of himself. Therefore, he pressured him a great deal and was often critical when some observers felt it may have better served the boy to just be encouraging.

If Conrad believed his yeoman's work for his father would be rewarded with any sort of permanent position at A. H. Hilton, he was wrong. In the fall, he was off to another school, St. Michael's College in Santa Fe, New Mexico, a move that, once more, he was dead set against having to make. He implored his mother that it was "a great waste of time. All the things I want to know I am learning at home." Mary Hilton was not moved, however, arguing that he would have plenty of time to learn his father's business—later. What Conrad needed at this time in his life, she reasoned, was a solid foundation. End of argument. Thus Conrad transferred to St. Michael's College, where he stayed for two years, once again spending summer vacations working in Gus's general store, but now at an increase in salary to fifteen dollars a month.

Along with Conrad's salary raise, at fifteen he shot up in height to six feet, making him almost as tall as his father. Though they could now look at each other eyeball to eyeball, the son's increase in stature did not alter Gus's attitude toward him; he was still a stern, overbearing taskmaster, giving Conrad more responsibility in running the store, but riding herd on him every step along the way and questioning his every decision and suggestion.

That summer, with all the hard work he was doing and lessons he was learning, Conrad Hilton would feel quite often with the passing years that something was lacking in his life. One day, he found on his mother's sewing table a copy of a book by Helen Keller, the twenty-three-year-old Alabama native, born deaf and blind. Late into the night in his room, he surreptitiously read her autobiography, *Optimism*, the message of which he found transformative. Keller wrote, "Optimism is the faith that leads to achievement; nothing can be done without hope," and, "Optimism is the harmony between man's spirit and the spirit of God pronouncing His works good." These precepts were in perfect alignment with those already instilled in Conrad by his mother. With a newfound courage gleaned from Keller's book, Conrad eventually announced to his parents that he would not be returning to school. His decision was final, he said, even though he was only fifteen. Gus responded without appearing to show the slightest sign of annoyance. "All right," he decided. "I guess you'll be worth twenty-five dollars a month on a full-time basis." And, surprisingly enough, his mother, Mary, went along with it too. "I believe now, looking back, that my parents took note of my conviction, and this encouraged them to change their minds," he would later explain. "I must say, I did make a good case for myself."

By 1904, Gus's skillful operation of his store enabled him to become quite wealthy, not just from the store's booming success, but also from smart investments, one of which was in the mining business. Known throughout the territory as "Colonel Hilton," he then added to his fortune by selling a coal mine for $135,000. Feeling flush and generous, he treated the entire family to a vacation trip to St. Louis for the World's Fair, celebrating the centennial of the 1803 Louisiana Purchase, and also the site of the Summer Olympic Games, the first to be held in the United States. Emboldened by the journey, Gus soon decided that a change of scenery was in order for his family. After researching the towns on the Pacific in Southern California, he decided that Long Beach, south of Los Angeles, would be an ideal place in which to settle down, with its warm climate and easier lifestyle. Upon their arrival, Mary immediately enrolled the children in school, convincing Connie to now finish his education. They lived there until Conrad finished high school. Meanwhile, Gus went back and forth to San Antonio, tending to his store, to which Connie (and the rest of the family) would return when his schooldays were over.

In 1907, the financial panic that came without warning hit the country and all but wiped out Gus Hilton's finances. Gathering his family about him, Gus spelled out the dire situation and asked for suggestions. Casting his eyes upon the floor, nineteen-year-old Conrad after a few moments of silence looked up, broke into a smile, and announced, "We should open a hotel. Let's take five or six of our ten rooms [of the house in which they lived] and make a hotel. This place needs a hotel!" Conrad further suggested that while his father ran the hotel, his mother and sisters could handle kitchen duty. He would be responsible for baggage. He further speculated that two and a half dollars a day for each bed would be a reasonable amount to charge guests. Much to his amazement, his father actually thought the idea might work! One might say that this suggestion was Conrad Hilton's first real brainstorm—the first of many, as it would happen.

Within six weeks, news of the new hotel spread throughout the area and all the way to Chicago: "[The word was that] if you have to break up your sales trip, break it at San Antonio and try to get a room at Hilton's," Conrad later recalled to author Whitney Bolton. "They serve the best meals in the West and they have a boy there who is a crackerjack at making things comfortable for you." He added, "Everyone got something out of our hotel. Travelers got cleanliness, comfort and a good table for their $2.50 a day, even though we served three bountiful meals. We all worked hard, and no one harder than my mother. I wouldn't take a million dollars for what those days taught me...and I'd give a million dollars for one of the suppers she served." Not only did Conrad manage the hotel, but he worked the desk, was the concierge, and did pretty much everything he could think of to keep the enterprise afloat. His father was pleased, though of course not exactly effusive with his praise. However, he indicated his pride in his son by giving him control of the store in San Antonio when he turned twenty-one. It would now be called A. H. Hilton and Son.

With the family solvent thanks to Conrad's bright idea, he enrolled at the New Mexico School of Mines at nearby Socorro, close enough that he could spend weekends in San Antonio or overnight if he were needed. What he learned in Socorro proved invaluable as he excelled at higher mathematics, providing "the best possible mental muscles necessary" for whatever career he would choose.

In 1911, when he was twenty-four, the Territory of New Mexico was admitted to the Union, and over Gus's strenuous objections—and also those of his brother Carl, who was now attending the Naval Academy in Annapolis, Maryland—Conrad entered the political arena. He was swiftly elected to a seat in the lower house of the new state's first legislature, serving one two-year term as New Mexico's youngest representative. He would go on to author eight bills, one having to do with prohibiting violence in motion pictures, another with proper highway markers. "It seemed that he could do pretty much anything he set out to do," said his son Barron, "and when he entered politics, which was a bit of a surprise turn for him, people began to see that he had big ambitions, that he didn't feel there was a ceiling to what he could achieve."

A handsome young man by this time, Conrad Hilton had a full head of brown hair parted on the right, a wide nose, penetrating blue-green eyes, and a full mouth. With his New Mexican drawl, he seemed polite and affable to all who crossed his path. Because he found working as a lawmaker slow and dull, his days in that field were now numbered, by his own admission—even though he hated proving his father right. His social life was anything but boring, though. He was out on the town every night, attending lavish balls at the state capitol, becoming a popular member of Santa Fe high society, and proving to be a proficient and much sought-after dancing partner.

Returning to San Antonio, more frustrated and more determined than ever to make it without his father's help and counsel, Conrad Hilton reasoned that since there was no bank in his small hometown, he would become a banker. Once again, Gus warned against it, arguing that the town was much too small for a bank, and besides, there were banks already established in nearby Socorro. Undeterred, and with about $30,000—$3,000 of it his own and the rest scrounged from friends and investors—Conrad opened the New Mexico State Bank of San Antonio in September 1913. Though he was just twenty-six, he believed that the locals would entrust their savings to his new bank. However, customers failed to materialize and by year's end the bank would close its doors. Another failure. Would his father always be right?

Restless for new challenges, in 1916, Conrad, at twenty-nine, took on the management of a musical group formed by his violin-playing sister Eva with two of her female friends, calling themselves the Hilton Trio. These girls were a real sight in their long, full skirts (which buttoned down the middle) wrapped by wide cloth belts, long-sleeved flouncy blouses, and enormous picture hats. Always the great multitasker, not only was Conrad their manager, but he was their agent and roadie as well. Though his father warned him that the undertaking was risky and likely to fail, Conrad was certain that people would flock to see the trio. Unfortunately, that didn't happen. Despite his best efforts, his first entrance into show business was a colossal failure, barely breaking even in the course of a year. Failing was bad enough, but failing in front of his critical father was much worse.

There seemed nothing more for Conrad to do but to return to the store, and since Gus had by this time given him stock in it, now perhaps he would be recognized as an equal partner not just in name but in profits. However, fate intervened and changed his course.

In 1915, the British liner the RMS *Lusitania* had been sent to the bottom of the Atlantic Ocean after being hit by a torpedo from a German U-boat. Two years later in April 1917, with Germany continuing its U-boat assaults on ships in the North Atlantic, including those of the United States, the country, which President Woodrow Wilson had managed to keep neutral, joined the Allied powers in the fight against Germany in the First World War. Conrad, having recently completed Army Officer Training School and been commissioned a second lieutenant, was eager for an assignment at the front lines. The Army had other ideas. Capitalizing on Hilton's experience in and knowledge of the dry goods business, the Army assigned him to the Quartermaster Corps, headquartered in Paris, a safe distance from the battles that still raged. By day, his duties were mundane and the work quite easy, and by night he became a fixture at the cafés and bistros off the Champs-Elysées. He was enormously popular and cut quite a figure in his officer's uniform, a good-looking fellow with a great smile and winning personality.

Being in France gave Conrad a new worldview and expanded his scope of experience outside of his humble beginnings. "Before, I had been a big frog in a small pond," he said, "now [in Paris] I realized I was just a tadpole in a big ocean." However, interrupting his joie de vivre, shortly after the Armistice was signed, he received a shocking telegram from his mother telling him that his father had died and asking him to come home.

Though Conrad hastily made plans to return to the States, he arrived too late. The funeral had already been held and his father buried. He was shattered that he was unable to pay his last respects to the often critical father he still loved very much and respected deeply. As it happened, Gus had been the owner of the town's first automobile, which, from photographs, looked pretty much like a broken-down old jalopy. It was in this Ford that he was killed on January 1, 1919, the town's first death by car accident when the vehicle failed to negotiate a turn in the road. Although Conrad knew full well that his father would have wanted him to take over the family business, he realized that San Antonio's boom days were over. If he were ever to make it big, it wouldn't be here.

Hotelier

*I*ronically, the automotive technology that had claimed the life of Conrad Hilton's father would be the impetus that would propel Conrad to his next venture—the oilfields of Texas. He wouldn't be a wildcatter, though. Instead, he would exploit the booming support apparatus that was springing up around the oil industry. "Black gold" was making millionaires overnight and Conrad wanted a piece of that action. Of course, his mother could have asked him to stay with her, but she wouldn't have thought to do it. As he later recalled, "Once again, my mother's faith was like a rock. One word from her that she needed me and I would have played out my hand in Socorro. But she gave me no such word. She could lose her husband, her companion of thirty-four years, and turn right around and send her oldest son, who had just come home, away again. She loved us both. She knew grief. But she did not know the meaning of fear or loneliness or dependence on human agencies because her protector would never leave her or forsake her. And so it was my mother who said very firmly, 'You'll have to find your own frontier, Connie.'"

With $5,000, his entire life savings, pinned to the inside of his coat, Conrad Hilton—now thirty-two—soon after struck out for Texas, landing in the small, blustering town of Cisco in the spring of 1919. By this time, the tall New Mexican had begun to lose his hair, but he still cut quite a figure in his natty three-piece suits, always with a silk tie that was perfectly knotted. "I thought, dreamed, schemed of nothing but how to get a toehold in this amazing pageant that was Texas," he later recalled. Here, he felt, he could finally fulfill that long-held dream to own a bank. Soon after arriving, he heard of one for sale in Cisco and met with the owner, who agreed upon a price. But as fate would have it, the banker reneged, upping the original, mutually established selling price. Frustrated and bitterly disappointed, Conrad retreated to a nearby hotel called the Mobley to ponder his next move.

The Mobley was a two-story, redbrick, down-in-the-dumps operation catering to the roughnecks who worked in the oilfields. "When I first saw it," he would recall, "it looked like a convenient place to sleep. Nothing more." Despite its dilapidated condition, Conrad was astonished to find that the place was fully occupied, with a waiting list of customers attracted to its low room cost. Hilton soon also discovered that the hotel's owner was renting out rooms by the hour in three shifts, in addition to the daily or weekly rate—and still he was turning people away!

Though the Mobley had the appearance of a flophouse, Conrad still saw great promise in it. He became even more enthused about the forty-room facility than he had been about possibly striking it rich in the oil industry. Therefore, when he learned that the Mobley's proprietor wanted to sell it and enter the oilfields himself, Conrad made an offer of $40,000.

However, he only had $5,000 to his name. His devoted mother, Mary—who had long ago come to the conclusion that Connie was a chip off the old block that had been Gus—along with the help of friends and the assistance of a bank loan would provide the balance for the purchase. This—his second foray into the hotel business, if one considers the hotel at the Hilton compound his first—would be the decision of a lifetime for young Conrad. He seemed to know it, too. When the deal was completed, he sent his mother a telegram: "Frontier found. Water deep down here. Launched first ship in Cisco."

From his earlier experience in the hotel business, there was one thing Conrad Hilton knew for sure was important: the careful utilization of space. To that end, he ripped out the lobby and sectioned it off into bedrooms. He then reduced the size of the front desk by half and added a retail shop. Removing three chairs and a sofa from another section of the lobby, he installed a newsstand. As carpenters moved into the Mobley and did their work, the place became a beehive of activity, which for some reason did not seem to bother the customers. They found it all exciting. Meanwhile, Hilton would move among his patrons with ease, mingling with one and all and constantly selling them on the virtues of his new venue. It worked. His "guests," as he called them, soon extolled the hearty meat-and-potatoes menu Hilton offered, the splendid service of his capable staff, and the accommodations he now offered at affordable prices.

It was with the Mobley that Hilton began to understand that a staff of contented employees usually resulted in a thriving business. He began to encourage regular meetings with his staff, listening to all of their concerns and taking care of each as best he could. Caring about his employees and viewing them as people with families and lives of their own rather than merely his charges would become an integral way of doing business for Conrad Hilton, and in years to come would account for much of his success as a hotelier. He soon outlined for his employees his personal guidelines for success, and then asked that they adhere to them. His code could easily apply today, almost a hundred years later, as one for better living. As he put it at the time, "Find your own particular talent; Be big; Be honest; Live with enthusiasm; Don't let your possessions possess you; Don't worry about your problems; Look up to people when you can—down to no one; Don't cling to the past; Assume your full share of responsibility in the world and, finally, Pray consistently and constantly."

With the Mobley, which he later called "my first love, a great lady," it seemed that Conrad Hilton was well on his way to success in the fickle hotel business. He forgot all about the idea of banking and decided that instead he would focus on his new passion. In doing so, his success would be like a juggernaut that could not be stopped. By 1923, Hilton had more than five hundred rooms in Texas in different small hotels he had purchased along the way, such as the Melba in Fort Worth. Because these were all dilapidated establishments that appeared to be on the verge of closing, Conrad was able to get them for a steal. He would then invest in renovating them with his own special touches—turning extra space in lobbies into rooms or, in some cases, bars; closets into gift shops—and before long they were turning a profit. As success seemed to be happening all around him, Conrad felt that he needed a slogan, something that would brand his hotels and the work he had put into them. After deliberating on it for some time, he came up with what he thought was the perfect catchphrase: "minimax." What did it mean? Minimum price for maximum service—a slogan he began to use on all of the advertising for his growing chain of hotels.

Once Conrad was making about $100,000 a year, he began to fantasize about building a hotel that would bear his own name. It didn't take long for that dream to come true, because after aligning himself with a team of financial advisers and backers, Conrad broke ground for the Dallas Hilton on July 26, 1924. He was thirty-seven. After leasing for a one-hundred-year term the ground upon which the hotel would be built, he used that purchase as collateral for a half-million-dollar bank loan, a staggering amount of money in 1924. He also invested $100,000 of his own money and another $200,000 from backers. Then, when he still didn't have the financial resources to fully complete the job, he somehow convinced the man from whom he had leased the land, a funeral director, to help him with some of the final details. It was as if Conrad Hilton could convince anyone to do anything for him. This would be the first of a series of hotels he would open in Texas in the next ten years, including hotels in Dallas, Abilene, Long View, Lubbock, El Paso, and Plainview. In 1927, he would even be named president of the Texas Hotel Association.

Losing It All

Conrad Hilton was having a good run, no doubt about it. Unfortunately, it wouldn't last. Everything would come to a crashing halt not only for him but for most people in October 1929 with the onslaught of the Great Depression. This turn in the country's fortunes not only increased the country's homeless population, but it forced many successful entrepreneurs to abandon their businesses and look for menial labor, anything to bring in a meager wage to support their families. Men much wealthier than Conrad Hilton found themselves in dire financial straits. Now there were many fewer traveling businessmen, and those that did still have jobs certainly couldn't afford to stay in hotels like Conrad's, choosing instead any flophouse they could find to put a temporary roof over their heads.

The Depression couldn't have happened at a worse time for Conrad. He was right in the middle of building the Dallas Hilton, and had already sunk a great deal of money into the project. As things went from bad to worse, in less than a year he found himself deeply in debt, having lost all but one of his hotels, the towering, grand El Paso Hilton (billed in one advertisement as "the Southwest's Finest Hotel. A Stone's Throw from Mexico. Radio in every room!"). At $500,000 in debt, he was all but ruined. The rapid speed by which things had taken such a turn was stunning. "I was heartsick about it," he would later recall. "But, of course, everyone in business was facing ruination at this time in our history. I had a sense that if I could just survive this, I could survive anything."

Conrad was still a determined man, even in the face of so much adversity. He believed that if he could at least keep the El Paso Hilton in business, he might actually be able to ride out the Depression. "He was the kind of man who always believed no bad situation to be permanent," said his son Barron. "He had become imbued with this kind of optimism back when he discovered Helen Keller's transformative book when he was a teenager, and he built upon it with the passing of the years. He also had great faith in America and in its ability to bounce back, and whereas many of his colleagues in the hotel business were certain that there was no going back, and the country would never return to its former glory, my father never bought into such negativity. It would take time, he suspected, but things would get better—if he could just hang on a little while longer." Meanwhile, Conrad had some of the rooms of the El Paso Hilton boarded up, he cut back on heating, electricity...whatever he could think of to lower his overhead.

When the lease payment became due on the El Paso, Conrad made a deal with a banker in Missouri who promised to give him the $40,000 necessary to keep the property. Hilton then took a prop plane—an extravagant way to travel at the time, but also the most expedient way in an emergency such as this one—to Missouri, only to find that the banker had changed his mind. Now Conrad was frantic. He knew that losing his only hotel would amount to his complete demise. He went back to Texas to begin brainstorming with a group of his suppliers—and his mother, who was living at the El Paso at this time. He promised that if they each contributed $5,000 to help him out of this tight spot, he would do business with them for as long as he was a hotel owner. Why was his mother present at the meeting? Could the others turn him down with Mary Hilton eyeing them, and willing to pitch in herself—which she did—to the tune of $5,000? Soon, the other seven businessmen in the meeting agreed to put up $5,000 each. Donald H. Hubbs, director emeritus of the Hilton Foundation, recalled that Hilton grabbed the money, "raced to the elevator, ran to the bank and made the lease payment. He said, had he not made that payment, he would have most certainly lost his empire right then and there."

Though he managed to save the El Paso, Hilton was still in big trouble. It was just one problem after another as things crumbled all around him. At one point, a sheriff showed up at the Dallas hotel with a judgment. "I've come to collect," he told Hilton. "Pay up or I'll tack this judgment in the lobby." Though it was a humiliating moment for Conrad, what could he do about it? "Tack away," he said blithely. "I'll go find you a ladder." A half hour later, the sheriff returned, saying, "You knew I would never be able to find a place to tack this, didn't you? The whole lobby is marble!" To which Conrad responded, "And you knew I would pay it as soon as I had the money to do so." The sheriff left, giving Conrad just a little more time to come up with the money, which he did, "but it wasn't easy," he later recalled. An even more mortifying moment occurred when Conrad owed just $178 to a furniture company and they took him to court for the debt. At that point, his attorneys strongly encouraged him to declare bankruptcy. Pounding his fists on his desk during more than a few meetings with those same lawyers, Hilton steadfastly refused. He insisted that the situation was just temporary, that he was going to wait it out.

"I've seen numbers in my research that suggest that over 80 percent of the hotels in America went bankrupt during the Depression," says Mark Young of the Conrad N. Hilton College of Hotel and Restaurant Management. "No one was traveling, no businesspeople especially, so the rooms were just sitting empty. All of the creditors, if they wanted to, could have called in all of their notes and totally wiped him out, but many of them realized that he was doing the best he could under horrible circumstances. They had faith in him, and plus he was a good barterer, like his dad. For instance, there was a dairy supplier in El Paso whose bill was due, and Conrad said, 'Look, if you'll just extend me more credit, as long as I'm operating a hotel here I'll buy all my dairy products from you.' And he did, for many years. He never forgot. We have so much correspondence from him to people saying, 'You helped me when times were tough, now I would like to help you. Would you like a job? Or would you like to buy stock in the company? What can I do to repay you for helping me?'"

Every day it seemed that Conrad was closer to complete financial collapse. "A very good story is that at one point he was $500 in debt and a bellman in Dallas gave him his life savings," recalled Conrad's granddaughter Linda Hilton (his son Eric's daughter). "And the bellman said, 'Mr. Hilton, this is my life savings, but I want you to have it because I know you're going to make this into something.' My grandfather said he would not take charity, but he would take it as an investment. He was such a visionary of where he was going and what he was doing. There was no doubt in his mind that he was going to get the next deal." (Incidentally, the bellman Linda Hilton spoke of eventually had his money returned to him by Conrad many times over. He received dividends on Hilton stock for the rest of his life.)

Soon, Conrad Hilton's intuition about the strength and resolve of his beloved country began to pay off; ever so slowly, America got back on her feet. As she did, Hilton's small empire also began to recover. Because he had so stubbornly refused to default on his many bills, he found his reputation greatly enhanced among creditors and future backers. He also found that he now had even greater alignment with important backers who knew they could trust him even at the worst of times, and this would remain the case for him moving forward. "They all wanted to sell to Conrad Hilton because he was the one who didn't declare bankruptcy," said Donald Hubbs, "and that's partly how he was able to acquire so many hotels in the future."

In 1939, Conrad would expand his influence to the West Coast with the purchase of the elegant and tasteful Sir Francis Drake Hotel in San Francisco—twenty-two stories tall with 450 rooms and a $300,000 luxury nightclub, built at a cost of $4.1 million. Hilton got it for a cash outlay of $275,000. He also now owned a hotel in Long Beach, California, and another in Albuquerque, New Mexico. Now that the Depression was finally over, there seemed to be no stopping Conrad Hilton.

It was 1940 when Conrad finally moved to Los Angeles. His siblings were doing well, too. While his brothers had continued with their educations, one sister married well and lived in a mansion outside of Boston; another had become an actress, and yet another was valedictorian of her high school graduating class.

A year after moving to the West Coast, Conrad established his company's first headquarters outside of Texas, with offices on Wilshire Boulevard in Beverly Hills. By this time, most interested Americans were well aware of the Hilton name and what it represented in terms of quality hotel accommodations at reasonable prices. Without a doubt, Conrad Hilton had become a major player—arguably *the* major player—in the hotel business, respected not only for his instincts and business acumen but also for the fact that he had not only survived but had gone on to thrive during a time when most American businessmen had no choice but to throw in the towel.

Georgia on His Mind

*H*e had never met anyone quite like her. But, then again, few people had.

It was a California winter's night early in the first week of December

1941 when Conrad Hilton and a date found themselves having a drink at the popular Ciro's nightclub on the Sunset Strip in West Hollywood. If one wanted to be seen in Hollywood, Ciro's was the place to go. All of the most famous of stars socialized with one another there—Joan Crawford, Cary Grant, and Barbara Stanwyck—with photographers stationed just outside the club's doors in order to preserve their celebrity sightings for the next day's newspapers. There was always a gaggle of fans patiently waiting out front with their autograph books open in the hopes of spotting their favorite movie star, and maybe even getting a signature. With this crush of people pushing and shoving for a better view as flashbulbs popped off all around them, it was always a mad scene at Ciro's.

As Conrad and his companion immersed themselves in the bustling nightspot, a stylish young woman and her handsome escort swept into the club, immediately drawing the attention of practically everyone in the small room. This was the era of the "grand entrance," and the new arrival certainly understood how to make one. Wearing a dark blue satin dress with turquoise embroidery, she moved confidently with feline grace. Although she was only five foot three, her voluptuous carriage made her seem taller and her high waist made her legs appear to be long. Her lovely face was surrounded by soft red hair in a bouffant style. With milky skin, high cheekbones, a straight nose, hazel almond-shaped eyes, and sensuous lips, this attractive woman certainly seemed as if she belonged among the elite in Ciro's, but in truth she'd yet to accomplish anything in Hollywood. Adding to her mystique, she was on the arm of dashing celebrity attorney Gregson (Greg) Bautzer, former fiancé of Lana Turner.

As the attractive couple walked into the club, they were followed by an equally eye-catching pair—actress Eva Gabor from Hungary and her date, G. Bentley Ryan, a partner in Bautzer's law firm. Eva had just begun her career as an actress, having recently made her debut in a small part in the Paramount film *Forced Landing*. Though she was quickly becoming well-known, it was not for her acting ability as much as for her beauty and charm. At twenty-one, she was an exotic young woman, blonde and shapely, with a thick Hungarian accent, a quick wit, a vivid intelligence, and a delicious sense of humor. Her march toward fame began at the knee of her ambitious, wellborn Jewish mother, Jolie (Jansci) Tilleman Gabor, a Budapest debutante and heiress to a jewelry fortune. Eva's father was Colonel Vilmos Gabor, a self-absorbed, domineering product of the

Hungarian military establishment, twenty-two years older than Jolie. By 1939, Eva, the first in the family to journey to the United States (with her then husband, Erik V. Drummer, from whom she was now separated), had obtained a Hollywood agent and a Paramount studio contract.

The woman who caught Conrad Hilton's attention was not Eva, though, it was her older sister, twenty-four-year-old Zsa Zsa,* the alluring redhead in the satiny blue dress. Zsa Zsa (born Sari) was the second of three daughters—the third being her older sister, Magda—born in Budapest, Austria-Hungary, in 1917. She had been in America for just three months, having also migrated from Hungary.

Zsa Zsa, beautiful and spoiled as a child, would be reared as if to the manor born, inheriting from her mother an overblown sense of entitlement that she would exhibit for the rest of her life. She had a Swiss private-school education, was given lessons in horseback riding, outfitted like a princess, tutored like a courtesan-in-waiting, offered singing, ballet, and piano lessons, and even spent an hour each day with a master of the epée. Jolie also saw to it that Zsa Zsa, as well as her sisters, Eva and Magda, was schooled in English, German, and French. "Zsa Zsa can talk about nothing in four different languages," Jolie would later say in an interview. Zsa Zsa landed her first role at the age of nineteen. She was discovered by the Austrian opera star Richard Tauber, who hired her to appear onstage with him in the Viennese production of *Der singende Traum* (*The Singing Dream*).

Because she had decided too late in life that she wanted to be an actress, Jolie Gabor would happily live vicariously through her ambitious daughters, especially Zsa Zsa. In 1936, she launched a campaign to obtain the title of Miss Hungary for Zsa Zsa. It didn't matter to Jolie that she viewed Zsa Zsa as having no discernible talent or that her daughter didn't even own an evening dress. She forged ahead anyway, using Eva's peroxide to temporarily turn her brown-haired daughter into a platinum blonde, raiding Magda's closet for a floor-length gown, then mus-

---

* In 1991, Zsa Zsa explained to Larry King how she got her name: "Zsa Zsa I got in Budapest. I was originally named Sari Gabor after a famous actress in Budapest [Sari Fedak] whose nickname was also Zsa Zsa." Technically, the spelling of her name is one Hungarian word, as in Zsazsa, and this is the manner in which she and her family members—and later Conrad Hilton—would write it.

cling Zsa Zsa into the wings of the stage and literally pushing her out into the lineup of finalists. Against all odds and with Jolie's practiced chutzpah, Zsa Zsa was crowned Miss Hungary of 1936, but had to surrender the crown since she was not yet sixteen. Now, in 1941, Zsa Zsa was in the process of obtaining a divorce from Burhan Belge, press director for the Foreign Ministry of Turkey in Ankara, leaving herself free to embark on a husband hunt that began with a trip to Hollywood to visit her sister.

Conrad Hilton had been sitting down while talking to Texan hotelier Joseph Drown, who in five years would open the Hotel Bel-Air in Los Angeles. When Conrad drew himself up to his full height, Zsa Zsa could not help but be impressed. In her 1960 memoir, her memory of the moment was vivid: "He stood there for a moment: A tall, erect, suntanned man with gray hair showing white at the temples in sharp contrast to his dark skin…looking like a wild Indian, with upturned greenish eyes, high cheekbones—a beautiful, distinguished figure who might have been a diplomat. I found myself thinking, this man I could marry."

Zsa Zsa would later add that Hilton had reminded her of the heroes of the Hollywood westerns she had fantasized about while growing up in Hungary, men like Tom Mix and Buck Jones, *real* American rough-hewn, take-charge types who could command her respect while also keeping her in line. She would write that she was crestfallen when Gregson Bautzer explained to her that Hilton was in the hotel business. That didn't seem like an interesting line of work, she wrote, and she secretly wished he had been a diplomat or perhaps even someone in politics. He was certainly stately enough to look the part. Nevertheless, for her—at least as she would recall it—it was love at first sight.

Not everyone would be taken in by Zsa Zsa's florid descriptions of the intense feelings she felt for Conrad the moment she laid eyes on him. Legendary gossip columnist Sheila Graham, for instance, would write acerbically that it was indeed love at first sight between the mismatched pair—"Zsa Zsa's first sight of Hilton's wallet." Graham may not have been far off the mark. In Jolie Gabor's autobiography, she reveals that shortly before Zsa Zsa left for America, Jolie had actually advised her daughter to marry a man in the hotel business. Zsa Zsa was intrigued. "Why?" she asked. Jolie explained that a friend of hers had married a hotel director in Carmel, California, and that he had provided the best life in the world for her. "She tells me the food is good and the accommodations are good and there is so much courtesy and so many parties," Jolie counseled her daughter. "She says it makes for a very good life. So, remember this." That Zsa Zsa was introduced to a "hotel director" just weeks after arriving in Los Angeles must have seemed to her like nothing if not an extremely good omen.

"Would you mind if I sat here?" Conrad asked Zsa Zsa before taking a seat right next to hers. Pleasantries were exchanged, and then, much to Zsa Zsa's surprise since he had arrived with a date, Conrad asked her if she would like to dance. She accepted the invitation without hesitation.

The two walked out onto the dance floor, and while they swayed in each other's arms, Zsa Zsa was dwarfed by Conrad, whose lean, muscular frame towered over her. She couldn't help but notice something elegant about him. At fifty-four, he seemed much more energetic and vital than any of the younger men in the room.

"They told me that a very pretty woman from Hungary would be here tonight," he whispered to her, according to her memory, "and, by golly! They were sure right." However, she didn't seem like a "Zsa Zsa" to him. "I can't pronounce Hungarian," he joked. In his mind, her name sounded more like "Georgia," and that would be—so he decided right then and there—the name he would call her from that evening forward. (Coincidentally, she had gone by the name of Georgia Gabor as a chorus girl at the Club Femina in Vienna when she was about sixteen.) She smiled coquettishly when he told her as much; she had been learning the role of a soubrette since she was a toddler.

After their dance, the couple spoke about Zsa Zsa's past, how she had just arrived from Hungary, and how much she already disliked Hollywood. The people were too phony, she said. She wasn't fond of the usually sunny weather, and didn't even like the look of the palm trees—too topheavy, she had decided. He laughed at her humor, "like a young boy," she would recall, "throwing his head back and roaring, uninhibited, enjoying himself completely."

There was another dance. Then another. After they finished their third and once again took their seats, the Budapest bombshell gave Conrad a teasing look and said, "I *seenk* I am going to marry you." There was a certainty in her flirting, expertly balancing brazen suggestiveness with a shimmering veil of aloofness. Here was a woman who was dazzlingly different from those whom Conrad had hunted and then discarded so easily. Here was a woman who appeared to be a bit of a huntress herself. For a moment, he was taken aback. "You *seenk* you're going to marry me?" he repeated with a chuckle, mimicking her accent. "All right, then," he decided, "why don't you just do that!"

The night seemed to fly by. Somewhere along the way, his date—the lady Conrad had shown up with—seemed to vanish. He never even inquired as to her whereabouts, so captivated was he by the girl he had just met. As they chatted, he suggested that Zsa Zsa accompany him on a trip he was taking to Key West to visit his brother Carl, who was now stationed there as a Coast Guard officer. But first he planned to stop in El Paso to attend a surprise party for his mother. Zsa Zsa, playing hard to get, said she had plans, but that she might be able to join him at least for the Florida part of the trip. The two promised to stay in touch.

That night, Zsa Zsa rushed back to Eva's small Hollywood apartment and announced, "This is the man I marry." Eva, who was brushing her teeth, stopped long enough to ask, "What man?" Zsa Zsa answered, "Conrad Hilton." Eva asked, "But isn't he too old?" Zsa Zsa smiled. "Oh no," she said. "I find him so beautiful." Eva had to laugh. "First a Turk," she said, "and now a Texan."

Meanwhile, Conrad drove his sleek black Cadillac convertible, with its snappy red leather interior, along the winding Sunset Strip and back to his Bel-Air estate. Upon arriving at his destination, according to what he would later recall, he decided to enjoy a brandy alone on one of the many courtyards before finally retiring for the night. By this time a peaceful hush had settled over the property, with all of its many workers and functionaries now fast asleep. His children were also in bed for the night. The only sounds were the rustling of the cypress trees in the soft breeze. Sitting under a clear Southern California sky studded with stars that sparkled like diamonds, Conrad couldn't help but smile. It had been a night he would never forget.

Loneliness at the Top

On December 7, 1941, three days after Mary Hilton's surprise birthday party, the Japanese attacked Pearl Harbor. With the country in turmoil, Conrad Hilton and his mother would spend the next few weeks in El Paso quietly waiting like the rest of the world to see what would happen next. He would later remember them spending much of his fifty-fifth birthday on December 25 in church, praying for peace.

On the twenty-eighth, Conrad went to New York on a business trip at the behest of Arnold Kirkeby, a good friend who was the founder of the Kirkeby hotel chain. (Many years later, Kirkeby would become known as the owner of the Bel-Air mansion used for exterior shots for the television show *The Beverly Hillbillies*.) "I've got this bug in my ear about the Hotel Pierre," he told Conrad. "What do you think about going into a little joint venture with me on it?"

Ordinarily Conrad would not have been able to resist at least closely examining the possibility of acquiring another hotel, but at this particular time he thought it best to be prudent. With the country at war and the battleground now extending to America's own shores, no one knew quite what to expect. At the least, he suspected that vacation travel would decline as the nation transitioned to a war economy. Conrad agreed to do an inspection of the Fifth Avenue hotel in order to gauge the possibility, but he really didn't take it seriously. Making it big in New York was still a major goal of his, though. All of his success somehow seemed insignificant to him when he thought of the valuable real estate in New York and how much he wanted a piece of that action. However, the time was not yet right, and for Conrad Hilton good timing was everything in business.

On New Year's Eve, Hilton found himself alone in a smoky, bustling Manhattan bar. It was ironic, because back in Los Angeles he was always the perfect host of any party, and he had many at his home, often to celebrate the opening of one of his hotels or some other business-related achievement. At such functions, Conrad could talk to almost anybody about almost anything, from the economy to sports to entertainment; real estate was his forte, though, along with politics and religion. Though he counted as friends many distinguished and important heads of state and government, one of the great paradoxes of his personality was that he was fundamentally quite shy. "I think he had friends for different purposes," said Donald Hubbs. "He'd have a friend to play golf with, a friend to ride horses with, a friend to do various things with, play cards, that sort of thing. But he didn't have a lot of close friends. He was, to a large extent, a private man." And now, on New Year's Eve in New York, Conrad once again found himself dreadfully alone.

As Conrad nursed his dry martini, the clock struck twelve and joyous couples all around him brought in 1942 with shouts of celebration, kisses, and embraces. Never had people been more completely and utterly annoying, he would later recall thinking to himself. "Hey! Happy new year, friend!" someone shouted at him over the din while slapping him on the shoulder. Conrad raised his glass. "Yeah, happy new year, *friend*," he said bitterly.

If anything, the celebration of New Year's Eve 1941 proved to be yet another in a recent string of soul-crushing, depressing moments for Conrad Hilton, and because he was alone in a room full of happy strangers, this one somehow felt even more discouraging than the others. While he had obviously done a lot with his life, all around him it was glaringly obvious that others had somehow done what he hadn't—they'd forged genuine relationships with spouses and partners with whom they were now happily sharing their lives. Maybe none of them had his money, but they seemed to have much more. When he put his life under heavy scrutiny, he didn't like what he saw. If only he had been at home with his sons, perhaps he would have felt better about things.

At about two in the morning, Conrad Hilton shuffled back to his hotel, his head hung low, feeling old, drunk, and unhappy. Sleep eluded him. A few hours later, once the East Coast sun had risen on the morning of January 1, 1942, Conrad picked up the telephone and called the woman he had begun to consider somewhat of a lifeline—Zsa Zsa Gabor in Los Angeles. She was elated to hear from him, even though the call had come at such a early hour. He instantly felt better, the heaviness of his hangover seeming to lift with just the sound of her voice.

"When are you coming back, Connie?" she asked, her English, if possible, somehow even more difficult to understand by long-distance telephone. "I miss you," she said, or at least that's what he thought she said. It sounded more like, "I *meese* you." Then she added, "I can't *vait* to see you."

"Well, Georgia, why don't you come down to Florida?" he asked, alluding to the trip he had mentioned when he first met her. "I'm headed there to visit my brother."

"But I can't afford to do that, Connie," she said. "I don't have the money."

"My dear, of course I will pay for it," he told her. "A round-trip train ticket. Please join me." (Airline travel was in its infancy at this time, seldom used even for cross-country trips.)

There was a pause. "You know, I'm not yet divorced," she told Conrad. He was surprised. This was the first he'd heard that she'd ever been married. "It's not right, Connie," she said. "I don't want you to *seenk* I am that kind of girl."

He had to laugh. Whatever kind of girl she was, he decided, he would see her soon enough. "Fine," he told her. "I understand, Georgia. We shall meet again very soon in this new year."

Upon hanging up, Conrad couldn't help but wonder about her. There weren't many women who would turn down such a generous offer. It did bode well for her, in his estimation. It would, at least thus far, appear that she wasn't just looking for a nice trip to the East Coast on his dime. However, he had to admit that the fact that she was married did bother him. How had it happened that, at her age, she'd already been wed and was on her way to being divorced? He had quite a few questions about her, but he also couldn't get her off his mind.

Soon Conrad would find himself in Florida with his brother Carl. Then it would be back to Los Angeles for business as usual. Only now he was beginning to sense that things could very well change in his life. At the very least, wondering about this new woman, "Georgia," and what she might one day represent made for more than a few moments of contentment as Conrad Hilton watched the scenery race by, his head resting against the window of a train's passenger car.

Buying the Town House

*I*t's a pretty good-looking building," Conrad Hilton was saying. "I think I want it. What do you think?"

"Well, how much is it?" asked his friend and adviser Arthur Foristall, who would go on to become Hilton's public relations strategist. He was a valued member of his board of directors.

"That's what I'm going to find out," Conrad said.

It was a brisk day in January 1942 and Conrad and Arthur were at Conrad's new huge Spanish-style home on Bellagio Road in Beverly Hills. His estate wasn't overwhelming in scope, but was still impressive and rich-looking; it spoke to the success Conrad had recently achieved. The two men were sitting in the study, a place where many memorable moments had already unfolded, whether it was a discussion about an important real estate purchase or a powwow with his sons about a problem in school, or maybe a discussion with them about the importance of prayer and the value of hard work. Whatever it was, if it merited a spirited dialogue, Conrad's study—the true inner sanctum of the home—was always the place for that to happen.

And what a study it was! He had come a long way. It was obvious that a great deal of care had been taken to make this space, a large room with dark wood ceiling beams and highly polished hardwood floors that were partially covered with expensive Moroccan rugs, as comfortable as possible. The centerpiece of the room was a massive stone fireplace and wooden mantel, upon which were carefully placed family photos in gold and silver frames. On an antique wooden table in the middle of the room sat an enormous bowl of fresh fruit. This display was replenished thrice daily; no piece of fruit was ever allowed to sit for more than a few hours. There were also huge bowls of colorful flowers on other occasional tables in the room, lending the premises a scent that wasn't exactly masculine but was clean and fresh just the same. The walls were painted a soft buttery yellow.

Conrad's large desk, made of rare and expensive agarwood, sat against one wall with a bank of three upholstered leather chairs facing it for the purpose of business meetings. However, for more personal moments with family and friends, the seating area in front of the fireplace—a pair of overstuffed sofas and matching chairs, each covered in cream-colored linen, with an antique coffee table and two end tables—was the preferred area of relaxation. The room always had a soft glow to it from period lamps in which Conrad preferred using amber light bulbs for a sense of tranquility, even during the day. Two of the four walls were covered with floor-to-ceiling African blackwood shelving, in which many hundreds of books were organized without their jackets for a uniform appearance. Conrad was a stickler for making certain that his books, many of which were extremely expensive and rare first editions, were stacked in an orderly manner. Only the same size books were to be situated next to each other. For instance, large coffee-table books were not to be placed among smaller ones. Also, everything was to be placed in strict alphabetical order by the author's name. However, true to the paradoxes of his personality, Conrad was not an avid reader. He practically never read books! On some of the tables in the room were stacks of magazines, everything from *Life* to *Time*, *Newsweek*, *Esquire*, and *Paris Match*—which he also wasn't known to read—as well as the latest important publications about real estate and the hotel business, which he did enjoy. There was also a stack of *Weird Tales* comic books, which belonged to Barron.

In the corner of the room sat a small Philco television set, a carved wooden cabinet about three feet tall with a six-inch screen in its center, six control knobs, and one small speaker. This was an unusual luxury for the times; American TV had just debuted in 1939. However, the set in the Hilton study was relatively useless since most stations had gone dark in 1942 because of the war. There was an occasional broadcast, but no one ever seemed to know when it would happen or for how long. One would turn the set on, and if anything but static showed up on the screen, it was considered a nice surprise. "It's just a glorified table with some sort of small window in it," Conrad would joke of the TV set that sat unplugged in the corner, one of just roughly 10,000 in the entire United States.

He had made it to the big time. This estate was really the high life, a far cry from any other place in which Conrad had ever lived, and for that matter, from any place he had ever even imagined living. His mother couldn't quite comprehend how far her son had come in such a short time, and when she would come to visit she would spend hours just walking around the estate in wonderment. His siblings had the same reaction. No one could believe how well Conrad had done for himself, yet somehow it all made perfect sense just based on what was known of his personality, his character, his temperament. He had earned his success, and he, along with everyone else in his life, was happy about it. But he couldn't bask in his victory for long; he was much too busy.

Conrad Hilton picked up the phone and dialed "O" for the operator. "Ma'am, I'd like to make a long-distance call to New York City," he said before giving her the number. He was calling his old friend Arnold Kirkeby in the Big Apple. Ten minutes later, the phone rang; it was the operator. She had completed the call. "So, my friend, how much do you want for the Town House?" Conrad asked when Kirkeby came on the line.

"Well, come up with an amount, Connie," Kirkeby said. "Just don't embarrass yourself or me by making it too low."

Hilton took a deep breath, smiled at Arthur Foristall, and took the plunge with a figure that was less than he expected Kirkeby to accept. "Tell you what," he said, his southwestern drawl more pronounced than ever, as was usually the case when he was trying to be polite, "I can probably give you, say, $750,000."

On the other end, Kirkeby laughed. "You've got to be kidding," he told Conrad. "Nine-fifty. That's what I want for it, $950,000."

"Are you joking?" Conrad asked. "I was just there, Arnie. The place is a ghost town. It's deserted. I think I can maybe bring it back to life, but even I can't perform miracles. So, who knows? If you don't sell to me, who's going to want it?"

That was true, Kirkeby had to admit. The building was all but empty. "Fine, then," he said, now sounding frustrated. "Nine, then. You can have it for $900,000. That's it, though," he warned. "That's my lowest figure."

"Eight," Conrad countered without hesitation. "I think eight is a nicer number, Arnie. I have always liked the number eight. So, let's say eight, shall we?"

"Good God, Connie," Kirkeby exclaimed. "All right, look, eight and a half. That's the best I can do for you. And only for you because we're friends. So take it or leave it, Connie."

"Okay, tell you what. Let me think it over," Conrad said. "Very nice talking to you, Arnie. Say hello to the wife, will you?" After hanging up the phone, Conrad looked at Arthur Foristall and gave him the thumbs-up. "But let's have ol' Arnie sit for a moment and wonder what's going to happen next," he said with a devilish grin. "Why ruin the suspense, right?" He then rose and went to the corner of the room, where he poured two glasses of sherry from a carafe on an end table. He handed one to Arthur. "To the Town House," he said, clinking his friend's glass. "Yes," Arthur agreed. "To the Town House."

The backstory of how Conrad made his most significant Los Angeles purchase to date is an interesting one. During the third week of January 1942—right after Conrad returned to Los Angeles after having visited his mother in Texas and then his brother in Florida—Arnold Kirkeby mentioned to him that he might be interested in selling one of his major holdings, namely the Town House. It was a thirteen-story brick structure of luxury apartments, mixing Mediterranean revival and art deco styles of design at the corner of Wilshire and South Commonwealth in the Westlake district of Los Angeles.

Actually, Conrad had first become aware of the hotel in 1937 when he was invited by the movie actor and astute businessman Leo Carrillo to his estate in Santa Monica Canyon. Built in 1929 by the oil-rich, socially prominent Edward L. Doheny family from architect Norman W. Alpaugh's blueprints, this prestigious property, which faced beautiful Lafayette Park on one side, had, as a result of the Depression, fallen on hard times. Was Conrad interested? Of course he was interested, he told Kirkeby. However, he wanted to do an inspection of the hotel first, which he did when he got back to Los Angeles.

The Town House, a striking structure with stately palm trees on its perimeter, made quite an impression on the tony boulevard with its upscale restaurants and department stores. However, when Conrad went inside and started asking around, he found that it was practically empty— another sign of the times. People were scared. The Japanese had gotten a little too close with their bombing of Pearl Harbor. There was fear that if they'd managed to devastate the country's naval fleet in Hawaii, perhaps the California shores were next. As a result, the economy in Los Angeles had never been weaker. The only bright spot was the burgeoning film industry, which continued apace its full-on film production despite the loss to the war effort of some of its major talent, from directors like Frank Capra, John Ford, John Huston, and William Wellman to stars like Carole Lombard, Jimmy Stewart, Tyrone Power, Clark Gable, Leslie Howard, and Robert Taylor.

Still, to Conrad, ever the optimist, this state of affairs couldn't last forever. Again, he wasn't about to allow a temporary situation to influence what could one day be a profitable idea. He noticed that the area was already beginning to hum with shipbuilding and airplane construction, with workers from around the state and across the country swarming into Southern California like bees to honey to fill the jobs in the defense plants.

When he got back to California from his trip to Florida, Conrad met Arthur Foristall, who was his spokesman but also advised him on business matters. After talking things over, Hilton called Kirkeby to make his offer. Then came the give-and-take that resulted in Kirkeby's counteroffer of $850,000 for the purchase of the property.

"Think he's had enough time to wonder?" Conrad asked Arthur.

"Sure," Arthur said, laughing. "Put the ol' guy out of his misery now, why don't you, Connie?"

Conrad chuckled and picked up the telephone. "Operator, a long-distance call to New York," he said. Finally, Kirkeby was on the line again. "My friend, you have a deal at eight and a half," Conrad said. Then, after a beat, he added, "I'll mail you a check today to bind the deal." He smiled at Arthur and hung up. "Easiest deal I ever made," he said. "You know, maybe I ought to do this more often."

With just two long-distance telephone calls, he had struck another major deal: Conrad Hilton had just purchased the Town House for $850,000. (Most of this amount would be the profit from his recent sale of the Sir Francis Drake, the storied San Francisco landmark.)

"Conrad Hilton was able to use certain events to the benefit of his business," notes Cathleen Baird, former director of the Conrad N. Hilton Archives at the University of Houston. "He realized with the prospect of a possible Japanese invasion—as many people thought—on the West Coast, property value was decreasing, and as a result he was able to negotiate the purchase of the Town House at . . . you could almost say . . . a bargain-basement price."

As soon as the Town House purchase was complete, Conrad would make significant changes to it, as he always did after buying any property. That was the way he made his imprint on a new acquisition, by personalizing it with his own special touch. To the Town House he added a swimming pool with white beach sand and an expansive tennis court, before ultimately transforming it into a hotel from its former status as an apartment building. (Of course, he also paid for the relocation of the few tenants still living there when he bought it.) It was an immediate success. Whereas its gross profit for 1941 had been $33,000, in 1942 under Hilton's ownership the Town House as a luxury hotel took in almost $200,000. From that time onward, it always earned at least a quarter of a million in profit. Hilton liked the property so much, he would establish corporate offices there and also provided certain units to friends to stay in when they were in town. It would become a preferred home base for him, his business associates, and any number of relatives.

Courting Zsa Zsa

*I*t had been about a month since meeting Zsa Zsa Gabor, and Conrad Hilton couldn't seem to get her off his mind. This was quite unusual for him. Women ordinarily did not hold his interest for more than a couple of dates, and if they became intimate, that was usually the kiss of death as far as the relationship was concerned. Afterward, he lost interest. He hadn't yet been intimate with Zsa Zsa, and maybe that's why he was still hooked.

When the Town House was finally his, Conrad drove over to Zsa Zsa Gabor's apartment, picked her up, and took her there. He wanted her to see what he had just acquired, his latest achievement. It was the first time in many years—since his marriage to Mary, in fact—that he would have the satisfaction of sharing with a woman something he was so proud of. Soon the two of them stood in front of the imposing building, she in a fur coat she'd borrowed from her sister, he in a sharp suit with his Stetson hat. In a photograph taken that day, they appear so formally attired, it might as well have been a holiday rather than just an ordinary Wednesday.

"So what do you think of it?" Conrad asked Zsa Zsa as the two gazed up at the structure. "I just bought it," he said in his southwestern drawl.

For a moment, Zsa Zsa seemed speechless. "This is *yours* now?" she managed to say. "This *mah-vellous* building is all yours?"

"That it is," Conrad answered, grinning with pride. If he had hoped to impress her, he had most definitely succeeded.

"What in the world are you going to do with it?" she asked. "Maybe one day you will let me live here?" she asked, batting her eyes at him.

"Perhaps," he said, nodding at her and smiling.

"Maybe we marry one day?" she said, looking hopeful.

"Maybe," he said, gazing at her. She was so intoxicating, he really couldn't get enough of her and the smell of her French soap. She had such a dazzling smile, such a terrific complexion, such perfect cheekbones, and all with a tight little—and bountiful—package that screamed out sex appeal. She represented his chance for real passion in his life, and he knew it. He wasn't going to let it go, either.

Attorney Gregson Bautzer, the friend of Zsa Zsa's who had been with her when she met Conrad, had warned her, "Don't ever mention marriage to him. He's a confirmed bachelor. Mention marriage and you'll never see him again." What Bautzer didn't know is that this enchantress had already mentioned marriage to Hilton, on the night they met, and that he had pursued her anyway, and now seemed interested in a future with her.

As if making up for lost time in his life, Conrad had begun sending roses to Zsa Zsa every day, followed by regular telephone calls every morning, making it his first duty of the day, much to the chagrin of Eva Gabor, Zsa Zsa's apartment mate, who as a working actress complained that she needed her sleep. (The two sisters slept in a double bed together in the small, cramped apartment.) Conrad not only took Zsa Zsa to daily lunches but to dinners almost every night. The two would then go out dancing after their meal, hitting all of the hot spots on Sunset Boulevard. He had never been out as many nights during the week at this time in his life as he'd been with Zsa Zsa, and instead of wishing he were home in bed resting for the next day's work, he was actually enjoying himself. (Again, poor Eva Gabor felt differently, with Zsa Zsa interrupting her much-required beauty sleep by coming home so late at night. Inevitably, Zsa Zsa and Conrad would make out in his white Caddy on the street outside Eva's apartment, with the lanky Hilton accidentally leaning on the car horn, thereby sending a loud blast of sound throughout the neighborhood. "Oh my God! That clumsy man!" Eva would exclaim. "I can't sleep at night and I can't sleep in the morning. Marry him, or I die!")

Zsa Zsa enjoyed every moment she spent with Conrad, lavishing him with praise, boosting his ego by her attention, and doing everything she could think of to be a perfect companion for him. Was she really just after his money? Of course she was. "How could I separate him from his money?" she would ask years later. "Would I have been interested in a man twice my age if he wasn't rich? I don't think so. Not at that time in my life, anyway. I was young and impressionable and new to Hollywood."

Many decades and many marriages later, Zsa Zsa Gabor would be described as "the most successful courtesan of the twentieth century."

Conrad suspected that his great wealth had at least *something* to do with her fascination. He knew that she wasn't just some innocent little waif. Even at her young age, she'd had her share of experiences with men of power and affluence. For instance, as a teenager prior to her arrival in the States, he learned, she'd even been romantically involved with Mustafa Kemal Ataturk, the first president of Turkey. Married to someone else and now on her way to divorce, she wasn't exactly inexperienced. "I want a man who is kind and understanding," she would one day say. "Is that too much to ask of a millionaire?" Conrad was just too swept off his feet by Zsa Zsa to really care whether or not she was just after his money, though. All he wanted at this point in time was Zsa Zsa Gabor, and any notion that she might not be right for him—or that she might have financial motives—he did not take seriously at all.

A few months after meeting her, Conrad decided to introduce Zsa Zsa to his eighty-one-year-old mother, Mary, who still lived in El Paso. It suggests just how important Zsa Zsa had become to him that he would want his mother to know her. He needed to go to Mexico in order to approve alterations being made to the new Palacio Hilton, an enterprise he would lease and operate in Chihuahua as per a deal he had closed the previous November. (The hotel was set to open in April.) Therefore he decided to stop first in Texas with Zsa Zsa.

Since childhood, the Gabors had been schooled on various kinds of seduction, and Zsa Zsa used her charm to weave a bit of a spell on Mary Hilton. A great storyteller even in her youth, Zsa Zsa told Mary many tales about her own mother, Jolie, and how much she missed her. She also talked about her family's many struggles in Budapest. Adolf Hitler's Nazi storm troopers had begun their onslaught for world domination in the mid-1930s, and it was feared by the Jewish Gabors that they would be among those targeted for concentration camps. Thus far, the war had not affected Hungary, and the Gabors were still doing quite well in their many enterprises, including jewelry and dress shops. They had a good life in Budapest, but it was limited, and as Zsa Zsa explained, that's why Jolie encouraged her and Eva to go to America. She missed her family desperately, Zsa Zsa said, and wrote letters to them on a daily basis. It was clear that she loved them very much.

Zsa Zsa also explained that her sister Magda was presently working in the anti-Nazi underground in disguise as a Red Cross worker, helping Polish prisoners of war make their way to Egypt to join General Bernard Montgomery's Eighth Army. She was deathly afraid that Magda would be discovered and killed, and she said the thought of it haunted her every waking hour. Such emotional stories, and Zsa Zsa's heartfelt telling of them, tugged at Mary Hilton's heartstrings. Soon she would be referring to Zsa Zsa affectionately as "that dear girl."

"In turn, Mary shared with Zsa Zsa stories of the Hilton family's early struggling days and their own humble beginnings, their first businesses, the gambles they had taken and the way those risks ultimately paid off for them," recalled one Hilton family member.

On the whole, Mary Hilton approved of Zsa Zsa Gabor. However, she warned Conrad that if he intended to take Zsa Zsa as his wife, he should reconsider. "And you know why," Mary Hilton told her son. "You will never be able to marry this girl," she told him. "So get that thought right out of your head, Connie. Get it right out of your head!"

Catholic Stumbling Block

The church will not let me marry Zsa Zsa," Conrad Hilton was saying, "and I'm not sure what to do about it." The hotel mogul had called an urgent meeting in the study of his Bel-Air mansion to discuss what was turning out to be a major stumbling block in his relationship with Zsa Zsa Gabor. Nicky, nineteen, was present for this confab, as were several business associates and a priest, Father Lorenzo Malone, who was also a trusted friend of Conrad's and a fellow golf enthusiast. According to the later recollection of one of those present at the meeting, Conrad seemed nervous and uneasy, and with good reason.

There were a couple of major concerns on the table. First of all, Zsa Zsa Gabor was not Catholic, or at least that's how it appeared to most people at the time. "I accept the teachings of the Catholic Church," she said, "and then I ignore them and do what I want." Hopefully, she was joking. Actually, she said that her mother was Jewish but that her father had converted to Catholicism. However, she couldn't prove it, and frankly, no one knew whether to believe her or not; the declaration seemed to come out of the blue one day during a discussion with Conrad about her religious background. It was at about this time that Conrad came to the realization that he couldn't necessarily rely on Zsa Zsa to be truthful. His gut now told him she was fibbing about a vitally important issue, her religion. In time, he would find that honesty meant little to her; a good story meant everything.

Actually, the question of Gabor's faith was not an insurmountable problem. Even though the Catholic Church at the time did not encourage so-called mixed marriages, such unions were still possible if performed by a priest not in the church but in the rectory, and also if the non-Catholic party agreed to raise all children as Catholics. A much bigger problem for Conrad in marrying Zsa Zsa was that the Catholic Church did not recognize the divorce from his first wife, Mary Barron. Therefore, as far as the church was concerned, he was still married to Mary. Any subsequent marriage would not be acknowledged by the church.

For Conrad, this stringent Catholic doctrine presented a major moral and spiritual dilemma. If he wanted to take Zsa Zsa as a wife, he would have to be married in a civil ceremony that would not be sanctioned by the church. He would then have to live with the consequences, which would include his not being able to partake in the Catholic Church's sacraments such as Holy Communion and Reconciliation (better known as Confession). Hilton was devout in his faith; would he be able to live with the idea of being so ostracized by the church? No. It was inconceivable. Therefore, to try to come to terms with the problem at hand, Conrad had called this meeting at his home.

"So, what do you gentlemen think of this?" he asked

"I think you have no choice in the matter," Father Malone offered. "You can't go against the church, Connie."

"I admit that I'm just not used to being told no," Conrad admitted. "But that's not it entirely. This is just an exploratory meeting anyway," he added, framing it almost as he would a business deal.

"Well, I suppose a canonical dispensation might be possible," offered Father Malone.

Conrad raised his eyebrows. "Is such a thing even possible?" he asked.

No one in the meeting knew for certain, but they quickly decided it was as good an idea as anyone could come up with under the circumstances.

"I don't know," the priest concluded. "It seems far-fetched, but maybe worth a try."

"Would you try?" Conrad asked the priest. "All I ask is that you at least see what can be done."

Father Malone said he would try.

Conrad Breaks the News to Zsa Zsa

The granting of a canonical dispensation simply so that a person who would otherwise not be entitled to do so could marry in the Catholic Church was almost never granted in those days. After Vatican II convened in the 1960s, such dispensations became more commonplace. But in the 1940s, it was practically unheard of. However, when Conrad met with certain officials of the church in Los Angeles, he was led to believe that his charitable contributions to the church might be so appreciated that there would possibly be a way to work around the red tape involved in a dispensation. Certainly, he had given huge sums of money to the church, and in 1940 he had donated more than $50,000 to Catholic charities—a staggering amount for the time. Therefore, Hilton left his meeting with the church officials hopeful that something could be worked out that would allow him to marry in the Catholic Church. He was elated. He knew there had to be some way around this matter. There was always a way, always an alternative—at least that had been his experience in life.

But then a week later Conrad received a telephone call from a friend of his, Father Kelly, telling him that there was not enough time to file the necessary paperwork if he wanted to marry in April, as he had said he did. Moreover, upon closer investigation, even if he delayed the wedding, it was unlikely that a dispensation would be possible.

The next morning, Conrad and Zsa Zsa took a walk through one of the lush gardens of his estate, just one of many that were filled with an abundance of vivid flowers planted in herbaceous borders. It was a sunny day with a bright blue sky that was lightly scattered with white clouds. "My dear, there's something I must tell you," he began.

"What is so wrong?" Zsa Zsa asked. Catching the tension in his voice, she knew it was bad news.

"It saddens me to say it," Conrad told her in a faltering tone, "but this is as far as we will be able to go in our relationship."

"What do you mean?"

"I can't marry you," Conrad explained. "It simply isn't possible." As she listened, Conrad detailed for her the laws of the Catholic Church relating to mixed marriages and, more specifically, explained that as long as his first wife, Mary, was alive, he was still married to her in the eyes of the church; their divorce was not sanctioned.

"But is there nothing that can be done?" Zsa Zsa asked. As she spoke, according to her memory, she bent over to admire a batch of colorful flowers rather than allow Conrad to see the tears of disappointment that had sprung to her eyes.

"No," he said firmly. "I'm sorry, Georgia. We can't get married."

The silence between them deepened. "Then I must go," she finally decided, never once looking at him directly.

"Please, let me show you the way," he offered.

"That won't be necessary," she responded. "I know the way." With that, she rushed off.

Once Zsa Zsa left his home, Conrad made up his mind that he would never see her again. Now, with her out of his life for good, he was engulfed by conflicting emotions. He couldn't help but be glad the matter had finally been settled, and in some ways he felt about it as he might have a hotel deal that couldn't be consummated. He was ready to move on to the next big deal. He had actually caught her in a number of small lies since her sudden revelation that her father had converted to Catholicism. For instance, he had become fairly certain that she'd lied about her age, saying she was eighteen when she was twenty-four. Later, she would say she was just sixteen when she met Conrad. It's safe to say that he would never know her true age. Still, women were known to lie about their ages all the time, he reasoned, and perhaps this was not a big deal. But Conrad had a strong moral compass. He liked to say that he *never* lied. Of course, that likely was not the case, but he did at least strive for honesty.

Was he in love with her? It had been so many years, to hear him tell it, that Conrad wasn't even sure he remembered what love felt like. However, he was fifty-five, and with this latest loss in his life, he began to sense his mortality like never before. For him, the big question was: Did he really want to be alone for the rest of his life? And if not, what were the chances he would ever find someone like Zsa Zsa Gabor again?

PART TWO

Mary

The First Mrs. Hilton

*I*t had been almost twenty years since Conrad Hilton felt about a woman the way he felt for Zsa Zsa Gabor. That he had an eye for the ladies as a young man, there is ample evidence. He had enthusiastically embraced the Santa Fe social whirl of balls, cotillions, and debutante parties when he was a young legislator, and was a much sought-after dancing partner for some of the city's most beautiful young women.

When Conrad was posted in Paris during the First World War, a safe distance from the front lines as a first lieutenant in the Army Supply Corps, he was a popular, striking figure in his bespoke uniform, with lovely young ladies in tow along the Champs-Elysées' bistros and boîtes, a boulevardier in the tradition of the great Maurice Chevalier. A devout Catholic, however, Hilton seemed to wear his religion on his sleeve, leading many to wonder if that was not the reason he'd managed to avoid a trip to the altar. It was almost as if he had decided that the ladies he sought were more suited to the ballroom than the bedroom. To many of his friends and associates, it seemed that he used the church as a shield against romantic commitment.

Fittingly, it was at church in Dallas that he first spied the woman who would soon end his days as a bachelor. Seated down front in the crowded sanctuary, she was conspicuous by the dark crimson hat she was wearing. Following the service, he lost her in the crush of people despite attempts to follow the red chapeau down the street, hoping the woman wearing it would lead him to her home. As he wrote in his autobiography, "There was something about the way she wore the hat, the way she carried her head that was attractive."

Having lost sight of the distinctive hat and its owner, Hilton wrote, "For a month of Sundays I amazed that congregation with my piety. I attended every mass from six 'til noon. But I didn't see her again." Then, while wrestling with the growing problems of trying to raise funds to build the Dallas Hilton, he was taking a stroll one day to clear his head when he encountered her, wearing a different hat and accompanied by an acquaintance of his, Mrs. Beauregard Evans, who made the introductions. "This is Mary Adelaide Barron," she said, "a relative of ours from Owensboro, Kentucky."

At the time, Mary Adelaide Barron—born in Kentucky on April 27, 1906—was a stern, serious-looking woman with strong bone structure and a robust frame. Her long, chestnut-colored hair was usually parted in the middle and pulled primly into a bun, just like the style worn by Conrad's mother—a woman whose name she also shared. She bore a distinct resemblance to Mary Hilton. At just eighteen, about half Conrad's age, she wasn't exactly eye-catching, but the camera didn't capture her full personality and charm. In reality Mary was a handsome young woman with expressive blue eyes, a small nose, thin lips, and a bright smile. Hilton recalled, "For a while everything took a back seat to the girl with the laughing eyes and soft Kentucky voice." Still, hers was a different background than Hilton's.

Mary was educated at Owensboro High School, though some family members have said that she didn't graduate. Her family (six brothers and two parents) was poor and moved about a great deal from one ramshackle farmhouse to another. Her father, Thomas Barron, raised tobacco and pigs for a meager living. Seeming undaunted by her lot in life, however, Mary Barron had an ebullient personality, often using salty language as she enjoyed her life to the fullest with many good friends.

"Conrad saw Mary as the kind of fun girl who could add levity to his dry lifestyle, which was all about high finance and complex business dealings," said Stanley Tucker, whose mother was a good friend of Mary's, having grown up with her in Owensboro. Tucker would become a close friend of Conrad's as well.

Before Mary left Dallas, she promised that when the hotel was complete she would return and marry Conrad. (As a sentimental gesture, she also gave him her red hat.) Once she was back, Hilton began to see his financial problems, which had once seemed insurmountable, begin to resolve themselves one by one. Breathing more easily now, he took off for Atlanta, where Mary Barron was visiting. After ten days, their pact to marry was sealed, and he returned to Dallas for the August 4, 1925, grand opening of the first hotel he had ever built from scratch, the Dallas Hilton. The hotel was a smash hit from day one. Forty-five days later, on October 19, Conrad Nicholson Hilton, thirty-eight, and Mary Adelaide Barron, nineteen, were married simply at a six o'clock mass at Holy Trinity Church in Dallas.

After the ceremony and bridal breakfast, Conrad took his new wife on a sightseeing tour of America, from Texas to Colorado, then on to California, where he introduced Mary to San Francisco, "whose elegant beauty had captured my imagination as a young army officer." Then they were off to Canada and down to Illinois, next stop Chicago, "for I wanted Mary to see another kind of American city, a swarming, hustling, commercial city that could also stir the imagination." At the LaSalle Hotel in Chicago, the Hiltons found a long line of frustrated tourists and businessmen attempting to check in to the popular and clearly overbooked establishment. Conrad, hoping to impress his new bride, whipped out a business card from his wallet and handed it to a bellboy. Before he knew it, he and his wife found themselves in a luxury room on a top floor with a stunning panoramic view of the city. Being Conrad N. Hilton, president of Hilton Hotels, had its advantages.

Upon returning to Texas, the newlyweds moved into one of Dallas's finest residences, the ultra-chic, eleven-story Beaux-Arts apartment-hotel the Stoneleigh Court. Some nine months later, they would become a family with the birth on July 6, 1926, of a son, Conrad Nicholson "Nicky" Hilton Jr. "If I listened to my wife, little Nick was something special," he would recall. "Actually I kind of thought so myself. He was not unduly red, had big eyes, curly hair and was quite a howler."

"Connie was so proud to have a boy," recalled Jarrod Barron, a cousin of Mary's who also became a close friend of Conrad's. "He wanted a son so badly. Nicky was his pride and joy from the beginning. Seeing him with that baby was something I will never forget. Mary used to say, 'God help me if I would have had a girl. I don't know how Connie would have reacted!'"

With the prospect of further increasing the family and a need for more room, the Hiltons bought a lovely four-bedroom home in the exclusive Dallas suburban residential community of Highland Park. Fifteen months after the birth of Nicky, they welcomed, on October 27, 1927, another son, William Barron Hilton, increasing the family to four. "Double trouble was what Connie called them," said Jarred Barron. "When Barron was born, he was over the moon with happiness. It was a good time, for sure."

Business Affairs

$\mathcal{F}$atherhood in no way impeded Conrad Hilton's ambitious quest to become America's foremost innkeeper. Before the end of the 1920s, he was well ahead of his goal of acquiring at least one hotel a year. "Besides Dallas, Abilene, and Waco," he recalled, "I had added Marlin (eight stories, one hundred rooms, costing $400,000), Plainview (eight stories, one hundred rooms, costing $400,000), San Angelo (fourteen stories, 40 rooms, costing $900,000), and Lubbock (twelve stories, two hundred rooms, costing $800,000)." Meanwhile, a family tragedy struck when Conrad's younger brother "Boy" (Gus Jr.) was struck down with tuberculous meningitis. His death rocked the family, and Conrad, of course, took it badly, saying he had lost his best friend. He did his best to support his siblings—and especially his grieving mother—through the loss and distracted himself with his work. Through it all, Mary proved herself a devoted mother, capably caring for their sons and pursuing her wifely duties, pressing Conrad's suits and baking his favorite dishes, such as tuna casserole. However, by the fall of 1929, storm clouds began to gather. It would seem that the stock market crash and the Great Depression signaled the end not only of Hilton's fortunes, as earlier noted, but also his marriage.

These were tough times, to be sure, and Conrad would be forced to take desperate measures in order to keep the wolves from the door. To that end, he began spending a great deal of time away from home, often in late-night meetings with board members, reviewing financial records and trying to come up with imaginative ways to remain solvent. At one point, matters became so dire that he considered borrowing against his life insurance policy. "Of course, you must do it," Mary advised him. "This bad spell will not last forever," she said, echoing his own philosophy. "And when it's over, you will come out on the other side bigger and better than ever." It was good to know, he thought, that he and his wife were in such accord, that she still had so much faith in him. Therefore, he borrowed against the policy and used the money to stay afloat, going from hotel to hotel and doing what he could in terms of cutting corners, leaving Mary at home with the children. It says a lot, though, that as happy as

Mary was that he took her advice, she was unhappy when he didn't show up one night soon after to be a fourth for bridge. Little things meant a lot to her, and his absence was just further evidence to her that he had other things on his mind.

Soon the money he had borrowed on the insurance policy ran out and Hilton was right back where he had started from, trying desperately to save his empire. Every day was an uphill climb. It wore him down. "Don't you dare give up," his mother, Mary, told him. "Some men jump out windows, some quit, some go to church. Some pray. Pray, Connie. Harder."

Meanwhile, as things continued to go from bad to worse, Conrad's wife became more and more restless. By this time, Mary had slimmed down and had adopted a more glamorous appearance, her hair now blonde and stylishly coiffed. She was worlds more sophisticated than the eighteen-year-old girl in the red hat who had first caught Conrad's eye. With the passing of just four years, she had become a striking woman, and she longed to be appreciated for it. Certainly, preparing Conrad's favorite meals and ironing his suits for business meetings were tasks that had lost their charm for Mary Hilton. Moreover, she now claimed that Conrad was distant and inattentive. She was right. For some reason, Conrad couldn't seem to connect to her on a deep, emotional level. While he was perfectly pleasant and respectful toward her, it was as if a wall existed between them. The truth, though, was that he was content with the relationship as it was, and addressing its limitations was not a priority for him. He felt that he and Mary shared enough happy moments to keep the marriage going, and for him the union had evolved into an amicable family partnership designed as a vehicle for the raising of children. He was comfortable with Mary, more at ease with her than he had ever been with any other woman.

Conrad first noticed that something was troubling Mary when he opened the El Paso hotel in November 1930. It had been a grand opening night, his sister Rosemary and her husband having traveled from New York for the occasion, as had his sister Eva from Boston. His mother was also present. That Conrad was able to open a hotel during such tough times was nothing short of a miracle, and would not have happened if not for some creative financing. So there was reason to celebrate. Everyone seemed to be having a well-deserved good time; everyone, that is, but

Mary. She appeared to be bored with the festivities and uninterested in knowing the people who worked with and for Conrad.

Judging from Mary's dissatisfied demeanor that evening, she seemed to have had her fill of the hotel business. At one point, she gathered her wrap and left the banquet room in a hurry, heading to their upstairs suite. It was then that Conrad's sister Rosemary approached Conrad and asked him if he thought that Mary was possibly bored with the hotel business. Actually, the idea had never even crossed his mind. Still, Rosemary cautioned Conrad to make sure Mary did not feel neglected, especially given her youth.

Though Conrad took his sister's comments under advisement, he really didn't know what to make of them. He felt he was giving Mary enough of his time, said he was even buying her dresses from stores during his travels just to show that he was thinking of her in his absence. He gave her different kinds of gifts, he said. His sister told him that it was likely Mary didn't care much about the presents he was offering her, and would much rather have her husband at her side than on the road, traveling, or at the office.

Making matters even more complex, though Conrad had just opened a new hotel, he couldn't afford his own home. It was probably bad planning, but in his defense he was doing the best he could under challenging circumstances. Therefore, he moved his family from their plush digs in Highland Park to a suite in the new El Paso Hilton. His mother, Mary, and his sister Helen—who had recently left her husband—were now living there as well, ordering a single sixty-cent meal and splitting it in two. (Mary didn't complain about it either, saying that in her view people ate too much anyway.) His wife, Mary, wasn't happy about any of it, though, stuck with two young boys—Conrad Jr. and Barron—in a hotel while her husband was at work. If he had the money to afford to buy this hotel, she couldn't help but wonder why he didn't have the money to put a roof over their heads. Moreover, how in the world had he been able to send his mother on that world cruise? None of it made sense to her, and as far as she was concerned, it suggested that Conrad was more devoted to the solvency of his hotel empire and the well-being of his mother than he was to her and to the security of their family. After they moved into the hotel, she made her views clear to Conrad; she was angry at him and worn down by the daily grind and struggle. "Like the Depression itself, what happened to Mary and me didn't come all at once," he would recall. "Little by little, the laughter went out of Mary's eyes."

"Many years later, Eric told me that because his father was gone all the time working, his mother was left feeling miserable and alone," said Patricia Skipworth Hilton, Eric's first wife. "It was an unfortunate situation that just kept getting worse."

Somehow, it seemed inevitable that infidelity might creep into the marriage. It was at a local charity event that Mary met the handsome Mack Saxon, a famous Texas football coach and onetime University of Texas team captain and all-conference quarterback. Tall, strapping, and good-looking, with dark wavy hair, deep-set brown eyes, and a winning smile, he must have been difficult to resist. Because nothing had changed in her marriage, Mary was drawn to Saxon. He listened to her problems, was present for meals, and even seemed to take an interest in her young sons. But perhaps more important to her, he appreciated her as a woman. "She knew it was wrong, she knew it would be devastating to Conrad if he were to find out about it," recalled one relative of Mary's. "However, she justified the relationship with Mack by telling herself that she was tired of being neglected, that she deserved more than what she was getting as Conrad's wife. So, yes, she strayed," confirmed the source. "She wasn't proud of it. But she did it."

"Mary would come to El Paso with Mack, and everybody knew something was going on between them, though we didn't know what," said Ken Heinemann, a player on Saxon's team. "Mack was a good-looking guy, attractive to women, who also had a little reputation as a drinker; we all knew that he caroused. Anyone who saw him with Mary knew it was trouble."

"Conrad and Mary tried to keep things going," recalled Stanley Tucker, whose father knew Conrad at that time. "Connie wasn't a quitter. He tried, and in all fairness to her, so did Mary. Then, much to everyone's amazement, Mary ended up pregnant in October 1932."

Nine months later, little Eric was born. However, in Conrad Hilton's diary he seems oddly indifferent toward the event. "Mary expecting a baby," he noted simply, conspicuously leaving himself out of the picture. He is just as unsentimental in his entry of July 1, 1933: "Eric Michael Hilton born at St. Paul's at ten a.m."* Then, immediately thereafter: "Must

---

* It's worth noting that this is the only mention of Eric Hilton by name in Conrad Hilton's 1957 autobiography, *Be My Guest*.

get something solid to show Greenwood. I know I can straighten that hotel out if I can only get a chance." Then, on September 5: "No time to stop off and see Mary or the baby. Called everyone I could think of as a substitute banker. My time's running out."

Though the idea of a divorce was anathema to the tenets of his beloved Catholic Church, Conrad Hilton had to wonder if he had any choice in the matter, considering the state of his marriage. While he wondered which course of action to take, Mary had already made up her mind: She no longer wanted to be with Conrad, she wanted to be with Mack. That said, Conrad actually seemed able to adjust to the new status quo. After he got used to the idea, he did what he had done when the attraction between him and Mary diminished: He adapted and made the best of the situation. He threw himself into his work. It actually wasn't so bad. At least now he could just focus on being a good businessman, at long last free of the guilt he'd felt about not being a good husband. The children seemed to like Mack Saxon, but they also knew who their real father was, so Conrad was satisfied with that as well. In a way most people might not have been able to fathom, the situation actually started to make some sense to Conrad. After all, he was accustomed to making the best of challenging situations. It was how he ran his business. Mary, however, had had enough. She announced that if Conrad didn't file for divorce, she would have to do it.

"Now, that was going a little too far," said Stanley Tucker. "His pride wouldn't have allowed it. Therefore, if they were to move forward with their lives, it would, unfortunately, have to be up to him. So Conrad filed for divorce." For his marriage to end in divorce proved a torturous proposition for a man who, by his own admission, started every single day on his knees in church. He would make no mention of the possibility of Mary's indiscretion anywhere in his memoir, choosing instead to keep his and her dignity intact, perhaps if for no other reason than for the sake of the three children who bore the Hilton name.

The divorce decree was granted on June 11, 1934—eleven months after Eric was born—thereby ending Connie and Mary's nine-year marriage. Mary waived her right to appear at the divorce hearing, being represented only by counsel. It was ruled that Conrad, who was present at the hearing, would have custody of all three children—Nicky was about to turn eight; Barron was seven—an arrangement that was considered quite unorthodox for the times. Judge Royall B. Watkins ruled that Conrad was "able and capable of caring for and educating the minor children and he is a proper person to have the care, maintenance, and control of said children." Mary would have only practical visitation rights, based on "all reasonable times and places that may be agreeable to Conrad Hilton."

The financial settlement with Mary Hilton seems paltry, even by 1930s standards. While she received household goods and furniture, the actual home in which she and Conrad had lived was granted to Conrad. Though he was worth well over a million dollars even if most of it wasn't liquid at the time, he would give his ex-wife alimony in the total amount of thirty-six hundred dollars, in payments of three hundred dollars per month.

It would seem, at least from all available evidence, that Mary didn't feel she had much choice but to accept the stringent terms of her divorce and subsequent child custody agreement. Of Conrad's first marriage, his second wife, Zsa Zsa Gabor, would, in years to come, testify under oath, "Mr. Hilton described his separation and divorce from his first wife, Mary Barron, as quite bitter and unpleasant. He stated that she had not done right by him, but he had used the lawyers and the courts to get what he wanted in the divorce. He stated, in substance, that if anyone crossed him, he knew how to get even." She also said that Conrad "bragged about his power and control with courts and stated that he could use them to obtain what he wanted or make them do what he wanted." Of course, as we will come to learn, Zsa Zsa, herself, would have her own tumultuous relationship with Conrad; her words should be judged accordingly.

Mary Hilton and Mack Saxon were married a year after her divorce from Conrad Hilton, on June 1, 1935 in Fort Worth, Texas. It was at that time that Conrad made the somewhat perplexing decision to surrender Eric to the couple. Conrad told relatives he felt it not fair to the child, who was two at the time, to try to raise him on his own, especially given his work schedule.

Considering that he obviously had the money to be able to afford plenty of help, some observers were confused by Conrad's decision to turn Eric over to Mary and Mack. But whereas he would in years to come have suspicions about the paternity of a daughter born to Zsa Zsa, there's no legal work, such as any codicils to his many wills, or other indication that would suggest that Conrad ever had similar questions about Eric. Whatever the reasons for his decisions where Eric was concerned, one thing is certain: At least during his early years, Eric Hilton lived separately from his father and siblings.

For his part, Conrad Hilton was never quite the same after the divorce from Mary. Going forward, he would always find it difficult to commit to and trust any woman. From most accounts, his relationships with women from this time onward would always be somewhat muted. He would lose interest quickly rather than take the time to develop a true emotional attachment. He would end it with her before she had a chance to end it with him. He did date on occasion, but nothing ever came of it. One of his relatives recalled of Conrad, "He was a proud man whose ego had been crushed by the dissolution of his marriage. Whatever it is that makes a man give his all to a woman—I mean, really and truly surrender everything to her and trust her with his heart—that was no longer there for Conrad."

He wanted that to change, though. He recognized the distinct void, and he wanted to fill it. Indeed, when the fascinating creature that was Zsa Zsa Gabor waltzed into his humdrum life, he felt something stir in him for the first time in many years, a kind excitement and anticipation that felt good, so good that he wanted to go with it, bask in it, explore it. It had been a long time since he was so interested in any woman. He didn't know what it meant. He just knew he didn't want to let it go.

PART THREE

Zsa Zsa

Conrad's Inner Turmoil

*I*n April 1942, after telling Zsa Zsa Gabor that they could not marry because of his religious convictions, Conrad Hilton spent the next three days sequestered in his palatial Bel-Air estate. He didn't want to see anyone, nor did he wish to talk to anyone on the telephone. He canceled all of his business appointments. As far as he was concerned, business could wait, which was rare. Confused, unhappy, and depressed, once he realized that he couldn't have Zsa Zsa as his wife, he wanted her more than ever. In a way, it made sense, considering his character and personality. If someone were to have told him that he couldn't purchase a luxury hotel in which he was emotionally invested, he would become all the more determined to make that property his own. It was just the way he trafficked in the world. Maybe he was spoiled, maybe he had a sense of entitlement, or maybe he was just a determined person. People thought a lot of things about him, none of which were opinions that mattered much to him. He had always lived his life on his own terms. However, he was now being prevented from doing just that, and by his own beloved religion. At an emotional crossroads, Conrad did what he usually did in times of great despair—he got down on his knees in his bedroom and he prayed.

Throughout his lifetime, Conrad had often stated that his "secret weapon" in business was his close spiritual relationship to his God. He had made each of his major hotel purchases only after a great deal of prayerful deliberation. He fervently believed he would be guided in the right direction if he simply asked for such guidance. "It's not enough to just pray," he once observed. "You have to be able to listen. Call it intuition or call it gut instinct. Call it what you will, but I recognize that little voice we all have in our heads as being the answer to our prayers. You have to be willing to listen, and then make decisions based on what that voice is telling you. A major problem, as I see it anyway," he continued, "is that many of us have not worked to cultivate that certain inner voice. We make snap decisions. We don't pray. Many of us don't even think. We just react to situations at hand. I have found that this isn't the way."

"A man knows his prayers have been answered if when he gets up off his knees he feels refreshed," Conrad liked to say. After praying about the dilemma regarding Zsa Zsa, he did find that he felt much better. His inner voice told him to follow his heart, that he deserved to be happy and that a way would somehow be made for him and Zsa Zsa to be together. "I'm going to marry Georgia and trust that God will find a way," he finally decided. His mind was made up; he wanted to be with her, and nothing— not even his religion—would stop him.

Had Conrad talked himself into believing he would be happy with Zsa Zsa, even if he were ostracized from the church that was so important to him? If so, was this a measure of just how powerful his feelings were for her? Or was it really just indicative of how powerful his feelings were about wanting that which he had been denied? Only he would know which—if either—of these scenarios was true. As often happens when a man is swept away by passion, he would have to admit in years to come that he really wasn't thinking straight. He was only sure of one thing: He wanted to pick up with Zsa Zsa Gabor where he had left off with her. "Georgia, I can't live without you," he said when he called her to tell her he had changed his mind. "*Sanks* God," she exclaimed. "I can't live without you either, Connie." And with those words, they were a couple once again.

At the end of March 1942, while the two were at the Mocambo nightclub in Hollywood with Zsa Zsa's sister Eva and a friend of theirs from Budapest, Andrew "Bundy" Solt, Conrad presented Zsa Zsa with two small jewelry boxes, a diamond ring in each. She was stunned and delighted. "I still wanted to sprinkle stars in a lovely lady's lap," he would later explain in his memoir, Be My Guest, of Zsa Zsa and of this "incurably romantic" time in his life, "and I must confess I had never met anyone so willing or qualified to receive them."

In one box, Zsa Zsa found a large gleaming diamond, the kind that would impress even the most seasoned collector of fine jewelry. It was breathtaking. In the other there was a smaller, much more conservative-looking diamond ring, not exactly eye-popping, but respectable just the same. As Zsa Zsa would later recall it, she wanted the larger diamond ring—of course! However, she knew that there were people in Conrad's life who were certain that she was only after him for his money. She and Eva exchanged quick, anxious looks. Of course, she knew which ring Eva would pick. But Zsa Zsa decided to take the opportunity to prove to

Conrad that she wasn't materialistic, and she sensed that her selection in this moment might suggest as much to his friends as well. The truth, though, was that Conrad wasn't exactly generous with his money when it came to her anyway. True, he bought her a few trinkets now and then, but he never went hog wild when it came to spending money on her. "I think, though, that this will change when I marry him," she told Eva. "Surely a man like that loves to spend money! And I love to spend money. So, we should be a match. Don't you think?" Eva wasn't so sure. "Zsa Zsa," she said, "a man most wants to impress a woman when he is courting her. If he isn't spending money on you when he hopes to impress you, when will he ever?"

In the end, Zsa Zsa picked the ring with the smaller diamond. "It nearly killed me," she would confess many years later, "because God knows I wanted the bigger ring." Conrad was pleased. "I *knew* you would pick that one," he told her.

"Does this mean you changed your mind about marriage?" Zsa Zsa asked hopefully.

He smiled at her. "Yes. We will marry in two weeks, my dear," he said.

It wasn't a proposal as much as it was a declaration. However, Zsa Zsa was thrilled with it just the same, and eagerly agreed to it. She said in a telegram to her mother that she was going to marry "a hotel manager. I *will* make a good life for myself now," she declared. Eva still wasn't convinced. When Zsa Zsa broke the news to her, she tried to be happy for her, but she wasn't able to do so. "I know what you want, dear sister," she said, according to her later memory, "and you will not find it with this man. Why? Because this is a cheap man," she said. "Just because he has money this does not make him want to spend it on a woman. I am telling you, Conrad Hilton is not the man for you."

Zsa Zsa was willing to take a chance that her sister was wrong. Shortly thereafter, on April 10, 1942, she and Conrad were married at the Santa Fe Hotel in New Mexico. Despite any reservations she had about the union, Eva stood up for her sister at the ceremony. Lawyers Gregson Bautzer and G. Bentley Ryan, friends of Conrad's who were there when the couple first met, were both present.

Zsa Zsa was twenty-five; Conrad was fifty-five. They had known each other for less than four months.

For Love or Money

On the same day he and Zsa Zsa were wed, Conrad Hilton finally closed the deal to buy the Town House in Los Angeles. "I made a package deal," he said, maybe only half joking about his double acquisitions. "I landed Zsa Zsa and the new hotel all on the same day!"

Also around this time, in 1942, the lease on the Dallas Hilton had expired and Conrad decided not to renew it. It was difficult for him to let the Dallas property go, however, because he had so many good memories attached to the city. After all, it was the first hotel built from scratch to bear his name. But it wasn't turning the kind of profit he wanted and there was little room for sentiment in business, at least as far as he was concerned.

There was good news in Chicago, though. The day after the wedding ceremony, Conrad took Zsa Zsa to the Windy City, where he was about to close a deal to purchase the opulent Blackstone Hotel, which stood across Michigan Avenue from the Stevens Hotel. After the two admired the Blackstone, Conrad took Zsa Zsa across the street to the Stevens.

A towering Beaux-Arts brick structure overlooking Lake Michigan, the Stevens had been opened in 1927 at a cost of $30 million (more than it had cost to build Yankee Stadium) by James W. Stevens. It was then operated by Stevens, his son Ernest, and other members of the Stevens family. At three thousand guest rooms and an equal number of baths, it was the largest hotel in the world, complete with its own hospital and operating room, movie theater, ice cream parlor, restaurants, pharmacy, beauty parlors, dry cleaners, bowling alley, miniature golf course (on the roof), and banquet facilities that could accommodate eight thousand guests at a time. As a result of the Depression, the hotel went bankrupt and the property ended up going into the receivership of the government. Conrad wanted nothing more than to own the hotel himself, but that wasn't possible at the time, not with the government's intention to sell the hotel to the United States Army Air Corps for $6 million later in 1942. The building would be converted into living quarters and instructional rooms for military training during World War II, with more than 10,000 cadets in residence.

The hotel—the actual premises—now belonged to the Army, but the Stevens Corporation itself, its assets and its liabilities, was still up for grabs.

It would be a solid investment for anyone smart enough to take it on, because when the war was over, the government was sure to let go of the hotel. Whoever owned the corporation would likely be first in line to buy the hotel itself. Of course, Hilton, with his gut intuition telling him that the war would soon end, wanted nothing more than the corporation behind the Stevens.

The trustees of the corporation asked for blind, or sealed, bids, meaning that any interested party would have to make his offer without any knowledge of the others being made. Conrad came in at $165,000. However, his intuition told him that was a lowball bid; he couldn't seem to shake that feeling. After thinking about it, praying over it, and listening to his gut, he submitted a new bid of $180,000. As fate would have it, he would end up being the highest bidder. Therefore, the corporation was his. However, any profit Conrad might make on a reinvigorated Stevens Hotel was still just a pipe dream. For now, he just owned a corporation that was in a lot of trouble—taxes were owed, bills left unpaid. He would do what he could do to keep it afloat until the Army was finished with the hotel, and then he knew it would be his.

As Conrad and Zsa Zsa stood on Michigan Avenue looking up at the enormous Stevens Hotel, a cold wind came in from the lake, causing Conrad's eyes to water. He looked at his new wife and, according to her memory, said, "I'm going to own that soon. Georgia, you watch. Before I'm finished, it's going to be mine."

That night, Conrad and Zsa Zsa had a wonderfully romantic evening of dining and dancing in Chicago. Later, they made love for the first time. Zsa Zsa would recall Hilton as being "strong, virile and possessive." Finally, she was his. After all the angst, the heartache, and deliberation, they had each other. It should have been a triumphant moment. For her it was; she was elated. She later wrote to her mother and told her that she was sure to be taken care of now. She had married a wealthy man, she said, and there was no way she would ever go without, "not as long as I am Mrs. Conrad Hilton." She wrote that she loved him very much and was happy to have found someone who could love her in return, "and also provide for me in the way that you have always wanted for me." So she had gotten what she wanted and was satisfied. To a certain extent, of course, Conrad was happy too, but to say that he was overjoyed would have been an overstatement. He was distracted, not present during this night in Chicago.

As they lay in bed, Zsa Zsa whispered that she hoped they would be together for the rest of their lives, or at least that is her memory. "That blonde secretary of yours," she said as she caressed his arm. "I don't like her, Connie. I think she's jealous of me. Would you fire her for me? I'm sure we could find you a better secretary."

He was preoccupied and not really listening. "Yes, dear," he said. "Of course."

Zsa Zsa recalled, "In the silence, in the darkness, I whispered softly, 'Conrad, what are you thinking?' And I waited dreamily to hear him murmur, 'Oh, my darling, I love you. I love you.'"

But instead, Conrad was quiet, just staring up at the ceiling, lost in thought with a small smile on his face. Zsa Zsa couldn't quite read his facial expression; it baffled her.

"What are you thinking, *dah-ling*?," she asked.

Conrad turned to his new bride and, at last breaking his silence, confessed, "By golly, Georgia! I'm thinking about that Stevens deal."

The Roosevelt

*I*n the spring of 1943, Zsa Zsa Gabor woke up one morning to find that Conrad Hilton was nowhere to be found. Though she searched from room to room, he was clearly gone. "Where is Mr. Hilton?" Zsa Zsa finally asked Wilson, Conrad's majordomo. "Oh, he went to New York, ma'am," Wilson answered. "But he didn't even tell me he was leaving," Zsa Zsa said, seeming crushed. The majordomo just shrugged. Zsa Zsa would later say that this was the first of many such occurrences—Conrad leaving town without so much as a goodbye. "Nothing hurt me more," she would later admit. "I began to see clearly that he truly didn't care about me as much as he did about his business."

Not that it was a good excuse to treat his wife so dismissively, but Hilton did have some rather important business in Manhattan.

Back in the mid-1920s, Conrad had launched an ambitious campaign to acquire, build, and/or upgrade hotels in Texas, his adopted state. This included properties in Dallas, Waco, Abilene, Lubbock, San Angelo,

Plainview, Marlin, and El Paso. At that time, the country's economy was booming, which he viewed as favorable for further expansion beyond the Lone Star State. By organizing Hilton Hotels, Inc. in 1932, he consolidated his properties into one group. As his acquisitions increased in number, he kept itching to move into the big time, with an eye toward the urban Northeast, specifically New York City. Now he had his eye on the Roosevelt Hotel in Manhattan.

By the time Conrad Hilton set his sights on the Roosevelt—named for President Teddy Roosevelt—it had been in business for nineteen years and had become a destination point for out-of-towners and notable figures from the worlds of society, politics, and show business. Located at 45 East 45th Street, it covered a city block along busy Madison Avenue. In speaking of the Roosevelt, Hilton referred to it as "this great hotel adjacent to Grand Central Station, half luxury, half commercial—a socialite, so to speak, with a working husband." In his mind there was nothing more beautiful than a towering hotel with a roster of satisfied guests.

Unfortunately, the hotel business in New York City was not booming in 1943, a consequence of the war and the Great Depression. But that situation was temporary. In the meantime, if there was any way to put together the capital to purchase hotel properties, Conrad's gut told him to follow through and buy. One by one, with each acquisition, it became easier to put together the equity necessary for the next one.

When Hilton acquired the 1,012-room Roosevelt Hotel in the spring of 1943 and announced the purchase to a close friend and business associate, his friend, J. B. Herndon, was only able to muster one word: "Why?"

"Because it's a fine hotel. And because I've got to practice," responded Hilton.

"What for?" Herndon wanted to know.

"For the Waldorf," said Hilton. "I'm not quite ready for that one yet."

Long before the term "multitasking" became part of our lexicon, it epitomized Hilton's octopus-like juggling act, keeping several projects going at the same time. While immersed in the demanding responsibility of putting together the financing he needed to complete the Roosevelt transaction, he was also frantically continuing to buy stock in the Waldorf-Astoria, of which Wall Street took note when word got out about the killing he would make on that stock. He'd bought the stock at 4½ and sold it at 85. It was more like a massacre than a killing.

If Mr. Herndon had his doubts about the wisdom of Conrad Hilton's ownership of the Roosevelt, they were nothing compared to the shock sustained by the faithful habitués of the hotel. About this, Hilton once recalled, "It was scarcely flattering to have everyone assume that I would ride my horse into the lobby or install spittoons in the famous Roosevelt Grill, yet on every hand, I received communications in various forms begging me to deal gently with my newest lady."

While naysayers chuckled about "that jasper from Texas," as it turned out, Conrad Hilton would have the last laugh. Under his guidance, the Roosevelt would be credited with an impressive list of firsts, changing forever the way hotels of the future would be operated: the first with baths in every room, the first to be air-conditioned, the first to incorporate storefronts instead of lounges (put in place to circumvent the law of Prohibition), and the first to install television sets in every room. He even chose the hotel's Presidential Suite as his home base when in New York City, a sign of the high regard he had for the Roosevelt.

When the deal was finally signed, Conrad called Los Angeles to talk to Zsa Zsa. It had been a week since they last spoke, not even a phone call since the day she woke up and found him gone. When she was cold and distant on the telephone, he didn't understand her attitude. In his mind, he hadn't done anything wrong. "You must realize that I have business to take care of and that I will sometimes have to leave to take care of it," he told her. All she was asking, she said, was for him to at least inform her in advance when he was leaving town. Was that too much to ask? It was difficult for Conrad to understand Zsa Zsa's concern. When he was married to Mary, he said, he would leave at a moment's notice and she didn't seem to mind. "But I am not Mary," Zsa Zsa reminded him. "Don't treat me as you would her."

Marriage: His

The first order of business for Conrad Hilton after Zsa Zsa Gabor moved into his huge Spanish-style estate on Bellagio Road in Beverly Hills was to establish certain ground rules for their new life together.

First on the agenda was Conrad's declaration that he and Zsa Zsa would sleep in separate bedrooms. Of the four large bedroom suites in the home, Conrad and Zsa Zsa would have one each. Nicky and Barron shared another, and the fourth was for guests.

Some people in his life found it perplexing that Conrad had spent so much time lamenting that Zsa Zsa couldn't be his wife, yet the first thing he did when he finally married her was to install her in a bedroom down the hall. Zsa Zsa was deeply disappointed by this arrangement; she wanted to sleep in the same bed with her husband. To her, it seemed only logical. Though he knew she felt the sting of rejection, Conrad wouldn't budge on the matter, explaining that he valued his privacy. He had been alone for so many years, he enjoyed his own routine and didn't want it interrupted. Besides, he was admittedly bothered by nearly everything done by women in the name of beauty. He didn't want his wife moisturizing her skin, doing her nails, or applying makeup in his presence. He found such rituals tedious and self-involved, and believed that a husband's bearing witness to such personal maintenance only served to detract from his wife's sex appeal. In the end, Zsa Zsa had no choice but to acquiesce to his wishes. "Conrad wasn't the type to share a room with a woman," she would later observe.

As a small consolation, Conrad gave Zsa Zsa license to redecorate her own enormous bedroom suite with its stunning view of the golf course in any way she saw fit. In that regard she went wild with expensive fabrics and pieces of furniture she later said were inspired by *Gone with the Wind*. Once she finished with her own suite, she eagerly began working on other rooms in the house. The only room she didn't have plans to totally redecorate was Conrad's, and that was because she was banned from entering it. It was inevitable, then, that the money she was spending on new furnishings would lead to a serious conversation about the household budget.

Conrad fully understood that Zsa Zsa enjoyed spending money, and he certainly had a lot of it to spend. The question for him wasn't whether or not he could afford to subsidize her extravagant taste, it was whether or not it made sense to him. He quickly realized that Zsa Zsa didn't understand the value of money, or at least his interpretation of the value of money. He had worked hard for his wealth and continued to work for it. What did she do to earn a living? Nothing, really. Sometimes Zsa Zsa spoke of wanting to be an actress, but she didn't seem to have much drive or ambition in that direction.

"Being Mrs. Conrad Hilton, *this* is my career and *sanks* God for it," she told her friend Andrew Solt. "I meant it, too," she would later recall. "I was satisfied to be the wife of an important man who was growing more important every day, to help him in his career, to run his home graciously, and to take my place in the society in which he lived."

To be fair, Conrad didn't expect her to do much else. He was perfectly satisfied if she just wanted to be a socialite, especially since she clearly wasn't going to be taking a motherly role with Nicky and Barron. However, he was only going to finance so much of her time in high society, and after he took a look at the books and realized how much she was spending, he pulled the plug on her redecorating efforts.

"But, Connie! I'm not done yet," she complained. "Oh, yes, my dear, you are," he told her.

The question of finances would always be at issue in Conrad's relationships with others, especially with family members. To him, it was a simple, black-and-white matter. He had earned his money fair and square, and he wasn't giving it away to anyone, even to family members. Some would say that he was incredibly cheap. In his own mind, however, that wasn't the case. Privately (never publicly, for he was too modest to do so), as proof of his generous nature he would offer up the names of the many charities to which he regularly donated. Would a cheap man be so philanthropic? He had few limits when it came to giving money to charities, especially to Catholic aid organizations. However, when it came to family members, as well as friends, he believed that they—all of them—should demonstrate a work ethic similar to his own, earn their own way, and not expect to benefit from his own station in life. Moreover, he felt it wasn't even *fair* to them to give them money. His financing of their lives would, he felt, be detrimental to them in the long run, eroding any motivation they might have to achieve wealth on their own, and also diminish their appreciation for the value of the dollar.

Fueling his philosophy about money, no doubt, was that Conrad had survived the Great Depression; he knew what it was like to lose everything and work hard to get it all back. Many of his generation would throughout their lifetimes place a premium on the American dollar.

Where Zsa Zsa Gabor was concerned, the discussion of domestic finances was one that would be resolved quickly, and not in her favor.

"There's too much trouble caused by women being foolish with money," Conrad told Zsa Zsa, according to his own memory (which, as well as a parsimonious view, suggests a rather chauvinistic one that perhaps was also not unusual for the times). "We're not going to have that trouble," he told her one night over dinner. She was seated at one end of the table, he at the other, with yards of space between them. A team of servants headed up by Wilson the butler dished out their food, expeditiously removing their empty plates as soon as they finished with each course.

"I don't understand," Zsa Zsa said. "What are you saying to me?"

"Georgia, I'm putting you on a budget," he told her. "From now on, you will receive a check from me at the beginning of each month for $250. You can spend it on clothes, hair, makeup, luncheons, tips, whatever you like."

She nodded.

"Meanwhile, you can charge any household items—furnishings, linens, food—to my store accounts."

She nodded again.

"But if you go over the allotted amount in personal expenses," he warned her, "that amount will then be deducted from the following month's allowance. I'll teach you sound business practices if it's the last thing I do," he said, his tone such as it might have been had he been lecturing a teenager. (To put this into a proper perspective, perhaps it should be noted that this amount would be equivalent to about $3,000 a month today, which seems not unreasonable for such extra expenses.)

"I am not a child, Conrad," Zsa Zsa said, now annoyed. "I am not your *daughter*. I am your *wife*."

Ironically, at this same time his teenage sons were often in negotiation with their father over just such matters. For instance, Barron had just given his father a handwritten letter detailing his own expenses and explaining why he needed more than a two-dollar-a-week allowance, or what he in his letter called "a raise in salary." He was spending seventy-five cents a week on milk and pie at recess, he noted. He was also spending fifty cents a week on telephone calls, and already that week he was twenty cents in the hole (which, in an arrangement like the one Conrad had with Zsa Zsa, would have to be deducted from next week's "salary"). He also explained that he was spending eighty-two cents a week on transportation. He detailed certain other expenses and came to the conclusion that he needed a three-dollar-a-week raise, to five dollars. His father, moved by his son's logic, gave him a raise of four dollars a week instead, which tripled the boy's allowance.

For Conrad, keeping his wife on a strict budget would not be as easy as keeping his teenage son on one. Or as he put it, "I tried to instill sound business principles into my beautiful Circe, but I might as well have practiced on a statue in the park."

For instance, one day Conrad noticed a charge for six chiffon housecoats. He became upset and confronted Zsa Zsa about the purchase. "Yes, I bought the housecoats," she admitted with wide-eyed innocence. "But they are for the *house*! And you said that *household* expenses could be charged to your account!" Even he had to laugh at that logic. When she tried to extend it to being able to buy presents on his account for "household friends"—namely, friends who visited the household—he wasn't sure what to think. "Glamour, I found, is expensive," he later recalled, "and Zsa Zsa was glamour raised to the last degree."

Humorous moments aside, Conrad would not be very lenient when it came to Zsa Zsa's budget. If she spent even five or ten dollars on something personal and charged it to his account, he would quickly deduct that amount from her next month's budget. She complained that it was impossible for her to keep up with the spending habits of the wives of Conrad's peers with whom she was social, and said that she found humiliating the fact that she was always pinching pennies while they seemed to have an unlimited supply of spending money. He told her she would just have to make the proper adjustments.

Another issue that was raised for Conrad was what he viewed as Zsa Zsa's inherent self-involvement. He was a man who lived his life trying to find ways to be of service, and through many philanthropic efforts fueled by his businesses, he sought to contribute to society. Whether it be the simple goodwill measure of speaking about prayer to a large assemblage, as he often did, or whether it had to do with making sure people in foreign countries were able to support their families by virtue of their jobs with his hotels, he truly cared about his fellow man; it wasn't an act. Therefore, it unnerved him that he was married to someone who, at least as he saw it, didn't really care much about others. As far as he could see, she cared only about herself.

No matter how many times Conrad tried to talk to Zsa Zsa about doing something for others—he even asked her to go to a homeless shelter and see what it might be like to feed the poor—there was no changing her. She knew little about world events except as they might affect her family in Hungary. She didn't have many real concerns other than disagreeing with the budget her husband had set forth for her. She liked to shop, and try as Conrad might to find something else that interested her, he couldn't seem to do it. Plus, she could be quite temperamental.

"It was a little like holding on to a Roman candle," Conrad would say of his marriage, "beautiful, exciting, but you were never quite sure when it would go off. And it is surprisingly hard to live the Fourth of July every day." He had indulged in his infatuation for her and misread that fleeting emotion for a deep and abiding love—likely because of his lack of experience in such matters. Compounding things, she said she wouldn't be intimate with him until they were married. If anything, that decision of hers kept him hooked. He must have known that it was a bit of a manipulation; he was a smart man, and she wasn't exactly an innocent little flower. Still, he fell for it. Now he couldn't believe the predicament in which he found himself. When he took stock of all he had given up to be with her—namely his religion—he couldn't reconcile his own naïveté.

Marriage: Hers

*C*onrad Hilton may have regretted his decision to marry, but to a certain extent, the same could be said of Zsa Zsa Gabor. According to her memory, within weeks of the wedding any physical intimacy between them suddenly came to an end. Once, according to what she would many years later tell her stepdaughter-in-law Trish Hilton (who would be Nicky's second wife), Zsa Zsa was feeling lonely and decided to try to entice her husband into a romantic interlude. "I screwed all of my courage together," she told Trish, "and went into his bedroom wearing a sexy black negligee. I was challenging him, wondering, 'Can I stop him from praying? Will he find me too sexy to resist?' I was Vivien Leigh teasing Clark Gable. When I walked in, he was on his knees, praying. 'No, no, no!' he said to me. 'Go to your own room and wait for me.' Can you imagine how that made me feel?" Zsa Zsa asked. "After that, he would always lock his bedroom door so that I could not walk in unannounced."

"That sounds true to me," confirmed Trish Hilton, who would go on to become a very good friend of Zsa Zsa's. "I think that by that time, Connie was really finished with the marriage. Zsa Zsa would not easily accept it. She had every right to try to entice him to change his mind."

It wouldn't be easy. Even when she thought he was being nice to her, it came with a twist. One morning, they were eating breakfast, Conrad in his royal-looking red velvet robe. ("I thought, this is a high priest sitting opposite me eating soft-boiled eggs," she would recall. "I could have been his handmaiden, not his wife.") He looked up at her and announced, "Georgia, I think the time has come to buy you a car." She lit up. This was good news! She and Conrad had seen a few automobiles in showrooms over the past couple of months, and she had suspected—hoped—that he was considering buying her one.

"Oh, that copper Cadillac we saw in the showroom the other day," Zsa Zsa said brightly. "How I would love that one." She said she thought it would go nicely with her hair, which for her was reason enough to want it.

Conrad frowned. Unbeknownst to her, just a day earlier when he mentioned to golfing buddies that he was thinking of buying his wife a car, one cynic predicted, "The little woman will want a Cadillac. I'm *sure* of it." The implication, of course, was that Zsa Zsa would ask for the most expensive car. Now that scenario seemed to be the case. Because many of his affluent friends were convinced that Zsa Zsa was a gold digger, Conrad had actually become quite sensitive to the idea. Simply put, he didn't want to look like an old fool in the eyes of his pals. "Well, I think a secondhand car would be best for you," he told Zsa Zsa. "Yes, that's what we shall do."

Her spirits dropped. "If that's what you think is best…," she said unenthusiastically.

In the end, Mrs. Hilton would wind up with Gregson Bautzer's used blue Chrysler, which she hated. To her it seemed unfair; after all, Conrad had *two* brand-new Cadillacs. Back in Hungary, Zsa Zsa and her sisters had been accustomed to being pampered by their mother. It would seem, however, that there wasn't to be a great deal of that going on in her life in America, at least not while she was married to Conrad Hilton.

Zsa Zsa couldn't help but take it personally. In her mind, if Conrad loved her, he would want her to be happy, and what made her happy was being able to spend money on extravagances. That's how she was raised, and even though she was still young she was too old to change. She didn't *want* to change. Why *shouldn't* she expect her husband to lavish her with presents? In her mind, money should be no object to Conrad Hilton; he could well afford anything her heart desired. His denying her only made her feel that he didn't really care about her.

Zsa Zsa tried to keep to her own business as best she could. "I threw myself into the job of becoming one hundred percent American," is how she put it. That meant taking English language lessons (trying to learn how not to pronounce her w's as v's—a practice she would never master). "I *vorked* on that forever," she explained. She also took golf lessons, tennis lessons, and horseback riding lessons, anything to stay busy. Also, she had grown attached to the Hilton estate, especially to the parties. They were always so entertaining, so aristocratic-seeming. For one party, Conrad hired a small orchestra to play a series of eighteenth-century Italian minuets while everyone, dressed very formally, danced with grace about the parlor. "Who in America does this sort of thing?" Zsa Zsa asked. "It's so sophisticated and lovely." She also enjoyed the estate's outdoors. It was stunning with its majestic palm trees and perfectly manicured walkways bursting with colorful flowerbeds at every turn. She had fallen in love with these glorious surroundings the first moment she set foot on the property.

When Eva Gabor announced that she was marrying her second husband, Charles Isaacs, an American investment broker, Zsa Zsa asked Conrad if she could host the wedding at their home on September 27, 1943. He agreed, but he asked her not to spend a fortune on the ceremony and reception. The two sat down and planned a budget. Of course, there was no way Zsa Zsa could resist giving her sister a wedding that was fit for a royal. Conrad was unhappy about the money being spent, so much so that he decided not to stay for the wedding.

Eventually Zsa Zsa found ways to get around the strict budget Conrad had imposed on her, at least where her own wardrobe was concerned. Resourcefully, she approached the world's most renowned designers and negotiated deals with them that allowed her to borrow their gowns for special occasions. As a result, she would manage to remain a shimmering fixture at parties and events. Many people didn't realize that many of Mrs. Conrad Hilton's most striking gowns were merely on loan. Designers in Los Angeles and New York were delighted to have one of their creations adorn the stunning Zsa Zsa. They well knew that she would be extensively photographed, and as a result the gown would be seen all over the country. Some designers even gave her the garment outright. Thus the legend of the ultra-glamorous Zsa Zsa Gabor continued to blossom. If Gabor established this custom, and it seems she did, today's red-carpet habitués have her to thank for it: Rarely do Emmy-, Oscar-, Grammy-, or Golden Globe–nominated females pay for the costly couture gowns they wear at these events.

"People think I have no right to be unhappy," Zsa Zsa later told her sister Eva. Eva would recall that the two of them were eating lunch in the spacious dining room with its burgundy brocade draperies covering leaded windows and its matching oversized furniture that could best be described as royal. The rectangular table in this room was massive enough to seat twenty-six people, twelve on each side and one at each end. Zsa Zsa and Eva must have seemed quite miniscule huddled together at one of its corners while picking at green salads brought to them by Inger, Zsa Zsa's personal maid. "But I *am* unhappy," Zsa Zsa said, lighting a Kool cigarette and then handing the pack to her sister. "I guess I am used to more attention," she said. "What kind of a man gives to the poor, but not to his wife?" she asked.

"The kind of man you should not have married," Eva said, driving the point home once again.

"There *is* no other man like this one," Zsa Zsa concluded with a sigh. "He has only one passion in his life. Hilton hotels."

A Frustrating Business Deal

*C*onrad Hilton had other things on his mind in 1943, matters that did not involve his wife's discontentment but rather problems having to do with the Stevens Hotel. Though it didn't happen often, there were times

when his finely tuned instincts for business let him down, and the story of
the Stevens exemplifies as much.

After the Army was finished with the Stevens, the place was left in a
total shambles. It had been used to house Army Air Corps personnel, not
as a high-class hotel but as a glorified barracks of sorts. Now, abandoned
by the government and back on the market, it hardly looked like a show-
place. The government had used its grand ballroom as a mess hall, so
one can only imagine the state in which Conrad found it when he did an
inspection of the property. He was sick about it, actually. This once grand
lady was now, in his mind, an old and ruined dowager, and there didn't
seem much that could be done for her. Though Conrad was first in line
to purchase it just by virtue of his ownership in the Stevens Corporation,
he decided against making a bid. It wasn't an easy decision. He had been
obsessed with the property for so long, it was difficult to let it go. The fact
that it was the biggest hotel in the world also came to bear for him—what
a coup it would be if it were his. However, his gut now told him that it was
no longer a sound investment.

But then, much to Conrad's great consternation, another businessman, Steve A. Healy—a bricklayer now suddenly turned entrepreneur—
swooped in and made the purchase himself. Though Conrad hadn't
wanted the Stevens, now that someone else had it his competitive nature
sprang forth and he wanted it too—more than ever. That Healy had no
hotel experience whatsoever somehow just made matters worse for Conrad. It was an enormous blow to his ego that someone inexperienced in
the business saw value in the Stevens when he hadn't, and had so quickly
acted upon it. However, since Healy was so green, perhaps the enterprise
would fail, or at least that was what Conrad hoped, and he would then
have another opportunity to buy it. That didn't happen, though. Quite
the contrary occurred: Healy somehow managed to restore the Stevens
to its former glory, and, thanks to his creativity and imagination—not to
mention the millions he would sink into renovations—it became a thriving hotel once again.

Still, Conrad couldn't let the Stevens go. Against his better judgment,
he made several bids to purchase the hotel from Steve Healy, thereby
tipping his hand that he truly wanted it, and in the process making Healy
even more determined to keep it for himself. Conrad couldn't rest easy

knowing that he had made a serious error in judgment where the Stevens was concerned, and that he had then compounded the damage by making so many appeals to Healy.

Because of his preoccupation with these negotiations, at least as Zsa Zsa saw it, Conrad had completely lost interest in her. He was depressed every day and couldn't hide it from anyone, and certainly did not attempt to hide it from her. He wanted to rise above such pettiness—so what if he hadn't gotten what he wanted? Must he always get exactly what he wanted when he wanted it? Unfortunately, when he asked this question of himself, the answer that always came back was a resounding and unequivocal "yes." He put everything he had into his business ventures and felt just as much unhappiness when things didn't work out as he felt happiness when they did. It was just the way he was wired, and there was nothing he could do about it.

The Plaza

One of those who had been most impressed with Conrad Hilton's Midas touch over the years was L. Boyd Hatch, the executive vice president of the Atlas Corporation, an investment trust headed by Floyd Odlum, often remembered as "the only man who made a great fortune out of the Depression." In 1943, Hatch approached Hilton to see if he was interested in joining Atlas in the purchase of the Plaza Hotel. Atlas had pockets as deep as the Grand Canyon, but knew virtually nothing about the hotel business. As Hilton recalls in his autobiography, "It would be ridiculous to say that such subtle tribute to my talents left me unmoved after my initial welcome to the hotel business in New York." He goes on to explain the proposition offered him: "[It] was that they take 40 percent of the Plaza deal [and] I take 60 percent and assume the responsibility of management. It suited me fine."

Atlas's interest in Conrad as an ally was a vindication of sorts for Hilton in the sense that back when he purchased the Roosevelt there had been a great deal of derisive press having to do with the consensus of some cynics that Hilton was in way over his head. He was a country boy, charged the skeptics. He had no business investing in hotels, especially given the country's topsy-turvy economy. Others felt that he was capable of owning and operating hotels in other parts of the country, but in New York City? No. He wasn't cosmopolitan enough to understand the nuances of high-society Manhattan, they claimed. Besides, what if he were to cheapen the austere surroundings of the classic New York hotels with his country-boy poor taste in décor? Though the suggestions were all quite insulting, Conrad took them in stride. He did nothing to substantially change the look of the Roosevelt or the way it operated, other than to finally make it turn a profit by guaranteeing terrific service and watching the books closely in order to cut back on excessive spending. Apparently he had proven himself with the Roosevelt, and now, with the help of the Atlas Corporation, he was on his way to owning one of the true crown jewels of the hotel business—the Plaza.

In October 1943, Hilton and the Atlas Corporation (along with a hefty first mortgage by the Metropolitan Life Insurance Company) bought the magnificent Plaza Hotel, a twenty-story Manhattan landmark, facing Central Park South (59th Street extended to the west) on the north and Fifth Avenue on the east. The price: $7.4 million (the equivalent of almost $100 million today). Hilton would plow another $6 million into upgrades. The luxury hotel, of French château style, was built in 1907 from the blueprints of architect Henry Janeway Hardenbergh, at a cost, according to Hilton, of $17 million (other sources place the figure at closer to $12.5 million).

The resistance and resentment that Hilton endured with the strollers and seat-takers in the lobby of the Roosevelt was nothing compared to the all-out war the dwellers of the Plaza seemed prepared to wage when they got wind of his ownership. Here Hilton was faced with a clientele that was much more conservative and more bound up in tradition. They were convinced that any connection Conrad Hilton had with their beloved but decaying hotel might signal the end of their world. And it was quite a world.

For generations, the likes of the Astors, the Vanderbilts, and the Goulds had made the Plaza the center of their business, political, and social activities and their residence of choice. It was a weekend destination for Young Turks from the Ivy League and a safe haven for well-heeled eccentrics and socially prominent denizens, who paid as much as $27,500 a year for their apartments (an exorbitant price for apartment rental in 1943). They were blind to the dilapidated condition of the hotel, with its peeling paint, its unattended woodwork, its tarnished metalwork, its grimy carpeting, its dull, sandblasted, pockmarked marble, its faded, dirty tapestries, and its out-of-commission plumbing and electricity. Every time Hilton tried to go about the business of refurbishing the old girl, however, petitions would be raised by its permanent tenants in an effort to stop the interloper from doing any work on the hotel.

Whereas Conrad had not let criticism of him and his roots bother him in the case of the Roosevelt, when it came to the Plaza he seemed particularly sensitive. One business associate recalled a meeting about the Plaza renovations at Conrad's Bel-Air home. Present were two of the family's attorneys and two representatives of Atlas. Recalled the business associate, "My memory of it is that Conrad was upset, and uncharacteristically so because he usually didn't get so worked up, at least not unless he found himself on the losing end of something."

"Why, I oughta just let the hotel just fall apart at their knees," he said of the Plaza residents who were unhappy with any alterations. "Because that's what's going to happen to it if we don't do something. The place is a wreck."

"Who cares what anyone thinks?" asked one of the Atlas representatives, according to one recollection of the meeting. "It doesn't make a bit of difference to me."

"Well, it does to me," Conrad said, raising his voice. "Public relations is important. I can't have those New Yorkers spreading the word that Conrad Hilton is a country hick who doesn't know what he's doing. It affects business. We need to remodel that place, but I don't know how to sneak any renovations by them. Perhaps . . . at night?"

It wasn't a bad idea. Of course, it would be next to impossible to do much of the renovations after the sun went down, simply because of the noise generated by such serious remodeling. However, as it would happen, a great deal of the makeovers (especially the polishing of old marble and the replacement of curtains and other fabrics) *could* be done in the middle of the night. Somehow, not having to constantly look at the workers as

they did their jobs did seem to ease tensions among tenants in the building. Throughout the entire process, remodeling the Plaza would prove to
be a delicate dance, one that would require tact, patience...and a great
deal of money. It also required a man in charge; after Hilton ponied up $6
million, he charged his longtime associate J. B. Herndon with effecting
the renovations.

Commanding Herndon's attention immediately were the lobby and
the Oak Room, which had been occupied by a broker paying $100 a week.
He was promptly relegated to the mezzanine and his office was turned
back into "that most mellow and inviting of New York bars." The lobby's
early décor was retained, its museum-quality brass lamps casting a glow,
bringing a shine to the floor and a gleam to the marble and woodwork.
In the basement below, the cobwebbed storage space became the Rendezvous Room. Turned from trash into treasure, it would come to gross
$200,000 a year, as would the Oak Room. Mindful that these changes
being made in restoring the Plaza to its former glory were giving the old
residents pause, Hilton kept the lobby's elevator doors within clear vision.
As the residents emerged and saw what was taking place, Hilton studied
the faces carefully. Soon he noticed that people stopped complaining,
and when all was said and done they began to come to him to tell him
how pleased they were with what he'd accomplished.

Now that the Oak Room, with its high Gothic arched ceilings, elaborate wooden crests, and square columns, was polished and scrubbed to its
original luster, its custom of years gone by was reinstituted: that it only be
open to men until the closing bell of the stock market sounded. Women
were welcome, but only after Wall Street had shut down for the day.
Famed architect Frank Lloyd Wright, a regular patron, was so impressed
by the stunning new look that he pronounced it "the finest single hotel
room in America." When Atlas and Hilton took over the Plaza, it had
61 percent occupancy. After its makeover, the historic edifice was almost
always filled to capacity. It was just another in a string of successes for Hilton, somehow making the disappointment of the Stevens just a little—
though not entirely—easier to take.

Conrad Hilton: a true, rags-to-riches, American success story. Here he poses with the monolithic Stevens Hotel in Chicago which, after he bought it, he renamed—what else?—the Conrad Hilton. (*Gamma-Rapho via Getty Images*)

Zsa Zsa Gabor upon her arrival from Europe in 1941. At the time, she was married to Burhan Belge, press director for the Foreign Ministry of Turkey in Ankara. By the end of that year, however, she would find romance in America with Conrad Hilton. (*Bettmann/Corbis/ AP Images*)

Conrad simply had to have Zsa Zsa, so much so that he married her without the sanctioning of the Catholic Church. He was fifty-five and she was twenty-five when they wed in April of 1942, having known each other less than four months. (*Globe Photos*)

Though Conrad and Zsa Zsa are seen in happier times here, their divorce in 1946 was difficult. Shortly after, Zsa Zsa would give birth to a daughter, Constance Francesca. It was because of Francesca that Conrad would accept Zsa Zsa in his world for the rest of his life. (*Globe Photos*)

William Barron Hilton was the first of Conrad's sons to marry, at the age of twenty, to Marilyn June Hawley. Here they are (far right) on March 19, 1958, embarking from Burbank Airport for a celebration for the new Habana Hilton Hotel. On the left is Conrad Hilton and Dorothy Johnson, a pioneer of nursing at UCLA. (*AP Photo*)

In October of 1949, Conrad purchased what most people considered the biggest and grandest of all hotels, the Waldorf-Astoria in New York City. It was most certainly the crown jewel of Hilton's international hotel collection. *(Photo by Martha Holmes//Time Life Pictures/Getty Images)*

Nicky Hilton—Conrad Jr.—believed he had found the love of his life in actress Elizabeth Taylor when he met her in September of 1949. He was twenty-three, she was seventeen. *(Photo by Murray Garrett / Getty Images)*

It wasn't long before Nicky decided to marry Elizabeth, despite overwhelming evidence that she wasn't ready for marriage. Here, the couple poses on Mother's Day in 1950 with Nicky's mom, Mary (Conrad's first wife, left) and Elizabeth's mother, Sara (right.) *(AP Photo)*

Best Man Barron (left) adjusts Nicky's boutonniere on his wedding day, May 6, 1950. (*AP Photo/HF*)

Nicky and Elizabeth leave the church after their wedding in Los Angeles. (*Everett Collection/Rex Features*)

Sisters-in-laws Elizabeth Taylor Hilton and Marilyn Hilton were very close. Here, Marilyn delights at a gift received during a baby shower hosted for her by Elizabeth (bottom right) in 1950. Marilyn was pregnant with her son, Steven, at the time. (© 1978 Bob Willoughby/mptvimages.com)

In years to come, Marilyn would appeal to Elizabeth to give Nicky Hilton an annulment in order that he might be able to marry in the Catholic Church. *(© 1978 Bob Willoughby/mptvimages.com)*

A joyous Elizabeth Taylor dances with Conrad Hilton in October of 1952 in the Cotillion Room of the Hotel Pierre in New York. The two remained friends after Elizabeth divorced Conrad's son Nicky. *(AP Photo)*

Eric was the third Hilton son to marry, on August 14, 1954, at St. Patrick's Cathedral in New York, to Patricia Skipworth. Here, the bride and groom pose with Eric's mother, Mary Saxon, and his dad, Conrad Hilton. *(Retro Photo)*

For her daughter Francesca's eleventh birthday, Zsa Zsa (seen here with her mother, Jolie) hosted a party requiring that boys and girls dress in formal wear. It was at this party that Zsa Zsa learned through an attorney that Conrad had suspicions about the paternity of Francesca. (*Leonard Mccombe//Time Life Pictures/Getty Images*)

The press junkets for the opening of Conrad's hotels were always star-studded, elaborate affairs. Money was never an object when it came to celebrating a new hotel acquisition. Here, the new Caribe Hilton pool and terrace are seen during the opening aquacade in San Juan, on December 12, 1949. (*AP Photo/ Puerto Rico News Service*)

July 14, 1953: An army of waiters bring forth desserts for guests at the opening of the Castellana Hilton in Madrid, the first Hilton International hotel in Europe. (*Time & Life Pictures/Getty Images*)

Conrad poses on the construction site for his new Beverly Hilton Hotel in Los Angeles on August 1, 1954. (*Time & Life Pictures/Getty Images*)

The completed Beverly Hilton Hotel—another of Conrad's architectural masterpieces—opened on August 10, 1955. (*Bettmann/Corbis/AP Images*)

Conrad Hilton worked very closely with the leading politicians of his day to further patriotism and religious values during the Cold War. He is seen here with President Dwight Eisenhower at the Mayflower Hotel in Washington on February 2, 1956. The occasion was the fourth annual prayer breakfast for members of Congress, the Cabinet, and other officials. From left to right are Hilton; Senator John Stennis, the president; Texas businessman and evangelist Howard E. Butt Jr., Senator Frank Carlson, and Senator Price Daniel. (*AP Photo*)

In a heated telegram, Zsa Zsa insisted to Conrad that only three people ever loved him—she herself, his son Nicky, and his secretary Olive Wakeman. "Please take yourself off this list," Conrad shot back. (*Globe Photos*)

Nicky Hilton finally found the love of his life when he met Patricia McClintock, better known as "Trish." They were married on November 26, 1958. (*AP Photo*)

Not only was Trish Hilton a knockout, she was a formidable woman who would do anything to love and protect her husband. (© 1978 Bob Willoughby/ mptvimages.com)

An Ominous Sign

"*W*hat is *this*?" Zsa Zsa Gabor asked, her eyes wide as saucers.

Conrad Hilton stood before his wife with an elaborately wrapped box, silver and gold paper artfully pulled together by an enormous matching bow. "It's for you, my dear," he said, handing it to her. "I know I can be a bit of a bore at times with all of my hotel nonsense. I'm hoping you'll forgive me, Georgia."

"Well, that depends on what's in *here*," Zsa Zsa said with a wink. She opened it quickly, gaily tearing the paper with abandon and tossing it all about like a little girl on her birthday. From the box, much to her delight, she pulled a full-length navy blue beaded and laced gown, by her favorite designer, Hattie Carnegie, from Vienna. "Wear it this evening and you'll be the most gorgeous creature in the room," he told her. "And wait! There's more," he said. "Look inside." Zsa Zsa reached into the box again, this time extracting two jewel-encrusted black silk opera gloves. "Oh, the perfect match," she said. She kissed him again.

"It's going to be a wonderful night, my love," he told her.

"Your night, Connie," she said. "You earned it. I'm proud of you, my husband."

He beamed at her. She really was quite lovely to look at, and she so enjoyed the role of Mrs. Conrad Hilton that there seemed little reason for her to show any ambition and go to Hollywood to audition for anything else.

The party Conrad Hilton hosted to celebrate his purchase of the Plaza Hotel took place one Saturday night in February of 1944 at, of course, the grand hotel herself. For the happy festivities, the main concourse of the lobby was festooned with red-and-blue streamers and balloons and packed to capacity with press people from across the country, as well as New York's finest, all the cream of the crop of Manhattan's high society. As the night wore on, Conrad and Zsa Zsa moved through the crowd effortlessly, accepting congratulations and making small talk. Zsa Zsa was in her element. Leave it to Conrad to buy her an ensemble he knew would perfectly match the party's décor. As well as the dress—a strapless little number with a wide swath cut from the middle so that both luscious legs were on full display—Zsa Zsa wore the elegant gloves, which ascended way past her elbows. Her hair, upswept and copper red, perfectly framed her gorgeous face and sapphire earrings. She was all personality—gracious, charming. He seemed proud to be at her side, eagerly introducing her to all of his business associates. "*This* is your wife?" asked E. F. Hutton, the American financier and cofounder of E. F. Hutton & Co. "How in the world did a guy like you manage to nab a dish like this?" he asked, ribbing the hotelier. "Just blind luck," Conrad said. "Well, I sure wish some of that luck would rub off on me," joked Hutton.

Based on their showing together on this important night, there seemed no reason why the Hiltons couldn't make a go of it as a couple— except for, perhaps, one. As Zsa Zsa recalled it, toward the end of the night, a priest approached them and began speaking to Conrad. Suddenly, Zsa Zsa felt invisible at his side. Conrad wouldn't introduce her to the priest. It was an awkward moment. Was it an oversight on his part? Perhaps he didn't recall the priest's name? Finally, Zsa Zsa extended her hand. "Father, I'm Mrs. Hilton, Conrad's wife," she said with a gracious smile. Conrad seemed to flinch. He recovered quickly, though. "Uh… yes, Father, this is my wife," he said haltingly. The priest seemed happy to meet Zsa Zsa. He expected that she was affiliated with St. Patrick's Cathedral and invited her to attend mass there anytime she liked. She said she would "*luff* to," and that was the end of it. He was then absorbed into the bustling crowd.

Zsa Zsa turned to Conrad. "*Dah-ling*, be a dear and fetch me a gimlet," she said with a frozen smile. Seeming happy to have an excuse to get away from her, Conrad took off and said he would return shortly. Actually, she just needed time to think. What had that odd moment been about with the priest? Should she address it, or wait until later? She decided to wait; why take a chance on having an argument on such an important night? However, when he returned with her cocktail, she simply couldn't help herself. "Why wouldn't you introduce me to that priest?" she blurted out.

"What, dear?" he said, feigning innocence.

"That was so strange, you not introducing me to that priest," Zsa Zsa told him, according to her memory of the conversation.

"Oh, that was nothing, Georgia," he said, pulling her closer to him. "I'm just so very tired." He kissed her on the forehead. "I love you," he told her. He then reminded her that he was proud to have her at his side, almost as if he suspected she might now think otherwise. "Let's just have a wonderful evening," he concluded.

Zsa Zsa studied her husband carefully. "Spare a cigarette?" she asked him. He produced a pack of Kools and lit one for her. She pouted. He put it between her lips and smiled at her. But she could tell that something was off with him. It was as if he was ashamed of her, or...she couldn't quite put her finger on it, as she would later recall it, but "it was almost as if he felt somehow *guilty* about being with me. Like he'd been caught with his hand in the cookie jar. I had a sick feeling in the pit of my stomach. I knew something was wrong."

The rest of the night went off without a hitch. It had a been a terrific party. Afterward, the Hiltons spent the evening in an enormous suite of the Plaza Hotel, together—and not in separate bedrooms. It was as if they were actually husband and wife...or at least it felt that way to Zsa Zsa Gabor. As long as she didn't think too long and hard about it, anyway.

A Priest's Visit

*F*rom there, things began to unravel quickly. Before leaving for New York, Conrad had mentioned that a priest would be coming by to talk to Zsa Zsa. She had almost forgotten about it, until one morning she awakened to a note: "My love, Father Kelly will come today to speak with you. Love, Conrad."

A heavy rain had been falling steadily since early morning, so when the priest showed up at the estate without an umbrella, he was soaking wet. Zsa Zsa took his coat and instructed Wilson the butler to bring him a towel with which he could dry his face. They then repaired to the parlor. Sitting down on two heavily upholstered chairs facing each other, the two stared into each other's eyes for what seemed like an eternity.

"I don't want you to misunderstand," the priest finally said, breaking the silence between them, "but you do realize that in the eyes of the church, you and Conrad are not married."

This was the first Zsa Zsa had heard of the problem presented by Conrad's faith since it was brought up to her before their marriage. She didn't know if Conrad had gotten the dispensation or not—he'd never said one way or the other—but she'd suspected that he hadn't.

"You know that Conrad's wife is still alive," Father Kelly said. Of course, Zsa Zsa knew as much. "Conrad loves you," the priest continued, "but you must realize that in the eyes of the church, he is not really married to you."

Now Zsa Zsa didn't know how to react. "What is it you are trying to say to me?" she asked, her eyes searching his face for answers.

The priest was silent for a moment. "Conrad suffers a great deal knowing that he is living in sin with you," he said. "Yet he cannot bring himself to speak to you about it."

"But..." Zsa Zsa was at a loss for words. "What are you saying, Father? Just tell me!"

"I am saying, my dear, that as long as Mrs. Hilton is alive, Conrad is not married to you. At least not in the eyes of the church."

As Zsa Zsa would later recall it, her throat tightened with a rush of emotion. "Are you saying we should divorce?" she managed to ask.

The priest stood up. "My dear, I have said what I came to say," he concluded, his tone abrupt. He appeared to have no compassion at all for her confusion. "And now I will take my leave," he said. As he stood up, he looked at Zsa Zsa in a way that suggested judgment, as if she had done something wrong, as if she was a sinner. Then, without another word, he turned and walked away from her. After retrieving his coat from Wilson, he left the premises.

What did all of this mean? Was her marriage over? As Zsa Zsa's eyes swept around the elegant room furnished with vintage antiques and priceless oil paintings, she wondered where she would go if Conrad banished her. She was surrounded by all of the finer things in life, and she liked it. She found great joy in being Mrs. Conrad Hilton—she loved the parties, the people, the lifestyle. It was her identity now, and without it she didn't have the faintest idea as to who she was.

After a few moments of self-pity, as Zsa Zsa would recall it, a burning, searing rage began to envelop her. She walked into the dining room where she knew she and her husband would later be eating dinner and, taking a look around, carefully selected an expensive crystal lamp she knew was a particular favorite of his. He often spoke of having purchased it abroad, saying that it had cost "a small fortune" but was well worth the price. She picked it up, considered it, and raised it above her head. Then, with all of her might, she hurled it to the floor. It broke into a million pieces, the small pieces of crystal cascading every which way. Hearing the cacophony, a battalion of alarmed servants led by Inger, Zsa Zsa's personal maid, appeared from seemingly out of nowhere. "Leave it right there," Zsa Zsa commanded Inger, pointing down at the broken lamp. "Don't you or any of the rest of you dare touch it. *You just leave it right there.*"

That evening, when Conrad returned home from a busy day at the office, Zsa Zsa didn't mention Father Kelly's visit. Conrad didn't mention it either. Instead, she brought him a dry martini, greeted him with a kiss on the cheek, and then went about her business as he went about his.

Later that night, Conrad casually walked into the dining room for dinner and was immediately stunned by the sight of the broken lamp on the floor, all of its little pieces scattered everywhere. Standing over the mess, he seemed frozen in place, his mind likely racing. But rather than say a word about it, he simply stepped over it and went to his chair on one side of the long, elaborately appointed dinner table. Soon after, Zsa Zsa walked into the room, fully made up and dressed to the nines in a bouffant black-and-white taffeta gown. She too gingerly stepped over the tangle of cords, metal, and crystal. Casually, she took her own seat at the other end of the table. The Hiltons then ate their meal, each eyeing the other, each not uttering a single word. After Wilson the majordomo expeditiously cleared away the plates, Zsa Zsa stood up and walked out of the room, her head held high, leaving Conrad alone, no doubt wondering what she was thinking…and probably suspecting that it wasn't good.

Up in Flames

*I*t was Sunday, March 19, 1944, when the Nazis invaded Hungary. Zsa Zsa was frantic with worry. She may have been self-involved and frivolous and not the kind of woman Conrad Hilton ever should have married, but she did have serious concern for her beloved family members. She hadn't heard from her parents or her sister in weeks, and she began to fear the worst. It was at this time that a series of life-altering events began to unfold for both spouses.

Because Zsa Zsa had contacts in the diplomatic corps in Washington who she felt might be able to assist her in getting her family out of Hungary, she asked Conrad if he would finance a trip to the nation's capital for her. He decided not to turn her down on a matter so urgent. Therefore, Zsa Zsa and Eva were off to Washington, where they would spend the next two months attempting to network with any congressman or diplomat who might be able to assist them in helping their family escape.

Meanwhile, in the summer of 1944, while Zsa Zsa was in Washington and Conrad in Texas on business—his sons Nicky and Barron were at military school—a devastating fire broke out at the Hilton mansion. Unfortunately, it was Zsa Zsa's wing that suffered the most damage—all of her precious photo albums, letters from her parents, and other prized possessions were lost to the blaze. Even more upsetting, the family's German police dog, Ranger, with whom Zsa Zsa had become particularly close, perished in the fire. "We will rebuild, of course," Conrad told reporters. "But much of what has been lost, my wife will never be able to replace." Understandably, Zsa Zsa took the tragedy to heart, finding symbolism in that it had been primarily her wing that had been destroyed, and not the rest of the house. In her mind, the fire seemed like nothing if not a metaphor for her marriage, as if her life with Conrad was going up in flames.

When it seemed matters couldn't get much worse for her, Zsa Zsa's luck finally took a turn for the better when she and Eva were introduced to Secretary of State Cordell Hull. Hull promised that he would do what he could to help get Zsa Zsa's family out of Hungary. He then urged her and Eva to go to New York to rest, telling them they had done all they could in Washington. In truth, he was alarmed by Zsa Zsa's appearance; she looked unwell and on the verge of a nervous breakdown. Zsa Zsa called Conrad to tell him that she was going to be in New York, and asked that he meet her there so that they could discuss their marriage. He agreed.

He Never Should Have Done It

*U*nfortunately for Conrad Hilton, as soon as he arrived in New York, he came down with the flu. Because he was so sick, he was forced to stay in a suite at the Plaza with Zsa Zsa, something he hadn't planned on doing. It was this twist of fate that would precipitate a final showdown between the unhappy couple.

While he was sick in bed, Conrad was forced to sit and watch as Zsa Zsa spent most of her day dressing and undressing for the day's big events—namely breakfast, then lunch, then tea, followed by what Conrad would derisively call "the main event," dinner. He couldn't believe how much time she spent putting on makeup, styling her hair, and trying on one glamorous outfit after another, then switching back and forth between all sorts of expensive jewelry, for the look most appropriate for each meal. "It took me by surprise to once again discover that beauty can be a full-time affair," he later recalled. He said that all of her many beautifying processes rather reminded him "of the rite of an ancient Aztec temple." With nothing else to do with his time, watching Zsa Zsa indulge herself became almost an obsession. It was like witnessing a bad train accident; he couldn't quite take his eyes off it.

Perhaps Zsa Zsa's self-indulgent behavior stung Conrad all the more because he had just recently established the Conrad N. Hilton Foundation, through which his charitable and philanthropic endeavors would now be channeled. A great deal of time and discussion was going into making decisions as to which charities would benefit from Hilton's largesse—and meanwhile, here was his wife, totally involved in herself and in her self-indulgent lifestyle. His hardworking mother, Mary, also came to mind, and how completely different she was from Zsa Zsa in values and priorities. Comparing the two women just made Zsa Zsa seem all the more superficial and silly. It appeared to him that his wife knew the cost of everything but the value of nothing. Eva had lately been suggesting that Zsa Zsa might try a career in show business, and Conrad had to agree with her. At least then maybe she could earn her own money and he might have some respect for her. As it stood now, he pretty much had no respect for her at all. She knew it, too.

Because there was a party on their schedule that was to be thrown in honor of the governor of New York, Thomas E. Dewey, the Hiltons had a choice to make: either stay at the hotel and try to tolerate each other, or go to the party and surround themselves with plenty of distraction. Even though he was sick, Conrad felt the party would be their best option. Of course, Zsa Zsa was game. She could always put aside any stress for a good party; plus, as she recalled it, she viewed the event as an opportunity to once again show Conrad that she could be an asset to him. She was a gorgeous woman at his side, a beautiful wife who was the envy of all of his colleagues; surely that had to count for something. And if there was one thing she knew how to do, it was to be social.

Conrad washed his face, donned a white shirt and jacket, black bow tie and pants, and was ready in about fifteen minutes. He then spent the next two hours waiting for Zsa Zsa to make her entrance.

Zsa Zsa finally emerged from the bedroom, a stunning vision in passionate red. She wore her slinky, formfitting crimson beaded gown—slit way up one side to show ample leg—as if she was born to wear it, as if there was no reason for it ever to have been made if not to adorn her curvaceous body. She also wore a small diamond tiara in her hair, which was no longer red but dyed blonde now. A pair of silvery starburst rhinestone earrings and matching brooch given to her by Conrad as a gift completed the perfect picture of 1940s glamour. Her hard work done, Zsa Zsa proudly stood before her husband for final inspection. "So, what do you *sink?*" she asked, spinning around a couple of times for him.

Conrad sized her up from head to toe. "I'm just wondering how much this has cost me," he said.

Zsa Zsa was speechless. She had spent hours getting ready for him, and *that* was his response? It made her angry, and he knew it. "Oh, you look beautiful, my dear," Conrad said, brushing her concerns aside. "But you always look beautiful. Can we please just go now?"

The evening went downhill from there.

The party at the Waldorf-Astoria was packed with New York socialites and a sprinkling of celebrities such as the actress Loretta Young and Zsa Zsa's sister Eva. However, it was Zsa Zsa Gabor Hilton who stood out from the rest in a gown that could not be overlooked. Conrad kept to himself, clearly not well, speaking to a few people. Because he had unknotted his tie, he seemed uncharacteristically disheveled, even in his natty white jacket. For her part, Zsa Zsa played the role of wealthy socialite wife to the hilt. It's what she did best, after all, her entire identity wrapped up in the being of Mrs. Conrad Hilton. "Pink champagne," she was heard saying, "we need much more pink champagne! Everyone drink up!"

"It's a great party, isn't it?" Eva asked her sister at one point. "Just think of all of the *money* in this room."

Actually, the thought had already crossed Zsa Zsa's mind. Looking around at all the well-heeled people in her midst, she wondered aloud if one could ever truly be rich enough. "And then I think to myself, no, you can *never* be rich enough, *ever*," she said, laughing. "*Sanks* God there's enough money to go around for *everyone* in America! *Sanks* God!"

Though Zsa Zsa did everything she could think of to cover for the fact that her husband was not at his best, Conrad didn't seem to appreciate it. Mostly he acted as if she was on his nerves. "What's the best scotch you have?" he asked a waiter, seeming distracted.

As soon as they got back to their suite, the Hiltons, predictably enough, had a terrible row. "*I tried*," Zsa Zsa told Conrad, according to what she would recall. She told him that she had done her part; she had been a good wife and partner at his side. Everyone loved her, she said. Everyone, that is, but Conrad. "You were the *only* one at that party who was not in love with me," she charged. He apologized, saying he wasn't feeling well. He left the room, changed out of his suit, and, according to her memory, returned wearing a short white terrycloth robe. He then sat down before her and began to smoke a cigar. "Let's just drop this thing until tomorrow morning," he suggested in a pleading tone.

Still dressed in her slinky red gown, Zsa Zsa paced back and forth before him, clearly not ready to let it go. "And then you send someone else—*a priest!*—to tell me that you want to divorce me?" she asked, now seeming to want to explore other areas of contention. "You send a *priest*?"

Conrad was speechless. In a boardroom, he certainly knew how to be confrontational when just such a moment presented itself. But in a marriage? No. Mostly, he didn't have the kind of passion for Zsa Zsa that it would have taken to work himself into the sort of furious lather that could even come close to matching her own. Not only that, but by his own admission, this was not a good day for him. Therefore, he just sat on the couch puffing on his Cuban and taking everything she had to dish out, all the while looking chagrined about it.

And *so what* if I want to look pretty?" she continued to rage as she stalked about the room. "*So* what? What have you ever done to make me feel wanted?"

He still couldn't find the words to respond. To her, it must have seemed as if there was nothing she could do to enrage him. What could she do to bring forth some passion from this man? It must have seemed useless to her.

"How could you do this to me?" Zsa Zsa continued, now facing him, her eyes blazing and her Hungarian temper on full, explosive display. "If you didn't *want* to marry me," she concluded bitterly, "you shouldn't have done it, Connie. *You just should not have done it!*"

He certainly couldn't argue with her there. Now, perhaps, more than ever, he likely realized that he never, ever should have done it.

What Would It Take?

*A*fter the big fight with Zsa Zsa in New York, Conrad immediately checked in to another suite of the Plaza. A few days later, he left the city and flew back to Los Angeles. By telephone, he then told Zsa Zsa that he was done with the marriage. There were a number of reasons for his decision. First of all, the religious conundrum having to do with his divorce from Mary had never really been reconciled in his mind. Also, that he now viewed Zsa Zsa as being shallow and self-involved did nothing to enhance her image in his eyes. Of course, his preoccupation with his work also figured into the equation. Hilton would later admit in his memoir that he preferred negotiating with businessmen for new hotels to negotiating with Zsa Zsa for ways to continue their marriage. Therefore, if she didn't file for divorce, he would do it. After all she had been through with him, she said, the last thing she wanted was for *him* to file against *her.* "I'll do it," she said, "and happily." After she did so, a property settlement and separation agreement was entered into on November 3, 1944, that saw to it that Zsa Zsa would receive $2,083.33 a month.

After Zsa Zsa returned to Los Angeles, Conrad tried to go his separate way from her. She made it difficult, though. He put her up in a suite at the Town House, but she was on the telephone with him constantly, arguing with him about one thing or another about the way things had gone between them. He kept giving her money in an attempt to assuage his own guilt, but it was never enough. She wanted more and she felt she deserved it, even though they had a separation agreement in place. There were some months when he would give her as much as $5,000 in the hope that she would just stop pestering him, but it never worked. As if out to prove the old adage that hell hath no fury like a woman scorned, she continued her verbal assaults on a nearly daily basis, seemingly determined to make him as miserable as she felt he had made her.

One day, Conrad received a telephone call from a close friend who told him that he had seen Zsa Zsa with another man at the Warner Bros. studio in Burbank. Together, they looked cozy in the commissary, holding hands—or so Conrad was told—and even sharing a kiss or two. Was Zsa Zsa having an affair?

Since she was officially separated from Conrad, it would seem that she had a right to do whatever she pleased; at least that's how most people might have viewed it. Not Conrad, though. He had his attorney hire a private detective and put him on her trail, following her for about a week. Sure enough, according to the attorney's recollection of events, the report came back that Zsa Zsa was involved with a successful movie studio executive. The private detective told the lawyer he believed he even caught Zsa Zsa with the executive in the man's cream-colored Mercedes-Benz convertible late one night, parked in an empty lot behind the studio. He produced a series of black-and-white photographs that, though shadowy, seemed to suggest that something was going on in that vehicle between Zsa Zsa and the studio exec. He also said that afterward, the two seemed to be arguing. The man suddenly bolted from the car and stormed down a nearby street into the darkness. Meanwhile, Zsa Zsa put her head on the steering wheel and appeared to sob uncontrollably.

"Get out of here right now," the attorney hollered at the detective. The notion that Zsa Zsa had been intimate with someone in an automobile genuinely upset Hilton's lawyer. "What the hell kind of a person are you, saying this about Mr. Hilton's wife? Even if it's true, you don't say that about a man's wife! What's wrong with you?"

"But that's what you paid me for," the detective said. He was dismayed, and, it could be argued, with good reason. What kind of news did the attorney expect from him, if not of the good and grimy variety? He had trailed Zsa Zsa every day for a week, he said, and he had much more to report. "That lady ain't no lady," he concluded. "Put it that way."

"Just get out of here," said the attorney as he slammed the door behind the private eye.

The lawyer decided not to give Conrad the lurid details or the photographs, just the information that his wife was likely involved with someone, and that maybe it wasn't going so well. When told this, Conrad decided to confront Zsa Zsa. He immediately raced to her suite at the Town House, and in front of a number of people, including a woman who was Zsa Zsa's personal secretary at the time, Lena Burrell, he laid it on the line with her. "Are you having an affair with some studio guy?" he demanded to know. "Tell me the truth this instant."

"Oh my God!" Zsa Zsa exclaimed, sizing him up. "You're an absolute wreck," she said. She suggested that he pour himself a brandy to calm his nerves. But he didn't need a drink, he told her. What he needed was an answer to his question: "Are you or are you not having an affair?"

"Of course not," Zsa Zsa said.

"She seemed unfazed by the question," recalled Lena Burrell of her employer. "I recall that she was formally dressed in a white strapless evening gown, prepared for a night on the town at Ciro's. She went into her purse, pulled from it her lipstick and compact, and began to apply the cosmetic, all the while looking into the mirror with what I think could only be described as the greatest of affection. This drove Conrad crazy. She once told me that nothing bothered him more."

"Must you do that now?" Conrad asked.

"What's it to you?" she remarked, still looking into the mirror rather than at him.

"One more time," he said. Then, punctuating each word with a period, he asked, "Are. You. Having. An. Affair?"

"No."

"I don't believe you."

"So what?" she asked, still acting disengaged. "Who cares? Our marriage is over, anyway."

"That still doesn't give you the right to lie to me," Conrad said, "and to make a fool of me." He looked more hurt and wounded than he did angry, which seemed to throw Zsa Zsa. Again, what would it take to upset this man? It was as if there was nothing she could do to make him explode. Why was he always in such perfect control, and what did it say about her as a woman that she was unable to make him furious with jealousy? It was maddening.

According to Lena Burrell, Zsa Zsa put her compact and lipstick back into her purse, took out a pair of embroidered and jeweled white opera gloves, and then walked over to Conrad. She stood as close to him as possible, raised her head to look up at him, and, in an even, dispassionate tone, reminded him, "I am a very beautiful woman, in case you haven't noticed." Many men were after her, she claimed, and yes, she *had* slept with quite a few of them. He might not have any desire for her, she said angrily, but others certainly did. "In fact, since we broke up, I have had more men than you will ever know," she declared, spitting the words out at him. "Now, if you don't mind," she said in finishing, "that will be all. *Husband.*" She smacked him hard on the chest with her gloves, and then turned her back on him.

"Mr. Hilton looked completely crushed," recalled Lena Burrell. "Who knew if what Zsa Zsa said to him was true or not? What was clear to me, though, was that she fully intended to hurt him with her words. He said, 'I will ignore what you have just said because I know you didn't mean it.' And she said, 'Oh, *really, now?*'"

Shaking his head, Conrad bolted from the room, slamming the door behind him so hard it rattled the walls. Zsa Zsa smiled to herself. "There," she said, seeming satisfied. "That should do it." After slipping her fingers into the gloves, she rolled them up her arms to her elbows and then turned to Lena Burrell with her wrists held outward so that the assistant could fasten the buttons. "Do you think it will be chilly this evening?" she asked. "Because if so, perhaps I should wear my platinum mink."

"Oh yes, do wear the mink," Lena said. "You look marvelous in it, Miss Gabor."

"I know I do," Zsa Zsa said petulantly. "That was not my question. You do have my medication now, don't you?" Zsa Zsa then asked, using her euphemism for the prescribed amphetamines she had begun taking of late.

"Yes, ma'am," Lena said. She reached into her purse and pulled out a large plastic bottle of capsules. When Zsa Zsa extended her hand, the secretary dropped two of the capsules from the bottle onto her palm. Zsa Zsa popped both into her mouth and swallowed. "Well, just look at that!" she exclaimed proudly after they went down. "Without even a drop of champagne. How about *that*, *dah-ling!*"

Zsa Zsa Is Institutionalized

*I*n the spring of 1945, Zsa Zsa and Eva Gabor finally received word from their mother, Jolie. She, her husband, and Magda had somehow made it to Lisbon and, thanks to Cordell Hull, would soon be on their way to the United States. Their arrival was still a few months away due to a paperwork delay, but at least they were en route to Manhattan. "I think you should go to New York and wait for them there," Conrad told Zsa Zsa. Even though he was angry at her, he was still trying to be supportive. "I will put you up at the Plaza for as long as it takes," he told her.

For the next few months, Zsa Zsa would live in a suite at the Plaza, and while there would do everything she could think of to escape the blues, including taking pills prescribed by her doctor not only to sleep but also to stay awake. Frustrated and bored, she also spent a fortune on designer clothing, on late nights out on the town, and on long-distance telephone calls. She was miserable, lonely, and worried about her future. "I wondered, if I could not be Mrs. Conrad Hilton, who would I be?" she recalled. "I was very much afraid."

When Conrad would speak to Zsa Zsa on the telephone, she seemed unreasonable to him, screaming at him in Hungarian and not making much sense. She wasn't eating, wasn't sleeping, and was consumed by worry. She actually seemed on the verge of an emotional breakdown. She had even taken all of her prized jewels and tossed them out the window of her suite, Eva told Conrad, blaming the baubles for her unhappiness. Eva was worried. Though not really a fan of Conrad's, she felt she needed his support, and so she decided to reach out to him.

"Oh no. What fresh hell is this?" Conrad said when Eva called to say she needed his assistance. When the two later met in his office to discuss the matter, Eva said that she felt something needed to be done for her sister, and it needed to be done quickly.

According to what she would later testify to during her sister's divorce hearing, Eva told Conrad that she had consulted with several doctors and was told that the only way to help Zsa Zsa was to admit her to a sanitarium for intense psychological treatment. "There's really no other alternative," she told Conrad.

Eva's logic made no sense to Conrad. Surely there had to have been some doctor somewhere who could tell them whether or not Zsa Zsa needed to be in a hospital or whether she was just play-acting. "He had a bad feeling that another reason Zsa Zsa would fake an emotional illness—besides wanting his sympathy—was to later use it as a way to secure more money from him in a divorce settlement," said his attorney Myron Harpole. "This does not sound like a charitable assessment of the situation, I admit. He was loath to make it. It was not like him to make it, and he would never have verbalized it to just anyone. However, I know that this is how he felt."

Eva Gabor told Conrad that she had already consulted with several doctors, and they suggested institutionalizing her. It was clear that Eva had her mind made up about it. Since he was separated from Zsa Zsa, Conrad felt that he should probably acquiesce to her sister's desires. However, he could not fully support her decision. He truly did not feel that Zsa Zsa needed to be institutionalized, and he wanted it on the record that this was her idea, not his. "I suppose you should do what you believe is best for your sister," he said, "but I cannot condone this," he told Eva before leaving her.

"Do you really care for her, Conrad?" Eva asked him.

"Of course I do," he said. "I will always love her. I'm just sorry it's going so badly right now. I want her to be well, Eva."

"I am sorry, too," Eva said sadly. "I truly am. But I don't know what else to do."

A week later, Eva called Conrad to tell him that Zsa Zsa had come at her with a knife in her apartment. They'd had an disagreement about something, she said, and the next thing she knew, Zsa Zsa was trying to attack her. She managed to get the weapon away from her, but now she was frightened. She was also more convinced than ever that her sister needed psychological help. Therefore, she came up with a master plan to get Zsa Zsa into a mental facility.

One morning soon after the attack, Eva and the sisters' friend Andrew "Bundy" Solt brought a bespectacled gentlemen to Zsa Zsa's suite and introduced him as a Rudolph Stein, a Viennese producer interested in meeting her so that he might cast her in an exciting new play. The gentlemen convinced Zsa Zsa that she should probably take a nap before discussing such important business, because she did seem to be exhausted, or at least that's what he told her. "You're a tired little girl," he told Zsa Zsa. At first she was insulted. But then she realized that she actually couldn't remember the last time she had slept, so she agreed to the nap. While she was lying grandly in her Empress Josephine bed, Mr. Stein pulled up a chair and sat down next to her. "There's nothing so urgent," he said, in a lilting, calming voice, "nothing at all. You must rest. You are tired. You are growing more tired by the moment." Then, as she listened to him repeat certain words and phrases in his ever-calming voice, she drifted off.

Rudolph Stein wasn't a Viennese producer at all, as Zsa Zsa would soon learn—he was a psychiatrist. Within hours, Zsa Zsa found herself committed in a sanitarium in New York, where she would stay for the next six weeks. Once there, things then went from bad to worse, as she has told it in her memoir:

> How shall I describe the nightmare of the next weeks, days and nights and horrors that might have been invented by Dante? I lived in a world of strait jackets, insulin shock treatments, endless injections—and always the unreal, terrifying realization that though I saw what went on and I knew and heard and understood the enormity of what was happening, no one would listen to me. No one came to visit me: Not Conrad...not Eva...no one. I felt rejected, utterly abandoned.

When she finally emerged from the sanitarium, Zsa Zsa Gabor practically didn't even know who she was. "I emerged a stranger in the world," she recalled. She was thin, unwell, and angrier than ever. Eva wasn't her target, though; Conrad was. She was convinced that the idea to have her committed was his, and she would never forget it, nor would she ever forgive him for it.

The Divorce

*W*ithin weeks of her discharge from the hospital, Zsa Zsa Gabor received word that her parents, Jolie and Vilmos Gabor, and sister Magda were on their way to New York from Lisbon. On the day of her mother's arrival in New York—her father and sister would arrive two days later on a different boat—Zsa Zsa and Eva met her at the dock, where the three enjoyed a wonderful and tearful reunion. However, the immigrant Gabors would come with no money, having lost everything in the takeover of their home country. They were all but penniless, the wealth and material goods they'd accumulated over a lifetime of hard work—mostly from the family's success in the jewelry business in Hungary—were now gone. Zsa Zsa once recalled that her mother, Jolie, arrived "with only a sable coat, some antique Portuguese silver and a hundred dollars in her pocket. As Eva and I rushed into her arms when the boat docked in New York Harbor, Mother removed the hundred dollars from her purse and, with a flourish, presented it to the porter who had just unloaded her bags." Jolie and family were so glad to finally be safe and sound on American soil that the fact that they'd lost everything in the process didn't really matter to them at the time. (Jolie and Magda would stay in America, but Vilmos— who was already divorced from Jolie—was not happy in the new country; he returned to Hungary and remarried there.)

It was Eva who summoned Conrad Hilton to tell him that her family had arrived from Hungary and had no place to stay and no money. Though he was still angry with Zsa Zsa, he was able to put those feelings aside and take a plane to New York to see what he could do to help the new arrivals. When he arrived, he found Zsa Zsa, Eva, Magda, and their parents all living in a two-bedroom suite at his Plaza Hotel. That wouldn't do, obviously; Conrad provided all of them with separate accommodations, starting with Jolie, who was put up in a grand three-bedroom, three-bathroom suite at the Plaza.

"He couldn't have been kinder and more compassionate," Zsa Zsa recalled of Conrad. "He then courteously examined the silver [Jolie had brought with her on the boat] and elected to buy it from her. He needed the silver like he needed to grow another three feet, but he was aware that Mother was too proud to accept money and wanted to help her. Using Conrad's money, she found a small store on Madison Avenue—between 62nd and 63rd streets—and opened 'Jolie Gabor'—selling exquisite costume jewelry modeled after the Maria Theresia pieces so popular in Europe." It would go on to become just the first in a successful chain of jewelry stores for the enterprising Mother Gabor. "Through the years, Mother made millions of dollars," Zsa Zsa would say, "also employing in her stores—she opened another in Palm Springs—Maria Callas' mother, and many impoverished members of European aristocracy."

Unfortunately, Conrad's generosity to Jolie Gabor had no bearing on his broken marriage to her daughter Zsa Zsa. He still wanted it to be over. It was then that the posturing began, as it often does in contentious divorces.

Zsa Zsa hired the most savvy lawyer she could find, hopefully to strong-arm Conrad into giving her millions of divorce dollars. She wasn't the only one with an adversarial streak, though; Conrad engaged in his own bit of gamesmanship. If Zsa Zsa wanted a good fight, he would give her one.

First, Conrad insisted that Zsa Zsa fire her lawyer and hire a different one to represent her—one of his own. He would pay the attorney himself. She said she was going to do no such thing. She wanted Conrad to pay for *her* attorney, which is not unusual in divorce proceedings. Annoyed by her defiance, Conrad retaliated by holding back the money he was supposed to give her under the separation agreement. Moreover, as per their settlement agreement, he had agreed to pay the rent on a hotel suite of her choice for a six-month period, and she had a choice of the Beverly Hills Hotel, the Town House, the Plaza Hotel, "or any other hotel selected by her in the United States." But after six months, she would be on her own. So Hilton just waited for the clock to tick away. He and his attorney knew that if there was no settlement in sight at the end of the six-month period and Zsa Zsa had no money coming in, she would be fairly frantic—and they were right.

In a letter to Conrad Hilton dated August 1, 1945, Hilton's lawyer, J. B. Herndon Jr., noted that Zsa Zsa was agitated because she had run out of money. In fact, due to the exorbitant legal fees she had incurred since the beginning of the divorce proceedings, she said she was ready to just abandon the fight. She asked when she might be receiving more money from

Conrad, as per their legal settlement. The lawyer told her that as far as he knew, no money had been sent and he had no idea when it might happen. "What I predicted has come to pass," wrote the attorney to Conrad. "She is desperate." By the time he concluded his conversation with Zsa Zsa, she was fully prepared to take a meeting with the lawyer Conrad had chosen to represent her in the divorce action. She said that she had some trepidation about doing so, however, because her present attorney had assured her that a substantial settlement would be forthcoming from Conrad if she could just hang on a little while longer. In response to that theory, Herndon told Zsa Zsa that her lawyer didn't know what he was talking about, that Conrad had no intention of giving her any money, and moreover, he didn't intend to negotiate with her lawyer at all. When Zsa Zsa asked Herndon if he might at least be able to secure a room for her at the Roosevelt Hotel, he turned her down. Herndon ended his letter to Conrad by writing, "My advice at this moment is to let her sweat. I think in a few more weeks she will be willing to settle without much difficulty."

Actually it would take an entire year with no money coming in, and with Zsa Zsa's rage toward Conrad mounting daily, before she would finally crumble and hire Conrad's lawyer to represent her.

On September 17, 1946, the final decree of divorce was to be handed down, as well as the terms of alimony.

On the witness stand at that final hearing, Zsa Zsa—referred to by her real name, Sari Gabor—testified that she and Conrad had no children. She testified that "a couple of months after the marriage," he had told her that he no longer wished to be married, and that he had repeated as much to her "quite often." She also testified, "He had a butler in the house for about five years before he married me, and he was busy and didn't like to take my orders. So I asked my husband to fire him, and he said he didn't like to fire him. If I didn't like it, I could go. But the butler would stay." She talked about the fire that burned her wing of the Hilton mansion, and stated that after the fire she stayed, for the most part, with her sister Eva. She said that she had asked if she could move back into the newly renovated mansion, but that Conrad turned her down. During the entire summer of 1944, she testified, she only saw Conrad twice. She testified that they had not cohabitated and had not reconciled.

Eva Gabor testified as well, saying that Conrad told her "several times" that "he doesn't like to be married." She said that Conrad "was tired

very often," not from working but rather "from playing golf." She talked
about Zsa Zsa's physical condition, saying that "she was very nervous, and
she looked very bad and couldn't sleep." She noted that it had been her
idea to have Zsa Zsa "taken to a hospital" but that Conrad didn't agree
with her because "he didn't think she was that sick. But as her sister I did
think." She concluded that the reason for her emotional state was that
"she was upset very much over the treatment by her husband."

Just as Conrad had predicted, it was on the basis of Eva's testimony
about Zsa Zsa's need for hospitalization that the judge ruled in favor of
Zsa Zsa's allegation of "extreme cruelty." He ordered that the amount of
money for her support and maintenance be raised as of October 1, 1946,
to $2,283.33 per month until she remarried or November 30, 1949, which-
ever came first. He ruled that she was also allowed to keep all of the insurance money she received from the fire at the Bellagio Road home, as well
as stocks she held in the Roosevelt and Plaza hotels. Also, Conrad would
have to pay her medical expenses for a year. Additionally, he would have
to pay all legal fees in connection to her obtaining immigration papers
that would legally permit her to remain in the United States, and 50 percent of all fees having to do with the immigration of Zsa Zsa's parents.

Conrad had already agreed to pay Zsa Zsa a lump sum of $35,000 in
cash, which he had paid back on November 3, 1944, and which was long
gone by the time the divorce decree was handed down. (That seems like a
small amount of money, and perhaps it is considering Conrad's wealth at
the time. But it should be noted that today the same amount—$35,000—
would be worth well over $400,000, which may also say a lot about Zsa
Zsa's spending habits.) "I did not grudge even a penny of it," Conrad Hilton said of the settlement. "It was true that a Gabor could bring much
laughter and gaiety in any man's life—if he could afford it, and if his faith
permitted."

"She made a stupid, stupid divorce," Jolie once recalled of her daughter. What irked the Gabor matriarch even more than any of the other
points of the settlement, though, was that Zsa Zsa didn't get a permanent
suite for life at the Plaza. "Not even a ten percent discount on any suite
anywhere in the world," Jolie Gabor fumed. "Wherever Zsa Zsa goes, in a
Hilton hotel, she must pay herself. Ridiculous." Or as Zsa Zsa liked to say,
"You never really know a man until you divorce him."

It could also be said that Conrad didn't really know the woman he was divorcing, because—unbeknownst to him at the time—Zsa Zsa was pregnant. Not only would she keep this news from Conrad, but she also chose not to divulge it to the judge who presided over the divorce. In doing so, she set the stage for what would amount to many decades of contention over money between her and a man who was well on his way to becoming one of the richest entrepreneurs in the country.

Buying the Stevens and the Palmer House

*I*n 1946, Conrad Hilton was fifty-eight. He and Zsa Zsa Gabor were officially divorced and he was determined to go on with his life and career. At the time, though, the pain of his divorce from Zsa Zsa was somewhat muted by a much-needed boost in his life—yes, the acquisition of yet another hotel.

Conrad had never given up hope that the Stevens Hotel would one day be his to have and to hold. Though he had just recently bought the Dayton Biltmore in Ohio, that purchase was, in his mind, just business as usual. It didn't excite him. He had pretty much decided that the only thing that would truly thrill him at this time when such a dark cloud was hanging over his head would be the purchase of the Stevens.

At the beginning of 1945, Conrad had made an important decision: He was going to take a train to Chicago and he wasn't going to leave the Windy City until the Stevens was his. Once he and a friend named Willard Keith got to Chicago, he began negotiating with the owner of the hotel, Steve Healy. In years to come, Conrad would regard these negotiations as the most maddening of his entire career.

At first, Healy said he wanted to make a profit of a half million dollars on the Stevens. He had paid $4.91 million, so he wanted roughly $5.5 million for it. That was fine with Conrad; the two men shook hands on a deal. But then Healy disappeared for a while and could not be found. When he finally surfaced, the price had suddenly gone up. Now he wanted to make a profit of $650,000. Frustrated but still wanting the hotel, Conrad agreed to the new price. Then, just as had happened previously, Healy made himself unavailable for future meetings. After the passing of a few weeks, Hilton was quite angry. When Healy finally showed up again, he said he now wanted to make a profit of a million dollars on the Stevens. Reluctantly, Conrad agreed. It speaks to how much Conrad wanted this hotel that he would acquiesce to Healy's demands. Ordinarily he would probably have walked away from the deal by this time. But then, sure enough, Healy vanished again! His behavior was so outrageous and unprofessional, Conrad didn't know what to make of it. "Who taught this guy how to do business?" he raged to Willard Keith. "Forget it," he decided. "It's not worth it." Though his friend didn't believe that Conrad would abandon his dream of owning the Stevens, he was happy for the storm to at least temporarily blow over. He suggested that they take a tour of the city and see if any other Chicago property might take Conrad's mind off the Stevens. It was then that Conrad Hilton laid eyes on the Palmer House.

The Palmer House was another of the grandest Chicago hotels, twenty-five stories, designed by the architectural firm of Holabird and Roche in 1925. Centrally located in Chicago's Loop, like the Stevens, it too was known for its dignified, austere décor. When Conrad walked into the lobby and took a look around, he made a statement not many people could make then, or even now. He said, "You know, I actually think I'd like to own this place." He didn't even know if it was for sale, but he knew he wanted it! For advice, he called upon his friend Henry Crown, a successful businessman who'd made a fortune with his Material Service Corp., which sold gravel, lime, and coal to builders in Chicago. In his meeting with Crown, Hilton said that he'd been negotiating to purchase the Stevens Hotel but was having no luck with the owner. He said that he'd come to the conclusion that the sale simply wasn't going to happen, and so he now had his sights set on the Palmer House.

"Well, is the Palmer House even for sale?" Crown wondered.

"I don't know," replied Hilton.

"Well, find out, my good man," said Crown. "And if so, why not buy both the Palmer and the Stevens?"

At that bold suggestion, Conrad had to smile. Henry Crown was a man much like himself, someone who saw no reason his wildest ambitions could not be attained. He had already made a fortune in the construction business and held interests in banks, electronics, and the oil business as well as in railroad and shipbuilding enterprises. He also owned real estate in Illinois, California, and New York. In just a few years, he would go on to own the Empire State Building, then the world's tallest skyscraper (which he would buy for $51.5 million in 1951). In his mind, there was no reason Hilton couldn't buy two hotels in the Chicago area; that is, if he could afford it—and of course Conrad could afford it (and if he couldn't he would find a way to do so).

It was Henry Crown who then introduced Conrad to Henry L. Hollis, the trustee for the Palmer estate. Hollis wouldn't say if the Palmer House was for sale or not, only that "we are not taking offers, nor are we refusing them." That was good enough for Conrad and for his associate Billy Friedman, an attorney who had helped him with the deal for the Sir Francis Drake Hotel and who would now be representing him on the purchase of either the Stevens or the Palmer House—or maybe both. After conferring with Friedman and several other business associates—including Willard Keith, who was president of Marsh & McLennan, Cosgrove & Co., an insurance firm in Los Angeles, and whom Hilton had summoned to Chicago to assist him with the dealings there—Hilton made an offer to Hollis of $18.5 million for the Palmer House, contingent upon his taking a look at the hotel's financial and tax records and the rest of the corporation's books. However, when it came to Hollis's attention that Hilton had also been trying to buy the Stevens, he balked, saying that the Palmer House trustees would not allow its hotel books to be viewed by anyone who could one day turn out to be competition for them. Hilton impressed upon Hollis that he had had no success in purchasing the Stevens and that as far as he was concerned it just wasn't going to happen. Hollis then said he would present Hilton's offer to the trustees of the Palmer House and see what happened, but he couldn't promise anything.

"That's fine," said Willard Keith, when Conrad told him about Hollis's position, "but please, Connie, let's not wait here in Chicago for an answer. It's too cold here, sir. Let's go back to California where we can thaw out."

Conrad shook his head no. "I said I was not leaving here without a hotel," he said, "and I'm not. If it's not going to be the Stevens, it's going to be the Palmer House. But I will have a hotel before I leave this damn frozen tundra."

"Fine," Keith said. "Whatever it takes to get out of here..."

"Say, I have an idea," Conrad said. "Why don't you set up a little meeting

with your friend Mr. Healy and find out what the hell is going on with him
and with his Stevens Hotel."

"Why?"

"Just curious," Conrad said. "Might heat things up a little in this
town," he said with a smile. "You never know."

As directed, Willard Keith arranged to see Steve Healy. Over drinks,
Keith said that Healy had blown it with Hilton where the Stevens was
concerned, that Conrad had gotten tired of his waffling and had abandoned the idea of ever purchasing the hotel. His mind was now set on
the Palmer House, Keith said, "and there was probably no changing it." If
it was a ploy, it worked. Now Healy wanted to unload the Stevens more
than ever. The next day he called Conrad with a new proposal. Going
back full circle to the original idea, he now wanted to make a profit of
just half a million on the Stevens. That was fine with Conrad, of course,
but how was he to know that Healy wouldn't disappear again and then
change his mind and up the price in the next twenty-four hours? Healy
said he was prepared to sign a contract immediately guaranteeing the
deal. The rest of the negotiation was quick and easy; before Conrad Hilton knew it, his dream of owning the Stevens had come true.

What happened next is quite remarkable.

After closing the deal on the Stevens, Conrad took a meeting with
Henry Hollis, the gentleman with whom he had been negotiating the
possible sale of the Palmer House. Reluctantly he explained what had
happened—that the sale of the Stevens Hotel had unexpectedly been
consummated. He said that he hoped Hollis wouldn't be upset and think
Hilton had been lying earlier when he said that the sale was not going to
happen—thus his interest in the Palmer House. At first Hollis was skepti-
cal. "The whole thing sounds suspect to me," he said.

"It's a matter of my integrity," Hilton told him. "It's important what
you think of me, and I don't want you to think I was lying."

Henry Hollis said he might actually still be interested in selling the
Palmer House, but considering all that had happened, he now felt he
deserved a better price for it. Conrad agreed—to the tune of almost $19.4
million, up from his previous bid of $18.5 million. Hollis accepted. The
two men shook hands. "And that was all there was to it," Hilton later
recalled. "No pens, pencils, papers, lawyers, witnesses."

Obtaining financing for the purchase of two hotels in the same city was no easy feat for Conrad. When he approached one of his chief backers, Samuel Doak Sr., president of the El Paso National Bank, with the plan, Doak wasn't at all enthusiastic about it. He felt that Conrad was stretching himself too thin by buying what Doak viewed as competing hotels in the same city.

Conrad had a few good arguments in his favor, perhaps the most persuasive being that he wouldn't tell Doak how close in proximity he should situate his bank branches if Doak agreed not to tell Hilton how close in proximity he should own his hotels. He also gave him enough information about the value of the land on which both hotels sat, as well as the money they generated annually, for Doak to reconsider. Besides, said Hilton, he really didn't need his backing. He had all the money he needed in his personal portfolio—not really, but it was a good bluff—but if Doak wanted in on the deal, fine. Of course, now Doak wanted in, and said he would help finance the purchase of both hotels. (It's worth noting here that Samuel Doak Sr. would in just a year's time be made a member of the board of the Hilton Hotels Corporation.)

At the last minute in trying to close the deals for the two hotels, Conrad Hilton found himself short a million dollars. He went to his friend Henry Crown for the balance. "We're friends," said Crown. "I admire the way you do business. You have nerve, but you're fair." He said he would happily help Conrad secure the money he needed, and he did just that, from First National Bank. A million dollars in 1945 would be worth roughly $11 million today—a lot of cash to raise with just a single telephone call to a good friend, underscoring once again that Hilton was a man who could put together a great deal of money at least partly based on his character and personality. Soon the Palmer House and the Stevens were both his.

Zsa Zsa's Daughter

On the evening of March 10, 1947—six months after her final divorce decree from Conrad Hilton was handed down—Sari Zsa Zsa Gabor gave birth at Doctor's Hospital in New York City to a daughter, Constance (named after Conrad) Francesca (after her great-grandmother) Hilton. "I will never forget how I felt the first time they brought Francie to me," she would recall. "When they put her in my arms, I was flooded with such warmth as I had never known. I still remember how powerfully my heart beat as I took her in my arms. I loved that helpless little thing as I had loved nothing in the world. I thought, this baby is a present from God, to calm me, to make up for what I have gone through in these last years."

That Zsa Zsa did not divulge the fact of her pregnancy at the divorce hearing back in September raised more than a few eyebrows. She would later claim that she knew she was expecting, but decided not to mention it because "the judge didn't ask me." Of the fact that she listed her age as twenty-one on the birth certificate, what can one say? She *was* Zsa Zsa Gabor, after all. (And she was also thirty.) She also listed her occupation as "house wife," which is perhaps as much of a surprise as the entry of her age.

When Francesca—she would always be known by her middle name— was born, Conrad Hilton did not openly question her paternity. Not exactly, anyway. Instead, James E. Bates, Conrad's attorney, called Zsa Zsa to ask for an important meeting with her. The two of them met in his office the next day, according to his and her later testimony about it. "She plopped her well-stacked 125 pounds down into a chair in front of me," he recalled, "and we got right down to business."

"Mr. Hilton and I are a bit curious to know why you have not demanded child support for Francesca," he observed.

Zsa Zsa studied the attorney carefully. "Because I don't need it," she said, choosing her words carefully. She added that she was "an independent, European woman," and was confident that she could raise their daughter on her own. "I don't want his money," she concluded.

"*You don't want his money?*" Bates asked incredulously. That certainly didn't sound like the Zsa Zsa known by James Bates. "Something is fishy here," he decided to himself, at least according to his later recollection. "You know, you can, if you wish to, that is, file a lawsuit against Mr. Hilton and demand child support from him," he told her, "and we may not even fight such an action." He said that they might be inclined to just settle the case, meaning Zsa Zsa would then end up with money for her daughter.

Now it was Zsa Zsa who felt that something was "fishy." Why would Conrad be *trying* to give her money? That certainly didn't sound like the

Conrad Hilton *she* knew. "As long as you tell Mr. Hilton that this is not my idea," she said, staring at the attorney sternly. "Because I don't ever want to hear that Zsa Zsa Gabor went after Conrad Hilton for child support. That's *not* what's happening here," she said. "Meanwhile, I need to think about all of this."

"Take all the time you want," James Bates said nonchalantly.

"I most certainly will."

That night, Zsa Zsa went home and racked her brain for an answer to the nagging question as to why in the world Conrad Hilton would be trying to give her money for child support. It made no sense to her. What was this really about?

Zsa Zsa was a smart woman. It wouldn't have taken her long to figure out that if she were to sue for child support, she might then be forced to prove in a court of law that Francesca was truly Conrad's biological daughter. In other words, she may have believed that he had devised a "backdoor plan" to get to what he believed might be the truth of Francesca's paternity. He knew Zsa Zsa was having sex with "many men"—at least by her own admission—and she figured that he probably felt he had good reason to believe that Francesca was not his child. Now she was angry.

"I finally understand what it is that you and Mr. Hilton are trying to do," she told James Bates the next day when she went back to his office.

"What do you mean?" he asked. "We are only trying to be of assistance to you, Zsa Zsa. Mr. Hilton still considers you family. Despite any recent ugliness..."

That Conrad Hilton still considered Zsa Zsa Gabor to be a member of the family would, with the passing of time, prove to be perhaps the greatest complication in both their lives, fertile ground for decades of paradoxes and contradictions in their relationship. Close to her parents and sisters, she was, like most Hungarians of her war-torn generation, an extremely family-oriented person.

If Conrad had cut Zsa Zsa off at this time, it might have saved them both many years of turmoil. He didn't, though. Coming from a large, close family, he too felt the urgency of familial bonds, and that Zsa Zsa insisted that Francesca was his child drew him in and made him feel connected to both of them—this despite any suspicions he may have had about Francesca's paternity. He would not remarry for decades, so in a sense, Zsa Zsa and Francesca would be the most recent addition to "family" he would have in his life. While it was true that Zsa Zsa would remarry many times over, her only child would be the one she had with Conrad. So, yes, these two disparate characters would be linked forever—for better or worse.

"Well, you can tell Mr. Hilton that I don't need his assistance," Zsa Zsa said, trying to keep her temper in check. "I will take care of our daughter on my own. He may think I just got off the boat, but I've been around long enough to figure him out. From now on if he wants to talk to me, he can call me himself. If we are, as he says, family, then no more meetings with *you*, Mr. Bates. Now, good day." She then stormed out of the attorney's office.

The big question, of course, was whether or not Conrad Hilton had sexual relations with Zsa Zsa Gabor during the time that they were separated, and in this case it would have to have been sometime in the summer of 1946. She claimed that they saw each other just one time between April and August of that summer, and that is when they were intimate. He said he did see her once, but that they most certainly did *not* have sex. They weren't even having sex when they lived together, he argued. Why would he fly all the way to New York to be intimate with her? Meanwhile, Zsa Zsa listed Conrad as the child's father on the baby's birth certificate, with his occupation "hotel owner." He didn't contest it. Complicating things further, he also did not feel much of an obligation to acknowledge the baby either. The fact of her birth—indeed, Francesca's name—is nowhere to be found in his autobiography, Be My Guest, which would be published in 1957 when the girl was about ten.

In his own reserved way, Conrad Hilton loved Francesca and wanted to protect her from scrutiny. After all, she was just an innocent child born to a warring couple. He sensed that her life would not be an easy one. Also, there's little doubt that he was also concerned about his family's name, as well as the reputation of his company. "Of course, he didn't want a public scandal," said his attorney Myron Harpole. "These were different times, different mores. These were the 1940s. He would have done anything at all to protect his family's good name. If you lived in the times, you would understand."

Simply put, Conrad encouraged Zsa Zsa and Francesca to feel that they were "family," mostly because he didn't want to force Francesca to live in a state of emotional exile. But privately, he would only take that kind of thinking so far. Without their knowledge, he did what he felt he had to do—he amended his last will and testament. A 1947 codicil to his will states, "It is my express purpose to leave nothing to the child born on or about March 10, 1947, to my former wife, Sari Gabor Hilton." Only he and his attorney knew of this new provision, however—and it would be more than thirty years before Zsa Zsa and Francesca would be made aware of it.

PART FOUR

Sons of the Father

Transition

Obviously, the marriage to and subsequent divorce from Zsa Zsa Gabor had taken an enormous emotional toll on Conrad Hilton. It had been draining. Making matters so much worse, the union had shut him out from the sanctuary of his religion, which had left a huge hole in his psyche. By the time he was divorced, he felt exhausted. A free man once again, he now hoped to put all the psychological turmoil behind him. Also, with this newfound freedom he could at last receive the sacraments of his faith once more, and that was no small comfort. Still, he was sad that it hadn't worked out. "I'm not even sure where it all went wrong," he would say. "I just never dreamed it would all end so badly. It had such a promising start. My God, I was crazy about her!"

After it was over with Zsa Zsa, Conrad Hilton did what most people expected he would do; he threw himself into his work. Now the owner of three of the best hotels in Chicago—the Palmer House, the Stevens (renamed the Conrad Hilton), and the Blackstone—and with two huge successes in New York City, the Roosevelt and the Plaza, Conrad Hilton turned his eyes 250 miles to the south, to Washington, D.C., where he set his sights on the Mayflower.

The Mayflower had quite a distinguished history. Construction on the hotel began back in 1922 by land developer Allen E. Walker, following the Beaux-Arts design of Robert F. Beresford of Warren and Wetmore Architects at a cost of $12.9 million. When it opened in 1925, it was nicknamed the "Grande Dame of Washington," and was said to contain more gold trim than any other building except the Library of Congress, evidence of which can be found in the ornate gilt columns standing guard in the hotel lobby. Located near the Dupont Circle neighborhood at 1127 Connecticut Avenue NW, it was deemed by Harry S. Truman to be Washington's "second best address."

Shortly after opening, the Mayflower hosted the presidential inaugural ball for Calvin Coolidge, a tradition that would continue for decades to come. Franklin Delano Roosevelt was a guest at the hotel when he worked on his historical "nothing to fear but fear itself" inaugural address. Truman, who succeeded FDR, resided there for the first ninety days of his presidency, following the death of Roosevelt, before moving to Blair House during the dismantling and rebuilding of the White House in 1948. Truman also announced his intention to run for the presidency from the Mayflower.

Conrad Hilton bought a controlling interest in the Mayflower in December 1946 for $2.6 million and later increased his stock for a total investment of $3.5 million (about one-fourth of the original construction cost). The Mayflower gave Hilton access to the powers of government much as his New York properties had put him at the center of the country's business and financial world, and much as the Stevens and the Blackstone had given him a huge presence in the most important city in America's heartland, Chicago. Now he was nothing if not a coast-to-coast presence, and his mantra seemed to be, "Give me more worlds to conquer."

In December 1946, just after Conrad closed the Mayflower deal, the Hilton family came together with other friends and business associates of the Hiltons for the eighty-fifth birthday celebration of Mary Hilton in El Paso. About a year later, Mary would suffer a heart attack while in Long Beach, where she was staying at the Hilton Hotel with her daughter Helen. For a couple of weeks, she would rally and then weaken again, her children at her side in the hospital the entire time. Finally, on August 27, 1947, she died peacefully in her sleep.

Not surprisingly, Mary Hilton's death hit Conrad hard. She was unfailingly there whenever he needed her, whether for financial aid—as had happened quite often—or for emotional support. Without her, he felt an anchor missing from his life. He believed that his success had true meaning when he could share it with his mother, and with her absence he knew that nothing would ever be the same. Still, he realized—to hear him tell it—that he had a clear responsibility to Mary to go on with his work and see to it that he not only continued to dream big dreams, but did everything in his power to make those dreams come true. "I have to do it for her," he said at the time. "After all she gave me, I owe her that much."

Mary Genevieve Laufersweiler Hilton was buried next to her beloved husband, Gus, in Socorro, New Mexico.

With his marriage over and his mother gone, now Conrad Hilton felt more alone than ever before. Of course, he had his sons, but Nicky was twenty-one and Barron twenty. Though he was close to them, both were becoming independent, with their own lives. Eric was just fourteen, but he was being raised by Mary and Mack; Conrad didn't see much of him.

It was at this time that Conrad began to keep company with the MGM film star Ann Miller. A beautiful, leggy brunette with a big, brassy personality, Ann was the epitome of Hollywood razzmatazz—an all-talking, all-singing, all-dancing Hollywood performer. She was a hell of a tap dancer, and because Conrad loved nothing more than being on the dance floor himself, he couldn't help but be drawn to this unflappable entertainer who claimed that she was able to do five hundred taps per minute. Along with her exuberance, Conrad also admired her level-headed determination.

At just twenty-four, Ann was fresh out of a stormy two-year marriage with steel mogul Reese Llewellyn Milner. She was just beginning a romantic relationship with William V. O'Connor, future chief deputy state attorney general of California and Governor Edmund Brown's right arm, and who, incidentally, had introduced her to Conrad.

After his divorce from Zsa Zsa Gabor and for many years to come, Conrad would regard Ann Miller as someone who would fill the void of flash and glamour that he had come to appreciate. She would often be at his side adding her glittery panache, especially at his hotel openings, where the two would take to the dance floor and thrill onlookers with routines carefully choreographed in advance. However, as she once insisted, "I was *not* having an affair with Conrad Hilton. We were always just good friends and, I might add, marvelous friends. We had a wonderfully warm relationship. He looked young, acted young. He was always the life of the party. But romance? Forget it."

Raising the Rich

Conrad Hilton had been raising his two sons, Nicky and Barron, as a single parent for many years; the exotic Zsa Zsa Gabor hadn't been much of a mother figure at all. The boys' biological mother, Mary Hilton

Saxon, was also not particularly accommodating at this time and some-times added stress to the equation. For instance, a tragedy was just barely averted in August 1940 when Conrad left Nicky, fourteen, and Barron, almost thirteen, in her care.

At the time, Mary and her husband, Mack, had fallen on hard times after Mack lost his school coaching job. Trying to help out, Conrad allowed the couple and little Eric to temporarily move into a suite on the ninth floor of the El Paso Hilton. One weekend, Mary asked if Nicky and Bar-ron could spend a couple of nights with her at the hotel; Conrad agreed and dropped the boys off. Mary and her sons then had a fun day together, and Barron and Nicky also spent time bonding with little Eric. But that night, Mary somehow fell asleep while smoking a cigarette; her bed went up in flames. After a bellboy noticed smoke billowing from a ninth-floor window, he summoned the fire department. Meanwhile, Mack Saxon—who was asleep in a room across the hall with Eric (since there weren't enough beds in Mary's suite for all of them)—was awakened by the smell of smoke. He raced into the hallway to find Mary standing there with Eric, choking and sobbing hysterically. He scooped her and the boy up and got them out of the suite as quickly as possible. Then he raced into her suite looking for Barron. When he finally found the boy, he rescued him as well. But where was Nicky? By the time Mack went back into the suite to search for Conrad's namesake, the room was so filled with thick black smoke that it seemed impossible to locate the boy. Luckily, Mack found a gasping Nicky standing in front of a living room window, desper-ately trying to open it for air. He grabbed the teenager and pulled him out of the suite, which by now was engulfed in flames. Though no one was injured, the frightening ordeal generated screaming headlines the next day in the *El Paso Herald*.

Had Mary been intoxicated? Was that the reason she fell asleep while smoking in bed? Conrad wasn't sure, but he suspected as much. From then on, he would severely limit the time she would be able to spend with her sons without his supervision. However, he stopped short of taking Eric from her and Mack; the boy continued to be raised by them. Eric was happy with the situation as it existed. After all, he was living the only life he had ever known and he was satisfied with it.

Whereas Nicky and Barron went to exclusive private schools and then military academies, Eric went to public schools. Whereas Nicky and Barron lived in an enormous mansion in Bel-Air, after the incident at the El Paso hotel Eric lived in a row home in a modest housing project in northern Virginia called Fairlington Villages. These were rental units built for the federal government's civil service employees and for the families of military personnel working in the gigantic Pentagon building. (After losing his coaching job, Mack Saxon had joined the Navy and began to work in its aviation physical training program at the Pentagon, thereby making him and his family eligible for housing quarters in Fairlington Village.) It was a simple, no-frills lifestyle, not exactly the kind one would expect to be lived by Eric, the youngest scion of America's greatest hotelier. Even though he didn't have much closeness with his youngest son, Conrad would still sometimes extend himself. For instance, he would sometimes fly Eric to the West Coast for a Hilton Hotels–related gala, or would include him on a junket for the opening of a hotel in another city.

He may not have always been present for Eric, but Conrad saw Nicky and Barron through myriad problems of teenage angst and rebellion. He did have some help. His mother-in-law, the mother of his first wife, Mary, came to live with them for a while and was helpful with the children. They were remarkable boys, actually, who enjoyed indulging their father in esoteric discussions about life and what it took to become successful in it. Conrad had told them that, based on his own experience, it was all a matter of prayer and hard work, that this was his "master plan" for great success. That didn't make complete sense to either of the boys at an early age. "But there has to be more than that, Pop," Nicky argued when he was about thirteen. "I also think there's something else at work," Barron agreed. "There's a missing ingredient there, Dad." The three spent many hours in Conrad's study talking about all of the possibilities and trying to figure out just what was missing from Conrad's equation for success, until finally the answer occurred to Conrad while he was on a business trip to New York. When he returned, he called the boys into the study and filled them in on what he now believed to be the missing element of his "master plan." "Dreams," he said. "You've got to *dream*. That's what's missing, sons. It's prayer, it's hard work, but it's also...dreams." The boys agreed and accepted the new theory.

Though both Hilton heirs had terrific senses of humor and were handsome and popular, neither was a particularly good student. Conrad was always tougher on Barron than he was on Nicky, though. It was as if he sensed that Nicky was doing the best he could, but just didn't have the faculties to excel in his studies, whereas he felt that if Barron would only apply himself he could be an A student. Limitations he could understand, a lackadaisical approach he could not. Nicky could goof off and Conrad seemed okay with it, but if Barron did the same thing, it was grounds for a major domestic crisis.

Conrad saw Barron's mediocre grades as a distinct character flaw. He hated the idea of mediocrity and wanted more than anything for his sons to excel. "All men are equal before God and before the law," he would later say in a graduation address at Michigan State College in East Lansing on May 19, 1950, "but it is nonsense to say that they are equal otherwise. There are a hundred ways in which people are not equal, in which they never will be equal, no matter how many laws are passed. Mediocrity is the price we pay for complete equality. If there is one thing our country needs today, it is to rid itself of mediocre—and find for itself—superior citizens, superior businessmen, superior fathers, mothers and wives, superior statesmen."

Conrad had what some might have considered a rather unorthodox way of handling Barron's pedestrian performance in school. As if reprimanding an unruly employee at the Hilton Corporation, he would schedule a meeting with Barron in his study to outline his rules and regulations for acceptable conduct, or as he explained in his memoir, Be My Guest, "our mutual responsibilities, allowances, duties, restrictions and privileges." After Barron reluctantly agreed to these stringent terms and conditions, each would be memorialized in a written contract, which both father and son would then sign. As far as Conrad was concerned, he now had an irrevocable deal with Barron. However, being a teenager rather than a company employee, Barron would inevitably dismiss the contract and do exactly what he wanted, much to Conrad's consternation. Actually, in some ways the relationship began to mirror the one Conrad had with his own hard-to-please father, Gus. Conrad had gone up against Gus every chance he got, and Barron did the same. In time, Barron's grades would improve, but he would never be a straight-A student. He would eventually end up dropping out of high school. Conrad certainly wasn't happy about it, but Barron's mind was made up. He didn't want to continue with high school, and for him that was the end of it.

As for Nicky, he just continued to maintain his below-par grades, sliding by without his father's attention or worry. "How come my pop gets all bent out of shape when Barron flunks something, but when I do, it's okay?" Nicky asked Everett Long, one of his best friends at the time. "It's like my pop doesn't give a shit if I graduate or not." Everett Long laughed. "Consider yourself lucky," he told Nicky. "You don't need the old man riding you anyway." Years later, Long would recall, "I remember Nick saying to me, 'I could murder someone and end up in jail and my dad would probably say, "Oh, gosh darn that Nicky!" But if Barron ended up in jail, my dad would die of a broken heart.'"

Predictably, Nicky soon became intensely competitive where Barron was concerned. If Barron had a girl, Nicky wanted a girl. If Barron got a new car, Nicky wanted a new car. It would be the pattern throughout their teenage years. Nicky just felt that Conrad preferred Barron, and so he would always work to try to reverse that situation, or at least be Barron's equal in all things. "Nicky could do anything he set his mind to, he just needed people to believe in him," said Robert Wentworth, who was also a friend of both Hilton sons. "He needed that kind of encouragement. I'm not sure he ever got it at home."

The boys may have been competitive, but they were also quite unusual youngsters in the sense that they both loved to express themselves, giving speeches when they were teenagers to nobody, really, other than each other and their father. Conrad would call these little speeches "stirring orations on important subjects." He wrote, "I could recognize my father's persuasiveness in this new generation. When Nick tried to convince me, his lone listener, 'Resolved: We Need Better Hospitals' or 'Resolved: We Have Too Many Schools,' I had visions of Gus and his cowbell storming about New Mexico for better roads."

After school, both Hilton sons ended up in the service. Barron had volunteered for the Navy as soon as he was old enough at seventeen, and soon found himself assigned to Pearl Harbor. Nicky served as a radar man aboard the battleship *North Carolina*. In one letter to Conrad, Nicky wrote that he realized that his personal wealth—or, more specifically, the wealth of his father—didn't matter one iota in the service. "You have to learn to take it and like it over here," he wrote. "It doesn't matter in the service how much money your dad has because you're in exactly the same boat with everyone else. If I was ever a smart aleck, or Barron either, and I guess we were, this is a fine place to get it kicked out of you."

In August 1945, when the war was finally over, Conrad was happy and relieved to have Nicky and Barron safely back home. However, neither son showed any interest in the hotel business. Likely because both had grown up in the huge shadow of their father's enormous success, now neither wanted to compete with him. True, when Barron was seventeen he worked as a doorman at the El Paso Hilton. He also worked in the garage at the Town House. But that was about as close to the hotel business as he wanted to get. He and Nicky—and even Eric—made it clear that they were not going to be following in their father's footsteps. Conrad was disappointed, but he tried his best to reconcile it, realizing, as he put it, "You have to let sons find their best path in life."

There was no denying that both Nicky and Barron were brimming with youthful potential and masculine allure. The Hilton brothers had grown into strikingly handsome men who oozed wealth and charisma. Nicky in particular had movie-star looks. His brown eyes were warm and inviting, as was his dazzling, porcelain-white smile. He added to his glamour boy appeal with impeccable grooming. His thick dark hair was always perfectly coiffed, groomed to perfection with expensive hair cream, comb-grooved, but with a careful, casual tousle—much like the teen idols of the day. He had yet to develop the full ladies' man image he would soon acquire, instead coming across as a younger, more innocent and boyish version of Burt Lancaster or Robert Mitchum. For his part, Barron was tall and slender with a regal bearing, dark curly hair, and an attractive intensity. He also dressed in impeccably tailored suits and exuded sophistication and charm.

Immediately after the service, Barron was able to enroll in the University of Southern California Aeronautical School—which did not require a high school diploma at the time—where he would go on to earn a twin-engine rating. However, he would drop out after just a year. "I didn't seem to get along with school," he would remember in 1981, "but I did well in arithmetic. It's somewhat embarrassing that I didn't really complete an education," he said. "I regret that to a degree."

Though he had dropped out of high school and then college, by the time he turned twenty-one, Barron Hilton's youthful days of irresponsibility and unreliability were relegated to his past. It was as if some mechanism in him switched on when he came of age, and suddenly he was his father's son: motivated, interested, invested, ready to make a fortune, and determined that he didn't have to have a full education in order to make it happen. Conrad agreed that Barron had what it took to advance in whatever profession he chose, and he was willing to give him a chance to figure out what that would be. It would probably be in the field of aeronautics, which was fine with Conrad. He knew that Barron would find his own way.

Unfortunately, Conrad didn't have the same confidence in Nicky. After the service, Nicky's ambition seemed to involve little more than enjoying his freedom and having a good time. Conrad also felt that Nicky was too idealistic. "Nicky was the kind of guy who just believed that everything was going to be okay," said Everett Long. "He wanted the best for everybody, even if he was in competition with Barron. He considered it a friendly competition. I'm not sure Barron felt exactly that way. I think Barron was a little tougher than that. Anyway, Conrad felt that Nicky was drifting. Eventually, he felt he had to step in and help steer Nicky in some sort of direction. He sent Nick down to Texas to work in the boiler room—the heating facilities—of his El Paso hotel for a short time. Then he coaxed him into studying hotel management in Switzerland at Ecole Hôtelière in Lausanne. Nicky didn't want to go, though, and fought it tooth and nail. His reasoning was that Conrad hadn't forced anything on Barron, why was he forcing this on him? Of course, the reason was because Barron seemed to have some sort of direction, whereas Nicky didn't."

After about six months of schooling, Nicky returned to Los Angeles, still no closer to having any sort of direction or goal. Conrad then offered him a job as a manager of the Bel-Air Hotel, in which Conrad had a major interest. Again, this was not Nicky's dream and he resented another attempt to push him into the hotel business. However, he figured that since Barron wanted nothing to do with it, it would give him a leg up in his competition with his younger brother for Conrad's approval. So Nicky took the job at the Bel-Air Hotel with reluctance, but soon realized he was actually good at it. He had a way with people, he had a great deal of charisma and personality, and he was funny and bright. "People gravitated to him and he was efficient in his job of managing that hotel," said Everett Long. "He had a lot of responsibilities and, for a minute there, I think he even had Conrad's approval."

An Offer He Could Refuse

On June 20, 1947, at just twenty, Barron Hilton married Marilyn June Hawley at St. Vincent de Paul Church in Chicago. "Her family had a home up in Lake Arrowhead," recalled Conrad's attorney Myron Harpole, "and that's where Barron and Marilyn first got acquainted. She was a wonderful girl. You couldn't help but fall for her."

At the time of her marriage, Marilyn—born in Los Angeles on February 11, 1928—was a pretty and stylish woman who wore fashionable yet simple clothes with classic lines. Her hair was dark blonde, her makeup usually consisting of little more than the red lipstick of the day. She certainly didn't have the flashy glamour of a celebrity, but her smile radiated great warmth. It was easy to see why Barron, who had grown up to be so serious and determined, would be attracted to such a striking, unassuming woman. Because of her great charm, friends like the actress Carole Wells remember her to this day as "beautiful."

The couple would have their first of eight children in 1948, William Barron Hilton Jr. Then, in 1949, along came Hawley Anne Hilton. By the time he was twenty-two, Barron was settled into a happy home life.

Just before he had his first son, Barron announced that he had been giving his future a great deal of thought and had come to the conclusion that he, like his older brother Nicky, who was working at the Bel-Air Hotel, wanted to work in the hotel business, and specifically for the Hilton organization. By this time, the Hilton Corporation had gone public, with its stock listed on the New York Stock Exchange; Conrad was the corporation's largest stockholder with more than $2 million in holdings.*

Conrad Hilton owned twelve major hotels by the time Barron decided

---

* "When Hilton went on the stock exchange, like any company there were upper-level employees who were able to buy the stocks at a little bit of a reduced rate before it went public," observed Mark Young, of the Conrad N. Hilton College of Hotel and Restaurant Management. "Someone wrote to Hilton and asked him why the rate was so exceptionally low. He wrote back explaining that he wanted not just the general managers and high-level executives to be able to buy, but also the cleaning staff, the cooks, the mechanics—the medium- and lower-level staff—to have the opportunity to buy as well. He believed strongly that people who worked for the company should have the opportunity to have some stake in it."

he wanted to be involved in the family's enterprise, nine of which were folded into the corporation and worth over $51 million. (The other three remained independent of it for technical reasons having to do with their financing.) It gave Conrad great satisfaction to know that the corporation's elected officers were all men who had started their climb up the ladder of success at around the same time he had, and who owed a lot of their success to his ingenuity, creativity, and business savvy. There was Red Ellison, for instance, who had once been a bellboy at the hotel in Abilene. He was the kid who had given Conrad $500, his life savings, when Conrad needed it most to keep the company going during the Depression. Now he was vice president in charge of the Western Division. There was also Bob Williford, former key clerk at the hotel in Dallas. Now he was executive vice president of the corporation and vice president in charge of the Central Division. There were many others as well, who had long been allies of Conrad Hilton's and were now rewarded with prime positions in the corporation. His assistant Olive Wakeman found herself promoted to executive secretary, which opened a position for personal secretary to Conrad Hilton, eventually given to Ruth Hinneman.

For Nicky, the news that Barron wanted to join the ranks in the hotel business wasn't the best. Now thriving at his position at the Bel-Air Hotel, for the first time Nicky had his father's respect on a professional level, and the old rivalry reared its head again. Nicky had even accompanied his father on an important business trip abroad intended to open communication channels between European and American hotels, which had led to the establishment of Hilton Hotels International in May 1946. As Conrad had explained it, the goal of this new company was to "expand internationally and thereby encourage both industry growth and tourism," with his corporate slogan being "World Peace through International Trade and Travel." Hilton believed his hotels could not only contribute to the economies of European countries but also provide a permanent reminder of the part America had played in the Allied victory with the establishment of the Marshall Plan and the Truman Doctrine. Along with the formation of the North Atlantic Treaty Organization (NATO), these two initiatives' stated aims were to help rebuild cities and economies after the devastation of World War II. Conrad also saw his efforts as a way to combat Communism, a growing menace to world peace and as insidious as the Nazi assault on Europe only a few years earlier. That he involved Nicky in these important matters meant the world to Nicky, and demonstrated that Conrad was beginning to take his eldest son seriously.

"Now, the hotel business was Nicky's thing," recalled Everett Long. "*He* was the son in the family business, not Barron. He wanted to know, 'Why is Barron all of a sudden interested? He wasn't before, why now?'"

This intense competition between the brothers was not the result of any genuine hostility between them. They had a deep and abiding love for one another. However, they displayed a fierce sibling rivalry that would last for their entire lives.

One day, out of the blue, Barron walked into Conrad's office to ask him for a job with the Hilton Corporation. Of course, Conrad was open to the idea. "I can start you out in a position at $150 a week," he said, according to his memory.

"You're joking, right?" Barron said.

"No," Conrad responded. "I think that's fair. I started at five dollars a month, but I think we can do a little better for you," he concluded with a wink. "Besides, that's what we started Nicky at, and that's where we'll start you at, whichever hotel we place you in."

Barron looked at his father as if he were daft. "But Nicky is on his own. I have a family," he said. "I have a child, my wife is pregnant with another. So we're talking about supporting three people. Plus, I have to have a cook. Oh, and I have to have a nurse, too. So that's *five* people I have to support, Dad!"

Conrad shook his head in astonishment, no doubt marveling at the temerity of the young man before him who felt entitled to not only his own cook but a live-in nurse as well. However, that's how he had raised his sons—with a staff of people on hand to do their every bidding. Therefore it was no surprise that they'd gotten used to living that way. Still, it was always a struggle for Conrad to reconcile the way he had been raised—with little—with the way he had raised his sons, and what they expected from life as a result of such a privileged upbringing. "I don't know what to tell you, Barron," he said. "We start people at $150 a week in our organization, and that's not going to change for you."

"Well, I can't work for any man for $150 a week," Barron said, getting up from his chair. "I need a thousand dollars a month, Dad. That's $250 a week."

"Sorry, son," Conrad said, holding his ground. "I can't help you," he concluded, standing up as well. The two men shook hands. As Barron turned to walk away, Conrad added, "If you think you can make a thousand dollars a month, go right ahead. But if you ever come back down to earth," he concluded, "come see me and we can always talk again."

"Sure," Barron said, seeming miffed.

As Barron left, Conrad sat back into his chair and smiled to himself. "Well," he later remembered thinking, "I guess you can't blame the kid for trying."

But Barron did exactly what he said he was going to do—he ended up making at least a thousand dollars a month, and usually much more, by going into the citrus products business with a friend and their Vita-Pakt Citrus Products Co. (The company is still in business today, though Barron long ago sold his interest in it.) It didn't take Barron long to go into that business, either. "Conrad was bowled over by Barron's success," recalled one Hilton relative. "He just always assumed that both boys would be in the hotel business at some point, and for Barron to make his own way like that, well, Conrad's admiration for him shot straight up through the ceiling." Or as Conrad once wrote, "I was pleased to think that if he and his wife had set out to better my own mother's and father's record, he had at least inherited some of Gus's ingenuity and business sense."

Not surprisingly, Nicky wasn't quite sure what to think of Barron's sudden success. Yes, he'd gotten what he wanted, which was Barron out of the hotel business. However, his brother was now his own man in more ways than one, and also making more money than Nicky. In the process, he'd earned even more respect from Conrad for making his own way and not relying on his father's largesse. Nicky wanted the best for Barron; he couldn't help it, he loved him. But still, the competition between the two brothers had just been ratcheted up to a whole new level.

The Question of Francesca

*I*t was July 1947. Newlyweds Barron and Marilyn Hilton were in New York staying at the Roosevelt Hotel when the telephone rang in their suite. According to what Barron would later recall under oath, the caller asked for "Mr. Hilton," and when told that he had Mr. Hilton on the line, he began to talk about an investigation he had been conducting. "As you instructed, sir, I've been looking into the matter we discussed," said the caller.

Investigation? At first, Barron was confused. "What are you talking about?" he asked.

"The investigation, sir," the caller said. "You know, the investigation I am doing into your divorce."

"Oh, wait," Barron said. "Hold on. You must want to talk to my father. Not me. I'm *Barron* Hilton."

"This isn't Conrad Hilton?"

"No, this is his son Barron."

"Oh," said the caller. "I'm terribly sorry." With that, he abruptly hung up.

After Barron put the receiver down, he sat staring at it for a moment. He was clearly disturbed. Marilyn had been quietly listening to the conversation. Noticing his confused expression, she came over and sat next to her husband on the bed. "What was that about, dear?" she asked.

"I'm not sure," Barron said, his brow furrowed. "Apparently, Dad has a detective investigating certain things regarding his divorce from Zsa Zsa."

"Really?" Marilyn said, looking perplexed. Perhaps it wasn't that unusual for a spouse to hire a detective during a divorce, but after one? And why would he keep the investigation a secret? "I wonder what's going on?" Marilyn asked.

"I don't know," Barron answered. "I cut the guy off. He thought he was talking to *Conrad* Hilton."

Marilyn collected her thoughts and sat quietly next to Barron for a long moment before speaking. "Do you think this has something to do with Francesca?" she asked delicately. It was as if her woman's intuition had just kicked in at that moment.

Barron shook his head. "No, it can't." Then, after a pause, he added, "I mean . . . *can it?*" It could not have been lost on him, nor on Marilyn, that Francesca had been conceived while Conrad and Zsa Zsa Gabor were in the middle of an acrimonious divorce, living apart and most of the time barely acting civil toward each other.

"I just don't know," Marilyn said. "But maybe you should talk to Conrad about it."

"Maybe," Barron said. He didn't, however, seem eager to do so. The subject of what had gone on behind closed doors during the end of his father's second marriage was an extremely uncomfortable one. There was no way he could ever imagine discussing sexual timelines and possible affairs with his devoutly Catholic parent.

Barron never would discuss the call with Conrad, other than to tell him that a private investigator had telephoned and began speaking to him erroneously. Barron would later say, "I assumed at that point that this could be the question, as to whether Francesca's birth would be a part of that investigation. However, it was just an assumption at that time. My father never did discuss this matter with me."

PART FIVE

Elizabeth

Beautiful Dreamer

*J*ust look at this girl, Pop," Nicky Hilton said. It was the summer of 1949 and Conrad Nicholson Hilton Jr. and his father, Conrad, were sitting in the study of their Bel-Air estate, Conrad holding court behind his large agarwood desk, Nicky sitting on the other side of it in a heavily upholstered leather chair. "I have to meet her," the twenty-three-year-old heir said as he handed his father a picture he had neatly clipped from a newspaper.

Conrad took the cutting from his son and examined it. "Yes, she's a real beauty, all right," he said, according to his later memory of the conversation. "Elizabeth Taylor, eh?" He handed the clipping back to his son. "Well, I'll bet you can't even get close to her," he said with a good-natured grin, "let alone meet her. I mean, she's a movie star. Come on, Nicky! How are you going to meet her?"

Nicky sat back in his chair and, staring at the photo, smiled to himself. "I'll bet I meet her, Pop," he said. "I'll just bet you that I do."

Conrad laughed. "Okay," he said, chuckling, "it's a bet, then." When Nicky left the study, Conrad sank back into his chair and smiled. "My Nicky, the beautiful dreamer," he said to himself.

As the months turned into years, an interesting dynamic had begun to develop between Conrad and Nicky. As much as he admired Barron's determination, and as flattered as he was that those traits mirrored characteristics of his own, there was something different and special about Nicky that appealed to him too.

Nicky was carefree and fun-loving, a real ladies' man. By the time he was twenty-one, he was living the kind of life Conrad had always wanted for himself but never had the nerve—or the personality—to make his own. After all, Conrad had worked from the time he was a young man. Now, at sixty-two, when he looked back on his life, he was of course proud of his business achievements, but he did have certain regrets. He realized that with all he'd accomplished he'd never had one of the most cherished things life had to offer: fun. His greatest source of entertainment had always been trafficking in big business, making deals, courting some grand hotel, and finally acquiring her and making her his own. However, in retrospect he felt a great sadness, a feeling of having missed out. For instance, he hadn't had a lot of women. He simply didn't have the time nor the inclination for romance other than the fleeting kind. When he did feel passion, it usually wasn't of the sexual nature. He had been married to one of the most sensationally beautiful women in the world in Zsa Zsa Gabor, yet when she wanted to make love he usually balked. Part of this could be ascribed to his religious convictions, of course. However, deep down, as he would later confide, he had to wonder if that was just an excuse, if he had simply lost interest in his wife after finally "acquiring" her. Why, he sometimes wondered, couldn't he be more like Nicky? Would Nicky have ever turned away someone like Zsa Zsa? Not likely.

As surprising as it would have been to Nicky had he known it, Conrad couldn't help but be just a little envious of him. "Nick was like a cat in heat," said a Hilton family friend. "Every gal he took out he screwed, and all were great beauties." Nicky was out on the town every night, getting into mischief with the opposite sex and spending his money wildly with no sense of responsibility. While it was sometimes maddening for Conrad to bear witness to Nick's lifestyle, he couldn't help but feel that Nicky lived fearlessly, and he had to admire him for it.

"If only I had just a little of whatever it is Nicky has that makes his life such a good time for him," Conrad told his attorney Myron Harpole, "I think maybe I would have been happier." When Myron commented that Conrad didn't seem to be particularly unhappy, he shrugged his shoulders and said, "Well, it's too late now to worry about it. But I have to confess, I do wish I'd had more fun. If you don't mind me saying so, maybe even some more romance. Does that make me sound like an old fool?" he asked. Myron smiled at him. "Yes, it does," he told Conrad. "An old fool, just like the rest of us."

Though Conrad Hilton couldn't turn back the hands of time, he could at least live vicariously through his namesake. How he loved hearing Nicky's wild tales! His stories were the source of hours of laughter and bonding between himself and his firstborn. Olive Wakeman would tell Myron Harpole, "You can always tell which of his sons is in his study with him behind closed doors. If the tone of the conversation is subdued and serious-sounding, it's between Conrad and Barron. But if raucous laughter and good-natured ribbing is heard, for certain the banter is between Conrad and Nicky."

Even though Conrad had bet Nicky he wouldn't be able to get near Elizabeth Taylor, let alone meet her, he would have to admit that, in his heart of hearts, he figured Nicky would win that bet. He rather hoped he would.

Enter: Elizabeth Taylor

*I*t didn't take Nicky Hilton long to prove his father wrong. Once he set his mind to doing something, he usually did it. As it happened, Nicky knew a friend who knew another person well connected in the movie business, and before he knew it, he was invited to actress Jane Powell's wedding party at the Mocambo nightclub on Sunset Boulevard (the same nightspot at which his dad had given Zsa Zsa Gabor her engagement ring). And there he found himself sitting shoulder to shoulder with the one and only Elizabeth Taylor. It was September 17, 1949, an evening Nicky would never forget.

Many years later *Vanity Fair* would call Elizabeth Rosemond Taylor "a real-life Helen of Troy." At just seventeen, she was ripe and ready to launch the first of her many thousand ships. She was already an accomplished actress, having appeared in more than a dozen major films, mostly for MGM, such as *Cynthia, A Date with Judy, Julia Misbehaves,* and *The Big Hangover.* By 1949, pretty much everyone in America knew the name Elizabeth Taylor, and it wasn't just her acting career that singled her out for acclamation, it was her rare, almost unparalleled beauty. Although she certainly wasn't statuesque, standing only a little above five feet tall in her stocking feet (her height would be exaggerated throughout her career), she had a regal bearing and a well-shaped body with full breasts and a tiny waist that she enjoyed showing off with plunging necklines and tight belts. She also had an inherent sexuality that even as a teenager she exuded effortlessly. Her beautiful face, while certainly one of the most photogenic in the history of motion pictures, was even more stunning in person, and made her truly ravishing. Women around the world would turn themselves into cut-rate Elizabeth Taylors in a futile attempt to duplicate her special allure: the jet black hair, flawless skin, pouty red lips, and perfectly sculpted eyebrows. But it was her bewitching, violet-blue eyes, so darkly lashed and blazing with a startling range of emotions, that really set her apart from mere mortals. It is now legend that when the still teenage Elizabeth would walk into the MGM commissary, everyone, even the most jaded stars, would stop eating, turn to look at her, and gasp. Then a hush would fall over the room as she made her way to a table, all eyes following her. That was the reaction Elizabeth Taylor elicited when-ever she entered any room. It certainly was the reaction she elicited from Nicky Hilton the night he finally met her.

Elizabeth had been working since she was a young girl, with her stage mother, Sara Taylor (herself a frustrated actress), constantly critiquing and fine-tuning her to almost mechanical proficiency. As a result, she felt that she had missed out on her childhood and teen years. At seven-teen, she thought she wanted nothing more than to break away from the mother who dominated not only her but also her brother, Howard, and their father, Francis, and start living a real, genuine life—not just one that was documented on film. However, when she told her mother that she wanted to stop making movies, Sara said it was impossible. "You have a responsibility, Elizabeth," she told her. "Not just to this family, but to the country now, the whole world."

It's safe to say that there was more than a little resentment and anger building in young Elizabeth by the time she met Nicky Hilton. She had just finished filming A *Place in the Sun* with Montgomery Clift and Shel-ley Winters, and she was exhausted. Although the film would not be released for almost two years, it would show Elizabeth to the world as an artist who could really act. Portraying the rich, spoiled Angela Vick-ers, she demonstrated a surprisingly wide range of emotions as she fell in love with a man far beneath her social class (played by Montgomery Clift, for whom she had truly developed feelings). In the movie, she drove Clift's character, George Eastman, to murder so that he could be free to marry her. It was a role through which the public would see a new depth and maturity in Elizabeth's acting, and the exhilarating working experi-ence did a lot to build her self-confidence. She was sick and tired of being manipulated by her mother, by the MGM movie studio, by the media, and even by a public that seemed to want to infantilize her forever.

After their initial meeting at the Mocambo, Nicky and Elizabeth had lunch at a Mexican restaurant on Melrose Avenue. He was so taken with her, he had flowers sent to her that same day. Their romance unfolded quickly from there. Before anyone knew what was happening, she was all he could think about, all he could talk about. He began to gift her with expensive jewelry, which even at her young age was one way to Elizabeth's heart. Those closest to the family felt that Nicky perhaps wanted to emulate his brother, Barron, and settle down, and maybe in the process win just a little more favor with his father.

"Pop, think we can have a little talk?" Nicky asked Conrad one evening after dinner. Conrad excused himself and his son from the table, and the two then went into the study.

"I want to marry Elizabeth," Nicky told Conrad once they were alone in Conrad's inner sanctum. "I love her and I want her to be my wife. I think we can be happy together."

According to what Nicky would later recount to his trusted friend Bob Neal,* Conrad wasn't sure what to make of Nicky's decision. "Why, Nick?" Conrad asked him. "You're both so young. This is so fast. You just met her!"

"But Barron was younger than me when he got married and you didn't question that," Nicky protested. That was undeniably true. But Conrad had felt that Barron was mature and prudent enough to handle marriage and children. He wasn't so sure about Nicky. He had the same opinion of Nicky that he'd always had—he admired his zeal for living and his appetite for fun, while at the same time questioning his ability to be responsible and to commit to one thing for long. He appealed earnestly to him to reconsider, to give it more time. But Nicky wouldn't hear of it. His mind was made up.

"Nick, you don't know what you're getting yourself into with this girl. I've been down this road, and I know how tough it is." He spoke of the difficulty of living a life in a "fishbowl" with Zsa Zsa and the unrelenting media curiosity that accompanied their marriage. And she was famous for her personality alone. Elizabeth Taylor was a movie star, America's

---

* Maxwell House coffee heir Robert Neal was a well-known man-about-town, once recognized by United Press International as one of the ten most eligible bachelors alongside Howard Hughes and Marlon Brando. A good friend of Peter Lawford's, he was Peter's best man when Lawford married Pat Kennedy, sister of the president. He also arranged their honeymoon cruise. He recalled that he and Nicky were so close, they used to call themselves "the Gold Dust Twins."

sweetheart, with the powerful machinery of MGM's publicity department behind her, turning out updated scoops on her life as they unfolded. The couple's every move would be documented in newspapers and fan magazines. They wouldn't have a moment of privacy. "Life with Elizabeth will be beyond anything you have ever experienced," Conrad said.

Conrad's fiery plea fell on deaf ears. Nicky was going to marry Elizabeth and he was sure they would make it work. He believed in her, and he believed in himself. Conrad felt he was being, as usual, idealistic and naïve. Nicky didn't care. "But I still need your approval," he told his father. "Please don't make me get married without your approval, Pop."

Conrad sighed. He knew he would have to acquiesce. Of course, he would have preferred to have more control over him, but he knew that Nicky would ultimately do what he pleased—and perhaps it would work out for the best. After all, Nicky had surprised everyone by stepping up to the plate and making a successful career managing the Bel-Air Hotel. "Of course you have my approval," Conrad said finally. "But," he couldn't help adding, "I think you're making a big mistake."

Nicky grinned broadly. "Then it will be *my* mistake," he said. The two men stood up and firmly shook hands, but only Nicky was smiling.

The Man Who Bought the Waldorf

Nicky Hilton's intention to marry Elizabeth Taylor would not be a priority in Conrad Hilton's life, not yet anyway. Something else big was on the horizon, the realization of what could only be described as a personal dream of his. Nicky wasn't the only one clipping pictures from magazines and using them for inspiration. Since 1932, Conrad Hilton had kept a small, dog-eared picture of a hotel under glass on his desk in his office at the Los Angeles Town House. He had seen it in a publication while crossing the country in a train, and couldn't resist it. Across its front he wrote, "The greatest of them all." It was a photograph of the splendid Waldorf-Astoria, truly considered at the time to be the world's premier hotel, a New York City landmark and one that Hilton had long wanted to own. He could barely afford to put a roof over his family's head—which was how they all ended up living at the El Paso Hilton—yet here he was fantasizing about owning the Waldorf-Astoria.

Of all the women in his harem, the Waldorf was the one Conrad knew he would cherish the most, and as far as he was concerned, all of the many loves of his life had been but mere forerunners to this one, the grandest dame of them all. Even with the string of successes Hilton achieved in the 1940s, he kept wondering if they constituted enough "practice," as he had once put it, for him to have a run at the real prize—the Waldorf-Astoria. Proudly it sat in all of its imposing art deco splendor at 301 Park Avenue, occupying the entire block between East 49th and 50th Streets. It was a forty-seven-story architectural marvel that had inspired countless glossy magazine features and photo spreads and hundreds of newspaper articles, with its celebrated history of luring thousands through its doors.

But that was in its heyday. Now the wisdom of owning the Waldorf-Astoria was questioned by many of Conrad's advisers on his board of directors. Nothing new there—they seemed almost never to agree with him. The hotel was in financial trouble; even though it was still considered the biggest and the best, it had fallen on hard times during the Depression and hadn't fully recovered. However, as with most of his acquisitions, Conrad had a strong intuition that the Waldorf could and would recover, and that when it did it would be more profitable than ever. What the hotel had going for it—besides its exquisite craftsmanship that would have been cost-prohibitive to replicate in 1949—was its prestigious name value. The Waldorf was world-renowned and had a stellar reputation. Many notables happily called it their home away from home. Winston Churchill, Pope Pius XII, and the crowned heads of many nations were impressed with not only the stunning architecture but also the impeccable service of the Waldorf-Astoria.

If one were going to visit New York at the time, the Waldorf-Astoria was still the most coveted destination. (At its original location, where the Empire State Building now stands, it was also the first hotel in the country to feature room service.) However, the prices were so exorbitant that most people simply couldn't afford it. "It was the host to kings," Conrad Hilton would write. "It made history. It made news. It made everything but money." Conrad believed all that could change, though, and of course he felt he was the man to do the job.

For Conrad, owning this hotel was essential. "He believed that if he could claim ownership of the Waldorf, it would be the one thing upon which he could always hang his hat," said Olive Wakeman a few years later, in 1963. "Call it ego, call it what you like, but Mr. Hilton felt the hotel already belonged to him, and all he had to do was cut through the red tape and deal with the other formalities that prevented it from truly being his. I don't think there was ever a doubt in his mind that, somehow, he would own the Waldorf-Astoria. That's the kind of man he was."

There were two companies governing the Waldorf at the time, with which Conrad would have to deal in order to acquire it: the Hotel Waldorf-Astoria Corporation, which owned the hotel and its name, and the New York State Realty and Terminal Company, which had been organized by two railroads, the New York Central and the New Haven, and which owned the land on which the hotel was leased. Since the New York State Realty and Terminal Company had put forth $10 million to build the hotel, it had final say over who owned it. So as well as purchase control of the corporation, Conrad would have to appeal to the Realty and Terminal Company.

The first hurdle to leap would have to do with the Hotel Waldorf-Astoria Corporation. Since it retained control of the building and the land, it was therefore in a position to deny any prospective purchaser the right to acquire the prized real estate. With a level of arrogance that some observers at the time felt set a new standard, the corporation members dug in their heels, claiming they were opposed to any prospective owner who had several irons in the fire, like Conrad. A new owner should be a man with nothing on his mind but the Waldorf. In other words, they were afraid that Hilton's commitment and attention to the hotel were lacking.

There were few businessmen as diplomatic as Conrad Hilton. He knew how to schmooze not only the stockholders leery of allowing him ownership of the hotel due to their sense that the hotel would be less special if it were "just another Hilton enterprise," but also his own board of directors, who viewed the Waldorf-Astoria as a white elephant that would do nothing but deplete the company's finances. No matter how many hotels Hilton owned and how successful he was with them, there was always resistance to his making big acquisitions. It speaks to the economic times, of course, but also to the ego of those who had designated themselves guardians of these hotels' legacies. There had been those who felt that Hilton's ownership of the Plaza would somehow ruin that grand dame's reputation, and he seemed to be facing the same sentiment where the Waldorf was concerned.

With the door slammed in his face by the Waldorf-Astoria Corporation, Hilton had to at least try to appeal to the New York State Realty and Terminal Company. He decided to first approach R. E. Dougherty, vice president in charge of real estate for the New York Central, figuring it would be better to plead his case to one man and arrive at something— even defeat—than continue to deal with what Conrad felt was an amorphous, soulless Waldorf Corporation. Accompanied by his trusted adviser Joseph P. Binns, Hilton began a long, wearisome campaign to convince Dougherty that he had no intention of converting the stately Waldorf into a run-of-the-mill way station, that he would keep alive the storied tradition that had made it one of the wonders of the hotel world. After all, hadn't he already proved what he could do with his acquisition of the Plaza and the Roosevelt, rescuing both from uncertain futures and returning them to their former glory? Dougherty conceded that Hilton had done a miraculous job in both instances.

Months passed in 1949 with no progress in the purchase of the hotel. In the summer, Conrad went to Europe to investigate opportunities there for hotels he might acquire as part of his new venture, Hilton Hotels International. Upon his return, he learned that another mogul was interested in the Waldorf-Astoria, or as he put it, "The Queen had, in my absence, acquired a second suitor, a wealthy fellow who had no other lady in mind." Now Hilton was afraid that he might never acquire the hotel unless he acted quickly. His corporation's board of directors was, as usual, not encouraging about the purchase and tried to block it in every way they could think of. Never one to be easily discouraged, Conrad decided to use his own money rather than the corporation's to finance part of the purchase, and to form a "buying group" of investors for the rest. In other words, he was acting independently of his own corporation—unusual, to say the least, but not surprising if one knew Conrad Hilton. He would find a way, especially when there seemed to be no way.

Within days, Conrad walked into the office of one of the chief stockholders in the Waldorf Corporation and presented a personal check to purchase 249,024 shares of stock at $12 a share. This purchase, if accepted, would give him a majority control of the corporation. The offer was accepted within forty-eight hours. Now it would be up to Conrad to cough up $3 million, the asking price for the hotel itself. Meanwhile, he kept whittling away at any resistance from the Waldorf-Astoria Corporation and the New York State Realty and Terminal Company, constantly meeting with its members, constantly reassuring them of his intentions and basically winning them all over.

With the wheels in motion for the purchase, and it being clear that Hilton was going to proceed with or without his own Hilton Hotels Corporation, HHC finally decided to participate in the buying group. Slowly but surely, with his corporation's investment as well as those of a number of backers, from banking institutions to insurance companies, Hilton began to amass the $3 million he needed to make the purchase. He was still $500,000 short when he sat down with his friend the entrepreneur Henry Crown. "What do you say you and I just go in with halves of the five hundred grand and get this hotel?" Crown didn't even hesitate, coming up with the $250,000 for his old friend. In the end, Conrad would pay $3 million for about 69 percent of the Waldorf-Astoria Corporation, and also assume a debt of almost $4.5 million. Thanks to his scrutiny of the bottom line, he would soon increase his holdings in the hotel from 69 percent to 100 percent.

On October 12, 1949, the deal was concluded; Conrad Hilton now owned the Waldorf-Astoria. For the rest of his life, he would be known as "the Man Who Bought the Waldorf." There was even a biography published about him in 1950 using that title by Thomas Ewing Dabney. Conrad would say that for the rest of his life, everything he did would be measured as having happened either "before the Waldorf" or "after the Waldorf."

Conrad's impact on the grandest of all hotels would be felt almost immediately. For instance, he would install vitrines—glass-paneled cabinets—in the lobby to showcase and sell objets d'art, thereby putting about $18,000 in the hotel's coffers every year. After a thorough investigation, he would disprove rumors that pilfering by employees was costing as much as $100,000 a year. He would also set up the operational side of the Waldorf on a basis whereby even partial occupancy would still yield a profit. His experience operating other hotels would tell him that if properly managed and cost-planned, the Waldorf could make a profit on 75 percent occupancy. In fact, he believed it could even be profitable on a 50 percent occupancy.

The same evening that Conrad Hilton made what was arguably thus far the most important purchase of his life, he stood under the formal canopy of the Park Avenue entrance of the Waldorf-Astoria along with his public relations man, Arthur Foristall. It was, as Conrad would later put it, "raining cats and dogs." The two men watched as an elegantly dressed doorman summoned taxicabs for hotel guests anxious to get on with their night. Despite the inclement weather, they all had smiles on their faces. Why not? They were staying at the Waldorf, after all.

"Can you believe your luck, my friend?" Arthur asked Conrad.

Hilton smiled broadly. "I'm not sure you could call it luck, but yes, this is absolutely unbelievable. Look at where we are. I feel blessed."

"What a life," Arthur said, shaking his head. "What an amazing life."

Conrad had to agree.

As the many patrons lined up to wait for their cabs, none of them were aware that they were in the presence of the mogul who now owned the hotel in which they were staying. Conrad just stood and watched with a smile on his face, allowing the moment to burn itself into his memory. This was what it was all about, after all. If not for the satisfied patrons of a hotel, what would be the purpose of his life?

"Rather makes it all worthwhile, doesn't it?" Arthur Foristall said as he watched the people go by, preoccupied with their lives and enjoying the Manhattan night scene.

"Well, at the end of this rainy night, they've all got warm beds to come back to in the best darn hotel in the whole wide world," Conrad concluded with a grin. "And you know what? It doesn't get better than that."

Fast Worker

*U*pon his return to Los Angeles in November 1949, some observers assumed that Conrad Hilton would retire. For the most part, these were people who didn't know him well and didn't understand his work ethic. But even his trusted assistant, Olive Wakeman, wondered what her boss would do now that he had topped off his career by acquiring the Waldorf-Astoria. "This is really the pinnacle, if you think about it," she said at the time to

Newsweek. "One has to wonder what's left to do in the hotel business?" As far as Conrad was concerned, though, there was still plenty to do. Like most enormously successful people, a new accomplishment only served to fuel his ambition. Still, with his great success, he did become a bit mellower, not as consumed by work as he had been in the past and a little more eager to enjoy his free time. Once he purchased the Waldorf, "he had a rule," recalled his son Barron, "which was, after six o'clock at night he didn't want to discuss business with anyone. At that point, all he wanted to do was think in terms of going dancing. This was a good time in his life, in all of our lives. When you're successful at what you love, it's a good time."

The first order of personal business for Conrad in the new year of 1950 was to focus on his family life, namely the future of Nicky. Conrad was still not convinced of the wisdom of Nicky's decision to marry Elizabeth Taylor, but he realized there wasn't much he could do about it. "Definitely, Dad would have preferred for Nick to lead a more stable life than the movie star experience he had with Zsa Zsa," his brother Eric would say many years later. "But Nick was an individualist. Just like children today, you can guide them and tell them what you want, but they're going to do what they want to do, especially if they're strong-willed like Nick."

It was clear to everyone that Elizabeth's mother, Sara Taylor, was excited about the prospect of her family being linked to the much-respected and upwardly mobile Hiltons. It wasn't as if the Taylors didn't have their own money, either. They were quite well-off, and had always been so even before relocating to the States from England. However, Sara Taylor was nothing if not ambitious for herself and her daughter. She loved the idea of successful American capitalism. If Elizabeth could marry well in the States, she would certainly not be opposed to it.

"As you know, Elizabeth is in the middle of filming a picture called *Father of the Bride,*" she explained during a dinner at the Hilton mansion to plan the nuptials. She said that the studio wanted the wedding to take place in conjunction with the release of the movie and asked Conrad if he had a problem with that strategy. Conrad was so taken aback by this revelation that he was at a rare loss for words. He asked Nicky what he thought. Nicky shrugged and downed another shot of Johnnie Walker Black, his drink of choice. Elizabeth also had no comment on the subject. It was Barron who blurted what was on his mind. "Why, that's the craziest thing I have ever heard," he said, chuckling.

Sara wasn't about to dignify what she considered an uninformed remark with a comment. Instead she turned to Conrad. "Mr. Hilton, you understand business," she said curtly. "Perhaps you should school your son on the ways of the Hollywood picture system." Elizabeth, she added, had a lucrative contract with the studio, and if MGM wanted to use the wedding as a vehicle to promote their picture, it was their prerogative. "I'm sure you, a businessman, have no problem with this. *Do you, Mr. Hilton?*"

"Well, I'm not the one getting married," Conrad answered, certainly not one to be cowed by Sara Taylor. "This is above my grade anyway," he said, using a slang of the times for "Don't ask me." He turned to his son. "Again, what do you think, Nicky?" he asked. Nicky gave his standard response in conveying indifference: a casual shrug.

Before the Taylors left the Hilton home, everyone agreed that they would allow MGM to do whatever it wished with the wedding. The parents of the bride were to pay for the wedding anyway, and since Nicky had no opinion one way or another, the Hiltons felt their only choice was to keep their input to a minimum. What they didn't know, though, was that the Taylors wouldn't be paying for the nuptials, either. In what they considered a fantastic advertising coup for their next Elizabeth Taylor vehicle *Father of the Bride*, MGM would foot the entire bill. Not to be outdone, Conrad would offer to pay for what promised to be a wedding reception to beat all receptions at the Bel-Air Country Club. (There would end up being more than seven hundred guests at this gala, with a receiving line that was so long it would take guests six hours to get from the end of the line to the front in order to greet the newlyweds.) Conrad also generously offered to pay for the couple's honeymoon, which was to be an extended cruise on the *Queen Mary* and a tour of Europe. In the end, the Taylors got away with not paying for anything.

Shortly after that planning dinner, Conrad discovered something about Elizabeth that he found somewhat alarming. It was actually Olive Wakeman who brought the matter to his attention. "Don't you think it's a little strange that this girl is just seventeen and already has one broken engagement?" she asked him.

Apparently, as Olive explained, just five months before she met Nicky, Elizabeth Taylor had been engaged to a man named William Pawley, who was ten years her senior. "It was in all of the papers," Olive told Conrad. "I'm surprised you didn't know!" Because of everything that had been

going on lately with the consuming New York and Puerto Rico businesses, Conrad said he was too busy to read entertainment-related articles
in the press. He asked Olive to find out what she could about the engagement. It didn't take long for his trusty assistant to come back with the
information that the engagement between Taylor and Pawley had ended
on September 17, 1949, which—coincidentally enough—was the exact
same date she met Nicky at the Mocambo! Pawley had been with Elizabeth at Jane Powell's wedding that same afternoon. He left Los Angeles
that night when Elizabeth broke off their engagement, which was how
she ended up going to the Mocambo alone. Once there, she met Nicky.

"Fast worker, that one, isn't she?" Conrad said of the young Miss Taylor.
"Is Nick aware of this?" Olive said she didn't know. Conrad then summoned Nicky and told him what he had learned. It was all news to him. He
couldn't believe Elizabeth hadn't disclosed the previous engagement,
especially since it had ended the same day he met her! "But she's only
seventeen," Nicky said. "When did she have time to be engaged to someone else? No," he decided. "I'm not going to doubt her. I just want to
believe in her."

"Well, if you ask me, I think it's a little suspect," Conrad told his son.
"A word to the wise...," he said, not finishing his sentence.

Nicky nodded. "Quite right, Pop. It is a little weird. I'll ask her about it."

When Nicky finally confronted Elizabeth, she said that she hadn't purposely kept anything from him. It had been in all of the newspapers, after
all. "It's not like I can ever have secrets," she told him. He was relieved
that she hadn't lied to him. "I just knew you wouldn't lie to me," he told
her. "I would never do it," she told him. "I love you, Nicky!"

Though comforted by the knowledge that she hadn't purposely with-
held information from him, the news of Elizabeth's previous engagement
at such an early age made Nicky wonder if perhaps the real reason she was
marrying him was because she was looking for liberation, and that any
man who could provide it to her would be an acceptable husband. Many
years later, in 1987, Elizabeth would admit, "I was desperate to live a life
independent of my mother." She often told Nicky that once she was Mrs.
Conrad Hilton, Sara would have less to say about how she lived. Nicky
didn't find this information at all reassuring.

Moreover, Elizabeth had a strained relationship with her father, Francis. He was a weak man who could never stand up to his wife and was not

exactly a strong influence. In some respects, Elizabeth seemed to be looking for a father figure.

Also, as it happened, Elizabeth was fighting another battle, this with her own natural adolescent urges. As she put it, "The morality I learned at home required marriage. I couldn't just have an affair. I was ready for love and I was ready for lovemaking." Nicky wasn't thrilled with that logic either. He wanted to believe that Elizabeth truly loved him and wanted more than just to get away from her parents and have sex, but he had to admit that he wasn't really sure.

In other words, a lot of reasons began to present themselves as to why she wanted to marry Nicky Hilton—and her actually being in love with him seemed pretty far down the list.

Nicky loved Elizabeth, though, for certain he knew that much. She was sweet to him, laughed at his jokes, seemed to want to be with him... and happily accepted the $10,000 four-carat diamond engagement ring he presented her. However, he couldn't shake the feeling that if not him, someone else...*anyone* else.

Nicky Takes Elizabeth to Texas

*W*hile Nicky had legitimate concerns when it came to marrying Elizabeth—and his father most certainly agreed that they were all potential problems—Conrad also had another worry. He was just recently out of a mixed marriage with Zsa Zsa Gabor and therefore all too familiar with the complications such a situation posed for any practicing Catholic. Elizabeth wasn't Catholic either. Her mother was a practicing Christian Scientist and she was intent on passing that religion down to her daughter. Conrad didn't want any more problems with the Catholic Church, and he wanted Nick to be married in the church. Therefore he told Nick that Elizabeth must take the religious classes necessary for her to marry in the church. He also wanted her to sign a document stating that she would agree to raise any Hilton child as a Catholic. It was the only way a marriage ceremony between her and Nick could occur in the church anyway. "I'm not sure I can do that, Pop," Nicky said when his father proposed the idea. "She's not going to like it." Conrad said he would take it up with Sara Taylor if he had to, so Nick knew that the best course of action would be for him to just convince Elizabeth.

Nicky was right; when he presented Elizabeth with the idea of raising their children as Catholics, she balked. Yet in the end she did sign the agreement—but because she waited until just ten days before the ceremony, there would be more than a little suspense about it. She didn't hesitate, however, to take the religious courses required for a Catholic wedding. In exchange, Conrad set aside $100,000 for their first child, and he also gave Elizabeth one hundred shares in Hilton stock to show his appreciation for her going along with his suggestion. Moreover, he told her that a suite in the Waldorf-Astoria would always be hers whenever she wanted one. For the moment anyway, everyone was happy.

On February 21, 1950, Conrad Hilton made the official announcement to gossip columnist Louella Parsons: His son Nicky was going to marry Elizabeth Taylor. The day of the announcement was a busy one. Elizabeth had finished filming *Father of the Bride* that morning—it was now scheduled to be released within two weeks of the wedding ceremony— and then later that afternoon the Taylors hosted a formal tea at their Elm Drive home in Beverly Hills, inviting all of the Hiltons as well as friends, family members, and, of course, studio executives. Compared to the Old World formality of dinner at the Hilton estate, it was quite a change for Conrad; the Taylors' Hollywood friends were much more raucous. "It was like going to the circus," Conrad later said, "there were so many characters. I'm not saying I didn't enjoy myself. I did. But, my goodness, what a bunch!"

At the end of March 1950, Mary Hilton Saxon, Nicky's now widowed mother, invited Elizabeth Taylor and her mother down to El Paso for a little get-together.* Nicky accompanied them on the trip, of course. As the three women discussed wedding plans in a suite at the Hilton Hotel, and then went on a shopping spree to Juarez, Nicky played golf at the El Paso Country Club. Mary thought Sara and Elizabeth were both wonderful. "They are just lovely," she said at the time. As Elizabeth and Nicky later posed for photos, it was clear that they made a striking couple, both

---

* Mack Saxon died of a heart attack in May of 1949 at the age of forty-seven. Following his death, Mary moved back to El Paso.

with wavy dark hair and well-drawn features, both uncommonly attractive, Nick with his dimples, Elizabeth with those eyes. Except for the fact that the Hilton men thought the Taylors were a little nuts, it all seemed as if it could work.

Being in El Paso also gave Nicky a chance to reconnect with his brother Eric, who was as excited as anyone else would have been in El Paso to meet a glamorous movie star. Much to everyone's disappointment, though, at first Elizabeth didn't want anything to do with Eric or any of his friends. She wasn't interested in knowing them. Though Nicky begged her to just try to be nice, she simply couldn't do it. "If she liked a person and felt she had common ground with that person, Elizabeth could be a terrific conversationalist," said Nicky's close friend Bob Neal. "But if she didn't, well, she could be rather bitchy. Nicky was pretty unhappy with her during that trip. 'He's my brother as much as Barron,' he told Elizabeth. 'So why aren't you as nice to him as you are to Barron.' Elizabeth shot back, '*Who said I was ever nice to Barron?*'"

"Eric won her over, though," admitted Eric's future wife, Pat Skipworth Hilton. "Nick asked Eric to babysit her while he played golf, and he did so. We used to laugh about it. 'What a terrible babysitting job for you,' I used to joke. Eric said that she was natural and easy to know, that she had a great sense of humor. I don't know what it was like at first between them, I just know that they warmed up to each other, and even remained friends for many, many years after."

When Nicky and Elizabeth returned to Los Angeles, they were besieged by photographers everywhere they went. Even though his father had warned him, Nicky wasn't prepared for the unrelenting zeal of the photographers. "How in the world do you deal with this bullshit?" he asked Elizabeth one night at the Biltmore Hotel as the media swarmed them. "Oh, you'll get used to it," she said with a fixed smile that never wavered.

"I think it'll be a problem," Nicky later confessed to Bob Neal over a couple of Pabst Blue Ribbon beers at the Polo Lounge of the Beverly Hills Hotel. Neal restated the obvious: that if Nicky married a celebrity he would belong not only to her but to her public as well.

"Screw that," Nicky said.

"You saw what your dad went through with Zsa Zsa," Bob Neal reminded him, according to his memory of the conversation. "But your father, he handled it with grace."

"Well, I'm not my father," Nicky said, his temper rising. He was in no mood to be compared to his father. He had already brushed off Conrad's warnings and didn't want anyone to see a connection between his marrying Elizabeth and his dad's union with Zsa Zsa. "I do things my own way," he said, jabbing his index finger into Neal's chest for emphasis.

"Hey, don't get teed off at me," Bob Neal said. "Let it slide, Clyde," he joked. "I got no beef with you."

A Party to Celebrate the Caribe Hilton

About a week after Nicky returned from Texas, Conrad Hilton hosted a lavish party at his home to celebrate the opening of the new Caribe Hilton in San Juan, Puerto Rico, Hilton Hotels International's first acquisition. It was a measure of how important Conrad Hilton had become as the premier American hotelier that the State Department and Department of Commerce had approached him with the idea of establishing American-operated hotels abroad in order to stimulate trade and travel. Coincidentally, at this same time, the Puerto Rico Industrial Company contacted a half dozen American hotel business owners with the idea of opening and operating an American hotel in San Juan. The government would build the hotel and then lease it to an American businessman to operate it, using American technology and know-how. Working with the State Department and the Department of Commerce, Hilton threw his hat in the ring. "My father actually responded to that invitation in Spanish," Eric Hilton recalled many years later, "and he was the only one who basically did that. I think that so impressed them [the Industrial Company] that they selected him."

In negotiating with the Puerto Ricans, Conrad said he felt they should not just build the hotel but should also furnish and equip it so that it would truly be theirs and not just another Hilton enterprise. After about a year of planning and construction at a cost of more than $5 million, the luxurious three-hundred-room Caribe Hilton opened on December 9, 1949. Two months later, in February 1950, *Hotel Monthly* magazine featured the Caribe in a splashy twelve-page pictorial, complete with floor plans. Suddenly, everyone in America seemed to want to visit Puerto Rico.

Now that the hotel was well off the ground, Conrad wanted to host a gala affair at his home to celebrate it with people who had not been able to make the junket down to Puerto Rico for the opening there. Dozens of Hilton Hotels International employees all dressed in formal wear mingled about in the spacious outdoors of the Hilton estate under heat lamps as uniformed waiters and waitresses served cocktails and foods popular in Puerto Rico. There was an atmosphere of jubilance not only because the Puerto Rican project seemed destined for success—and in three years' time it would recover the government's $9 million investment—but because it was thought that the Caribe Hilton would inspire developers around the world to seek out Hilton expertise in opening their hotels in other countries.

When Conrad, who had been in San Francisco for a meeting, finally showed up at his party a little later than expected, Zsa Zsa Gabor cracked, "Yes, well, he no doubt saw a hotel he liked along the way and decided to buy it. He doesn't mind making people wait for him, as I found out the hard way." She could not resist being cynical about Conrad. However, because she was considered "family"—and also because she was so entertaining to have at a party—Zsa Zsa was almost always on the guest list. "Look around you," Nicky told his former stepmother as he gently wrapped his arms around her slim, sequined waist from behind. In a photograph taken that night, Nicky looked as dapper as ever in a white shirt and jacket, an untied silk bow tie, black slacks, and glossy alligator shoes. "We're on top of the whole goddamn world, Zsa Zsa!" he said to her. "Why not just enjoy the view?" Her face lit up when she realized it was him. "Oh, Nicky, I am just *joking*," she said. "Now, you know Zsa Zsa loves a good joke, don't you? Come, do the cha-cha with me," she said, turning around and pulling him out onto the dance floor. "Let's make everyone here incredibly jealous of our beauty!"

Along with Zsa Zsa, other attendees of the black-tie party included dancer Ann Miller, actor Jimmy Stewart, and actress Natalie Wood—but not Elizabeth Taylor. However, Elizabeth's mother, Sara, showed up—but on the arm of someone other than her husband, Francis. No one knew quite what to make of that other than to think it an interesting development. When at one point Conrad noticed Sara and Zsa Zsa comparing notes, all he could do was look to the heavens and shake his head. He turned to one of his staff members and said, "Do me a big favor, Dave. Get me a Dewar's neat, will you? And fast."

Watching Conrad interact with his employees was always fascinating. He had such an incredible memory; he was somehow able to remember the names of people he had met only once or twice along the way. If someone told him a story, it would be long remembered. Hilton would often approach an employee to ask how a personal problem that had been shared with him months or even years earlier had been resolved. The staff members of all of his hotels had great respect and even love for him because they knew him to be reasonable and fair. Thus it was easy to understand why the applause was so deafening when, toward the end of this celebratory evening, Nicky Hilton introduced his father. Conrad strode proudly onto a stage that had been constructed for a vocalist and full orchestra. Taking the microphone, the distinguished entrepreneur began to address the crowd by first thanking them for coming to his "humble home" to celebrate the occasion.

"The world is changing," Conrad told his guests, "and we in this country at this time are fortunate enough to be able to bear witness to it." He then talked a bit about the booming airline industry and how it had made travel so easy. "When I was a boy, we would take a train from Texas to New York and it would take days," he said. "Now? Hours on a plane. Yes, my friends, the world is shrinking," he concluded. "The happy result of the ease by which Americans can now travel is that the hotel business has benefited greatly. More travelers equal more business," he continued, "not just for our Hilton hotels, but for the entire industry. We are not an island," he reminded his employees and friends, "we are a part of a bigger system, and if that system profits, I promise you, we shall all profit."

He then spoke a little about the new hotel in Puerto Rico and his hopes that its success would help to further develop tourism there, "a safe haven for travelers from all parts of the world." He concluded by saying, "Hilton Hotels International is a wholly owned subsidiary of the Hilton Hotels Corporation, and long may it prosper for all of us and all of America." As the crowd cheered, he added, "I can promise you that we have but just begun!" (With the passing of time, Hilton Hotels International would soon open hotels in Madrid, Cairo, Rome, London, and Istanbul.) Conrad then called his sons Barron and Nicky to the stage, both of whom took a bow. After walking offstage, the three Hilton men sequestered themselves in a corner to enjoy three celebratory snifters of a good French brandy. Conrad was seen patting Nicky on the back and laughing heartily, likely at one of his jokes.

About an hour later, dozens of people took to the dance floor as the orchestra played a set of fast-paced, rhythmic Latin songs. It wasn't long before the crowd moved to the sidelines in order to make room for the host and his MGM star companion. "Oh, my goodness, it's all just *marvelous*," Sara Taylor enthused as Conrad Hilton danced across the floor with Ann Miller and everyone around them clapped merrily in time with the music. "I've never seen anything like this before," she exclaimed. "These Hiltons certainly know how to live, don't they?"

Nicky and Elizabeth Marry

The wedding ceremony honoring Nicky Hilton and Elizabeth Taylor finally took place at the Church of the Good Shepherd on May 6, 1950. It was, as expected since it was orchestrated by the MGM Studios, beautiful and extravagant. Spencer Tracy and Joan Bennett, Elizabeth's parents in *Father of the Bride*, seemed almost as happy as Sara and Francis Taylor. The church was filled with celebrities, including Janet Leigh, Rosalind Russell, Fred Astaire, Ginger Rogers, Esther Williams, Gene Kelly, Debbie Reynolds, and, of course, Zsa Zsa Gabor and Ann Miller. Elizabeth, who had turned eighteen on February 27, looked stunning in her white wedding ensemble (designed for her by MGM's wardrobe mistress Helen Rose and a virtual replica of the dress she wore in *Father of the Bride*), while Nick was as dashing as ever in his black tuxedo. Even the bridesmaids' yellow organza gowns were designed and paid for by MGM; Marilyn Hilton, Barron's wife, was one of the bridesmaids. Everyone seemed so young and filled with joyous naïveté. "I was just enthralled by it all," said Margaret O'Brien, who was an MGM child star of fourteen at the time and had recently appeared alongside Elizabeth in the studio's film *Little Women*. "It was absolutely gorgeous and I think every little girl my age hoped to one day have that kind of fairytale wedding." The church was not only filled with Hollywood dignitaries but also with dozens of Hilton Hotel executives and their spouses. "I was terrified," Elizabeth later recalled, "and so was Nick. I remember taking out my handkerchief and mopping the sweat off his face during the ceremony. I wanted to run, I was so scared. I really had no idea what was coming."

After the ceremony, there were so many screaming fans waiting outside the church that there was hardly room for the pressing media. It short, it was a madhouse. Meanwhile, Conrad and his first wife, Mary, who was accompanied by her youngest son, Eric, stood in the receiving line with Sara and Francis Taylor, acknowledging guests and thanking them for coming.

After some of the hoopla died down, Nicky and Elizabeth seemed to relax, their future together seeming more promising than ever. "I remember looking at Elizabeth and Nicky and thinking how lucky they were," recalled Ann Miller, "and how beautiful it all was, a marriage made in heaven. They were the most gorgeous couple in the world and they had the world by its tail."

Conrad had to agree; he would later say he had never seen a couple as "handsome" as his son and new daughter-in-law. Over the din, he turned to Mary and, as he would later recall it, said, "They have everything, haven't they? Youth, looks, position, no need to worry about where their next meal is coming from."

Mary wasn't so sure. Leaning into Conrad so that he could hear her over the chaos, she said, "Maybe they have too much. I don't think it's going to be easy for them."

"Oh, nonsense," Conrad said with a nudge and a gentle smile.

Perhaps he hoped to alleviate his ex-wife's fears with a jokey remark, but one thing was certain: Conrad had plenty of his own concerns, especially when a couple of days later Sara Taylor called to say that she wasn't at all happy with the wedding photographs. In the true tradition of a Hollywood agent, she requested that Nicky, Barron, Eric, Conrad, and Mary get dressed in the exact same outfits they wore for the wedding and meet at her home so that photos could be taken again. "Just pretend that it's last week," Sara gaily suggested. They did as they were asked, but to say that the Hiltons weren't exactly thrilled with the idea would be an understatement.

Honeymoon from Hell

*I*mmediately after the wedding, the new Mr. and Mrs. Conrad Nicholas Hilton drove up to Carmel, California, in Nicky's red Mercedes-Benz convertible. There, the couple would spend the next three nights at the Carmel Country Club. They seemed happy, but Nick was seen drinking a great amount of alcohol, which made some observers wonder about his true feelings. He was worried. He confided in one friend that though he was relieved the wedding was over, he was now beginning to wonder just what he had gotten himself into, because the country club was overrun with photographers and press people all vying for shots of the newlyweds. Meanwhile, to fill the weeks before their honeymoon—heaven forbid the Hiltons should have some free time!—MGM arranged a busy itinerary, which included many photo sessions and press conferences. Nick spent most of that time dodging these press events in any way he could. At one point he skipped out on a media dinner and holed himself up at his dad's home. "Screw this," he told Conrad and Barron as soon as he walked through the door. He was agitated. "She loves this stuff," he told Conrad of his new wife. "You oughta see the way she eats it up. They're all over her, taking pictures, kissing her ass. But me, they just ignore. What's the point?" he asked, pouring himself a shot of his preferred libation.

"First of all, the drinking has got to stop," Barron told his brother. It was clear that Nicky was already drunk. "It's ten in the morning and you're already loaded," Barron said.

Nicky told his family members that he had expected a certain amount of media intrusion, but that this was far more than any man could take. "You have to live through it to understand what it's like," he said.

It would have been easy for Conrad to give Nicky the "I told you so" routine, but he genuinely felt badly for his young son. "You have to take it in and then ignore it, Nick," he said. "What have I always told you: Be big," he added. "You have to be bigger than they are. Now, go back and join your wife. You can do this, son. I know you can."

In two weeks' time, Nicky and Elizabeth boarded the *Queen Mary* for their "perfect" honeymoon cruise. Nicky by now knew pretty much what to expect and tried to steel himself for a trip that would doubtless be filled with curiosity seekers, fans, photographers, and journalists. Nothing, though, could have prepared him for the circuslike atmosphere that awaited him. It actually started with boarding. Nicky had a couple of suitcases with him. However, Elizabeth's load was another matter altogether; she brought new meaning to the concept of overpacking. "She was traveling with seventeen trunks," said Nora Johnson, the daughter of director Nunnally Johnson, who was on the ship, traveling first class. "She also had a maid and an entourage of, I would say, a dozen people."

Instead of getting an opportunity to bask in the first blush of young married life and explore their sex life, like most honeymooning couples, Elizabeth and Nicky had no privacy at all. Everywhere they went on the enormous ship, they were followed by either photographers—who had been allowed access to the cruise—or other vacationers who couldn't take their eyes off them. Although the Duke and Duchess of Windsor were also on board (occupying the bridal suite), it was the new Mr. and Mrs. Hilton whom everyone wanted to see. Everywhere they appeared, throngs gathered to get a good long look at them, but especially at Elizabeth. Even the crew of the ship surrounded the movie star, pleading for an autograph "and practically knocking over Nicky in the process," recalled Melissa Wesson, who was also on the cruise on her honeymoon.

The cruise chaos was maddening to Nicky. Elizabeth was his new bride, yet she seemed to belong to everyone but him. To Nicky, it felt as if people were listening at the door of their stateroom, or trying to look through cracks to get a glimpse of them—and he was probably right. "I didn't marry a girl," he declared angrily. "I married an institution."

Out of frustration, Nicky began to distance himself from Elizabeth and the chaos that surrounded her. He turned cold toward her, staying out all night drinking and gambling in the casino, leaving his new wife alone waiting for his return. In time there would even be stories of Nicky having pushed and shoved and been otherwise physically abusive toward Elizabeth on the deck of the ship. Somewhere along the line, he had developed a terrible temper. He certainly proved on this cruise that he could be explosive. "I thought he was a nice, pure All American boy," Elizabeth told the writer Paul Theroux in 1999. "Two weeks later, wham! Bam! All the physical abuse started."

"He wasn't that way as a kid," said Bob Neal of Nicky. "It was gradual. After he got out of the service, we noticed that little things started pissing him off.

I think he was just unhappy, or restless…or…well, we couldn't understand it. Back then, you didn't analyze people as much as you do today. Back then, you just took it in, thought that it was strange, and moved on. You didn't sit around trying to figure people out. But now, looking back on it, I think he was incredibly disappointed himself. I think he wanted a lot for himself, he believed in himself so much, and every time he took a misstep, it made him hate himself a little more—and thus the temper. That's my theory, anyway.

"He also began drinking too much, and I also think this bad habit started in the service. There were signs that Nicky was getting worse, especially during the honeymoon with Elizabeth."

"He loathed being known as Elizabeth Taylor's husband," Marilyn Hilton would recall of Nicky many years later. "He did not like being called Mr. Taylor. He was the I'm-the-boss-and-you-do-as-I-say type. He had a terrible temper and could be a real bastard," she continued of her brother-in-law. "But he also could be sweet and gentle and really wonderful."

"She left Nick three or four times on their honeymoon while in Europe," Marilyn Hilton would say of Elizabeth.

Others saw another side to the story.

"Imagine being stuck on a cruise ship for three months with a woman who's really, really pissed off at you," said one of Nick's close friends. "She started hitting him out of frustration when he didn't do what she wanted him to do, and that wasn't the best way to deal with Nicky, believe me. He'd hit you back, for sure."

Bob Neal added, "By the time they got to New York, Nick was sick of all of it and, I dare say, sick of Elizabeth too. 'She's so goddamned demanding,' he told me when he got back to Los Angeles. 'You can't please her. I don't think anyone in the world is as spoiled as she is. You would not believe how bitchy she is too.' So it's safe to say they were not getting along at all. Or, as he told me, 'It was three months of hell.'"

After the honeymoon was over, Elizabeth Taylor stayed in New York for a couple of weeks, likely trying to come to terms with the ordeal she'd just been through on the high seas. Meanwhile, Nicky Hilton returned to Los Angeles. "Nick was resentful, hot-tempered, and handled himself accordingly," recalled Conrad. "Sometimes his temper flared and he stalked out. By the time they came home on the Queen Elizabeth," Conrad added sarcastically, "the papers were printing tall tales of a separation."

Those tales weren't quite as tall as Conrad suggested.

Elizabeth Suffers a Miscarriage

*T*he moment he got back to Los Angeles, Nicky made a beeline to Conrad's house. When he opened the door to his father's study, he found him in there with a battery of attorneys, in the middle of a meeting. Conrad remembered Nicky looking "absurdly young."

"I'm sorry, Pop. I'll come back," Nicky said, apologizing. "Business first."

"No," Conrad said. "*Family* first." He then asked the lawyers to please leave him and his son alone. What followed was a difficult conversation. Nicky said he hadn't wanted to disappoint his father; he truly hoped he could make a go of it with Elizabeth, the way Barron had with Marilyn. Now that it was becoming painfully clear to him that such would not be the case, he was feeling sad and incredibly defeated. He was also bitterly disappointed in himself. "I'm really sorry, Pop," Nicky told Conrad. "I've made a real mess of things. As usual." He also told his father that much of what had been reported about his behavior on the ship was exaggerated. "It's not true, and those writers *know* it," he said, slamming his fist on his pop's desk. "It doesn't matter though; they'll print whatever they want to print."

Conrad understood. He'd been through the same sort of thing with Zsa Zsa. "You know what's true and what isn't," he told Nicky, according to his later memory of the conversation. "You just have to hang on to the truth. And what have I always told you, Nicky: Be big. You have to be big."

Nicky nodded his head. Later, Conrad would say, "I did my best," but there was simply no way to cheer his son up that day. Compared to the happy union his brother Barron had been enjoying for years with Marilyn, Nicky's relationship with Elizabeth was a real disaster. He felt like a failure. In a sense, though, that was something else he had in common with his father. Certainly Conrad felt like a failure as well in that he had had *two* bad marriages. He wasn't nearly as judgmental of Nicky as Nicky believed. He understood Nicky—maybe even better than he understood Barron.

Deeply conflicted, Nicky didn't seem to have much capacity for diplomacy, especially where Elizabeth was concerned. Instead of trying to reason with her, he would just scream at her, which didn't make the situation any better and actually just made it worse. "She would then jump on him like an angry cat," said Bob Neal, "punching and scratching, really enraged. Then Nicky did what Nicky would do. He'd say, 'Get the hell away from me, you crazy broad, you,' and he'd smack her just once and she'd go flying. She would cry, 'How could you?' He would then feel terrible about himself, so disappointed in himself. Then, a couple days later, it would happen again. It was an awful cycle."

In the fall of 1999—almost fifty years after she and Nicky Hilton were divorced and thirty years after Nicky was dead and gone—Elizabeth Taylor would tell writer Paul Theroux in an interview for *Talk* magazine that she finally walked out on the marriage after Nicky caused her to have a miscarriage. She explained, "He was drunk. I thought, 'This is not why I was put on earth. God did not put me here to have a baby kicked out of my stomach.' I had terrible pains. I saw the baby in the toilet. I didn't know that I was pregnant, so it wasn't a malicious or on-purpose kind of act. It just happened." Elizabeth became so upset in the telling of the story, wrote the writer, that she was forced to leave the room to compose herself. When she returned, she apologized, explaining, "I have never spoken about this before."

As it happened, after Elizabeth and Nicky returned from their honeymoon, Elizabeth began filming the sequel to *Father of the Bride*, called *Father's Little Dividend*, in which her character introduced in the first movie becomes pregnant. Her stand-in for the move, Marjorie Dillon, recalls of Elizabeth's miscarriage at the time, "It was an early pregnancy—she wasn't far along. One day, she fainted on the set and had to be rushed home. Nicky's uncle was an obstetrician and he came to the house, but Liz had already miscarried. She was in bed and wanted Nicky to stay with her, but he had already made plans to go deep-sea fishing. He gave her a kiss and said, 'I'll be back in a couple of days. Marge will spend the night with you.' I did, of course, and that's when she cried and cried."

Divorce—Hollywood Style

I want you to end this marriage," Conrad Hilton told Nicky one day at the end of November 1950, according to what Nicky later said. "Sometimes," Conrad told his son, "a woman can bring out the worst in a man. Believe me, I know what I'm talking about." He did. After all, how many times had Zsa Zsa Gabor driven him to the brink of fury? Though he was always able to control himself—he didn't have the temperament for violence in any way, shape, or form, and he also rarely lost his temper—he was surprised just the same at how angry she could make him. In many ways, he didn't like the man he had become as Zsa Zsa's husband, and from what he could tell, Nicky was going through the same thing as Elizabeth's spouse. "End it, son," he told him. "Get the hell out now, while you still can."

"I don't have to," Nicky told him. "I got a call from some hot-shot lawyer yesterday. She's divorcing me!"

Conrad shook his head sadly. "Well, here we go again," he said. "Another divorce the church isn't going to recognize, only now it's going to be your cross to bear."

"I know, Pop," Nicky said. "The only difference is that I will never go through this again. I'll never marry again. I can promise you that."

On December 1, 1950, MGM announced that Elizabeth and Nicky were separating. A statement from Elizabeth said that "there is no possibility of a reconciliation." Three weeks later, Elizabeth filed divorce papers, charging that throughout their brief marriage Nicky had treated her "in a cruel and inhumane manner." She also cited "great and grievous mental cruelty and mental pain, suffering and anguish." She did not stipulate any charge of physical abuse. For his part, Nick's lawyer filed an answer denying all charges of cruelty.

On Friday, March 9, 1951, barely three months after it was announced that they were divorcing, Nicky Hilton and Elizabeth Taylor were back in touch. He picked up the telephone that morning to find Elizabeth calling him. She was now romantically involved with director Stanley Donen, she said, but she missed him very much. Nicky couldn't believe his ears. That she missed him was perhaps not surprising, but that she was already in another relationship did give him pause. Their divorce wasn't even final yet! He was reminded of the fact that he had met her on the day she ended her engagement to William Pawley. Or as Conrad had said of Elizabeth, "Fast worker, that one."

Elizabeth's latest romance with a film director gave even more credence to Nicky's fear that had it not been him standing next to Elizabeth at the altar, anyone else would have sufficed, just as long as she was obtaining some measure of freedom from her mother and MGM. As far as he was concerned, he'd been duped by Elizabeth, and he wished he'd never met her.

Now the reason for his unhappiness and confusion was on the phone with him. She missed him, she said, and he had to agree that he missed her too. Despite their combative relationship, at the core of it all they really did love each other. If only things could have been different, they mused. He *wanted* to see the best in her. That's just the way he was wired; he looked for the best in people. She said she was sorry for the way it had gone on their honeymoon, and if it had been up to her, she would just as soon have been alone with him, "somewhere...anywhere." After piling on endearment on top of endearment, sentiment on top of sentiment, the next thing Nicky knew, he and Elizabeth were trying to figure out how to spend time together.

As it happened, Nicky was to host a party in Palm Springs on Saturday night honoring a physician who was in town from Chicago, and while he was in the desert he hoped to take in some golf. Perhaps she could accompany him? She was delighted with the invitation and eagerly agreed. Within a matter of hours, he found himself sitting next to her in his red convertible, driving through the desert from Los Angeles to Palm Springs with the top down, her raven-colored hair blowing in the wind as she nuzzled into his shoulder. Impatient for each other, they stopped on the side of the road and, almost invisible in the ink-black desert night, made fierce love to one another in his car under desert stars. Now that the pressure and angst of their marriage had subsided, she was much harder for him to resist, and apparently she felt the same about him.

An hour later, once they arrived in the Springs, the couple checked into the Thunderbird Ranch and Country Club in nearby Rancho Mirage—the first eighteen-hole golf course there. Was the divorce still on? Yes, they decided. They should not be together. He had learned an important lesson about marriage; it was not to be entered into lightly. It could be said that, at least based on Taylor's future matrimonial track record, this was a lesson she would never learn. For now, though, she was happy, as was he. That night, in a quaint ranch-style cottage—far away from the prying press and from overzealous fans—Nicky Hilton and Elizabeth Taylor, still for all intents and purposes Mrs. and Mrs. Conrad Hilton, were together...and completely alone, the way he had always wanted it.

PART SIX

Spoils of the Rich and Famous

America's Dad

On November 21, 1950, Conrad Hilton addressed the National Conference of Christians and Jews at his Waldorf-Astoria hotel in New York City. He called the speech "The Battle for Freedom," and as he would later observe in his autobiography, *Be My Guest*, it "came from a heart filled with a deep and abiding love for and faith in our country and our way of life."

"The essence of Communism is the death of the individual and the burial of his remains in a collective mass," Conrad intoned to those attending the conference at the Waldorf. Continuing the train of thought, he added, "This is a crucial time in the destiny of our nation, in the destiny of mankind. The remaining free peoples of the world must be strengthened and defended. In this struggle for freedom, at home and abroad, our greatest weapon, both a sword and a shield, will be our love of, and faith in, God."

Conrad Hilton had agonized over this speech for a number of weeks, later admitting that he felt his delivery perhaps "lacked persuasion and the professional polish to put it across." Yet he never questioned his qualifications to render such a speech. He always felt a true and sincere calling to showcase his patriotism as well as his faith, and was never shy about doing so.

Apparently it was Hilton's friend the hotelier Henry Crown who helped persuade him that his "Battle of Freedom" speech was well worth sharing, that it deserved to be heard. As the oft-told story goes, Crown met with Conrad at his home to debate whether or not Hilton should have a platform for more than just the buying and selling of hotels, but to actually impact the country—maybe even the world—with his thoughts and views about politics and religion. Crown and Conrad talked at length about Conrad's mission—and that was the word Conrad often used, "mission," when it came to sharing more than just his hospitality with the nation. Hilton had a real need to speak out against Communism, and he believed that he could be a persuasive spokesman in that regard. This isn't to say that he was a boastful or even extremely outgoing man. He wasn't. But when it came to speaking out for his beloved country, he wasn't the least bit hesitant. His biggest concern was that if he was going to be viewed as someone to whom people should pay heed, he wanted to be sure that his message was well crafted. If he had any apprehensions about his speech, they had to do with whether or not it was strong enough.

As it turns out, Conrad's fears were unfounded. Not only would his speech resonate with those present to hear it, but "The Battle for Freedom" would soon be printed and reprinted in newspapers and magazines across the country, resulting in thousands of letters coming in to him, as Hilton later noted, "from every corner of the land and from people in all walks of life." He recalled, "The receipt of these letters was one of the great inspirational experiences of my life. I was profoundly impressed with the depth of feeling which they expressed."

Hilton would call one of those many letters "as important as any I have received in my life." It was from a young boy named Daniel Paolucci, who wrote, "I have read your talk in the *Herald Tribune*, and I think it was wonderful. Especially that our faith in God was our only hope. You are right, and I think if everyone would fall down and pray we would have real peace." It was thus that Hilton would be inspired to compose a speech that would eventually become first known as "Uncle Sam's Peace Prayer," and then better known as "America on Its Knees."

Hilton, with his unapologetic dedication to the American ideal and his devotion to God, saw prayer as the primary solution not only to obtaining peace but also to neutralizing the insidious agenda of Senator Joseph McCarthy from Wisconsin. With his campaign against alleged Communists, McCarthy had created a kind of demagogic terrorism that shook the principles upon which this country was founded. (The reckless manner by which the senator continued to make accusations of disloyalty without much proof, or based on very slight evidence, would become known as "McCarthyism.") Not only did Hilton hope that "America on Its Knees" might encourage national patriotism, he also hoped it would influence Americans to stand strong in the face of McCarthy's fearmongering.

In "America on Its Knees," Conrad intoned, "We pray that you save us from ourselves. The world that you made for us to live in peace, we have made into an armed camp. We live in fear of war to come. We're afraid of a terror that flies by night and the arrow that flies by day. We have left your altars to serve the false gods of money and pleasure and power." Hilton prayed for God's guidance to "fill us with new faith, new strength and new courage, that we may win the battle for peace. Be swift to save us, Dear God, before the darkness falls."

"America on Its Knees" was broadcast nationally on May 7, 1952, and later published on July 4 of that year. Hilton also appeared on Ralph Edwards's television program, *This Is Your Life*, that same year to deliver his prayer, standing on a stage by himself in a striped tie and black jacket, looking more like a minister than a hotelier.

Later, in an address given at the meeting of the American Hotel Association on October 10, 1952, in St. Louis, Conrad noted, "Within twenty-four hours after 'America on Its Knees' was in print, I was deluged with letters and requests for copies of this pictorial message. From almost every country in the world, from every state in the Union, from the old and the young, from rich and poor, from military and civilian, from cynics and the unsophisticated, from philosophers and advertising men, from rabbis, ministers and priests, from wise men and crackpots from every level of society, from children of eight to oldsters of ninety-two, came requests for one hundred and sixty thousand reprints, and messages that sometimes brought tears to my eyes."

Stewart Armstrong, who would go on to work with Nicky Hilton in the Inns Division of the Hilton Hotels Corporation, recalled, "As affable as he was, you couldn't be in a room with Conrad Hilton and not feel the weight of his growing influence. I know that Nicky was conscious of it, too. 'I try not to think about it,' he once told me. 'I already don't feel like I'm worthy to be at the same dinner table with the man; how am I supposed to feel when I see him on television or hear him on the radio reciting that prayer for so many millions of citizens? It's daunting,' he told me. 'So I try not to think about it.' But I also know that Nicky was extremely proud of his pop. There were many times when I was with him and Barron and Eric, and the sons would say, 'Can you believe this thing?' talking about the impact Conrad was having on the entire country. 'How in the world did this happen?' Eric would say. 'It seems unbelievable. I mean, he's just...Dad.' But while that was true at home, on the national stage Conrad Hilton had become a lot more than that, influential in ways that none of us could ever have anticipated at the time. In some ways, you might say he had become America's Dad."

Casa Encantada

*I*n December 1950, around Christmas and his sixty-third birthday, Conrad Hilton purchased the grand estate that would for the next three decades be known as Casa Encantada, or House of Enchantment. This was an opulent two-story, 35,000-square-foot modern Georgian mansion, which sat on eight and a half lush acres at 10644 Bellagio Road in Bel-Air.

Before he made the final decision to buy the estate, Conrad asked to be able to spend a morning there alone to meditate and pray in its surroundings. Despite the place's enormity—seventeen bedrooms and twenty-six bathrooms!—Hilton still felt a great sense of peace on the premises, with its floor-to-ceiling windows inviting the outdoors into each and every room. He simply knew he had to own it. The home, which was perched on a hill overlooking the Bel-Air Country Club, had cost more than $2 million to build during the Depression in 1938, which would be about $20 million by today's standards. Conrad bought it at a steal for just $250,000, furnished. This purchase afforded a jubilant conclusion to what had been a difficult 1950 for the Hilton family, primarily because of what Nicky had gone through with Elizabeth Taylor. As soon as Conrad bought the estate, Nicky moved into it. It was so big, father and son rarely even saw one another.

"In a word, it was spectacular," Zsa Zsa Gabor once said of Casa Encantada. "Conrad had great taste, I will say that much for him. It was a palace." Indeed, according to photographs taken of the property when Conrad lived at Casa Encantada, the home was lavishly and tastefully furnished. In the entrance hall were found fourteenth-century bronze statues of Devi and Siva from India. A pair of Ming vases from ancient China stood in the foyer. Blanc de chine vases from Denmark adorned the parlor. The drawing room featured eighteenth-century panels painted by Jean-Baptiste Greuze, a favorite artist of Conrad's, who died in 1805. An eighteenth-century Viennese clock was a stunning centerpiece in the enormous, high-ceilinged drawing room with its panoramic view of the country club. A grand semicircular staircase led from the first floor to the second. Upstairs, Conrad's master bedroom suite looked as if it had been decorated for a king, boasting gold silk walls with matching bedspreads and draperies, along with gold cashmere carpeting. In one corner of the room stood a green Italian marble fireplace.

Conrad would say that every time he looked around at the ostentatious surroundings, he couldn't help but think of his beloved mother, Mary Laufersweiler Hilton, and how absolutely amazed she would have been by such a palace. He also knew that she would have thought it was much too excessive for her son—and he would have agreed—but still, she would have been impressed. She likely would have marveled at how far the family had come from the small adobe home in New Mexico in which she had raised her children.

Many visitors would say that Casa Encantada looked more like one of Conrad's jaw-dropping hotels than it did anyone's home. Once, when Conrad's granddaughter Linda (Eric's daughter) was a small girl, she took a wrong turn in the house and was hopelessly lost. "Somehow, I got separated from the pack," she recalled many years later. "Probably something shiny caught my eye, and then I was lost. I really didn't think anybody was ever going to find me." As she walked from one enormous room to the next, the young girl became more and more frightened. Compared to the modest eight-room home in which she and her family lived in Texas, this house with its sixty-one rooms provided quite a culture shock. At one point, Linda stumbled upon one of the elevators, but she was afraid to get into it because, as she would recall, it reminded her of a coffin. "It was all so freaky," she recalled, laughing at the memory. "I just remember being lost in this big, big house and hoping to somehow catch up with everybody else. I just remember that you had to stay close when there was a party, or you'd never be seen again."

The *Los Angeles Times* once noted of Casa Encantada that it was "one of the finest homes west of the Mississippi." But maybe Nicky Hilton put it best when he said at the time, "I look around here and I think to myself, 'Jesus Christ! Will you just look at what my pop has been able to do with his life?' I mean, if *this* isn't the good life, I don't know what is."

"He's Getting Worse"

*T*he surroundings may have been plush, but that didn't necessarily mean that everyone living at Casa Encantada was happy. "I don't care, just give me a cup of coffee, pour some brandy in it, and get off my back," Nicky

Hilton—now twenty-three—hissed one morning. He didn't look well. It appeared that he hadn't shaved in at least a week. His dark hair, usually so meticulously styled, was disheveled and looked unwashed. There were dark circles and bags under his eyes. Wearing a short white terrycloth robe, he had a lit cigar hanging from his lips. Slumped in a chair at a table in the massive kitchen of the Hilton estate, he glared at the chief maid of the household, Maria de Amaté, through glassy eyes.

Maria and her husband, Juan, a groundskeeper, lived on the premises. Their little girl, Connie, was often seen playing in a sandbox with the children of other maids and butlers, most of whom didn't live at the estate but often came to work with their parents. On this morning, Maria was working with another maid, Delores Hall, in the kitchen when she found Nicky, looking as he usually did these days—melancholy and hungover. She had merely asked what he wanted for breakfast when he snapped at her. "Yes, Mr. Hilton," she said, ignoring as best she could his abrupt outburst. She then poured him a cup of hot coffee.

"What are you so nervous about?" Nicky asked irritably. Apparently he noticed a slight tremble of her hands. But she wasn't at all nervous. Maria suffered from severe arthritis, especially in the mornings, and was just having trouble holding the heavy, coffee-filled pot. "Look at you," Nicky said with an air of disgust. "What are you doing still working here if you can't even pour a pot of coffee?" That was enough. After all, *he* was not the lord of the manor. Maria put the coffeepot down on the table with a thud. "You may get away with talking to the others around here like that," she said. Though she spoke with an accent, her voice was steady and firm. "But you will respect *me*, Mr. Hilton. I won't have you talking to me like that."

Nicky wilted with regret. He bowed his head and lowered his voice. "I'm sorry, Maria," he said hoarsely. "Rough night, you know?"

Rough night indeed. Nicky had spent it arguing with another woman, this one a maid working at the Bel-Air Hotel, her name being Virginia Larson. A tall brunette from New York, she was young and shapely—Nicky said she had "a great rack"—with a dazzling smile and a flirtatious way about her. Every time Nicky would see her in the hallway, he would exchange long, smoldering looks with her. However, as an employee of the hotel, she was strictly off-limits, or at least that would have been the case under normal circumstances. However, Nicky was hurt, lonely, and feeling sorry for himself.

He was still distraught and angry about the end of his marriage. He was also upset at himself for not handling all of it better. He had let his family down, but he had also let himself down. Now he felt he deserved a good time, and he decided that Virginia was just the woman to give it to him.

As he later explained to his friends, he went looking for Virginia and found her cleaning one of the rooms on her assigned floor. They'd never even had a conversation, that's how little they knew each other. He just walked into the room, closed the door behind him, and pinned her up against the wall. "No, not here," she protested. Too late. He was already having his way with her. "I didn't even give her a chance to take off her cute little maid's uniform," he said later, "which made it somehow even better." He later said that she was a willing partner. He knew as much, he claimed, because after they finished, she kissed him fully on the lips and said she would like to see him again, but "maybe next time you can at least take a girl out to dinner first."

However, the next day, Virginia complained to a few of the other maids that Nicky had forced himself on her. She said that she was thinking about lodging a complaint with his father. When Nicky heard this troubling bit of gossip, he decided to confront her. The two then had a big quarrel about what had occurred between them—his view of it and hers, which now were vastly different—and when she threatened to tell Conrad about their illicit rendezvous, he smacked her hard across the face and called her a liar. He instantly regretted it, he said, but—again—it was too late. The damage was done. Now there was no way she could continue working at the Bel-Air Hotel. It was too much of a risk. Therefore, he took her down to his office, wrote out a big fat check, threw it at her, and sent her on her way, telling her to find employment elsewhere. She seemed so happy with the amount he'd given her and so amenable to leaving her job that as soon as she sashayed out the door he wondered if he hadn't been set up. Now, the next morning, he was just tired, hungover, and sorry he'd ever succumbed to the likes of Virginia Larson.

Maria de Amaté realized that for Nicky Hilton, every day seemed more hopeless than the one before. Sometimes he managed to go to work at the hotel, but there were many days he would rise, have his breakfast, and then simply go back to bed. As often happens, one day of discontentment led to another and another, until finally he was deep in a rut, drinking too much alcohol, popping too many pills. "Don't tell my pop I'm here," he would instruct Maria before closing his bedroom door. "If he asks where I am, just tell him I'm at work." He would not emerge again until the next morning, pale and miserable, and then would repeat the same routine.

Later that afternoon, Conrad and Barron were having a meeting in the study and came out looking for Nicky. "Have you seen my son?" Conrad asked Maria. He had called the Bel-Air Hotel and was told that Nicky hadn't come in that day. Now Maria found herself in a predicament. Nicky had specifically instructed her not to tell his father when he was in his bedroom during the day. Yet she worked for Conrad, not Nicky. While she had some sympathy for the young man, there was no question that her allegiance was to Conrad. "He's in his room, sir," she said quietly. Conrad looked miffed. "But he should be at work," he said with a tinge of frustration. He and Barron left the kitchen, headed for Nicky's bedroom suite on the second floor. A few moments later, Maria heard loud banging on the suite's door, then angry, muffled voices. Ten minutes later, Conrad and Barron came back down to the kitchen.

"He's getting worse," Barron said.

Barron saw the sadness in his father's face and waited for a response. "I know," Conrad said at last. "But he's a strong kid. He'll get over it. It's the divorce. He just needs more time."

"Okay, Dad," Barron said, looking a little hopeless. "Maybe you're right."

When Conrad left the room, Barron sat down at the table, poured himself a cup of coffee, and lit a cigarette. Now it was his hands that were trembling. The pressure of not knowing for certain how to handle his older brother's desperate situation was getting to him. He looked at Maria de Amaté sadly. There was nothing either of them could think of to say. "That will be all," Barron finally said, dismissing the maid.

A Baroness Named Betsy

"Let's make a promise," Nicky Hilton was saying. "Let's promise to never have another drink again." He gazed lovingly into the green eyes of the beautiful blonde seated next to him at the bar of the Bel-Air Hotel. "Baby, if we can feel like *this* without drinking, then why bother having even another drop?" he said, holding her hand. "This is already as good as it gets," he concluded. "We don't need liquor!"

"Oh, I agree, Nicky," cooed the blonde. She had earlier confessed to him that she too had a serious drinking problem. "Never another drink for either one of us, then," she whispered to him. "Seal it with a kiss?"

He leaned over and kissed her fully on the lips. "Consider it sealed," he said.

It was the summer of 1951 and Nicky Hilton had finally begun to feel a bit better. He was now finding comfort in the arms of another young lady with an exotic past and show business aspirations. One day, while surveying the pool area at the Bel-Air Hotel, his eyes had fallen upon a shapely blonde lounging poolside. Her shocking pink bikini—unusual in America in those days—had distinguished her among the other beauties sunning themselves that early afternoon. Nicky made a beeline for her and began to pour on the charm.

"You know, sweetheart, I run this place," he said, standing above her. "So if there's anything you need," he added, "anything at all. Just ask for me. I'm Nicky Hilton."

"*The* Nicky Hilton?" she asked, sitting up in her lounge chair. She lowered her cat-eye sunglasses and took him in.

"The one and only," he answered with a lopsided grin.

"Spare a smoke?"

He pulled a pack from his vest pocket, lit one, and handed it to her. She inhaled fully and then, exhaling deeply, languidly lay back down on her recliner. "So, what's a handsome, rich boy like you doing working in the middle of the day?" she asked, gazing up at him dreamily.

"Making it possible for beautiful girls like you to show off here at the pool," he said, seeming transfixed by her body.

"Do you make a habit of undressing girls at the pool with your eyes, Mr. Hilton?" she asked.

"*Mr. Hilton* is my father," he said with a sly smile.

"Well, does your daddy know that you undress girls at the pool with your eyes?" she asked with an arched eyebrow.

"Actually, my *daddy* encourages it," he shot back with a wink.

"My kind of *daddy*," she said.

One thing led to another until, finally, he asked her out. She was eighteen-year-old Betsy von Furstenberg and she accepted. It was Betsy, then, to whom Nicky would vow to never have another drink. "It was the kind of thing you promised when you were in the first blush of romance, when you're head over heels and you think life couldn't get any better. Unfortunately," she hastens to add, "the promise we made to each other lasted only about a week. Then, unfortunately, we both picked up where we left off."

Born Elizabeth Caroline Maria Agatha Felicitas Therese, Freiin von Fürstenberg-Hedringen in Arnsberg, Germany, she was a baroness by birth, her father was a count from Germany, her mother from Union Springs, Alabama. Her parents met while her mother was vacationing on a yacht in the south of France.

After moving to America, Betsy attended the Hewitt School in New York. A model who had often graced the covers of French fashion magazines as well as three issues of *Look* magazine (photographed by Stanley Kubrick), her goal was to become a successful actress. After changing her name to Betsy von Furstenberg, she had made her stage debut in New York at the Morosco Theatre in the play *Second Threshold*. The show ran from January to April. After it closed, Betsy moved to Los Angeles to pursue a career in film with MGM, which immediately positioned her for stardom with a cover story in *Life*. Then she met Nicky Hilton. Like Elizabeth, Betsy was an actress who at times appeared sexy and alluring yet on other occasions was able to project a winsome, innocent quality that hid a much tougher core. "I could drink any fellow right under the table," she said with a laugh. "We *all* drank back then. Nicky and I were probably not the best influences on each other because we were both heavy drinkers from the start. Plus we were both taking Seconal, which was the recreational drug of choice in Hollywood at that time. I mean, everyone was on it. Marilyn [Monroe] was living on it! I soon learned that Nicky and I had that drug in common. Mixing it with alcohol was deadly, but we did that too. Before long, we were enabling each other like nobody's business."

Though they didn't know anything about her alcohol or drug issues, Conrad and Barron were still ambivalent about Nick's relationship with Betsy. Of course, she hadn't reached anywhere near the kind of fame and notoriety Elizabeth had attained, but this was Hollywood and anything could happen overnight. Betsy seemed to be on her way, and thus both Hilton men saw trouble on the horizon for Nicky.

"Oh no, not again, son," Conrad said loudly. His voice could be heard as he approached from many feet away, according to Bob Neal, who was lying by the pool with Nicky at the Hilton mansion that afternoon. He and Nicky were baking in the sun in their swimsuits, alongside a pair of girls in matching white bikinis, when Conrad's voice boomed toward them. Both young men looked up, and to their amusement they saw that Conrad was wearing a brown suit, matching cowboy hat, and heavy western boots. (He also wore his star sapphire ring on his right hand, a favorite of his.) "A little hot out here for a get-up like that, isn't it?" Nicky asked lazily as he lay back down and offered his face to the sun. Conrad ignored his observation. "Barron told me about this girl you're seeing," he said, stepping toward Nicky so that his shadow was cast over his son's face. "I understand she's in show business." Nicky said nothing. "Please don't get in too deep, that's all I'm saying," Conrad added.

Nicky didn't look up at his father. He tipped the fedora he was wearing down below his eyes. "I like her," he said simply. "And I haven't been happy since Elizabeth. Betsy makes me laugh. She's fun. And she's got a classy chassis, too, Pop. So just leave it alone, all right?"

"I'm just saying, maybe take it slow, okay, kid?" Conrad asked. "There's no hurry, right?"

Nicky's answer was silence. He wouldn't allow himself to be drawn into a discussion about Betsy; he kept his hat covering his eyes. Finally, he said, "I get it, Pop, okay? We got other dames here today, don't we? Obviously I'm not in that deep, right?"

"All right. I'm just a little worried about you, that's all," Conrad said before taking his leave.

After he was gone, Nicky tipped his fedora up above his eyes, looked at Bob Neal, and said, "Sometimes it would be nice if he would just see the best in me, instead of the worst. I mean…would that be so bad?"

Bob Neal thought it over. "Actually, you might want to do the same for him, Nick. Would *that* be so bad?"

Nicky grinned at his friend. "*Asshole*," he said with a swift, playful punch to Bob Neal's arm.

The Shadow of Her Smile

Oh, baby, I'm so sorry about what happened last night," Nicky was saying to Betsy. The two were on the telephone. Betsy was so hungover she was finding it hard to focus on the conversation. It had been a rough night of partying on the Sunset Strip.

"What do you mean?" she wanted to know

"Have you looked in the mirror?" he asked, his voice well modulated and controlled. If ever a relationship could be viewed as toxic—a term certainly not used to describe such pairings in the 1950s but one that today certainly does apply—the one between Nicky Hilton and Betsy von Furstenberg qualified. Both were drinking too much, both were addicted to Seconal, and, by her own admission, both were physically abusive of one another. On this morning, she got out of bed, walked over to the vanity, and gazed at her reflection in the mirror. Much to her surprise, she had a black eye. She didn't even remember how it happened. "Well, one thing led to another," Nicky explained when she came back to the phone, "and the next thing I knew, you slugged me and, well, I slugged you back," he said. "I got a shiner, too. Can you believe it?"

"Oh well," she said with a sigh. "Give me a call later and we'll have a nice quiet dinner and talk it over, okay?"

"Okay, baby," he said. "Sorry. Bye."

"It actually was no big deal," Betsy would recall many years later, "which shows you how bad things had become. It had just been another night in our life together, one of us as bad as the other, both dragging each other down. I enabled him, he enabled me. I look back on it now all these years later and wonder how we ever got through it. But in our defense, drinking was much more accepted back then. Nobody saw anything wrong with it. It was actually considered to be glamorous and a big part of living the good life, to have cocktails all the time."

In September 1951, Nicky and Betsy announced their engagement, saying that that they planned to wed aboard a yacht in the Caribbean in January. Though Betsy told gossip columnist Louella Parsons, "I'm too thrilled to talk," it's not likely she ever really felt she and Nicky were destined for marriage. "I'm not sure he even asked me to marry him," she recalled many years later. "It was more like, we were drinking one night and leaving a club and the media was all over us asking about our future, and one of us flippantly said, 'Oh, we're engaged.' The next thing we knew it was in all of the papers, 'Elizabeth Taylor's Ex-Husband Is Marrying a Baroness.'"

If Only

*A*fter her divorce from Conrad Hilton, Zsa Zsa Gabor married actor George Sanders. She was not happy, though, and felt that he was unkind. When he received his Oscar for Best Supporting Actor in *All About Eve*, he didn't even thank her or so much as mention her name in his acceptance speech. That night, after the show was over and everyone had vacated the venue, Zsa Zsa sat alone in the dark, cavernous Grauman's Chinese Theatre. Feeling sad and worthless, she listened to the sounds emanating from backstage—actors and actresses, producers and directors and others connected to the film industry celebrating their victories and commiserating over their losses, but reveling in their camaraderie just the same. "I could hear their laughter and their merriment," she would recall. And she thought to herself, "If I only had a career. If only I had…power."

It was a compelling thought, the idea of her attaining power during this time. In the 1950s, women generally didn't think in terms of finding their own power. Men were thought of as being powerful, women feminine. Of course, in show business, there were any number of women who could be aptly be described as being overtly powerful—great actresses such as Katharine Hepburn, Joan Crawford, Bette Davis, even, to a certain extent, Marilyn Monroe. It's likely that when Zsa Zsa spoke of wanting power she was thinking in terms of having some influence in the entertainment world—like her husband, George Sanders—and perhaps even parlaying that power into a lucrative career so that she didn't have to be so dependent on any man for her survival. This isn't to say that she would ever be the kind of woman who would be independent of a man; that wasn't who she was either. "What I wanted was to look into the mirror and see someone I could be proud of," she once explained. "I knew no one would take me there, I would have to do it on my own."

Lately, Zsa Zsa had been talking about trying for a serious career in show business; she just wasn't sure how to go about it. Sanders was less than encouraging, believing her to have no discernible talent. He agreed that she was quite witty, but he didn't see how she would be able to utilize that character trait in show business. She was uncommonly beautiful, he had to concede as much, but so were many other women in Hollywood. Beauty would not necessarily distinguish her, or so he thought. It was ironic, then, that while George Sanders was out of town for three months making the movie *Ivanhoe* in England, his brother, Tom Conway, called upon Zsa Zsa to assist him in what can only be called a "show biz emergency."

Tom Conway was on his way to the taping of a local Los Angeles–area television program he was appearing on called *Bachelor's Haven*, a panel show where celebrities answered questions sent in to the TV station from the lovelorn. There was an opening on the panel of three; would Zsa Zsa like to appear on it?

This was actually the perfect star vehicle for Zsa Zsa Gabor. It required what she knew she could do best—be gorgeous with her stylish wardrobe, be funny with her continental accent, and be quick with her Hungarian wit. "I can do this," she decided. "I *want* to do it." But still, she didn't know if she could pull it off; she was terribly fearful, especially since she had never been before a television camera.

Zsa Zsa's mother, Jolie, who happened to be visiting, did everything she could think of to encourage her daughter. Still, Zsa Zsa was unsure. Therefore, Jolie picked up the telephone to recruit the one person she felt could convince Zsa Zsa to take the chance of a lifetime, someone who had spent most of his days taking big chances—Conrad. Even though the two had suffered a contentious relationship of late, Jolie knew that deep down they still had a deep, soulful connection. Still, when she told Zsa Zsa that Conrad was on the telephone, Zsa Zsa balked at speaking to him. She thought he had called to pick a fight with her. "Oh my God! I can't speak to *him* now," she said. "He'll just upset me." However, her mother insisted. "He is *family*," she said. "Now, you speak to him!"

"Jolie explained to me what's going on," Conrad told Zsa Zsa once she got on the line, "and I think you should do the program. Trust me."

Zsa Zsa could not have been more surprised. Never would she have expected his encouragement, especially after some of the terrible things they'd said to each other in recent years. "I can't believe you are telling me this," she said. "Really, Connie? You *sink* I should?"

"From the moment I met you," he told her, "I knew you were something special. There's no one like Zsa Zsa, my dear. You are one of a kind, for better or worse," he added with a chuckle. "I think it's time to let America in on our little secret. So, I say do it, Georgia."

She was immediately brought to tears, especially by his calling her "Georgia," which he hadn't done in years. She thanked him profusely and made up her mind: She was going to give it a try. What did she have to lose?

Zsa Zsa Finds Her Niche

*I*f ever a woman was an overnight sensation, it was Zsa Zsa Gabor, thanks to *Bachelor's Haven*. Wearing a stunning black off-the-shoulder Balenciaga gown, a large diamond bracelet, matching earrings, and a twenty-carat solitaire, she was an instant hit, not just because of her glamorous appeal but also because of her wicked sense of humor. "My goodness, look at those diamonds," the show's host, Johnny Jacobs, said. "Oh, these?" Zsa Zsa said dismissively, holding her hand out for inspection. "These are just my *vorking* diamonds." From that moment on, she had the audience in the palms of her silk-gloved hands. "All I know is that my career was handed to me on a silver platter," she would say.

Though the show was a West Coast broadcast, reports of Zsa Zsa's snappy, irreverent answers and her quick sense of humor soon spread across the country, thanks to newspaper and radio coverage. After the first segment, she was asked to become a regular on the program.

One woman wrote in to the show, "I'm breaking my engagement to a wealthy man. He gave me a beautiful home, a mink coat, diamonds, a stove, and an expensive car. What shall I do?"

Zsa Zsa shot back, "Give him back the stove."

Another woman complained that her husband was a traveling salesman, "but I know he strays even when I'm home. How can I stop him?" she asked. "*Dah-ling*, shoot him in the *legs*," Zsa Zsa suggested.

Still another man wrote in that he was a bachelor who had a great many oil wells, and he wondered if he should marry since he had just turned fifty. Zsa Zsa thought it over for a moment and answered, "For this man, life is just beginning. He is just now becoming interesting. I do not *sink* I should give him advice. In fact, I *sink* I should see this man…*personally.*"

She continued to bring down the house; the *Hollywood Reporter* dubbed her "the most beautiful girl to ever be on a television screen." She would even be nominated for an Emmy for her work on *Bachelor's Haven.*

"Looking back, I realize that all I did was do what I have always done: flout convention and say what I really think, no matter the consequences—and poke fun at myself while doing it," Zsa Zsa recalled. "Noël Coward used to say that he had a talent to amuse. It seemed that I had a talent—of sorts—to shock in a comical way and to ad-lib without the help of script writers. I found it was much better being myself than trying to be someone else. So, no matter what I was doing or how I was doing it, it was always honest, always…me."

In October 1951, Zsa Zsa appeared on the cover of *Life* magazine, looking gorgeous in a studio-posed black-and-white photograph. This was a huge career boost, of course, though she was used to being in the press. Along with *Life*, she would also find herself on the cover of *Collier's, Paris Match*, and the *London Picture Post*, all in one month's time. The primary reason for all of the attention this time, though, was not because of one of her marriages or some personal scandal, but rather a result of her work on *Bachelor's Haven.* To commemorate the publication of the *Life* magazine spread, Zsa Zsa hosted a spectacular party at her home—and offered each of the guests a signed copy. "*Mah-vellous*," Conrad said, imitating her accent, when Zsa Zsa gave him his magazine. She was visibly happy to have his approval. "Are you proud of me?" she asked him. "I certainly am," he told her. "You found your niche, my dear. Now make lots and lots of money." That sounded like a good plan to her.

From this time onward, it would be a rapid rise to the top for Zsa Zsa Gabor, beginning when MGM offered her a film role in *Lovely to Look At*, the adaptation of the Broadway musical *Roberta.* It wasn't a big role—she played Mignon, the French maid—but it made a huge impression on the public, as well as on her bank account, because she was paid $10,000 for the job, a huge amount of money at that time. All of her lines were in French, with English subtitles. (Conrad's companion Ann Miller was also in the film.) Zsa Zsa would then have starring roles in no less than eighteen more movies throughout the 1950s, including the role as singer Jane Avril in a performance many still consider to be her best, the Academy Award–winning *Moulin Rouge* (directed by John Huston), as well as *Lili, We're Not Married*, and *The Story of Three Loves*. In 1958, she would become known for starring in the campy science fiction cult film *Queen of Outer Space*.

There's never really been anyone quite like Zsa Zsa. "It's funny, I met Courtney Love the other day at the market," her daughter, Francesca, has said. "I was getting her autograph for my stepdaughter, and I told her my mother is Zsa Zsa Gabor. She said, 'Oh my *God*! How *cool* is that?'"

Filling Elizabeth's Shoes

*T*hough the sky seemed to be the limit for the ever-ascending Zsa Zsa Gabor, the same couldn't be said for her former stepson Nicky Hilton and his lovely fiancée, Betsy von Furstenberg. Within a couple of months, Betsy got the full picture of what a future with Nicky would be like...and it wasn't good. "He was so complex," she said. "On one hand I had never met anyone who believed so strongly in others. As competitive as he was with Barron, I could truly see that he wanted the best for him, and for his dad, and for all of his friends. He was so sweet like that. But the problem for me was that he had no motivation," she remembered. "He still had his important position at the Bel-Air Hotel, but he was hardly there and I can't even imagine how he kept the job. I was no help. I was too young. I didn't know what to do."

The memory of Elizabeth Taylor was proving to be another kind of problem. She was not the sort of woman a man easily forgets. "He was tormented by the failure of his marriage to Elizabeth," Betsy said. "He once told me that she was his first love and that he didn't think he would ever be able to get over her. I felt he had somewhat romanticized the relationship, that it hadn't been as good as he believed it had been in retrospect. Whenever we would fight, he would call me by her name. I was walking in her shadow.

"I remember once we went to a movie theater for an opening and we found out she was there as well, sitting somewhere behind us. Nicky didn't want to run into her. 'Let's just wait for her to leave,' he said, almost begging me. So we waited and waited, but as it happened, she was waiting us out too! Finally, the theater was nearly empty and she was still sitting with someone, waiting for us to come up the aisle, I guess so that she could have a good look at me. We said hello, and that was it. From that moment on, the evening was ruined for us because Nick fell into a deep depression. I did begin to feel that I would always just be filling Elizabeth's shoes."

In early 1952, when MGM opted not to renew Betsy's movie contract, she decided to return to New York to appear in a show there called *Dear Barbarians*. She would be back and forth between Manhattan and Los Angeles for the next six months, but it was clear that her relationship with Nick was on the wane. He was sad, but he said that he had given up on finding happiness. "Maybe I'm just not meant to be happy," he told his friend Bob Neal.

"How can you say that, Nick?" Bob asked. "You have the world by the balls! You're living the *dream*, pal," he exclaimed. "You got money. You got power. Your family is sitting on top of the whole world. The rest of us, we're all down here wishing *we* were Hiltons."

"Are you trying to make me feel better... *or worse?*" Nicky asked.

"You just have to get out of this goddamn mausoleum," Bob told him, according to his memory of the conversation. "You have to bounce back, man. Listen to me. Elizabeth Taylor is not thinking about you. I guarantee it. No way is that crazy broad thinking about you, Nick. She's out getting laid somewhere. And you know it's true."

"Shut up, Bob," Nicky said angrily. "Don't say that about Elizabeth."

"Look, I'm just telling you the truth," Robert said.

Nicky nodded. "Yeah, I know," he conceded sadly. "But shut up anyway."

Assault

*I*n the spring of 1952, Conrad Hilton hosted a party at his home to celebrate the acquisition of his first hotel in Europe, the Castellana Hilton in Madrid, which would finally open on July 14, 1953. (In its first year of operation, the Castellana Hilton would bring in more than $1 million worth of U.S. tourists.)

While a dozen flamenco dancers performed outside to the sounds of a thirty-piece orchestra, more than a hundred formally dressed Hilton employees from around the world feasted on a sumptuous buffet of Spanish cuisine. Wearing a dapper black suit, Conrad held court, along with his sons Barron and Nicky, also in finely tailored suits. Even Eric had flown up from Texas. "This was a time when men were *men* and women were *women*," is how Betsy von Furstenberg, who was present, put it. "The gentlemen were always impeccable in their black or gray suits with crisp white shirts and black ties, the women gorgeous in their cocktail dresses with waists cinched so tightly we could hardly breathe. Everyone smoked. Everyone drank. Everyone drove off in cool cars. Everyone was sexy." The star-studded affair boasted a guest list that included Frank Sinatra, Grace Kelly, James Stewart, and Doris Day. "About three hours into the party, Nick was pretty drunk on Dewar's," recalled Betsy, "as, of course, was I."

Barron looked at Nick with disapproval and wanted him out of the party. He was afraid Nick would embarrass himself and his father. "You've had too much to drink, Nick. Now, let me see to you," Barron said as he pulled Nicky along by the elbow. But Nicky wasn't having it. "I'm not a child," he kept saying, "stop treating me like one." Betsy followed the two of them into one of the upstairs bedrooms.

"You're in bad shape, Nick," Barron said, according to what Betsy recalled. He asked Nicky to stay in the room and sleep it off.

"Get bent!" Nicky shouted at his brother, using 1950s slang for "drop dead." He added, "I'm not drunk, Barron. I know when I'm loaded and I'm not loaded. So get away from me!" From the way he slurred his words, he was clearly inebriated. He insisted that he was going to go back downstairs, because "Pop needs all of us down there, not just you, Barron. Me and Eric, too. Why are you trying to get all the attention?"

"You can't represent Dad this way," Barron reasoned. Again, he asked him to just stay in the bedroom and sober up. Barron then summoned the maid, Maria, on the intercom system to ask her to bring a pot of black coffee to the room. Afterward, Barron tried to lead Nicky to a chair, gently pulling him along by his arm. But suddenly Nicky broke free. He then spun around and, in one quick motion, punched Barron right in the face with a powerful left hook. It was so quick and sudden, the three of them—Nicky, Barron, and Betsy—just stared at one another for a stunned moment. Almost instantly, Barron's nose began to bleed. As soon as Nicky saw his younger brother's white shirt become streaked with red, he crumbled. "Holy shit! I'm so sorry, Barron," he said. He began to cry. "I can't believe I hit my own brother." Upset, Barron left the room.

Though Betsy sat down next to Nicky and tried to console him, it was impossible. "I can't believe I did that to Barron," Nicky said, his head sunk low to his chest. "He'll never forgive me."

"He's your brother," Betsy said. "Of course he will forgive you."

"But how can I forgive myself?" he asked, distraught. "I'm better than this, Betsy. I'm a *Hilton*. I'm better than this."

"Look, things got out of hand, that's all," Betsy said, trying to calm him down. "It's okay, Nicky. It's okay."

Though it obviously was not okay, for Nicky Hilton it was at least a wake-up call. The next day, he ended it with Betsy once and for all. "We're not good for each other, baby," he told her, sitting with her in his white convertible with the red interior. "I need some time alone to pull myself together."

She knew he was right. She had wanted to end it herself several times, but didn't have the nerve. "I'm just going to worry about you so much," she told him, her eyes filling with tears. "Just the thought that you'll be out here doing whatever it is you'll be doing, and I won't know you're okay. It kills me, Nick."

He smiled at her. "I feel the same way about you, baby."

"If I call you in the middle of the night and tell you I'm in big trouble, Nick, will you come?" she asked. "Will you show up?"

"In a heartbeat," he answered. "I'll be there so fast, Betsy, your pretty little head will spin."

They kissed. She got out of the car. And that was the end of that.

Now more determined than ever to straighten out his life, Nicky again made the decision to stop drinking, and also to stop with the pills. "That's it," he told Conrad and Barron. "I can't let what happened the other night ever happen again. I'm done. I'm going to get clean."

Magic Words

See, this is what happens when you're bangin' women with no sense," Robert Wentworth was telling Nicky Hilton. It was about a week after the disastrous Hilton party and the two friends were chatting in the parlor of the Hilton estate. Wentworth was referring not only to Elizabeth Taylor but also to Betsy von Furstenberg. "These crazy broads, Nick, I'm telling you, they will ruin you, pal," he said. "You got to set your sights higher. You got to get a better class of dame, Nick!"

Nicky had to agree. "My old man always says that growing trouble is like a snowball rolling down a mountainside," he said, taking a drag from a cigarette. "It just gets bigger and bigger until you put a stop to it. I got nothing to show for any of it but misery. Then I gave my own brother a knuckle sandwich!"

"Guess we can't really blame that on Betsy, though, can we?" Robert asked.

"No, Bobby. We can't," Nicky agreed. "She's a good kid. She really is."

For Nicky Hilton, it simply may have been a case of too much too soon. He was blessed with exceptional good looks and great wealth. He was given a stellar position at a prime location in his father's business at an early age. As with everyone born with a silver spoon, he could have gone down one of several paths. Barron—with all the same privileges— got married, started a family, and had begun to build his own fortune. But Nicky succumbed to more wild and glitzy temptations. Still, as Robert Wentworth recalled it, "Elizabeth was history. Betsy was history We just chalked them up to having been two crazy broads from the unpredictable life and times of Nicky Hilton."

"You know, Bobby, I think maybe I was a little rough on Elizabeth," Nicky suddenly said. Wentworth was surprised to hear him admit as much since he never had in the past. "Something just got a hold of me," Nicky continued. "She made me so crazy. I'm not proud of the way I dealt with it. I'm ashamed of myself."

"Well, you can't let it happen again, Nick," Robert said. "It's not good and you know it."

Nicky nodded but didn't say anything. He seemed lost in thought for a few moments. Then he smiled. "You know, we were at a party once," he said, now in a daydream about Elizabeth, "and she looked so beautiful. I remember I was across the room just staring at her and thinking what a lucky bastard I was. And she winked at me and mouthed something to me. I couldn't figure out what she was saying; her lips were just moving. So I walked over to her, and I said, 'What are you trying to say, baby? What is it?' And she leaned in and whispered in my ear, 'I'm not wearing any panties.'" He chuckled and slapped his knee. "God damn it! I just wanted to take her right then and there. Know what I mean?"

The two friends shared a good laugh.

"Well, a man can never hear *that* enough, I guess," Robert Wentworth concluded.

"Yeah," Nicky agreed, laughing. "Those are some magic words, all right."

Mamie

*T*here's something about this one, she's different," Nicky Hilton was telling his friend the actor John Carroll. "She's smart. She's a knockout, too. I really like her." He and Carroll were sitting in Nicky's apartment at 882 North Doheny Drive in Hollywood. It was the end of February 1954. After the physical altercation with Barron, Nicky decided to move out of Conrad's home and take an apartment. He said he needed distance from his father, and a small apartment in Hollywood seemed the perfect refuge for him. Incidentally, Marilyn Monroe lived in the same complex, having moved there from the Beverly Hills Hotel in 1953. The apartment building, which had been built just two years earlier, was quite comfortable but modest, especially in contrast to his father's opulent estate. No one knew for certain how many rooms were in Conrad's Casa Encantada, but there was no question as to how many were in Nicky's apartment—three: a living room that doubled as a bedroom, a kitchen, and a bathroom.

"You're not getting serious about another dame, Nick," John Carroll warned him. "Don't forget our new rule."

Nicky laughed. "Yeah, the new rule is: They're all fine, as long as you don't take any of 'em seriously."

The two men clinked glasses.

The new woman in Nicky's life was yet another Hollywood knockout, this time up-and-coming Universal Pictures starlet, twenty-three-year-old divorcee Mamie Van Doren. Born Joan Lucille Olander, of Swedish, German, and English heritage, she hailed from the small town of Rowena, South Dakota. Discovered by Howard Hughes on the night she was crowned Miss Palm Springs, Mamie made a few appearances in bit parts of RKO movies before signing with Universal in January 1953 and making her film debut for that studio in the Tony Curtis movie *Forbidden*, and then appearing in another Curtis vehicle—this time in a starring role—in *The All American*.

Mamie came into prominence during a time in 1954 when Marilyn Monroe mania was sweeping the country, if not the entire world, thanks to blockbuster movies like *Niagara*, *Gentlemen Prefer Blondes*, and *How to Marry a Millionaire*. Every studio was grooming their lustiest, bustiest, and blondest starlets and hauling them out to compete with 20th Century-Fox's hottest commodity—Marilyn. Mamie's champagne blonde hair, curvaceous figure, and sex kitten persona conveyed some of the Monroe mystique. Universal had high hopes of turning her into their version of a sizzling blonde box-office bonanza. In some photographs, when properly coiffed, made up, and costumed, Mamie actually looked as if she could be Marilyn's double.

It was Universal publicity department head Al Horowitz's idea to bolster Mamie's visibility by having her escorted to the Los Angeles premier of *The Glenn Miller Story*, starring Jimmy Stewart and June Allyson, on February 17, 1954. When he called Nicky with the suggestion, Nicky—blasé by this point when it came to Hollywood glamour gals—asked to see a picture of Van Doren before agreeing to the PR gimmick. Horowitz cannily sent by messenger a few glossy cheesecake photos of Mamie at her most enticing to Nicky's Hollywood apartment, and within hours heard back from Hilton declaring that, hell yes, he'd be interested in a date with the new stunner on the block.

"The night of the premiere, Nicky picked me up in his white Cadillac convertible with red leather," Mamie recalled many years later. "I was excited, dressed to the nines in my white, strapless Ceil Chapman–designed, beaded dress with a little jacket."

As was his style when out on the town, Nicky also looked his best. He could have been mistaken for a movie star himself, decked out in his white tuxedo jacket and bow tie. "He had flawless skin, a great body, beautiful eyes, a full head of hair," Mamie remembered. "He was so handsome. We were the perfect Hollywood couple, really. I remember the klieg lighting the sky over the Pantages Theatre when we arrived, and there were police barricades on both sides of Hollywood Boulevard with fans just pushing and pushing against them as Nicky and I walked up the red carpet and into the theater. It was so exciting. 'Mamie! Mamie!' they were all screaming. But then we were eventually seated close to the stage, maybe three rows from the front. It suggested that maybe I wasn't quite as big a star as I had been led to believe by the crowd's reaction to me. The really big names were always seated much farther away from the screen. I was embarrassed."

"Oh my," Mamie said self-consciously as she and Nick settled into their seats. "Maybe you said yes to the wrong starlet. I mean, look where we're sitting, Nicky."

Nicky gallantly took Mamie's hand and, with a little squeeze, whispered, "We're going to enjoy ourselves despite these seats." Then he put his arm around her and, flashing his winning smile, said, "Hell, Mamie. You're with a Hilton! Let's live it up!"

After the premiere, the couple enjoyed the rest of the night at Romanoff's, a Beverly Hills restaurant popular at the time because it was frequented by Hollywood's elite. Nicky, a pro in front of the cameras by this time, coached the show business neophyte on how to comport herself for the inevitable next-day newspaper photos. "He told me where to pose for the camera and how," she recalled. "He held my hand throughout the night, the perfect escort. Finally, he said, 'You know what, babe? Let's blow this pop stand.' We then got into his car and drove all over the city with the top down, the cool night air against our faces, talking, laughing, smoking one Kool cigarette after another and getting to know one another. Finally, he drove me back home to the house in which I lived with my mom. He asked if he could call me sometime, and I said yes and gave him my number. He was such a gentleman, giving me a nice kiss at the door. Then he got into his car and drove off. I thought, 'My goodness. That was really the perfect date, wasn't it?'

"In the days to come, we had many long conversations," she recalled. "I got it right away that he absolutely adored his father. He spoke about his dad's success and about the hotel business and about how proud he was of him. I thought, how nice to know a son who has such a great relationship with his father. He adored his brother too, just idolized him, as much as he was in competition with him."

Bob Neal recalled an evening at the Hilton mansion with Nicky when Mamie's name came up. Conrad's and Nicky's friends John Carroll and Robert Wentworth were present, as were Conrad, Barron, and his wife, Marilyn. They were all playing cards in the parlor, drinking coffee, and watching television. "I want you to meet this girl," Nicky told his father and brother. "I think I'm getting serious about her." Conrad stared at his son without saying a word. No one else spoke either. Conrad glanced over at Barron, as if waiting for his second son to say what was on everyone's minds. "Not another actress," Barron finally said, taking his cue. "We're not playing *that* scene out again, Nick, are we?" Nicky responded by saying he felt they weren't being fair. This girl was not like the others, he said, and when the family had a chance to meet her, they'd understand. After a few moments of awkward silence, Conrad finally spoke up. "Is she Catholic, Nick?" he asked, not even looking up from his cards.

"Well, not everyone's Catholic, Pop," Nicky answered.

"Okay," Conrad said. He then folded his cards, bade everyone a good night, pushed out his chair, and left the table.

"What followed was a reasonably levelheaded discussion amongst those of us present of the wisdom of Nicky repeating his history with another actress," Bob Neal said. "It wasn't hostile or difficult. Nicky seemed open to all views, which were pretty much in agreement that he shouldn't do it. Then, at the end, Marilyn spoke up and said, 'Well, to be fair, I think we owe it to this woman to at least meet her.'"

As it happened, Barron and Marilyn Hilton had recently bought a sprawling Tudor-style beachfront mansion in Santa Monica, a home formerly owned by MGM's head of production, Irving Thalberg, and his wife, actress Norma Shearer. (Two of their neighbors on Sorrento happened to be Peter Lawford and his wife, Pat Kennedy.) Shearer actually had the house soundproofed so that Thalberg, who was an insomniac, wouldn't hear the waves crashing onto the sand, the surf was that incredibly close. "Marilyn lived in constant fear that one good storm would end with her antique dining room furniture floating out into the sea," recalled Bob Neal. "Luckily, that never happened."

To celebrate their new home, the Hiltons were planning an elaborate housewarming party. "Why not bring Mamie to the party?" Marilyn offered. Barron didn't think it was a good idea; he didn't want to stir the pot. However, Marilyn felt that if Nicky had such strong feelings for someone, the family should at least get to know her.

Marilyn's Party

About a week later, Barron and Marilyn Hilton hosted a gathering for about a hundred of their friends and business associates. By this time, Marilyn had completed a fascinating metamorphosis from a pretty but simple young lady into a truly stunning woman. Her blonde hair was now professionally styled weekly and her shapely body draped in only the finest, most expensive designs from boutiques on Rodeo Drive. Her glossy new appearance combined with the innate charm that had always been integral to her personality made for a "new" Marilyn Hilton that was a real knockout. For this night, she orchestrated a Hawaiian-themed party, with all of the guests asked to arrive dressed in Polynesian styles. Hanging tiki lights gave the backyard a magical look, with paper lanterns, hibiscus leis, and lotus blossoms completing the theme. As the smell of barbecued ribs wafted through the air and records by Eddie Fisher, Rosemary Clooney, and the McGuire Sisters played on the outdoor sound system, Marilyn moved with grace through the crowd. She was wearing a flower-patterned silk sarong, her hair pulled into a French twist with large gardenias framing her face. The perfect hostess, she would take the time to share at least a moment with each and every person who was present.

"When she talked to you, she zeroed in on you like you were the only thing that mattered," recalled Bob Neal. "You felt you were in the company of someone unique, worldly. She could also be quite demanding. I saw her impale a couple of waiters with an icy glare, putting them in their place. I overheard her tell Conrad's butler, Wilson, who was on loan to her, 'You are being paid to *work*, not converse with the guests.'"

Nicky's date, Mamie Van Doren, wore a white silk dress cut so low no man or woman could take their eyes off her bountiful bosom. At one point in the evening, she and Marilyn Hilton performed a sexy little hula dance to the accompaniment of a trio of Polynesian musicians who'd been hired for the festivities. "The party spilled out onto the beach under the stars," recalled Louella Parsons, who was also present, "and it was quite a lovely affair, typical of the Hiltons' grand, rich lifestyle."

Mamie recalled that while she was enjoying a slice of Hawaiian pineapple cheesecake, John Carroll informed her that Nicky had become quite serious about her. "I actually think he wants to marry you," Carroll told her. "So, play your cards right, sweetheart, and you can have it all. All this? It could be yours." Mamie listened with a noncommittal smile. "I remember thinking, my goodness, if I *was* that kind of girl, it wouldn't have been difficult to break into the winner's circle and end up with a piece of Hilton fortune, the way his friends were pushing me to marry Nick," she recalled. "I thought they might have been a little more protective of him, considering the kind of money that was at stake. After all, they really didn't know me. I *could* have been a gold digger, for all they knew."

Among the many guests were, of course, Conrad Hilton and his date, the vivacious Ann Miller. However, Conrad seemed to do everything he could think of to avoid meeting Mamie Van Doren. Clearly, he did not want to make her acquaintance. At one point she walked over to him, and just as she opened her mouth to introduce herself, he turned from her and said to a passing bartender, 'Say, my good fellow. They serve scotch in Hawaii, don't they? So, how about a shot of your best." Then he quickly became engaged in a conversation with someone else, leaving Mamie to just walk away.

Marilyn Hilton felt differently; she told Nicky that she approved of Mamie and hoped they could all see her again one day. Nicky wasted no time in taking advantage of the powerful ally he now had in her. When he asked her to intervene with Conrad, Marilyn agreed to talk to her father-in-law about arranging a meeting with Mamie.

Two weeks later, Conrad reluctantly agreed to have dinner with Mamie and Nicky at Casa Encantada.

Dinner at the Manse

*W*hen we pulled up at the Hilton mansion, I simply couldn't believe my eyes," recalled Mamie Van Doren. "I had never seen anything quite like it. It was out of this world. It seemed as big as any Hilton hotel, the furnishings opulent in a way that would make your head spin. I remember thinking about Nicky's little apartment on Doheny, which I had been to several times, and I couldn't help but wonder why in the world he lived in such a small place when his father had this gigantic mansion."

After about an hour of sitting in the elegant drawing room waiting for an entrance by Conrad—with Nicky nervously puffing on a Cuban cigar the entire time—Wilson, the butler, approached Nicky and Mamie to tell them that dinner was to be served. "What? But my father hasn't even come out to greet us yet," Nicky said in protest. At that, Wilson said, "I'm sorry, sir, but Mr. Hilton has instructed me to have you and your guest join him in the dining room." Nicky shook his head in annoyance and said, "Fine. If those are his wishes. Thank you, Wilson."

"We then walked through a complex maze of rooms to the dining room, which was as big as an airport hangar," Mamie recalled. "And in the middle of the room was a massive rectangular marble table that, I believe, had twelve chairs on each side, and one at each end. At the far end of the table sat Conrad Hilton in an impeccable suit and tie, appearing quite handsome and quite royal. He stood up, looked at me with distant eyes, and said, 'Welcome to my home, my dear.' Then he sat back down. I don't believe he said one word to Nicky. Nicky then showed me to my seat, which was in the middle of the table, where a lovely setting was in place, a solid gold plate with silverware. Then Nicky took his seat at the other far end of the table, facing his father. There was so much space between us, it didn't feel like we were even in the same room together. Maids and butlers came in and out doing this and that, arranging things and acting dutiful and somewhat nervous. There was so much food arranged on the table, I couldn't imagine that it was just for the three of us! The best way to describe the experience is to say that it was like having dinner in an English manse in the early 1900s. Very formal and quite intimidating if you weren't used to that way of life."

"So, my dear, how do you like the motion picture business?" Conrad asked Mamie as a maid dished out a lobster pâté appetizer. Conrad never looked directly at Mamie. Instead he kept his gaze straight ahead, at Nicky.

"It's interesting," Mamie said uncomfortably. "You meet so many people, you know?"

Conrad continued to stare at Nicky, who then awkwardly parroted Mamie's answer. "It's interesting for her, Pop," he said. "She meets so many people, you know?"

"Indeed," said Conrad. "And how, may I ask, did you happen upon the motion picture business, my dear?" he asked, still not taking his eyes off Nicky.

"Well, Howard Hughes helped me a great deal," Mamie said. His gaze still fixed on Nicky, Conrad acted as if he hadn't heard her.

"Howard Hughes sort of discovered her, Pop," Nicky repeated nervously.

"Indeed," Conrad said with an arched eyebrow. "I'm sure he did."

And on it went, with Conrad asking questions of Mamie but never actually acknowledging her presence, and Nicky answering for her. "Needless to say," Mamie recalled, "I did not feel welcomed."

After dinner, Nicky and Conrad found themselves in an adversarial discussion about a ballpoint pen business in which Nicky had recently become invested. The idea was to have large ballpoint pens placed in the rooms of Hilton hotels all over the world, which guests would then pay for on an honor basis, leaving behind a dollar for a set of two. Though Conrad's intuition told him it was a bad idea, he had decided to go along with it in order to support his son's vision. However, so far, the concept was not turning a profit. Conrad chose this moment to bring his disappointment in it to Nicky's attention. "People are just taking the pens without paying for them," he told Nicky. To Conrad, it made sense; in his mind, when a person picked up a pen to use it, the next thing he usually did was put it in his pocket and walk away with it. It wasn't stealing, Conrad said, it was instinct.

"But these pens are too long to put in your pocket," Nicky argued. He explained that they were writing pens, the kind one would use at a desk; they had no click-on tops. So Nicky didn't believe people were stealing them.

"But charging a dollar for two pens?" Conrad asked. He wasn't sure about the price, he said; he *was* sure, though, that *he* certainly would not spend a buck for a couple of pens. "And have you taken a look at the books?" he asked. According to the financial statements, Conrad noted, it definitely appeared that people were pilfering the pens.

Nicky shook his head at the suggestion that he didn't know what was going on in his own business. Maybe out of frustration, he unknotted his black bow tie, unfastened the top button of his crisp white shirt, and then let the tie just hang from his collar. He didn't like being told in front of Mamie that his first stab at an entrepreneurial venture was failing. "It takes time to start a new venture," he told his dad defensively.

"Quite right," Conrad said, conceding the point. "But my gut tells me this isn't going to work."

Nicky didn't respond.

(In the end, Conrad's intuition would be proved right; Nicky's venture would soon go belly up.)

After this somewhat tense discussion with his father, Nicky tried to lighten the mood by taking Mamie on a tour of the massive estate. Conrad decided to tag along. As Nicky showed Mamie one room after another, Conrad didn't say a word, still seeming somewhat miffed about the earlier disagreement. Finally, the trio found themselves outdoors.

"Say, I want to show you the new pool house," Conrad finally said to Nicky, breaking his silence. He led the couple down a long pathway through the sprawling floral gardens, past the glistening blue pool, and finally to a nice cottage that looked as if it had just been built. Smiling for the first time that evening, Conrad told Nicky that he had had the guesthouse remodeled specifically for Nicky's use. He said he felt his son could be happy living there, and would have a measure of privacy as well. So," Conrad concluded, "what do you think, son?"

"I don't know, Pop . . . ," Nicky said. He seemed extremely uncomfortable.

"Well, let's go in and take a look around, shall we?" Conrad offered.

After opening the front door with a large, ornate key, Conrad stepped inside the cottage and into its parlor, followed by Nicky and Mamie. The living room was opulently furnished, as if having been prepared for a photo shoot that would appear in a magazine devoted to the lifestyles of the rich and famous. There was even a pool table. "I had never seen anything quite so beautiful," Mamie said. "I remember thinking, 'This is a pool house? You have *got* to be kidding me!'"

"So what do you think, Nick?" Conrad asked again after they had gone to each room and were now back where they had started, in the living room.

"Nice, Pop," Nicky said, leaning against the black-felted pool table. He then turned his attention to the table, set the balls up in a rack, removed the triangle, and selected a cue stick off the wall rack. Bending over the table, he sized things up and then took his best shot. The balls went scattering, four of them flying swiftly into side pockets. He nodded his satisfaction and put the stick down. Then, turning to his father, he said he was impressed with the job Conrad had done on the remodeled guesthouse but, in the end, he still preferred his own little apartment in Hollywood. Conrad studied his son carefully. "Well, I insist that you move in here," he said, his tone now firm.

As Conrad spoke, Nicky began to look self-conscious, and as Mamie would later recall it, "he seemed so small and weak to me as he stood there with his father, this imposing, powerful presence." Shuffling his feet, Nicky managed to say, "Okay, Pop. I'll think about it."

"Fine, then," Conrad concluded. "I will arrange to have your things packed and brought here right away." Now seeming pleased, Conrad looked at Mamie and said, "I have rather a headache, my dear, so I will take my leave. So very nice to meet you." She extended her hand to him. He kissed it gallantly. Then he walked away, leaving her and Nicky standing in the living room of the cottage.

"Wow," Mamie exclaimed.

"Yeah, I know," Nicky said, shaking his head in dismay. "Wow."

That night, after Nicky and Mamie made love, the two lay naked on top of the bed, chain-smoking cigarettes and chatting about their strange experience at Conrad's home. "I'm awfully sorry about it," Nicky told Mamie. He said he felt he should apologize for his father. "He means well. But..." His voice trailed off.

"Well, I think you might love it in that little cottage," Mamie said, according to her memory of the conversation. She added that she could even redecorate it for him, if he wanted her to do so.

"No, I don't think so," Nick said, taking a puff. Lost in thought, he exhaled a plume of white smoke upward to the ceiling. He said he wasn't moving because he believed his father's true motivation was just to keep an eye on him. "It's his way of controlling me," he concluded.

"Well, I think he just loves you, sweetheart," Mamie said, curling up close and relaxing into him. "Like me."

He kissed her tenderly on the forehead. "Yes. But he thinks I'm a loser," Nicky said, suddenly seeming sad.

"That's not true," Mamie said.

"It is," he said. "He respects one thing. Strength."

"But you *are* strong."

"Then I need to prove it by keeping my own apartment," he decided.

She said she understood.

Nicky then became lost in a distant memory. He was thirteen and he and his father were in a department store attempting to buy him a new suit for a birthday party. Conrad and a superior-acting store clerk were going from one department to another picking out jackets and shirts and ties for Nicky while the teenager sat in a chair and waited impatiently. Finally, Conrad stood before his eldest son, his arms overflowing with clothing, beads of perspiration dripping from his forehead. "I looked up at him," Nicky recalled with a little smile, "and I said, 'Wow, Pop. You sure worked hard on this goddamn thing, didn't you?'" He laughed. "I love him so much," Nicky said. "All I want to do is please him. That's about all I want to do."

"Laying there in that moment, I suddenly felt that I really understood Nicky Hilton," Mamie Van Doren recalled. "He respected his father so much, yet he felt that his father didn't respect him in return. I suddenly got it that the reason Nicky drank so much was because he knew that his father had such low expectations of him. Nicky wanted a lot, but constantly fell short of the mark, and it got to the point where he started thinking maybe his father was right about him. After all, *Conrad Hilton* couldn't be wrong, could he? He was totally dominated by Conrad. Because of that, I knew he and I would be hopeless. If he valued his father's opinion so much, and his father didn't approve of me, I knew I wouldn't stand a chance with Nicky. After that night, I gave up on the idea of having a future with Nicky Hilton."

PART SEVEN

The Big Boon

The Hilton Junket

*W*ith the passing of the years, things seemed to get worse for Nicky Hilton, but not so for his father. Conrad Hilton continued to make an indelible mark on American history as a true pioneer of its hotel industry.

In 1954, Hilton bought the Statler hotel chain with its eleven hotels for $111 million, which at the time was the largest real estate deal made since the historic Louisiana Purchase 150 years earlier. The following year, he further streamlined his hotel operation by creating a central reservation office, which he called Hilcron. Though no one had ever heard of such a concept, Conrad had created a system whereby customer reservations could be made at any of his hotels anywhere in the world simply by calling a telephone number or sending a telegram to a central address. That same year, 1955, Conrad also innovated the concept of air-conditioning in every room, which was unheard of at the time. Also in 1955, Conrad opened the Hilton Istanbul, the first modern hotel built in post–World War II Europe. It would be responsible for a 60 percent increase in tourism in Turkey during its first year of operation. At about this same time, he also opened the Continental Hilton in Mexico City and the Beverly Hilton in Los Angeles.

The opening of the Beverly Hilton in August 1955 was, as usual, a star-studded affair that involved a solid week of carefully orchestrated, splashy activities. Money was never an object when it came to these events. "We have the finances to spend on impressing people, and there's nothing wrong with it," Conrad had told his staff. "The sky's the limit," he exclaimed. "Whenever we open a hotel, it's to be considered a cultural event."

The opening of the Beverly Hilton provides a textbook example of what these affairs were like during Conrad's heyday. On August 4, 1955, members of the media as well as Hilton employees from all over the world and personal friends were flown to Los Angeles and then taken to the new Hilton hotel at the busy intersection of Beverly, Santa Monica, and Wilshire Boulevards. Upon his arrival, each person was handed a specific itinerary of exciting upcoming events, which would commence on the fourth and end on August 12.

For instance, according to the schedule, among the events on the evening of the sixth was a "Dinner Preview and Tasting" at the hotel's L'Escoffier restaurant. The next night, after a full day of press conferences and speeches, a special cocktail reception was held at Conrad's home from seven to nine. It was attended by many celebrities, including, of course, Conrad's companion Ann Miller—sporting a striking emerald necklace given to her by Conrad—and other show business luminaries such as Debbie Reynolds, Charlton Heston, Dean Martin, Diahann Carroll, and Lena Horne. Also present were notables from many walks of business who had become regular invitees to such events, such as Henry Crown, who owned the Empire State Building, and Y. Frank Freeman, president of Paramount Pictures. To make sure the event generated an appropriate amount of media buzz, newspaper columnists such as Louella Parsons and Cobina Wright were also on hand.

On August 8, Hilton's invited guests were taken on a full tour of the new hotel before enjoying another full day of luncheons and dinners.

The next day, two more extravagant luncheons were scheduled, one hosted by Paramount Pictures Corporation and another by 20th Century-Fox Studios. That same day, August 9, everyone was taken to Disneyland at 4 p.m. Afterward, a "Black Tie Victory Dinner" was scheduled in the Bali Room of the Hilton.

On August 10, "the flag raising ceremony and official opening luncheon for gentlemen only" was scheduled. That afternoon, a "luncheon for ladies only" was held at Conrad's Casa Encantada, hosted by Olive Wakeman. Also helping to host the affair was Marilyn Hilton, making a stylish impression in a Persian lamb sweater, a gift from Barron. Zsa Zsa Gabor—now divorced from George Sanders, mostly as a result of her public and stormy affair with Dominican Republic playboy Porfirio Rubirosa—even stopped by to greet the ladies, looking smashing in a beaded cashmere sweater. After the luncheon, there was "The Hilton Champagne Ball" and then "The Hilton Barbecue Party," followed by "The Hilton Private Event" (white dinner jacket required) and then "Conrad's Special Evening Event" (black tie only).

"You were swept off your feet by these activities," recalled Margaret O'Brien. "It was exciting and fun but also a lot of work. Sometimes it felt like a job! But the extravagance was overwhelming. Money was being spent like there was no tomorrow. Everything was first-rate."

The merriment culminated on Sunday, August 14, when the Beverly Hilton was finally opened to the public, with a dapper Conrad Hilton standing at the end of a bright red carpet in a sharp-looking tuxedo, personally welcoming the first couple of hundred guests to his newest establishment.

"I'm not sure that anyone does this kind of thing today," said veteran actress Ruta Lee, who attended many such Hilton functions around the world. "There was always a celebration somewhere, and if you were on the list, you were always on the go, taking off on a chartered jet for some exotic location or another.

"The kind of organization it took to pull off just one of these events was staggering, and Conrad would do two, three, sometimes four a year," Ruta Lee added. "The buzz in Hollywood was always, 'Are you going on the next Hilton junket?' And if you weren't, you did everything you could think of to get on that darn list. Luckily, I was on the list. But to tell you the truth, pretty much every celebrity in town was on it! You would look around and think to yourself, my God, who isn't here?"

Though these Hilton junkets usually went off without a hitch, the occasional unexpected event would occur. For instance, the opening of the Hilton Hotel in Rome was interrupted in June of 1963 by the death of Pope John XXIII. That junket would have to be called off and rescheduled at a tremendous cost. A ballet company from the British Isles hired by Conrad to perform was canceled just in the nick of time before boarding its flight to Rome. As a result of the cancelation, a chef was stuck with twelve hundred desserts—peaches stuffed with ice cream, wrapped in batter, and baked lightly with crushed almonds. "We threw away a shitload of peaches that night," Nicky said with a laugh when recounting the story.

In 1956, an earthquake occurred in the midst of the Mexico City junket, which so frightened members of the press that many of them asked to be whisked out of the country as soon as possible. One reporter was so shaken up, she had to have psychiatric treatment. She sent Conrad the bill. And he paid it!

The Hilton junket in Hong Kong happened to fall in the middle of the so-called Three Years of Great Chinese Famine (1958–61), a time of widespread food shortages, drought, and terrible weather conditions. Many members of the media and other socialites who had been invited decided to pass on it. Those who did show up were met with a daily ration of two gallons of washing water, one quart of drinking water, and two pints of toothbrushing and/or shaving water. "It wasn't the best week of my life, put it that way," is how entertainer Debbie Reynolds recalled it.

The Berlin Hilton opened the same week in November 1958 that Soviet premier Nikita Khrushchev decreed that the United States had six months to vacate West Berlin. Despite the ensuing unrest, Conrad decided to go ahead with the junket.

As it happened, Khrushchev would turn out to be the least of Hilton's problems. A dancing bear had been hired to perform in the hotel's main ballroom to kick off the festivities. Unfortunately, in the middle of his performance the animal caught a whiff of fresh pheasant being cooked in the kitchen for dinner. Without warning, the bear broke away from his trainer and galloped out of the ballroom and down the hall, following the scent and frightening everyone in his wake. The food and beverage manager, hearing the sounds of people screaming, "Get out of the way!" bolted from the kitchen to see what was going on, and in doing so ran right smack into the arms of the bear, which had just rounded a corner. At that moment, the trainer managed to secure the animal, who seemed as stunned as the poor hotel employee. When the whole thing was over, the food and beverage manager couldn't contain his anxiety; he burst into tears and fainted dead away. He then had to be carried away by three members of the Hilton security team, past a crowd of stunned hotel guests, into the elevator and up to his room. "Never a dull moment at a Hilton junket," is how Hedda Hopper put it in her report of the chaotic mishap.

At the Nile Hilton opening in Cairo in March 1959, a blustery sandstorm interrupted the proceedings, blowing away the large Bedouin tent that had been erected in the middle of the desert for a press corps dinner. In the process, more pounds of roast lamb than Conrad cared to remember were dusted with hot sand fresh from the Sahara. "Don't remind me!" he once said with a laugh when asked about that particular junket.

Of that Cairo junket, singer/actress Anne Jeffreys recalled, "The propeller plane—there were no jets, of course—was overloaded with stars, and as stars will do, we had overpacked for the occasion. Therefore, Conrad was forced to hire another plane to follow us, which was filled only with our luggage.

"When we arrived, we were bowled over by the beauty of Cairo, until we realized that none of the electrical outlets worked for American equipment. I had just washed my hair to prepare for the opening night ball and had gone to dry it, when I found that the dryer didn't work! So I called my best friend, Ann Miller, in the suite next to mine and told her about it, and she said, 'Oh my God! The same thing just happened to me. What shall we do?' Because it was such a hot day in Cairo, we decided to use the weather to our advantage. Both of us went out onto our balconies, and there we were—a blonde and a brunette with about three yards of hair between us—swinging our wet locks over the Nile River, trying to get them to dry. Ann asked, 'We'll never forget this moment, will we?' And we never did!"

"I have so many memories of the Middle East junket," added actress Jane Russell. "For instance, I still can't believe that I had the chance to climb a pyramid, on my hands and knees! Me and Anne Jeffreys and Hugh O'Brien. We got about halfway up, which I think was equivalent to about forty stories. Your jaw would drop, it was that amazing, and all thanks to Conrad's largesse. I remember that we went straight from Egypt to Athens for the opening of the Hilton there. Who would spend this kind of money today? I actually can't imagine a businessman doing today what Conrad Hilton did back then."

As well as personal fun shared by celebrities, there were important socioeconomic strides made during Hilton junkets. For instance, in 1958, Conrad Hilton opened the Havana Hilton and made national headlines when, during his keynote speech at a luncheon with Cuban officials and businessmen—which, incidentally, he delivered in purest Castilian, having mastered the Spanish language—he dealt another blow to Communism. He noted that "ordinarily labor works for capital; the usual thing is for employees to work for employers. But in the building and operation of our new Havana Hilton we have reversed the picture; the employers are working for their employees."

Conrad was referring to the fact that Hilton Hotels did not own the Havana Hilton, but had leased it from the Cuban Catering Workers' Union. It was an unusual Cuban-American business relationship where the workers had a stake in the property and were encouraged to become owners of shares in the business, a real stake in the enterprise. They would be partners rather than just workers. Conrad described it as " a new weapon with which to fight Communism, a new team made up of owner, manager and labor with which to confront the class conscious Mr. Karl Marx." He noted that Marx never owned, managed, or worked an enterprise in his entire life, "but from his world of inexperience he has managed, for a whole century, to convince hundreds of millions of people to be at each other's throats." He said he was happy to say that "the project we are dedicating today gives the lie to Marx, Communism and all they stand for."

"Hilton openly attacked Communism for the first time in a foreign country when he spoke in Havana," wrote Vincent Flaherty, who had attended the luncheon, for the *Los Angeles Examiner*. "Hilton is out of Cuba now, but that beautiful 30-story hotel he dedicated remains as a mute but powerful reminder of all he had to say."

Barron Climbs the Ladder of Success

*E*ver since he was denied a job back in the 1940s by his father because his salary demand was too steep, Barron Hilton had been adamant about finding his own way, carving his own niche. However, his wife, Marilyn, had asked him to at least think about joining the family enterprise. "It's your legacy," she told him at one family dinner, according to a witness. "In the end, you know you and your brothers are going to have to take over the business when Dad [Conrad] dies, so I don't know why you are being so hardheaded about it," she said, always a practical woman. "You may not think there is a premium on money and power right now," she said, "but I can assure you that others do, and they will be coming after the Hilton Corporation when Conrad dies; that is, unless his sons are in charge," she said. "Hotels are this family's life's blood. You must know that by now."

In the end, Marilyn Hilton prevailed. When Conrad offered it to him, Barron took the corporate job of vice president in charge of television. "We became one of the first chains in the country to offer TV sets in every room," he would later recall. At this same time, Barron also took interest in an idea Conrad had of investing in what would eventually become a huge enterprise in this country—the credit card business.

Several credit card companies, including American Express and Diners Club, had begun to flourish in the late 1950s, though it wouldn't be until the 1960s and '70s before the general masses began to use them. In 1958, Conrad began to conceptualize the Carte Blanche credit card business. Barron was intrigued enough by the idea to accept his dad's appointment as president of the company. This would be an opportunity to be a part of the Hilton empire while putting his own stamp on an important new endeavor—he could be his own man, even while working in his father's domain. Of course, another key factor in his decision to join the ranks was that he wanted to make his father proud. "That was always a running theme with all the sons when it came to Conrad," said one Hilton relative. "Making Connie proud. It killed them to think that Connie might not be proud of them. I actually think they would have turned on each other if it meant making Dad proud, that's how important it was to them."

"Money has gone out of style," Barron said at the time. "Credit and convenience are the biggest consumer needs today."

However, it was tough going for Barron in his new position. Likely because Carte Blanche was so ahead of its time, it would lose $2 million in the next six years, this even though it was considered to be a more prestigious card than American Express or Diners Club. It had a small base, because, as some argued, the qualifications for the card were so stringent. Soon the board would sack Barron as the company's president, a big embarrassment to him. But then, as a board member, Barron was still in the position to make a successful sale of the company to Citibank for a profit of $16.5 million in 1965, and, as he would later put it, "all of a sudden I was a hero in the company again." (Though Hilton would buy it back in 1979, the card would eventually be phased out in the 1980s.)

Whether working with Carte Blanche or involved in other Hilton business pursuits, from 1958 onward, Barron Hilton would always have an important role in the family business. Eventually, in 1966, he would succeed his father as president of the domestic Hilton Hotels Corporation.

"He was serious, not a funny or lighthearted person," said one of Barron's former employees. "When he walked into a room, it was the same feeling as when his father walked into a room. He commanded respect because of the way he handled himself. He was friendly, don't misunderstand. But whereas you felt you could talk to Nicky, you didn't feel that Barron was approachable. He was intimidating. When he was with his wife, it was even more off-putting because, together, they were like royalty. He was tall and good-looking and she was gorgeous and sophisticated, and they carried themselves with a kind of mystery. You felt the Hilton money and power when you were around them. They just looked and acted rich."

Nicky's Fast-Paced Life

*F*or several years and until the present time, I have clung tenaciously to the hope that my son, Conrad Nicholson Hilton, Jr., would settle down and go to work with the serious purpose of making his own way through life, acquire a gainful occupation and become a useful citizen of this country," Conrad Hilton wrote in his will of 1955. The will then stipulated that Nicky be given a $500,000 trust fund in the event of Conrad's death—but with one proviso: "It is not my intention that the provisions made for him in my will be used in a wasteful or extravagant mode of living, but it is my purpose and my profound wish that my said son so conduct himself and order his life that he may, if he chooses, enjoy to the fullest extent the provisions I had made for him in my will. Therefore, I hereby commit to my trustees absolute discretion to and full power over the accumulation and application of all income and principal of the Trust Estate created in my will for Conrad Nicholson Hilton, Jr." In other words, if Nicky did not live up to his father's expectations, the trustees of his estate could choose to withhold his trust—or perhaps not even allow him to have it at all. Even in death, Conrad would have the final word over whether or not Nicky had lived up to his fullest potential.

In 1956, Nicky was named vice president in charge of the Inns Division of the Hilton Corporation, responsible for the management of three airport-adjacent Hilton-owned hotels, in San Francisco, New Orleans, and El Paso.

Always the visionary with an eye toward expanding his vast empire, Conrad had the foresight to realize that as more people began to travel by air, there would grow to be a huge need for quick, sometimes just overnight accommodations. He began to invest heavily in a chain of establishments near airports that many would have considered modestly priced motels rather than superior hotels. However, Conrad loathed the word "motel," because it suggested low-quality accommodations—thus his usage of the word "inn." Starting with the San Francisco Airport Hilton, the venture would be wildly successful. That these properties weren't of the same ilk as the glorious Hilton hotels found around the world didn't make them any less important to the Hilton Corporation's bottom line.

Because he was so honored that his father had finally seen the best in him and offered him the Inns position, Nicky took the job seriously. "I think it did him a world of good in terms of his self-esteem," said Wyatt Montgomery, who worked as an assistant to Nicky in the Los Angeles Inns Division office. "I found him to be efficient, Hilton-like in his demeanor, professional," recalled Montgomery. "But he did drink too much, there was little doubt about that. He tried to make sure it didn't interfere with his job, but I have to say that there were more than a few days there when he dragged himself in to work.

"When Conrad went to Monaco to personally represent President Eisenhower at the wedding of Grace Kelly to Prince Rainier, Nicky took advantage of the time his father was gone to lay back and not do much," added Montgomery. "He was single, he was young and handsome, his dad was golfing buddies with the president of the United States...I think he just felt entitled."

Actress Carole Wells Doheny became a close friend of Nicky's and recalled the first time she met him. "It was at La Rue's restaurant in Beverly Hills," she said, "and present were Bob Neal, the actor Peter Lawford, and hotelier Henry Crown, who had backed Conrad in his early ventures and was a key player in Conrad's success. Nicky was smart, handsome, and I just remember thinking, 'Wow, what a great catch.' He had a zest for life. I knew he had a reputation as a heartbreaker and when I met him I thought, 'Okay, I get it. I definitely get it.' I had also heard that his family—worried about the image of the Hilton hotels—was keeping a close eye on him."

Wyatt Montgomery recalled a day in January 1957 when Marilyn Hilton came to visit Nicky in his Los Angeles office without an appointment, explaining that she happened to be shopping for hats in the neighborhood and thought it might be fun to take Nicky to lunch. To some employees, it was starting to seem as if family members were checking in on Nicky. When Wyatt told Marilyn that perhaps she should have called first, she looked at him as if he had lost his mind. "Do you know who I am?" she demanded. "Of course I knew who she was—*everyone* knew who she was," Wyatt recalled many years later. Marilyn didn't look up as she tugged on her gloves. "I'll wait here while you fetch my brother-in-law," she said with practiced imperiousness. She then took a seat in the small waiting area as Montgomery went down the hall to Nicky's office.

Wyatt knocked on Nicky's door. There was no answer. However, since he knew Nicky was in there, he went to his desk and called his boss's extension. After several rings, Nicky finally picked up the line sounding out of breath and anxious. "Mrs. Barron Hilton is here to see you," Wyatt told him. Nicky was flabbergasted. "Oh no! What is *she* doing here?" he wanted to know.

A minute later, the door to Nicky's office burst open and out stumbled a disheveled woman in a fur coat furiously patting down a mussed hairdo with well-manicured hands. "I took a good look at her and, much to my astonishment, it was Natalie Wood," said Wyatt Montgomery. "I couldn't believe my eyes." Natalie had been a star since her childhood appearance in *Miracle on 34th Street* and had reached iconic status with her role in *Rebel Without a Cause* opposite James Dean. By 1957, the nineteen-year-old doe-eyed, dark-haired beauty was instantly recognizable. "I didn't even know he was dating her!" Montgomery continued. Without saying a word, Natalie rushed by Marilyn, who sat with her mouth wide open. Once she was gone, Marilyn looked at Wyatt Montgomery and asked, "Wasn't that Natalie Wood?" He shrugged and said, "Sure looked like her to me."

In fact, Nicky—ever the eligible bachelor at the age of thirty-two—was seeing both Natalie Wood and Joan Collins at this time.

Joan Collins had been imported to Hollywood from the United Kingdom in 1954, as 20th Century-Fox's answer to Elizabeth Taylor. She was immediately put to work in films like *The Girl in the Red Velvet Swing* and *The Opposite Sex*, and critics were always quick to point out her arresting good looks. Joan did bear a striking resemblance to Nicky's former wife, and for decades she would be described as "the poor man's Elizabeth Taylor"—much to her chagrin. In reality Joan was very much her own person—a striking, fiery, startlingly confident young woman. Years before the sexual revolution, she was known as much for her sexuality as for her beauty and biting wit.

With Joan, Nicky found a kindred spirit who also enjoyed fast '50s sports cars with fins, lots of flowing champagne, and intense nightclubbing, followed by heated sexual marathons. When Joan would call the office and demand to see him, Nicky would pretty much drop everything and run to be with her. "She's a hell of a lot of work," Nicky told Wyatt Montgomery, "but she's worth it."

In May 1957, Nicky asked Wyatt to send Joan Collins flowers for her twenty-fourth birthday. Wyatt chose an elaborate floral arrangement and signed Nicky's name to the card. Nicky then sat by the telephone all day, waiting for the payoff: a thank-you call from Joan, and perhaps an invitation to go to her home to help celebrate. Every half hour, he would bolt out of his office and pepper his assistant with questions such as, "Did she call?" and "What did you send?" and "Were they nice flowers?" and "Then why hasn't she called?" Joan never did call Nicky. Finally, at the end of the workday, Nicky had Wyatt place a call to her. "She came on the line and immediately started bitching him out for not having called her first thing on her birthday," Wyatt Montgomery recalled. "'But, Joan, I sent flowers,' he exclaimed. And just before I disconnected from the line I heard her say, 'Nicholas, do you know how many people send me flowers? It's not as if I have time to read all the cards. I'm a busy woman!' After he hung up, he came out of his office smiling and shaking his head. 'What a bitch,' he said, laughing. 'That woman takes the cake!' He loved it, though. He found her amusing.

"She came into the office one day, I'll never forget it. I was at my desk working and Joan Collins swooped right by me without saying a word, looked at me with a superior expression, walked into Nicky's office, and slammed the door behind her. An hour later, she emerged, head held high, shoulders back, big bosom popping out of her tight black corseted dress. Again, she walked right by me without saying a word. But as she sashayed down the hall, she must have sensed that I was staring at her caboose because, without turning around, she said in her clipped British accent, 'Enjoy the view. Pity it won't last forever.'"

It says a lot about Nicky's appeal that even his first wife, Elizabeth Taylor, who would later claim that he had been physically abusive to her during their marriage, still included him in her life. The two would some-times meet at the home of Dr. Lee Siegel and his wife, Noreen Nash, especially in the period after her marriage to Michael Wilding, before and during her marriage to Mike Todd and just before the one to Eddie Fisher, which would have been 1957 through 1959. "They would come to the house and sit at the bar, and just be so darling together," recalled Noreen Nash. "I felt a chemistry between them still. I think it would be safe to say there were no hard feelings there, even though the marriage obviously didn't work. There was a connection between them neither could deny. If you knew Nicky, you knew there was something so intriguing about him that just kept drawing you in."

It was his relationship with his mother, Mary, though, that meant the world to Nicky. "I love all my sons," Mary told Nicky at a party for one of her grandchildren. "But you and I, we're not like the others," she told him. "We have our little flaws, don't we? And I guess that separates us from the rest, doesn't it?"

According to a witness to the conversation, Nicky looked at his mother as if he didn't know quite how to respond to her astute observa-tion. They didn't have these kinds of open conversations often. It was as if the occasion of her grandson's birthday had made Mary feel nostalgic, and maybe even a little wistful. She'd had such a hard life; Nicky's heart went out to her. He opened his mouth as if he wanted to say something, but words failed him.

Eric: From Out of the Shadows

*I*t was August 14, 1958, the final day of a week of festivities celebrat-ing Conrad Hilton's latest acquisition, the Beverly Hilton Hotel in Los Angeles, which had just opened its doors for business. The lobby bustled with people, some checking in to the hotel and others just meandering about with their heads tilted back as they stared at the eye-popping sur-roundings. In the background could be heard the sound of a full orchestra rehearsing Johnny Mathis's popular song "Chances Are," the music drift-ing out of a nearby banquet room. A young couple dressed in formal attire seemed unable to resist the dreamy melody. They quite literally fell into each other's arms and began to dance in perfect unison. Enraptured by one another in the moment and oblivious to the stares of onlookers, they swayed together with a delicate but tangible sensuality. It was a spontaneous moment so surreal and so beautiful, onlookers forgot themselves and gawked openly at the sheer magic of it. If anything, this was just the kind of romantic scene Conrad Hilton always wanted to represent his hotels. The strains of pretty music, the flatter of good lighting, the elegance of expert décor, all of it intrinsic to projecting the feeling that staying at a Hilton hotel was a unique and enchanting experience, one with which no other hotel could possibly begin to compete.

As the scene unfolded, a dashing, robust young man in a crisp white tuxedo and black bow tie stood nearby and spoke in an animated fashion to a small group of people, all of whom seemed enthralled by everything going on around them. Waving his hand in one direction, then another, he said, "As you can see, my father has spared no expense to distinguish this Hilton from the others. We have thirty-three hotels in twenty-seven cities around the world," he continued proudly. "But you might say that *this* one is the crown jewel of all Hilton hotels. After all, this one is right here in Los Angeles, the show business capital of the world. You'll probably see a few celebrities walking around here and there," he said with a grin. He spoke with confidence and authority. "If so, feel free to ask for their autograph or even a picture. Just tell them my dad, Conrad Hilton, sent you." Everyone around him nodded and grinned with satisfaction. He was so charming and articulate, it's likely that none of them could have imagined a better spokesman for the Hilton brand. Then, with supreme timing, an announcement came bellowing over the hotel's intercom system. "Elizabeth Taylor calling for Eric Hilton," said the female voice. A mild shock wave was transmitted through the crowd. Then, a few seconds later, again: *"Elizabeth Taylor calling for Eric Hilton."*

The man in the tux smiled at the contingent with whom he was talking and said, "Oh, that's me. I have to take that call. Would you excuse me, please?" The bewildered crowd began chatting excitedly to each other. "Is that operator sure she has the right Hilton?" one asked as Eric Hilton rushed off to take the call. "That's odd, isn't it?" noted another. "No, not really," remarked a third person, this one a well-dressed brunette with a pearl necklace around her neck and matching earrings. "Just another day in the life of my husband," concluded Patricia Skipworth Hilton as she ran after her spouse.

While it may have seemed strange to most outsiders that Elizabeth Taylor would maintain any sort of relationship with Eric Hilton, it wasn't that unusual to those in the Hiltons' inner circle, especially given that Elizabeth had never stopped communicating with Eric's brother Nicky. "Eric was like Nicky. He was the kind of man who, once you met him, you wanted to continue knowing," said his first wife, Patricia—better known as Pat. She explained that after Nicky gave Eric the responsibility of "babysitting" Elizabeth seven years earlier when he first brought her to El Paso, Eric and Elizabeth became fast friends. They decided not to allow her high-profile divorce from Nicky to interfere with that friendship. In years to come, Elizabeth would become legendary for remaining loyal to the people she liked; once you became her friend, you remained her friend for life. "They would see each other whenever Eric was in Los Angeles," said Pat Hilton. "Elizabeth also called the house [in Texas] quite often. She thought Eric was a riot. They had the same sense of humor. Eric thought she was fun, a lot of laughs. I never met her, though, not once," Pat allowed. "She was a friend of Eric's that predated me, not really a friend of mine. I can't tell you how many people I met over the years who would tell me, 'Oh, your husband, Eric, is my closest friend,' and this would be someone I had never heard of in my life! But that was just Eric."

There had always been an air of mystery surrounding Eric Michael Hilton, the youngest son of Conrad and Mary Hilton. It was as if he were deliberately being kept in the shadows.

At about this same time, Conrad named Eric—who was twenty-five in 1958—resident manager of the Shamrock Hilton in Houston. Conrad had picked up the Shamrock four years earlier, a lavish hotel with televisions in every one of its eleven hundred rooms, air-conditioning, Muzak piped into the hallways, and a 165-foot glistening swimming pool. Managing the place was a mammoth undertaking for someone of Eric's age, but Conrad said that he felt the time had come to slowly ease his youngest son into the family business. (Actually, Nicky had also cut his teeth at the same hotel, as vice president of the Shamrock for a short period of time.) Since the death of Eric's stepfather, Mack—Mary Hilton Saxon's second husband—back in May 1949, Conrad seemed to have more of an interest in forging a closer relationship with Eric and his family. In a short time—1960—Eric would receive an even bigger assignment as general manager of the Hilton Hotel in Aurora, Illinois.

Wyatt Montgomery recalls Eric Hilton as being "a hell of a nice guy, good-looking, with a winning personality and a big smile for everyone. As adults, he and Nicky had grown very close. The two would take off in Nicky's flashy red convertible with the white leather interior, go to the Santa Monica beach, maybe have dinner in Beverly Hills. I always felt the closeness they shared was because both viewed the other as underdogs in the family. Barron wasn't an underdog, that's for sure. Barron was always top dog.

"But in the end, the three of us, we're not so different," Nicky told Eric one day at the office, according to Wyatt Montgomery.

"I don't know. I think we're different," Eric observed.

"Not really," Nicky continued. "After all, the three of us are just trying to do the same thing, aren't we? We're all just trying make our father proud."

Eric had to agree.

Like Nicky, Eric was certainly never at a loss for female companionship either. One of Eric's many girlfriends was the popular actress Margaret O'Brien, who won a Juvenile Academy Award as the outstanding child actor of 1944 for her unforgettable performance as Tootie in 1944's *Meet Me in St. Louis*. She recalled, "I was seventeen and Eric twenty-one when he and I dated.

"I met him while doing an appearance at the Mayflower Hotel in Washington, which of course his father owned. He was my first offscreen kiss, with Jeffrey Hunter being my first onscreen. Then I went on with my film career and we drifted apart. But I have the sweetest memories of Eric Hilton."

Perhaps another reason any possible romance cooled between Eric and Margaret O'Brien was because he had become so smitten with the lovely Patricia Skipworth, daughter of El Paso insurance man E. T. Skipworth.

Pat Skipworth was about five foot six, slender with a willowy figure, her chestnut brown hair worn full and loose around her pretty face. She had a finely drawn, aristocratic nose, deep brown eyes, and a wide mouth that, when turned up in a smile, filled her face with a certain radiance. She looked smart in anything she put on, so much so that some thought she could have been a high-fashion model. She knew just how to wear clothes and had a great sense of personal style, one that evolved even more after she met Eric.

Eric and Pat first met while attending El Paso High School in Texas. "I'll never forget it," she recalled with a laugh. "I was sitting in the passenger's seat of a green 1945 Buick with my girlfriend in the driver's seat when Eric and two other boys piled into the backseat. Eric said, 'Hey there! How are you girls doing?' But I was much too shy to turn around. So all he saw was the back of my head. After we dropped them off wherever they were going, my girlfriend said to me, 'Oh my God, that boy Eric Hilton is so *adorable*! How could you not turn around and say hello to him? Did you see how blue his eyes are? He's a real dreamboat!'"

A week later, Patricia finally got a formal introduction to Eric at school. However, she didn't make much of an impression on him. The next day she saw him again, and he didn't remember ever having met her. Every time the two would run into each other and be introduced, Eric would act as if it were the first time. "He would extend his hand and say, 'Hello, I'm Eric Hilton,'" Pat recalled with a chuckle, "and I would think, 'Dear Lord! I am not registering with this boy at all, am I?' It drove me crazy throughout my sophomore and junior years."

When Pat moved to what she refers to as "the other side of the mountain" and began attending Austin High School, she stopped seeing Eric around town. But then, after graduation in 1951, the two ran into each other again at the El Paso Country Club, where Eric volunteered to call out bingo games. "I was with my mother when someone reintroduced me to Eric and—again—he acted as if it was the first time. I turned to my mom and said, 'You see? *This* is the boy I told you about. The one who never remembers me!'"

Despite his apparent lack of interest, Pat saw something in Eric that intrigued her, a kindness and warmth in his eyes that inexplicably made her feel tender toward him. With her curiosity and attraction peaking, she began to arrange "impromptu" meetings with him, making sure she would be in places she knew he frequented in hopes of possibly striking up the conversation with him that would finally break through his inscrutable indifference and make him remember her. That it wasn't working was maddening. "My mother would always know when I'd been in the same room with Eric," Pat recalled, "because I would come home and slam the front door real hard in complete frustration, shaking the whole house. My mother would say, 'Oh my God! Pat must have met Eric Hilton. Again!'"

Finally, Pat and Eric both found themselves attending Texas Western College, the college in which Eric would enroll for two years and which is today known as the University of Texas at El Paso. "One day, a friend of Eric's sat down at a table in the Student Union Building where I was eating lunch," Pat recalled, "and he said, 'My friend Eric Hilton can't seem to get a date. Do you know anyone?' And I thought, 'Um...*hello?*' I didn't believe for a second that he couldn't get a date! Perhaps he really *had* noticed me! Sure enough, the next day he called and asked me out. And that was it; we began to date."

Interestingly, after his initial indifference, Eric fell hard for Pat. Within just two weeks, he wanted to marry her. While there was no doubt that she was infatuated with him, Pat couldn't help but feel uncertain about his suddenly ardent feelings. "I didn't know what to say," she recalled. "It was all so sudden. I hadn't even thought about getting married. But I later learned that Eric was a determined man, which I guessed was a Hilton trait. He wouldn't take no for an answer. So we continued dating and he continued trying to talk me into it and, well, I guess you could say I was drawn in by him.

"As well as his good looks, it was his personality," Pat recalled of her initial attraction to Eric Hilton. "He was just so funny. To this day, he has a wonderful sense of humor. So I think that's what did it for me. It wasn't his father's wealth, or anything like that. God's honest truth, I never gave that a second thought." Finally, as she recalled, it was her mother who made the decision. "You are marrying Eric Hilton, and that's the end of it," she told her daughter. "You know you love him. You've been in love with him since way back when, when you were slamming doors for him!"

The wedding took place on August 14, 1954, at St. Patrick's Cathedral in New York City. Along with Pat's parents, Conrad Hilton was also present, as well as Mary Saxon, and Barron with Marilyn, and Nicky. "It was a lovely ceremony," Pat recalled. "Conrad and Mary seemed proud of Eric, and everyone got along well. I was excited to join a family that had done so much good for the country. Eric and I began our lives together, and he continued with his career. We used to joke that he started at the top of the hotel business—that is, on the roof of the El Paso Hilton, sweeping up after the pigeons! Then he started working as an engineer in the basement. He had just been accepted into the Cornell Hotel School when he was drafted. The next thing I knew he was off to Japan...and I was off with him."

Conrad made a rare exception to his steadfast rule about lending money to family members, fronting Eric the money that paid for Pat to go to Japan and live with him while he was in training to be a radar specialist. "Conrad was considerate enough to make sure we weren't separated so early in our marriage," Pat recalled. "He loaned Eric the money to rent us a nice apartment there, and a year later I found out I was pregnant. Our firstborn, Eric Jr., was born in Tokyo. [The couple would have three more children: Beverly, Linda, and Brad.] After Eric was discharged, we moved back to Dallas and continued our lives together.

"It was hard in the beginning," Pat recalled of her nearly thirty-year marriage to Eric Hilton; they would divorce in 1983. "We rented and moved around a lot. We were poor. Conrad believed that people should work for a living. If he was giving out handouts—and I'm not saying he was, but if he was, it wasn't to Eric," she said, laughing. "We paid him back the loan he gave us for my move to Japan.

"Eric had to work *hard* for his money, all sorts of jobs at Conrad's hotels, from doorman to cook to elevator operator. It didn't matter, he wanted to do it—desk clerk, steward—he did everything he could, as long as it was at a Hilton hotel. We had a tiny little house and Conrad could come down from Los Angeles and visit from time to time. I can't say that he and Eric had a close relationship. Not that it was strained; it was more like they didn't really know each other well. It felt formal, though cordial. [Conrad] was always nice to me. I figured that his relationship with Eric was set in stone before I came into the picture, and so I stayed out of it.

"As for the brothers, I thought of Eric as the gentler of the three," she continued. "When I first met Nicky and Barron, I was a little struck by how different they were from Eric. Whereas they were aggressive, commanding personalities, Eric was much more laid-back and mellow. He said it was because his brothers had his father as a role model while growing up. 'I had my mom and my stepdad,' he told me. 'We lived a normal life in the suburbs. My brothers had all the trappings of wealth, I didn't.' He had no bitterness about any of it. 'I wouldn't trade my life for my brothers,' he always said. But Eric was pretty much always the eternal optimist. 'I get that from my father,' he would tell me."

A Troubling Conversation About Francesca

*I*t was March 10, 1958, Francesca Hilton's eleventh birthday. She was a happy little girl with wavy shoulder-length brown hair. She loved her mother, and as little girls often do, thought of her as the center of her whole world. Zsa Zsa did her best, but being maternal did not come easy for her. It wasn't as if she made herself available, even for a morning ritual such as coming down from her room for breakfast with her child. "Come *down* for breakfast!?" Francesca once exclaimed. "She had breakfast *in* bed. And I was usually in school by then, anyway." Parenting was a constant struggle for Zsa Zsa. Self-involved, she had trouble making time for her daughter. She was conscious of it, too. It wasn't as if she was oblivious to her shortcomings as a mother. However, she felt that her burgeoning career was so demanding, there was no way to find a happy balance between it and her responsibilities as a mother. Many of her films were made in Europe, so she and Francesca spent a great deal of time there, and she reasoned that Francesca was getting a well-rounded worldview as a result. Plus, at this time she was involved in a messy on-again, off-again relationship with the notorious playboy Porfirio Rubirosa, which totally consumed her. She would *try*—and in her mind, that was the best she could do.

When it was time to celebrate her daughter's birthday, suffice it to say, no one threw a party quite like Zsa Zsa. Every year, Zsa Zsa would come up with a different theme for Francesca. She took great pleasure in hosting anything but the ordinary party for her daughter—admittedly as much to celebrate herself as a mother as to celebrate Francesca's birthday—so one year it would be a western theme, another year a Spanish theme, a circus theme, a masquerade theme, and so forth. Because these theme parties usually ended with at least fifty screaming, crying children tearing her Bel-Air house apart—as often happens when that many kids are together for hours at a time—it was Zsa Zsa's idea that for Francesca's eleventh, the party's theme would be "formal." "All children want to be grown-ups," she said. "This time, for one night, they can be grown up." Therefore, all of the girls would be asked to wear ball gowns and long white gloves— which they would not be allowed to take off for the entire night—and the boys would wear tuxedos; their little bow ties were to remain intact as well. Zsa Zsa reasoned that if the children were dressed like adults, maybe they would actually *act* like adults and the party wouldn't end up a big, chaotic mess.

With the passing of about a week's time, though, Zsa Zsa couldn't help herself; her imagination began to run wild with ideas for the party:

"What if we had a twelve-piece orchestra so that the children could dance?"

Done.

"And what if Eddie Fisher performed?"

Done.

"And what if Pat Boone sang 'Happy Birthday' to Francie, because he's her most favorite star of all?"

Done.

Celebrities loved Zsa Zsa Gabor. She was fun, well connected, and could get pretty much anyone to do anything for her. The media loved her too. Once word got out about the kind of sensational party she was to host for Francesca's birthday, *Life* magazine decided it was an important enough cultural event to warrant a photographer and a reporter for a three-page spread, which would appear in its March 31 issue.

Unsurprisingly, the party was a smashing, over-the-top, bombastic success. "Why, this is just so... *unusual*," Marilyn Hilton told Zsa Zsa, as butlers served ginger ale and grenadine cocktails from silver trays. "What a novel idea! How ever did you come up with it?"

Zsa Zsa smiled. "Well, if you're going to throw a party, you have to make it worthwhile," she said. "Otherwise, you can't expect *Life* magazine to show up, now can you?" How could anyone disagree?

Life's story later noted that the "18 guests, dressed like well-bred miniatures of their movie-colony elders, showed up on a rainy evening at Miss Gabor's Bel-Air home. When the evening threatened to segregate into sexes, Francesca, a chip off the old block, murmured to the girls, 'Let's go in and meet the boys.'"

Later, Zsa Zsa was photographed while doting on Francesca—who was wearing a white-and-pink short-sleeved bouffant ball gown—and helping her open dozens of elaborately wrapped presents presented by the offspring of celebrities like Van Johnson, Dick Powell, and Deborah Kerr, all of whom came with their famous parents. As songs like "Picnic" and

"Sugartime" by the McGuire Sisters played on the sound system, Zsa Zsa was interviewed not only by the reporter from *Life* but also one from the Associated Press. "My sweet daughter, she is the apple of my light," Zsa Zsa said, of Francesca, commingling the metaphors "apple of my eye" and "light of my life." She continued to rave, "As you can see, we are one big, happy family. Connie is right over there," she said. She then pointed to a tall man in a cowboy hat looking around with a bewildered expression, as if he had never seen any children's party quite like this one. "My divorce from Connie has not affected his relationship with our daughter at all, not one bit," she said. "And there's Nicky, Barron and Marilyn, too," she told the reporter.

After dinner was served—fried chicken and mashed potatoes—all of the children and adults assembled on the wooden floor Zsa Zsa had laid down on top of the brick-paved library for a stage. It was where the orchestra had already assembled. Zsa Zsa walked onto the stage wearing a strapless bouffant floral-printed evening gown, cut about as low as possible. She then told a few jokes that seemed a little inappropriate considering the party's age group, but the famous parents certainly enjoyed them. "I'm a *great* housekeeper, as you can see," she said, motioning around to her surroundings. "I get divorced. I keep the house!" And this one: "I believe in large families. Every woman should have *at least* three husbands!" Asked about the diamond brooch she was wearing, she said it was a gift. "I don't take gifts from perfect strangers," she allowed, "but, then...nobody's perfect." She knew how to get a laugh.

Finally, turning serious, Zsa Zsa announced, "It is my great pleasure to introduce a good friend of mine. I'm sure you watch his television program every week, don't you? Ladies and gentlemen, Mr. Eddie Fisher!" Eddie then came out to great applause to perform a few of his big hits, such as "Heart" and "I Need You Now." Afterward, the cake, as big and as ornate as any royal wedding cake, was brought out as the guests all sang "Happy Birthday" to Francesca. Then, right on cue, the telephone rang. Surprise! It was Pat Boone, calling from New York. As it happened, he wasn't able to rearrange his schedule in order to appear in person, so it was decided that he would sing "Happy Birthday" to Francesca long-distance. "Why, this is the best birthday *ever!*" Francesca enthused after hanging up with her "most favorite star of all."

At around ten o'clock, the guests began to filter out. Francesca and

Conrad then stepped outside to enjoy some private time together. They began to play in the expansive yard as Zsa Zsa stood in the kitchen watching through an open window with attorney Gregson Bautzer, a very good friend of hers who was at the party along with his wife, actress Dana Wynter. (Bautzer had been Eva Gabor's date the night she and Zsa Zsa met Conrad for the first time, many years earlier. He had also attended Zsa Zsa's wedding to Conrad.) With one hand, Conrad tossed a red ball in Francesca's direction, while with the other he nursed a Dewar's neat. Though the little girl would sometimes catch it, she usually missed the ball. She would good-naturedly run to retrieve it and then pop it into the air to return it to her dad. It was relaxed and very natural.

"Will you just look at those two," Zsa Zsa said to Gregson with a satisfied smile. "They get along so well, don't they?" she added, lighting a cigarette. "Family is *so* important, don't you agree, Greg?" Then, speaking loudly to her daughter through the open window, she cautioned, "Now, Francie, don't you dare get those gloves dirty! They're pure silk! I just bought them at Magnin's!"

"Yes, they're really great together," agreed Gregson as he watched father and daughter at play.

"I know this birthday party is a little much," Zsa Zsa admitted. "But all I want is for Francie is to have a beautiful life. I think every young girl deserves that much," she added with a reflective smile, "and a father is *so* important to a child. Don't you agree, Greg?"

"I do," he answered. "And my God, that Connie is such a fool sometimes," he added, shaking his head.

"Why do you say that?" Zsa Zsa asked.

"Well, you know, sometimes he says that Francesca is his daughter, and sometimes he says she is not," Gregson answered. The remark was casual and off the cuff, as if he was just thinking aloud.

Zsa Zsa faced Gregson directly. "What do you mean by that?" she asked, suddenly stiffening. "When has Connie ever said that Francesca is not his daughter?"

"Oh...I mean..." Suddenly, Gregson was at a loss for words; he began to sputter. Ordinarily a very smart, discreet lawyer, he had spoken out of turn. Now he was definitely on the spot, and likely annoyed with himself about it, too. "What I mean is that...sometimes he feels like a father and...sometimes...he doesn't. That's all."

"But that's not what you *said*," Zsa Zsa countered, her expression now stern. "What you *said* is that he sometimes thinks Francesca is not his daughter. *That's* what you said."

"Well, has he ever said anything like that to you?" Gregson asked Zsa Zsa.

"No," Zsa Zsa answered quickly. "Not once has he ever said anything like that to me. And just look at them," she continued. "He is so nice to her and she loves him so much." She added that Conrad was always present for all of the girl's parties, and as far as Zsa Zsa could tell, he truly cared for Francesca. "Why, we're *family*," she concluded, according to her distinct memory of the events.

"Look, let's just have a fun day and not worry about it," Gregson said, trying his best to end the conversation. "I was talking through my hat, anyway. Let's forget it." He then leaned in to her and added, "Take a look around, Zsa Zsa. This is the high life, baby. You got it made, sweetheart. Enjoy it! Who the hell cares what Conrad Hilton thinks about anything?" And with that, Gregson Bautzer left the room as quickly as his legs could take him.

Now alone, Zsa Zsa Gabor turned her full attention to Conrad and Francesca, still playing in the backyard and acting for all intents and purposes like father and daughter. Only she would know exactly what was going on in her head in that moment, but to hear her tell it many years later, as she sat smoking her cigarette and staring at her ex-husband and her daughter, Zsa Zsa was more than a little concerned.

Natalie Wood's Advice

*A*re you sure about this? Because this is a big decision. You need to think about it carefully."

It was late in the evening of November 4, 1958. Natalie Wood—the famous actress who once dated and was still friendly with Nicky Hilton— was trying to reason with a dark-haired eighteen-year-old girl named Trish, offering her advice about her love life. As it had happened, Natalie's fling with Nicky had overlapped with her love affair with Robert Wagner, a handsome actor known for his pretty-boy looks and exaggeratedly groomed pompadour. Natalie and Robert had married the year before, shortly after her affair with Nicky ended. Now Natalie felt she could offer some insight into what Trish could expect in a relationship with the Hilton heir.

The two were sitting on a not very comfortable Victorian-era black-and-gold settee in an ornately appointed suite at Manhattan's Waldorf-Astoria in which Natalie was staying with her new husband. Nicky and Trish McClintock had also checked into the hotel for a weekend of fun and socializing in New York City. They'd been dating for a couple of months, and despite the age difference—Nicky was thirty-two—Trish had fallen head over heels in love with him. Just days earlier she had agreed to marry him. It had all happened so fast, no one in either of their lives seemed able to understand the relationship. Trish's father was particularly upset about it. After all, at thirty-eight, Frank Grant McClintock was only six years older than Nicky. It didn't matter to Trish, though. She knew what she wanted—what she felt she needed—and it was Nicky Hilton.

The two young ladies were settling into their chat after what had been an eventful night. Earlier, Nicky, Barron, R.J.—as Robert Wagner was known—and the actor Nick Adams (who would later star in a TV series called *The Rebel*) joined them for dinner at an upscale restaurant. Although they all had a few drinks and were no doubt feeling a bit high, no one seemed to be inebriated by any means. By the time they returned to the Waldorf, however, Nicky and Barron had a serious case of the giggles, as if the alcohol had finally kicked in and was making them giddy. Eventually Nicky and Barron began to engage in some juvenile horseplay. Suddenly, Barron slipped on a newspaper and fell backward. It was such a freak accident, it took everyone by surprise. One moment, Barron and Nicky were laughing and mock fighting, and the next, after a loud thud, Barron was flat on his back. It looked serious; everyone was concerned. Nicky immediately sobered up and sprang into action. He helped Barron into the elevator, secured a cab, and got his brother to a nearby hospital as quickly as possible, leaving his fiancée, Trish, behind in the suite with Natalie, R.J., and Nick Adams.

When Nicky and Barron returned to the suite, the group learned that their concerns had some merit. Barron had broken his leg. Relieved that it wasn't anything more serious, Nick Adams wearily said good night. Then Barron went to his room, and Nicky and R.J. went off to enjoy the view from one of the terraces, leaving Natalie and Trish to their cups of coffee and girl talk.

The evening's events had brought Natalie's concerns about Trish's romance with Nicky into sharp focus. At just twenty, Natalie Wood wasn't much older than Trish, but because she'd been involved in the cut-throat world of show business since the age of five, she was much more experienced. And because of her previous relationship with Nicky, she was aware of the dark side behind his charismatic, playful demeanor. "So, how are things going between you and Nicky?" Natalie wanted to know.

"It's wonderful," Trish said, according to her memory of the conversation. "He's just great."

"You know, he really is," Natalie agreed, looking a bit troubled. "He's a wonderful man. But he does have a problem, you know? Are you sure you're ready to handle this kind of thing?"

"What do you mean?"

"You haven't seen him drink?" Natalie asked.

Actually, as it happened, this night marked the first time Trish had ever seen Nicky have an alcoholic beverage. She wasn't that concerned about it.

"Sweetheart, it's a problem," Natalie added. She then said that she and Nicky had once dated, so she knew him quite well and felt that his drinking was not a small matter. She said it was "a lot for any woman to handle." Being candid, she had to admit that she didn't know if Trish was ready to cope with such trouble.

Trish didn't know what to think. Her silence was a disheartened one. Natalie was an actress, she reasoned, and perhaps she was just displaying her flair for the dramatic. "Okay, well, if he has a problem, I will deal with it," Trish said finally.

"What's the attraction?" Natalie asked.

"I have never met anyone who has such strong faith that people will ultimately do the right thing," Trish answered. She added that she first fell in love with Nicky's idealism, and then with him as a man. "I love him," she said, "and that's all that matters."

Natalie smiled. "Oh my," she said, shaking her head at Trish's naïveté. "Love isn't enough." She reached out and took both of Trish's hands in her own and told her that she used to believe the same thing, "that when you love a boy, that's enough," she said, a bit wistfully. But she added that she'd since learned the hard way that this was not always the case. "Love is *not* enough," she concluded. "You need much more."

Trish held her ground. "Well, I'm not leaving him," she said. "I see all he can be, and I want to help him get there," she added.

Natalie shrugged as if to suggest that she had tried her best and was now ready to let it go. She then suggested that Trish at least take her time and not rush into marriage. Trish said she would do just that. "Fine," Natalie concluded as she set her eyes on the fancy cake platter set before them. "Now, let's have some of that nice coffee cake, shall we?"

In her heart of hearts, Natalie Wood must have known that her advice to Trish would go unheeded. Just as she had to learn her own hard lessons, so would Patricia "Trish" McClintock. For Trish, sitting in a glamorous suite at the Waldorf-Astoria while listening to advice about her love life from one of the world's most famous actresses—a woman who three years earlier had been nominated for an Oscar for her work in *Rebel Without a Cause*—was just the first of many years' worth of head-spinning moments she would experience as the fiancée, and later wife, of Nicky Hilton. Trish would spend the next eleven years doing everything she could think of to prove Natalie wrong . . . to prove that love really *was* enough.

Trish

*P*atricia "Trish" McClintock was seventeen when she met Nicky Hilton one Saturday in the summer of 1958 at the Del Mar racetrack in Del Mar, California. From a well-to-do family whose wealth had been made in the banking and oil businesses, Trish was accustomed to trafficking in the circles of high society. Her parents were both college-educated; her mother had dated Joseph Kennedy, the oldest Kennedy brother, who was killed in the war, and her grandmother was assistant treasurer of the United States. Born elite, Trish was raised with maids and servants at her

feet in an enormous Oklahoma mansion. Her education was an expensive and private one at the Ethel Walker School in Connecticut, from
which she received glowing grades. Her vacations were spent traveling
through Europe with her recently divorced mother, who was now remarried to Broadway actor and producer (of *South Pacific*) William Horace
Schmidlapp, who had been married to film star Carole Landis for three
years until her suicide (a Seconal overdose) in 1948. Sometimes, Trish
would find herself in California, where she and her grandparents would
loll away the hours on Wednesdays and Saturdays at the racetrack in
box number 203 (which happened to be directly below one shared by
FBI director J. Edgar Hoover and his protégé, Bureau Associate Director
Clyde Tolson).

Trish was the kind of woman men looked at twice. About five foot
four, with bright brown eyes and shoulder-length brunette hair, she was
shapely and carried herself with great élan. She was stylish, not just with
her clothing but in the way she comported herself. She had what the
French call "je ne sais quoi," that ineffable quality that made people take
note of her. This isn't to say that she was a Hollywood-style glamour girl,
though. She wasn't. Rather, she had a homespun quality about her. She
was approachable, not aloof, a girl-next-door type.

One Saturday, Trish's grandfather—who was a member of the Federal Reserve Board and, as president of First National Bank in El Paso,
was also Conrad Hilton's banker—spotted another board member at
the races in the company of Nicky Hilton. Introductions were made all
around, which was how Trish McClintock ended up meeting the tall
and darkly handsome—and older—Nicky Hilton. "Here's some money,"
Nicky told the young ingénue as he handed her a crisp one-hundred-
dollar bill. "Now, go bet on whatever horse you like." Was he trying to
impress her? If so, it hadn't worked. "I'm not taking your money," she
said, more intrigued than insulted. "You can give me two dollars to bet
if you like, but not a hundred." Then, catching herself, she quickly said,
"Wait! I don't need your money! I have my own!" He laughed and said
he liked her spunk, her lack of pretense. She had to admit to herself that
she found him interesting. "But he was too old for me," she would recall
many years later. "He was thirty-one when I met him. I thought that was
old. At seventeen, I had never dated anyone over the age of twenty. I'd

certainly never gone out with anyone in his *thirties*." The two spent the afternoon gambling together, however, and getting to know each other. The following Wednesday they saw each other again, and then again on the next Saturday. "But there was no interest from me at all," she recalled. "Not in the least. We would talk and he would flirt and I was not interested.

"At the end of the day on Saturday, he said, 'I have a party I'm going to on Saturday night and I'd love for you to be my date'," Trish recalled. "'It's Natalie Wood's party,' he said. So that piqued my interest. And then he told me it was a Gay Nineties theme. I told him I would have nothing to wear to such a party, and he said, 'Don't worry about it. You and Natalie are the same size. I'll tell Natalie to get one of her costumes from Warner Bros. for you.' I thought all of this was exciting and said yes, I would go."

Trish's excitement would be short-lived, however. When Trish told her father. Frank Grant McClintock, of Nick's invitation, he objected. "He said, 'Forget it. You are not going out with a man who is old enough to be your father.' And that was that. I was seventeen. What was I going to do? My father had such a fit, I had to call Nicky and tell him the date was off. He was disappointed. But not so disappointed that he didn't continue to pursue me."

For the next few months, Trish and Nicky would continue seeing each other at the racetrack, but never dated. He would turn thirty-two in July; she would turn eighteen in August. Finally, on September 14, 1958, Trish returned to New York, where she was scheduled to begin her freshman year at Briarcliffe College. She would stay with her mother and stepfather while in the city. The next day, Nicky telephoned her. He missed her, he said, and wanted to continue their relationship, even if by long distance. Before long, he was courting her in New York.

"One thing led to another," she recalled, "and before I knew it, I had gone from being not that interested to being completely in love. It was sudden and surprising. When I realized how I felt, it was like being on board a fast-moving train, everything moving quickly. I was young and excited and it felt romantic and new. Finally, just before Halloween 1958, Nicky asked me to marry him."

"The Woman to Give My Children Life"

Nicky Hilton had never before met anyone like Trish McClintock. First of all, she didn't drink. She most certainly didn't do drugs, and she didn't swear. She was also a virgin. "She's practically a nun," was how Eric Hilton put it at the time.

After the succession of glamorous, sophisticated women in his life, Nicky's friends and family were baffled by his choice of Trish McClintock as a partner. He was used to being in the company of much more experienced women. Though Trish was quite pretty, she wasn't what one might think of as a bombshell. She didn't emanate the confidence or sexuality of his previous romantic conquests, a wide range of self-possessed beauties from Elizabeth Taylor to Mamie Van Doren to Betsy von Furstenberg to Natalie Wood and Joan Collins. Trish was unaffected, a genuine innocent. "She's a breath of fresh air," Nicky told Bob Neal about Trish McClintock. The two were throwing back Pabst beers in a bar in West Hollywood in October 1958, just before Nicky would ask for Trish's hand in marriage.

"She's not your type, though," Bob observed. "She doesn't have that *edge* your girls usually have."

Nicky smiled. "Yeah, well, if you look at my track record with girls, it's not so great, is it? I think it's time for a change."

"But is there passion between you two?" Bob asked, pushing a little more. "I just don't see it, Nick."

Nicky took a drag from his cigarette as he considered his friend's statement. "Passion is overrated," he countered. "I had passion with Elizabeth and look what that got me. Now I want something more. She's the one," he concluded. "I think she's the woman to give my children life." Because it was such a poetic way to put it—"give my children life"—Bob Neal would always recall the moment with vivid clarity. "He really meant it," Bob would say many years later. "I think it came from a deep place in him."

It was as if, at the age of thirty-two, Conrad "Nicky" Hilton was finally growing up and looking for something more significant in a partner than just the temporary thrill of sexual fireworks. He had recently begun talking about having children and said he was searching for a woman who would not only be a romantic partner for him, but a suitable mother for his children. "Can you see Elizabeth Taylor as a mother?" he asked Bob Neal. "No way. [Actually, Elizabeth had three children by this time, and from all reports, she was a pretty good mother.] But can you see *Trish* as a mother? Absolutely. When am I ever going to find another girl like her?" he asked.

Also distinguishing Trish McClintock was that she didn't know much about Nicky's past and therefore held no judgment about him. "At first, I didn't really know anything about him at all," she now allows. "I never knew, for instance, a thing about his marriage to Elizabeth Taylor. I didn't even know that he had been married to her until I read about it in stories that ran in the press after Nicky and I announced our engagement. That was—honest to God—the first time I had ever heard a thing about his involvement with Elizabeth.* And even after that, Nicky and I never discussed her. He never discussed any of his ex-girlfriends with me. And I was just as happy that he didn't. I didn't want to know the details, and he never told me any of them.

"But after our engagement, I started hearing rumors about this one and that one, and to tell you the truth, I didn't know whether to believe the stories or not. I would have been horrified, at the time, to learn that these rumors were true."

If Nicky Hilton ever had the benefit of starting over with a clean slate, it was with this woman. It wasn't that Trish had decided to trust him; she was so inexperienced it never occurred to her *not* to trust him. Considering how high-profile his past exploits had been, Nicky probably was correct in thinking that he would likely never find anyone else so blind to his past.

"She didn't judge him," said Bob Neal. "She made him feel like a winner at a time when he was tired of feeling like a loser. I understood it. It was like everything that had happened in the past was finally in the past, and he now had a chance to write a new future. Also, he finally had alignment in terms of how his family felt about his romantic life, because

---

* Trish's comments make sense, considering that she was just ten when Nicky and Elizabeth married.

all of the Hiltons fully supported Trish. They felt that she was just what the doctor ordered, that she could keep Nick on the straight and narrow because that was the way she lived her own life. Conrad decided to accept the fact that Trish was Episcopalian and not Catholic. I think at this point he felt she had so many redeeming qualities, he could live with her faith."

Trish's character was a pleasant counterpoint to her sisters-in-law, Marilyn and Pat. Whereas Marilyn was regal and Pat stylish, Trish was more the babe-in-the-woods type. What the three wives had in common, though, was their intelligence and determination. They were not weak-willed women; they had strongly held opinions. Of course, their husbands didn't always pay attention to their viewpoints. In this era before the women's liberation movement, many wives found that their husbands weren't eager to hear their views about business, and the Hilton sons were no exception in that regard. Whether or not the fellows heeded their wives' advice, though, they were going to hear it anyway. None of the Hilton wives were silent or demure.

"We all attended the party in New York [at the Colony restaurant] where the engagement was announced to the press," added Robert Wentworth. "I just remember Nicky's mother, Mary, being happy and generous toward Trish."

"Does she make you happy?" Mary Saxon asked her son Nicky at the Colony party. Mary, who was now fifty-two, was sitting at a table with Pat and Marilyn when Nicky came over, took a chair next to her, and kissed her on the cheek.

"She makes me happy, Mom," he said.

Mary smiled at him. "Does this mean you'll finally be giving me more grandchildren?" she asked him. "Because, as you can see, I'm not getting any younger."

Nicky laughed. "I don't know how we can avoid it," he answered. He then stood up. "Mom, may I have this dance?" he asked her.

"Oh my!" Mary exclaimed as she rose from her chair. "You know, I do love to dance," she enthused as she and her oldest son took to the floor together.

Nicky and Trish Marry

*A*fter Natalie Wood's admonition to her, Trish McClintock was concerned enough about her future with Nicky Hilton to at least raise the subject with her mother, who said that she wholeheartedly agreed with her father that Trish should not marry Nicky. Trish's mind was made up, though. She was going ahead with the wedding. However, her father, Frank Grant McClintock, was so unhappy about the upcoming nuptials that he wouldn't even allow her to marry in his hometown of Tulsa. He explained that he would be too embarrassed in front of his personal friends and business associates to have his daughter walking down the aisle with a man close to his own age, and the fact that her bridesmaids would be around her age and Nicky's groomsmen approximately his age didn't make matters any easier to accept. Instead, he would host an engagement dinner for about a thousand people in one of the elegant banquet rooms of the Southern Hills Country Club in Tulsa.

After the engagement was announced, Trish felt that she needed to clear the air with Nicky once and for all. "Look, I've heard some stories about this starlet and that starlet," Trish began tentatively, according to her memory. "And I don't know what you could see in me after some of the women you have had. But I have to tell you, Nicky, that if you ever cheat on me, *ever*, I will walk out on you and never return."

Nicky was stunned. Trish's direct approach took him by complete surprise. "Okay," he finally said. "I get it. I understand."

Emboldened by Nicky's submissive response, Trish took things a little further. She said that she needed him to know that she did not come from a family of abuse, and she wasn't used to it, nor would she tolerate it. Therefore, if he ever hit her, it would be over between them. Nicky couldn't help but become a tad defensive. After all, this was quite a indicting suggestion for Trish to make. "But I would never do that, Trish," he protested. "Why would you ever think that?"

"I'm just saying," she told him, holding her ground. She would later recall that in spite of her stern demeanor, "my heart was beating a thousand beats a minute." She didn't want to lose him or scare him away. "You just have to know that this is how I feel," she concluded.

Again, Nicky didn't argue with Trish. "Okay, don't worry," he told her, now smiling sheepishly. "I love you, Trish. We're going to have a family. We're going to be happy."

And she believed him.

The wedding between Nicky and Trish—at least the one that most people in New York society circles would know about—would take place on Wednesday evening, November 26, 1958, as a civil ceremony at the Plaza. However, there was actually a secret wedding prior to the main event. "I have never told anyone this," Trish Hilton said in 2012. "I kept it a secret all of these years, even from my own father."

Hilton history repeated itself: Nicky was not able to marry in the Catholic Church, since his divorce from Elizabeth Taylor had not been sanctioned by the church. As Trish Hilton explained it, only one judge was available on the day of their wedding who could perform a ceremony that would be Catholic in nature, and he was only available at seven in the morning. Since Nicky couldn't marry in the church, the least he could do, in Conrad's eyes, was have a Catholic judge perform a Catholic ceremony, even if it wasn't recognized. So at seven o'clock the morning of her wedding, Trish and Nicky, accompanied by Trish's mother and Warren Avis (the Michigan car dealership owner who founded Avis Rent a Car) in place of her father, were secretly married by a Catholic judge at his home outside of New York. "I went along with it," she recalled. "Nicky said it was necessary, so that was enough for me. My father was already against one marriage. I didn't know how he would react to *two* of them, so we kept it from him. After the ceremony, I said goodbye to Nicky and we went our separate ways until that night. Then I got all dressed up and acted as if the first marriage hadn't taken place, and we did it again. It was a little odd. But it was important to Nicky and Conrad, so we did it that way."

Conrad Hilton arranged for Trish to have her hair styled by Lilly Daché, who was a legend in the millenary world, best known for her turbans. She also ran a hairstyling salon in New York. She was told to strip Trish of her simple, girl-next-door quality and make her look a little older and more sophisticated. So without consulting Trish, the stylist went right to work. "I always had long, dark hair," Trish recalled. "And everyone was so excited that this woman, who apparently never styled anyone's hair but the most rich and famous, was going to work on me. And this woman, she just cut, cut, and *cut* until, before I knew it, I had the shortest hairstyle I had ever seen on anyone. I absolutely hated it. There was no prior discussion about it," Trish recalled, laughing, "she just did what she wanted to do and I just sat there and let her do it! So, because of that, I hate all of my wedding pictures. It took me years to grow my hair back out."

At the evening ceremony, Barron stood as Nicky's best man, accompanied of course by Marilyn. Eric was present, along with Pat. Even Zsa Zsa Gabor and her daughter, Francesca, who was twelve by this time, were present.

Of course, Conrad was present too, along with Ann Miller and Nicky's mother, Mary Hilton Saxon. Trish was walked down the aisle by her unhappy father, Frank Grant McClintock.

"It was a beautiful wedding," John Carroll, who was present, recalled. "Trish went all out with the white long-sleeved satin gown, the veil, all of it. It was a Dior. She told me that she and her mother had picked it out at Bergdorf Goodman. She was actually one of the most beautiful brides I had ever seen."

After the wedding, Conrad held court at the reception at the Plaza. From the head table, looking before him at mostly Hiltons and friends and just a smattering of McClintocks, he raised his glass of wine. "I would like to raise a toast," he said with a proud smile. "Here's to family." Mary—of course also at the head table and seated right next to Conrad—beamed at her former husband as she raised her glass. Zsa Zsa did as well, and she too was at the head table. Some thought it odd that the toast was to "family" and not to the bride and groom, but as it happened, Conrad spoke first, before the best man, Barron. He apparently didn't want to infringe on Barron's toast.

"Yes, to *family*," Eric added as he lifted his glass.

"To *family*," everyone else chimed in, raising their glasses.

"And to Nicky and Trish," Barron finally piped up, "long may they be happy. We love you very much, Trish. Welcome to our family."

Everyone then joined in on the toast, which incidentally would mark the first time Trish had ever tasted alcohol.

Later, Nicky, Barron, Eric, and Conrad, all three of whom looked elegant in well-tailored black tuxedos, sequestered themselves in a corner so that they might have a private moment together, a challenge because there were so many guests pressing in around them wanting to congratulate Nicky. "I want you boys to know that I'm proud of you," a beaming Conrad was overheard telling his three sons. "You know, I must tell you, I've come at this thing from every angle," he said, sounding serious. "And I have come to the conclusion that despite all of my accomplishments, you boys have done something that I have not been able to do."

"Uh-oh. I think I know where this is going," Nicky said with a laugh.

"Yeah, so do I," Eric added with a grin.

Then, after a beat, Conrad deadpanned, "Each of you boys have, at long last, found someone who will put up with all of your bullshit."

As the four Hilton men laughed and slapped each other on the back, Nicky glanced over at his new wife, Trish, who had begun to tentatively approach the coterie. Of the six hundred people who had been invited to the ceremony, she actually knew maybe ten of them. Never, she would later recall, had she ever felt more awkward and out of place than at her own wedding. "Hey you! Get in here, Trish," Nicky said as he pulled his new bride into the little huddle. "You'll get used to all of us in time," he said with a grin. "I promise."

PART EIGHT

For Love or Money

Zsa Zsa Is Not Wanted

$\mathcal{W}$hile Conrad Hilton was in New York for Nicky's wedding, he thought it would be a nice gesture if he took his daughter, Francesca, to the swanky Plaza Hotel for lunch. Of course, as owner of the Plaza, at Fifth Avenue and Central Park South, he took special pride in the grand hotel. As he told Zsa Zsa, according to her recollection, "I want to show off my daughter to everyone who works there. So be sure to buy her a pretty dress for the occasion." Zsa Zsa was delighted that Conrad wished to spend time with Francesca and that he had initiated the visit. It was a rare occasion; Conrad didn't often take the little girl on private outings. At twelve, Francesca could not have been more excited to have the opportunity to spend quality time with her father. "It was all she could talk about for three days," Zsa Zsa recalled. "'Daddy is taking me to lunch. Daddy is taking me to lunch.' It's all I heard."

On the afternoon of the luncheon, Conrad arrived in his sleek black limousine in front of the Park Avenue entrance of the Waldorf-Astoria, where Zsa Zsa and Francesca were staying free of charge, courtesy of the owner. It should be noted that Conrad almost never paid for Zsa Zsa's accommodations at his hotels, always a point of contention between them. However, because she was a wedding guest, her room was paid for, as were those of all the guests.

Conrad waited in the vehicle for a few moments before one of the passenger doors finally opened and in stepped lovely little Francesca, so proud and excited in her new dress. As she sat down, Conrad told her how pretty she looked in her outfit, which was a Gabor-esque, flouncy pink-and-white affair—very much in Zsa Zsa's taste, selected by her for the occasion and purchased at Bergdorf Goodman. As Conrad paid Francesca the compliment and the driver began to close the door, suddenly Conrad heard that all too familiar shrill, Hungarian-accented voice. "*Vait! Vhat* are you doing? *Vait* for me, you fool!" Zsa Zsa Gabor quickly slid into the car. Obviously Francesca wasn't the only one who had dressed for the occasion. Zsa Zsa was carefully put together with a fas-

tidious hairdo, perfect makeup, and an expensive white silk dress, accessorized with a wide-brimmed white hat and matching shoes and purse.

"What is this?" Conrad asked. "What are you doing?"

"Why, I am going to lunch with you and our daughter," Zsa Zsa said
casually, as she smoothed her dress and settled into the seat. "And just
look at you," she exclaimed, "why, you are just as handsome as ever," she
said, flirting with him.

Conrad ignored the compliment. "You, my dear, are not invited,"
he said. "This outing is strictly for me and Francesca." He smiled at the
delighted child.

"Oh, don't be *silly*, Connie," Zsa Zsa said. "We're *family*, aren't we?"
Besides, she said, Francesca went nowhere without her, and Conrad knew
it. Then, knocking on the partition that divided the passenger section
from the driver, Zsa Zsa instructed the driver to step on it, lest they be
late for their reservation at the Plaza. At that, Conrad calmly reached up
and tugged at a switch that lowered the partition. "We're not going anywhere until I say so," he informed the driver. After he raised the divider
again, he turned to Zsa Zsa and asked her to get out of the car.

"I am not leaving," Zsa Zsa told Conrad. "Don't be ridiculous. This is
a nice day for all of us, Connie. Don't ruin it." She opened her pocket-
book, took out her compact and lipstick, and started to apply lipstick to her
mouth. Of course, this only made him angrier. "Must you do that now?" he
asked, annoyed. "Please, I want you out of this car, now," Conrad insisted.

The two former spouses stared at one another for a moment. "Fine,"
Zsa Zsa said, closing the compact and putting it and the lipstick back into
her purse. "But if I go, Francesca goes with me," she said.

"So be it, then," Conrad said. He then turned to Francesca and, as
gently as he could, apologized to her and said he would reschedule the
outing. "It'll just be an old man and his best girl, I promise," he said.

Francesca began to cry. "But, Mommy, *please!*" she begged. "Just go.
Daddy and I will see you later."

Now it was a real scene, a crying child and her warring parents all
stuck in the backseat of a limousine together. Fed up, Zsa Zsa had enough.
"*Quiet*, Francesca," she shouted with a loud clap of her hands. The girl
went instantly silent. "Come on, sweetheart," Zsa Zsa said, hushing her
tone. "We're *both* leaving. We are not wanted here."

Opening the passenger door, Zsa Zsa stepped out of the car. She grabbed her stunned daughter by the arm and pulled her out of the car. As soon as both mother and daughter had exited the vehicle, Conrad slammed the car door shut behind them. The limousine lurched away from the curb and began to drive slowly down busy Park Avenue, leaving a disgruntled mother and her wide-eyed daughter standing there. Seconds later, it stopped. The vehicle backed up. The passenger door opened. Conrad extended his hand, and Zsa Zsa and Francesca got back into the limousine. The door closed, and the car drove off, headed in the direction of the Plaza Hotel.

"The Most Beautiful Woman"

*N*icky and Trish Hilton's honeymoon happened to fall at exactly the same time as the opening of Conrad Hilton's latest acquisition, the $7 million, fourteen-story Hilton in West Berlin. As usual, a large press junket had been planned by Conrad and his staff to celebrate the opening. When it was decided that the newlyweds would join the excursion and begin their honeymoon in Germany, Trish learned just how Hilton wives were outfitted for such outings. "Nicky dropped me off at a boutique in Beverly Hills, where I joined [sisters-in-law] Marilyn and Pat," she recalled. "The proprietor had been notified in advance as to where we were going and what we would need. It was then that I realized that Hilton women were always well dressed. Chanel was a favorite designer of Conrad's, so for this junket it was Chanel for all of our day and evening wear. It would be Chanel for just about all of the junkets we would attend for years to come. I guess you could say wearing Chanel was one of the many perks of being a Hilton girl."

It was in Berlin that Trish first had the opportunity to see Nicky at work, acting as one of the hosts for the opening along with Conrad, Barron, and Eric. "I was impressed," she recalled. "He was professional, charismatic. I remember thinking I had married someone special, someone people respected. I also started seeing the kind of prestigious family I had married into, the way they moved about with influential people from around the world. The money. The power. For an eighteen-year-old, it was a little overwhelming. But it was also exciting to be at the center of this excitement, especially in Berlin. For instance, while Nicky was giving a presentation during one of the many black-tie dinners, my partner at the table was West Berlin's mayor [Willy Brandt]. It was a heady experience."

Unfortunately, that first evening in Berlin would also mark the first time Trish would see Nicky drunk. While Natalie Wood had warned her about his drinking problem, she hadn't yet been confronted with it. But as this celebratory night wore on, she soon realized that Nicky and his friend Bob Neal had both become inebriated. "I remember looking at Nicky and thinking, I have to act fast. I have to get him out of here," she recalled. "So I walked over to him, picked up his ice cream parfait, and spilled it right into his lap. I acted as if it was an accident. Then, under the guise of having to help clean him up, I got him out of there as quickly as I could and up to his room." In the moment, Trish felt that she had proven to herself that she would be able to handle just about anything that came her way as a Hilton wife, no matter how unexpected. "I didn't see it as a problem, not yet," she recalled. "After all, it was just the first time I had seen him drunk. I was just proud of myself for having taken care of it so expeditiously."

Upon returning to the States, the newlyweds purchased a modest three-bedroom, two-bathroom home in Beverly Hills on Alpine Drive. Soon after, nineteen-year-old Trish Hilton learned that she was pregnant. The couple was ecstatic, as were Conrad, Barron, and Eric, who seemed to sense that the impending birth would mark a defining moment in Nicky's life. It certainly did seem as if he had turned his life around. He wasn't drinking or taking pills, he was responsible at his job, and he seemed to be happy in his life. Conrad saw to it that Trish had one of the best obstetricians in Los Angeles, the same one who had delivered Lucille Ball's children. "My pregnancy was so wonderful," she recalled. "I remember it as being a happy time."

One morning, at a Hilton Corporation board meeting, Nicky stood up to make an announcement. He'd never looked better, wearing a navy blue cashmere jacket and black pants with a crisp white shirt and navy tie. "It's official, gentlemen," he announced to the executives seated on both sides of long conference table. "We have a new acquisition," he continued, now gazing at his father at the head of the table. "He's a bouncing baby boy.

And his name is Conrad Nicholson Hilton the third." As everyone at the table applauded the good news, Nicky rose and walked over to his father, who also stood up. He had finally done something Barron had somehow neglected to do—name a son after Conrad. Of course, maybe it would have been inappropriate for Barron to have done so with one of his many children, since it was Nicky who had been named after his father. As it was, Nicky would be the one to bring forth Conrad Nicholson Hilton the third. He and Conrad embraced, holding each other for just a moment before Conrad broke loose. "Okay, enough," he said. "We've got work to do," he concluded with a grin. "Looks to me like the next generation of Hiltons is growing by leaps and bounds. Let's give them something to remember us by, shall we?"

A year later, Trish and Nicky welcomed another son, Michael, named after Nicky's friend Miguel Alemán Valdés, who had been the president of Mexico from 1946 to 1952 and was now president of the national tourist commission.

Nicky and Trish's friend Carole Wells Doheny—married to Laurence Doheny of the wealthy Doheny family of Los Angeles—recalled the couple's first years of marriage as being blissfully happy. "Nicky seemed to fall more in love with Trish with the passing of time," she said. "He became more emotional, more sentimental, especially after the second baby came. I can also tell you that he never cheated on Trish. He and I were close and I would know—and he never did. He was utterly devoted to her."

Carole Wells Doheny recalled one evening in particular during a skiing vacation in Aspen, Colorado, that she and her husband took with Nicky and Trish. She says it was a night when she realized just how much Nicky had changed. She and Nicky were relaxing on a couch in the den of the chalet the couples had rented for the week, having drinks and passing the hours. Trish was lying on the carpet in front of them, chatting happily away and playing with the two boys. Wearing tight black jeans, a red silk blouse, and a wide silver belt that perfectly accentuated her hourglass figure, Trish had never looked more striking. As she spoke, Nicky just looked warmly at her. Then, when Trish became preoccupied with one of the babies, Nicky turned to Carole and said, "Isn't Trish beautiful?" Carole had to agree. Then Nicky added, "I think she's the most beautiful woman I have ever known." Considering the number of stunning women Nicky had known in his lifetime, Carole felt that his observation of Trish was quite the compliment. "What a wonderful thing to say," she told him. Nicky grinned at Carole and, still gazing lovingly at his wife, concluded, "I'm a lucky man, Carole. And I've never known it more than I know it right now in this very second."

Zsa Zsa Teaches Trish About the Hiltons

*D*ah-ling, Zsa Zsa is here now. So, don't you worry about a thing!"

It was Tuesday, December 16, 1958, and Zsa Zsa Gabor had just come to the rescue of an anxious Trish Hilton. Trish was frantic with worry as she attempted to plan her first important dinner party as a Hilton wife, which was scheduled for the evening of the eighteenth. Even though she had certainly entertained in the past, this night was to be special because all of the Hiltons would be together for the first time in the new Beverly Hills home she shared with Nicky. Nicky had told her not to give it a second thought. Just whip up something simple, he told her. "No big deal."

With just two days to prepare, Trish didn't know how she would be able to make the kind of good impression she so desperately wished to make on her affluent new family members. "I don't think I can do it," she told Nicky, close to tears. "I need a least a *week!*" Nicky laughed. "I'll tell you what; call Zsa Zsa for help," he suggested. "If anyone can put on a good party, it's her." Trish was reluctant. She barely knew Zsa Zsa Gabor, having only met her a couple of times. She couldn't imagine why the Hungarian star would want to help her. But Nicky told her that if she called Zsa Zsa and just said the word "party," she would "come a-runnin'. Not only that, she'll *want* to help," he said with a grin, "because we're family. She was my stepmother, after all. I mean, in some crazy way." The idea of Zsa Zsa Gabor as anyone's stepmother made Trish smile and relax a little; she suddenly felt better.

About an hour later, Trish called the telephone number Nicky had given her, and within thirty minutes Zsa Zsa Gabor was seated with her at her dining room table. Over streusel cake and coffee, the two women got to know each other a little better before finally getting down to business. Of course, they talked about Conrad. Zsa Zsa told Trish about their early courtship days and how thrilling that time was in her life and how sorry she was that the marriage had to end. She said she was sure things would work out better for Trish and Nicky, but offered a little advice. "Husbands are like fires," she said, "they go out when left unattended." Finally it was time to get down to business. Zsa Zsa whipped out a small spiral notebook from her purse. "Okay, now what exactly is it you want to do, dear?" she asked.

"Well, Nicky said to just keep it casual," Trish explained. "So, you know...*simple*, I guess."

Zsa Zsa laughed heartily. "Oh, my dear, there is nothing *casual* or *simple* about the *Hiltons!*" she exclaimed. She added that even if it was to be an intimate gathering, Trish should still make it memorable. After all, she would have "only one chance to make a good impression on *this* kind of family." Then, taking quick stock of things, Zsa Zsa decided that if she really wanted to impress, Trish needed a majordomo, a chef, and a maid. However, the problem was that Trish and Nicky had no such staff in their employ—in fact, they had no help at all! Therefore, Zsa Zsa offered to send members of her own household workforce who held those positions.

"So, what would you like to serve?" Zsa Zsa then asked.

"Um...spaghetti?" Trish asked.

Zsa Zsa doubled over with laughter. "*Spaghetti!*" she exclaimed. "Oh, no, no, *no!* You do not serve *spaghetti* to the *Hiltons!*" Steaks should be on the menu, Zsa Zsa decided, because the Hiltons liked "hearty American foods. *Potatoes! Corn! Vegetables!* All of the typical American foods. Just no hot dogs," she said with a laugh. As she spoke, she continued to add to her list: French bread, red wine, "a nice salad," and cheesecake with strawberries for desert. "Oh, and champagne," she added. "*Pink* champagne." Finally she looked up from her notepad and announced, "You and I will do this together, my dear. It'll be fun! I've been a part of this family for a long time, and I know just what we all like."

"Well, then you must come to the party," Trish offered. "Say you'll come. Please."

"Oh no, absolutely not," Zsa Zsa said. She explained that if she were present alongside members of her own domestic staff, the family might conclude that it was *her* party, not Trish's. And this was to be Trish's big night. "Just act as if you did it all yourself," Zsa Zsa suggested. "Let it be our little secret." Also, she hastened to add that when she and Conrad were in the same room together, it could sometimes be explosive, "and you aren't ready to experience *that* just yet, especially not at your first party," she concluded with a cackle. Besides, she said, she was already scheduled to appear that night at the red carpet premiere for the new Frank Sinatra film, *Some Came Running*, directed by Vincente Minnelli. If she didn't show up, she concluded, it would be to the disappointment of many people. "Plus," she added gaily, "I'm wearing my new chinchilla!"

For the next day or so, Trish Hilton and Zsa Zsa Gabor planned Trish's dinner party down to the very last crouton, and they became good friends in the process. It was to be a friendship that would last for more than thirty years.

"Now I must see the dress you will wear," Zsa Zsa told Trish on the morning of the party. Trish went upstairs to change and reappeared in a floral-printed bouffant dress with a tightly cinched waist. "Oh, you look so *luffly*," Zsa Zsa enthused as the new Hilton wife descend the stairs. She complimented Trish's good taste, and even seemed somewhat surprised by it. She then walked over to Trish and with her fingertip traced the area just below Trish's neck and above her cleavage. "Do you see this part right here?" she asked. "This is the sexiest part of a woman," she told her new charge. "It's not the breasts, though I do love the breasts," she continued. "It's the fleshy area right *above* the breasts and below the neck that is sexiest. Such a beautiful spot on a woman."

Zsa Zsa gathered her things to leave. After telling Trish to have a *"mah-vellous* time," she promised to have flowers delivered that afternoon—specifically red roses, which she said were Marilyn Hilton's favorites. She hugged Trish and was then quickly out the door, on her busy way to prepare for the movie premiere, but not before one last parting thought. "Do not let Conrad intimidate you," she said. "He's just a man like any other, do not forget that."

That evening, Trish hosted her first dinner party as a Hilton. "Of course, as expected, Conrad was present, as was Nicky's mother, Mary," Trish recalled. "Barron and Marilyn were also there, as was Eric and his wife, Pat. There were a few other business associates present as well. In all, there were ten guests, including me and Nicky. It turned out to be a perfectly lovely evening; Zsa Zsa's staff handled every moment beautifully."

"Say, don't I know these people from somewhere?" Conrad asked Marilyn at one point as he studied the maid's face carefully. Of course,

Marilyn knew exactly who the household staff belonged to, having been to Zsa Zsa's on many occasions. However, she would never give away Trish's secret. She and Trish shared a conspiratorial look. "No, Connie," Marilyn said. "I believe these people were just hired by Nicky and Trish." Conrad smiled. "Funny how all maids look alike, isn't it?" he asked with a chuckle.

The next day, Zsa Zsa Gabor came to Nicky and Trish's for a late breakfast, which Trish prepared as a small way of thanking her for her assistance. Nicky joined the two women for the meal—eggs Benedict, hash browns, cottage cheese, coffee, and an assortment of fruits. "It was obvious that Nicky and Zsa Zsa had a special relationship," Trish recalled. "Zsa Zsa had known him since he was a kid, so really she was like a mother to him in some ways, though she liked to think of herself as an older sister. They had a lot in common, I found, especially in terms of how they believed they were viewed by Conrad."

"You know, your father has no respect for me whatsoever," Zsa Zsa told Nicky at one point. She was not her effervescent self; she looked tired and a little hungover, likely from the previous night's festivities.

"Oh, no, Zsa Zsa, that's not true," Nicky said.

"Oh, *please*," Zsa Zsa said. "He thinks I'm a joke." Zsa Zsa then said that Conrad had no idea what she had done with her career, how hard she had worked to make something of herself. In his mind, she said, it was all just "silly nonsense." She said that she faced the exact same dilemma with her third husband, George Sanders, who had told her she was much too stupid to ever have a career, and when she finally did have one, he would never so much as even acknowledge it. As for Conrad, she recalled once saying to him, "You know, Connie, I was nominated for an Emmy award." Now she asked Nicky, "Do you know what he said back to me?"

"What?"

"He said, 'Well, you didn't *win* it, now, did you?'" She shook her head incredulously. Then she asked Nicky a difficult question. "Tell me the truth," she said, leaning in to him and looking quite serious. "Do you feel that he respects *you*?"

The question seemed to make Nicky self-conscious. "I think so," he answered, hedging. He also added that everyone in the family had worked hard to earn Conrad's respect.

"*But why?*" Zsa Zsa asked, exasperated. "Why is it that *everyone* in this family wants Conrad Hilton's respect?" She said she thought it was strange, the way they were all vying for his approval. "As I told Trish yesterday, he's just a man like any other," she noted. She added that he was not a god, contrary to what many people in the family seemed to believe.

Nicky mulled it over. "I guess we just want him to acknowledge that we learned a little something from his example," he said thoughtfully. "Because it's true, isn't it?" He added that, in his view anyway, everything the Hiltons would ever achieve was intrinsically connected to who Conrad was and would always be in their lives. "Even you, Zsa Zsa," Nicky said with a patient smile. "Don't you think Pop influenced you to create this big, sensational life for yourself?"

Zsa Zsa nodded. "I suppose that's true," she said, somewhat reluctantly. She added that she used to think to herself, " 'Oh my God, if I could just have the kind of life Conrad Hilton has.' He would always say, *'Be big, think big, do big.'* I guess I must have listened, because look at me now," she exclaimed with a wide gesture of her arms and hands. "Who is bigger than Zsa Zsa?" she observed grandly.

"No one," Nicky said with a grin. "No one I know, anyway."

"*Exactly,*" Zsa Zsa said. "If only I had a little humility, I'd be *perfect,* now wouldn't I?" she asked. At that Nicky doubled over laughing. Watching the two of them, Trish couldn't help but join in the laughter.

"I remember thinking, 'What a family I have married into,' " Trish Hilton would recall. "Yes, there was something sad and poignant about the way they were all hopelessly vying for Conrad's attention and approval. But at the same time, there was something inspiring about their unity in it. They had this bond, this kind of 'for better or worse' family bond that made me just want to be a part of it. It wasn't exclusive. Once you were in the Hilton family, It was *inclusive,* at least that's how I saw it. It was 'all for one, one for all.' Even when they were *against* each other, you still felt they were somehow *for* each other."

"Oh, he will make you *crazy,*" Zsa Zsa told Trish in speaking of Conrad Hilton. "Trust me, dear. One day you will come to me and you will say, 'Zsa Zsa, he has really done it. He has finally made me crazy.' "

"Probably sooner than you think, too, Trish," Nicky added with a wink.

Success

*I*n December 1962, Conrad Hilton turned seventy-five, a milestone birthday in anyone's life, and for some a time to adapt to a slower pace of living and spend more time exploring leisure activities. Not so for Conrad Hilton, though. He was still full of vigor, ambition, and curiosity—still involved in the day-to-day decision making of his company, attending all of its board meetings, and constantly looking to the future in terms of potential acquisitions. Of course, he suffered from certain conditions that are usually unavoidable manifestations of aging. He had arthritis in his knees and bursitis in his left shoulder. His mind wasn't as sharp as it had once been; he sometimes forgot the names of people. His eyesight had begun to fail him; he now allowed Olive Wakeman to read to him the daily profit-and-loss reports from his hotels. But he was still thin, mostly agile, and usually able to cut a rug with the best of them, which he never failed to demonstrate at Hilton press junkets around the world.

Conrad did have pangs of sadness regarding his fading youth, however. The main reason for his wistfulness was the lack of romantic love in his life. He had been married twice and had a myriad of beautiful female friends, but his true love, the person he could view as a soul mate with whom he could share himself on every level, had never materialized. But on the whole, he'd long ago made peace with his life. He was proud of himself and what he had achieved in his seventy-five years. After all, the Hilton name was now as emblematic of American culture as Pepsi-Cola and American Express.

Conrad owed a great deal of his success to the country's postwar economic boom. The amazing progress that had been made in jet air travel in the 1950s made the world a smaller and more accessible place, and there was nothing like feeling right at home at a Hilton hotel no matter where one traveled. Globally, it's almost impossible to calculate how much money Hilton hotels have generated. For instance, the Castellana Hilton in Madrid brought more than a million dollars in tourist revenue in its first year of operation in 1953. The Istanbul Hilton increased tourism in Turkey by 60 percent in its first year of operation in 1955.

By the end of 1962, hotel occupancy in America was down 30 percent from the immediate postwar high of 90 percent, but Hilton was still at the top of his game, even with room rates and salaries increasing across the board. That isn't to say that he didn't have competition, though. The Sheraton hotel chain had the Hilton chain beat by nine hotels—a total of sixty-nine properties in the world. But it had fewer rooms (29,000) and a much smaller overseas presence (just fourteen abroad, eleven of which were in Canada). "It's an American operation, for the most part," Nicky Hilton would say of the competition. "Which is fine and good. And which is not what we are." Pan American Airways also had a chain of hotels called Intercontinental Hotels, with nineteen properties around the world. But again, theirs was such a small presence compared to that of the Hiltons, and no competitor company was expanding anywhere as rapidly as the Hilton chain.

From San Francisco to New York, Berlin to Trinidad, Puerto Rico to the Nile there were Hilton hotels. In 1962 alone, Hilton hotels opened in Tehran, London, Portland (Oregon), Rotterdam, Rome, Athens, Hong Kong, Tokyo, and New York City (where the $57 million New York Hilton had just opened, of which the Hilton Hotels Corporation actually owned only 25 percent and ran the hotel on a management contract). Plans for 1963 included openings in Milwaukee, Honolulu, and Montreal (at the airport, which constituted the property as an "Inn" and was therefore in the purview of Nicky Hilton).

Also being planned in 1963 were junkets for the Hong Kong and Tokyo Hiltons, both scheduled for June. By the end of 1963, the Hilton Hotels Corporation would own, lease, or manage sixty properties in nineteen countries around the world, with more than 40,000 rooms and 40,000 employees. It should be noted that unlike Chicago's Palmer House or the Conrad Hilton (formerly the Stevens) or Houston's Shamrock Hilton— all examples of hotels owned wholly and outright by Conrad Hilton—the hotels overseas were either leased or run on a management contract.

Also worth noting is the level of confidence the Hilton name had earned around the world by the beginning of 1963. For instance, tourists had once been reluctant to visit the Nile, fearing the local drinking water. But once they realized that they could check into a Hilton hotel—where they could avail themselves of reliable plumbing and electricity, direct-dial telephones, and other creature comforts, not to mention special perks like air-conditioning in each room and refrigerators in the bathrooms that generated their own ice cubes—most reluctance to travel to the area seemed to be lifted. The Nile Hilton had brought in more than $12 million in foreign tourism since its opening. Along with the fact that people of every nationality worked at Hilton hotels around the world, it was impossible to escape the conclusion that Conrad Hilton had brought people together from all walks of life, earning money together and spending it as well—thus the slogan Conrad had adopted for his international hotels: "World Peace Through International Trade and Travel." Or as his friend Henry Crown put it to *Life* magazine in 1963, "Next only to the Peace Corps, Connie Hilton's hotels around the world have done more for the U.S. than any other thing. And the State Department ought to be the first to say so."

Though 1963 would always be remembered as a tragic and even traumatizing year in this country because of the November assassination of President John F. Kennedy, it was still a booming year for the travel and hotel industries. It would end with the Hilton Hotels Corporation's assets totaling a staggering $289 million—an amount that would today be equivalent to a little more than $2 billion. That sum included all of the domestic and international hotels, as well as the inns and other subsidiaries such as the Carte Blanche credit card business, of which Barron Hilton was in charge. Conrad and his family controlled about a third of the company's stock, and the rest was divvied out to investors, the biggest being Conrad's longtime friend hotel mogul Colonel Henry Crown.

Sibling Rivalry on the Rise

*I*t gives me the greatest of pleasure to first introduce the new chairman of the Executive Committee of Hilton International. My son, Nicky Hilton," Conrad Hilton intoned. "Or as I like to call him, Conrad Hilton Jr."

It was the evening of October 1, 1966, and Conrad Hilton was hosting another of his lavish parties at Casa Encantada, this one to announce the promotions of his two eldest sons, Barron to president and chief executive officer of the Hilton Hotels Corporation's domestic division, and Nicky to the position of executive in charge of the international subsidiary of the Hilton Corporation. So vital and arresting did Conrad look in his white tuxedo jacket and black tie, it was difficult to reconcile that he was rapidly approaching his eightieth birthday. Though Conrad was still chairman of the board of the Hilton Hotels Corporation, he had recently stepped down as president and chief executive officer—thus the vacancy filled by Barron—to devote most of his attention to the company's all-important international division, now headed up by Nicky.

The gathering over which Conrad presided on this Saturday evening took place on one of his estate's many lavishly landscaped courtyards under a night sky aglow with stars, the towering glass buildings of Westwood shimmering in the distance. This was not a raucous celebration. Rather, the event was designed to project the dignity of true accomplishment in the world of business. That said, there was still a strong sense of success and achievement in the air; everyone was quite excited. These were the best of times, and everyone seemed to realize it. As a little more than a hundred guests, all in formal wear, enjoyed the refined tranquility, a ten-piece orchestra provided the perfect backdrop of pleasant but unobtrusive cocktail party music.

In his new position, Nicky Hilton would be responsible for all of the Hilton-leased hotels abroad in twenty-five countries. Actually, Nicky began his work with the international division at the start of 1966, but the official announcement would not be made until this night in October. It was a tremendous responsibility, but one his father—and the corporation's board of directors—had decided the forty-year-old Hilton scion could handle. Ever since his marriage to Trish McClintock seven years earlier, Nicky had worked hard to rehabilitate his image not only in Conrad's eyes but in those of his younger brothers, Barron and Eric, as well. Nicky was more devoted to the company than ever; Hilton hotel business rarely left his thoughts. In recent years, he had done an excellent job of heading up the company's Inns Division, increasing its profit margin by more than 30 percent in the last three years. Meanwhile, in his private life, he had grown to truly love Trish and his sons, Conrad and Michael, who meant the world to him.

The party to announce the dual promotions of Nicky and Barron was attended by many of the Hilton Hotels Corporation's officers and board members, such as billionaire hotelier Henry Crown and his wife, Gladys, to whom he had been happily married since 1946. Conrad's first wife, Mary Saxon, mother of Eric, Barron, and Nicky, was present, as was his second wife, Zsa Zsa, along with Francesca. (Six months earlier, Zsa Zsa had divorced her fifth husband, Texas oil baron Joshua S. Cosden Jr. "We were both in love with him," Zsa Zsa explained at the party. "I fell out of love with him, but he didn't!")

As uniformed waiters passed through the crowd with tall Baccarat crystal flutes of Veuve Clicquot and a variety of seafood hors d'oeuvres, Nicky Hilton—looking Rat Pack suave in a perfectly tailored black jacket and matching pants with a crisp white shirt and black bow tie—walked up to the makeshift stage to join his father in front of the microphone at a wooden podium, the front of which was emblazoned with the Hilton Hotels insignia.

"Those of you who know me well probably believe that this is the last thing in the world you'd expect from me, the idea of being a big shot with my pop's company," Nicky said with a grin. "Don't forget, I'm the guy who once described myself in the press as a professional loafer," he added. Everyone laughed—everyone, that is, except for Conrad. A flicker of annoyance crossed his face.

"Seriously, I want to thank my father for this vote of confidence," Nicky continued, turning to face Conrad. "I promise, I won't let you down, sir," he said. Then, as if suddenly overcome by a strong and unexpected wave of emotion, Nicky took a step toward Conrad and wrapped his arms around him in a tight embrace. The hug just lasted a moment, though, before Conrad pulled away and made his way back to the microphone. "And now," he said, "I would like to introduce the new president and chief executive officer of the Hilton Hotels Corporation's domestic division, and that would be my son Barron."

Barron had recently made headline news in August 1966 by selling his San Diego Chargers football team for a record $10 million to an investment group headed by former White House press secretary Pierre Salinger. Barron and Conrad had picked up the American Football League team back in 1959 when it was based in Los Angeles. In 1961, Conrad made the decision to move the team to San Diego. Though the Hiltons both liked a good challenge, this one was to be a losing battle. They would have only one profit-making year in the nearly seven years they would own the club, in 1964. Still, the sale price was $3 million higher than the previous high paid for the Los Angeles Rams of the NFL back in 1962. When Barron was named president and chief executive officer of the Hilton Hotels Corporation's domestic division back in March—the American counterpart of the subsidiary now being headed by Nicky—there was simply no time for this "mad money" sports investment; it made sense to sell.

As Barron Hilton strode confidently through the crowd, the applause for him was more enthusiastic than it had been for Nicky. Then there was a bit of a surprise when, as Barron was halfway through the crowd—almost as if the moment had been choreographed—his wife, Marilyn, mother of his eight children, suddenly emerged. Wearing a diaphanous pink silk floor-length gown, the bodice of which was embroidered with pearls and sequins, she joined hands with Barron. Beaming, the couple walked up onto the stage together, Marilyn's gown billowing elegantly in the breeze, like that of a goddess ascending Mount Olympus. As she stood stately at Conrad's side while Barron accepted the crowd's generous applause, some guests couldn't help but think that perhaps Trish should have been on that stage as well, at Nicky's side. However, as Trish would later recall it, "In a hundred—no, *a million*—years, it would never have occurred to me or to Nicky to do such a thing!"

"This is quite a honor, of course," Barron said, taking the microphone. "As many of you know, I accepted this position back in March. Why, you may then wonder, are we just now making the official announcement?" he asked dryly. "Well, the truth is that my father wanted to have time to change his mind." The audience laughed; it was a good joke.

Barron had been hard at work in his new position for some time. One of his first decisions had been to cut decorating costs 25 percent by limiting the colors of carpets in all hotel rooms to four basic shades that would match all the décor. If that seems like a menial decision, it wasn't. He saved the company millions of dollars. Like his dad—who Barron says "understood the hotel business from the inside out [and] knew firsthand what it was like to clean a room, launder the sheets, and serve the guests"—he understood that little things often mean a lot in the hotel business.

As Marilyn stood proudly behind him, Barron spoke eloquently about the Hilton brand and his plans for the company. "We are, all of us here, in the hospitality business," he said, "and it should always be our intention to satisfy and entertain our guests to the best of our abilities." His fifteen-minute speech was so articulate and well considered, Nicky's few words somehow seemed meager and unprepared in comparison. Nicky actually seemed to shrink just a little in Barron's presence. "Those of you who know me well know that my father is my hero," Barron said as he wrapped things up. "There will never be another like him. So let's hear it for Conrad Hilton." As the crowd applauded, Barron walked over to Conrad and shook his hand firmly. The two did not embrace. Rather, it was formal and businesslike between them—a demeanor with which Conrad seemed more comfortable.

"May we have a few glasses of champagne up here?" Conrad asked one of the waiters. After he, Barron, and Nicky had flutes in hand, the Hilton patriarch asked Eric to join him at the podium. Eric Hilton—now thirty-three—was successfully managing the Shamrock Hilton Hotel in Houston, whose out-of-town transient business was up 10 percent, due in part, according to what Eric explained to interested partygoers, to the opening of the Houston Astrodome a year earlier. He and Pat still lived in Texas; Conrad had flown them up for the festivities.

Once all four Hilton men stood before the crowd, along with Marilyn, Conrad raised his glass in Barron's and Nicky's direction. "To William Barron Hilton and Conrad Nicholson Hilton Jr.," he announced. "I want you to know that you've made all of us proud. We wish you the best of luck in your new appointments." Everyone then raised their glasses toward Barron and Nicky.

With Marilyn shimmering majestically at Barron's side, Nicky's visible discomfort seemed to grow. Apparently it hadn't occurred to him to include his wife onstage. He now must have realized he was being outshined, not only by his younger brother's extremely polished and rehearsed speech, but also by Barron's thoughtful gesture of including Marilyn in his moment of accomplishment and honor. Quickly going into damage control mode, Nicky approached the microphone. Although his timing was perhaps a bit off with the toast already having been made, he did the best he could. "They say that behind every successful man is a strong woman," he began hesitantly. "Well, I happen to have the strongest woman in the world behind me, and I think she should also be up here in this moment. Trish, come on up here," he concluded with confidence.

Trish's tall and slender body moved with facile grace as she walked up onto the stage. Wearing a simple but tasteful white skirt and black beaded blouse, she stood in stark contrast to Marilyn's dramatically stylized high-fashion appearance. Once onstage, she kissed Nicky. She then embraced Barron, Eric, and finally Conrad. When she got to Marilyn, Marilyn gamely reached out and kissed her on both sides of her face, in the fashion of society women, and then held her hand. Now that he had evened out the playing field, Nicky seemed to regain some of his confidence. He walked over to his wife and kissed her fully on the lips. The crowd again broke out into rousing applause.

Nicky was determined to hold his own when it came to contending with his younger brother. On this occasion, he certainly rose to the challenge—with the help of his lovely and unassuming wife, Trish. "All right, enough of this old fogey music," Nicky said as he whipped off his black tie and unbuttoned his white shirt. "Do you guys know the twist?" he asked the musicians. Of course they did; by this time, it wasn't exactly a new dance craze. As soon as they started playing, Nicky pulled Trish out onto the dance floor to show the old fogies how it was done. Soon, the other partygoers joined in—jackets, coats, and purses were tossed aside along with the stiff formality so characteristic of life at the Hilton manse—and before anyone knew it, Conrad and Zsa Zsa were twisting the night away and laughing merrily in the middle of the dance floor. It was a night no one would ever forget.

Francesca's Summer of Discontent

$\mathcal{T}$hough Conrad Hilton's daughter, Francesca Hilton, had been in attendance with her mother, Zsa Zsa Gabor, at the gala to celebrate her half brothers' promotions within with the Hilton Corporation, guests recall her as having not been social or even happy. Nineteen-year-old Francesca was still having problems with her mother.

Zsa Zsa loved her daughter in her own way, and the feeling was mutual. But as Francesca got older, the two continued to argue, as always, about Zsa Zsa's selfishness and her reluctance to give more of herself. Zsa Zsa still had a demanding career and was involved in every aspect of it. She cultivated the persona she had created, and was very protective of it. Nothing was more maddening to her, for instance, than when she was mistaken for her sister Eva, who was now one of the stars of a hit television show, *Green Acres*. Suddenly, Zsa Zsa wasn't viewed as being quite as "original" as before—people actually thought she and her sister were interchangeable: same Hungarian accent, same zany sense of humor, same hourglass figure, and same bouffant blonde hairstyle (which Zsa Zsa accused Eva of having stolen from her). Even their own mother, Jolie—who had always preferred Zsa Zsa and made no secret of it—wrote in her memoir, "They look the same, sound the same, and act the same. They are often mistaken for each other and both hate it. Even I mix them up."

It would be a tough battle for Zsa Zsa Gabor to stay relevant in the 1960s (and into the 1970s), by outdoing herself on talk shows—such as Merv Griffin's and Mike Douglas's—and being ever more provocative with each appearance. After all, it was television that now provided her with her greatest exposure since the impressive film career she had carved out in 1950s did not continue into the new decade. Although she was still making movies, the plum roles just were not there for her. More and more she found herself as a guest star on *Bonanza* or *Gilligan's Island*—even as an archcriminal on *Batman*.

There were problems at home, too. For instance, Zsa Zsa had a way at times of making Francesca feel inadequate. She strongly wished for her daughter to adopt the "Gabor mystique." To that end, she urged Francesca to groom herself more stylishly, to dress more provocatively, and, most of all, to keep her weight down. But Francesca wasn't a painted-doll type. She was an earthy young woman, trying to find her way in the world and come into her own as an independent-thinking person. She knew her mom well, though, and loved her very much despite her flaws.

The spring of 1966 was a difficult time for Francesca. She had spent it in the Hamptons with her aunt Eva, to whom Francesca was particularly close. Meanwhile, Zsa Zsa was having a busy year promoting two movie releases, *Picture Mommy Dead* and *Drop Dead Darling* (retitled *Arrivederci, Baby!*). Plus, she was having a difficult time with the men in her life; she'd just divorced husband number four, Herbert L. Hunter, chairman of the board at Struthers Wells Corporation in New York City, and had just married her fifth, the aforementioned Texas oilman Joshua Cosden Jr. Despite the miles between them, mother and daughter could not seem to stop arguing with each other on the telephone. Conrad wasn't exactly sympathetic. One correspondence from him that summer, dated April 30, 1966, seems a bit troubling in its brash tone. He thanked Francesca for a letter she had recently written and noted that he was getting back to her as quickly as possible. He cut to the chase quickly, however, wanting to know how much weight she had lost and what she currently weighed. He closed with, "My love to Zsa Zsa and more for you," but before finally signing off with "Love Daddy," he reminded Francesca to get back to him about her weight.

One can only imagine how such a letter might have struck Francesca, who, like many teenagers, must have been a little self-conscious about her weight. Zsa Zsa found her so disagreeable, she cut off her allowance. Then, when Francesca decided she didn't wanted to return to Zsa Zsa's Los Angeles home at the end of summer, her mother suggested that she call Conrad. Thus Francesca reached out to Conrad on Thursday, May 5, 1966. He happened to be in New York City on business, staying in his suite at the Waldorf-Astoria. Francesca telephoned him there.

Olive's Appeal to Zsa Zsa

Though Conrad patiently listened to Francesca as she filled him in about what was going on in her life, he really had no solution for her. History had shown that whenever it seemed Francesca was dangerously close to asking for real assistance, Conrad would distance himself from her and from whatever situation was troubling her. If Zsa Zsa wasn't always motherly to Francesca, it could be also said that Conrad wasn't exactly fatherly. This time was no exception. When he felt the conversation becoming dangerously uncomfortable, he said, "I'll put Olive [Wakeman, his assistant] on the line. Maybe she can help."

Francesca explained to Olive that her mother had cut off her allowance. Also, she was at a loss as to what to do that coming summer, whether she should even bother returning to Los Angeles. She and Olive brainstormed some ideas, but nothing came of them. Olive then offered to get in touch with Zsa Zsa, with whom she had a cordial relationship, and talk to her, but Francesca felt that it would do no good. By the time she hung up, Francesca not only felt hopeless, but was also extremely upset, as was Olive. Olive felt she had no choice but to appeal to Zsa Zsa.

Actually, it was because of Zsa Zsa that Olive had been hired by Conrad back in the late 1940s. She was the woman with whom he had replaced the secretary Zsa Zsa had so objected to, the blonde she'd asked him to fire on their wedding night. A devout Catholic, Olive had been working for the Jonathan Club in Los Angeles for eleven years in charge of administrative duties when Father Lorenzo Malone of Loyola College recommended her to Conrad. ("Your need is greater than theirs," the priest told Conrad.) A petite and stylish woman who wore her brown hair in an officious short bob, she posed no threat to Zsa Zsa early on in her marriage to Conrad, and thus the two always got along. Olive now hoped that her relationship with Zsa Zsa could withstand a bit of her intrusion into personal areas where perhaps she didn't belong. She sat down and typed a letter to Zsa Zsa on "Hotel Waldorf-Astoria Corporation—Office of the President" stationery.

In Olive Wakeman's letter to Zsa Zsa Gabor on May 5, 1966, she told Gabor that she really didn't know what else to do but to write to her, even though she feared that Zsa Zsa would think "I am butting into your business, but I believe that you know that I love you enough that anything I ever do or say is what I think might be helpful to you." She continued by writing that Francesca had called, that she had spoken to Conrad for a few moments before he told her that she "had better talk to me." She said that Francesca felt that Zsa Zsa "didn't want to be bothered with her any more," and that Zsa Zsa had hung up on her several times. She wrote that Francesca had mentioned going to London in the summer, and since she would not have a place to stay, Francesca had suggested that maybe she could work at the London Hilton and stay there. Olive added that she had to tell her that the company's employees did not live at the hotels in which they worked, so that idea was not feasible. Then, according to Olive, Francesca had put forth the idea that if she could not go to London and if Zsa Zsa didn't want her in Los Angeles, perhaps she could stay with her father at Casa Encantada for the summer. "I hated terribly to explain to her," Olive wrote, "how odd he is about this, that he did not let the boys live with him after they grew up, and he would not let his sisters visit with him any time and as he got older he seemed more and more to want to be alone."

In fact, Nicky did once live with Conrad, after his divorce from Elizabeth Taylor. Then, after he moved out, Conrad refurnished the guest house at Casa Encantada for him, though Nicky chose not to move back into the estate at that time. While Conrad most certainly did want his sons to be independent, it wasn't likely that he would have turned them away if they really needed a place to stay. He wasn't one for company, that was true, but his sisters had actually visited quite often. He was fine with that, too, as long as they didn't stay long. However, Francesca was apparently a different story. He really didn't want her at Casa Encantada.

"I do hope that I did not hurt her," Olive, who found herself stuck right in the middle of this Hilton domestic dispute, wrote to Zsa Zsa. "She was sweet, but she seemed upset and a little bewildered and confused. I do wish I could help her more, but I know that you realize that I do all that I can and that my hands are tied."

Olive closed sweetly by asking for Zsa Zsa's forgiveness "if I have interfered. But thought you might like to know." She signed it, "with love, Olive."

"Zsa Zsa Who?"

*W*hen Zsa Zsa Gabor received Olive Wakeman's letter, she responded to it immediately. "My dearest Olive," she wrote, "in no way would I ever feel that you are intruding in my life or in that of my daughter's, Francesca." She continued by saying that she was actually relieved that Francesca had gone to Olive for help. Moreover, she was grateful to Olive, she wrote, for acting as "an intermediary between [Francesca] and her father, because God knows it has never been easy for me to play that role." She noted that raising a child "in this day and age" was especially challenging given her status as a single mother with a busy show business career. However, she hastened to add that she did not wish to make excuses for herself or her daughter. In fact, as soon as Conrad returned to Los Angeles, she wrote, she intended to call him and make an appointment so that the two of them could sit down and discuss Francesca's problems. "Thank you again for caring about Francie," she added. She signed the note, "All of my affection, Zsazsa." In a postscript, she wrote, "Let's do have lunch soon, Olive. There is much to catch up on. You may have heard that I have had one or two husbands since last we dined."

Once Zsa Zsa knew Conrad was back in Los Angeles, she called, as promised, to make an appointment to see him. After several unreturned calls, she decided to take matters into her own hands and visit him at Casa Encantada, showing up without an appointment. She was told by Conrad's butler, Hugo Mentz (who had replaced Wilson some time earlier), that Conrad wasn't home. He was at the office. So Zsa Zsa hightailed it over to Hilton's office at 9990 Santa Monica Boulevard in Beverly Hills.

When Zsa Zsa walked into Conrad's office, she found Olive Wakeman at her usual station in the reception area right outside Conrad's door. The two greeted each other warmly; Zsa Zsa complimented Olive, saying she looked "*luffly*." She then explained that she had just gotten back from Europe two days earlier and was leaving again in the afternoon. She was therefore in a bit of a hurry. "Be a dear, won't you, and tell Connie that the dragon queen is here," she said, laughing. She was certainly in a good mood.

"Of course."

Olive then walked into Conrad's office. "Zsa Zsa is here to see you," Olive announced to Conrad, who was sitting behind his desk. He looked up at her wearily. "Zsa Zsa who?" he asked. "Zsa Zsa *Gabor*," Olive clarified with a chuckle. "Who else?"

Because the door was open, Zsa Zsa was able to hear Conrad's question. It alarmed her. Was he serious? Did he not know who she was? Likely he was just being facetious or maybe even sarcastic, but that's not how Zsa Zsa took it. "Something is wrong with him," Zsa Zsa said to Olive when she came out of Conrad's office. "Tell me this instant, what is wrong with Connie?" she asked, being dramatic.

"Why, nothing at all," Olive said.

"But that was strange, Olive," Zsa Zsa continued, not wanting to let it go. "He didn't know who I was, did he? Oh my God, is he going senile?" she asked urgently. "Tell me, Olive," she demanded. "I am family. I have a right to know."

Olive shrugged. "Oh, Zsa Zsa, *please*," she said, now exasperated. "I don't know what to tell you," she added, clearly wanting to stay out of it. "But he will see you now."

Olive escorted Zsa Zsa into Conrad's office. "My dear *Connie*!" Zsa Zsa exclaimed, greeting him. "Look how *handsome* you are," she said, flirting with him, as always. She sat on the corner of his desk, crossed one leg over the other, and made herself comfortable. Olive closed the door, leaving them alone.

Since there were no witnesses to their private discussion, it's not known exactly what was said. However, Zsa Zsa would later claim that Conrad refused to listen to her plea that Francesca stay with him, "even for a week." He would not be swayed from his feeling that Francesca was her mother's responsibility, and he wasn't going to allow the status quo to be altered in any way. There was nothing she could do to change his mind, she said. Therefore, because Eva Gabor had business on the West Coast and had to vacate her home in the Hamptons, Zsa Zsa would have to take Francesca with her back to Europe. According to what she would later recall, before they left the States, Zsa Zsa sat down with Francesca and tried to reason with her. "I am your mother and whether you believe it or not, I do love you very much," she told her. "I don't want to see you constantly get hurt by trying to get your father on your side. "You must accept the relationship you have with him as it is. Just as I did a very, very long time ago."

The Simple Life

*I*t was a chilly afternoon, the first week of November 1966, in a suburban West Los Angeles neighborhood. A woman in a long gray wool coat and yellow babushka walked very slowly up two flights of stairs to the door of a modest-looking stucco apartment building. Though she was just fifty-nine, she seemed much older than her years, each step very labored and deliberate. Despite her simple clothing, she had a distinct air of breeding about her, a certain dignity that commanded respect. She was followed closely by a well-dressed young lady who watched her carefully, both hands at the ready in case the older woman should stumble backward. After the two stopped at the door, the older woman began to rummage through her purse in search of her keys. After finally finding them, she slowly opened the door to a quaint two-bedroom unit. "Home sweet home," she said with a smile.

Though neatly kept, the place was humbly furnished, as if being rented by someone who could barely afford to make ends meet. There was a twin bed in one of the bedrooms, along with a bureau, two dressers, and two lamps. In the second bedroom was nothing but a daybed, a table, and a lamp. There were four windows—one in the living room, the kitchen, and in both bedrooms. "I sure wish I had a window in there," she said, motioning to the tiny bathroom. "But I've learned to live without."

"Living without" had been this woman's custom for many years. It was always difficult for neighbors to reconcile that this simple dwelling was the home of the first wife of one of the wealthiest, most influential, most famous men in the world. This was the home of Mary Saxon—Conrad Hilton's first wife and the mother of the three young men he proudly called his sons.

"I like it here," Mary Saxon said matter-of-factly to her daughter-in-law Trish Hilton as she took off her coat and hung it on a gold hook behind the front door, "even though this place isn't much to look at." Mary pointed out that the brown shag carpeting was new, "maybe three months old, and oh, the battle I had with the landlord to get that put in," she said with a laugh. "And then he wanted to charge me! Well, you can be sure I didn't pay. Not one red cent," she said with indignation. The walls around her were painted dark green. A couch, coffee table—upon which was a stack of Daily Racing Form newspapers—and two matching side chairs all looked as if they had seen better days.

The centerpiece of the living room was a black-and-white Zenith television in a wooden cabinet supported by four spindly wooden legs. "Have you seen this?" she asked, walking over to it. She said it was new, bought by her son Eric as a birthday present. He had intended to buy her a color set, she explained, but she told him, "Absolutely not!" She wouldn't think to have him spend his money on such a thing. "Color TV is so ridiculous," she exclaimed. "If I want to see color, I'll look out the window. This one is just fine."

On top of the television set was an arrangement of photographs in simple gold and silver frames, all of which were carefully placed on a large white doily. Mary pointed to Barron and Marilyn on their wedding day, and to Eric and Pat on theirs, and commented on how lovely everyone looked. Then, picking up one of the frames, she said, "This is of me and Mack when we got married. I miss him so much." Clutching the framed photo to her bosom, she mentioned that she and Mack had once been expecting twins. "But I lost the babies," she said sadly. This was a shock. In all of the time she had been a Hilton wife, Trish had never once heard that Mary had miscarried twins; apparently it was a tragedy people in the family just didn't discuss. "I had no idea," she said, at a loss. "Well, it was a long time ago," Mary told her. Abruptly, she put the picture back in place, picked up another and handed it to Trish. It was of Trish and Nicky shortly after their marriage. "Just look how beautiful you are, my dear," Mary remarked.

Trish Hilton took the framed picture from Mary. Holding it in front of her, she peered at it closely for a long moment and was drawn back to a very special time. "My God," she exclaimed. "This seems like a life-time ago. Nicky was so handsome, wasn't he?" she observed. "Still is," Mary said matter-of-factly as she gently took the picture from her daughter-in-law and put it back in its proper place.

"And as you can see," Mary said, as she extended her hands to the rest of the display, "I have pictures of all of my beloved grandchildren here as well." She then ticked off the name of each smiling child as she pointed to the corresponding image, announcing each name with great satisfaction as if to prove that she was up to the task. She loved all of her grandchildren, she said, each one bringing her much joy. "And there you have it," she concluded, standing proudly in front of the television cabinet and gazing down at all of the collected Hilton family history, "every single person I have ever loved in my whole life is right here on top of this TV. Isn't that something?" As the two women took in the display, Trish couldn't help but notice that one family member was noticeably absent from the display: Conrad.

Some people who knew Mary Saxon felt that Conrad Hilton could have done more for her after their divorce so many years earlier. Of course, the primary reason they felt that way was because he was a man worth at least $100 million by 1966; he could well afford to subsidize a grander life-style for Mary than what she was now living in West Los Angeles. It was easy to feel that something wasn't quite right when comparing the glorious estate in which Conrad lived to Mary's simple and modest apartment. It wasn't that he held a grudge against her for the way their marriage had ended, either. It was just that he had worked hard for his wealth and he wasn't giving it away to anyone—even his own children, let alone one of his ex-wives.

Mary Saxon never asked Conrad for money anyway. "The boys gave her everything she wanted," her daughter-in-law Pat Skipworth Hilton recalled. "She'd call one of her sons if she ever needed anything—and it wouldn't be money as much as some necessity. Like, when she needed an air conditioner, she called, I think, Nicky, and he bought one for her and put it in. The boys kept a close eye on her, as did we wives." It was Nicky, though, the son who was most like her, who took the best care of her. "She never wanted for anything," said one of her relatives. "Nick took care of her because Nick was her favorite."

"She was like no other mother I had ever known," Trish Hilton recalled of her mother-in-law. "She loved going to the races. She loved playing cards. She could shoot dice. She loved a good joke, loved to laugh. I don't know what she was like as a young woman, but as an older woman I thought she was marvelous. She didn't have a venal bone in her body. I sensed that she had a hard life, though. I think she had her regrets. I would sometimes wonder, if she had to do it all over again would she change anything? But never would I return her to a place of pain or sorrow by asking her such a personal question. We were close. I loved her very much."

"It's Going to Be Okay, Brother"

*I*t was Trish Hilton whom Mary Saxon called one fateful Sunday morning, November 20, 1966. Nicky had just left the house to play golf when Trish picked up the telephone. "Something's not right, Trish," Mary told her. "I'm in terrible pain!" Alarmed, Trish told Mary to go and lie down immediately. "I'll be right over, Mary," she said, already grabbing her hat and coat.

When Trish arrived at Mary's apartment, the door was ajar. She walked in with great hesitation and took a quick look around. Thinking she would probably find her on the couch, her heart skipped a beat when Mary wasn't there. She was on her way to Mary's bedroom when she passed the spare room and, glancing in, noticed Mary sitting on the daybed, staring straight ahead. "Oh my gosh! Are you okay?" she asked her mother-in-law. "What's going on?" Mary didn't answer. She just shook her head. Trish ran into the kitchen and called for an ambulance.

Fifteen minutes passed before the paramedics finally arrived. After they placed Mary onto the stretcher, they began to strap a white sheet around her. "No, not this arm," she said, pulling her right arm out. Mary took Trish's hand in her own. "Now, you tell my boys that I love them," she whispered to Trish. "Will you do that for me?" she asked. As a tear slid down her face, Trish promised that she would do as Mary asked. Mary nodded and smiled wanly as the stretcher was loaded onto the ambulance. Just as the door to the ambulance was closing, she waved goodbye to her daughter-in-law.

Filled with fear, Trish followed the speeding ambulance to St. John's Hospital in Santa Monica, where Mary was quickly admitted. Thirty minutes later, a doctor came out to the waiting room asking to speak to "a relative of Mary Saxon's." He looked burdened, his face morose and stark. Trish raised her hand and stepped forward. "That's me," she said. "I'm her daughter-in-law. Is she okay?" she asked anxiously. "Can I take her home now?"

"I'm sorry to tell you that your mother-in-law has suffered a massive heart attack," the doctor said with a flat demeanor.

"Well, will she be okay?" Trish asked.

He shook his head. "I'm sorry, ma'am," he said. "We don't expect her to make it through the night."

"Just like that?" Trish asked in disbelief. For a moment, she was unsteady on her feet. "But it can't be!" she exclaimed. "She was fine just yesterday! We went shopping. She was just fine!"

After a few more moments with the doctor, Trish Hilton did what she knew she needed to do; she began to make the telephone calls she most dreaded. First, of course, she called Nicky, tracking him down at the Bel-Air Country Club. She tried to keep it simple, telling him that his mother had been admitted to the hospital and that he should get there as soon as possible. Then she called Barron, who was at home with Marilyn, and told him the same thing. Finally, she called Eric, who was in Houston where he and Pat lived. Because he was so far away, Trish felt compelled to give Eric all of the bad news at once, that his mother had suffered a heart attack and would likely not survive. He broke down and asked to be kept apprised of the situation.

"Did you call Pop?" Nicky asked as he burst into the waiting room about thirty minutes later. No, Trish hadn't called Conrad. She explained that she thought the call should come from Nicky. He agreed. "Oh, honey, I'm so sorry all of this had to fall on your shoulders," Nicky told his wife as he embraced her. While in his arms, Trish braced herself to tell Nicky the full truth. "Nicky, your mother's not going to make it," she blurted out, pulling away from her husband and looking at him directly. He just stared back at her, his eyes wide with shock and disbelief. "The doctor said she's...dying," Trish continued, examining his face closely for a reaction. "Oh no," was all Nicky could say as his eyes instantly filled with tears. "Not Mom," he said. "She's too young, Trish! She's only fifty-nine!" Suddenly, Nicky looked like a little boy to Trish, lost and afraid. She took him into her arms and held him close. "Now, you must go and call Conrad," she whispered in his ear. "You have to call your father, Nicky. Now, go." After she released her hold on him, he walked slowly to a pay phone in the corner, his head hanging low.

While Nicky was on the telephone with Conrad, Barron and Marilyn arrived at the hospital. Both seemed frantic. "What's happened?" Marilyn asked Trish. "What's going on?" As Trish explained the situation, Marilyn stood staring at her with her mouth open. Meanwhile, Barron, standing behind his wife, slowly crumpled into a chair. He buried his face in his hands.

Nicky hung up the pay phone and walked toward his family members with an oppressed and bleary expression. "Guess what? Pop's not coming," he said, looking bewildered.

"Really?" Marilyn asked. She and Barron shared a secret look. "But... are you sure, Nicky?"

"Yeah, I'm sure," Nicky said. "He asked me to keep him posted," he added. An uncomfortable silence followed. "Well, then, that's what we'll do," Barron finally concluded, trying to stay positive. "We'll keep him posted, just like he said."

As the family waited for word, the decision was made by the hospital staff not to move Mary Saxon to a hospital room. The doctors were certain that death was imminent; they felt it better to just leave her in the emergency ward. Nicky, Trish, Barron, and Marilyn stayed nearby, taking shifts for the next few hours, visiting Mary in the small cubicle where she lay on a tiny bed in a drugged sleep. Occasionally she would stir, but never did she speak. Finally, when all four Hiltons were together in the nearby waiting room, a grim-faced doctor emerged to give them the bad news that Mary Saxon had died. "No!" Nicky exclaimed. "No! It can't be!" he said. He choked on his words and broke down. Barron just shook his head sadly as Marilyn hugged him.

Trying to stay strong, Trish walked over to Nicky, put both of her hands on his shoulders, and looked him squarely in the eyes. "You should go and say goodbye to your mom," she told her husband. "You have to say goodbye."

"No, I can't do it," he said, crying. "Don't make me do it, Trish. Please. I can't do it."

Barron walked over to his older brother and put his arm around him. "We can do this, Nick," he said. "It's okay. We can do this." Pat and Marilyn watched sadly as the two brothers steeled themselves to bid farewell to their mother. "Come on, Nick," Barron continued, his tone even. "Mom needs us," he said. "It's going to be okay, brother."

As the Hilton sons slowly walked toward the small curtained cubicle, their heads hung low, Barron repeated, "It's going to be okay, brother. It's going to be okay."

PART NINE

In His Father's House

Nicky Causing Problems

The death of his mother saw Nicky Hilton plummet to the deepest, darkest pits of despair. Mary had been a great ally, a true confidante, and now she was gone. In response to the loss, his demons took over; Nicky turned to liquor and pills to alleviate the pain, especially Seconal. At the time, Seconal was widely prescribed to high-profile people with particularly stressful careers. Because Nicky had been taking the drug for so long, Trish didn't see it as a problem. She felt he was in good hands because his doctor, Lee Siegel, was a good friend, as was Siegel's wife of forty-seven years, Noreen Nash Siegel.

"Nicky suffered terribly from insomnia," Noreen Nash Siegel recalled, "and my husband was treating it as best he could. Though the Seconal would relax him, I think maybe it was prescribed too much back then. It's important to note, though, that Nicky wasn't just scoring drugs on the street to get high. He was under a doctor's care. My husband was doing the best he could for Nicky. Many times, he gave him pills that were half sugar and half sleeping ingredient. He sent him to a hypnotist at one point to deal with the sleep issue. He loved him and he was in many ways a father figure to him. He wanted to help him. But it was a tough battle."

A memorable turning point had occurred a couple of years into Nicky and Trish's marriage during a vacation in Acapulco. Nicky combined Seconal with alcohol to the point where he became so sick, a frightened Trish flushed all of the pills down the toilet. It was the worst thing she could have done, as she later learned. "It forced him into a withdrawal he couldn't handle and the next three days were sheer hell," she recalled. "He was having convulsions and I thought he was going to die. Finally, a Mexican doctor prescribed some more Seconal, which we gave Nicky in low doses until he finally came around."

"Though he was still functional," recalled Stewart Armstrong, who had been Nicky's assistant when Nicky was heading up the Inns Division of the Hilton Hotels Corporation, and who had maintained a close friendship with him, "there was a definite shift in his efficiency after Mary died. I remember Trish saying to me, 'It's a bad time, but I know Nicky will pull it together. I'm just afraid that Connie won't see it that way.' She was right: Connie did *not* see it that way. Adding to the pressure was that Nicky and Trish had just purchased an opulent stone colonial estate in Holmby Hills for $450,000 [the equivalent of more than $3 million today]. So the financial pressure was on as well."

Along with his new position at the company came a whole new set of responsibilities for Nicky Hilton at a time when he was ill-prepared to handle them. There were many days—more days than anyone could count—when he simply didn't show up for work. "I'm taking the day off," he would say. "I'm allowed to. My pop owns the company." Barron would have to cover for him. "Barron, above all else, didn't want Conrad to know when Nicky didn't make it to the office," said Bob Neal.

"I remember one time when Nicky was nowhere to be found and Barron was at the office doing Nicky's work when Conrad showed up unexpectedly," recalled Bob Neal. "Barron said, 'I gotta go,' and he took off and exited through a back entrance so as not to run into his father. I thought he was trying to avoid Conrad. Later, from wherever he went, Barron called Conrad at the office and told him that Nicky was with him, covering once again for his brother. He had left the office just to be able to create an alibi for Nicky."

Try as he might, though, Barron would not be able to keep Nicky's absences from Conrad for long. "Once, Nicky was gone for an entire week," recalled Bob Neal. "We had no idea where he was. We feared the worst—that he was dead in some alley somewhere. Barron and Marilyn were frantic with worry. We had no choice but to tell Conrad. But we said that he had decided to take a vacation, not that he had just disappeared. As it would happen, that wasn't such a great idea. 'How dare he take an unscheduled vacation?' Conrad asked. The old man was almost as upset about our excuse as he might have been had we just told him the truth: that Nicky had vanished."

Finally, after more than a week, Nicky showed up at the office as if nothing was unusual. When Conrad came through and saw Nicky, he immediately lit into him, asking him how he could fly off on a vacation without telling anyone in advance. "What vacation?" Nicky asked. "I was just busy. I wasn't on any vacation. What are you talking about?" That was all Conrad needed to hear. "Do you know how much business you missed?" he asked. "This isn't playtime," he scolded Nicky. "Important international business is being conducted here on a daily basis, and you are responsible for it." Though Nicky felt badly about the time he had taken off and promised to make it up to his father, Conrad was far from satisfied.

"It was unprofessional behavior, and Conrad couldn't accept that," said Noreen Nash. "There was so much money on the line! Millions. *Hundreds* of millions. I mean, this was the absolute upper echelon of big business and power. There was no time for fooling around."

"Maybe we've just given him more than he can handle," Barron suggested during one conversation with Conrad about Nicky in the presence of several staff members. Nicky had shown up for work every day for three weeks, but then he was gone for four straight days.

"The problem is that he's not consistent," Conrad said. "I don't know what to do..." He seemed completely bewildered.

The TWA Merger

I'm happy to say that Hilton International has had its best year ever," Nicky Hilton announced at a Hilton Hotels Corporation board of directors meeting. It was the first week of December 1966. Nicky sat at the head of one end of the conference table, Barron at the other—the long, imposing polished mahogany surface separating them—with a dozen company executives sitting six on each side. Conrad was to the right of Barron. Nicky, as head of the international division, was in the process of giving his annual summation to the firm's highest-level employees.

In the last five years, Nicky explained, revenue from the international division had exceeded $143 million. But in 1966 alone, the year Nicky had taken charge of the operation, the division had generated a stunning $122 million. A total of 4.8 million guests had stayed at the thirty-five overseas Hilton hotels in the past year. There were eleven more hotels under construction and twenty-five others in various stages of planning. "Why, that's absolutely incredible," Henry Crown, one of the board's directors, enthused. Nicky's smile exuded confidence and accomplishment. "Nineteen sixty-seven could be our biggest year yet," he concluded. He then outlined some of his marketing plans for the coming year and other efforts to make certain that when tourists made their vacation plans, they included a Hilton hotel on their itinerary. After Nicky was finished, Barron gave his brother a big thumbs-up. Conrad, on the other hand, seemed inscrutable. He sat quietly, deep in thought, his face immobile, his only contribution to the meeting being an occasional slight nod.

While it was certainly true that the division was prospering under Nicky's leadership, Conrad felt that he knew a larger truth: Much of the momentum had to do with Hilton's good name and with the kind of upward trajectory that couldn't be thwarted even by the head of a division who was often absent from work. Imagine how much could be achieved if Nicky was actually present all of the time? At least that's the question Conrad couldn't help but pose to some of his associates. Barron wasn't sure what to think, and neither was Eric. They loved their brother and wanted to give him as much latitude as possible. However, Conrad seemed to have reached the end of his rope where his namesake was concerned.

Nicky seemed blissfully unaware of the effect his work ethic was having on his father. The night of the board meeting during which he spoke of the company's 1966 record, he had dinner with Trish and their friend Carole Wells Doheny at Chasen's in West Hollywood. He was in great spirits. He said he had a lot of big plans, new ideas for international expansion. "I think the next year will be a big one for us," he added.

"You two love the idea of being Hilton's international representatives, don't you?" Carole said to the Hiltons. She couldn't help but notice the glow on both their faces.

"I never thought I would," Trish said. "But, yes, it *has* been amazing." Trish added that she enjoyed the traveling, the opening of hotels abroad, the excitement of meeting new people. Somehow, she concluded, it suited her and Nicky. "I don't know why..."

"I know why," Nicky chimed in. "It's because we're such a great team," he concluded, looking at his wife with great admiration.

"Oh, I don't know," Trish said bashfully. "You're the star of this family," she told her handsome husband. "You always have been."

"It's so true, Nicky," Carole agreed. "Why, you're like a...a... a *Kennedy!*" she exclaimed. "You have so much charisma, so much magnetism."

Nicky blushed. "It's not me," he observed modestly. "It's just luck. We're in the right place at the right time."

The end of the 1960s was a booming time in history as far as the American travel industry was concerned. Airplane travel was at an all-time high, especially now with the addition of jumbo jets to every airline's fleet. The far reaches of the world were now easily accessible by anyone with the money for a plane ticket and a hotel room.

Taking advantage of the increase in air traffic, Pan American World Airways had broken new ground in the travel business by establishing a subsidiary called the InterContinental Hotels chain. The plan was for the airline to direct its passengers to hotels it had either leased or purchased around the world—thirty-six in all—providing not only a convenience but a price break on the purchase of travel tickets. The InterContinental chain was a real thorn in Conrad's side, because it specialized in the same areas of expertise as Hilton, sometimes purchasing but mostly leasing hotels abroad, assisting local developers in the design, construction, and renovation of these hotels, and then managing them. So far, by 1967, InterContinental had not made any headway in domestic hotels, so at least Conrad still had that leverage over them. Still, he had to admit that the competition's merging of air travel with hotel accommodations was a good idea. Always a visionary and industry leader, he couldn't help but feel great annoyance that it hadn't been *his* idea.

Conrad was somewhat appeased when, toward the end of 1966, representatives from TWA—Pan American Airways' chief competitor—contacted him to explore the possibility of going into business with him. TWA had taken a good look at the growing Hilton International enterprise and viewed it as a possible asset. In obtaining it, the airline wouldn't have to create its own subsidiary to compete with Pan American and InterContinental; it could just align itself with the Hilton brand and compete that way. It was an interesting proposition, and with almost $200 million on the table, Conrad, his instinct for business growth still intact, was intrigued.

"Tired of Being Misunderstood"

$\mathcal{B}$y the end of the 1960s, Conrad Hilton's multifaceted feelings about his oldest son had become even more conflicted. Maybe it was understandable. After all, Conrad had been putting up with Nicky's erratic behavior for most of his namesake's adult life. Now in his old age, he was just plain sick of it.

Bob Neal recalled a troubling November evening in the winter of 1966 when he witnessed firsthand the great tension between Conrad and Nicky. The two men were in the living room of Nicky's enormous mansion watching a Walter Cronkite broadcast about the Kennedy assassination three years before. J. Edgar Hoover had just announced that all evidence pointed to Lee Harvey Oswald as having acted alone. "That's bullshit," Nicky said. "There were at least two shooters, maybe three. It's some kind of cover-up." As the two friends watched the program and discussed conspiracy theories, a crystal carafe of scotch sat in the middle of the coffee table before them, their two empty glasses on each side of it. When Trish walked into the room to announce that Conrad had come by unexpectedly, Nicky rolled his eyes and, turning to Bob, sarcastically muttered under his breath, "All hail." On cue, Conrad walked into the room, straight as a board, still agile and determined in his gait. Taking one look at the display of carafe and glasses on the coffee table, he stopped and looked at Nicky. "Not overdoing it, right?" he asked. "Tomorrow's a work day."

"Pop, I've had exactly one drink," Nicky said wearily.

"You sure about that, kid?" Conrad asked, now standing in front of his son, arms folded, blocking the view of the television set.

"Sit down, Dad," Nicky said, trying to lighten the mood. "Take a load off, why don't you?"

Conrad didn't want to sit. Instead, as he towered over his son, he began to ask him questions about a business deal concerning the Hilton hotel in Paris. However, Nicky wasn't in the frame of mind for business, nor was he prepared for a meeting. In a measured tone, he told Conrad that all of the paperwork relating to the Paris hotel was back at the office. He said he didn't have it memorized. "You'll have to wait until tomorrow when we're at work," he told his father, all of this according to Bob Neal's vivid recollection of events.

"You know, when I was your age, everything was right up here," Conrad said, pointing to his head. He then recalled that when he started in business, he always knew every detail of everything that was going on, because "back in my day, that's how we operated."

Was Conrad purposely trying to pick a fight with Nicky? Maybe not. But Nicky was offended anyway. "What are you trying to say?" he demanded.

"Nothing," Conrad answered. "I'm just having a conversation with my son, that's all."

Nicky stood up to face his father. "Look, I know I'm a disappointment to you," he told him defensively. "But see this, right here?" he asked, gesturing to himself. "This is the best I could do with what I had to work with."

Conrad stood in place looking at Nicky with a furrowed brow as if trying to completely digest what he'd just heard. Then, seeming upset, he turned and strode toward the door.

Nicky visibly crumbled. "Wait, Pop," he pleaded. "Hold on a second," he said as he ran after him. "Wait!"

It's not known what happened between Conrad and Nicky after they left the living room. However, whatever transpired in the next fifteen minutes was likely not pleasant, at least judging by Nicky's demeanor when he returned and sat back down on the couch next to Bob Neal. He seemed utterly defeated. "I shouldn't have lost my cool," he said as he buried his face in his hands. "I just feel like I'm such a failure in his eyes." He poured himself another scotch.

"But that's not true," Bob Neal said. "Don't be so down on yourself. Your old man thinks you've done a great job, or he wouldn't have promoted you."

Though Nicky tried to listen to his friend's words of encouragement, they seemed to slide right off him. "I'm tired of being misunderstood," he concluded with tears in his eyes, "by my old man, by my brother, by everyone. It's wearing me down." He buried his head in his hands for a moment as if he was about to unleash a torrent of tears. But he didn't. Or...maybe he couldn't.

The two friends then talked about aging and how upsetting were the consequences of the time. Nicky said that he never imagined his father would change so much as he aged. "He was always a man you could reason with," Nicky said. "Now he's just so cantankerous." Then, in a moment of sheer wisdom and understanding, he added, "I think he's afraid. I get it, Bob. He's afraid of dying. But...*hell, man.* So am I," he concluded. "I'm not ready to go either, pal."

Bob assured his friend that he had "plenty of years ahead." At that, Nicky smiled. "You know what I'm looking forward to?" he asked with a mischievous grin. "I'm looking forward to the day when I'm eighty and I can give my sons what-for and they just have to put up with it because, well, they got no choice—and the hell with both of 'em because that's just the way it works! Right?" At that, both men laughed, touched their glasses, and threw back another shot.

Nothing Personal

*I*t happened in the middle of January 1967. That's when Conrad Hilton and Charles C. Tillinghast Jr., chairman of the board of TWA, agreed in principle on a merger between TWA and Hilton International. The deal would call for TWA to issue for each share of Hilton International a combination of .275 of a share of TWA common, and a half share of a new issue of TWA preferred. This exchange of stock would benefit the Hilton Hotels Corporation with at least $250 million, and the understanding that the Hilton name would remain on its hotels abroad. Many—but certainly not all—of the executives working for the company would keep their jobs. However, Hilton's international division would now be wholly owned not by Conrad Hilton but by TWA.

Frank G. Wangeman, an executive of the Hilton Hotels Corporation at the time of the merger, recalled, "As a senior vice president, and subsequently a director of the Hilton Hotels Corporation, I retained a policymaking role. Thus did I witness the transaction that Conrad Hilton would forever regret. Trans World Airlines came to us and said, in effect, 'If you sell your overseas business to us, with our international know-how, we can make that company grow faster for your shareholders.' So he went for it."

This was bad news for Nicky Hilton. Basically, since he ran the foreign division, it meant that he would either be out of a job or seriously demoted. Everything was about to change in his life, and as Conrad's attorney at the time, Myron Harpole, put it, "The Cain and Abel story of Barron and Nick was about to escalate to a whole new level."

"But," Myron Harpole hastened to add, "Mr. Hilton also had reasons that did not involve Nicky for wanting to sell the foreign properties. For instance, the Havana Hilton had been taken over by Castro, and then they had an attack on the hotel they owned in Cairo. He told me that he was beginning to become concerned about the vulnerability of his hotels in foreign locations. That worry also played into the decision, as well as, of course, any disappointment in Nicky."

Myron Harpole was not involved in these delicate negotiations, but as Conrad's attorney at the time, he was well aware of what had transpired around them. "Barron thought it was good business, the money was good," he recalled. "Conrad wholeheartedly agreed. Unfortunately, the consequence of this decision would be the deprivation of a role in the company for Nick. I think now, in retrospect, given Nick's temperament and insecurities, perhaps more consideration could or should have been given to what such a decision would have meant to his pride and self-worth. But Nick wasn't controlling his personal life all that well, and that made him vulnerable. Nicky was so idealistic, I'd have to say that he truly did not see it coming."

The notions of power and money had never been as important to Nicky as they were to Conrad and Barron. It was always approval that Nicky sought. "But you couldn't really be a successful Hilton without placing *some* premium on power and money," observed Noreen Nash. "Conrad and Barron thought alike when it came to that. Barron used to say, 'Along with money comes power and along with power comes money.' Nicky was more emotional, more sensitive. He let his heart rule many of his decisions. Not Conrad and Barron. They were tougher. They were of the same mind."

"Nicky and I were in Africa opening the Hilton hotel in Rabat when those negotiations took place," recalled Trish Hilton. "Because I had studied French, I was able to give the opening remarks in celebration of the hotel completely in that language. Nicky was so proud. We were like a royal couple, hosting one of the most successful press junkets in Hilton history. However, Barron and Conrad were not there. Though Nicky and I both felt it odd, Nicky took it as a vote of confidence. 'They must think I'm doing pretty good if they're putting me out here on my own,' he said. Unfortunately, that's not what was going on at all."

"I love you," Nicky had told Trish on New Year's Day 1967 as they toasted each other. Neither had any idea of what was in store for them. In that moment, they were just ecstatically happy in their marriage, and that's all that mattered to them. "I want you to know it, Trish. And I want you to believe it every day," he concluded, "for the rest of your life."

Trish was moved by her husband's sudden burst of sincerity. "Why are you saying this to me now?" she asked him, her eyes brimming with tears.

"Because I should have said it a long time ago," he told her. "I'm sorry if I ever made you feel otherwise." He added that he knew what it was like to be let down by a loved one. "I know what's that's like, Trish," he said. "And I'm sorry."

Nicky had not been a perfect husband, that much was certainly true. He had a quick temper, and of course, his addiction to Seconal and alcohol had taken on the role of a mistress in his marriage: It was always present, always intrusive. Still, Trish fought what she refers to as "the good fight," and did whatever she could to support and love her husband. Whatever his faults, he never cheated on her and he never physically abused her, just as he had promised so long before. She had never met anyone who believed in her as much as he did. He worshipped the ground she walked on, felt she could do no wrong. Therefore, she wanted to be there for him. In the coming months, Nicky Hilton would find that he needed Trish more than ever.

Showdown

I think it was about the first week in February of 1967 when we learned that Conrad and Barron were about to sell Nicky's division," Trish Hilton recalled. "No one discussed it with us. Nicky saw an article about it in *Time* [the issue dated January 27, 1967], and that's how he found out about it. There wasn't anything we could do but just sit back in shock and look at each other...and wonder...*why*? It was such a crushing moment, so disillusioning on so many levels. 'You are the strongest man I know. *You will fix this*,' I told Nicky. 'You're goddamn right I will fix this,' he said. He was upset."

Not surprisingly, Nicky set up an immediate meeting with Conrad and Barron. Bob Neal was also present; he had shown up with Nicky, and Nicky said he wanted him to stay as a "witness." That Nicky felt he needed a witness suggests that he was perhaps beginning to think in a more tactical way about his future with the company. The four men were seated in Conrad's office—Conrad behind his desk and Barron, Nicky, and Bob seated across from him.

"*What the hell*, Pop?" Nicky began, turning to his father.

According to Bob Neal, Conrad and Barron glanced at one another as if waiting to see who would answer first. Barron took the lead. "Look, it's just a good business move," he told his brother. "It's not personal. You've got to believe that, Nick." He added that the three of them could discuss the strategic reasons for the decision at another time. For now, he said, he and Conrad just wanted Nicky to understand that "this is not a personal thing against you."

"Are you kidding me?" Nicky asked angrily. "*It's not personal?*" He reminded Barron that the family had hosted a party not even a year earlier where it was announced that he was running the international division. Speeches were made, toasts given. The next day, he reminded them, press releases were issued to the media. He had then started the job, as promised. "Now, it looks like you're saying, 'Never mind all that,'" he observed. "'Turns out Nick Hilton couldn't do it after all. Sorry for the misinformation.' To me, that's *very* personal."

"Nick, you aren't listening," Barron insisted. "Again, this isn't about you," he reiterated. "This is about the company."

"Maybe we should all just cool down a little," a worried Bob Neal injected. He reminded them that they were family, that they loved each other. "Come on, Barron," Bob said, turning to him. "This is *Nicky*. This is your brother."

"This doesn't concern you, Bob," Barron said, now seeming insulted.

Trying to get things back on track, Nicky said that he believed the merger to be a terrible idea. However, if it was their decision, he would have to live with it. His big question to them, he said, had to do with why he had been left out of the loop.

"We *wanted* to bring you in," Barron explained, "but you were nowhere to be found, Nick." He added that he and Conrad would never have intentionally made such an important deal behind his back. Nicky had been completely unavailable, Barron claimed, and he knew it. At that, Nicky looked at his brother blankly, as if he didn't know how to respond. Had he been all that unavailable? In the moment, it was as if he couldn't seem to remember.

"As we have repeatedly told you, Nick, this isn't about you," Conrad said, rising from his chair. He said that the three of them could discuss the matter later—preferably without Bob Neal's presence—after they had a chance to cool down. "For now," he concluded, "that will be all."

"That will be all?" Nicky asked, looking defeated. He rose from his chair and turned to Bob Neal. "Let's get out of here," he announced. "I don't have to listen to this."

"But wait!" Neal protested. "There's got to be something we can do," he said, trying to act as peacemaker. "We can't leave it like this!"

"No. I'm done, Bob," Nicky said, shaking his head. Then, as he stood in the doorway, he looked at his father and brother and concluded, "I've worked hard for this company. I deserved to be in the loop, that's all I'm saying." And with that, he stormed out of the office, Bob Neal following close behind. Barron ran after them. "Nick, wait up!" he exclaimed.

Nicky stopped just as Barron caught up to him. "I'm worried about you," Barron said, putting his hand on his brother's shoulder. "Come to the house later tonight so you and I can talk this thing out. Bring Trish. Have dinner with me and Marilyn. Maybe eight?" Nicky looked at him and nodded, now seeming calmer. It was as if just a single caring gesture from Barron was all that was needed to defuse the situation and alter Nicky's mood. Now he just seemed exhausted. "Okay, Barron," Nicky said, nodding. "I'll see you tonight."

Barron grinned at him. "And don't be late," he added, patting Nicky on the shoulder.

"Yeah, right," Nicky remarked, smiling halfheartedly.

"See to him then, will you please?" Barron asked Bob Neal as he ran off to catch up with Conrad.

A Done Deal

$\mathcal{A}$fter he had time to get over the upsetting meeting with his father and brother and then marshal his strength for the battle that was clearly ahead, Nicky Hilton went about the business of trying to align himself with the necessary number of board members who might be able to veto any sort of merger with a majority vote. As it happened, Nicky's greatest ally would turn out to be Conrad's close friend, longtime confidant, and business associate Colonel Henry Crown. Crown, former owner of the Empire State Building and a long-standing member of the board of the Hilton Hotels Corporation, also felt strongly that selling the international division was a big mistake, and he told Conrad as much. A slight, short, gray-haired man with a gray mustache, Crown had recently been offered by Howard Hughes a chance to take controlling interest in TWA. He turned it down simply because he felt TWA was not a solvent investment.

"Gentlemen, let's be reasonable about this thing," Nicky said in one board meeting about the matter, according to someone who was present. "Forget about any personal feelings," he said. "You want to talk about business? Fine." He continued by noting that foreign travel was booming at this time and was only going to get bigger. The Hiltons needed to stay in the game.

"Quite right," Henry Crown said. He added that the Hilton brand was huge overseas. Divesting at this time would be a huge mistake.

"But the expectation is that TWA stock will rise," Barron said, defending the merger, "and all of us will be the better for it."

"I have taken many risks in my life, gentlemen," Conrad finally said. He added that while he did see this present move as just such a risk, he also saw it "as a winning situation."

"But what's on the table is us losing the rights to the Hilton name overseas, Pop," Nicky argued. He noted that Conrad had worked hard to make the company's brand international. "Why in the world are you doing this?" he asked.

"TWA is in the process of negotiating to compete with Pan American with new routes to China, and we have hotels there waiting," Conrad answered. "And TWA is getting ready to roll out their new fleet of enormous Boeing 747 jets in the next few years. People are flying, Nick, and planes are carrying them..."

"My point exactly," Nicky countered. "And we have the hotels in each country for them to stay in. So why are we handing it all over to TWA?"

No matter how many different ways the merits of the merger were explained, they made little to no sense to Nicky, Henry Crown, and several of the other board members. However, any meetings about the matter seemed to be little more than a formality. It really was a done deal.

Trish Enters Conrad's Den

Trish Hilton was still determined to help her husband at all costs. Frightened, intimidated, and feeling out of her league, she gathered her courage to meet with her father-in-law, Conrad Hilton, at Casa Encantada. Appealing to him would take nerve, because she well understood that Conrad came from an age cohort that did not take women seriously in business. It was a simple generation gap. He had an old-fashioned way of thinking about females in the workplace, and at almost eighty, he wasn't likely to change his mind about it. Would he listen to advice from a woman? He did have Olive Wakeman in his life, Trish decided, so maybe it was worth a try. "But I probably should have known better," Trish Hilton would say many years later. "I'm sure I *did* know better, and that's why I didn't tell Nicky I was going. He would have tried to talk me out of it, telling me it was inappropriate."

As soon as Trish walked into Conrad's mammoth drawing room, she realized for the first time that Casa Encantada seemed a tad run-down. "It definitely needed a woman's touch," she later recalled. "It was as if Connie hadn't changed the furniture at all since he moved in. It was still majestic, with the elegance and grandeur of an estate found, maybe, in the south of France. However, you could plainly see that no female had ever lived there. A woman would have been more conscientious about the state of the furnishings. Even the drapes looked as if they needed to be replaced. As I looked around, I realized that the whole place needed a fresh coat of paint."

"Thank you for being on time," Conrad said as he greeted Trish. "You know how I am, Trish. I don't like to be kept waiting." He was smartly dressed in a finely tailored suit, his Old World formality on full display, not only in his sartorial splendor but also in his very proper demeanor.

"Of course, I know that, Connie," Trish said as she embraced her father-in-law.

"Never been late a day in my life," he continued with a chuckle.

Trish and Conrad then took two leather chairs facing one another. She took a deep breath, cleared her throat, and began to give the speech she had been rehearsing all morning. "I know you love your son," she started carefully. "So, I'm asking you, please don't do this to Nicky."

"Exactly what is it you think I am doing to Nicky?" Conrad asked with a frown, all of this according to Trish's vivid recollection of events.

"Well, the TWA takeover," Trish answered. "It's happening, isn't it? I mean..." She faltered. Conrad sat with an impassive face and allowed Trish a moment to collect herself. She then concluded that in her view, the merger was a very bad idea. Nicky was agonizing over it, she said.

"But how does this concern *you*, Trish?" Conrad asked. His curious expression suggested that he really wanted to hear her answer. Nicky was her husband, Trish explained, and thus everything that concerned him concerned her. "And this is his whole life," she said.

"Well, I'm not so sure about that, my dear," he said. "But, be that as it may, if you don't mind my saying so, I feel that you are very far out of your depth here."

"Why?"

"Because you and I have never once discussed business," he answered, "and I don't think it's appropriate to do so now."

"But..."

"Please. I don't wish to offend you," he quickly added. He was simply being as candid with her as possible, he explained.

"But...I..."

"I love my son very much," he continued. "And I promise you, I will take care of my son, just as I have always taken care of my sons. Now," he announced as he stood up, "it's been wonderful seeing you again, dear." He kissed her on the cheek. "I'm sure you know your way out, don't you?" he added, holding both of her hands "All my love to those little rascals of yours." Conrad then regarded his daughter-in-law with a raised-eyebrow expression suggesting that as far as he was concerned, their time together had come to an end.

"No. Wait a second," Trish said, summoning up all her moxie and trying to be firm. This meeting had not gone at all the way she'd hoped, and she wanted to get it back on track. "I am only thinking about your son," she continued. She said that she loved Nicky, would do anything for him, and was very worried about him. Conrad seemed unfazed. Business was business in his mind, and it had nothing to do with anyone's personal agenda, even a family member's. "Are we finished now, dear?" he asked. "Or is there more you would like to say?" He stood looking at her for a few more seconds with a patient smile. "No," she conceded. "I suppose I said what I came here to say."

"Very well," Conrad concluded. He grinned, nodded, and then walked away from her, leaving her alone in the expansive drawing room. A few moments later, Hugo Mentz joined her. "Would you like me to show you out?" he asked, his German-accented voice seeming more formal than ever. He led Trish through a labyrinth of rooms to the marble entryway and toward the large, imposing eight-foot oak doors. After Trish took two steps outside, she turned around to say goodbye to him. But before she could say a single word, the butler abruptly closed the doors behind her with a booming thud.

Nicky Considers Suing His Family

On May 9, 1967, TWA's takeover of Hilton International was complete. With this change, it became official that Nicky Hilton had lost his position with the international subsidiary. TWA named him a board member, but with limited responsibilities. Meanwhile, Conrad would continue on as president of the Hilton Hotels Corporation and Barron as head of the domestic division—no changes there. As far as Barron was concerned, the sky was now the limit for the Hilton brand. Literally. In a speech before the American Astronautical Society in Dallas in May 1967, he discussed what he called "The Lunar Hilton"—an underground one-hundred-room hotel that would be built just below the moon's crust.

"In almost every respect it will be physically like an earth Hilton," Barron explained, adding that construction would start as soon as the notion of mass space travel caught on, which, he admitted, "might be a while." As far-fetched as it may have sounded, he was only half joking. "Look, my father had many ideas in the 1940s and 1950s that people thought were out of this world," he explained. "And today those same ideas are commonplace. We Hiltons think big. That's always been our way."

While Barron's ambitions were reaching dizzying heights, Nicky had never felt smaller or more insignificant. "We heard that Nicky was drawing up legal action alleging that Barron had caused Conrad to become disaffected with him," said Conrad's longtime lawyer Myron Harpole. "It would have been a case against Barron, and possibly Conrad—likely the entire firm. He was talking to high-powered lawyers, who were, of course, getting back to us on it, keeping us posted on his intentions. If he filed a lawsuit like the one he was promising, it would have been a complete disaster for the family and for the company. Barron and Conrad wanted to avoid it at all costs, but they had to acknowledge that Nicky was very upset. There was no telling what he would do."

Nicky's friends tried to talk him out of litigating against his own powerful family. They didn't see how a lawsuit would help him and suspected that it would just make things much worse. "Your old man and your brother gave you every chance in the world," Stewart Armstrong told Nicky one day during a particularly heated exchange. "Do you know how many hundreds of millions of dollars they handed over to you when they put you in charge of the international division? You're the one who threw it all away," he charged, all of this according to his memory of the conversation. "Be a man, Nicky. Take some responsibility for your actions." Not surprisingly, Nicky didn't see it that way. "I didn't start with the pills and liquor until *after* they stole my company out from under from me," he said in his defense. "*Excuse me*," his old friend told him, "but I was there. Remember? That's pure bullshit, Nicky, and you know it. You fight your family in court, I guarantee you will lose everything."

"My call, then," Nicky said. "I got nothing left to lose, anyway. I will burn their entire world *to ashes*," he concluded bitterly. "Welcome to the dark side, my friend. Because that's what we're looking at now."

"You have a family. A wife. Two sons," Stewart reminded him. "Don't think for one second that you are the only person with something to lose here."

Undaunted, a few days later Nicky met with prominent show business attorney Arthur Crowley, who took the meeting at Nicky's home and was astonished by Hilton's debilitated condition. The last time he had seen him, many years earlier, Nicky was a handsome lothario who didn't seem to have a care in the world. Now he looked like a battered old man. Bitter and unhappy, Nicky made it clear that he wouldn't stop until he had justice. "I felt that he was hurt, feeling betrayed, and was lashing out," Crowley would later say. "I told him that before he considered litigation, he needed to clean himself up, go to a rehab center, and try to put the pieces of his life back together. Then, if he got clean, we could consider our options. I wasn't going to have him fight his family in the shape he was in. He would have been a terrible witness for himself."

"Oh, screw that," Nicky exclaimed, exasperated by the attorney's sensible advice. He said he didn't need "a shrink." He needed a lawyer.

"Look," Arthur Crowley said. "The world spins fast, kid. Life is short. So, straighten this shit out, Nick," he said. "You're a Hilton. You're better than this. I'm not going to stand by and watch you destroy yourself and your family, too. I'm just not going to do it."

"Well then, to hell with you, man," Nicky said, now fed up. "Just get out, all right?"

Though Nicky received about $100,000 in stock as a result of the sale, it wasn't much considering the amount generated by the international division, and it didn't matter to him anyway. Over dinner one evening, he unburdened himself to his friend Noreen Nash, wife of his doctor, Lee Siegel. "How could they do this to me?" Nicky asked Noreen. They were sitting at the bar in the Siegels' home, nursing martinis. He looked tired, his face drained of all vivacity. Nicky put his head on Noreen's shoulder, like a little boy might do with his mother. "I would never do this to them," he said quietly, likely referring to Conrad and Barron. "I just never would, Noreen. You know me!"

"I don't know what to say," Noreen told him. She recalled being at a complete loss. "Maybe, like they said, it's nothing personal," she offered. "Maybe it really *is* just business." She was grasping at words to try to help relieve his pain, but she knew the truth: It really *was* just business...and business being business had little to do with personal relationships, especially in a powerful family like the Hiltons. In her opinion, Nicky had let down his father and brother, and they were now making him pay the price. Still, she couldn't help but wonder why Conrad and Barron didn't just come out and tell Nicky that he had been his own undoing. But then, in thinking about it, she came to the conclusion that they probably felt Nicky wouldn't have been able to handle the truth. He was already in such a downward spiral, how would he cope with the fact that he had done it to himself? "I felt that maybe, in their own way, they were protecting him," she said. "And I still think there is some truth to that."

From Kings to Paupers

While it was expected that TWA's stock would rise as a result of the merger with Hilton International, that did not happen. After the takeover, it went into a nosedive, dropping from $87 a share at the time of the change to, a year and a half later, just $43 a share. "The major problem was OPEC," hotel mogul Donald Trump would observe. Of course, Trump wasn't involved in the situation—he was twenty-one at the time and still in college—but everyone who has ever studied the hotel business knows about this unsuccessful Hilton venture. "Oil prices started to skyrocket, and that proved to be devastating to the airlines. The stock would never recover," Trump added. "I think it bottomed out at five dollars a share in 1974."

Meanwhile, Pan American World Airways and the InterContinental Hotels chain continued to thrive, not really feeling much competition from the new TWA-Hilton alliance. Also, other airlines such as American and United continued to flourish because, said industry observers at the time, they had iron-willed CEOs dedicated to their brand as carriers and were not distracted by other ideas, such as getting into the hotel business.

Though foreign travel continued to boom in the late 1960s and would become even more lucrative in the 1970s, Conrad Hilton and the Hilton Hotels Corporation would not benefit from such growth. Because of the merger with TWA, Hilton lost all rights to his name overseas. In years to come, it became painfully clear that Nicky Hilton had been right all along. Even Barron would, many years later in 2010, admit, "Not every deal worked out well in the short term, such as our sale of Hilton International to TWA in 1967."

Frank G. Wangeman, senior vice president of the Hilton Hotels Corporation at the time, recalls the merger as "our blunder of 1967. It proved a mistake," he said. "TWA's airline business soon ran into financial problems, while Hilton International—indeed, the entire international hotel industry—enjoyed tremendous growth. We simply had not realized what a prize we had in the international division."

Myron Harpole put it this way: "This was a big misfire on both Mr. Hiltons' parts—Conrad and Barron—and we all knew it. *They* knew it."

In strategizing the merger with TWA, Conrad and Barron suspected there might be certain problems with a number of the foreign hotels, and they were correct. The hotels overseas had long been run by Hilton International using a lease agreement. The Hilton firm didn't actually own the hotels; it just managed them. Now, of course, the management would be taken over by TWA. It wasn't a surprise that the boards of directors of some of the hotels became resistant to the change. After all, Conrad Hilton had a system in place for managing hotels, one that had worked for years. Though TWA promised to adhere to those same standards and practices, some of the hotel's officers felt that the merger was a violation of their contract with Hilton International. The result was a messy tangle of lawsuits, many of which would end up in Nicky Hilton's lap since he was now on the TWA board of directors and, as such, still responsible for some of the Hilton International business. "He wasn't happy about it," recalled Frank G. Wangeman, years later. "Whereas he was once in charge of the whole shebang, now it seemed that his job was to put out fires we had caused by the merger."

"Look at all of this bullshit," Nicky said to Stewart Armstrong when Armstrong came to visit him one day in his office. The top buttons of Nicky's collar were undone, his tie was loosened, and his shirtsleeves were rolled up, as if he had been toiling at work for many long hours. An ashtray on his desk was overflowing with cigarette butts. He pointed to a large stack of paperwork. "All of this because of the takeover."

"What's the problem?" Stewart asked.

"What *isn't* a problem?" Nicky asked, agitated. "I told them this was a bad idea. But of course no one listens to me..."

"What do you mean?"

"What I mean is that this is a family business and Conrad Hilton is the head of this family, so no one cares what I think," Nicky answered. "And now...*this*."

Nicky explained that he was currently acting as a mediator between TWA-Hilton International and Tokyo Electric Express Railway, LTD, which went by the name Tokyu. Tokyu had just announced that it was pulling out of its twenty-year contract with Hilton International to run the Tokyo Hilton because it did not agree with the TWA merger. "We wanted to go into business with Conrad Hilton and that's what we did," said one spokesman. "We have no interest in being in business with TWA." Moreover, Tokyu was a stockholder in Japan Airlines, which was TWA's competition in Japan. Nicky told Stewart that Tokyu had given plenty of notice that they were going to end their contract with Hilton International if the merger was finalized. Therefore it didn't come as much of a surprise to anyone when they did just that. There was nothing left to do now, Nicky explained, but for Hilton to sue Tokyu for breach of contract.

From his haggard appearance, it was obvious that Nicky hadn't been sleeping. Though Stewart didn't ask, his gut told him that Nicky was probably on Seconal. "You look like shit, Nick," he told him.

"Man, we had it made," Nicky said, ignoring his friend's critical observation. "We were kings overseas," he said, his voice filled with discouragement. "We had power. We had money. We had it all. Now we're just... *paupers*."

Stewart Armstrong suggested that Nicky didn't need the income, due to the stock he had made on the merger, "so what's a rich boy like you even doing here? Stop trying to sell this goddamn dream, Nick. Let it go."

Nicky stared off into the distance. "I was about fifteen," he said, suddenly lost in a memory. "And my dad had this chauffeur who doubled as a butler, his name was Wilson," he remembered. "He knew everything about cars, that guy." Nicky then recalled the time that he and Barron convinced Wilson to teach them how to disassemble one of Conrad's favorite automobiles, a 1931 cabriolet. With a chuckle, Nicky remembered that the three completely dismantled the engine. However, the Hilton boys lost interest in the project before Wilson could teach them how to put it back together. A week later, Conrad came back from a business trip to find the engine parts of his prized cabriolet scattered about in one of the garages. At dinner that night, he looked sternly across the table at his young sons and said, "I hope you boys learned a little something about cars while I was gone, because I want you to put that cabriolet back together."

"So me and Barron and Wilson worked like the devil on that thing for about a week," Nicky recalled with a smile. "Somehow, we managed to do it! We were so proud, we couldn't wait to tell Pop."

Conrad walked into the garage with a big smile on his face, Nicky remembered. He got into the vehicle and put the key in the ignition. Within seconds, white smoke began to seep from the motor and green liquid began pouring out of it. He quickly turned off the ignition, got out of the car, cleared the smoke away from his face, and, coughing, said, "Nice try, boys. That's all I ask. That you at least *try* to get the job done."

The two men had a laugh. "My pop needs me," Nicky said, now back to the business at hand, "and Barron needs me. I think maybe this is another chance..." His voice trailed off.

"Another chance to do what?" his friend asked him.

"I don't know," Nicky said halfheartedly. "To try to get the job done, I guess."

Trish Tries Again with Conrad

*I*t was November 4, 1967. From just outside the front door, she could hear the phone ringing inside the house as she tried to fit the key into the lock. She hurried inside as the phone continued to ring. Quickly dropping her armful of groceries on the kitchen counter, she ran to the nearest extension and picked up the receiver.

"Is Mr. Eric Hilton there?" asked the voice on the other end of the phone.

"No, he's not," answered the woman. "This is his wife, Pat."

"Would you be Nicky Hilton's sister-in-law, then?"

"Yes," she answered, her panicky feeling rising. "Yes, I am. Is he okay? Is Nicky okay?"

"I'm sorry to tell you that your brother-in-law is in the hospital," said the caller. She identified herself as a head nurse in the emergency ward of Palm Springs General Hospital in Palm Springs, California, where the Hiltons owned a family vacation home. "Do you have a way of getting in touch with your husband?"

Pat, who was in the Houston home she shared with Eric, explained that her husband was in Dallas on business. She could reach him, of course. "But what happened?" she first wanted to know.

This was the phone call Pat Hilton had been dreading. By this time, Eric had been promoted to southwest sales manager of the Hilton Corporation, a job that entailed a great deal of travel between the home office in California and hotels in the Southwest. On his frequent visits to Los Angeles, he would spend as much time with Nicky as possible. So he and Pat were well aware of Nicky's deteriorating condition.

"I'm afraid that your brother-in-law tried to harm himself," the hospital employee told Pat. She caught her breath. "Would you please contact your husband for us?" she asked urgently.

"Yes," Pat answered. "Yes, I will."

Now quite shaken, Pat tracked Eric down in Dallas and gave him the upsetting news. They wondered why Nicky hadn't called Trish, but didn't know the answer to that question. Therefore, Eric immediately called Trish. He assured her that Nicky was fine and that he would give her more details as soon as possible. He then took a flight from Texas to California; he showed up at the hospital the next morning. It was then that Eric learned the shocking news that Nicky had slit his wrists. Eric would spend the week in Palm Springs, waiting for Nicky to be released. Then the two of them retreated to the Hilton vacation home, where Nicky tried to recover and come to terms with his desperate act. Once he got home to Beverly Hills, Nicky took his heated emotions out on the one person closest to him, and likely the one who cared the most for and about him—his devoted wife, Trish.

"It's difficult to describe how quickly things unraveled from there," Trish Hilton recalled. "The suicide attempt shook up our whole world. I wanted him to understand how much he had to live for, how his family now was me and the kids, not so much Conrad and Barron. Little Conrad was seven, Michael was six. They needed their daddy more than ever. I didn't know what to do."

Although her appeal to Conrad Hilton about the TWA merger had not worked, Trish still felt the need for his assistance. But first she called her friend Zsa Zsa Gabor to ask for advice.

"Oh, my poor dear, didn't I once tell you that Conrad would drive you crazy?" Zsa Zsa asked. "And it's happened, hasn't it?" Zsa Zsa noted that as he'd gotten older, Conrad had only gotten more stubborn. "And he is making us all crazier than ever, isn't he?" she asked. "That old goat!"

Trish had to admit it was true. But then again, everything going on right now was driving her out of her mind. She told Zsa Zsa that she still believed she could get through to Conrad and reach him in some nostalgic, tender place. She continued to hope that if he recognized the full truth about his son's condition, he would take charge of Nicky and somehow get him back on track. After all, there was no one in the world Nicky respected more than his father, no matter their battles.

"Then you must try again," Zsa Zsa said. "You owe it to Nicky to do everything you can to save him."

"I will do whatever I have to do," Trish affirmed. "I don't want to lose him."

"You are such a good wife," Zsa Zsa concluded. "*Sanks* God for you. You're a fighter, Trish, and I admire you. If you learn anything at all from me, learn this: Do not stop until you get exactly what you want. Period."

After talking to Zsa Zsa, Trish decided to call a strategy meeting at her home, bringing Conrad together with three of the doctors who had been treating Nicky: Dr. Judd Marmor and Dr. Rex Kennamer, both physicians, and Dr. Robert Buckley, a psychiatrist.

The meeting took place in November 1967. Conrad, who would soon turn eighty, showed up in a natty black suit and tie. Everyone invited to the meeting took a seat in Trish's tastefully furnished parlor.

"I would say that Nicky has a fifty-fifty chance of surviving if he goes to a rehab facility," said Dr. Kennamer, "and if he doesn't, he has no chance of survival at all." Conrad took a moment to let that upsetting news sink in, and then, with a very worried expression, asked the doctor to repeat himself. After he did, Conrad thought it over for a moment. "He's forty-one, now, isn't he, Trish?" he asked. Trish confirmed as much. Conrad then wondered aloud about the wisdom of having a meeting such as this one behind his back, as if he were a child. "Shouldn't he be here too?" he asked.

"He's too sick," Trish explained. "We're here to find a solution to try to help him."

"I sometimes wonder if a man who doesn't want help can ever actually accept it," Conrad said, shaking his head in despair. "Rather reminds me of something my mother used to say," he recalled. "She used to say, 'You can't drag a man kicking and screaming to his glory.'"

"I tend to agree that sometimes that's true, sir," said Dr. Kennamer. "But if we can just settle on some course of action for Nicky, maybe we can help."

Conrad sighed deeply. He said he completely understood. However, he also explained that he had been dealing with the problem of Nicky for many years. "I'm a very old man now...," he added, not finishing his sentence. Trish raised her eyebrows in surprise. It was the first time she had ever heard her father-in-law acknowledge his advancing years. In that moment, she suddenly saw the futility of having asked Conrad, a father who had already been through so much with his son, to come to some decision as to how to now deal with him. Now she was sorry she had even asked Conrad to attend the meeting. It was as if she had set him up to disappoint. Conrad looked at Trish helplessly. "You're his wife, dear," he said. "What is it *you* would like to do?"

Trish looked down at the floor. "If not rehab," she said, "maybe just a stay at Cedars." She added that she believed Nicky would probably go to a hospital more readily than he would to another treatment facility.

"Fine," Conrad said as he rose. "I agree with that, then. You'll speak to him, then, about doing it, won't you, Trish? Thank you so much, gentlemen," he added as he shook the hand of each doctor. He then spent a few moments talking with the doctors and thanking them for their help. Afterward, Trish accompanied Conrad out of the parlor into the entryway, where he retrieved his long wool coat, and then out the front door.

Once outside, Trish noticed Conrad's sleek black Cadillac idling in the driveway and, standing next to it, Hugo Mentz, in a distinctive chauffeur's suit complete with cap. "I want to thank you again for everything you have done for Nicky," Conrad said, his eyes filling with tears. "It's nice to see you again, Trish," he added as he embraced her. "Give those kiddies of yours a squeeze for me, will you?"

It was while Trish's arms were wrapped around Conrad that she noticed the brittle and sharp bones in his back. He felt so fragile to her, it was as if he would snap in two if she squeezed too hard. She had always viewed him as being so youthful and energetic; it had never occurred to her that the recent years had taken such a toll on him. Had she been so consumed by her own problems that she hadn't even noticed that her father-in-law had aged so? Conrad had always been so strong and confident. The cruelties of aging had made him, in that moment, seem frail and isolated. It hit her as they stood in the driveway and hugged one another, the emotion in her coming forth so strongly it was all she could do to keep from crying. She suddenly realized that for all he had accomplished, he was alone. He had no wife. He had no companion. Of course, he had his children, but they were grown and had their own lives. He had worked hard for most of his life and had all the money in the world, but as he approached the end of his days, he stood before her old and alone. She had to wonder, what did it all mean? All of that success, all of those triumphs, all of the victories... and for what? With no one to care about him or worry about him the way she cared about and worried about Nicky, Trish suddenly felt sorry for Conrad. Her heart went out to him. "Take good care of yourself, Connie," she told him as she broke their embrace. "Call us if you need anything, okay?"

"Oh, you know me, dear," Conrad said as he slowly eased himself into the backseat of the car. "I'll be just fine." The chauffeur closed the door behind him.

As Trish turned to walk back into the house, she stopped for a moment and looked back over her shoulder. Conrad had lowered the car window and was now smiling broadly at her and waving goodbye. For a second, she didn't know how to react. It was as if neither of them had a care in the world, as if they had just enjoyed a lovely afternoon in each other's company. Then, in a moment as incongruous as any she had ever known, Trish Hilton did the only thing she could think of to do: She smiled and waved back.

Marilyn Hilton's Plea to Elizabeth Taylor

They hadn't seen each other in many years—so many they had actually lost count—but there they were, seated across from each other at a small table in a dark corner of the Polo Lounge of the Beverly Hills Hotel: Marilyn Hilton and her former sister-in-law, Elizabeth Taylor. It was in

October of 1968 that Marilyn called Elizabeth's secretary to ask if it would be possible to have an important conversation with Ms. Taylor. "It's quite urgent," she said. "A family matter."

By this time, Elizabeth Taylor had taken four husbands since being married to Nicky Hilton back in 1950: Michael Wilding, Mike Todd, Eddie Fisher, and her present spouse, Richard Burton (whom she would later divorce, and then remarry). As it happened, when Marilyn called Elizabeth she was in Los Angeles for the funeral of her father, Francis L. Taylor. She had planned to be on Burton's yacht, *Kalizma*, sailing on some far-off sea with her husband and members of their family for the holiday, but those plans were scuttled upon the news of her seventy-two-year-old father's death. Since she was in Los Angeles, she was able to meet with Marilyn in person for lunch.

According to family history, by this time Marilyn had come to believe that Nicky needed something to make him feel alive again, something to live for—which was why she came up with the idea of asking Elizabeth to agree to an annulment of her marriage to him. He would then be able to marry Trish in the Catholic Church, which Marilyn knew would mean the world to him. Now it was just a matter of getting Elizabeth to agree to annul a union that had occurred almost twenty years earlier.

In truth, Elizabeth didn't hold a grudge against Nicky after their divorce, and even for years after. For reasons known only to her, it wasn't until much later that she began to harbor resentment toward him and began talking publicly about the abuse she suffered at his hands. Elizabeth told Marilyn that she was sorry about Nicky's problems. She was also feeling raw at this time, because of the death of the father with whom she'd had an ambivalent relationship. She'd always felt she would have more time with Francis to settle their differences, but now that could never happen. Also adding to her burden was that because of a tubal ligation and then a partial hysterectomy she'd undergone back in September—she called it "the destruction of my womanhood"—she and Richard Burton would not be able to have children of their own. Even though she was already a mother of four, she was heartsick. Therefore, the notions of parenting and of children weighed heavily on her mind. The idea that if something wasn't done to help Nicky his two little boys might grow up without their father was something she felt she couldn't allow to happen.

That said, to annul a marriage that had caused her so much heartache was, Elizabeth felt, comparable to acting as if it had never even happened, that it wasn't an important and, in some ways, defining touchstone in her life. She had suffered greatly during that marriage, she said, and she felt it unfair for everyone to just wipe the slate clean and act like that union to the Hilton heir—and her torment as a result of it—hadn't happened. "I don't know how I feel about this," she finally decided. "I need to think about it, Marilyn. You are asking quite a lot of me."

Elizabeth Makes a Decision

$\mathcal{T}$oward the end of October 1968, just a week after Marilyn Hilton's plea to her and around the time of the premiere of her movie *Secret Ceremony* with Mia Farrow, Elizabeth Taylor called Marilyn Hilton to render her decision. Before giving it to Marilyn, though, she wished to remind her of a time long ago when Marilyn had been of assistance to her.

Elizabeth reminded Marilyn that when she had married Nicky, he was living in a suite at the Bel-Air Hotel. It was small and suitable for one, and Nicky knew it. Still, he hoped that Elizabeth would accept it temporarily while he looked for a bigger place. However, when he brought Elizabeth to the suite, she took one look around and said, "Absolutely not." It was too tiny, she complained, "and I won't even have room for all my wedding gifts!" Because Nicky didn't want them to move in with his father, it was decided that they would move in with Barron and Marilyn for just a month.

Maybe not surprisingly, the time Elizabeth and Nicky spent with Barron and his wife was difficult—and it wasn't even really a full month, because Elizabeth kept going back and forth between the Hilton home and her mother's in Beverly Hills. Right away, Elizabeth was unhappy with the Hilton household staff and took it upon herself to fire a couple of them for not treating her properly. That this eighteen-year-old guest in their home had the temerity to dismiss members of their staff seemed unfathomable to Marilyn. She, of course, turned right around and rehired the employees. But somehow the gossip columnist Sheila Graham got wind of the situation and wrote about it in her column, concluding, "Servants don't usually leave considerate employers." Nicky was embarrassed. "Elizabeth is dragging the Hilton name through the mud," he told Bob Neal. "I feel bad for Marilyn. When was the last time *she* was ever in a gossip column?"

Though Marilyn was upset with Elizabeth for her treatment of the Hiltons' domestic staff, she didn't hold it against the young starlet. In fact, she had a great deal of empathy for her where her marriage was concerned. The two sisters-in-law had many heartfelt conversations about Nicky, and Marilyn—who was only twenty-two herself, four years older than Elizabeth—was always there for Elizabeth with a ready handkerchief to wipe away her tears.

Now, all of these many years later, Elizabeth said she was sorry for the petulant and spoiled way she had acted as a guest in Marilyn's home. She also regretted dragging Marilyn's name into the press. She explained that she had been "a silly young girl," and now realized she'd had no right to be such an ungrateful guest. "I have always remembered how kind you were to me back then," she said, "and now I would like to help you in any way I can." For her part, Marilyn said that Elizabeth had already more than returned the favor when in 1950 she hosted a lovely baby shower for her when she was pregnant with her second son, Steven. Indeed, the two women did have some rather warm history between them.

"I just don't want to hang on to any anger where Nicky is concerned," Elizabeth said, all of this according to a close friend of Marilyn Hilton's who was privy to these communications with Elizabeth. "I don't think it's good. Maybe one of the reasons Nicky is in so such trouble," she opined, "is because he is holding on to unhappiness from his own past." Given what had happened with Nicky's international division, Marilyn couldn't very well disagree. Elizabeth further said that she wasn't sure it would even be possible to obtain an annulment. She wasn't familiar enough with Catholic Church doctrine, she admitted, to know one way or the other.

It would not be easy and there wasn't much time in which to do it, but Marilyn knew that her influential family had not only the power but the money to make things happen. "You just let me and Barron take care of all of the pesky details," Marilyn told Elizabeth. "As long as you will agree to sign the papers when they show up, we will handle everything else."

Elizabeth agreed.

A Grasp at Happiness

*Y*ou'll never believe what has happened," Nicky Hilton was telling Trish. It was the first week of January 1969 and the two were sitting together in the middle of the small Coldwater Canyon Park in Beverly Hills. There were just two small picnic areas with a couple of tables under a shaded arbor. Trish had packed a small lunch for them—two chicken salad sandwiches, some fruit, and a couple of small cartons of milk. They sat facing each other at one of the picnic tables.

By this time, Trish Hilton had decided on a last-ditch, tough-love approach to Nicky's problems: She had filed for divorce and asked him to move out of the house. "I didn't know what else to do," she would explain in subsequent years. "I had a consultation with Dr. Judd Marmor. He said, 'Trish, you're going to lose this man. I would give you nine-out-of-ten odds that if he doesn't get help, he's going to die.' He thought that if I made him leave and told him he could not come back until he went into a treatment facility, he would finally realize how much was at stake, and he would straighten himself out. I was twenty-eight. I listened to what I was told. I told Nicky, 'I love you enough to know that I can't help you. You need treatment.' I regretted it, though. Suffice it to say, this was a mixed-up time for all of us Hiltons."

But certainly not for anyone more than for Nicky as he moved into a small split-level home off of Laurel Canyon Boulevard in the Hollywood Hills. To keep an eye on him, Trish sent with him their cook, an African American woman named Mary whom Nicky liked very much. Trish also vowed to visit him every day, and on this winter day in the park he seemed genuinely happy. He had asked Trish to meet him so that he could give her some good news.

"What's going on?" Trish asked. "What's happened?"

"It's Elizabeth," he said, beaming. "She has given me an annulment. Finally, after all of these years!"

Trish was stunned. "But...but...how?" she managed to say.

The annulment had not been finalized. How could it have? It had only been a short time since Marilyn obtained Elizabeth's permission to proceed. What likely happened is that Marilyn told Nicky about the *possibility* of an annulment and he had misunderstood and thought that the process was completed, when actually it had just begun. It didn't matter, though. The result was the same: Nicky seemed to have a brand-new lease on life. "Marilyn is a saint," he told his wife. "She's an absolute *saint* to have done this for us!" he exclaimed.

"I'll bet Barron had something to do with it, too," Trish offered.

Nicky stopped and mulled that possibility over for a moment. "Do you think?" he asked, his dark eyes wide with astonishment. "Do you think Barron would do this for me?" The anxious expression on his face suggested that he truly wanted to believe it.

"Of course he would," Trish said. "He loves you so much, Nicky." Moreover, she said that Elizabeth and Marilyn would have needed some assistance with something as complex as an annulment. "They would need Barron," she said.

It had been Nicky's nurse, a man named Elliot Mitchell, who had most recently tried to convince Nicky to do whatever he could to make amends with, at the very least, Barron, if not also Conrad. Then, in an effort to smooth things out, the nurse took a meeting with Barron at the Hilton Hotels corporate office in Los Angeles. He told Barron that he believed Nicky didn't have long to live. Barron then contacted Nicky by telephone, and the two had an emotional, heart-to-heart conversation. Later that day, when Elliot Mitchell returned to Nicky's side, he found him crying in bed.

Now, just a short time later, it seemed that Barron had helped his wife, Marilyn, do something for Nicky that was, in Nicky's view, quite monumental. Nicky was so incredulous, he couldn't stop shaking his head in disbelief. "Marilyn did tell me something about a big contribution to the Catholic Church," he said, trying to put the pieces together in his head. He and Trish looked at each other in amazement and then, laughing, said in unison, "*Barron!*"

Though Trish was happy about the news, she didn't quite understand how an annulment held any relevance for them. After all, they'd been married for ten years. Nicky explained, though, that an annulment would mean the two of them could finally marry in the church. "This is *huge* for us, Trish," he said, beaming. "It's a new start for us."

Though Trish wasn't convinced that it was as easy as Nicky seemed to believe, it was difficult for her to resist getting caught up in the moment. As her husband went on about their exciting future together, he began to remind her of someone she once knew. Who was it, though? She couldn't quite put her finger on it. Just whom did he call to mind? It was driving her mad. Then it hit her, and when it did it was such a surprise, she felt the hackles rise on the back of her neck and goose bumps on her arms. He reminded her of...*Nicky Hilton*—the Nicky Hilton of days gone by, the one she hadn't seen in years, the one with whom she had fallen in love. It was as if news of the annulment had brought him back to himself and he was suddenly the man he'd once been—full of life and excited about the future. "Maybe we can have that happy ending we deserve," Nicky told his wife, holding her hands and gazing lovingly into her eyes.

"Do you think?" Trish asked hopefully. "Do you really think so?"

He nodded. "I do," he said with a loving smile. "Just wait and see."

It wasn't meant to be, though. Within just a month, Nicky Hilton would be gone from Trish forever.

The Death of Nicky Hilton

$\mathcal{T}$he funeral took place at St. Paul's Church in Los Angeles on Saturday, February 8, 1969. *Time*, in its obituary, called Conrad Hilton Jr.—Nicky—"a director of his father's 41-national hotel chain and inveterate playboy." Of course, much was made of his infamous marriage to Elizabeth Taylor. There was also a passing reference to the fact that "he later remarried, only once," but there was no mention at all of Trish McClintock Hilton's name. Maybe it wasn't surprising. After all, throughout their ten difficult years of marriage, Trish had always felt alone and unrecognized in her battle to save Nicky Hilton from himself. He was just forty-two when the battle was lost.

The night before the service, a rosary was said for Nicky at St. Paul's. Trish had requested that the casket be open because she had heard a rumor that Nicky had shot himself in the head. It wasn't true, and she wanted there to be no doubt about it. As mourners milled about in the small chamber in which the rosary was to be said over the casket, Barron and Eric walked with Conrad—one on each side, holding him gently by his elbows—up to Nicky's dead body.

Finally, Nicky looked at peace, young and rested. In repose, his face had a sweet innocence to it. He was handsome in a black suit with a white silk tie. As the three Hiltons stood next to the brass casket, Conrad bent over and kissed his son lightly on the forehead. He then lingered over the body for a few moments, his body heaving up and down, overcome with emotion.

"Come on, Dad," Barron was overheard telling him. "Nicky's okay now. Let's go sit down." Conrad shook his head no. He said he wanted to stay next to the casket as others came up to pay their final respects. Always the great host, he said that Nicky would want him to be there to greet the mourners. It was perhaps the last thing he felt he could do for his son. With his death, he wanted to stand near him, be his voice. However, his remaining sons didn't think it was a good idea. He simply wasn't strong enough. They gently led their shaky father away. "It's okay, Dad," Eric said. "Let's just sit down. It's okay."

After everyone left the church, Trish knew she would be seeing Nicky for the last time. She couldn't bear to say her goodbyes alone and called upon her friend Carole Wells Doheny to stand nearby for moral support. Filled with complex emotions, Trish spent an hour with Nicky's body. As she stared down at him, events from his turbulent life played out in her mind. She couldn't get over the fact that Elizabeth Taylor had called both Eric and Barron to extend her condolences. After all she had been through with Nicky, there was still something that bonded Elizabeth to him all these many years after their troubled marriage. Obviously, Trish could relate. Nicky looked so restful and natural lying in the casket, Trish couldn't believe he was gone. "Oh my God, Carole," she gasped, turning to her friend. "He's really dead. It's true. It's true!"

The next morning, sitting in the front pew of St. Paul's with Trish for the requiem mass were Nicky's young sons, nine-year-old Conrad III— also called Nicky—and seven-year-old Michael. Also seated in the front row were his grieving friends Stewart Armstrong, Bob Neal, John Carroll, and Robert Wentworth. In the second row were Nicky's father, Conrad, his brothers, Barron and Eric, and their wives, Marilyn and Pat.

After the service, Conrad wandered around the church, seeming alone and lost. While everyone was making plans to go to Holy Cross Cemetery, where Nicky would be laid to rest in the family plot near his beloved mother, Mary, the millionaire tycoon had somehow wandered off. Ironically, there seemed to be no plan in mind for a man so well-known for orchestrating the most complex hotel openings around the world. "Do you think there's a car for me?" Conrad finally asked a police officer.

"Should there be, sir?" the office asked him.

"I would think so," Conrad said hoarsely. "You see, I'm the father of the deceased."

Witnessing the scene as it unfolded, Nicky's old friend Robert Wentworth walked over to Conrad to help. "This gentleman is Mr. Conrad Hilton," he told the police officer, "owner of the Hilton Hotels Corporation and father of Nicky." The officer raised his eyebrows, nodded, and then went to find out which car would be carrying Conrad to the cemetery. While he was gone, Robert Wentworth took Conrad by the elbow and moved him to a nearby chair, where he had him sit.

"He was in a bit of a daze," Robert recalled of Conrad. "He asked me if I had any children. I told him I had two sons, age ten and twelve. He looked at me with a weary expression and said, 'Enjoy their youth. Those are the most precious years. I have to say, I enjoyed Nicky's youth,' he continued. 'I so loved watching him grow up.' At that point, the officer reappeared to say that Conrad would be riding in a car with Barron and Marilyn. His instructions were to take him to them. Conrad stood up, turned to me, and extended his hand to shake mine. He thanked me for being a good friend to his son for so many years. 'You know, I was always a little jealous of you fellows,' he told me. 'You had so much fun, didn't you?' he said. My heart went out to him as the officer led him away and helped him into a black Caddy."

It had been a massive heart attack that finally claimed Nicky Hilton's life on the morning of Wednesday, February 5. Weeks later, Barron and his sister-in-law Pat would dine together in Los Angeles and have a serious conversation about Nicky's passing. Pat knew she had great latitude with Barron; she could be candid with him. "You know, the thing that hurt him so much was that he felt you took his company away from him," she told Barron. "You took the international division away from him," she said. "Why did you do that, Barron?"

"But I had nothing to do with that, Pat," Barron said in his defense. He elaborated that it had been a board decision, not one he had made unilaterally. He insisted that Nicky understood as much.

"Are you sure?" Pat said.

Barron lowered his head. He was clearly distraught. Finally, he managed to say that if his brother did have a problem with him, he had "forgiven him," adding, "We put all of that aside before he died." He said that he and Nicky had reached an accord. "I loved my brother very, very much, Pat," he concluded.

As Pat looked at her brother-in-law, she recognized that he was as overwhelmed by everything that had happened in recent years as anyone else in the family, and maybe even more so. Resting her hand atop his, she told him that she believed him and was sorry for his loss. "I'm just so happy we could talk about this," she said. "It's been killing me," she concluded.

"Me too," he said sadly.

During the weeks following Nicky's death, Trish Hilton kept replaying the moment she heard of his passing as she tried to make sense of his death. It was 9:30 in the morning when she got the call about Nicky from his accountant, Richard Cohen. Her mother and stepfather were visiting and it was all they could do to keep her from running into the street in hysterics, overcome with grief. She believed then, as she does today, that it wasn't really a heart attack that caused her husband's death. She believes that Nicky accidentally overdosed, and then perhaps suffered a heart attack as a result. Considering all he had been through with alcohol and drugs, her gut told her that they were the real culprits behind his death.

As she had done every night, Trish had visited Nicky the evening before his death. He seemed better than he'd been in recent months, the news of the annulment from Elizabeth Taylor still fresh and still seeming to motivate him toward real change in his life. "I'm sorry," Nicky told Trish. "I've made a real mess of everything, haven't I?" He seemed so bewildered, she didn't know quite how to respond. "I am someone you never have to apologize to," she told him. She tried to assure him that he was going to get better. "You're a Hilton," she continued, trying to be strong. "And while we Hiltons do sometimes make mistakes," she continued, "we never give up."

He chuckled. "So I've been told," he said. Nicky then bowed his head as if he was so ashamed of the way things had turned out, he couldn't even bear to look at his wife. In response, Trish lowered her own head and then leaned in so that her forehead touched his. They sat in that position for a few moments, not saying a word to each other. It was as if there were nothing left to say. Silence was a relief. Finally, Trish sat back and studied her beleaguered husband of the last decade, the father of her two boys. Though he was just a shadow of the handsome man she had long ago met at a racetrack, there was still something about him—a twinkle in his eye, or maybe it was the way he smiled—that continued to remind her of the man she had fallen for so very long ago. He had never lost his little-boy quality. "So...okay," she said, coming out of her daydream. "See you tomorrow, then?" Trish asked.

"Yeah," he answered, seeming tired.

"I love you, Nicky," she reminded him.

"I love you too," he said, forcing a smile.

"See you tomorrow," she said again.

"Yes. For sure. See you tomorrow, Trish."

The Wake at Casa Encantada

*A*bout a hundred people showed up for Nicky's wake at Conrad Hilton's home, Casa Encantada. Eric Hilton and his wife, Pat, stood nearby as Barron spoke to some of those present. Trish Hilton had chosen not to attend the gathering, deciding instead to go back to her own home and spend the time alone with her two children. "We Hiltons believe that God has a plan for all of us," Barron Hilton said. "It's not our place to question God. All we can do is abide by his will, as difficult as that may be." As Barron spoke, his father sat in a corner, staring vacantly into space while chatting with his longtime family friends Carole and Larry Doheny. Marilyn, Barron's wife of twenty-two years, watched him with great concern. "He's just trying to stay in control," she said to Pat Hilton. "He's a man. And worse yet, a Hilton man. And Hilton men have to believe they have everything under control. But this is so hard on him..."

Pat nodded her head in agreement. As Eric's wife, she knew that Marilyn was certainly accurate in her assessment of Hilton men. "That splendid Hilton pride," she observed with a bit of a smile.

Barron really was not that hard to understand. Quite simply, he believed in the Hilton brand with all of his heart and would do anything in his power to protect it. In his mind, the reputation of the company was always of paramount concern. Barron was a company man. Some would say he was cold, distant, not sentimental. Others would say that he was pragmatic and single-minded, pretty much like his father. "How can we best honor what Conrad Hilton has put into place?" was the question that he would ask his children on a regular basis. In fact, he was grooming his son Steven from almost the beginning to take a leadership position in the company. (Steven M. Hilton is today chairman, president, and CEO of the Conrad N. Hilton Foundation.)

By the end of the 1960s, no one could argue with Barron's track record. As president and chief executive of the Hilton Corporation, Barron saw the company's profits double in a three-year period, from $6.6 million in 1966 when Barron was promoted, to $12.2 million in 1969. In that same period, revenues rose 18 percent to $231 million. By 1969, the chain owned, managed, or franchised sixty-seven hotels and inns in fifty-six U.S. cities, with an occupancy rate 10 percent above the industry-wide average of 61 percent. This increase was despite the fact that the average room rate at a Hilton hotel had increased 21 percent, from about $17 a night to about $21. On the New York Stock Exchange, Hilton shares reflected the company's fortunes by leaping from 7 in 1966 to 57½ in 1969—a gain of 80.7 percent. While it was true that the company had lost a fortune by divesting itself of its international division, a decision that both Barron and his father would lament, Barron was never one to live in regret. Instead, he outlined plans that included $50 million worth of expansion at U.S. airports and in Hawaii, where Hilton hotels ran an 80 percent occupancy rate.

Barron, like Conrad, was a man who paid great attention to the day-to-day operations of his hotels. He had reduced the size of the company's payroll, upsetting many employees but enhancing the corporation's bottom line. To save on food preparation costs, he decided to no longer use fresh eggs for salads and sandwiches. Instead, he now bought frozen hard-boiled eggs in footlong rolls. Once thawed, they were ready to slice and serve. Also, by centralizing the purchase of housekeeping items under a subsidiary, Hotel Equipment Corp., Barron saved the parent company money on everything from carpets to cutlery. "Everything is about the bottom line," he said in 1969. "That's where I keep my eye, all the time."

Marilyn and Barron certainly enjoyed an affluent lifestyle, thanks to his position at the company and his salary of about $100,000 a year. That wasn't much; today it would be worth roughly a half million a year. However, it was in his share of booming Hilton stocks where Barron had enjoyed his biggest financial gains. He and Marilyn and their eight children lived in a palatial estate in Holmby Hills with a swimming pool, tennis court, putting green, sauna bath, and film projection room. They also owned a half dozen automobiles, including a black Rolls-Royce convertible, as well as their own private jet and helicopter. Often Barron would fly about the country visiting as many as a half dozen hotels in a single day. In 1969, he was mulling over the idea of buying his own airline that would operate charter flights from major U.S. and European cities to his resort hotels.

"I don't think I have ever seen a marriage quite like theirs," Trish Hilton would say of Marilyn and Barron, who would be married for fifty-six years. "I never heard of them having a fight. I once asked Marilyn what the secret of her long marriage was, and she said, 'I accept him for who he is, and he does the same for me.' What more does any spouse need other than such total and absolute acceptance?"

"I'm the luckiest man in the world," Barron told a small group of friends and relatives at Nicky's wake. "Somehow, God has blessed me with a wife who puts up with me, understands me, and supports me unequivocally," he said as he continued to hold court, with everyone listening intently. His kind words about his supportive spouse made some feel uncomfortable about the fact that Trish was not present for her husband's wake at Casa Encantada. Did she blame the Hiltons for what had happened to Nicky? It certainly seemed that way. "I shudder to think what might have happened to Nicky if Trish hadn't come along," Barron said, maybe picking up on the awkward moment. He said that Trish had been, as he put it, "a godsend," especially during recent times.

As everyone spoke, Zsa Zsa Gabor fanned herself and looked unwell. She was grief-stricken by Nicky's death. He meant a lot to her. At one point, she was so inconsolable that Francesca, now twenty, was seen talking softly to her, holding her close. As all of this was going on, Conrad just sat in a corner and listened, occasionally nodding but looking sad. Though Barron and Eric Hilton would both continue to work for the Hilton Corporation, their primary concern for the next decade would be the welfare of their aging father. Both had noticed that Conrad was now quieter, more reflective than he'd been in the recent past. Eric would share with Pat his concern that Nicky's death had somehow extinguished the fire that had always been in Conrad's belly.

Nicky's widow, Trish, empathized with Conrad's great sense of loss; of course, she felt it too, keenly. "Things were never quite the same for me after losing Nicky," she says. "My heart was broken, and the next ten years would be difficult. I had a hard time dealing with it, and then raising my children as a single parent."

Trish says that she did remarry, an attorney from Wayzata, Minnesota. "I don't think I was in love with him, though," she recalled, "as much as I just felt that my children—who were getting to be fifteen, maybe sixteen—needed a father. However, it didn't work out, and we divorced after about six years. I didn't have any more children, and I never would—not without Nicky."

To this day, Trish, who lives in Palm Beach, Florida, receives a courtesy discount on accommodations at any Hilton Hotel. "I have what they call a fifty-dollar stay, which, obviously, means I don't have to pay more than fifty dollars for any room, anywhere." These days, she counts Barron Hilton's daughter Hawley, who also lives in Palm Beach with her husband, as one of her dearest friends. They see each other on a weekly basis. Of course, Trish remains close to the sons she had with Nicky, Conrad III and Michael Otis. It's also worth noting that Conrad N. Hilton III is on the board of directors of the Conrad N. Hilton Foundation.

"I must say that in the last twenty, twenty-five years, I have been very happy," Trish Hilton said. "I haven't had what you would call an exciting life after Nicky, but it's been peaceful and I've been content. After all of the pain I went through with Nicky, I somehow came out of it a better person. I will never forget Nicky Hilton, though," she concluded wistfully. "He will always be the great love of my life."

PART TEN

Secrets

Conrad's Warning to Zsa Zsa

$\mathcal{D}$uring the final years of Nicky Hilton's life, Conrad Hilton was also coping—as always—with turmoil presented by circumstances surrounding another child, his daughter, Francesca, as well as her mother, Zsa Zsa Gabor. In August 1971, things took a bad turn between Conrad and Francesca, and it's likely that at least some of the reason for the disintegration of their relationship had to do with the ongoing irritation of Zsa Zsa.

First, a little backstory.

In October 1968, Zsa Zsa was in the middle of negotiations for a massive advertising campaign for Smirnoff vodka. Unhappy with the work being done by her representation, she asked Conrad to step in and close the deal for her. She offered to give him 10 percent of the total she would be paid. In response, he told her that because he wasn't a licensed theatrical agent, he would not be able to officially represent her. However, he offered to assist her agent in closing the deal.

For a period of about three months, Zsa Zsa was on the telephone with Conrad almost every day, constantly asking one question or another. Finally, when it was over and the deal was struck to the tune of $250,000, a huge amount of money for the time, (equivalent to more than a million dollars today), she was grateful. Conrad didn't take a percentage either, which she felt was extremely generous of him. For the final campaign, Zsa Zsa was photographed dripping with rubies and diamonds in a bouffant cream-colored gown. *"Don't darling me if it's not Smirnoff"* ran the ad copy under her stunning photograph. "Your guests expect Smirnoff Vodka just as Zsa Zsa does!"

In some ways, Zsa Zsa felt that the Smirnoff negotiation had brought her closer to Conrad. He disagreed, to the point where he was just tired of her and needed some time away from her. However, she had gotten accustomed to calling and chatting, and she rather enjoyed it.

This same thing had happened five years earlier when Conrad helped Zsa Zsa negotiate a $100,000 deal to endorse the new Paper-Mate Pen with ad copy that read, "Zsa Zsa Gabor says, 'C'est Magnifique . . . no more ink-stained hands or clothes with my Paper-Mate Pen!'" At that time, after the deal was consummated, Conrad stopped returning her calls or responding to her many messages. Now he again decided on that course of action.

Conrad's silence bothered Zsa Zsa more than anything. Every time he didn't call her back, her anger ratcheted up a notch. Finally, after three weeks, she was fit to be tied, or, as she put it, "tied to be fit." Of course, it wasn't really his phone etiquette that exasperated her so much. It was everything else she felt he had ever done to her, all sorts of incidents from their troubled past colliding with one another in her head, building and building and building until she was fairly ready to explode. If he wasn't going to speak to her, fine. She would send him a telegram—and what a telegram it would be!

In Zsa Zsa's telegram of October 29, 1968, she charged that Conrad was not a good father to Francesca, and that Francesca didn't know how to feel about him. She hoped that Francesca would be included in Conrad's will, she noted, because "it would only be right." In Zsa Zsa's estimation, there were only three people in his life who really loved him—she, Olive Wakeman, and his son Nicky. (It was interesting that she left Francesca off the list.) Then, truly hitting below the belt considering the TWA merger, she said that Conrad's behavior toward Nicky and even Olive had given them both "nervous breakdowns." She added that he was "very cheap" and that, as his ex-wife, one would think that she could at least stay at his hotels without charge. She went on to indicate that he wasn't so miserly when it mattered to him most, and, she alleged, he had *paid* the pope a million dollars to be dubbed a Knight of Malta. She reminded him that "I am no longer the naïve little girl you married so long ago. I am a grown woman now. Stop treating me like a child." She closed by reminding him that since his first wife, Mary Saxon, had died, Zsa Zsa was still married to him in the eyes of the church. Therefore, he should have "some respect" for her. She stated that she was sending her attorney a copy of the telegram, and, moreover, she would forward to him any response from Conrad, "so you should watch what you say to me because he will be reading it, not just me."

By the time Conrad Hilton finished reading Zsa Zsa's long telegram, he was fuming—no surprise there. He had just assisted her with the Smirnoff deal, made a nice fortune for her, didn't ask for a single penny in return—and this was how she repaid him? "Gratitude was never her strong suit," he said to his attorney, Myron Harpole. "When will I learn?"

Conrad immediately dictated his own angry missive to Olive Wake-man, who feverishly typed it up. It was sent by special delivery to Zsa Zsa's home at 938 Bel-Air Road in Los Angeles.

In Conrad's letter to "Zsazsa," dated October 29, 1968, he acknowl-edged receipt of her "libelous telegram" and said that he now wished to set the record straight with her. However, before he did so, he wanted to give her fair warning that she should carefully consider the wisdom of dragging Francesca into their battles. He didn't want to hurt Francesca, he wrote, and he hoped that Zsa Zsa would think about her daughter's future before further antagonizing him. No one, he noted, knew better than she did about what really transpired all those years ago in New York when Francesca was conceived, and, he added, "I have preserved the proofs of what I say here." Though Conrad didn't specify what he could prove, he warned Zsa Zsa not to push him to bring forth his evidence. In fact, he suggested that she might want to have a talk with her attorney, Don Rubin, to fill him in on what had happened and then ask for his counsel. Regarding Zsa Zsa's threat to give Rubin a copy of the telegram she had sent, Conrad countered with a promise of his own that he was going to forward his response to his own lawyer—the same one who had finalized their divorce. He further stated that his attorney would be eager to meet with hers anytime.

Conrad then went on to address some of the specific points Zsa Zsa had made in her telegram:

Where his hotels were concerned, he said, her real problem was that she just wanted to stay in them free of charge. Even when he gave her a discount, she wasn't happy. She had, he reminded her, taken months to pay a recent bill for her time at the Beverly Hilton.

He also wrote, "You speak about only three people in the world who love me as far as you know. It is you, Olive and Nick. Please take your name off of this list." He also added that it was not true that he had given Olive and Nick "a nervous breakdown."

What seemed to have upset Conrad most—at least according to the tone of his missive—was Zsa Zsa's allegation that he had paid the pope millions of dollars for the title Knight of Malta. He wrote that this was "a big lie."

He then addressed Zsa Zsa's allegation that the Catholic Church still recognized his marriage to her, especially now that his first wife, Mary, was dead. In fact, he reminded Zsa Zsa that the church hadn't recognized their marriage years ago, and it still didn't. He reminded her that they had been wed in a civil ceremony in Santa Fe, not in the Catholic Church.

Conrad finished his letter by saying he was sorry to have to take such a harsh tone with Zsa Zsa, but she had left him no choice. He closed by writing, "For the sake of Francesca, I think you should be very careful in your statements in the future."

A Shocking Revelation

Conrad Hilton and the rest of the family spent the next two and a half years—1969 into 1971—dealing with Nicky Hilton's death and its aftermath. The Hiltons did what they could to go on with their busy and productive lives, coping with their grief each in their own way and without much discussion about it. With the passing of this time, however, the tense situation between Zsa Zsa and Conrad did not get any better. She spent most of the time working in Europe, but she was still a constant pressure in his life with heated phone calls and telegrams, the usual Zsa Zsa Gabor turmoil over one thing or another.

On Friday, August 13, 1971, Conrad was himself scheduled to go to Europe on business. The night before his departure, he reviewed his itinerary with his assistant, Olive Wakeman, who now lived in a stylishly appointed guesthouse on the property of Casa Encantada. As they spoke, butler Hugo Mentz came into the study to announce that Francesca had shown up at the house and wished to speak to Conrad. Conrad was delighted; he had wanted to say goodbye to her anyway.

Though he had his problems with her mother, Conrad tried his best to maintain some sort of peaceful relationship with Francesca, who was now twenty-four. He still kept her at arm's length, but when he was in her company he acted warmly toward her.

As she got older, Francesca continued to be much unlike her notorious mother, Zsa Zsa. She wasn't over the top or extravagantly adorned, yet she was pretty, smart, and funny. She had an ironic sense of humor and always made Conrad laugh, especially when she joked about her eccentric mom. It was easy to make fun of Zsa Zsa, after all; the Hungarian glamour queen certainly gave Francesca plenty to work with in terms of comedy material. Being the daughter of Zsa Zsa Gabor continued to be difficult, though. After Nicky's death, Zsa Zsa pulled herself together and went on to replace Julie Harris on Broadway in the show *Forty Carats*. Happily, she was a smash hit in the show—her only Broadway appearance—but it did take its toll on her already turbulent relationship with Francesca. Zsa Zsa was more preoccupied and busier than ever, even after the show closed; she also introduced her own fragrance that year, called Zig-Zag.

On this day in August, mother and daughter had apparently endured a real blowout. By the time Francesca showed up at her father's home, she was distraught and in tears. As soon as she saw him, she ran into Conrad's arms.

"What's the matter, my dear?" he asked, startled at her troubled emotional state.

"It's Mother," Francesca said through her tears.

"What happened?" Conrad asked, holding her.

"It's not important," Francesca answered, all of this according to her later testimony. "I just need your help, Dad. Can I *please* move in here with you?"

This was actually the third time Francesca had sought to move into Casa Encantada, the first having been back in 1966, and then again in 1968. She was denied by Conrad both times. She had never even so much as stayed in the house overnight on any occasion. After having already been so rejected, one can only imagine how difficult it was for her to again broach the subject.

Conrad pulled away, seemingly taken aback at being asked the question once again. Looking surprised, he said, "But you know that's not possible, Francie."

"But why?"

"Because...because..." He fumbled for words. "Because there's just not enough *room* here in this house," he finally stated. It was a flimsy excuse and they both knew it. Francesca stared at him for a moment. "But it's just you here with Hugo, Maria [his wife], and Olive," Francesca said, "and this place is so huge!" (Actually, besides Hugo, Maria, and Olive, there were eight other servants also in residence at the property.)

"Well, I'm very sorry, dear, but it's not possible," Conrad said, hold-

Nicky and Trish with their two sons, Conrad III and Michael Otis, in April of 1962. *(Allan Grant//Time Life Pictures/Getty Images)*

Rat Pack Cool, father and sons: (left to right) Barron, Conrad, Nicky, and Barron Hilton at the Aurora Hilton Inn in March 1960. *(Hospitality Industry Archives, Conrad N. Hilton College, University of Houston.)*

Zsa Zsa and Francesca (with their Spaniel puppy, Paul McCartney) at London's Heathrow Airport, September 1968. *(Tony Wallace/Associated Newspapers/Rex Features)*

Nicky Hilton—seen here with his staff—became head of the international division of the Hilton chain in 1966. (*Bettmann/Corbis / AP Images*)

As bellhops and a desk clerk look on, Nicky greets guests at the Bel-Air hotel. (*Bettman/Corbis/AP Images*)

Barron Hilton and his lovely wife, Marilyn, always made such a stunning couple. Here they pose at a party for opera star (and, later, gossip columnist) Cobina Wright. Nicky Hilton is in the background. (© *1978 Wallace Seawell/mptvimages .com*)

Nicky and Conrad, formally dressed for another hotel opening. When Conrad made the decision to sell the company's international division, it caused a serious breach with Nicky. However, the two reconciled before Nicky's sudden death, in 1969. (*Photo by Donald Uhrbrock//Time Life Pictures/Getty Images*)

Conrad fell in love and took a third wife, Mary Frances Kelly—better known as "Frannie"—on December 21, 1976, four days before his eighty-eighth birthday. Frances was sixty-one. (*Stella Kelly*)

Zsa Zsa and Conrad. There may have been years of tension between them having to do with money and power, but they did share many laughs. (© 1978 Wallace Seawell/mptvimages.com)

Chip off the ol' block: Conrad shortly before his death, with his son Barron. (© 1978 Gunther/mptvimages.com)

Conrad Hilton died on January 3, 1979, at the age of ninety-one. He had led an incredible life, there was no doubt about it. However, years of turmoil would follow his death, caused mostly by his last wishes that family members not prosper from his wealth. (AP Photo/Wally Fong)

The first to contest Conrad's will was Francesca Hilton. (Bill Howard/Associated Newspapers/Rex Features)

Aligned with Francesca in her fight against the estate, Zsa Zsa would give three lengthy legal depositions. Shattering her enigmatic facade, she exposed her most private secrets in the hope that Conrad's will might be overturned. *(© 1978 John Engstead/mptvimages.com)*

Zsa Zsa and Francesca on August 16, 1983. By this time Francesca had lost her case against the Hilton estate. Mother and daughter had been through a lot—but they still had each other. *(Ron Galella/Wire Image.)*

Barron Hilton—seen here on Capitol Hill with President Ronald Reagan in January 1985—would fare much better than Francesca in his own claim over Conrad's will. (*AP Photo/Budd Gray*)

The Hiltons—the Next Generation—at the World Music Awards in Monte Carlo in May 2010: Barron's son Rick Hilton (far right) and his wife, Kathy, are seen here with three of their children: Barron, Paris, and Nicky. (*Anthony Harvey/Picture Group via AP Images*)

Paris Hilton launches her fragrance, Tease, dressed as Marilyn Monroe, in Los Angeles in August 2010. (*Picture Perfect/Rex Features*)

Three generations of Hilton men: Barron (far left) with his son Rick (far right), with Rick's son—Barron's grandson—also named Barron. (*Amanda Edwards/ Getty Images*)

Sisters Paris and Nicky Hilton pose at a gala on December 5, 2012. (*Mitch Levy/ Globe Photos*)

The most famous Hilton today is socialite and fashionista Paris Hilton, photographed here with her grandfather Barron Hilton, at Dan Tana's restaurant on April 14, 2010, in Los Angeles. Many people have said that Paris has the entrepreneurial spirit of her great-grandfather, Conrad Hilton. (*Jean Baptiste Lacroix/ WireImage*)

Conrad Hilton, 1887–1979. (*Bachrach/Getty Images*)

ing his ground, all of this according to Francesca's testimony about the conversation. "You know, Francie, you have always lived with your mother, and you have always been her responsibility," he concluded.

"But..."

"I'm sorry, my dear, but that is my final word on the matter."

"I was also hoping that maybe you could lend me a little money," she added, pushing forward anyway.

"No," he said in an even tone, trying his best to control himself. "I'm very sorry."

At that, Francesca became emotional. "It's so unfair," she said. She began to detail the long and troubled history she had with Conrad and how he often had not been there for her when she needed him. Now he had a real chance to prove himself to her, she said, and if he loved her, the time had come for him to show it. She was desperate, feeling alone... and putting him on the spot.

Conrad stared at Francesca, seeming at a loss. And that's when it happened. For her entire life, Conrad had never explained his reasons for keeping Francesca at bay, mainly because he wanted to protect her, because he loved her, and because he knew that she had been born into a troubled, damaged situation that was not of her making. Francesca was an innocent victim in all of it, and he felt that she shouldn't have to suffer. Family mattered to him, and she and her mother were part of the family. Of course, some in his inner circle felt that he was also protecting himself and his hotel chain from any hint of scandal, and it stands to reason that this could also have been the case. But now Francesca had backed him into a corner like never before as she demanded to know the reason for the distance he had placed between them for as long as she could remember. Suddenly, likely as much out of frustration as from anger—and, who knows, but maybe his feelings about Zsa Zsa had something to do with it too?—Conrad finally broke down. "I'm not even sure I'm your father, *that's* why," he declared. "*I'm not even sure I'm your father!*"

Francesca stood before Conrad, shocked and confused. "What are you saying?" she asked. "*Of course* you're my father! Why would you say that?"

"I don't think we should discuss this any further," Conrad said, trying to shut things down. Clearly, he did not know how to handle the situation. He then said what he often said when he didn't know what to do about Francesca: "Why don't you talk to Olive?" And with that, Conrad left the room as quickly as his legs would take him.

Olive Wakeman had been standing behind Francesca, watching as the volcanic scene unfolded. She rushed over to the young woman and embraced her. But Francesca just stared at Olive, pale, empty, and drained. "There must be something *wrong* with Dad," she finally said as she slowly came back to her senses. She noted that in all of their years together, Conrad had never before said anything like that to her. They'd never really quarreled. He was certainly never unkind to her. "Is he okay, Olive?" Francesca asked, concerned. "Is he sick?" she asked. "He must be sick," she decided.

"He's been under a lot of pressure, dear," Olive said as she walked Francesca down the hallway. "Come back tomorrow," she said, as she showed Francesca to the front door. "We love you, Francie. It's going to be okay."

Francesca's Requests

The next morning, August 14, Conrad Hilton left for his European trip. He was upset about what had occurred with Francesca, and before taking his leave, he told Olive Wakeman that he needed time not only to think but to pray over the entire matter. He seemed angry at himself for having blurted out what he had to Francesca. Rarely did he lose his temper. He said he couldn't even remember the last time he had done so. Even during all of the explosive times with Nicky, he had managed to keep it mostly in check. Even when Zsa Zsa pushed him to the limit, he couldn't remember a time when he truly lost it with her. He had never been the kind of man to allow his emotions to get the best of him. In fact, he'd always prided himself on being able to find a way to keep his head about him when others around him were losing theirs. Why, then, had he let things get so out of control with Francesca? When he discussed the matter with Myron Harpole, the attorney said, "Well, I don't blame you, Connie. Two words: Zsa Zsa. You don't need a carbon copy of your ex-wife in this house." It was the wrong thing to say. *"That's not true, and you know it,"* Conrad said, pounding his fists on his desk in another rare display of anger; yes, this *was* a touchy subject. He was right, of course. Francesca was certainly nothing like her mother.

When Olive mentioned that Francesca would be coming by the house again today to talk to her, Conrad asked her to see what she could do to make "Francie" feel a little better. Olive promised that she would try.

That afternoon, Francesca arrived at Casa Encantada. Olive greeted her warmly. The two went into the kitchen, sat at the table, and enjoyed light seafood salads for lunch. "So, what exactly do you need, Francesca?" Olive asked.

Francesca seemed exhausted, as if she hadn't slept in days. She said that what she really needed was to get out of her mother's house. It was too difficult living with Zsa Zsa, she explained, and that's why she wanted to move into Casa Encantada. However, she now realized that her father didn't want her there, she continued, "so, I was thinking that perhaps I could get a small apartment somewhere. Just a one-bedroom."

Olive nodded patiently.

"And maybe Dad could get me a small car so I don't have to use one of Mother's," Francesca said. "And maybe he could give me an allowance of a thousand dollars a month until I can get on my feet?" she asked. She waited for a response, but one was not forthcoming. Olive knew this terrain well. She must have also known how these requests would be taken by Conrad. "Okay, I will see what I can do, then," she said.

"Would you, *please*?" Francesca asked urgently. "It's not a lot to ask, is it?"

Olive didn't want to commit to anything, even to a vague opinion about the requests. She just nodded and tried to appear as understanding as possible.

"Just in Case"

On Sunday night, September 19, 1971, Conrad Hilton returned to the United States. The next morning, Francesca called to see how he was doing, how his trip had been, and whether or not he had talked to Olive Wakeman regarding the requests she'd made a couple weeks earlier. He said he hadn't had the opportunity to talk to Olive, but that he would do so later that day. He would get back to her, he promised. He still felt very badly about the altercation with Francesca and hadn't come to any sort of peace around it. He simply wished it hadn't happened.

That afternoon, when Conrad finally sat down with Olive, she told him about Francesca's requests. "She wants us to subsidize an apartment for her," Olive said, specifically using the word "us," perhaps thinking it might take some of the edge off the request.

He didn't say anything. Olive waited a beat. "And she wants us to buy her a small automobile," she added. She waited.

Nothing.

"And she would like a monthly stipend of a thousand dollars." She waited.

Nothing.

"Call Bentley," Conrad finally said. He was referring to his longtime attorney, G. Bentley Ryan, "and see if he can get over here, will you, please, Olive?" Olive rose from her chair and went into the other room to do as she was told.

Less than an hour later, Bentley Ryan appeared at Casa Encantada. The three adjourned to the study, Conrad behind his desk, his assistant and attorney sitting on the other side of it. "I'm afraid things have gotten a little out of hand with Francie," Conrad said, this according to Olive's later testimony. "It is not her fault, though. None of this is her fault," he conceded. He then filled Bentley Ryan in on what had happened with Francesca prior to his European business trip. Ryan seemed quite surprised by the story. He said that the unpleasant scene was probably "inevitable," but still, it made him sad.

"Well, what do we do, now?" Bentley asked.

"Hell if I know," Conrad said.

"We could just give Francie what she wants," Olive suggested. Then, advocating for her like never before, Olive pointed out that Francesca didn't "deserve" the trouble she now faced. She offered to go with her to find an apartment in order to make sure it was a reasonable rent, and she would also make certain that any automobile purchased was affordable. She could take care of all of it, she said. Just leave it to her.

"No, Olive," Conrad decided, "though it's nice of you to offer.

Instead," he added, "would you take a letter?" Of course, she had her writing pad with her. Conrad then dictated a lengthy letter to Francesca.

In Conrad's missive to Francesca, dated September 20, 1971, he began by noting that despite the work that had piled up on his desk in his absence, he had still taken the time to talk to Olive about her. However, before addressing Francesca's requests, he wanted her to know that the conversation he'd had with her before his trip had troubled him deeply. In thinking about it while he was gone, he realized that it was the first time the two had had any sort of "highly unpleasant" exchange. It had been nagging at him, he said. He then got to the point of his letter.

Conrad was aware, he said, that Francesca had asked him to subsidize an apartment and an automobile for her in order that she might be able to obtain some freedom from Zsa Zsa. Also, he understood that she had requested a stipend of a thousand dollars a month. But after thinking about it, he said, he had decided *not* to grant her requests. He explained that "I am neither morally and certainly not legally obligated to you for any reason, whatsoever." While he was quite aware, he said, that his decision might "destroy our friendship," he sincerely hoped that this would not be the case. He had enjoyed her company over the years, he said, and often reflected on their times together, such as a trip they had once taken to New York during which Francesca had revealed herself as being particularly smart and insightful. Still, his mind was made up, and he wasn't going to justify his position to her. As was well-known by all, she had always been Zsa Zsa's responsibility, and he didn't want that to change. He believed—though he admitted that he couldn't be absolutely sure—that Zsa Zsa had the finances to support Francesca, and that she wished to continue to do just that.

In closing, Conrad noted that if Francesca could accept his decision and never again demand money from him, he would be more than happy to continue a relationship with her such as the one they had enjoyed prior to their recent difficult meeting. He added that he had only the best of wishes for her and no anger toward her. "On the contrary, I send you my love," he wrote, "which I hope will be reciprocated." He signed it, "Daddy."

After Conrad finished dictating the letter, there was only silence. It was as if Olive and Bentley didn't know what to say about it. Finally, Bentley spoke up. "You sure about this, Connie?" he said.

"Yes," Conrad said. "I'm sure." Then, thinking ahead should Francesca one day pursue the matter, Conrad decided to dictate *another* letter to Olive, this one addressed to her and to Bentley. "And I'm afraid this particular letter will test the bounds of your discretion," he told them before beginning his second dictation.

In Conrad's second correspondence, this one to Olive and Bentley— also dated September 20, 1971—he noted that he had just dictated a letter to Francesca with their assistance. He said that nothing in that first letter should alter any aspect of his will where Francesca was concerned. He added that Olive and Bentley well knew, since they had both been present in his life at the time, that "I am not and could not be the father of Francesca." He further explained that the only reason he had ever allowed Francesca and Zsa Zsa to use the Hilton name was because he didn't want Francesca to grow up feeling that she was an illegitimate child. Moreover, in an effort to make her feel loved, he had always addressed her as "daughter." But in fact, he maintained, he was *not* her biological father, and also had never adopted her. Therefore, if the issue was ever raised in the future, he wished to have Olive and Bentley testify to his feelings about the paternity of Francesca, and as to why he had made the decisions he'd made regarding her, going all the way back to her birth. As far as he could remember, he concluded, Francesca was born "almost a year and a half after I separated from Zsazsa and after which I had no sexual relations with my former wife." He signed it, "Conrad N. Hilton."

After the second letter was dictated, Olive sat in her chair and read it over repeatedly as if trying to reconcile it. With so many closely held secrets now being memorialized on paper forever, it must have been hard for her to take it all in. "Why don't you go into the other room, type that up, and then bring it back to us," Conrad suggested, pulling Olive out of her thoughts. Though personally upset about what had happened with Francesca, Conrad decided to handle it as he would a business matter, obviously fearing that, one day, it might become just that.

When Olive left the study, Conrad and Bentley just sat staring at each other, neither saying a word. It was as if there was nothing left to say. A few moments later, Olive returned with the letter, now typed neatly on Hilton Hotels Corporation stationery. She handed it to Conrad for his final review. He read it carefully. Then he read it again. He signed it.

He folded it. He opened his top desk drawer and took out an envelope. He put the letter in the envelope, sealed it, and handed it to G. Bentley Ryan. "Hold on to this," he told the lawyer. "Just in case."

"Just in case of what?" Ryan asked.

"Just in case," Conrad repeated. He looked hard into his attorney's eyes as if to convey that no further explanation was needed.

The Challenge

*I*t was February 1973. More than a year had passed since Conrad Hilton's letter to Francesca Hilton and the one he then dictated to his assistant and lawyer for safekeeping, "just in case." While Francesca's reaction to his missive is not known, Zsa Zsa made her position clear about it. She was upset that things had gotten so out of hand. Who knew what had possessed Conrad that night? she told Francesca. There was no telling what was going through his head. Maybe he was just tired. Maybe his age was showing, she suggested. Or maybe he had been pushed too hard and just misspoke. At a loss, she finally offered, "People are complicated, Francie. Your father loves you. That's all I know. Now, for the sake of our family, please, you must let this go."

Summoning all her resolve, Francesca did as her mother suggested: She went on with her life and did whatever she could to keep the peace with Conrad. "Our relationship was exactly as it had been before our heated discussion," Francesca recalled. "He never again said or did anything which caused me to believe he doubted that he was my father. He continued to refer to himself as 'Daddy,' and continued to treat me as his daughter."

Now it was the evening of February 21, 1973. Conrad Hilton, eighty-five, was standing in the library of Carole Wells Doheny's home in Brentwood, California. He had come to offer his condolences over the tragic suicide death of her husband, Larry.

It had happened a week earlier. Carole had been visiting with Barron and Marilyn Hilton on Valentine's Day when she became alarmed that she could not reach her husband by telephone. Because he had suffered three heart attacks in the last year, she was frantic with worry. She raced to their home, where she found him dead. He had taken a purposeful overdose of prescription medications.

Now, barely a week later, a still shaken Carole Wells Doheny was surprised to find Conrad Hilton at her door, asking to speak to her. She hadn't seen much of him in recent years. "Oh, my dear Connie, you look like you could use a drink," she said. "No, thank you," he told her. "I'm fine, my dear."

Carole, with her two young sons in tow—Sean, three, and Ryan, one—studied Conrad with great apprehension as he moved uncertainly across the floor to a nearby chair and sat down. "So what do you think about this Watergate scandal?" he asked Carole. He was of course referring to the break-in at the Democratic National Committee headquarters at the Watergate office complex in Washington six months earlier, and President Richard Nixon's subsequent attempt to conceal his involvement. "Do you think Nixon is in trouble?" he asked. Carole said she didn't know, but it was certainly possible. Conrad then said that he had friends in Washington who had told him that more would be revealed in the coming months, and he was afraid that it wasn't going to be good for the president. In just five months' time, recordings would be discovered in the White House that would ultimately implicate Nixon in the cover-up.

Finally, after a few more minutes of small talk, Conrad got to the point of his visit. "I just wanted you to know how much it devastates me that Larry has left you with these two lovely boys," he said as he watched her sons play in front of the fireplace. He said that he could never have done it, he could never leave his sons without their father. "Imagine the great despair Larry must have felt to have done such a thing," he observed.

With the loss of Nicky still weighing so heavily and the problems caused by Francesca still ongoing, the subject of fathers and their children was clearly on Conrad's mind. He allowed that it was terrible for a child to lose a parent, but for a parent to lose a child was "simply unbearable." With that comment, Conrad's eyes welled with tears. Obviously, the passing of the years had not diminished his grief in the least. He shook his head in despair. "I wish I could go back," he said. "I would do things very differently."

Carole couldn't help herself; she simply had to ask the question: "What would you do differently, Connie?" she wondered.

"Of all my sons, Nicky always shone the brightest," Conrad began with a nostalgic smile. Bathed in the soft light emanating from the fireplace, he seemed more fragile to Carole than ever before. He said that Barron and Eric were both like him, always with their noses to the grindstone. He was especially proud of Eric at this time, he noted, because immediately after Nicky's death, Eric became instrumental in the creation of the Conrad N. Hilton College of Hotel and Restaurant Management (still supported today by the Conrad N. Hilton Foundation). Ground had already been broken for the Hilton University of Houston hotel. Eric had proven himself as a Hilton, Conrad said. And of course, Barron was his father's son in every way. "But Nicky," he concluded, "for all his faults, *he* really knew how to live."

Conrad then talked about Nicky's untamed, controversial youth, his turbulent marriage to Elizabeth Taylor, and his reputation with the ladies. He shared with Carole many stories and secrets about Nicky that she promised never to reveal to a single soul—and she never has. He also talked about his son's successful second marriage to Trish and how throughout it all—the bad years and the good—he had remained conflicted about Nicky's work ethic. "Zsa Zsa always felt I was in competition with Nicky," he continued. "That wasn't true, though," he concluded. "How could I ever compete with Nicky? He had it all over me, didn't he?"

Carole nodded. Though Conrad never really answered the question of what he would have done differently, she understood his torment. "I guess the great irony is that you wanted his life," she said, "and all he ever wanted was your approval, Connie. That is just so sad." She instantly regretted stating the obvious, especially when Conrad bowed his head and, much to her astonishment, began to shed tears. So moved by Conrad's unabashed display of heartache was Carole's son Ryan that the tot took several jerky steps toward the old man and stared up at him. Then, just as he was about to tumble backward onto his bottom, he wrapped his little arms around the hotelier's leg to steady himself. "Well, my goodness! Will you just look at that?" Conrad exclaimed. It was a powerful moment, compelling and appropriate in its symbolism. Regarding with affection the youngster at his knee, Conrad ran his fingers through the boy's soft hair several times. "Maybe I should have spent more time with Nicky when he was this lad's age," he said. He said that it was easy to lose sight of family when "you're all in business together. I have always understood the fundamentals of power," he said, "but the fundamentals of *family*, those are..." His voice trailed off.

Carole rose and walked over to Conrad. Standing behind him, she gently put her hands on his shoulders. She observed that, as parents, they had always done the best they could for their children. She knew in her heart of hearts that her husband loved her and his boys, and it was that knowledge that sustained her, she said, patting Conrad's shoulders. "Nicky loved you, too, Connie," she continued. "All of your children do. You must know that."

"Oh, yes, I do," Conrad said. He then revealed to Carole that he'd had a brief conversation with Nicky the night before his death during which the two proclaimed their affection for one another. He said it was strange, as if Nicky knew he was not long for this world. "He told me he loved me and I told him I loved him, too," Conrad recalled. He said that he then hung up the phone while wondering to himself how many years it had been since they'd said that to each other—and he didn't know the answer to that question.

"Then you must remember that last conversation," Carole told Conrad, "because it will help you get through the years ahead." Still standing behind him, she pulled Conrad in closer. "Your friends and family will help you, Connie," she told him. "We are all here for you."

Joined in their mutual grief, Carole and Conrad spent the next couple of hours gazing absently at the flames while remembering their lost loved ones and talking about the importance of family. From talking to him that night, she recognized that one thing about Conrad Hilton had not changed: He was still a man of great faith who believed that his sins were forgiven as swiftly as they were acknowledged and then confessed to his God. He also believed that, by the grace of his Lord, it—*all of it*—would somehow be made better. In other words, it was in God's hands now. That said, she also knew that he would mourn the death of his son until the day that he too would be gone from this world. There was nothing she could do about that, either. That would be Conrad Hilton's cross to bear.

PART ELEVEN

Frances

At Long Last Love

$\mathcal{A}$re you ready?" Conrad Hilton asked the attractive woman at his side. The two were in the backseat of his sleek black 1976 Cadillac Fleetwood.

"I am," she replied enthusiastically.

"Okay, here goes." He grinned. "Hail Mary, full of grace," he started, now bowing his head. "The Lord is with thee."

"Blessed art though amongst women," she continued, her head also lowered, "and blessed is the fruit of thy womb, Jesus."

It was a Sunday morning in November 1977 and life had taken an unexpected turn for Conrad. Married to two enormously different types of women and divorced for many years, Conrad was about to embark on a new life's journey he dared not hope for at this late stage of the game—real romance. About to turn eighty-eight in December, on this day Conrad found himself cozying up to an elegantly mature and still pretty woman who was more than twenty-five years his junior, Mary Frances Kelly, age sixty-one. The two were being driven to a Catholic church in Beverly Hills by her brother, William P. Kelly, who was visiting from Illinois and had volunteered to take them to mass. The couple, who had been dating for more than a year, customarily enjoyed playing out a little ritual on their way to church; both devout Catholics, they would recite a prayer familiar to both of them as a way of beginning their day of worship.

"Holy Mary, Mother of God," Conrad continued, "pray for us sinners—"

"Now and at the hour of our death," she added.

Then, in the spirit of comfortable solidarity, they concluded, "Amen." At that, they raised their heads and smiled unabashedly at one another. He leaned over to give her a quick peck on the cheek. "It's going to be a wonderful Sunday, isn't it?" Conrad asked, smiling.

"That it is," she agreed. "That it is."

"Keep it down back there, you kids," admonished Bill from the front seat. He winked at Conrad through the rearview mirror.

"Well, you know how we youngsters are," Conrad said. "Incorrigible." He seemed to enjoy nothing more these days than just being lighthearted. After all of the darkness that had plagued him in recent years, it felt good to be playful once again, especially since he wasn't really working these days.

During this period, Conrad Hilton was still involved in many Hilton Corporation decisions, but it was Barron who was really running the company from their three-story office building in Beverly Hills at 9990 Santa Monica Boulevard, across the street from the Beverly Hilton Hotel. "Conrad would come into the office just about every day," said Virginia "Gini" Tangalakis, who worked as an assistant to Hilton attorney David Johnson from 1973 to 1980. "I remember he would show up in a black Cadillac driven by his butler, Hugo, and always with his fluffy white poodle, Sparky, following him on a leash up to his office on the third floor, where you would also find Barron and Eric. He was always immaculately dressed in a blue business suit, once in a while a gray one, but primarily he wore some shade of blue. He treated the staff so well. Mr. Hilton had a private chef named Wilhelmina, an African American, grandmotherly type, who came in every day to prepare hot lunches for the staff. We would be served every day in an enormous conference room, the food all laid out on a boardroom table buffet style, with linen napkins and porcelain plates, for all of us working in the office. The girls all had a crush on Mr. Hilton, despite his advancing age. He was just so charming. He would walk with a little shuffle through the office and everyone was just in awe of him."

The last corporation board meeting where Conrad actually presided had been back on August 14, 1975. As long as he still had an impact on certain aspects of the company's operation—as corporate chairman, he attended all of the board meetings and was sure to register his views—he was satisfied. He was proud of his son Barron and thought he was doing a terrific job. In 1975, Barron made the decision to sell half the company's equity in six major hotels to Prudential for $83 million. In what is still viewed as one of the first major management leaseback deals in the business, the Hilton Corporation would run those hotels and in return collect a percentage of the profits. Conrad wholeheartedly approved. He had been using similar leaseback strategies overseas for years, but never to build operations domestically.

With Barron in charge, Conrad no longer had the constant chaos of the hotel business to keep him occupied. He felt a definite void in his life. Actually it was an emptiness he had experienced for decades. It had just been easier to brush aside when he was the ultimate man in charge. Now it was much more difficult to distract himself from his longings.

Conrad had obviously achieved a great deal in his life, but it had always frustrated him that both of his attempts at having a fulfilling relationship with a woman had ended in failure. Failure was not something he could easily bear. While he could always plan and strategize his way out of a business dilemma, solutions to the complexities of love and romance had eluded him.

Hilton family lore has it that Conrad prayed for the void in his life to be filled—and that this was when Frances Kelly came along. She had been a good and trusted friend for at least thirty years. But she had been more a background figure in his life, their friendship solid but quiet. After having known her for so long, he had never viewed her as a romantic partner. "But then they had a few casual dinners and one thing led to another," recalled Bill Kelly, "and they just sort of tumbled into a relationship. Fran said it felt natural, so much so that they didn't fight it. They just welcomed it."

"They were incredibly happy," Bill Kelly, who was four years Frances's junior, would recall. "The perfect match. It took us all by surprise, but Frannie—that's what we called her, Frannie—was a wonderful woman who, I think, turned out to be a good influence on Conrad at a time when he most needed it."

Frannie

*I*n 1977, Mary Frances Kelly was sixty-one years of age. She was tall and stately, with piercing blue eyes and short, wavy dark hair that was quickly graying. In stark contrast to most of the women in Conrad's social circle, she favored clothing that was for the most part conservatively tailored: long, straight skirts, and classic button-down blouses. She sometimes accessorized with simple jewelry, but she was by no means flashy or ostentatious. She had a distinct air of breeding about her, a certain dignity that commanded attention and respect. She was soft-spoken, but direct. Though she appeared to be fragile, she actually had a strong, formidable core that often surprised people. When her long-standing friendship with Conrad finally blossomed into romance, she was delighted. She didn't mind that it had taken so many years for them to "find" each other. Instead, she was just amazed that they had finally discovered their true feelings for one another.

Frances Kelly was born on January 29, 1915, the daughter of Scottish-born parents, William Patrick Kelly and Christine Crawford, who had immigrated to America in the early 1900s. At the time of his death in 1936, her father was a vice president and comptroller of the International Harvester Company, a successful farm equipment manufacturer, a position also later held by her brother, Bill.

Raised in tony Highland Park, Illinois, near Evanston, twenty miles outside of Chicago, Frances came from a family that is described by her relatives today as having been "well-to-do." She attended the Catholic Marywood School for Girls, where she was valedictorian of her class. She then enrolled in the School of Speech at Northwestern University, and afterward attended the Royal Academy of Dramatic Art in London with dreams of becoming an actress. When World War II broke out, she and her sister, Patty, volunteered for service in the American Red Cross and served in the South Pacific. After Patty returned to the States, Frances stayed on with the Red Cross and was among the first Red Cross workers stationed in Japan.

In 1946, Patty married John Rutherford Fawcett Jr., who was still in the Army and stationed in El Paso. Because she suffered from polio as a baby, Patty swam every day as therapy at the El Paso Hilton. At the time, Conrad's sister Helen Buckley and his mother, Mary Saxon, happened to be living at the El Paso Hilton. Since Helen had also been in the Red Cross, the three women became good friends.

When Frances's father died at the age of fifty-two, Frances and her mother, Christine, decided to move from their fifteen-room home in Highland Park, citing the weather as a major factor in their decision. "Patty knew Conrad's sister, Helen Buckley," explained Bill Kelly. "So when Helen learned that Frances and Christine were moving to Los Angeles, she said, 'Well, you really have to meet my brother Connie. He lives there!'"

It was the late 1940s when Frances and her mother finally settled in Los Angeles. Frances became manager of convention sales for United

Airlines, her job being to promote and organize conventions for the employees of hotels nationwide. Because her work involved the hotel business, it gave her plenty to talk about when she and Conrad finally met in 1948. It was their easy, unthreatening conversation—free of any agenda—that compelled them to remain fond friends for thirty years before their first date. Conrad was such a staple in Frances's life that there were many youngsters on her side of the family who called him "Uncle Connie."

Frances's niece and namesake, Frances Kelly Fawcett Peterson (the daughter of Frances's sister, Patty), recalled, "When I was about six months old, Aunt Frannie took me and my mother with her for a vacation with Uncle Connie at his home in Lake Arrowhead—and that was around 1960. I also remember that when I was four, we went to Germany and had to leave from New York, so Uncle Connie put us up at the Waldorf. I distinctly remember a huge spray of roses on the mantelpiece in the suite, all bright red, from my Uncle Connie to my mom, Patty. So, yes, he was a good and longtime friend of the family's."

In November 1963, shortly before the country would be staggered by the assassination of President John F. Kennedy, Frances Kelly received a highly amusing telephone call from Conrad Hilton's German-born butler, Hugo Mentz. "Please come and take Mr. Hilton to mass," he pleaded with her. "The poor man can't even go to Communion without some widow trying to pick him up at the Communion rail!" Frances laughed at Conrad's "dilemma" and agreed to be his church companion. "So for many years after that, they went to church together," recalled Frances's niece.

Like Conrad, Frances was a staunch Catholic, and deep-seated faith helped forge the bond between them. She had never met a man with so much faith, a man so devoted to his God. She knew also that his religion had been a constant in his life from the time he was a little boy.

In the early 1970s, when Frances Kelly Fawcett Peterson was a college student, she would spend many of her summers with her aunt Frannie in Los Angeles. "Every morning before work, my aunt would get up and go to church with her best friend, Helen. Occasionally, Uncle Connie would join them. In addition to that, four nights a week we would go to Uncle Connie's for dinner. Although it was usually just the three of us, it was a very formal affair; I had to wear a long dress, very Old World and mannerly." Even with such longtime friends, Conrad insisted on an element of ceremony, regardless that he was hosting small, intimate social occasions. "Dinner was served promptly at eight. I remember that Uncle Connie would fine us twenty-five cents if we were late," said Frances. "He was determined to keep a schedule. There was always an air of ceremony. For instance, once I went into the kitchen and Hugo the butler and [his wife] Maria [one of the housekeepers] were *horrified* to see me there. Uncle Connie explained that you just did not go into the kitchen when the staff were working.

"We would have cocktails in the den, watch the news, and then talk politics and current events. I remember a news story about a man who had shot his wife and five children and then committed suicide. Uncle Connie was upset about it. 'We just don't know enough about the human brain,' he said, 'and what would cause a person to do something like that.' He then mentioned that he'd just recently given $10 million to the Mayo Clinic to do research on the human brain. He was always so interesting, so informed and so charming. For me, as a young girl, it was all fascinating, everything he had to say. I hung on his every word. After drinks, we would have dinner in the dining room, which overlooked the grounds [of Casa Encantada]. It was truly a beautiful setting."

By 1977, Conrad was quite lonely, as had been apparent to many people in his life, such as his old friend, actress Debbie Reynolds. "I had been to Casa Encantada probably a dozen times for parties in the late sixties and early seventies," she recalled, "but by the end of the decade, not so often. I just had a sense that something wasn't right. One day, I was driving my car through Bel-Air and I thought, 'I wonder how Mr. Hilton is doing?' I was all dressed up and on my way to a luncheon but I decided to stop at Conrad's home on an impulse. I drove up to the enormous gates and rang the buzzer and asked for Hugo, on the chance that Conrad might see me. I just felt nostalgic for him.

"The gates opened and Hugo came out to greet me. I walked into the house and Mr. Hilton yelled down from one of the balconies, 'I'm up here, Debbie. Ice the champagne, Hugo. We're going to dance!' He came down in the elevator, and for the next three hours I sang to him and we just danced, danced, and danced. We had a glorious time. He had such a smile on his face by the time I left, just like the old Conrad. 'Thank you so much for coming,' he told me. 'This has meant the world to me.'

"I sensed that, while he was older, he still was hungry for female companionship. I felt that strongly. He still had a lot of life in him, a lot to give to some lucky woman."

It was in 1977, then, after many years of good friendship, that Conrad Hilton and Frances Kelly finally began dating. Besides their shared passion for religion, Connie and Frances were also happy to discover they had a great deal more in common. For instance, they loved to dance around the house to the music of varsovienne—music and dance, originating in Warsaw, Poland, that combined elements of waltz, mazurka, and polka. (It was danced in America to the tune of "Put Your Little Foot Right There.") They also enjoyed reading and were avid golfers. Moreover, Conrad belonged to the Los Angeles Country Club, while Frannie belonged to the Bel-Air Country Club, and they enjoyed taking each other to dinners at their respective clubs (with Frances's niece and namesake always tagging along). On lazy Sunday afternoons, the couple could think of nothing better than a long drive together through the hills of Brentwood and Bel-Air, with Frances driving because Conrad as he got older didn't like to get behind the wheel. It was as if the loneliness in their later years had sparked something in both Conrad and Frances and allowed them to view each other through different eyes. This turn of events was a big surprise for everyone on Frances's side of the family. Stella Kelly, Bill's wife and thus Frances's sister-in-law, observes, "I started to notice that whenever Frannie would walk into the room, Connie's face would absolutely light up. When I saw that, I knew it was love."

A Gentle Nudge

*H*er excitement practically leapt through the telephone line.

"You'll never believe it," Frances Kelly was saying. She was on the telephone with her brother, Bill, calling him from the main kitchen of Conrad's estate, Casa Encantada. "Conrad has asked me to marry him."

"Well, I'll be! Congratulations, Frannie," Bill exclaimed. "That's great news!" Then, just as suddenly as her joyous proclamation had nearly floored him, her tone changed.

"But I have my reservations," she said.

He couldn't imagine what such reservations could be. Obviously his sister and Conrad got along; they had a wonderful relationship, at least as far as he could see. It seemed to him that Conrad couldn't get along without her. Just recently, the siblings, along with Bill's wife, Stella, had gone on a vacation to Marbella in southern Spain, where they owned a condominium. They didn't have a telephone in the unit. Yet somehow Conrad managed to get in touch with Frances by tracking her down at a golf course. He told her how much he missed her, and pleaded with her to return to Los Angeles. "Forget it, Frannie," Bill told her. "We're here now, and we're not turning around and going back for anyone!" He knew then that Conrad Hilton would likely never let Frances slip away from him again.

"You know, he's one of the wealthiest men in the world," Frances said, her voice a whisper. "People will think I'm marrying him for his money!"

Bill had to laugh. Knowing his sister as he did, he realized that nothing could be further from the truth. "Who cares what people think?" he said.

"I do!" she shot back.

Frances Kelly had been a single woman her entire life. Of course, she'd had her romances over the years, one with a gentleman from South Carolina almost culminating in marriage. However, when that didn't work out, she all but gave up hope of finding a husband. She decided then—and this was when she was in her early fifties—that she didn't necessarily need a spouse, that she was perfectly content with her life as it was. Being single wasn't so bad. Some were surprised by her status as a spinster, though. She seemed like a good catch for any man.

Frances had worked most of her adult life and now valued her job with United Airlines. She had her own money, was financially secure, and lived in a small, albeit nicely furnished three-bedroom apartment in Westwood, near UCLA, with her mother. Her life was predictable and safe. But from the time Conrad came into the picture as a possible romantic partner, nothing was the same for her. He made her feel alive. He was funny, full of surprises. She was well aware that recent years had been difficult for him, but she would never have known as much based on the way he was when they were together. When Frances was with Conrad, he seemed strong and resilient, not at all fragile. "Everyone breaks," he told her one day, quoting author Ernest Hemingway, "but most are stronger in the broken places."

Although through the years Zsa Zsa Gabor would perpetuate the image of her ex-husband as being stingy, Conrad was by far the most generous man Frances had ever met. He lavished many expensive gifts on her during their courtship, mostly jewelry. There seemed no end to his extravagant gestures. Only a week before proposing to her, he arranged for a fifteen-piece orchestra to play classical music for them as they dined on one of the terraces of Casa Encantada. That experience alone was beyond anything she had ever heard of, or even imagined possible! And although she had lived a comfortable life, the opulence of his mansion was like no home she had ever seen, and it left her speechless. She would never forget the expression on her mother's face the first time she accompanied her to a cocktail party at Casa Encantada. On the evening of the party, her mother, Christine, went into one of the many well-appointed bathrooms to freshen up. So astonished was she by the many solid gold fixtures in the room, when she exited she joked with Conrad, "When you have trouble in that bathroom, who do you call? A plumber? Or a jeweler?"

"Frannie, don't be ridiculous," Bill told his sister during their phone conversation about Conrad's marriage proposal. "Just accept it."

"I don't know. I have a lot of questions."

"The only question you need to ask yourself," Bill offered, "is: 'Do I love him?'"

"Yes," she answered without hesitation. There was no doubt about that in her heart. She loved him very much, and she was quite sure he loved her as well. "But is love enough?" she asked.

"Hell if I know," Bill said, laughing. He was a pragmatic man. In his world, people simply fell in love and got married. They didn't examine complex emotions, pick them apart, and try to understand them. He'd been happily married to his wife, Stella, for many years and just wanted the same for his sister. "I say let people think what they want," he concluded. "You and Conrad know the truth, and that's all that matters."

Bill's simplicity on the matter seemed to cut through Frances's qualms, clearing out the overanalyzing that had clouded her decision making. "Okay," Frances decided. "I'm going to do it. I'm going to say yes! Can you believe it?" she asked, barely able to contain her growing excitement. "Can you believe that I am going to marry Conrad Hilton?"

Best Friend's Advice

*E*very morning for more than twenty years, Frances Kelly and her best friend, Helen Lamm, would attend 6:30 mass at St. Paul the Apostle Catholic Church in Westwood. Helen had worked for Fawcett Publications from 1940 to 1955, first as a secretary and then as the coordinator of celebrities for commercial endorsements. Now she was an employee of Kelly Girl, the successful temporary employment agency.

Helen had met Frances at a Kelly Girl convention at the Beverly Hills Hotel back in 1960. The company had hired a spokesman from United Airlines to lecture its employees on how a woman should pack for a trip. This idea may sound a bit strange today, but back in the 1950s and early 1960s, traveling by airplane was still a daunting adventure for the average American. With travel becoming such a major part of the lives of everyone, advice on how to pack for a trip was actually something people found useful and valuable. The woman sent by United to give the talk? Frances Kelly.

"A woman should be able to travel the entire country with a single suitcase," she told the group while standing behind a lectern. Addressing her mostly female audience, she demonstrated the most efficient ways to fold clothing, where to put high heels in the suitcase, and how to pack as many outfits as possible in one suitcase.

As songs like Bobby Darin's "Beyond the Sea" and "Mack the Knife" played on the hotel's sound system at the Beverly Hills Hotel pool, Frances and Helen shared cocktails and life stories under the sun and became fast friends. They remained so all of these years later. Their daily church ritual was a big part of their friendship. All of that changed, though, when Frances met Conrad. Now, suddenly, Frances was going to mass with *him* every morning.

"Of course I thought it odd," recalled Helen. "But I had met Connie—though I always felt odd calling him that, and preferred 'Mr. Hilton'—and had many dinners at his lovely home with Frannie. I knew how much she liked him; they were so darling together. I thought, 'How wonderful that she has met a new friend'; it's so difficult to meet new friends at our age. That's all I thought it was, a nice friendship."

One afternoon in the spring of 1976, Frances telephoned Helen to suggest that they go to mass together the next day, "like old times." When Helen picked up Frances at her apartment at 512 Kelton Avenue in West-wood, she couldn't help but notice the unwavering, radiant smile on her face. Ordinarily, Frances was a lighthearted person who enjoyed life to the fullest, but on this day, according to what Helen would remember, Frances seemed particularly "jaunty." Helen suspected something was up, but the two old friends attended mass as usual. Afterward, they sat in the car for a moment in the church's parking lot. Frances was beaming by this time, seeming ready to burst with some sort of good news. "I have something I have just been *dying* to tell you," she said.

"What's that, Frannie?"

"You know that gentleman I've been going to mass with—Mr. Conrad Hilton?" Frances began.

"Yes?"

"Well," she said, pausing for a moment. "I am going to marry him!"

Helen could not have been more surprised. "What!" she exclaimed as she leaned over to embrace her friend. "I knew you were friends, and I knew you liked him and he liked you, but I had no idea..."

Frances's smile grew even broader.

Helen was silent for a moment. "*How* did this happen?" she finally managed to say.

"I don't even know how to explain it," Frances began. She said that what she felt for Conrad was different from the way she had ever felt about any other man. "And at my age," she said, shaking her head in disbelief. "Why, I'm sixty-one!"

"Well, how old is he?"

"He's..." She hesitated. "I think he's, perhaps, eighty-seven or eighty-eight?" She posed it like a question rather than an answer. "Is that too big an age difference, Helen?" she asked. "Please tell me. Am I being an old fool?"

"Oh, *pish-posh*," Helen answered. "You are never too old to fall in love."

As in her telephone conversation with her brother, Frances's exuberant mood quite suddenly shifted. Her nagging doubts had returned. "You know, his lifestyle is nothing like anything I have ever experienced," she observed. She wondered if she would be able to fit into his world of wealth and privilege, power and prestige. For instance, when Conrad wanted to go somewhere, he just boarded his own private jet and took off. He had told her that he hadn't been on a commercial airliner in thirty years! "I don't know if I could live like that, Helen! You know how we are," she concluded. "We're just ordinary girls."

"Speak for yourself!" Helen shot back, feigning umbrage. She then turned serious and looked her friend directly in the eyes. "Let me ask you one question, Frannie: Why should you settle for an ordinary life when you can have . . . an *extraordinary* life?"

Frances had to admit that her good friend had a point.

"Well, then I say *yes*! Do it, Frannie," exclaimed Helen. "Marry this man before he changes his mind," she joked.

"Yes, that's what I'm going to do," Frances concluded, her courage once again boosted by a close and trusted person in her life. "God help me, Helen, because it looks like I'm going to be a blushing bride at the ripe old age of sixty-one."

"Please, can I ask you just one favor?" Helen asked.

"Sure."

"Don't wear white, Frannie! *Please!*"

At that, the two best friends burst into laughter.

Family Concerns

*W*hile Frances Kelly's friends and family were unequivocally happy that she was marrying Conrad, that view wasn't exactly shared by some of those in Conrad's family—at least not at first. When Conrad introduced Frances to Barron and Marilyn and to Eric and Pat, they all found her to be perfectly charming. No one wanted Conrad to be alone, as he had been for so many years, and they were all happy that he had finally found someone with whom he could share his life. However, this wasn't the typical scenario of an elderly single parent having a last shot at love. No matter how lonely Conrad had been, there were legitimate practical concerns to a potential union for him. What would it mean to the corporation, to its assets, and to its heirs if Conrad were to now suddenly marry? While it was a delicate subject, it was one that could not be avoided and had to be addressed early on. "Some people worried that [Frances] might be a gold digger," recalled Tom Parris, a former Hilton Hotels Corporation vice president. "Certain members of the family were upset."

"My mom told me that, yes, there was worry when Frances began dating Conrad, mostly from Barron, not so much from Eric," said Anna Fragatos, whose mother, Evelyn, was also a close friend of Frances in Los Angeles. "After all, he was worth a half billion dollars. Was she a gold digger? That was the question a lot of people were asking at the time."

According to well-placed sources in the Kelly family, a meeting was held at Barron's home to discuss Conrad's engagement shortly after he asked Frances for her hand in marriage. Because Barron Hilton wanted Conrad to be happy and have love in his life, he took no issue with his father's wanting to remarry; he had met Frances and felt she was a kind person. Still, he felt it prudent to err on the side of caution and have some legal document in place protecting the family and the company in case of divorce. After all, there were hundreds of millions of dollars at stake. It stands to reason that as head of the company, Barron would be concerned.

Another issue was Conrad's age; he was going to turn eighty-eight in December. There was a question as to the logic of complicating his will at a time so close to what was likely to be the end of his life. According to the Kelly family, the question was posed: Why couldn't Frances just move into Casa Encantada and she and Conrad live happily as companions for however many years they had left together?

Marilyn had already discussed with Conrad the possibility of simply living with Frances, gently bringing up the subject over lunch with him just a week earlier. It turned out that he had a good reason, he said, for wanting to marry Frances.

Now that his first wife, Mary, was gone, his union to Zsa Zsa was totally invalid—at least according to the tenets of the Catholic Church, which had never recognized it anyway. Conrad was now free to marry in the church once again, which was something he wanted more than anything else at this time in his life. He said it would mean the world to him. "So I think we have to let him have it," Marilyn said. "I mean, how can we deny him this wish?"

It was decided then to proceed with caution and to be discreet. Though no one wanted to upset Conrad or insult Frances, there was nothing wrong, it was concluded, in having a reasonable prenuptial agreement in place and ready for their signatures.

The Thorn in His Side

I've enjoyed quite a few accomplishments in my life," Conrad Hilton was saying. "But do you want to know what I think was a *real* achievement?" he asked with a twinkle in his eye. He was sitting at the bar in his home with his future brother-in-law, Bill Kelly.

"What's that?" Bill asked.

Conrad waited a beat to deliver the punch line: "The fact that I got out of my marriage to Zsa Zsa Gabor for only $35,000." (This figure does not include five years of monthly alimony already paid to Zsa Zsa.)

"But that's a hell of a lot of money, Connie," Bill exclaimed.

"Well, at the time it really was," Conrad said. "It's peanuts today. But believe you me, she has never let me forget it," he said. "That woman has been a thorn in my side for thirty years now."

"Well, ex-wives will do that," Bill said with a conspiratorial grin.

Conrad nodded his head. He then fell silent for a moment, seeming to slip down into his thoughts. "The fact that I married her is a mystery to me now, I have to admit," he finally said. "It was the biggest mistake of my life. But at the time, I just wanted her so badly. I just had to have her," he recalled. "However, you know what they say," he concluded with a wince. "Be careful what you wish for..."

"You just may get it," Bill finished.

At that, the two men clinked their glasses.

With his marriage to Frances Kelly quickly approaching and the reality of wedded happiness at long last within his grasp, Conrad Hilton couldn't help but feel wistful about his two earlier marriages. However, it really wasn't his marriage to his first wife, Mary, that occupied his thoughts these days. Rather, it was the one to Zsa Zsa that frequently haunted him, especially after he became serious with Frances. With his new marriage in the offing, the subject of Zsa Zsa kept coming up for one reason or another, such as when Conrad joked about his settlement with her to Bill Kelly.

On one of Conrad and Frances's Sunday drives together, they came upon the house Conrad had owned in Bel-Air back in the days when he was married to Zsa Zsa. He mentioned to Frances that he liked the simpler ranch house better than massive Casa Encantada because it was "cozier" and suited him more. "And see that tree right over there?" Conrad told Frances as they drove slowly past the estate. "That very tree was watered by the tears of Zsa Zsa Gabor when I told her I couldn't marry her."

For her part, ever since her divorce from him in 1946, Zsa Zsa Gabor, who was fifty-nine in 1976, still harbored a great deal of resentment about marriage to and divorce from Conrad, but, true to her nature, had managed to turn some of it into comedy. "Conrad Hilton was generous to me in the divorce settlement," she would say. "He gave me five thousand Gideon Bibles." (She once used that line in her Las Vegas act, with Conrad in the audience. "So why didn't you read one, then?" he cracked out loud from his seat, to the delight of the crowd.)

By 1976, Zsa Zsa had been married seven times—once before Conrad, and five after him. The sixth marriage, to Jack Ryan, creator of the Barbie doll, ended in 1976 in an acrimonious divorce. Three days after her divorce from Ryan, on August 27, 1976, Zsa Zsa married Irish American attorney Michael O'Hara, her seventh and present husband. The couple lived in Bel-Air.

Zsa Zsa was still famous as a talk show guest, but the money she made appearing on such programs was negligible—a few hundred dollars an appearance, at best. That said, she was still a wealthy woman, worth about $6 million at this time, due not only to her earlier career but also to settlements along the way from a string of well-to-do husbands.

Though she'd been married many times, Conrad hadn't married again since his union to Zsa Zsa. Now that his first wife, Mary, was gone, Zsa Zsa always figured that when Conrad passed away she would be the widow apparent. It was her hope, then, that there would be some provision for her in Conrad's will. It would have been more than welcome. However, she had her own money and she didn't actually *need* his—and she had always maintained as much. It was her daughter, Francesca—who was twenty-six at the time—about whom she was most concerned. It was for that reason that she never pushed Conrad too far, never pressed him too hard on the issue of money. She would bide her time, careful never to alienate him and jeopardize her daughter's possible inheritance—though at times she certainly did come close.

This uneasy truce changed dramatically when Mary Frances Kelly came into the family. Now, with word of Conrad's engagement spreading,

Zsa Zsa realized that she would no longer be the most recent wife, that she would be nothing more than the second wife—of thirty years ago! One day in his office, in front of witnesses, Zsa Zsa peppered Conrad with questions about his fiancée. For instance, she wanted to know Frances's age. Conrad answered honestly. At sixty-one, Frances was two years older than Zsa Zsa. "My goodness, Connie! It's so *May-December*, isn't it?" Zsa Zsa asked. "Well, I think you are an old fool to get married at your age," she added. Conrad shot back, "And *I* think your romantic experience does not qualify you for an opinion."

It could be said that Francesca was at this time on thin ice where Conrad was concerned. He had already expressed doubt as to her paternity—and that was when her mother had a real (or, it could even be argued, imagined) place in his life. Now that he was engaged to Frances, the question became, how would the new arrangement impact Francesca and her inheritance?

Of course, logically, one would think that Frances's place in Conrad's life should have had no effect whatsoever on Francesca's inheritance. However, in fairness to Zsa Zsa, it had long ago become necessary to suspend all logic and reason when it came to the subject of money and how Conrad Hilton saw fit to distribute it to family members. Always true to his antithetical nature, Conrad was quite philanthropic when it came to his favorite charities, while at the same time relatively parsimonious with his own relatives. Simply put, Zsa Zsa was worried that the money she expected to secure Francesca's future—and maybe a little of her own, too—might now go to Frances and to members of *her* family. Indeed, it was around the time that Frances came into the picture that Zsa Zsa began to become even more concerned about her only daughter's interests.

The Marital Agreement

During the early days of Conrad Hilton's courtship with Frances Kelly, rumors began to circulate within the family that he was thinking of marrying her. Barron made it clear right off that he believed some sort of prenuptial agreement should be in place. This was not unreasonable.

However, Conrad Hilton, for all his business savvy, was adamantly opposed to any such agreement. He simply wanted to marry Frances and, as he put it to one family member, "let the chips fall where they may." Sources in Frances's family say that when Conrad and Frances sat down with one of the Hilton lawyers who had drawn up the prenuptial document, Conrad flatly refused to sign it. "Oh, just sign the darn thing," Frances reportedly told him. "It's okay, Connie. Truly it is." Still, he would not sign it.

At the time, there were some who felt that Conrad wasn't thinking clearly, blaming it on his advancing years. Others just took him at his word when he said that he didn't want to embarrass or humiliate his fiancée by entering into a contract with her. He said that he believed her when she said she didn't want anything from him but his love, and he didn't want to act as if he were challenging her in that regard. While that may have been a romantic way to look at things, with possibly hundreds of millions of dollars at stake, the Hilton Corporation's board of directors—not just Barron—had good reason to want that prenuptial agreement in place.

Again according to Hilton/Kelly family history, one of the Hilton Corporation's lawyers met with Frances on his own, with Conrad not present. This attorney asked Frances if she would mind at least signing a declaration that would limit the money she would receive upon Conrad's death, and also provide for her afterward. The document was called an "antenuptial," which was basically another term for "prenuptial." She said, yes, of course. To the Hiltons, her agreeing to sign such a declaration spoke volumes about her intentions where Conrad was concerned.

According to informed sources, the document Frances Kelly was asked to sign called for her to receive a lump sum of $1 million upon Conrad's death. She would also receive $50,000 a year for the rest of her life. However, one of her lawyers felt strongly that there should be some sort of cost-of-living escalation to the $50,000. What if Frances lived twenty years longer than Conrad? Fifty thousand dollars would not be worth nearly as much in that case. She wouldn't hear of it, though. She didn't want to appear to be negotiating a "deal" and was perfectly fine with the terms as they had been outlined for her by the Hilton camp. According to the agreement, in exchange for the million dollars she would receive at Conrad's death and the $50,000 a year for life, Frances "relinquished, disclaimed, released and forever gave up any and all rights, claims or interest in" Conrad's property, including "community property right, rights as an heir or widow, rights to family allowance, rights in case of death or rights to act as an administratrix of the estate." It was an ironclad deal.

When Conrad was told that Frances had agreed to sign the antenuptial, he wasn't at all surprised. He didn't want to push it, though. He took his copy of the agreement—still not signed by either party—and tucked it safely away in his desk drawer. Then he forgot about it.

Conrad and Frances Marry

*W*hen Frances agreed to marry Conrad, the only thing she asked was that it not be an extravagant, overblown ceremony and reception. She wanted a small, intimate wedding, not one that would make newspaper headlines and inevitably generate more attention and unfair speculation about her motives. Conrad agreed; all he really wanted was a church wedding, anyway, he told her. Therefore, they planned a small ceremony at St. Paul the Apostle Catholic Church in Westwood, in December 1976.

On the morning of the ceremony, the premarital agreement had still not been signed. The couple raced to the church, excited about their nuptials and not thinking twice about any legal document. "Have you signed the agreement?" one of Conrad's attorneys asked as soon as he and Frances arrived at the church. "What agreement?" he asked. Not only had they not signed it, they didn't even have it with them! Never fear, though; the attorney happened to have a copy folded in his breast pocket. He presented it to Conrad with a pen. "This is not the time for this," Conrad protested. "Why, this is my wedding day!" Frances took in the moment and said, "Oh, Connie, please, let's just sign the darn thing." The lawyer gave them a pen, and the couple then put their signatures on the agreement.

Conrad Hilton then took his third wife, Mary Frances Kelly, during the simple ceremony they both wanted at St. Paul the Apostle Catholic Church on Ohio Avenue in Westwood. It took place on December 21,

1976, four days before his eighty-ninth birthday. No family members flew from out of state to be in attendance, except for Eric Hilton (but not his wife, Pat). Barron, Marilyn, and a few other Hilton family members who lived in Los Angeles were also present. (By this time, Frances's mother, Christine, was deceased.) The marriage license noted that the groom's "Present or Last Occupation" was "Chairman" and that his "Kind of Industry or Business" was "Hotel." The bride's was "Salesperson for airlines." The couple was married by the Reverend John T. Carroll, associate pastor of St. Paul's. The newlyweds were then especially delighted with the wedding gift presented to them by Barron and Marilyn: a beautiful Eastern European ceramic Madonna figure, with the infant Jesus wearing a crown.

One happy result of finally having the love of his life at his side was the softening of the hard edge Conrad had developed in later years—and the return of his sense of humor. "You want to know the real reasons I married Frannie?" he told her best friend, Helen Lamm, over dinner one night shortly after the wedding at Helen's condominium in Brentwood. "First of all, she gets a great discount on airlines," he said with a twinkle in his eye. "And secondly, she's got great connections! That girl can always get me a good hotel."

PART TWELVE

House of Hilton

Life at the Mansion

*L*ife for Mr. and Mrs. Conrad Hilton unfolded easily and effortlessly. The couple had a natural camaraderie that surprised even their closest friends. They started their marriage with a trip to Manhattan—one that was comically ill-timed. They stayed, of course, at the Waldorf-Astoria. Connie had been bragging that it was "the greatest hotel in the world," which, of course, he'd been doing for decades. On their weekend there, however, the electricity went out in the building, rendering the Waldorf completely dark. The kitchens were, obviously, useless—no room service!—and no elevators either! Eventually, Frances had to descend ten flights of stairs to get the couple some food, and then go back up the stairs to their room. "The greatest hotel in the world?" she asked when she finally returned, out of breath. "Maybe you should pay the electric bill around here," she suggested as she flopped onto the bed, exhausted. It was a story they both loved to tell.

As Conrad and Frances continued their lives together, of course they learned more about each other, deepening their understanding of one another from the complex to the mundane. For instance, the Hiltons had their thrifty natures in common. Both had grown up in the Depression era and, like many people of that time, they valued the American dollar. At one point early in the marriage, a friend of Conrad's suggested that he buy her a Mercedes. She had come into the marriage with a relatively new beige Pontiac. However, she usually drove the Cadillac Fleetwood owned by Connie. "So how much is a Mercedes?" Conrad asked. He was told it would cost about $20,000. "Are you crazy? Forget it," Conrad said. "Frannie is fine with the Pontiac." To put this story in perspective, $20,000 in 1977 would be worth about $75,000 today.

Frances would have frowned at the idea of a Mercedes anyway. She was wearing a diamond engagement and wedding ring that, according to her family, couldn't have been more than two carats. "She was thrifty," said her sister-in-law, Stella, with a laugh. "She didn't waste food, for instance. You couldn't throw away a tomato with a rotten spot on it, because she would say, 'That's so wasteful! Don't do that!' Frannie wouldn't throw anything away. I'd say to Bill, 'You have to tell her to get rid of that old coat,' or 'Tell her that skirt is out of fashion.' Otherwise, she'd keep it forever. Of course, her mother was the same way. It's Scottish to not be wasteful."

For his part, Conrad accepted Frances's little idiosyncrasies, such as the fact that she had never cooked a meal in her life—at least not a good one. "There are three things that may lead to our divorce," he told her one day.

"Which are?" she asked.

"Breakfast, lunch, and dinner," he answered.

Of course, it was a joke. In truth, Conrad certainly had enough servants working at Casa Encantada to prepare all manner of meals for them.

Among those now working at the mansion was a woman Conrad hired to be Frances's personal assistant, Phyllis Davis Bradley. In 1976, Bradley was fifty-eight years of age. She had just moved to Los Angeles from London, where she was born and raised. Bradley actually started her career as a live-in personal secretary to Zsa Zsa Gabor, but, as she put it, "That didn't last long. One day we had a huge disagreement about something ridiculous and, much to my horror and astonishment, she hurled a plate of food at me. I was outraged and told her I would not tolerate that kind of behavior from her. Later that day, after my errands, I drove up to the mansion and found all of my belongings packed in boxes and stacked neatly at the front gate. Bewildered, I rang the intercom buzzer. Miss Gabor came on and demanded to know, 'Who is out there?' I said, 'It's me. It's Phyllis.' And she said, 'I don't know anyone by that name. Now, go away!' At that point," she concluded with a laugh, "I could only assume I had been fired."

She continued, "I had met Mr. Hilton through Miss Gabor. When I had no place to live, I called his office to ask for help. He offered to allow me to live in a guesthouse at Casa Encantada for two weeks until I found a new place, which was so kind of him.

"About a month after I finally relocated into a new apartment, I got a call from Mr. Hilton asking if I would be interested in working for his new wife as a personal secretary. When I met the new Mrs. Hilton, I was bowled over by her good grace and easy temperament. Compared to the six months I spent with Miss Gabor, I knew I would be happy. Mrs. Hilton and I were about the same age, peers. Despite the difference in our stations, I considered her a good friend. I know she felt the same about me."

Phyllis Bradley recalled, "Mrs. Hilton and I made quite a few changes to the décor shortly after she moved into Casa Encantada. We had been told that a woman had never been in residence there. Mr. Hilton had purchased the estate after his divorce from Miss Gabor and always lived alone. Therefore, after more than twenty-five years, it was definitely in need of a woman's touch.

"Because some of the rooms were so dark, the first thing we did was change out the curtains and carpeting, switching to lighter and softer fabrics. Most of the furniture was customized replicas of French Empire furniture, which the original owner [Hilda Weber], had commissioned back in 1938. But some of the pieces were just outdated American furnishings. Mrs. Hilton replaced a lot of it with much finer pieces, many of them original French antiques. We worked with an expensive Beverly Hills interior decorator on many such upgrades, which was always a point of contention for Mr. Hilton. Oh, how he used to fuss about that decorator! He would ask me, 'Phyl, what does he do, exactly?' And I would say, 'Well, sir, we pore through magazines and he gives us ideas.' And Mr. Hilton would say, 'But, my dear, I can give you ideas for *free*; why do we have to pay *him* for ideas!' But in the end, Mr. Hilton was happy with the changes we made to his home. It was Mrs. Hilton's intention to continue with the redecorating efforts, one room at a time.

"It was such a good life, I will never forget a second of it," continued Phyllis Bradley. "The parties Mr. and Mrs. Hilton hosted at that mansion were marvelous. The money that was spent...the best of everything— the best foods, the best clothes...the best, the best, the *best*...all so expensive. Or, as Mrs. Hilton used to say, 'Everything is just so *dear*.' That was apparently a Midwest phrase for expensive.

"'I don't need all of this,' Mrs. Hilton often told me. 'This is Connie's life, not really mine. I just have to play the role of well-to-do socialite as best I can.' She also told me that she'd never been happier. 'These are such big moments in my life,' she told me, 'and I don't want to miss them. I want to be present for each and every one.' Mr. Hilton seemed to be having the time of his life as well. 'No matter how long we are married,' he used to tell me about Mrs. Hilton, 'she will always be my bride. It is such a privilege to wake up in the morning and see her face.' I will never forget the twinkle in his eye when he would say that to me: 'It is *such* a privilege.' Mrs. Hilton told me they never went to bed without him first telling her that he loved her. 'He never misses a night,' she told me. I thought that was so lovely."

"Spoiled Fruit"

$\mathcal{T}$he invitation for the party celebrating the first anniversary of Conrad and Frances's wedding was quaint, with a warm and welcoming, home-made feel to it. It had Frances Hilton's personal touch all over it, there was little doubt about it. By this time, Frances felt comfortable enough in her role as Conrad's wife to inject some of her personality into their life at the mansion.

The front of the invitation featured a drawing of a man sitting in a chair, with a cut-out photograph of Conrad's head attached to it. The text next to the illustration said, in cursive handwriting:

"I think," said he, "I'll marry her (with joy and great elation) for then I'll have United's free and friendly transportation."

Below Conrad's image was an illustration of a woman crocheting, with a photo of Frances's head attached to it. The text next to it read:

"I think," said she, "I'll marry him (with equal jubilation) for I am tired of—and quite abhor—this old-maid situation!"

On the next page was illustrated a contented couple sitting next to each other on a couch in front of a fireplace with Christmas stockings hanging from it. The text beneath it read:

And so they wed, and it will be
One year they've flown "united,"
And both of them indeed agree
That they are quite delighted

They want their friends and family
To share their happiness
And celebrate that special day
When Fran to Con said, Yes!

A third page set forth the date for "our anniversary day"—December 21, 1977—and an invitation to a "cocktail buffet" from 6:30 to 9:30 at Casa Encantada, 10644 Bellagio Road, Bel-Air.

This amusing invitation certainly said a great deal about Frances's no-frills personality and the sort of informality she brought to Conrad Hilton's life. "All of that was her idea," recalled her personal secretary, Phyllis Bradley. "It was in sharp contrast to everything around us. She wanted to bring as much simplicity to the formal environment as possible."

The invitation was homespun, but the party really was anything but. It was, as usual at the estate, Old World formal. As guests entered the mansion, their coats and wraps were immediately whisked away by two maids. Then, as music by a four-piece string ensemble played softly in the background, Hugo Mentz, the butler, stationed in the entryway, informed the newcomers that "Mr. and Mrs. Hilton are receiving in the foyer." Once in the foyer, the guests found a receiving line. At the end of the line, under the long, winding staircase that led to the second floor, stood Conrad and Frances. Frances looked lovely in a diaphanous, cream-colored silk cocktail dress with a pearl choker fastened at her neck; Conrad wore a brown silk suit with a red handkerchief in his vest pocket. The Hiltons had positioned themselves in front of an oblong glass entry table that rested on an enormous pedestal of dual marble horse figurines. On top of that table sat a large, colorful floral arrangement. There, the couple— Frances's right arm entwined with Conrad's left—graciously greeted each partygoer, enjoying a moment or two of small talk with every person. In many cases, this minute or so would be the only time a guest might actually have with the hosts.

The last of the receiving line guests had just walked away from the Hiltons when one of the security guards who regularly patrolled the premises made his way to Frances and discreetly whispered something in her ear. "Excuse me, darling," she told Conrad. He smiled at her and then turned to talk to someone else. From Frances's cool demeanor, no one could have guessed that trouble was brewing.

Frances followed the guard through the parlor to the entryway and then out the front doors, headed to the valet station, which was down at the bottom of the long, winding driveway. It took her a couple of minutes to get down there, that's how far the walk was from the front door. Once there, Frances found an extremely agitated Zsa Zsa Gabor arguing with Hugo Mentz and a woman who was holding a clipboard. She watched critically as the scene unfolded. "Why, *I'm* the one who hired you," Zsa Zsa was saying to Hugo, "and *this* is how you treat me?" (For the record, Conrad hired Hugo Mentz in 1959, thirteen years after his divorce from Zsa Zsa; she actually had nothing at all to do with it.)

"Thank you, but I will handle this, Hugo," Frances said as she approached.

"That's quite all right, Mrs. Hilton," the haughty majordomo told her. Everything was under control, he said. Like many long-term employees, he had a system in place for how to handle things.

"No," Frances insisted sternly. "*I will handle it, Hugo,*" she said, raising her tone in response to his insubordination. "Now, please go back up to the house."

Hugo looked startled at this new voice of authority. He then did as he was told.

Anna Fragatos's mother, Evelyn, who was one of Frances's more affluent friends, happened to be pulling up in her turquoise Corvette convertible just as the scene was unfolding. The following day, she recounted it in detail to her daughter.

With Frances now at her side, Zsa Zsa told the girl holding the clipboard that it didn't matter whether or not her name was on the guest list. "Don't you know that I was married to Conrad Hilton?" she asked. "We are *family*. We have a *child* together!"

As soon as Frances Hilton realized the volatile nature of what was occurring, she didn't waste a second attempting to contain it. In full view of Evelyn Fragatos, the third Mrs. Hilton walked directly to the staff member in charge of the guest list and told her that there was no mistake, that Zsa Zsa was not on the list by design. "Why don't you and I go and have a little chat," Frances said, turning to Zsa Zsa.

In her first year of marriage to Conrad, Frances had only had limited exposure to Zsa Zsa. The first time they met was in November 1976. That was when Zsa Zsa burst into the kitchen while Conrad, Frances, and members of their family were eating breakfast. Frances appeared particularly prim and proper that morning in her finely tailored skirt and white jacket with conservative blue-and-white polka-dot blouse buttoned all the way to the top. Zsa Zsa, of course, was dressed much more theatrically in a red-and-white polka-dot blouse and enormous white picture hat. She stood directly in front of the seated Frances. "You must be *her*, then," Zsa Zsa said, as she took in Frances's outfit from head to toe. "Tell me. Is that from the new *Paris* line?" she asked, her tone dripping with judgment. Conrad bolted up, took Zsa Zsa by the elbow, and pulled her out of the room before she could say something truly hurtful. After that morning, when Zsa Zsa would come to Casa Encantada to meet with Conrad, she would be generally cordial to Frances whenever she saw her passing through. However, on the evening of the anniversary party, Zsa Zsa seemed as if she were looking for trouble.

Frances took Zsa Zsa by the hand to an area farther away from onlookers. Once there and out of earshot of witnesses, the two women engaged in what appeared to be an animated conversation. Judging by the way Zsa Zsa's arms were flailing about, it was clear that she was arguing with Frances. Meanwhile, Frances seemed relatively calm in the face of Zsa Zsa's temper. Finally, loudly enough for everyone to hear, Zsa Zsa screamed out, "*Enough!* I have had enough of your insulting behavior!" She then turned and bolted away from Frances and back to her car, which was still parked at the valet station. Meanwhile, Frances—still accompanied by the security guard, who was now holding her arm and steadying her—calmly began to make the long walk back up the driveway toward the main house and finally to its large, eight-foot-high oak front doors.

"Who does she think she is?" Zsa Zsa said as the valet opened the door to her Bentley. "She is a very thin and very withered creature, that's who she is," the buxom Zsa Zsa fumed. "What could he possibly see in her? She looks like, like..." Zsa Zsa hesitated, fumbling for the perfect words. Then she called out for all to hear, "...*spoiled fruit!*" For a moment, while Zsa Zsa simmered in her anger, it looked as though she didn't want to get into her vehicle; it appeared as if she were considering following Frances up to the house. Thinking better of it, she announced her intentions. "I will return with my daughter," she told the valet, who had nothing to do with barring her entrance. "I will come back with Francesca," she declared, "and you *will* let me in!" She then got into her vehicle and screeched away.

Clearing the Air

Zsa Zsa did not return to the party with Francesca, as promised. Conrad had no idea of the scene that had been caused by her, either. The next day, when Frances finally told him about it, he was upset but not surprised. In fact, he couldn't help but wonder if perhaps he was at least partly responsible.

Back in 1919, when Conrad bought his first hotel, the ramshackle Mobley, he had authored a code of living for his employees, one tenant of which was, "Assume your full share of responsibility in the world." But had he done that when it came to his problems with his second wife? He was elderly now, maybe approaching the end of his life. No longer young and naïve, he had vast experience—he'd been married, divorced, raised children—and he felt he should now know better how to deal with this truly maddening person in his family.

What was at the root of all of this familial turmoil? Conrad was certain that it was simply that Zsa Zsa wanted money from him. But what he didn't seem to understand was that, as much as she would not have rejected anything he might have offered her, it was her daughter's inheritance about which Zsa Zsa was most concerned.

Conrad thought that he should finally have a heart-to-heart talk with Zsa Zsa. Therefore, the day after the party, he telephoned her and suggested that she come by his office so that they could clear the air. The next morning Zsa Zsa appeared, bright and early. She sat across from him at his desk, next to Conrad's attorney, Myron Harpole. After she settled in, she asked why Harpole was still present. "I've decided that he shall be my witness," Conrad said sternly. Zsa Zsa rolled her eyes. "And they say *I'm* dramatic," she remarked.

Details of the subsequent meeting would be recalled years later not only by Zsa Zsa Gabor—in a sworn deposition—but also by Myron Harpole.

"I want you to understand that the Hilton Company is a large corporation run by a board of directors and by stockholders," Conrad told Zsa Zsa. Hilton said that it wasn't just him sitting behind a big desk with an adding machine, counting the millions being made by his hotels around the world. "So, just barging in and screaming, '*I want money*,' isn't going to get you money," he told her.

"But I have never done that," Zsa Zsa protested. "Never have I barged in here and screamed that I want money from you." But as his ex-wife and the mother of his daughter, she hastened to add, some might feel that she did deserve some measure of generosity. At the very least, she concluded, Francesca deserved it. "I just want what's best for our daughter," she said, "and maybe for me, too. Do you remember how much you gave me in our divorce?" Zsa Zsa asked. "Well, I do," she answered for Conrad. "Only $35,000. You said sign here, I signed. And that was that. Now I just want what's coming to me."

"Oh, don't worry about that, my dear," he said, showing a bit of an edge. "You will get exactly what is coming to you."

After a little more discussion about the past, Conrad shifted the conversation to the present. There were serious problems all over the world, he told Zsa Zsa, and the corporation had found many good ways to help assist the poor and disenfranchised. Perhaps she might consider contributing something for the betterment of others, Conrad suggested, and possibly use the Hilton name as a vehicle in that regard. The last time he had mentioned such a thing to Zsa Zsa was almost thirty-five years earlier in 1944 when they were married. At that time, he had suggested that she volunteer at a homeless shelter. Because she wasn't interested, the subject was dropped. Why, knowing her as well as he did, Conrad would pick this time to once again try to convince her to be philanthropic was a bit of a mystery. Perhaps he just thought it was worth a try, that he had nothing to lose and that maybe Zsa Zsa would have everything to gain in terms of satisfaction and fulfillment. "I am just telling you this," he told her, "because I care... Georgia."

It was the first time Conrad had called Zsa Zsa "Georgia" in probably thirty years. According to Myron Harpole, she appeared to be moved by his use of the sobriquet. "I forgot that this was your name for me," she said, suddenly looking very sad. "It was so long ago, Connie. My God. What happened to us?"

"We still have time," he said, smiling at her. "We can try. Maybe start a charity yourself. Maybe that could be the first step..."

Zsa Zsa didn't answer. She just stared at him, lost in thought, as if caught between the past as it had once been with him and the present with all its confusion, anger, and unhappiness.

"Okay. So, what about that charity idea?" Conrad asked, trying to get things back on track. The two were truly at cross-purposes. She wanted money from him. But he wanted her to give of herself. It must have made no sense to her, especially since becoming involved with any Hilton-related charity would likely not provide her any income.

"Obviously, the meeting was not going well," recalled Myron Harpole. "'Okay, my dear, I guess you have made your point,' Connie said, now seeming too tired to continue the discussion. As he rose, he said that the meeting was over. 'I suppose it is,' Zsa Zsa agreed, also rising. 'Fine,' she announced, 'then we shall discuss this another time.' She said that she was on her way to Beverly Hills to have a sable coat fitted, so she would take her leave. Besides, she said, she wasn't quite sure she felt welcomed, anyway. 'You know, Connie, you could at least apologize for *some* of the things that happened between us,' she then said. 'Not *everything* was my fault.' Connie and I looked at one another, and he raised his eyebrows as if to say to me, 'Good point, eh?' He sighed. 'I *am* sorry, Zsa Zsa,' he said. 'For any time I ever hurt you,' he added, 'please know that I am truly sorry.' I felt that he really meant it, too. Somehow, it felt…big."

After a moment, a surprised Zsa Zsa asked, "Really? Do you really mean that, Connie?"

"I do," Conrad said. He looked at her wearily as if he was ready for her to go. "I guess no man is rich enough to buy back his past," he concluded, quoting Oscar Wilde.

"Fine, then," she said.

"So…will that be all?" he asked, trying to end things.

The two were about to part ways. But not yet. If they were going to "clear the air," as Conrad had earlier put it, Zsa Zsa still had a bit of unfinished business. According to what Myron Harpole would recall, she walked over to Conrad, tilted her head up, and put her mouth very close to his ear. "In all of these years, you have never respected what I managed to do with my life," she said. She wasn't heated or even upset, she was just quite firm, as if wanting to clearly convey something she'd had on her mind for years. "I want you to know that I am a self-made woman," she continued. "No man ever did one goddamn thing for me. I have had to

fight to survive every single goddamn day of my goddamn life. So, *please . . .
stop . . . judging me!*" And with that, she gathered her things. "*That* will be
all," she said as she turned and walked away from him.

Barron, Eric, and Francesca

*O*f course, the hotel business matters," Barron Hilton was saying as he
spoke to a reporter for the Associated Press during an interview at his
massive estate in Holmby Hills. "But family comes first."

It could certainly be argued that Barron's father, Conrad, didn't always
place family first, even though the notion of family was extremely important to him. He did his best with his sons—Nicky, Barron, and Eric—but
even they would have had to agree that he didn't spend as much time
with them as they would have liked. He was a busy man building a vast
empire; his time was limited. With that empire already built, though,
Barron didn't want to go down the same road with his own family. He
learned from many of Conrad's missteps and did things his own way. He
managed to sustain a happy marriage, for instance, to a wonderful woman
who was ever loyal to him. "She is everything to me," he said of Marilyn
in 1977, to whom he had been married for thirty years.

Though Barron and Marilyn had led a life of privilege and power for
many years, somehow they never allowed it to affect their family in a negative way. Their children were anything but spoiled. That was one of the
lessons Barron learned from Conrad and one that he applied to his own
family life. Just as Barron had to earn his own way and was never handed
anything on a silver platter by his father, his children were taught that
they shouldn't depend on their potential inheritance to get by, either.
Rather, they should chart their own course and start doing so as soon as
possible.

By 1977, Barron and Marilyn's brood was growing up: Barron Jr. was
twenty-nine; Hawley was twenty-eight; Steven was twenty-seven; David
was twenty-five; Sharon was twenty-four; Richard was twenty-two; Daniel was fifteen; and Ronald was fourteen. "They each have their own personality, their own character," Marilyn said of her children. "But in each

of them, I see their father. They're ambitious, like Barron. They're curious, like Barron. Of course, all of that is like Connie, too. So in our case, the apple doesn't fall far from the Hilton tree at all."

Certainly, where Barron was concerned, Conrad's influence was obvious. "Barron took a fine company in Hilton and developed it into one of the truly great hotel companies in the world," observed Bill Marriott, chairman and CEO of the competition, Marriott International. "The thing about Barron is that he was already a great businessman before he got into the hotel business." Like Conrad, Barron operated from his gut. He tried not to allow emotions get in the way of business decisions, but it wasn't always easy. Again, like his father, he trusted people and believed in them. However, by the 1970s, the hotel business was different from what it had been during Conrad's heyday. "There were a lot of sharks out there," said one of Barron's friends. "He had to grow to be a little tougher than Connie because the times were different. But Barron was up for it. By 1977, he was someone who commanded a great deal of respect amongst his colleagues."

In the 1970s, when the National Gambling Commission held hearings on proposals to legalize gambling outside of Nevada, one of the first witnesses it called was Barron Hilton. Consequently, in 1971, the Hilton Hotels Corporation became the first company registered with the New York Stock Exchange to operate gambling facilities. Since taking over the reins of the Hilton Corporation, Barron—who was forty-nine in 1977—had become one of the most respected and most powerful hoteliers in the business. In 1966, the year he became its president, the company's profits were about $6.6 million. By 1977, they were up to nearly $10 million. By this time, the Hiltons owned or leased 148 hotels, including Las Vegas's Flamingo Hilton. Barron was earning about $150,000 a year, but as always, his major income came from stock dividends, not his salary. In his spare time, he enjoyed flying his own glider while at his 460,000-acre High Sierras ranch. He would soar at altitudes up to 18,000 feet, much to Marilyn's consternation, who couldn't help but worry about her husband when he indulged in this hobby. "But soaring," Barron would say, "is a feeling you just can't beat."

His was a good life. Barron Hilton was smart, savvy, and in many ways his father's son. "He tried to be friendly to the staff, but I think he had a difficult time relating to us," said Virginia "Gini" Tangalakis, who worked as a legal secretary for the Hilton Corporation in the 1970s. "You'd get into the elevator with Conrad Hilton or Eric Hilton and they would ask about your family, about your life, about your day. But you'd be in the same elevator with Barron and he'd stiffly observe, 'Well, they say the stock market is up today. How do you like them apples?' And you really wouldn't know how to respond. He was more formal, reserved. I also recall that he had an enormous and lovely oil painting of Marilyn Hilton hanging on the wall behind his desk, which made me think, 'My goodness, how much he must love his wife!'"

Barron's brother Eric had also proven himself a force to be reckoned with as he continued his work for the company. He didn't demand the same kind of formality as his father and brother. "In the office, it was always 'Mr. Hilton' when referring to Conrad and Barron," recalled Gini Tangalakis, "but when Eric came in, all of the secretaries and other staff members were on a first-name basis with him. It was always, 'Hi, Eric! How are you?' Or, 'Eric's on line one.' Never 'Mr. Hilton.' He was always in a good mood, always cordial, a salt-of-the-earth kind of guy."

Eric and Pat remained happy in their marriage as they raised their four children in Texas.

Of course, the Hilton men shared a great deal of regret when it came to Nicky, but they had all moved forward with their lives as best they could, getting along with one another and fully enjoying the spoils of great success. Only one family member was usually missing and considered by some to be a complete enigma: Francesca.

As always, Conrad's daughter, Francesca, remained a background figure in the family. By the time she was thirty in 1977, she had completed her transition into what could be considered the anti-Gabor. She wasn't flamboyant or ostentatious like her mother and other female relatives, though she did share their sharp wit. "I didn't want to be all glamorous, and I didn't want to be another Gabor," she told Geraldo Rivera in 1995. "I didn't want to look like . . . you know . . . I wanted to be *me*. And they always wanted me to dress a certain way. But I rebelled. That's their thing, not mine." She also didn't seem to have the same interests in business of her father, nor of her brothers.

At one point, Francesca Hilton was finally given a summer job behind the registration desk at the Beverly Hilton Hotel in Beverly Hills. "[The customers] would always ask your name so they could scream at you if it didn't work out," she recalls. "When I gave them my name they'd say [sarcastically], '*Surrrre*.' I'd go, 'Listen, do you want me to take this reservation... *or what?*'" As it would happen, that particular job was about as close to working for the Hilton organization as Francesca would ever get, and it didn't work out. It's not known whether she was fired or quit, only that the job didn't last long. Of course, Barron, Nicky, and Eric had all started their careers at menial jobs within the Hilton organization. But they were given opportunities to prove themselves and work their way up, and their careers eventually flourished. They each had the support of their powerful father, as well as the encouragement of each other. Even Eric—who could be considered third in terms of his status among the sons—had eventually gained the backing of his father and his brothers, which helped to motivate him toward great success in his life. Francesca never benefited from such support. She had her mother, but Zsa Zsa was a mercurial figure who could never really be counted on for anything. She tried to be present when she was supposed to be, but for the most part she lived her life on her own terms and was never eager to set aside her own agenda for someone else's. By the time Francesca turned thirty she had long ago learned that she could not depend on anyone. In this family dynasty, she was most definitely on her own, like it or not.

Francesca's Idea

*A*lthough Conrad Hilton had customarily rejected her requests for financial help over the years, Francesca Hilton continued to turn to him from time to time. Sometime in January 1978, she decided to ask him if she could possibly borrow a thousand dollars. Francesca summoned up her courage and explained that she was interested in beginning a career as a photographer, she felt she was good at taking pictures, and she needed her father's assistance in purchasing equipment for her new endeavor.

Francesca spoke with such enthusiasm, Conrad was pleased that she finally seemed to have found a career about which she could be passionate. Therefore he made a rare exception and actually agreed to lend her the money. Not surprisingly, he was extremely specific about the timeline in which she would have to pay back the loan. She would have just six months to return him the money. He was so emphatic about the terms, he went so far as to outline the loan agreement on paper.

Six months passed. Though she tried her best, Francesca had only paid back half of the loan to Conrad. When she appealed to her mother for the other half, she was flatly turned down. The loan was Francesca's responsibility, Zsa Zsa said, and she was not going to bail her out. Francesca then suggested that if her mother would just lend—not give—her $500, she would immediately hand it over to Conrad. She would much rather owe the money to her mother than to her father, and she would then pay Zsa Zsa back within the next six months. Again, the answer was no. If Francesca couldn't pay Conrad back, Zsa Zsa reasoned, what guarantee did she have that she would pay *her* back?

In June 1978, the editors of *People* magazine heard that Francesca was attempting to launch a career as a photographer. This news seemed to present an opportunity for the magazine to finally obtain photographs of Conrad and his new wife, Frances—none had been published up until that time. The magazine's editors told Francesca that if she could take those pictures, they would be interested in purchasing them. It was an exciting proposition. Not only could it launch Francesca's career with a reputable publication, but she would be paid more than $500 and would have money left over after paying back her father. Francesca made the trek up to Casa Encantada to present the idea to Conrad.

The two sat in Conrad's study as she made the pitch. "This would be a great way for me to break into the business, Dad," she enthused, according to her later testimony. She explained that she cared about him much more than any other photographer who would just come in and take pictures for the money. She promised that they would be wonderful photographs, and assured him that he would have full approval not only over each shot but also over any story in which they would appear. She added that she would earn more than enough money to pay back what she owed him. Conrad didn't have to mull it over long. "Absolutely not," he decided. Francesca was bewildered: *"But why?"* Conrad explained that he didn't feel it was fair for *him* to have to work in order for *her* to earn money. Keeping his temper in check, as usual, he said he could think of nothing worse than spending the entire day posing for pictures. In his mind that was definitely work.

For a moment, Francesca was at a loss. Finally, in her own defense, she reiterated her intention: She was only taking the job in order to pay him back what he had lent her. But as he rose from his chair, he told her to just forget about it. She didn't have to pay him back at all, he declared.

"But I'm not trying to get out of paying you back, Dad," she said. "I'm just…"

"I understand, and that will be all, Francesca," Conrad announced formally, as if ending a Hilton board meeting. "Good day, my dear," he added, as he patted her on the shoulder and then took his leave.

The Great Adventure of His Life

*I*n the fall of 1978, Conrad and Frances Hilton began planning their second wedding anniversary party, which would take place at their home in December, shortly after Conrad's ninety-first birthday. He was in fine spirits and in relatively good health, given his age. He still went into the office six days a week, if only to make a pest of himself to Barron. "He'd rather I only come in a couple times a week," Conrad told one secretary of his son, "but why make it easy on the boy?" he asked with a wink. "He was actually quite active in the year 1978," Barron Hilton would recall. "I discussed with him our business on a day-to-day basis. He was particularly interested in what our earnings reports were indicating. He constantly was on the phone with the stockbrokers determining the value of Hilton stock."

Though he stayed busy, after a lifetime of work Conrad had slowed down. He was suffering from permanent heart dysrhythmia, for which he was taking a daily dose of digitalis. Sometimes his knees hurt and his ankles would swell. He also had hearing loss. His doctors had a hearing aid made for him, which he tried a couple of times but eventually discarded. "What I don't hear is probably for the best," he joked. He was also beginning to lose his sight, recalled his attorney Myron Harpole. "Many a day would pass with Frances just reading to Conrad," he said. "They both enjoyed it very much."

While a renowned nutritional therapist, Patricia Bragg, continued to advise Conrad on diet and exercise, as she had done for the last ten years, there was only so much she could do. At ninety, it was becoming more and more difficult to stave off the effects of aging. Still, when Conrad overheard someone tell Barron, "Your old man looks damn good for his age," he took offense. "I am not an old man," Conrad said, bristling. "But you're right about one thing. I do look damn good for my age."

It was also true that as he got older, Conrad became more stubborn, or, as he put it at the time to his brother-in-law, Bill, "I'm too old to care what people think of me. So I say what I feel, and I find it refreshing. Don't you?"

One evening in the study at Casa Encantada—the same study in which so many important family meetings had been held over the years—Conrad, along with his sons, Barron and Eric, and his brother-in-law, Bill Kelly, enjoyed a nightcap as they did at the end of many evenings. While they sipped their Harvey's Bristol Cream sherries, Conrad, who was wearing a comfortable silk robe, twill-striped pajamas, and leather slippers monogrammed with his initials, regaled his family members with stories of his legendary past, details of the great adventure of his life.

Conrad talked about his childhood in New Mexico, about his parents, Gus and Mary, and about his early days in the hotel business. He spoke about his first hotel, "a fleabag of a place," he said with a laugh. "Cost me something like $40,000. But, truth be told, I only had $5,000 to my name." He recalled that his mother put up the rest, "my first investor," he said with a smile. He remembered that Mary had always said that Gus was the dreamer, and that she was the more conservative of the two. Had he taken after her, she claimed, Conrad would have been satisfied with just his first couple of acquisitions. He added that when he bought the eighteen-story Spanish baroque Breakers Hotel back in 1938 in Long Beach, California—the eighth hotel in his chain—he and Mary sat in the elegant Sky Room atop the hotel, and as they gazed out at the stunning view, she asked him, "Now that you have hotels in three states, are you satisfied, Connie?" He quickly answered "No, Mother!" She laughed and said, "You see! Your father all over again."

He also spoke about Nicky. "That boy could make me madder than a wet hen in a thunderstorm," he said, laughing. "But how I miss him." And he talked about his wife—his "bride," Frances—and how fortunate he was to have found her so late in life. He said that she had brought him "new hopes and new beginnings." Finally, he concluded, "I have had an amazing life. I pretty much have achieved everything I set out to do, haven't I?"

"You certainly have," Bill offered. "Your boys should be proud."

Conrad looked at his "boys," Barron now fifty-one and Eric forty-five. With a trace of a smile, he wagered that they were probably a bit tired of him by now. "After all, I've been around for a long time," he said. "We Hilton men have been through an awful lot together."

"We love you, Dad," Barron said suddenly. The mood Conrad had set with his storytelling had become so sentimental, Barron was all but swept away by it. He had tears in his eyes. "Every day with you, Dad—every single moment—I have treasured so much," he blurted out. "You have always been my hero. I love you, Dad." This was very unusual behavior. Because of Conrad's Old World formality with them, the sons usually kept these sorts of emotions to themselves. Not tonight, though. "I feel the same way," Eric piped in, seeming on the verge of tears. "You're my hero, too, Dad. I love you."

Conrad gazed at his sons with an astonished expression. Then, turning to his brother-in-law, he cracked, "What the hell is going on here, Bill? Am I dead?" he asked, laughing. "Is this my eulogy?"

Understanding Zsa Zsa

*F*rances Hilton and Zsa Zsa Gabor were two very different women in many ways. Still, where Frances was concerned, that was no reason some understanding between them could not be reached. The constant emotional upheaval caused by Zsa Zsa was wearing Conrad down, and Frances knew it. She wanted to see if she could do something about it. "Frances wanted to try with Zsa Zsa," said Anna Fragatos, who remembers a conversation in which Frances said, "People think she's some sort of shark, and Connie wants me to stay away from her. He told me, 'Be careful with her. She circles before she attacks.' But I think I can get through to her. She's *family*. I have to try." Frances set up a luncheon with Zsa Zsa in an effort to get to know her better. "It was to be Zsa Zsa, Frances, my mother,

Evelyn, and Marilyn Hilton," recalled Anna Fragatos. Later, Evelyn Fragatos would relay the events of the day to her daughter.

The four women—Frances, Zsa Zsa, Marilyn, and Evelyn—came
together for lunch at the Polo Lounge of the Beverly Hills Hotel sometime in the winter of 1978. Zsa Zsa hadn't been anxious to go. According
to one source, she told her sister Eva, "Hold on to your *vig, dah-ling*, I am
dining with the noble Lady of the House of Hilton and her handmaidens,
and believe me, those rich harpies hate me!" Still, she must have felt it
important, because she showed up. "Oh, my dears," Zsa Zsa said when she
found the ladies waiting for her in front of the Polo Lounge, "you all look
so *beautiful*." Eventually, the women repaired to the Polo Lounge, taking
a comfortable back booth. Perhaps as a bit of a peace offering, Zsa Zsa
then presented Frances with a gift—a pretty, hand-painted silk scarf in
tones of magenta and pink. Frances loved it and immediately wrapped it
around her slim shoulders.

For the next two hours, over finger sandwiches, scones, and tea, Zsa
Zsa presented a different variation of the Gabor mystique. According to
Evelyn Fragatos, she only made one joke: "I wasn't born," she said, when
talking about her early beginnings, "I was ordered from room service!"
Other than that one great line, she was quite serious. Her demeanor
forced the ladies to take note as she regaled them with fascinating stories
about her colorful life and times, the way she had taken her persona and
used it to her advantage on television and in movies; her many marriages;
how she had never been able to find true happiness; and how—at least
according to what she said—every one of her marriages had ended with
her having to pursue the ex-husband for money. Now, she said, she was
in a loveless marriage to Michael O'Hara. They led separate lives and
even had separate bedrooms, she said, which explained why he seemed
to never be around. She said that, as a proud woman, it was not easy for
her to admit as much, but it was true just the same. "The only thing I've
ever really wanted was a beautiful love story," she said, "and I've never
had one."

"She said she was not an unreasonable woman," according to Anna
Fragatos. "She explained that the reason she was fighting so hard for her
daughter was because Conrad was getting old and she realized that once
he was gone, the Hiltons would likely never have anything to do with her
or Francesca ever again. 'And you *know* it's true,' she said, looking directly

into Marilyn's eyes. She said she could live with it if Conrad didn't leave her any money, but her heart would break into a million pieces for her daughter if he didn't make provisions for her. 'She's the best thing Connie and I ever did together,' she said. 'Yes, I'm selfish. So what? I'd like to see my daughter happy. *This* is why I fight now.' Then she made an astute comment. She said, 'It's just not fair for Connie to take out on Francesca what he feels about me.'"

Frances, Marilyn, and Evelyn listened intently and tried to understand. Caught up in her impassioned plea, they felt the sincerity behind Zsa Zsa's fervent delivery. Her reasoning made some—though not complete—sense to them. "Of course, Marilyn had heard most of these stories before over the years," said Anna Fragatos. "My mother said that she suspected perhaps the luncheon performance was a bit of a manipulation on Zsa Zsa's part. Zsa Zsa *had* come on a little strong. Not only that, my mother pointed out that Zsa Zsa was an affluent woman with plenty of money of her own with which to take care of Francesca. She was a multimillionaire. Why, then, was she so hell-bent on Conrad's money? Those reservations were all voiced in the days after the luncheon, though. In the moment itself, I believe that the women were quite moved, especially Frances."

Frances suggested that perhaps she and Zsa Zsa could figure out a way to work together so that Zsa Zsa and Connie could have a better relationship. She felt it had to start there, that the two of them had to at least learn to get along if they were ever to have a reasonable discussion about Francesca's inheritance. "I would like that," Zsa Zsa said eagerly. "Do you think it's possible?"

"I do," Frances said. "We must remember, we're all family. But you have to be willing to let go of the past, Zsa Zsa."

"Zsa Zsa and Frances then agreed to keep talking in the weeks and months to come in order to, hopefully, find a way to not only coexist in Conrad's world but to enhance Zsa Zsa's and Francesca's relationships with him as well," said Anna Fragatos. "The women then spent another hour chitchatting, laughing, and getting just a little tipsy smoking cigarettes and drinking pink champagne. 'All of you are invited to my house for dinner some night soon,' Zsa Zsa told everyone as they were getting ready to leave. 'I will cook my famous Hungarian goulash,' she added. 'But get there before eight,' she cautioned, 'because the maid is always drunk after eight.'"

When the four women parted company, Frances Hilton felt that she had a much better understanding of Zsa Zsa Gabor. "You have really gone beyond the call of duty where this thing is concerned," her secretary, Phyllis Bradley, told her. "It's all having to do with ancient history and hurt feelings, isn't it?"

Frances agreed. Certainly, all of the melodrama between Conrad, Zsa Zsa, and Francesca predated her time at Casa Encantada, and, yes, it was extremely complicated. "But I am learning that understanding a woman like Zsa Zsa Gabor is like baking a cake from scratch," Frances Hilton concluded. "It's very messy."

Death's Door

*I*t was just before his ninety-first birthday on December 25, 1978, that Conrad Hilton first became ill with what the family thought—*hoped*—was just a chest infection. He was admitted to St. John's Hospital in Santa Monica for a few days and then released. Still, he wasn't fully cured. At home, he was still weak and lethargic. The family kept a watchful eye on his condition, but Conrad quickly took a turn for the worse.

On December 31, doctors readmitted him to St. John's with a full-blown case of pneumonia. Still, most of the family thought he would recover. After all, he had never really been seriously ill a day in his life. Barron and Eric refused to believe that, even at ninety-one, it was their father's time. Francesca was also certain that the Hilton patriarch would fight his way back to health. Frances wasn't so sure, and neither was Zsa Zsa Gabor.

Zsa Zsa was upset about Conrad Hilton's illness. Some in the family felt that it wasn't just his time she saw slipping away, but also her chance at securing something substantial upon his death. Others took a more charitable view and wondered if she didn't want to make amends with him before it was too late. After all, as Conrad lay in his hospital bed, Zsa Zsa talked to his relatives about the "unfinished family business" she had with him, adding urgently that there was "little time to waste." Even those aware of how assertive she could be were taken aback by how adamant she was to see Conrad one last time. Everyone seemed to agree, though, that Conrad was in no shape to endure an unpredictable visit from his combative second wife. Therefore, Zsa Zsa was asked to stay away from the hospital and wait until Conrad was released and recuperating at home before seeing him.

When Zsa Zsa telephoned Frances to ask her for personal permission to visit Conrad, Frances wasn't sure what to think. She was inclined to give Zsa Zsa the benefit of some doubt, especially after her pleasant luncheon with her a few months earlier. However, she felt that she should acquiesce to what had already been decided by the Hiltons not to allow Zsa Zsa to see Conrad. Frances said that she would talk to the Hiltons and see what she could do. She was likely referring to Barron, Marilyn, and Eric, but it's also possible that there were members of the Hilton company's board of directors involved.

The next day was January 2, 1979. Throughout the morning and into the afternoon, different members of the Hilton family as well as some of Conrad's close friends solemnly came and went from his room at St. John's Hospital. He seemed to be getting worse. And then late in the day, a surprise visitor showed up: Zsa Zsa Gabor, carrying with her a small Christmas tree. As usual, she was dressed to the nines. Hair coiffed and makeup fastidious, she was exquisitely bejeweled and sporting a stylish crimson-colored suit. Years later, she would recall in her autobiography, *One Lifetime Is Not Enough*, that she looked into the room and saw Conrad. "His toupee was on but he didn't have his false teeth in, and seeing him that way—Conrad who had been so big, so strong, and so powerful—was one of the saddest moments of my life," she wrote. "I thought to myself, It is Christmas," she continued. "Why should he die in the hospital? Why should he die alone?" The truth, though, is that he was not "alone"—and she never got into his room. (It's also worth noting that Conrad had stopped wearing a toupee after he began seriously dating Frances. At that time he didn't feel the need for it any longer. So he likely did not have it on in his hospital room.)

According to a number of witnesses, Frances happened upon Zsa Zsa just as she was about to enter Conrad's room, miniature Christmas tree in tow. "Oh my goodness! Zsa Zsa, why are you here?" Frances asked, alarmed by her presence. "I specifically told you I would talk to the Hiltons about you. But you didn't give me a chance!"

"But I thought we had an *agreement* that I could see Connie," Zsa Zsa said, standing in the hallway and still clutching her little Christmas tree as if it were a party invitation.

"No, Zsa Zsa. We had no such agreement," Frances said. Now she was getting upset. The notion of Zsa Zsa trying to push her way into Conrad's room like an uninvited guest at a show business gala had really unnerved her, especially after she said she would try her best to get her in to see him. Once again, Frances's tough core—usually hidden under her lady-like exterior—sprang forward, her protective lioness instinct coming to the fore. She stood in front of the door with her arms crossed. "I'm sorry," she said, "and don't mean to be unkind," she continued, "but I simply can not allow you to go into that room." She met Zsa Zsa's determined gaze with a steely one of her own. "Not until I have had a chance to talk to the Hiltons, just as we discussed."

"Well, I'm sorry, too. Because, yes, I *am* going into that room," Zsa Zsa said.

"Oh no, you are *not*," Frances countered. She suggested that the two of them go for a cup of coffee to calm down, because Conrad wouldn't want them to be arguing at this time. For a moment it looked as if Zsa Zsa was weighing her options. But then she said, "No, Frances. I *need* to see him."

"At that point, a doctor, two nurses, two friends of Mrs. Hilton's, and I had run down the hall to come to her aide," recalled Phyllis Bradley. "We gathered protectively around her. Now Miss Gabor was outnumbered. 'Why, this is outrageous,' she said, looking around her. 'Who are you people to prevent me from seeing my Connie?' she asked. 'I have known him longer than any of you! I have known him since I was a young girl! And *you*,' Miss Gabor said, turning her attention to me. 'You should at least have *some* loyalty to me. After all, you used to work for me!' I said, 'That is, until you *fired* me for no good reason.' Flabbergasted, she exclaimed, 'Oh my God. You bring that up now?'"

Zsa Zsa must have known she was fighting a losing battle. "Okay," she abruptly decided. "I leave." Then, turning to Frances, she added, "I'll never forgive you for this, you...you...you..." It was as if she were—at long last—*finally* at a loss for words. She finished with, "...you *frump*!" Then Zsa Zsa Gabor turned on her heels and clacked down the hallway, still holding her little Christmas tree, head held high, but seething nevertheless.

Conrad Hilton: Rest in Peace

Conrad Nicholson Hilton died at 10 p.m. on Wednesday, January 3, 1979, at the age of ninety-one.

As well as his children—Barron, Eric, Francesca—and his wife, Frances, "Connie" was survived by three of his sisters: Eva Hilton Lewis, Helen Buckley, and Rosemary Carpenter. Among his three sons, he had fourteen grandchildren.

Conrad Hilton had enjoyed a singular lifetime full of triumphs. Not only was he revered by everyone from Hilton employees with the most menial of jobs to high-level directors of his Hilton Corporation, but he had also been lauded over the years by fellow hoteliers with whom he'd competed for business. He was true to his word and honest in a business world where the norm was to be deceptive and cutthroat. More than just a hotel magnate, he'd also been commended for his religious and political views by American presidents as well as dignitaries from around the world. His patriotic and spiritual influence was felt strongly, especially in the 1950s when the threat of Communism was foremost on the minds of most Americans. Conrad Hilton actually made Americans *care*—about their country, about their faith, about each other.

A funeral mass was held for Conrad at his parish, St. Paul's Church in Westwood, California. A memorial mass was also held at St. Patrick's Cathedral in New York, attended by dignitaries and politicians from around the world.

Conrad Nicholson Hilton was buried in Calvary Hill Cemetery in Dallas.

The Way He Wanted It

When Conrad Hilton died, he left behind a liquid fortune of approximately $200 million, which in today's dollars would be worth roughly $6 billion. Besides that amount, he held at least $500 million in stocks.

Hilton had, throughout his storied life, dedicated himself not only to his work in the hotel business, but also to his many philanthropic endeavors through the Conrad Hilton Foundation. He was a man who had always believed—and everyone in his life knew it—that no one deserved a free ride. His sons, Nicky, Barron, and Eric, had all worked within the company and had all benefited financially from their jobs. They weren't given anything by their father—they had to earn it. He let them find their own way, succeed or fail on their own merits. So it wasn't much of a surprise to his heirs that they would receive just a minuscule portion of Conrad's fortune.

Conrad's last will was written and executed six years before his death on October 31, 1973.

First things first: Zsa Zsa. She had campaigned long and hard for a place in her second husband's will, hopefully for herself but definitely for her daughter, Francesca. So how did it turn out? For her, not so well. Conrad declared that he was unmarried at the time his will was executed, and further affirmed that he was legally divorced from his last wife, Sari G. Hilton (Zsa Zsa). He also stipulated that he had already entered into a property settlement agreement with her, referring to the terms of their divorce so many years earlier. Therefore, she was to receive nothing more. That die had been cast as early as 1973—many years before Conrad had even thought of marrying Mary Frances Kelly. Therefore, Frances's presence in his life had done nothing to influence his decisions where Zsa Zsa was concerned. Conrad had once promised Zsa Zsa that she would get "exactly" what was coming to her, and apparently with his death, the time for that promised to be fulfilled was at hand. She got nothing.

Conrad further acknowledged that he had "only three living children, namely William Barron Hilton, Eric Michael Hilton and Constance Francesca Hilton," and that he had made provisions for them in his will. Before getting to those provisions, however, it was his desire, according to the will, that he be buried next to his brother August Harold Hilton in Dallas. Further, all of his automobiles, jewelry, and personal effects should be divided between Barron and Eric.

Finally, it was time to divvy up his fortune to his heirs.

For Barron—$750,000, not in cash but in shares of stock in the Hilton Hotels Corporation or Trans World Airlines or both.

For Eric—$300,000, again not in cash but in shares of stock in the

Hilton Hotels Corporation or Trans World Airlines or both. (That's $200,000 less than he had willed to Nicky all the way back in 1955, in his will of that year!)

Considering the vastness of his estate and their importance to his company, these were obviously not large sums for his sons. There was also a provision of the will that gave Barron Hilton an option to buy his father's shares of common stock of the Hilton Hotels Corporation at the value appraised by the estate. Barron immediately announced his intention to purchase a large block of shares by using a ten-year promissory note. However, as it would happen, this transaction would turn out to be easier said than done. Barron would be in for a long, protracted legal battle where this effort was concerned.

Conrad's widow, Frances, was not named as a beneficiary of the estate. It was stated that she had signed a marital agreement before her marriage to Conrad, and though the amounts were not stated in the will, her family maintains that she was given a lump sum of $1 million, and $50,000 a year for life.

"To my daughter," Conrad's will states, "Constance Francesca Hilton, the sum of one hundred thousand dollars." Again, considering his fortune, it doesn't sound like much money, but $100,000 at the time would be the equivalent of almost $3 million today. It's also worth noting that after so many years of controversy about her paternity, Conrad did seal forever the answer to the question, at least as far as the world was concerned. In death, he referred to Francesca as his "daughter," just as he had always done in life.

Two of Conrad's sisters, Helen Buckley and Rosemary Carpenter, received $50,000 each. His fourteen grandchildren—from Nicky, Barron, and Eric—each received $15,000. (Perhaps it's a measure of Conrad's increasingly tight hold on his money that his grandchildren benefited *less* as Conrad accumulated more. According to his 1955 will, his grandchildren were to receive $25,000 each, $10,000 more than they were given in the 1973 will—and he was certainly worth a lot more in 1973.) Moreover, a total of twelve nieces and nephews received $10,000 each.

Olive Wakeman, "my valued friend and administrative assistant," was bequeathed $75,000.

Conrad's trusted butler, Hugo Mentz, received $30,000.

To a nun, Sister Francetta Barberis of Washington, D.C., Hilton bequeathed "my star sapphire ring."

To the California Province of the Society of Jesus, Conrad willed $100,000.

Everything else—*everything else*—was to go to the Conrad Hilton Foundation to then be earmarked for charity. Basically, all totaled, Conrad Hilton had willed to his heirs and friends a little more than just $1.5 million of his $200 million estate ($700 million if including stocks)—or as the attorneys for the Conrad Hilton Foundation would succinctly put it in one legal brief, "He chose to devise less than 1% of his entire estate to his relatives and close associates or employees, and give the balance to charity."

An eloquent missive from Conrad followed, addressed to the directors of the foundation that bore his name:

> There is a natural law, a Divine law, that obliges you and me to relieve the suffering, the distressed, and the destitute. Charity is a supreme virtue, and the great channel through which the mercy of God is passed on to mankind. It is the virtue that unites men and inspires their noblest efforts. Love one another, for that is the whole law; so our fellow men deserve to be loved and encouraged— never to be abandoned to wander alone in poverty and darkness. The practice of charity will bind all men in one great brotherhood.
>
> Be ever watchful for the opportunity to shelter little children with the umbrella of your charity; be generous to their schools, their hospitals and their places of worship. For, as they must bear the burdens of our mistakes, so are they in their innocence the repositories of our hopes for the upward progress of humanity. Give aid to their protectors and defenders, the Sisters, who devote their love and life's work for the good of mankind, for they appeal especially to me as being deserving of help from the Foundation.

He mentioned specifically the Sisters of Loretto, "as it was this order who first established educational institutions in my home state of New Mexico." He also mentioned the Sisters of the Sacred Heart as "another order that I have assisted in Chicago, but there are many deserving support in other fields, particularly hospitals."

Conrad Hilton's words were powerful and moving, his intention quite clear: Charity—not family and not friends—was to receive the bulk of his estate. He had drafted thirty-two wills and codicils since 1946, all under the legal advice of the same attorney, James Bates. None of those wills had ever left large sums of money to family members. Rather, all of them had left the vast majority of his wealth to charities. It was always the way he wanted it.

PART THIRTEEN

The Fight of Their Lives

Francesca Contests the Will

*D*espite the relatively small amount of stock in the Hilton Corporation bequeathed to them by their father, Barron and Eric Hilton would most certainly remain financially solvent. Both already held considerable stock and other annuities in the company, which were worth many millions. According to Conrad Hilton's lawyer Myron Harpole, Barron was worth about $26 million at the time of his father's death—in other words, he didn't really need that $750,000 in stock. Actually, it would seem that the division of stock bequeathed to the sons by their father was more a formality than anything else. It would have been much more advantageous to Barron, Eric, and their own heirs if Conrad had actually given them *control* of his huge empire, but he didn't and there wasn't much they could do about it. It was as if Conrad had decided that his sons should be the custodians of the dynasty that he had built—but not necessarily the owners.

Conrad Hilton was a complicated man. Most observers were perplexed by his reasoning when it came to his family and his vast empire. True, he wanted the company to remain in the family and continue to flourish, yet he did *not* want his sons to have complete control over it. Most people don't know how Barron and Eric felt about this judgment—neither would ever think to speak out publicly in a critical way about their father. As coexecutor of the estate along with James E. Bates, Barron was well aware of the specifics of the will at least a year before his father's death, and he made no effort to change Conrad's mind about any of it, at least according to his later testimony. It's also likely that he warned Eric in advance, lest his younger brother get his hopes up where the estate was concerned. Neither brother, however, had the kind of close relationship with Francesca where they would confide in her. Therefore, although she was painfully aware of Conrad's frugal nature, Francesca was still dismayed at the relatively small amount of her inheritance. Along with her surprise came disappointment and then anger. It was as if, even in his death, she was being slighted by the man she had called "Daddy" for her entire life.

At the time her father died, Francesca Hilton was thirty-one. She was a strong-willed, outspoken woman, like her mother, and in many ways like the man she had always looked to as a father figure. She'd spent most of her life seeking acceptance from Conrad and the other Hiltons, and it could be argued she never really got it. Now she decided that her only course of action was to contest the will, one of the points her mother made clear in a meeting with one of Hilton's attorneys, her good friend Gregson Bautzer, shortly after the reading of the will.

"Now do you see?" Zsa Zsa asked Gregson as the two spoke of recent events. She was very upset, holding the thick last will and testament in her hand and repeatedly smacking it on the lawyer's desk as she spoke. "For years, everyone has been saying, 'Oh, that Zsa Zsa, she's so *ridiculous*," she continued. "Oh, that Zsa Zsa, she's so *money hungry*. Well, I guess I knew him better than anyone, didn't I, Greg?"

"You have to calm down," the attorney told her. As Conrad's lawyer and Zsa Zsa's longtime friend, Bautzer once again found himself in a tough position. He reminded her that Francesca needed her full support during this difficult time. "You've always been hard as nails, Zsa Zsa," he said. "Now is not the time to fall apart."

"It's just that my daughter doesn't deserve this embarrassment," Zsa Zsa said, trying to compose herself. She conceded that while she and Conrad certainly had their fair share of problems, "Francie was never to blame for *any* of it. You have always been on our side, Greg," she added. "You *know* this isn't right."

"You raised a tough, smart kid," Gregson said. He believed Francesca could get past this present unpleasantness. "After all, it's only money, Zsa Zsa," he remarked.

"Oh, please don't be so patronizing," Zsa Zsa said. "It's not becoming to either one of us. And besides," she added, "this is the real world we're living in, not some fairyland." She observed that money usually equated to power, especially for women. Money also meant independence. "Money matters a great deal," she declared, "and the only people who don't think so are people who have it." When Bautzer noted that Conrad had not completely excluded Francesca from his will, Zsa Zsa made the point that he had bequeathed her only $25,000 more than Olive Wakeman. "And how does that make sense?" she asked, raising her voice. "You tell Conrad's people that we will fight this thing," Zsa Zsa said as she gathered her things to leave. "If it's a family war they want, they will get it. Wills can be broken," she concluded. "And Francie will do just that," she added. "I assure you, she will."

No matter her determination, taking on Conrad Nicholson Hilton's estate would not be easy for Francesca. After all, the estate had what seemed like an endless supply of money and high-powered attorneys to litigate such legal wrangling. Francesca had nowhere near the same resources available to her. As it would happen, fighting for what she believed should be her rightful inheritance—at least $50 million, or, in the words of her attorney Robert D. Walker, "to be treated in the fashion a daughter ought to be treated"—would come at a steep price to her privacy. This would be no private affair. Named as defendants in the case would be *all* of the other beneficiaries: As well as her siblings, Barron and Eric, that would include all of their children (and Nicky's too); all of Conrad's grandchildren; his sisters; his nieces and nephews; his other close associates such as Olive Wakeman and Hugo Mentz; and dozens of nuns and priests and other people associated with the many charities now benefiting from Conrad's estate. In effect, it meant that all of those people would be, by law, privy to the many filings associated with Francesca's case, including copies of the thirty-one prior wills and codicils of Conrad Hilton, many of which declared the embarrassing fact that he did not recognize her as his daughter.

Unbeknownst to Francesca, in all of the wills Conrad Hilton had prepared between 1947 and 1955, he stated clearly that she was to receive no money from his inheritance, not a dime. He vaguely referred to her as "the daughter born to Zsa Zsa Gabor." But then, in 1955, when Francesca was eight, Conrad apparently warmed up to her and had a change of heart, because in his will of June 3 that year, he decided to be more generous. He acknowledged her as his daughter and left her $50,000 in trust. In years to come, Hilton would repeat that $50,000 bequest to Francesca. Then, in his will of October 1960, he would double that inheritance to $100,000, remove the trust, and make the amount an outright bequest. However, Zsa Zsa Gabor and Francesca Hilton would be unaware of any of these private decisions until the dawn of the legal action they were about to mount.

Additionally, Francesca would have to be deposed—as would her mother—about her private relationship with Conrad. Copies of those lengthy and revealing depositions would then be readily available not only to each and every defendant in the case and their many attorneys and associates, but also to anyone else interested as a matter of public record. Still, despite this enormous invasion of her privacy, Francesca decided it was worth it. She wanted to fight. No. She *needed* to fight.

For the next few years, Constance Francesca Hilton would spend hundreds of thousands of dollars engaged in this legal war. Zsa Zsa, of course, agreed with her daughter's position. Mother and daughter now found themselves aligned in the fight of their lives, not just for money for Francesca, but also for recognition.

Besides the cost to Francesca Hilton's privacy, the fight would come at another huge risk. In many wills written by wealthy people, it is stipulated that when one of the recipients contests the will, that person is immediately written out of the will if he loses the contest, and completely forfeits his or her inheritance. Such a provision existed in Conrad's will. As always, he wanted his word on the matter to be final. Therefore, if Francesca were to lose her case, she would end up with nothing, not even the $100,000 Conrad Hilton had left to her.

"Insane Delusion"

$\mathcal{T}$he thrust of Francesca Hilton's contesting of her father's will, according to her original filing of March 13, 1979, was her theory that because of Conrad's unwavering devotion to his faith, he began to suffer from the "insane delusion" in 1971 that he was not her father. That was the year the two had their big argument at Casa Encantada. It was after that heated confrontation, according to her theory, that he first asserted he was not her father and suddenly "changed from a caring and loving father to a fear-ridden old man who renounced his only daughter." Moreover, "As a result of his age, illnesses and cerebral accidents which had impaired him physically and mentally, [Conrad Hilton] on October 31, 1973 [the date of his last will], did not know and comprehend the nature, extent and value of his estate and bequeathed 'one-tenth of one percent' of his estate to her, his daughter."

Today, of course, a simple DNA test could quickly determine whether or not a person is a child's parent. But back in the late 1970s and early 1980s, DNA testing for the purposes of proving paternity had not yet been pioneered. The process of DNA fingerprinting was not developed until 1984, by Alec Jeffreys, and didn't become available for paternity testing until 1988. Prior to that time, a blood test—ABO blood typing—could have been used to *exclude* Conrad Hilton from being Francesca's father in that all the markings in the blood typing would be inherited characteristics. However, it could not be used to confirm whether or not he *was* her father. It's a moot point, anyway. Conrad never asked to be tested, and he never was tested. Myron Harpole says that James E. Bates "had a thick file that he kept for years that was for entirely the purpose of filing a paternity case against Zsa Zsa Gabor where Francesca Hilton was concerned. However, we never did it."

Obviously Francesca had no inkling as to the evidence that would now be collected by the Hilton estate's many lawyers to indisputably discount her theory about Conrad's "insane delusion." For instance, at the end of 1979, those attorneys presented the hotel mogul's many previous wills, some of which illustrated quite clearly that Conrad had disowned Francesca—and well before 1971. These long-buried documents turned Francesca's theory on its head. Now, with her argument—that Conrad's ambivalence toward her started in 1971—significantly weakened, Francesca had no choice but to amend her complaint. To that end, she then stated that she believed Conrad had actually begun to suffer from an "insane delusion" *not* in 1971, when she first heard him doubt his paternity of her, but way back in 1947, right after she was born. She said she now believed that he disavowed her at that time because she was born into a marriage (to Zsa Zsa Gabor) he was ashamed of, a union that was not sanctioned by the church.

Francesca Hilton's depositions would be taken on September 12, 13, and 14, 1979. The principal examination of the first day and a half was conducted by Ralph H. Nutter and the balance by Myron E. Harpole. "As I recall it," said Myron Harpole, who from the firm Witter and Harpole represented Barron and Eric Hilton, James Bates, and Olive Wakeman, "one of the biggest hurdles faced by Miss Hilton was defining the term 'insane delusion.' It was a legal terminology her attorneys had implemented, and one she didn't seem to fully understand or, at the very least, couldn't fully explain."

During her deposition, Francesca testified about the night in August 1971 when she had the argument with her mother that caused her to then flee to Casa Encantada and into her father's arms. This was the night she asked him for money and shelter. "On previous occasions when he turned down a financial request," she stated, "he had done so calmly and easily—simply stating, in substance, 'No, I won't do that,' and 'That's too much money,' or words of similar meaning. He had never displayed any anger or ill feeling, but rather had simply turned down my request. However, on this occasion, he became visibly upset, vehemently stated that my support was my mother's responsibility and made a series of statements, the substance of which was that he didn't believe he was my father (or wanted me to think he didn't believe he was my father)."

QUESTION: Besides a request for money, what else did you ask of him?

ANSWER: I inquired of my father whether or not I could temporarily reside with him at his residence in Bel-Air until I could locate another place, and he responded, in substance, there was no room in the house.

QUESTION: You are saying that when he said there was no room in the house, that indicated to you that he was no longer of sound and disposing mind and memory?

ANSWER: Well, I am not a psychiatrist or a doctor, but in view of the fact that I suspect that you have all seen the size of the house, it does seem a little strange since it is quite large.

QUESTION: Had you ever lived with him in that house before?

ANSWER: No. But I can't say that one line alone made me totally believe that he was not of sound mind.

QUESTION: What else?

ANSWER: The feeling that he gave me was that he possibly felt he wasn't my father. It was strange. As he indicated [in his follow-up letter to her] this was the first time during our relationship we had ever had any situation that was unpleasant. I believe that I took him a little bit off guard because I don't think he had ever really seen me upset before. I don't know whether he said this [about

her paternity] because, you know, maybe he just didn't
want to give me the money and that was his way of
not giving it to me.

QUESTION: It was an emotional conversation on both sides. Is that
right?

ANSWER: Yes.

QUESTION: So, Miss Hilton, did you believe in August of 1971 that
. Conrad Hilton suffered from an insane delusion that
you were not his child?

ANSWER: Well, let's put it this way: When he said to me that he
thought he might not be my father, I didn't know what
to think, really.

The subject of Conrad's state of mind was then broached. "From time to
time over a period of approximately ten years prior to the demise of my father,"
Francesca had previously stated in one of her answers to interrogatories, "I had
conversations with my mother, the date and place of which I cannot clearly
recall, which indicated that my father was no longer of sound mind."

QUESTION: Can you give us an instance of a conversation you had
with your mother during which Conrad Hilton's state
of mind was called into question?

ANSWER: As an example, my mother indicated to me she had
on one occasion during 1973 gone to my father's office
and was waiting in the reception area while Olive
Wakeman announced her, and my father said, "Zsa
Zsa who?" [Note: This incident actually occurred in
1966. However, it's not unusual in depositions for specific dates to become confused.]

QUESTION: He said "Zsa Zsa who?"

ANSWER: Yes.

QUESTION: So the only conversation you can remember is this
one where it refers to "Zsa Zsa who?"

ANSWER: Yes.

The biggest problem with Francesca Hilton's case was that it seemed—
at least based on her answers at her depositions—that her lawyers had not

fully prepared her for an intense examination. Said a frustrated Myron Harpole during his day of questioning, "I just want to know how, in her mind, she permitted this contest to be filed with these allegations in it? I want to know what was in her mind."

In a more organized presentation to counteract Francesca's theories, one of the first witnesses the estate called was Barron Hilton. Under oath, he testified that the paternity of Francesca had been for decades the sub-ject of concern and speculation for his father and some members of his inner circle, such as his assistant Olive Wakeman. However, he said that the delicate subject was, by Conrad's insistence, off-limits to him and his brothers. He testified that he, Nicky, and Eric were always encouraged by Conrad to "recognize, accept and love Francesca as our sister." Not once, said Barron, did he and his father ever discuss whether or not Fran-cesca was actually his biological daughter. Still, there was always "general discussion within the family that Francesca was not the daughter of my father. It was just generally understood that that was the case." He testi-fied that "my brother, Nick, for an example," was someone with whom Barron often discussed the question of Francesca's parentage, "as well as my wife and my father's sisters."

To prove that Conrad Hilton was of sound mind when he filed his final will in 1973, the estate called forth the witnesses to the signing of his will and an assortment of friends and employees who were with him during that time in his life. All would testify that Conrad was in good health, with no physical or psychological infirmity. For instance, he knew the people in the room; no one helped him sign or date the will; he was actively working; and so on. Barron Hilton, Frances Hilton, and Olive Wakeman would corroborate that testimony—all extremely forceful and credible witnesses. "Mr. Hilton always stated that he had no secrets from me, and I don't know of anything he did not discuss with me," testified Wakeman.

To rebut it, Francesca Hilton could offer only her and her mother's opinions that something was "just not right" with Conrad Hilton, that he had slowed down and had shown signs of what they described as possible dementia.

It's likely that Francesca really did feel that her father was slipping. After the verbal altercation with him at Casa Encantada, she was quite clear, according to Olive Wakeman's own deposition, that she feared a possible loss of intellectual acuity. There was no other explanation she could come up with as to why Conrad would suddenly disavow her as he had that awful evening. After all, as far as she was concerned, he had always called her his daughter, had always signed his letters to her "Daddy," and had always acted as if she were his offspring. Something had obviously happened. What was it? The answer to this question was basically the linchpin of her entire case. But—at least based on all of the available evidence—it would appear that the only thing that happened was that Conrad Hilton had completely lost his temper and, in a moment of heated emotion, blurted out something he had been concealing for many years.

Zsa Zsa's Deposition

*I*t was on June 14, 1979, that Zsa Zsa (Sari) Gabor Belge Hilton Sanders Hutner Cosden Ryan O'Hara was scheduled to give the first of three depositions, at 10 a.m. at the Beverly Hills Hotel, though she didn't make it to the hotel until well after noon. "Of course, I remember Mrs. O'Hara's depositions," said attorney Myron Harpole, using Zsa Zsa's married name at the time; she was married to Michael O'Hara. "Say what you will about her, one thing was true," he recalled. "She had charisma and personality like no one I had ever met. She just vibrated with it. You could not take your eyes off her. She was absolutely magnificent. I hadn't seen her in a few years, but she hadn't changed at all." Indeed, at sixty-two, Zsa Zsa was still a real beauty, with charm to spare. "Immediately, she captivated everyone's attention," said Myron Harpole.

"You will not believe the time I had getting here!" Zsa Zsa exclaimed as she took her seat at a round table in the middle of the small living room. Holding court, she then told a humorous story about being stuck behind a "Tour of the Stars' Homes" bus in her Bel-Air neighborhood. Apparently the driver had been commandeering the middle of the road for miles, preventing Zsa Zsa from getting around him. Then finally he stopped and, according to Zsa Zsa, announced to his passengers on his bullhorn, "The great movie star Zsa Zsa Gabor is right behind us!" She exclaimed, "The next thing I know, all of these little Chinese people begin stampeding off the bus and surrounding my Bentley! It is a nightmare. They are putting their pieces of paper in my face, they are asking for autographs, they are taking pictures and they are shouting at me...*in Chinese!* Why, I barely got out of there *alive!*" Everyone burst into laughter at her story.

"Zsa Zsa, this is Ralph Nutter," Myron Harpole told her with a smile. "He also represents the Conrad Hilton estate," Harpole explained, "and he too will be asking you questions today."

From her seat, Zsa Zsa took in Nutter, sizing him up from head to toe. He was a middle-aged man with a round face and horn-rimmed glasses, wearing a conservative gray suit, a white shirt, and a black striped tie. A former Los Angeles Superior Court judge and the author of the Los Angeles Superior Court Rules for Writs and Receivers, he'd seen pretty much all there was to see in the judicial system. "We then got to the business at hand," said Myron Harpole. "Once the pleasantries were over, Zsa Zsa became very serious and focused. This was not child's play for her. She started by producing Francesca's birth certificate and baptism certificate. Constance Francesca Hilton was born on March 10, 1947, and it was Zsa Zsa's immediate testimony that between April and August of 1946, she only saw Conrad one time, and that he telephoned her, as she recalled, 'a couple of times.'"

After talking a bit about her early impressions of Conrad and touching on their marriage, the questioning got serious and Zsa Zsa talked about the night she conceived Francesca, which she said happened in July 1946.

QUESTION: Exactly where was Francesca conceived?
ANSWER: At the Plaza Hotel in New York.
QUESTION: What do you remember of it, Mrs. O'Hara?
ANSWER: This is embarrassing and inappropriate.

After a brief recess during which Zsa Zsa conferred with her attorneys, the deposition continued.

QUESTION: I will repeat the question for the record. What do you remember, Mrs. O'Hara?
ANSWER: I remember that something was wrong with Conrad's leg at the time. I think it was broken. He had a cast of some kind on it.

QUESTION: So, what happened?

ANSWER: He came in from Los Angeles and said he wanted to see me. I was staying at the Plaza with my parents. And I remember he drove up in a white convertible with red leather interior and he was very happy to see me on the curb waiting for him in front of the hotel. Then, he went one way and I went another. Late that night, he came to my suite and that's when it happened.

QUESTION: What happened? If you don't mind, Mrs. O'Hara?

ANSWER: We were intimate. Francesca was conceived.

QUESTION: You said he had a cast on?

ANSWER: Yes. But it did not hinder him to make love to me. This is terribly embarrassing.

QUESTION: Just a few more questions, Mrs. O'Hara. You say it did not hinder him?

ANSWER: He did not take off all of his clothes. Not completely. He could not take off his pants completely because of the cast. Oh, this is terrible.

QUESTION: Go on.

ANSWER: He pulled down his pants as far as he could, and that's how he did it.

QUESTION: What happened then?

ANSWER: He left.

QUESTION: He did not spend the night?

ANSWER: No. He left.

QUESTION: And then?

ANSWER: Six weeks later, the doctor told me I was pregnant.

QUESTION: So, on or about the 6th day of August, 1946, you knew that you were pregnant, did you not?

ANSWER: That I remember. Most every woman would.

QUESTION: And at the time of the interlocutory divorce hearing on September 17, 1946, you knew you were pregnant, did you not?

ANSWER: Yes, I did.

QUESTION: You did not tell the judge that you were pregnant, did you?

ANSWER: He didn't ask me.

QUESTION: You did not tell the judge that you wanted equalization payments for the baby?

ANSWER: I was a European person. I was hurt. I didn't want money. Conrad said, "This is what I give you. Now sign."

QUESTION: Have you ever made any requests for funds from Conrad Hilton since 1946?

ANSWER: Never.

Zsa Zsa further testified, "I did not have relations with any man other than my husband, Mr. Hilton, anytime in the summer of 1946, or even after, until long after Francesca was born." She affirmed that Conrad was "very pleased" when she had the baby, and that he assisted in locating and purchasing a home in Manhattan for her because he knew she couldn't live in a hotel with the baby.

As for Conrad's relationship with Francesca, Zsa Zsa said, he always treated her like a daughter, making it a point to mark the familial events of her life such as birthdays and graduations. She recalled that when Francesca was a little girl, Conrad would take her by the hand and walk her proudly into L'Escoffier—the stylish French restaurant that for years was on the penthouse level of the Beverly Hilton. Father and daughter would then enjoy a private luncheon. She said that he also took her and Francesca to "a very nice lunch" at the Beverly Hills Hotel on the day of Francesca's confirmation in 1960. He even sometimes invited Francesca to Christmas Mass with him, following which just the two of them would open his presents, she said. Also, "He was obviously pleased when friends and acquaintances would comment upon the family resemblance between himself and Francesca." She added that Conrad had always made it clear to her that Francesca was her responsibility, not his, and that she was fine with it.

QUESTION: Did Conrad Hilton ever tell you that he believed Francesca was not his?

ANSWER: No. As I said before, I would have killed him.

QUESTION: Is it possible that you don't remember incidents from the 1940s?

ANSWER: No. The important things I remember.
QUESTION: But do you have any problem recalling incidents that occurred in, say, 1944?
ANSWER: Yes, sometimes. So do you!

Regarding Francesca's allegation that Conrad suffered from an "insane delusion," Zsa Zsa testified that while Conrad obviously wasn't insane, he "wasn't well since at least '66 or '67." Zsa Zsa was never entirely comfortable about linking the notion of "insane delusion" to Francesca's case against the estate. Privately, she told one of her associates before her deposition, "Of course, Connie was mad. You have to be mad to do what he did with his life, to take the chances he took, the risks he took, especially during the Depression. The worst thing you can be in this insane world is the only sane person in it. People think I'm crazy, and I hope I am! God help me if I wasn't; I would never have made it here from Hungary!" Still, for the purposes of her daughter's case, she would go along with the theory. To that end, she said that Conrad had begun to forget people's names and that his general memory had begun slipping. She then cited the incident that occurred in 1966 when she went to see Conrad in his office to discuss Francesca and she heard Conrad ask, "Zsa Zsa who?"

"That [incident] told me that he was not himself. He wasn't the same Hilton I used to know. He had never been old, but he became old. He had been such a young man, but no more. He always had a sparkle in his eye, and unfortunately that was gone. Sometimes, he was coherent and sometimes he wasn't with it. Barron said so, too. Barron Hilton kept telling it to me."

QUESTION: What else did you notice?
ANSWER: He walked differently. He walked like an old man. Stooped over. He started going down the hill. All of a sudden he didn't wear his toupee. No. Take that out.
QUESTION: Excuse me?
ANSWER: About the toupee, take that out. Take that toupee bit out.
QUESTION: I'm sorry?
ANSWER: Can we take that out? I don't want to say that.

QUESTION: But if it is something you noticed...
ANSWER: I don't like it. It's terrible. Take that out.

Eventually, Gabor's attorney convinced her that the remark should not be stricken if it was true. She said it was true.

At the end of the first four-hour session, Zsa Zsa was exhausted. When told by Ralph Nutter that she would probably have to come back for more questioning, she became annoyed. "But how much more can I tell you?" she asked him. "I have already given you my whole life!" Myron Harpole added that there would likely be just a few more questions. "Fine," Zsa Zsa decided. "Then I will do what I have to do for my daughter. I don't care how many more times I have to come down here and answer your embarrassing questions, I will do it," she concluded. "Connie always thought I was weak. Well, I just hope he is watching me now."

In the end, Zsa Zsa Gabor would be further deposed on July 9 by attorneys Nutter and Harpole, and then again on July 10 by Harpole alone.

Smoking Gun?

*I*n her sworn testimony, Zsa Zsa Gabor claimed that she and Conrad Hilton had engaged in one single night of passion at the Plaza Hotel in New York City in early July 1946, during which her daughter, Francesca, was conceived. Zsa Zsa's tale of an almost scatterbrained, hurried tryst with Conrad half dressed while in a leg cast had a whiff of the kind of highly amusing anecdote she loved to tell late night talk show hosts. It's safe to say that no one on the Hilton estate's side believed a word of it. But then, much to everyone's astonishment, Francesca Hilton's team of attorneys located a gentleman named Willard Kramer, an insurance man who was able to testify to at least some of the specifics of Zsa Zsa's unusual story. Kramer had been a golfing buddy of Conrad Hilton's in the 1940s. His testimony—at least the way Francesca's lawyers viewed it—could well help win Francesca's case. Willard Kramer was deposed by Robert D. Walker of the firm Belcher, Henzie & Biegenzahn on July 1, 1979.

QUESTION: In the spring of 1946, did you have occasion to remem-
            ber any kind of injury that Conrad Hilton had to any
            part of his body?

ANSWER: Yes. It was to his knee. I don't recall whether it was
            broken or lacerated or strained, but he wore a cast on
            his right knee. I don't remember how long he wore
            it, but it was cumbersome. It interfered with our golf
            game, but he and I still traveled extensively during
            that period when he had the cast on his knee.

QUESTION: So you recall traveling with Mr. Hilton at this time?

ANSWER: Yes. I have a rather good recollection of having flown
            with him to New York. I think it was the day before
            Easter, which was in April of that year. We arrived in
            New York by plane after midnight. We stayed at the
            Plaza Hotel which at that time, or later, became one of
            the Hilton Hotels acquired by him. We shared a suite
            of rooms in the building. We arrived there on Easter
            Sunday in the very early morning hours. We went
            to the hotel by limousine. We got to the hotel after
            midnight.

According to his testimony, the morning they arrived—which would
have been Easter Sunday—they rose and went to mass at St. Patrick's
Cathedral. "It had been the only reason we flew to New York," he said.
"Connie's custom was to attend Easter Sunday Mass at St. Patrick's. He
was very excited about it. We went by taxicab because of the cast on his
leg, and then by taxicab back to the hotel."

QUESTION: When you came back to the hotel, did you meet
            anyone?

ANSWER: Yes, standing on the steps of the hotel facing Madison
            Avenue was the ex Mrs. Hilton and her mother and
            father.

QUESTION: Now, the ex Mrs. Hilton, what is her first name?

ANSWER: Zsa Zsa.

QUESTION: I see. That is the woman who is known as Zsa Zsa
            Gabor.

ANSWER: That is correct. To me, it was rather obvious that she
was waiting for us to come. She knew that we were at
church, and we would be coming back, and, of course,
it is a presumption on my part, but it looked to me as if
she was prepared to wait there to receive us.

QUESTION: Okay, tell us what happened then.

ANSWER: She invited us, both Connie and myself, to come to
her table inside the Plaza, which was a very colorful Easter Day, for a cocktail. We declined and said
that we would later come after we had been upstairs
to freshen up, and we did. We came down from our
rooms. We went to her table. We had a cocktail.

Just as it seemed Kramer's testimony might go a long way toward helping to prove some of Zsa Zsa's claims, the case took yet another surprising
turn.

QUESTION: All right. Now, did Conrad Hilton say anything to you
about or with regard to Zsa Zsa Gabor on this occasion
that you now recall?

ANSWER: Well, all I recall is that he didn't want to be in her
company by himself. He said, "Willard, whatever you
do, don't let me be alone with Zsa Zsa today." I said,
"All right, Connie. I will keep a close eye on you."

QUESTION: So, to your knowledge, was Conrad Hilton ever alone
with Zsa Zsa Gabor on that trip to New York City?

ANSWER: To my knowledge, no.

Willard Kramer's testimony that Conrad Hilton was never alone with
Zsa Zsa Gabor substantially weakened his impact as a witness for Francesca. That said, there was an even bigger problem. In 1946, Easter Sunday fell on April 21. But Francesca was born on March 10, 1947, a full
eleven months later. Therefore, one of the two witnesses—Kramer or
Gabor—was mistaken (or lying) about the date Conrad Hilton was in
New York wearing a cast.

To clarify things, Zsa Zsa needed to once again be interrogated at
the Beverly Hills Hotel, this time on July 10, 1979. Questioned by both

Robert D. Walker for Francesca and Myron Harpole for the estate, Zsa Zsa—more impatient and short-tempered than before—repeated her story of making love to Conrad while he was wearing a cast exactly as she had earlier told it.

QUESTION: Mrs. O'Hara, is it possible that this event you described occurred in April of 1946?

ANSWER: No.

QUESTION: Why is that?

ANSWER: Because I remember it very specifically. How could I not? It was when my daughter was conceived. It was in July of 1946.

QUESTION: Can you be specific in terms of the date?

ANSWER: How can you be specific about a date from 30 years ago? No, I can not. I know it was in July of 1946. That I know.

QUESTION: What would you say to a witness whose testimony it is that you were never alone with Conrad Hilton when he came to New York either in April of 1946 or, as you claim, July of 1946?

ANSWER: I would say you are a liar. That is what I would say.

QUESTION: How would you respond to a witness who claims that Mr. Hilton said, "Please do not let me be alone with my ex-wife," and who then proceeded to make certain that Mr. Hilton's wish was then granted?

ANSWER: Was he with Conrad Hilton 24 hours a day? Did he sleep next to him in his bed all night long? How does he know where my husband was every single moment of the day and every single moment of the night. It's ridiculous. Please.

QUESTION: So, is it your testimony then, Mrs. O'Hara, that Mr. Hilton slipped away for a rendezvous with you?

ANSWER: No it is not. Stop putting your words into my mouth. I don't know if he slipped away. I only know that we were together. That is what I know. And it was in July of 1946. That is what I know.

The question remained: Was Conrad Hilton in New York in April 1946, or was he there in July? If in April, it would not be have been possible for him to have fathered Francesca, since she was born the following March. But if in July, then, yes, it would have been possible.

It wasn't until weeks after both Gabor's and Kramer's depositions that Conrad Hilton's attorneys were finally able to locate his travel itineraries for 1946. Had they found them earlier, it might have saved a lot of trouble, though still not answering all questions conclusively. The startling discovery was made that Conrad had been in New York in both April *and* July. Now it appeared that both Zsa Zsa Gabor and Willard Kramer had been telling the truth. The only question was whether or not Zsa Zsa was telling the *whole* truth: Had she and Conrad really been intimate in July 1946?

A Surprise Visitor

*I*t was a sunny afternoon the last week of July 1979 when Frances Hilton was rudely awakened from a sound nap by a loud rapping on her front door. It had been six months since the death of her husband. She was now living in a fairly nice—but by no means extravagant—three-bedroom apartment on Comstock Avenue in Beverly Hills. The home was tastefully furnished, a few antiques here and there, but mostly plain retail furniture. Frances was quite comfortable there, having turned one of the bedrooms into a study, the other into a master for her own use, and the third for guests. About a month after she moved in, Steven Hilton, Barron's son, visited her and noticed that the apartment needed some repairs. "This has got to be done now," he said, and he took care of it immediately. A few weeks later, Barron came to visit with a gift—a mink coat. She had never had one, and Barron just thought she deserved one, so he bought it for her. His father would have been happy about it. Barron always realized how much Frances meant to his father. He even wrote a letter to Bill Kelly to tell him that he believed Frances to be "my father's one true love." Therefore, the Hiltons would always treat Frances as a treasured member of the family. She would never really want for anything, but as was her custom, she would never really ask for anything either.

"Who is it?" Frances said as she stood behind her front door.

"Why, it's me, *dah-ling*," came the voice from the other side. "It's Zsa Zsa!"

Could it be? Was it possible? And if so... *why*?

Frances cracked the door open with more than a little trepidation and... there she stood: Zsa Zsa Gabor—bouffant platinum blonde hair, shimmering blouse, slim-fitting slacks, spiked heels... the whole Gabor-esque picture. As Frances would later recall it, she couldn't quite believe her eyes. In that moment, it was as if her two worlds had suddenly collided—the extravagant life she had once led as Conrad Hilton's wife and the simpler one she now led as his widow. Instinctively, she reached out and embraced Zsa Zsa. "My goodness," Frances exclaimed. "This is such a surprise."

"For me, too," Zsa Zsa said, laughing.

As it would happen, in the days following Zsa Zsa Gabor's deposition in Francesca's case, she couldn't get Conrad Hilton off her mind. After all, at one time he had meant the world to her; they had so much history. When she heard that he had died, she went to pieces. People in her life were surprised at just how devastated she was by the news. Now it appeared Zsa Zsa had some unfinished business with his widow. After Frances welcomed her into her living room. Zsa Zsa took a place on the sofa; Frances sat next to her. She offered her a cup of tea, but Zsa Zsa declined.

Phyllis Bradley recounts what Frances Hilton later told her about this surprise visit from Zsa Zsa. "Mrs. Hilton told me that Miss Gabor started by asking if she had given her deposition yet," Bradley recalled. "At first, Mrs. Hilton didn't know what she was talking about. Then it hit her—Francesca's lawsuit. Frances was scheduled to be deposed in just a week's time. Miss Gabor warned her that the attorneys would probably ask her to recall every little detail about this visit, so they should probably be careful about what they discussed. She said that she had become smart about such things of late and joked that she could be a lawyer herself, with all that she had been through with what she called 'these goddamn *depquisi-*

tions.'" (As it would happen, Zsa Zsa would be proved right; the attorneys *would* ask Frances about this surprise visit and Frances would be asked to provide a clear and concise account of it in order to determine if Zsa Zsa had left any threadbare clues as to Francesca's paternity—which apparently she had not.)

After she settled into her chair, Zsa Zsa took in her modest surroundings. "So, they wouldn't let you stay at the mansion, would they?" she asked.

"Well, no," Frances answered. She explained that the Conrad N. Hilton Foundation actually owned Casa Encantada. Attorney Donald H. Hubbs had told her that the foundation would list the house completely furnished—the way Conrad had bought it—for around $15 million (the equivalent of about $50 million today). "It was definitely time for me to leave," Frances said. She added that she was sure Conrad wouldn't have wanted her rattling around in that enormous mansion all by herself with just servants for company.

"You couldn't take any of the furnishings, either?" Zsa Zsa asked.

Again according to her deposition, Frances told Zsa Zsa that if she wanted to keep any furnishings from Casa Encantada, she would've had to purchase them from the foundation. Zsa Zsa found this arrangement puzzling. She wondered why the widow should not be allowed to keep her deceased husband's furniture. "Maybe in the real world," Frances observed wryly, "but not in this one." She added that even Barron and Eric had to purchase any pieces that had sentimental value to them. After some more small talk, Frances finally asked, "So, why are you here, Zsa Zsa?"

"I don't know, to tell you the truth," Zsa Zsa answered. She looked a little lost, as Frances would describe her. "But you were always so kind to me," she said. "I guess I want you to know that I'm very sorry I was so mean to you, dear. It has really bothered me."

Frances was surprised. She certainly never expected an apology from Zsa Zsa Gabor! She told Zsa Zsa that she probably had a great deal on her mind at the time, and that this was likely the reason she had often been so abrasive. Zsa Zsa agreed, but said she now realized she could have just been nicer to Frances. She specifically referred to the scene she had caused in front of Conrad's hospital room when he was dying. "Do you know that I was actually quite proud of you that day?" Zsa Zsa asked Frances. She said she admired how Frances had stood her ground. Of course, she was angry at the time, she admitted. "But I also thought, 'My God, this woman is completely underrated, isn't she?'" she observed. "'She's tough, like me. She's strong, like me.' I thought, 'It's no wonder Connie married her.'"

Frances conceded that, in retrospect, she felt terrible about the way she had handled things at the hospital. She now believed she should have just let Zsa Zsa in to see Conrad, "but it was such an emotional time," she explained. "I think I just got caught up in it." She added that "in some ways I ended up being someone I really didn't want to be."

"You did what you believed was the right thing to do for the family," Zsa Zsa concluded. "I understand. I fight for family, too. I always have."

Zsa Zsa then spoke about her tortured relationship with Conrad. "To be loved is a strength," she observed, "but to love, *that* is a weakness." Conrad had represented an important reminder of her first days in America, she said. He was like a father to her, which, she observed, perhaps explained why she had so desperately sought his approval for so many years. "I have not been able to stop crying about his death," she confessed, sadly. "I've just been so upset."

Zsa Zsa then spoke of the meeting she and Conrad had about a year before he died when he apologized to her for ever having hurt her. "It just meant the world to me," she said. "My God, I never thought he would do that! Never!" She also said she'd had a telephone call with Conrad about a month before he died, during which she told him that she didn't know how she would ever survive his death. True to his nature, he told her that she would just go on, that she would pull herself "up from her bootstraps" and continue with the business of living. She should not give him a second thought, he said, because that's just how he would want it. Characteristic of their relationship, the two then got into a bit of a tiff because Zsa Zsa felt Conrad was trying to control the way she should grieve his death, telling her just how to be sad.

"So does this mean you are no longer angry at him?" Frances asked.

Zsa Zsa couldn't answer the question; she was ambivalent. She allowed, however, that she would always have strong feelings for Conrad Hilton because, as she put it, "completely letting those feelings go would be like cutting out the roots beneath me."

"Okay, I go now," Zsa Zsa then suddenly announced. "I've taken too much of your time." According to Frances's memory, Zsa Zsa stretched out her arms to her as the two women stood in the doorway. The unlikely friends then shared an embrace. "You know, I don't ordinarily like women," Zsa Zsa told Frances with a smile. "But you, I like. I know why he loved you," she concluded as she broke away from the hug. And with that, Zsa Zsa Gabor turned and walked away.

Frances closed the door behind her.

* * *

Mary Frances Kelly Hilton, Conrad's third wife, would survive her only husband, Conrad, by twenty-eight years. She would die of lymphoma on May 30, 2006, in Santa Monica, California, at the age of ninety-one.

"Frannie" would be survived by her brother, William P. Kelly—Bill—as well as his wife, Stella, and many nieces, nephews, and close friends, including her best friend, Helen Lamm, and her former personal secretary, Phyllis Davis Bradley.

"Frances became quite ill in the last years of her life," recalled her sister-in-law, Stella. "When she was ill, we wanted her to move to Illinois to live with us, but she was independent. She loved her little apartment and wanted to stay in California. However, the money Conrad had willed to her was running out fast. My husband, Bill, wrote to Barron to say we were having problems supporting Frannie. Barron didn't hesitate for a second making sure Frannie was taken care of for life."

"The Hiltons all loved Frannie very much and treated her like a member of the family until the day she died. She was one of the loveliest human beings I had ever known," concluded Stella Kelly. "Not a day goes by that we don't miss her."

A memorial mass for Mary Frances Hilton was set at St. Paul's the Apostle Church in Westwood, the same church at which she and Connie attended mass every morning. Frances had originally intended to be buried next to Conrad in Dallas. However, her family convinced her to be buried in the family plot in Lake Forest, Illinois, so that they could visit the grave.

Judge's Decision

*T*he case of *Francesca Hilton v. The Estate of Conrad N. Hilton* would not end up before a jury. Instead, Los Angeles Superior Court judge Jack W. Swink granted the defendants what is called a "summary judgment," a decision based on legal issues without a trial. "In other words," explained Myron Harpole, "we, as Hilton's lawyers, presented our evidence to the judge to prove that there was no need for the matter to go to trial, that the end result was obviously going to be a determination in our favor. Meanwhile, Francesca's side appealed to him that the case had not been proven by us at all, and that it should go before a jury [for a trial that was slated to take place on May 16, 1980]. After both arguments were presented, we moved for summary judgment. The judge ruled in our favor."

Neither Francesca Hilton nor Zsa Zsa Gabor was in court for the two-hour argument by both sides, on March 28, 1980.

In his decision, Judge Swink ruled that Conrad Hilton knew exactly what he was doing when he wrote his will of 1973, given that it so closely mirrored the many wills he had written prior to that time; he had never given a great deal of money to *any* family member. In Francesca's case, Hilton had actually increased the amount of her inheritance from virtually nothing (in wills from 1947 to 1955) to $50,000 (in wills from 1955 through 1960) to, eventually, $100,000 (in wills from 1960 through 1973). In all of those wills, he also gave the great bulk of his estate to charity.

It had been Francesca's attorneys who had turned the case into one about her paternity. As far as the Hilton estate was concerned, Conrad had publicly acknowledged her as his daughter to the world, and privately acknowledged her as his daughter in his will, and that should have been the end of it. However, Francesca's attorneys sought to prove that even though Conrad had done so, he harbored a secret, unreasonable doubt as to whether or not he was her father. As to this nagging question, the judge ruled that Conrad had not suffered from any "insane delusion." Rather, his doubts about her paternity were based "on logical suspicions," which he had entertained for many years as a result of the shadowy circumstances of Francesca's birth. In the end, the conflicting testimonies of Zsa Zsa Gabor and Willard Kramer only went toward convincing the judge that Conrad had good reason to wonder. "It would still come down to not whether he was the father or wasn't the father," the judge wrote in his ruling, "but what his *belief* was. Was his doubt a figment of his imagination? And the Court would answer no to that. Was it a belief that came out of thin air? And the Court would answer no to that, as well."

Most persuasive to the judge was the letter Conrad Hilton had dictated to his assistant Olive Wakeman and lawyer G. Bentley Ryan in August 1971 in which he specifically stated that he had not believed from the beginning that Francesca was his daughter. This was the letter he had his attorney put away for safekeeping, "just in case."

"His foresight in dictating this letter was quite prescient," wrote the judge. " 'If this matter ever comes to court,' he had written, 'I am asking you two dear friends, who witnessed this dictation, to testify to the reasons why I have permitted the relationship to exist between Francesca and myself.' "

Moreover, many people testified that Conrad was of sound mind when he signed the will. Therefore, there was no question about it, the judge decided: Conrad Hilton knew exactly what he was doing when he wrote his will and he bequeathed Francesca an amount of money he decided was appropriate. The judge then ruled in favor of the Conrad N. Hilton estate.

"This case was an attack on the moral values and work ethic of Conrad Hilton," Hilton attorney Ralph Nutter then declared. "He believed his children and grandchildren should work for a living and that was a virtue, hardly an insane delusion."

Obviously, Francesca Hilton was disappointed by the judge's decision. She took it hard. "For years, she had fought for recognition, and that's what this case was really about—recognition and acknowledgment," said one close friend of hers. "But, in a sense, the judge ruled that she *had* been recognized in the will. She *had* been acknowledged in the will. She just hadn't been given a lot of money, and that was Conrad's right. You can imagine how she felt about that. You can also imagine how Zsa Zsa felt about it."

Unsurprisingly, Zsa Zsa was quite upset. Taking a very theatrical turn, she told the attorney Myron Harpole, "We haven't even *begun* to fight yet. You just wait and see." It was a sunny California day and the two were sitting poolside on the patio of Zsa Zsa's sumptuous estate, under an oversized umbrella As the attorney presented her with a stack of documents requiring her signature, Zsa Zsa spoke about her daughter's difficult legal battle. "Francesca says she wants to appeal," she observed. "And I think she should," she concluded. She said that even though she was angry that Francesca had lost her case, she was gratified to know that the estate had not been able to prove that she wasn't Conrad's daughter. "And they tried, too, didn't they?" Zsa Zsa asked bitterly. "Embarrassing me with their questions about my sex with Connie. But the truth is the truth." When the lawyer reminded Zsa Zsa that the fight really hadn't been about paternity, but rather about Hilton's will, Zsa Zsa scoffed. "Yes, it was about Francie's inheritance," she agreed, "but please don't be naïve," she added. "For years, the Hiltons have been whispering amongst themselves that Francesca is not Conrad's daughter, robbing her of her true heritage." She added that when Francesca had children, it was inevitable that the battle for recognition would be passed on to an entirely new generation, "and I simply won't have it," Zsa Zsa concluded. "I am not going to have my grandchildren go through the same thing my poor daughter has gone through all of these years. So, yes! Francie should definitely appeal."

In fact, Francesca agreed with her mother; she had come so far, she felt she had no choice but to take it all the way. Therefore, in the spring of 1982, she mounted an appeal.

Unfortunately, she would lose on appeal as well.

Then, as if to add insult to injury, Francesca would also be forced to forfeit the $100,000 Conrad Hilton had bequeathed her. As per the terms of his last will and testament, any unsuccessful contester had to sacrifice any inheritance. "Jim Bates insisted that we put that provision of the will into effect," Myron Harpole recalled. "Therefore, Francesca Hilton was deprived of any inheritance. She didn't get any money at all."

PART FOURTEEN

Heir Apparent

Barron's Option

*D*oubtless, one of the primary reasons James E. Bates, coexecutor of Conrad Hilton's estate along with Barron Hilton, was adamant about enforcing the clause in Conrad's will that would disinherit Francesca for contesting it was because of the complications her legal action had created for Barron and the Conrad N. Hilton Foundation. Francesca wasn't entirely responsible for the ensuing chaos—but she certainly hadn't helped matters. As a result of her contesting of the will, it could not immediately be admitted to probate. It wouldn't be until March 1983, when Francesca lost her appeal, that Barron's concerns were finally able to be fully considered.

It's commonly believed in the business world that Conrad Hilton's will did Barron a great disservice. Even Donald Trump—a good friend of Barron's—noted in his book *The Art of the Deal*, "The assumption had been that Conrad Hilton would pass on his near-controlling interest in the company to Barron—or at the very least that he'd spread it among family members. Instead, Conrad Hilton used his will to disenfranchise his children. He just left Barron a token number of shares of stock. The result was to make Barron just another high-level corporate manager who lacked the power of a major stockholder."

Trump's assessment was at least partly accurate. However, the situation wasn't quite so cut-and-dried, luckily for Barron Hilton.

Conrad Hilton owned the largest block of stock held by the Conrad N. Hilton Foundation, a controlling amount of 27.4 percent, or 6.78 million shares—which was worth about $500 million at the time of Conrad's death. The rest was divided among board members, with Barron holding just 3.6 percent. Hilton's will granted Barron an option to purchase a described portion of stock in the estate "at the values as appraised in [Conrad's] estate." These assets were, basically, anything above that which a charitable corporation (in this case the Conrad N. Hilton Foundation, the beneficiary of most of Conrad's assets) was permitted to hold, as defined by the Tax Reform Act of 1969. According to that act, the estate was only allowed to hold 20 percent of Conrad's Hilton Hotels

Corporation stock. If Barron could pull together the money, he would be allowed to purchase any excess stock, which was the remaining 7 percent and was worth millions of dollars. He had, according to the will, ten days to exercise this option. However, there were some immediate questions about this particular option (which, incidentally, became known amongst the players in this case as "Barron's Option").

The board of directors of the Conrad N. Hilton Foundation and its lawyers—such as Myron Harpole, who was hired by James E. Bates to defend the foundation—maintained that Conrad Hilton's intentions were clear not only by virtue of what he stipulated in the will, but in large part because of what was widely known about him. He was someone who never intended for his family members to attain great wealth by virtue of their lineage to him, and that much was generally agreed by all. Therefore, when he bequeathed $750,000 worth of stock to Barron, that was his sole intention—or so the foundation argued. Beyond that, they maintained, Conrad had no further intention where Barron was concerned.

Another opinion also held by some of the foundation's attorneys, and one that was not so openly stated at the time, was that James E. Bates—who was Conrad's personal attorney and friend from 1944 until his death, and who drew each of Conrad's wills and codicils since 1947—had made a serious error by even including Barron's Option in the will. "Jim Bates was an excellent lawyer, but not a tax attorney," Harpole allowed. "He also did not allow a review of the will by any of us who actually were tax attorneys. Therefore, Barron's Option was a serious error on his part. We argued that Jim Bates—according to his own interpretation of the Tax Code of May of 1969—had ill-advised Conrad. We believed that Conrad was led to believe that there would be no excess stock at all, and thus there would be nothing for Barron to purchase. That scenario was much more in line with Conrad Hilton's personality and with what we believed was his intention where his son was concerned."*

---

* Donald Hubbs, in an interview with the *Los Angeles Times* in 1986, suggested that he was actually the one who proposed to Bates the language in the will that was ultimately disputed. Also, during the ensuing litigation, Hubbs testified that Conrad Hilton asked his advice as a tax expert on whether he should sign the will with the provision granting Barron Hilton the option. Hubbs said he advised Conrad Hilton to sign.

A Windfall for Barron?

*T*hings got worse for the Conrad N. Hilton Foundation and much better for Barron Hilton when he was finally able to fully exercise that option in November 1983, four years after Conrad's death. It was then that he and his lawyers fired the first of a few surprising salvos.

First, Barron's team argued that because of various tax code complications arising from Barron's position as both a shareholder of Hilton and a director of the foundation, the amount of excess stock now available to him had been ratcheted up to a full 100 percent—the controlling interest—of Conrad's stock in the company. He could buy it all if he wanted to—and he most certainly *did* want to—and he could make a profit on it too. Within that four-year period, the stock's value had skyrocketed.

Barron's attorneys then fired their next salvo. They argued that not only did Barron have the right to purchase all of the stock in question, but that he should be able to buy it at its so-called date of death value as of December 1979, meaning what it was worth when Conrad died ($24 a share), *not* what it had appreciated to by 1983 ($72 a share). The result? Barron would be paying $170 million for $500 million worth of stock, a profit of *$330 million*. The actual payment for the stock would go back to the foundation, but the profit would be Barron's and Barron's alone. "It's called a great deal," Donald Trump observed. "It may also be called trying to rewrite your father's will."

There was just no way, the foundation argued, that Conrad Hilton ever intended for Barron Hilton to make hundreds of millions of dollars in profit, especially on excess stock he didn't even realize would exist. The foundation argued that Barron was taking advantage of the huge windfall he was able to make because of a big mistake—or at the very least, a big loophole—in the will. In other words, they charged that he was undermining the intent and purpose of his father's will.

"I knew Conrad pretty well. I was his lawyer for thirty years," said Myron Harpole, "and I spent a great deal of time sitting behind my desk, staring at the ceiling and just asking myself, 'Is this *really* what Conrad would have wanted?' And the answer that kept coming back to me was,

'No way. Not Conrad. No way. I *knew* Conrad. We *all* knew Conrad. No way.'"

James E. Bates's deposition went a long way toward supporting Myron Harpole's theory:

QUESTION: Describe Conrad Hilton's motivation where his will was concerned.

ANSWER: One of his objectives was to not leave unearned wealth to relatives and members of his family. He believed in a strong work ethic. His desire was to have all of his relatives, his children, get out and go to work and earn their own living. He thought that and discoursed many times about the destructive effect that unearned wealth might have if it was inherited by young people before they had learned to work and understand how to handle it. So throughout all this period of time one of his objectives was to leave a minimum amount of wealth and to leave the entire residue of his estate, that was all this period of time getting ever greater and greater, to charity, and he wanted the bequest to charity administered through the foundation that he had set up for that purpose and incorporated for that purpose.

QUESTION: Had that ever changed?

ANSWER: He never to my knowledge ever changed the primary objectives which was not to leave inherited wealth to the destruction, possible destruction of members of his family, but to give everything that he had accumulated back to the public through the charitable bequests that he had described time and time again in his series of wills.

James E. Bates also suggested in his deposition that, like Francesca, Barron was really just angry because he hadn't gotten as much money from his father as he had hoped. Barron said that theory was hogwash. He stated that he "never for a moment questioned my father's interest in leaving his wealth to charity instead of to family. Indeed, my father instilled those same values in me." That said, he also believed that Conrad would never begrudge him the opportunity to make a profit if that opportunity presented itself.

Barron's attorneys further theorized that Conrad was afraid that if Barron didn't have the option provided in his will, an outside buyer could come in and try to purchase any excess stock, thus making the company vulnerable to a hostile takeover. Indeed, Conrad had frequently stated to friends and associates that he did not want his hotels to go the way of the Stevens Hotel and the Statler hotels, which lost their continuity and identity after the deaths of their founders.

Since the foundation felt that James E. Bates had botched things up for them, it moved to reclassify itself as a so-called supporting organization, also known as a public support group, in accordance with the Internal Revenue Code. This step was a means of avoiding having to sell all or part of its hotel stock as "excess business holdings" under that troublesome federal tax law. If it were forced to sell any of those shares, the will gave Barron the option to buy them—and that's exactly what they were trying to avoid. As a public support group, the foundation argued that it was now entitled to use its "power of sale" to buy back from itself the *entire* amount of stock—*including* the part Barron wanted to purchase at a profit. The result would be *no* stock for Barron, and, thusly, *no* profit for him either. In other words, it seemed—at least in Barron's view—that the foundation was doing everything it could think of to defeat Barron's Option.

Barron Hilton's deposition:

QUESTION: It is your opinion that your father knew what he was doing?

ANSWER: He would not have given me an option if he didn't intend that I be able to use it.

QUESTION: How do you know that?

ANSWER: Because I know my father. He would not have structured it that way. He would have found another way to structure it. He would not have given me an option if he knew that the Foundation would find a way to work around it, thereby depriving me of the option. It's clear to me that instead of accepting gratefully that it will receive from my father all of his wealth which existed at death, the Foundation wants to destroy the option my father gave me for no reason other than the fact that the option has turned out to be worth a good deal of money due to the delay in closing the estate. The Foundation wants *all* the money.

The Francesca Factor

$\mathcal{T}$he foundation is trying to wear me down," Barron Hilton complained. He and his wife, Marilyn, were having a meeting with two business associates at the Hilton home in Bel-Air. It was the end of 1984. By this time, Conrad Hilton had been gone for five years, and the matter of his will was still not resolved. Barron was now fifty-seven, but looked older than his years, the lengthy legal battle over his father's estate having taken its toll.

"I don't understand how these people who have known you since you were a kid could do this to you," Marilyn said. She was hurt, and those close to Barron felt she had good reason. After all, the foundation was comprised of people who had known Hilton for decades, such as Olive Wakeman; Spearl "Red" Ellison, the former bellboy who had once loaned Conrad $500 and who then worked his way up the ranks of the organization; Vernon Herndon, Robert Groves, and Thomas Wilcox, all longtime Hilton Hotels Corporation executives; Robert Buckley, the former doctor of Conrad's son Nicky; and even Barron's brother Eric. All were dedicated to preserving what they believed to be Conrad's wishes. That said, none really had the power of Donald Hubbs and James E. Bates. For instance, most certainly if Eric had had his way, the present disagreement would have been quickly resolved, and likely in favor of his brother.

"Well, as they say, it's just business," Barron remarked wearily.

"But how dare they try to impose their will on your father?" she continued. She said that he, of all people, would know what Conrad had intended with the will.

"Jim Bates has it in his head that he knows better than me," Barron said.

"The nerve!" Marilyn exclaimed.

One of the more interesting aspects of the present conflict over Conrad's will was that it pitted longtime allies against each other. For instance, Myron Harpole had long represented Barron (and had just done so in the case filed by Francesca), but now he was representing the foundation *against* Barron. Not only that, but James E. Bates had also represented Barron Hilton for many years, was a close personal friend, and, along with Barron, was coexecutor of the estate. The battle over Conrad's stock now also pitted him against Barron. Many people long associated with the foundation were longtime associates and friends of Conrad's and Barron's—such as Conrad's tax adviser and now the president of the foundation, Donald Hubbs. Because of their positions with the foundation, however, they were all forced to align themselves against Barron. (Despite these tense times, Hubbs remained Barron Hilton's business partner in Eastridge Development Co., a $19 million real estate venture, split 80/20 between Hilton and Hubbs. Hubbs was still also involved in Hilton's Vita-Pakt Citrus Products company.)

"They act like my dad didn't know what he was doing," Barron added. He further stated that Conrad was obviously a very smart man and must have realized that there was a good chance the stock he provided with the option would appreciate. One of the associates, according to his memory of the meeting, brought up the fact that for a time after Conrad died, the stock actually plummeted, and that if the stock had continued to depreciate, Barron would have taken a big hit. "It's the nature of the stock market," he said. "Sometimes you win, sometimes you lose." Marilyn then made the point that the reason the stock had appreciated was solely because of Barron's management skills. She added that since Conrad's death, no one associated with the foundation had contributed in any way whatsoever to the continued success of the Hilton hotel business. It was all because of Barron's efforts that the stock now had such excellent value, at least in her estimation. "They should be *thanking* you," she said, "not punishing you."

"You know, this is really the result of the Francesca Factor, don't you?" one of the other associates offered.

"Interesting," Barron said, nodding his head.

"The Francesca Factor" is what the Hilton camp had begun to term Francesca Hilton's impact on the dispensation of the estate. Because

Barron's fight was not about the wealth that Conrad had accumulated, but about the post-death appreciation of a large portion of stock, some observers felt that Francesca had actually done Barron a huge favor. After all, it was because of the delay she had caused that the stock had so much time to appreciate. But the truth, as Barron saw it, was that had he been able to exercise his option and buy the stock in January 1979, immediately after Conrad's death, it would have appreciated under his stewardship anyway, and the profit would have been his without question. "The Francesca Factor did us no favors here," said the associate. With a chuckle, Barron remarked that if Francesca only knew of the chaos she had caused, she would be "just a little bit delighted." He actually had no beef with her, though. She had fought for what she believed was right, and she gave a good fight, too. That's what Hiltons do; Barron said he respected her for it.

At this point, one of the associates present then took a leap and posed what was by now an unpopular thesis among those in Barron Hilton's close-knit circle. "Is it possible that James Bates just screwed this whole goddamn thing up?" he asked. "Is it possible that Conrad never intended for you to make a profit like this?"

Barron didn't explode; that wasn't like him, anyway, just like it was never like his father to lose his temper. He mulled over the question. "I'm not sure it matters," he said, his tone level. He said that his father taught him to take advantage of every situation that could potentially provide a profit. They now had a big opportunity to do just that, and they had no choice but to take advantage of it. "I, for one, believe that my father fully intended it," he concluded. "But it doesn't matter one way or the other. I'm not walking away from it."

They then all started talking about Conrad, sharing their memories of him. It was clear that everyone still missed him terribly. "I was maybe thirteen," Barron recalled with a soft smile, "and, you know, my dad was a very busy man. But Nick and I had this lemonade stand with which we planned to make a fortune," he said with a laugh. Barron then explained that he and Nick offered Conrad the opportunity to share in the potential profits of their exciting new venture. They would give him a third of every ten cents made. However, he would have to be the one to actually make the lemonade. Conrad decided it would be a good investment. "So, as busy as he was, there was my old man, in the kitchen, trying to figure out how to make a decent lemonade. Finally he came out with a pitcher. He proudly poured the lemonade into a glass and handed it to me. I took a sip. I spat it out. I looked up at him. And I said, 'Boy, that's really *lousy*.'" Everyone had a good laugh. "Yes, those were the days," Barron said wistfully. "Those were certainly the days."

Each Other

I did the best I could," Francesca Hilton said. "Now I have to just put it behind me."

It was the fall of 1984, almost two years after her appeal was denied, but it was still sometimes on her mind, as it was on her mother's. Francesca was speaking to Zsa Zsa over dinner at a restaurant in West Hollywood. Zsa Zsa, now sixty-seven, had just come from a fitting and photo session related to an upcoming event at the Beverly Wilshire Hotel. Therefore she was in full Zsa Zsa Gabor regalia—an expertly tailored pink bugle-beaded pantsuit, her hair, now more platinum than blonde, perfectly coiffed, lots of expensive jewelry. Diners at other tables couldn't take their eyes off her.

Zsa Zsa's most recent marriage—her eighth—to character actor Felipe de Alba a year earlier, had been annulled just twenty-four hours after the ceremony because she didn't know that her union to husband number seven, Michael O'Hara, hadn't been legally terminated. "It's so sad about Felipe," she remarked with a twinkle in her eye. "Do you know how many men I will have to sleep with just to get over him?" It seemed that there would always be some sort of high-stakes drama unfolding in the life of Zsa Zsa Gabor—and she would always have a great line to go along with it.

Though Zsa Zsa managed to thrive no matter the circumstances, recent years had been difficult for Francesca. In the end, though, it could be said that Francesca proved herself to be as much a Hilton as anyone else in the family, just by virtue of the tenacity and persistence she demonstrated in her quest for acknowledgment. In that regard, Conrad might have been proud of her. True, he never would have approved of her taking legal action against his estate, but he probably wouldn't have begrudged her right to fight for what she believed was hers. After all, he was always a man of his own convictions, whether in business or in his personal life. As far as Francesca was concerned, she was still—and always would be—the daughter of Conrad Hilton. It had never been proven otherwise, had it?

Also at the table with Zsa Zsa and Francesca was Zsa Zsa's new personal assistant, a young man named Timothy Barrows. "If you don't mind me asking, exactly how much did your father leave you, Francesca?" Barrows asked.

Francesca shot him an irritated look. "*Excuse me,*" she said, "but... *who are you, again?*"

"Oh, he's my new secretary," Zsa Zsa answered for Barrows. She explained that he was her fourth in just six weeks; she was having "*terrible* luck with the help." Then, turning to him, she snapped, "Mind your own business. Just sit there and be quiet!"

"Well, look, it was his money and his right to do whatever he wanted with it," Francesca said, trying to be objective about situation, all of this according to Barrows's memory. "What's done is done."

"Well, I for one am not satisfied," Zsa Zsa said. "I still think there must be *something* we can do..."

Francesca shook her head. "You know, life doesn't always have to be a battle, Mother," she said. "A war to be won." Though she was trying to be positive, Barrows would remember that the expression of sadness on Francesca's face suggested that the pain of this conflict was still deeply embedded in her heart.

Zsa Zsa nodded. "Maybe you're right, Francie," she concluded, now seeming a little defeated. Then, after a beat—"I'd like to make a proposal to you," she said, taking her daughter's hand. "Let's make a promise to never fight again." From the sincere expression on her face, Zsa Zsa seemed to genuinely mean it. She added that she was "just too old and tired" to argue with her own daughter these days. "You and I, we belong to each other," she concluded, her eyes filled with sudden warmth. "We're all we have, Francie. So, what do you say?"

Francesca looked at her mother with mock astonishment. "I would say you have had *way* too much to drink," she shot back with a cackle. "And I would say, woman, you are *dreaming!*"

"And I would say...*cheers to that*," Zsa Zsa Gabor exclaimed, raising her glass of wine.

Mother and daughter then shared a hearty laugh. Yes, they'd been through an awful lot together. But they still had each other.

Eric and Pat Divorce

*B*y 1985, six years had passed since the death of Conrad Nicholson Hilton. During that time, his son Eric was divorced from Pat after twenty-nine years of marriage and four children; the divorce was finalized in 1983. "We grew apart," is all Patricia Skipworth Hilton wishes to say about the breakup of her marriage. "Eric is a wonderful man and I would never have a negative thing to say about him, ever. I admit, though, that it was sad. The end of a long marriage is always difficult, but what can one do? Life does go on."

Pat Hilton remains single and lives in Houston. "I have a very happy life," she says. "The days as a Hilton wife are far behind me, but I have fond memories of my sisters-in-law, Marilyn and Trish, and my brothers-in-law, Barron and Nicky. Oh yes, we were at the center of *everything*, or at least that's the way it felt to us at the time. These days, I'm happy to have a much more quiet life here in Texas.

"Eric and I are still friendly," she allows. "After all, we have children, and family is important to the Hiltons. So we have always made a genuine effort for the children."

Today, Eric Michael Hilton, who is eighty-one, sits as a director of the Conrad N. Hilton Foundation. In March 1997, he retired as Hilton Hotels Corporation vice chairman. "Eric's contribution to the success of Hilton Hotels Corporation is significant," said Barron at the time. "His accomplishments in the areas of domestic and international strategic planning and property development have been important to the continued growth of the company our father, Conrad N. Hilton, founded more than seventy-five years ago. Eric was involved in many of the corporation's major transactions throughout his career, including Hilton's reentry into the international market when the luxury Conrad International brand was introduced in 1985."

Eric also serves on the advisory board of the Conrad N. Hilton College of Hotel and Restaurant Management at the University of Houston. Presently, he is married to Bitten "Bibi" Hilton. Eric also remains close to his four children by his marriage to Pat: Eric Jr., Beverly, Linda, and Brad, all of whom lead lives outside of the public arena.

Barron Is Denied

*B*y the mid-1980s, Barron Hilton—who remained happily married to Marilyn—had begun to make quite an impact on the gambling business with the Hilton hotels. Whereas in 1970 gambling had accounted for none of the company's operating income, by 1985 it was almost 50 percent, thanks largely to its Las Vegas holdings, the Las Vegas Hilton and the Flamingo Hilton. Recently, though, to add to his ongoing troubles with his father's estate, Barron faced a major public embarrassment.

By this time, legalized gambling had taken off in Atlantic City, with most of Nevada's major hotels—Caesars, Bally, Sands, Harrah's, and the Golden Nugget—doing profitable business at the shore. To get in on the action, Barron spent $320 million building a majestic 614-room hotel and 60,000-square-foot casino on an eight-acre site in Atlantic City. It was the biggest undertaking in the Hilton Corporation's history. But on February 28, 1985, the New Jersey Casino Control Commission surprised most industry observers when it denied Barron his application for a license to operate a casino in Atlantic City. It practically never happened that someone of Barron's stature was turned down by the NJCCC. He was already licensed in Las Vegas, and he promised to bring big business to the city, as well as all of the goodwill of the Hilton name. Therefore it seemed inconceivable that he would be denied. He had to have the approval of four commissioners, and though he won a majority of three to two in his favor, it was still a loss, and an embarrassing one, too. Barron issued a statement saying he was "shocked and stunned."

"This was a bitter pill for him to swallow," said Tim Applegate, senior vice president and general counsel for the Hilton Corporation. "It was a surprise, hard to accept. Not a good moment for Barron...for any of us."

"You have to remember that, for Barron, everything he ever did was measured by whether or not Conrad would approve of it," said another of Hilton's associates. "It was always about honoring his father. No matter how successful he became with it, it was still Conrad's company, at least as far as he was concerned. Therefore, he felt a responsibility to keep it operating smoothly and to keep clean its image. When he and I met the day after his license was denied, Conrad's name kept coming up."

Barron and his associate were at Barron's home on Brooklawn Drive in Bel-Air having breakfast with Marilyn and some other family members and a few others. Barron seemed disheartened, which was unusual for him. No matter how difficult things became in his life, he always managed to at least appear unruffled. But lately it had just been one challenge after another. Between his battles with the foundation over his father's will and now with the NJCCC over his license in New Jersey, he had a lot on his plate. "We've been putting off building in Atlantic City since, what, 1981?" he asked his associate. "High interest rates, an uncertain market ... I was just never sure about Atlantic City, was I?"

"Look, this is still a good idea," the associate argued. He urged Barron not to doubt himself.

Barron sat back in his chair, tilted his head back, and stared at the ceiling. "Maybe we were a little too eager," he said. He said he didn't think his father would ever have put the cart before the horse. Probably Conrad would have gotten the license first, he mused, *then* built.

"Well, your father was a lot more conservative that you are," the associate argued. He also noted that the competition in Atlantic City was so cutthroat, "you have to get in there quickly and do whatever you're going to do." He added that things were now very different in the hotel business. Back in Conrad's day, the competition was somewhat in alignment with him, he observed. "You didn't see guys like Henry Crown trying to undercut him," he added. "Today, these guys are out there nipping at your heels. You got your Donald Trumps, you got your Steve Wynns ... Why, it's a different world."

Barron agreed. Still, he said, he couldn't shake the feeling that Conrad was looking down at them and asking, "What the hell were you guys thinking?"

Marilyn laughed. "Oh, Conrad would have *plenty* to say," she concluded, smiling. Not about her husband either, she said, looking at him warmly, "but about those fools in the Casino Control Commission!"

The major reason the NJCCC rejected the Hilton Corporation's application for a gaming license was the company's relationship with a particular business associate. Conrad and Barron had made it a rule to stay clear of mobsters. It couldn't always have been easy. After all, gangsters controlled many of the unions, such as those connected to the liquor industry and to other supplies or services the Hiltons needed to entertain guests in their hotels. Once the Hilton Hotels Corporation got into the gambling business, however, avoiding such shady characters would have become even more difficult. In fact, the company had a relationship with a Chicago attorney named Sidney Korshak who apparently had ties to organized crime figures. According to press reports at the time, the Hilton company had been paying Korshak $50,000 a year as a "special labor consultant," and that's the reason the NJCCC turned down the request for a gaming license in the Garden State.

New Jersey gaming official Joel R. Jacobson stated, "In my judgment, the relationship of the Hilton Hotels Corporation with Sidney Korshak is the fatal link upon which I primarily based the conclusion that this applicant has not established its suitability for licensure in New Jersey." After that rebuke, Barron did what he probably should have done much earlier: He cut off his relationship with Korshak.

As Donald Trump sees it today, Sidney Korshak was only part of the problem the Hilton Corporation faced in New Jersey. "At the risk of sounding pejorative, I think another rather big issue was overconfidence," he recalled. "There was a definite feeling that Barron deserved the license and that he was doing the commissioners a favor by applying for it. Of course, that kind of daring goes along with the Hilton brand, with being so successful. But the commission didn't see it that way, and never does. It always thinks it's doing you a favor by granting, not the other way around."

Barron Hilton planned to open his grand hotel in May 1984, but now, just three months before that target date, he had no gaming license in New Jersey. It was a bad situation. This was when Donald Trump came into the picture.

Donald Trump Makes an Overture

*D*onald Trump was thirty-eight years of age in 1984 and already well regarded as a real estate mogul in New York City before his entree into the Atlantic City gaming world with Harrah's at Trump Plaza. He had a great deal of admiration for Conrad Hilton and for what he had done for the hotel industry. Zsa Zsa Gabor recalled that she was in New York in 1984, staying at the Plaza, when Trump—whom she had never met—telephoned her. "We ended up chatting for nearly an hour," she recalled. "He was nice and I had the feeling he was quite wonderful. Above all, though, he wanted to know all about Conrad. He said that he admired him very much and had always wanted to be another Conrad Hilton."

Trump recalled, "I admit that I wasn't thrilled with the idea that Barron Hilton was building a hotel in town, especially since the Boardwalk hotel I owned [with Harrah's] wasn't performing as well as I would have liked. I knew that Barron was soaking a fortune into his new enterprise, and I also knew he was, like his dad, a tough competitor. But then one day [on February 14, 1984], I got a telephone call from a colleague who said, 'You will never guess what just happened to Barron Hilton. He got turned down for his license in Atlantic City.' My source said that Barron might now just try to sell the whole facility rather than go in for another hearing. That got my attention."

Because Barron was scheduled to open his hotel imminently, he had already hired well over a thousand employees and intended to have more than four thousand by the time he opened. "It was a disaster in the making," Trump recalled. "All those people working there with no money coming in? I felt bad for Hilton. I decided to give him a call. We had never met, so it was more like a friendly call from one colleague to another to commiserate over a dilemma."

During the phone call, Donald told Barron he was both surprised and sorry that he had been denied a license in New Jersey. Barron said he appreciated Donald's empathy. "I don't know what you have in mind for that hotel in Atlantic City," Trump told Hilton, "but if you ever decide you want to just sell it, I might be interested if the price is right." Hilton thought Trump's proposition sounded interesting. He didn't yet know what he was going to do, he admitted. "Let me discuss it with the board and the family and get back to you."

According to Myron Harpole, Barron was actually contemplating the notion of filing for a new hearing—he wasn't just going to go away with his tail between his legs, and as he told Harpole at the time, "I believe my dad would fight this with everything in him." However, Harpole recalls that most members of his board of directors felt this wasn't the best strategy. After all, they argued, if Barron were to be turned down a second time, it could prove to be devastating not only in the company's stock market showing but also in the court of public opinion. Moreover, a second rejection might make the property seem even less valuable to any prospective buyer—should that buyer even exist. No, Harpole says the board told Barron that the property should just be sold and they should cut their losses while they still had the opportunity to do so.

Sure enough, a potential buyer really was out there sniffing around—and not just at the new Atlantic City Hilton, but the entire Hilton hotel chain.

Hostile Takeover?

*B*arron Hilton had previously argued that one of the main reasons his father had wanted him to have the option of purchasing any excess stock held by the foundation was in order to prevent anyone else from doing so and thereby taking over the Hilton chain. That's exactly what seemed to be happening by the spring of 1985.

A few days after Barron was denied his license in New Jersey, hotel mogul Stephen Wynn—the then forty-three-year-old chairman of Golden Nugget, Inc., which owned two of the most profitable casino hotels in business in Atlantic City and in Las Vegas—launched a takeover bid for the Hilton Hotels Corporation by making a surprising bid to buy Conrad's 27.4 percent block of shares, the same shares that Barron and the foundation had been fighting over for many years. Wynn offered to pay $488 million, or $72 a share. Barron's top offer up until this point had been just $24 a share. Wynn's probable intention was that if he should succeed in this bid, he would then attempt to buy out the other shareholders at the same price, at a cost of about $1.8 billion. Then the company would be all his.

Barron Hilton likely thought that Wynn was a young upstart who didn't have nearly enough capital to pull off such a major and hostile takeover. At this point, Hilton Hotels had earned more than $100 million over its last four quarters and owned $1.2 billion in assets, whereas Wynn's company had earned just $20.6 million in the same period with assets only two-thirds as big. Whether or not Barron had the full support of some of the other shareholders at this time was questionable because of the dispute over Barron's Option. If those particular shareholders were annoyed enough with Barron, they could actually side with Wynn, and Hilton could end up losing his whole company. Given these possible scenarios, it was as if Steve Wynn had become a major threat overnight.

Another big problem for Barron Hilton at this time was that his image was taking a bit of a thrashing in the media. For instance, *Forbes* pointed out Barron's role in the company's divesting of its international chain—Nicky's division—back in 1969. The magazine also reported critically about Barron's handling of the Carte Blanche credit card business and the millions he had lost in that particular endeavor. (The publication neglected to mention that Barron sold the company to Citibank for a tidy profit of $16.5 million in 1965.) The press didn't really have a lot to pick through in terms of Barron's mistakes, though. If that was the best *Forbes* could come up with—two incidents in a career spanning almost forty years—then it could be argued that Barron was in pretty good shape. Still, because of his idea of building a hotel in Atlantic City before he had a license to open one there, Barron's critics were eager to note that he could lose as much as $50 million in the summer of 1985 from revenues that might have been generated by the Atlantic City Hilton.

Steve Wynn seemed to want to use the tide in the media against Barron to help plead his case to the Hilton shareholders, telling *Fortune*'s Terry Moore that it didn't bode well for Barron that he was run out of New Jersey without a gaming license and without clearing his name in regard to his association with Korshak, thereby making the Hilton chain much more vulnerable to a hostile takeover. "Here's a company that gets 40 percent of its income from gambling and has been adjudicated as unsuitable in one of the biggest gambling markets in the world," Wynn told Moore. "As a shareholder, I would be concerned." (Wynn owned about 1 percent of Hilton's stock.) He also told the *New York Times*, "It's a black mark on Hilton."

Then, much to the Hilton Corporation's dismay, "John Van de Kamp, who was the California attorney general, took Steve Wynn's side," recalled Myron Harpole, "and tried to assist Wynn in his takeover attempt. Now there was an even greater chance that Barron could lose the entire pie."

"Look, I have no sympathy for Barron Hilton," Steve Wynn said candidly. "I felt comfortable making this offer; it is not a personal attack. And I'm not taking advantage of a tax loophole to take the company away from some charity."

According to Myron Harpole, Barron Hilton was unhappy about some of the negative press and felt that Steve Wynn was at least partially responsible for it, even by just playing into it. Barron likely wasn't sure what to make of Wynn. Wynn was slick and polished. Like Trump, he talked a good game. But he lacked Trump's people skills. If he had that same skill set, he might have appealed to Barron on a more personal level and as a result might have fared better with him. "Barron was a lot like his father in that he was the type to sit down, make a call, shoot the shit, and find out what was what," said one of his business associates at the time, "not just make a dramatic play for someone's company. In that respect, Barron had more admiration for Trump. He appreciated Trump's telephone call, for instance. Little things mean a lot, even in big business. The fact that Wynn was pushing so hard made Barron feel like, yeah, he'd probably rather to do business with Donald Trump."

Trump Meets Hilton

*I*n early March 1984, Benjamin Lambert, one of the Hilton board of directors with whom Donald Trump was friendly, suggested that Trump attend a party he was hosting for the Hilton board of directors at his New York home, just prior to its annual meeting in Manhattan. He suggested that Donald and Barron should take the opportunity to meet, and, he added, who knew what might result from such a meeting? "So I went to the party," Trump recalled, "and I finally had the opportunity to meet Barron Hilton. Right away, I felt he was an amiable fellow, if not also extremely cautious. We went out onto the patio to chat."

During their conversation, Barron confided in Trump that he was still frustrated by the Casino Commission's decision. Though he had considered reapplying for a license, he wasn't yet sure how to proceed. "I think there was a little bit of, 'Screw 'em if they don't want me' kind of thinking going on," Donald recalled. "He *was* Barron Hilton, after all. As we spoke, I stood there wondering what Conrad would have done in that situation. I knew for sure what I would've done. I would've fought. I think that's how Barron felt, too. But I also think his fighting spirit was compromised due to the fact that he was facing battles on more than one front."

"I've been squeezed in a vice a hundred times before," Hilton told Trump, "but not like this." He said that, on one side, he had his father's estate fighting him "tooth-and-nail," and on the other side, he had the New Jersey Casino Commission doing the same thing. Donald sympathized with Barron's quandary. He asked exactly how much Barron had "soaked into this thing in Atlantic City?" Barron paused. "Three hundred and twenty million," he answered abruptly. He waited for a reaction. Donald acted unfazed, but actually that was a lot of money at the time, even to Donald Trump. A year earlier, it had cost him $220 million to construct the Boardwalk, and that had been his biggest gamble to date. "Well, I would say that that's a pretty good figure," Donald remarked with raised eyebrows.

"Yeah, tell me about it," Barron agreed. The two men spoke for a little while longer before ending their impromptu meeting. "It's a real honor to meet you," Trump told Hilton, and he meant it. He added that he had a great deal of respect for both Barron and Conrad, and for what they had done for the hotel business. "I'm impressed with what you've done, too," Barron told Donald. Shaking hands, the two famous hoteliers agreed to stay in touch.

Many years later, Donald Trump would observe, "My experience is that sometimes in business it's good to just sort of lay back and see where the tide can take you. So that's what I did with Barron. Later, my friend Ben Lambert told me that Barron felt comfortable around me.

"I understood Barron," Trump continued. "I know that kind of guy because I *am* that kind of guy. For Barron, personality and character are important. It's not just the deal that matters, it's the people in it. In fact, the best of deals fall apart because the people in them have a deficit of character. Barron and I were on the same page in that regard, and I also felt that this was probably how Conrad Hilton did business as well."

Trump to the Rescue

*M*any industry observers believed that Steve Wynn had a hidden agenda, that he didn't really want the entire Hilton company but rather just Barron Hilton's Atlantic City property. It was thought that maybe by making preliminary moves toward a hostile takeover, Wynn was hoping to set the stage for a negotiation somewhere along the lines of, "I'll set aside my offer to move in on your company if you'll just sell me that one valuable hotel in Atlantic City." It would seem that Barron Hilton was one of those who sensed this agenda. It wasn't long before he decided to do something about it. Donald Trump recalled, "I got a call from Barron's people saying, 'Guess what? Barron is interested in selling the Atlantic City property to you.' I was delighted."

Trump's first offer was about $250 million. Barron had already told him that he'd invested $320 million in the hotel, so Donald didn't really think he would go for the offer; he wasn't going to take that much of a loss. Trump then did the sensible thing—he raised his offer to a full $320 million. In cash. Manufacturers Hanover Trust would lend him the money; he would have it in hand in a week.

Maybe the Atlantic City property really was on Steve Wynn's mind, because the day after he learned that Hilton was considering selling it to Trump, he filed a lawsuit against Hilton charging securities violations. Meanwhile, one of Wynn's Golden Nugget executives stated to the press that "Hilton is putting his tail between his legs and running away from New Jersey without vindicating his name." Then Wynn made an offer for the Atlantic City Hilton—$344 million. That was even more than Trump's bid! Maybe not surprisingly, Barron rejected it. Beyond any personal feelings, Trump's offer was all cash, whereas Wynn's was a package of promissory notes and an undeveloped parcel of land in Atlantic

City. Barron wasn't that impressed with it. One thing was also certain—
Barron knew that, sans the valuable Atlantic City property, the Hilton
company had just become a little less attractive to Steve Wynn. Wynn's
attorney Bruce Levin confirmed that Trump's purchase, if consummated,
would most definitely force Steve Wynn to reevaluate his offer.

"I like this guy, Trump," Barron told the foundation's attorney, Myron
Harpole. "He reminds me of my father. He's a salesman, like Conrad Hilton, isn't he?"

"I agree," said Myron. "I think maybe he's got something Wynn doesn't
have. I don't know what it is..."

Both men had been influenced by Conrad's credo that relationships,
as well as business, mattered. Many in the Hilton group sensed that Donald Trump was of a similar philosophy. Trump, for all of his well-known
braggadocio, seemed like an upright man.

The next day, Barron Hilton accepted Donald Trump's offer. Trump
then had no trouble getting a license for his new hotel and casino, which
was called Trump's Castle and would open on June 17, 1985. "I bought Barron Hilton's Atlantic City hotel sight unseen, meaning I didn't do the usual
walk-through to see what I was getting myself into. The good Hilton name of
quality workmanship is what I was counting on, and I was not disappointed.

"What I remember most was that first inspection after it was truly
mine. I was amazed at the quality of the work Barron had put into it.
Everything was tip-top shape, the best of the best, money being no object.
It was spectacular. I remember thinking, 'All right, I get it, now. What I
am seeing here is the Conrad Hilton influence, and it's impressive.' All of
those many years later, you could still feel the presence of the old man."
(In March 2006, Donald Trump paid what might be considered the greatest of compliments to his friend, Conrad's son Barron. He named his
third son after him—Barron Trump.)*

---

* It bears noting that Barron Hilton did finally secure his gaming license in Atlantic City
in 1991, ironically enough taking over Steve Wynn's Golden Nugget. When Barron purchased the property, Frank J. Dodd, who was a new member of the commission, said, "It was
a major blunder to deny a casino license to Hilton [in 1985]. The industry has since fallen
on hard times in Atlantic City; the decision sent out a hostile signal to investors about how
arbitrary and unreasonable New Jersey gambling officials could be. I don't think I would
have denied him a license. That was a major turning point in the history of Atlantic City. It
sent out a bad signal." (Barron would rename the hotel the Atlantic City Hilton. However,
still disenchanted with Atlantic City, he would sell the property a short time later.)

On April 25, 1985, the threat of Steve Wynn's takeover of the Hilton company receded when James E. Bates and a majority of other foundation board members rejected his bid, calling it "inadequate." There was never much of a groundswell for Wynn, anyway. He had never mounted a successful public relations program, other than one that involved making critical pronouncements about Barron. Therefore, the other Hilton board members didn't see how he could do much better with the company; he never laid out a good strategy for them. The bottom line was that it had been a red-hot matter for a few weeks, and then, just as quickly, it cooled.

Barron Hilton had managed to avoid a hostile takeover of the company from someone who at the time apparently didn't have the financial wherewithal or the persuasive power to pull it off. But who knew what the future might hold with a more influential opponent? As long as the in-house battle existed over Conrad Hilton's stock in the Conrad N. Hilton Foundation, there was always a chance that someone else could enter the picture, attempt to purchase that block, and also entice a majority of shareholders with a better offer, thereby managing a complete takeover. Barron realized that in order to protect his (and his father's) best interests, he needed to find some way to end his battle with the foundation as soon as possible.

Resolution

*I*t would not be until the spring of 1986, after a three-week trial before Los Angeles Superior Court judge Robert Weil, that a final—and surprising—order would be issued in the matter of Conrad Hilton's will. Judge Weil ruled in favor of the Conrad N. Hilton Foundation. His harsh ruling read, "The entire residue of the estate is distributable to the Foundation, and *no part* of said residue is subject to the option contained in Paragraph Eight (a) of decedent's will in favor of William Barron Hilton."

In his decision, Judge Weil found that when the option permitting Barron to purchase excess stock was included in Conrad's will, no one, including James E. Bates or Donald Hubbs, "perceived or realized that by creating this option it was possible that Barron Hilton could receive

100 percent of the shares of the estate." The judge observed that Conrad Hilton was a "very wise man" and that "if he had intended to give Barron Hilton all his stock, he would have done so."

Myron Harpole recalled, "I had succeeded 100 percent in protecting what I believed to be the interests of Conrad Hilton and of the foundation bearing his name—at least for the moment."

The foundation, now victorious, was anxious to move forward and let bygones be bygones. Barron wasn't quite so eager. He decided to take his case to the U.S. district court in the spring of 1986, and it was there that he would finally prevail. "The presiding judge, Thomas J. Whelan, was very much on the side of Barron and his lawyers," recalled Myron Harpole. "He decided to nullify the decision of the superior court. So Barron managed to get the whole thing reversed; excellent lawyering, one could say, on the parts of his attorneys."

At the core of the court ruling in Barron's favor was the foundation's conversion to a public support organization, which the judge ultimately decided was invalid. His decision concluded that the foundation could not take those kinds of dramatic actions after Conrad's death to change its status, thereby invalidating Barron's Option.

"We think this is a shocking opinion," said foundation lawyer Thomas J. Brorby at the time, "and is clearly contrary to Conrad Hilton's will."

Barron countered by saying, "I regard this as a significant victory."

With that nullification in hand, Barron Hilton then formally appealed the original ruling. At long last, he would win his case in the court of appeals in California in March 1988.

Finally, in November 1988, this battle—almost ten years long—would conclude with a settlement that would see the foundation give Barron Hilton the bulk of the disputed shares of stock, about two-thirds of them. "By this time, the total wealth on the table was about $2 billion," recalled Myron Harpole. "In the end, Barron ended up with four million shares, worth about three-quarters of a billion dollars. The foundation received 3.5 million shares [placed in the Conrad N. Hilton Fund], and the remaining shares [about five million] were placed in the W. Barron Hilton Charitable Remainder Unitrust. According to the arrangement, Barron then received 60 percent of the W. Barron Hilton Charitable Remainder Unitrust's share dividends and the foundation received 40 percent until 2009, after which those trust assets reverted to the foundation."

In the end, Barron didn't have to pay for his newly acquired three-quarters of a billion dollars' worth of stock—not what it was worth when Conrad Hilton died and not what it was worth in 1988. In order to do so, he would have had to recruit a large group of fellow investors who would have been entitled to as much as perhaps two-thirds of the stock. "He would have had to have come up with a fortune to afford that much stock, and then the taxes on what he had to raise would have killed him," recalled Myron Harpole. "This is why they established the W. Barron Hilton Charitable Remainder Unitrust, a legal tactic that allowed Barron to win the stock and not have to pay for it. Some felt this maneuver was actually a clever way of rewriting Conrad Hilton's will," concluded Harpole. "Barron disagreed, of course."

Myron Harpole is still not, all these years later, convinced. He still feels that Conrad did not wish for Barron to achieve great wealth by virtue of his option. "Conrad had favored Barron in other business deals, so Barron was worth about $26 million at the time of the dispute," he reiterates. "It wasn't as if he was being left penniless by his father. But as a result of the dispute over the will—and also because of some additional technicalities and stock appreciation—Barron walked away with about a half billion dollars. However, I understood Barron's reason for contesting the will," he concluded. "There was just too much money at stake. He couldn't very well walk away from that kind of money. He was a Hilton, after all. Conrad's son. The best and brightest of the bunch. So he did what Hiltons do, he fought hard and he won fair and square. You have to hand it to him, because there's a big difference between the $750,000 he had when he started the battle and the half a billion he ended up with when he finished it."

Barron still felt that, through it all, he was merely carrying out his father's wishes, even if some of them had been badly misconstrued by portions of his will that were ambiguously written. "My father's two objectives, retaining control of the stock in family hands and benefiting charity through the Conrad N. Hilton Foundation, can now both be achieved," Barron Hilton said at the time of the settlement. "I am confident that my father would be pleased with this accord."

PART FIFTEEN

Fini

Zsa Zsa's Lapse in Judgment

*A*fter the death of Conrad Hilton and the unsuccessful contesting of his will by his daughter, Francesca, the histrionic nature of Zsa Zsa Gabor's life continued seemingly unabated. In August 1986, after her divorce from Felipe de Alba, she married Frédéric Prinz von Anhalt.

Frédéric Prinz von Anhalt—born Hans Robert Lichtenberg in Wallhausen, Germany—says he was adopted as a grown man in 1980 by Princess Marie-Auguste of Anhalt, daughter-in-law of Kaiser Wilhelm II. He is twenty-seven years Zsa Zsa's junior. To hear him tell it, he came to America with the express purpose of meeting Zsa Zsa, which he did after he paid a photographer $10,000 to introduce him to her and snap their picture together. One thing led to another, and—as often happened in Zsa Zsa's unpredictable life—they ended up man and wife.

Though she always managed to put on her resolute Zsa Zsa face for the public, by the end of the 1980s certain cracks had begun to appear in that façade. In 1989, for instance, she was convicted of slapping a police officer in Beverly Hills. She was forced to pay $13,000 in fines and also spend seventy-two hours in jail. It would seem that the constant stress of just being Zsa Zsa was taking its toll, as evidenced by the copy of an advertisement for a skin cream she was promoting at the time, "Zsa Zsa's Beautifying Night Creme." It read, in part, "The anxiety, the mobs of reporters, the strangers always calling—it's awful! Yet, you could never tell on my face. I always look *mah-vellous* and beautiful. But, *dahling*, you *know* how Zsa Zsa is suffering."

Maybe part of her agitation had to do with her ambivalent feelings about Conrad Hilton, which continued into the new decade. She was eventually able to accept—as she would later say—that he had omitted her from his will. However, Francesca's inheritance was still difficult for her to reconcile. When Zsa Zsa thought about the long, tangled journey she, Conrad, and Francesca had shared for so many years, it made her angry. Indeed, with the passing of time, it would seem that she became more—not less—bitter.

In 1990, Zsa Zsa Gabor was seventy-three and apparently determined to even the score on all counts—thus her memoir of that year, *One Life-time Is Not Enough*.

Comparing to her smartly written autobiography of 1960, *Zsa Zsa Gabor: My Story*, the reader is overwhelmed by the gossipy nature of *One Lifetime Is Not Enough*, as well as its many inconsistencies. For instance, in the 1960 book she wrote, "One evening I greeted Conrad with a warm kiss. Nicky said with a grin, 'Dad, what must a fellow do to get a kiss like that from Zsa Zsa?' Conrad and I both laughed it off." The 1990 book reads, "On one occasion, Conrad presented me with a box of chocolates, I kissed him. And Nicky—not able to control his jealousy—said, 'What does a man have to do, Dad, to get a kiss like that from Zsa Zsa?' Conrad whacked him so hard that I was afraid Nicky might suffer a concussion!"

One of the conquests Zsa Zsa conjured up in her book was with Nicky Hilton. She claimed that after her divorce from Conrad, she engaged in a three-year love affair with Nicky that continued into his marriage with Elizabeth Taylor. "Nicky Hilton was the first of a series of men I would have in common with Elizabeth Taylor," she wrote.

Nicky's wife, Trish Hilton, doesn't believe that is true. "Do you think my husband would have had a three-year affair with his former step-mother and forget to mention it to me? Of course not. I loved Zsa Zsa. We were good friends; I saw her all the time, as did Nicky. It would have come up between us, this so-called affair. She would never have told me such a thing to my face, though, because she would have known that I would have seen through it."

It got worse in *One Lifetime Is Not Enough* when Zsa Zsa set her sights on the one man who had vexed her for decades, Conrad Hilton. He had always had the last word, at least as far as she was concerned. Even from the grave, he had managed to have the last word about Francesca. Not anymore. Zsa Zsa now claimed in her book that Francesca was actually not conceived during a spontaneous Manhattan tryst in July in 1946, but rather as a result of Conrad having raped her.

"One day he sent a limousine for me, with instructions that I visit him in the Plaza," Zsa Zsa wrote. "I obeyed, simply because by now obeying Conrad Hilton had become a habit for me. When I arrived at his suite, I discovered that Conrad was in bed, his leg in a cast after an accident. First, we had coffee. Then (incredible as it sounds, but quite believable if you had known Conrad, his forceful nature and his intense virility), he raped me. Nine months later, our daughter Francesca Hilton was born."

Zsa Zsa's new version of events surrounding Francesca's conception was a lurid twist to an old tale. She certainly never mentioned rape the three times she was under oath about Francesca's conception.

Zsa Zsa's story could only jeopardize Francesca Hilton's already tentative place in the Hilton family. Perhaps the best course of action—that is, if Francesca wanted to be looked kindly upon by the family—would have been to immediately disavow it. How could she, though? It came from her mother, after all. They still loved each other very much, even if they did have a lifetime of differences between them. Once again, Constance Francesca Hilton found herself in an all too familiar place: caught in the middle of an ugly war between her irate mother and the distant man she had always called "Daddy." Therefore, where this allegation was concerned, she turned to humor. "Don't ask me," she joked. "I wasn't there."

It's difficult to imagine why a woman of distinction like Zsa Zsa Gabor would have wanted such a tasteless book to be representative of her life and times. No matter her flamboyant or controversial nature, she had never been lacking in class and refinement, which makes the fact that she authored this book all the more perplexing. "Yes, I think she was angry," says Trish Hilton in trying to understand Zsa Zsa's motivation, "but I also don't think she took the book that seriously. I think, for her, it was just a collection of sensational stories for entertainment and attention. I could just hear her saying, 'Oh, *dah-ling, please!* Why, no one actually *believes* this stuff. This is just for *fun!*'" concludes Trish Hilton. "Giving her the benefit of doubt, I long ago chalked this book up to a terrible lapse in judgment."

* * *

As of this writing, Zsa Zsa Gabor is ninety-seven years of age. She and Frédéric, who is seventy, have been married for twenty-eight years. Von Anhalt continues to court media attention. For instance, on February 6, 2012, he hosted a ninety-fifth birthday party for Zsa Zsa at the couple's Bel-Air home, even though Zsa Zsa was bedridden and seemingly incapacitated. He allowed a few celebrities—such as Larry King and his wife, Shawn Southwick—to go into her room and pose with her for photographs of questionable taste. Judging from them, Zsa Zsa did not seem to know what was going on around her.

Zsa Zsa Gabor is now a complete invalid, bedridden in the Bel-Air home in which she has lived for nearly forty years. She suffers from dementia, has had one leg amputated and half her body paralyzed as a result of a stroke. "She doesn't even know she gets food through the tube," von Anhalt told the *New York Post* in September 2012. "It will only upset her," he says. "She was so glamorous always, and she is so vain." It's a heartbreaking ending for a strong and powerful woman who once proclaimed, "I do not want to get old. Please, God, take me before that happens. There's nothing beautiful about aging. It's a cruel thing to happen to a woman such as myself."

Francesca: "The Original Hilton Heiress"

Today, Zsa Zsa Gabor's only daughter, the formidable Constance Francesca Hilton, is divorced and has no children. At sixty-seven, she lives in Los Angeles. Occasionally she performs as a comedienne at the Comedy Store on the Sunset Strip, where she demonstrates a sharp wit and humorous point of view about her life and times. "I am the original Hilton heiress," she has said during one of her monologues. "I'm older, wiser, smarter—and I'm *damn* wider! My mom is Zsa Zsa Gabor," she continued. "My father was Conrad Hilton. Some of you have our towels. *Keep 'em!* Keep anything you steal!" And later: "My niece is Paris Hilton. She called me the other day and said, 'Francesca, can you pick me up? I'm just too drunk to drive.' I said, 'Girl, I'd pick you up, but I'm too drunk to drive myself.' "

Though Francesca likes to joke that she and Zsa Zsa "are best of friends now that we're the same age," there has been no shortage of heartache for mother and daughter since Zsa Zsa's marriage to Frédéric Prinz von Anhalt. For the last twenty years, there have been many lawsuits and a myriad of other legal actions between von Anhalt and Hilton, most of them in recent times having to do with the care of Zsa Zsa.

For years, von Anhalt had allegedly prevented Francesca from seeing her mother and, according to her, would not share medical, psychological, or financial information with her. In a 2011 statement, Francesca said, "By isolating me from my mother, not only does her current husband deprive her of my love and companionship, but he goes against estate planning documents that appear to reflect her wishes that he not be in sole control of her affairs." In 2012, Francesca won, by court order, the right to regular, private visitations—one hour, once a week, alone, without von Anhalt present but with the presence of a caretaker, lawyer, or officer. She is now also entitled to a full accounting of how her mother's money is being spent by von Anhalt. As of this writing, von Anhalt remains his wife's temporary conservator.

Because of her mother's illnesses, these have been anything but easy times for Francesca Hilton, a woman who, it would seem, has always had it rough. "Zsa Zsa's ongoing health problems have been so hard on her," says one of Francesca's closest friends. "Sometimes she wants her mom. Things happen in the course of her life and, you know, she just needs her mom. It's that simple. But she doesn't have her. Not really. So it's very painful."

"She squeezes my hand," Francesca has said of Zsa Zsa. "She knows me. She mouths a few words. She once called me 'the Brat,' so that's how I announce myself. I say, 'Mother, the Brat's here.'"

As for her present relationship with the Hiltons, Francesca remains on friendly terms with some members of the family; she and Barron speak occasionally and she has also assisted the Conrad N. Hilton Foundation with certain charity events. "I think she has spent a large part of her life trying to find her path," says the foundation's head, her nephew Steven Hilton.

"People who know her well realize that Francesca has not only survived a very challenging life, she has thrived despite it," concludes her publicist and good friend Ed Lozzi, "and so they wish her well. I think people have always rooted for Francesca Hilton. They still do."

Paris

*I*f Conrad Hilton's historical hotel chain does not immediately come to mind when the Hilton name is mentioned these days, it's likely because of the impact on our culture that's been made by the most well-known, controversial, and successful of the current Hilton generation: Conrad's great-granddaughter Paris.

Paris Whitney Hilton was born in New York City on February 17, 1981. Her sister Nicky was born two years later. Two brothers were added to the family, Barron II in 1989 and Conrad III in 1994.*

Richard Howard Hilton, better known as Rick, is Paris's father. The sixth child of Barron and Marilyn, he was born in 1955. Hilton would go on to make a fortune as the chairman and cofounder of Hilton & Hyland, a high-end real estate brokerage firm headquartered in Beverly Hills. He has a degree in hotel and restaurant management. "You could say that he is a chip off the ol' block that is Barron," says a good friend of Rick's.

In November 1979, the end of the year of Conrad's death, Rick married Kathleen Elizabeth Avanzino, today better known as the socialite (and also actress) Kathy Hilton. (Kathy's half sisters Kim and Kyle enjoyed success in TV and movies in the 1970s and 1980s, and more recently in the reality show *The Real Housewives of Beverly Hills*.)

Kathy was a young mother—twenty-two when Paris was born, and at times her inexperience showed. For instance, Pat Hilton—Eric's wife—recalls that she was in Los Angeles (from Houston, where she and Eric lived) visiting her sister-in-law Marilyn when she first met Paris, who was about nine months old. "Kathy brought her over to Marilyn's and was excited to introduce me to the baby," she recalled. "She called her 'Star,' as I remember it—a nickname for her. She handed the infant to me and said, 'Here, Pat, why not hold Star for a little while?' I was thrilled to do so, she was such a happy, beautiful baby. But then Kathy just disappeared. The next thing I knew, Marilyn and I had Paris for the entire day."

Between the two of them, Marilyn and Pat had raised twelve Hilton

---

* Nicky's son Conrad Nicholson and Rick's son Conrad Hughes are both known as Conrad III.

children, so it wasn't as if they didn't know how to handle an infant. "Still, you would have thought she might have left *some* instructions for us," a dismayed Pat told Marilyn as the two women took turns cradling the crying infant, "maybe feeding times?"

Marilyn laughed. "Well, look, she's young," she said. "She doesn't know any better. She probably figured as Paris's grandmother I wouldn't mind."

Pat agreed. "Still," she said, "back in our day, we wouldn't have thought to just leave a baby for the entire day without at least warning the people you were leaving her with."

"Well, back in *our* day, *a lot* of things were different," Marilyn said as she changed little Paris's diaper. "Back in our day, as I recall it, we pretty much never left the house when we had that first baby, did we? I was a nervous wreck when I had Barron Jr." She recalled that she was twenty when she had her first child, two years younger than Kathy. She added that she didn't really feel comfortable leaving Barron Jr. for an entire year, "and then, by that time, I had Hawley, and then, a year later, Steve, and then five more in rapid succession" she remembered. "So it's safe to say I *never* felt comfortable leaving the house," she added, laughing. "And we had help, too! Things are sure different today. Women are different."

When Kathy returned, the two Hilton wives took her to task for leaving Paris with them and not first asking if they minded babysitting for the day. "Oh my gosh, I'm so sorry," Kathy said, seeming mortified. "But I just had some things I had to take care of."

"Believe me," Marilyn told her daughter-in-law with a patient smile, "for the next eighteen years you will have many things that will need to be taken care, *none* of which you will ever have time to take care of, because," she concluded while handing her granddaughter back to her mother, "this child comes first."

By Paris's eighteenth birthday in 1999, she had attended seven private and/or parochial schools before being expelled from the Canterbury Boarding School in Milford, Connecticut, for "violating school rules." She later earned her high school diploma equivalency via the GED (General Educational Development). Like her grandfather Barron, she wasn't a good student, but there was something about her that was special, unique. Her mother always knew it, too—as the nickname 'Star' suggests—and encouraged her to, as Paris once put it, "think outside of the box. There are a lot of things a Hilton can do," she told me. "You have the name, you have the looks. But do you have the imagination? Do you have the creativity? Do you have the ambition? My answer to all three questions was: yes, yes, and *yes!*"

When Paris was nineteen, T Management, Donald Trump's talent agency, signed her to a modeling contract. "I guess you could say that I believed in her when most people didn't," Trump says. "Paris actually wanted to be a veterinarian when she was a little girl. But I saw her as something else. She was always incredibly unique, an interesting look. There was something about her that evoked a 1960s modeling sensibility. She had done a few things before coming to me, but I like to think that we buffed up the diamond that is Paris Hilton." Other agencies Paris worked for included Ford Models in New York and Premier Model Management in London. "I was so taken aback when I saw that Paris looked so much like Conrad," says Conrad's niece Frances Peterson. "Conrad had those beautiful, crystal clear blue eyes and so does Paris. It's uncanny. It just struck me how much she looks like her great-grandfather."

With the passing of just a few years, the tabloid press soon began to refer to Paris and her sister Nicky, along with girlhood friends Nicole Richie and Kim Kardashian, as "celebutantes" or "celebutards." Though she secured her place in gossip columns through her hard-partying ways and rumored affairs with celebrities, it was the release of a scandalous sex tape in 2004, *1 Night in Paris* (with then boyfriend Rick Salomon), that gained her instant notoriety. "It was the most embarrassing, humiliating thing that has ever happened to me," she has said.

The Hiltons took an immediate stand against the tape, issuing a collective statement about it: "The Hilton family is greatly saddened at how low human beings will stoop to exploit their daughter Paris, who is sweet-natured, for their own self promotion as well as profit motives. Paris is working hard on her career. The release of a private tape between a younger girl and an older boyfriend is more than upsetting. Anyone in any way involved in this video is guilty of criminal activity and will be vigorously prosecuted."

Though many lawsuits were exchanged, the settlement between the parties was never revealed. It's been reported that Paris finally received a portion of the profits made from the tape, though she has denied that this is true. She does admit, however, that the sensational tape and its aftermath caused members of her immediate family to seek therapy together to figure out how to navigate the rocky terrain ahead, both personally and professionally. "It was not some random guy in that tape," she recalls. "It was someone I was with for years, so the betrayal was the hardest part. He took something away from me, my reputation, basically. People thought I was a slut, and some still do. It's something I'll have to one day explain to my children. So, no, I will never forgive him. But I have moved on, because that's what Hiltons do. We survive."

One advantage to the publicity—both good and bad—was that it went a long way toward establishing Paris Hilton as a household name. She knows how to use the media, and is not adverse to allowing it to use her in exchange. The release of the tape coincided with the debut on Fox TV of her reality series, *The Simple Life*, costarring Nicole Richie, garnering 13 million viewers, and earning its two stars international recognition.

In her youth, Paris kept the Los Angeles cops and courts busy with charges of speeding, reckless driving, DUI, a parole violation, driving with a suspended license, failure to enroll in a court-ordered alcohol education program, and marijuana and cocaine possession, the latter causing her to be banned from entry into Japan because she was considered "undesirable." She served time in jail, with an early release. She has also written two autobiographies (one of which, *Confessions of an Heiress*, was a *New York Times* best seller); a book about her Chihuahua, *The Tinkerbell Hilton Diaries*; and in 2011 starred in a reality TV program called *The World According to Paris*.

While Paris's occasional film and TV work contributed to her pop-culture high profile, her real focus has been to establish her brand name as a fashionista with an astounding number of business platforms in her ever-expanding empire, including fragrances (ten at last count), handbags, watches, footwear, sunglasses, pet products, stationery, bedding, and clothing she either designed or endorsed, sold in fifty-five Paris Hilton Stores worldwide and earning her more than $10 million a year. Credit for much of Paris's success should go to her mother, Kathy, who has often been a smart businesswoman and savvy negotiator on her daughter's behalf. It's also safe to say that Paris herself has exhibited over the years the kind of business acumen demonstrated by both her grandfather and great-grandfather. Her fragrances alone have reportedly earned $1.5 billion in the last decade. In 2013 she signed a major DJ contract with a famous nightclub in Ibiza. And in October of that same year Paris released a new single and video, "Good Time," on Cash Money Records, produced by Afrojack (and featuring Lil Wayne); a new album is scheduled for release in 2014. "It's just part of my brand," she told Piers Morgan of CNN. "I see myself as a businesswoman and a brand. And singing is just something that adds to my brand." Her net worth is said to be as much as $100 million.

"Rather Silly"?

*J*ust having the last name Hilton, people assume that everything was handed to me and that I've never had to work a day in my life," Paris Hilton told a writer in 2006 when she was promoting her album, *Paris*, which was released on her own label, Heiress Records, in association with Warner Bros. "But the truth is that I have worked hard, I've done it all on my own. I like to think that I was influenced by my great-grandfather to make a place for myself. Yes, obviously I have had the advantage of the name, and the family genetics. But all of the Hiltons have a big pair of shoes to fill. None of us will ever be Conrad. None of us will ever be Barron. We just do what we can, and that's all that's ever been asked of us by my parents and other relatives."

When she says that she's had to work hard to get ahead, she's likely referencing the fact that, as is well-known in her family, a mere biological connection to the Hilton fortune does not guarantee a free ride. Like his father and grandfather, Paris's father, Rick Hilton, made it a practice never to give his children "mad money" with which to live their lives. He's been just as stringent about that rule as his ancestors. Paris learned she had no choice but to make something of herself. The alternative was an upper-middle-class lifestyle—and she was not cut out for upper-middle-class. Paris Hilton is, in many ways, a self-invented, independent woman. In that regard, it's difficult to resist the temptation to compare her to Zsa Zsa Gabor. Though the two are distantly related, from all accounts, they have never met. "I think she's rather silly," Zsa Zsa said of Paris in 2007. "She does too many things for publicity."

Like Paris, Zsa Zsa Gabor wasn't known for her acting or singing either. Like Paris, she was known for being known...she was famous for being famous. However, Zsa Zsa had the ability to sit with the host of a television program and engage in witty, provocative, and entertaining repartee. She had no pretense; she was purely herself, whether on camera or off. She knew how to tell a good story, and people loved hearing her tell it. For her part, Paris is more at ease when it comes to responding to questions shouted out at her by paparazzi, and in an age when the attention span of a point-and-click generation is often limited to just a few moments before interest is completely lost, Paris's brand of quick-wittedness is more than enough to keep her in the news.

It has also helped Paris—as it did Zsa Zsa—that she is uncommonly beautiful and knows how to take a good picture. Like Zsa Zsa's, her love life has also been somewhat turbulent, which many people find compelling. But Paris has also made much, *much* more money in her lifetime than Zsa Zsa ever made. Her vision is greater than Zsa Zsa's ever was, and it's safe to say that even Zsa Zsa Gabor—who was influenced to "think big" by Conrad Hilton—never could have imagined a life for herself quite as "big" as that of her ex-step-great-granddaughter, Paris Hilton.

In lieu of millions of dollars just handed down to them, Hilton heirs have the opportunity to use the Hilton name to do whatever they can with it. If they are creative enough to parlay the name into great wealth—like Paris Hilton—more power to them. If not—like most, if not all, of her cousins—that's their choice too. At thirty-three, Paris has more than secured her future. A less controversial figure than she once was, she seldom makes headlines these days, causing some to wonder if a fickle public has had enough of her. However, according to those who know her best, Paris Hilton has simply grown up and is now making better life choices.

As of this writing, Paris Hilton is in a steady long-term relationship with a successful model, the Spanish-born, twenty-two-year-old River Viiperi. During an appearance on *The Wendy Williams Show* on May 2, 2013, she said that she hoped to start a family with him. "I think that's the meaning of life, to have children and have a family one day," she explained. "I am so in love. I feel so lucky to have met him. He's one of the kindest, most loyal men I've ever met in my entire life, and he treats me like a princess."

How Did Conrad Do It?

Rick Hilton's family has kept a high public profile in recent years. Along with Paris, Nicky (whose full name is Nicholai Nicky Olivia) and her brothers, Barron II and Conrad III, are in the public eye.

Nicky, born on October 5, 1983, has run a couple of successful clothing lines and has designed a line of handbags. She has also worked extensively as a model. In 2006, she even dabbled in the hotel business by opening two Nicky O Hotels, one in Miami and the other in Chicago, careful not to use the name Hilton on it. "I've been around hotels my whole life," she told *People* magazine in 2006. "I know a good hotel when I see one." Unfortunately, she learned the hard way that it's a tough business; the hotels didn't last long.

"Nicky is actually a savvy woman," says one person who worked with her in her hotel enterprise. "She talked a lot about her great-grandfather Conrad, and her grandfather Barron, and also her dad, Rick. These men have had a big influence over her and her sister, Paris. Having worked with Nicky, I can tell you that she's a smart businesswoman who has made a fortune for herself, if not in the hotel business certainly with her lines of clothing. She and Paris understand how to create and develop a brand. They understand marketing and promoting, and if that isn't all from the canon of Conrad Hilton, I don't know what is."

Like her sister, Nicky has also made headlines with her personal life, such as when she married childhood friend Todd Andrew Meister in 2004, a marriage that was eventually annulled.

Nicky's mother, Kathy, hosted a network reality television show for NBC in 2005, *I Want to Be a Hilton*. In the series, fourteen young people, male and female, engaged in competitions relating to art and culture, beauty and fashion in order to gain the opportunity to live a glamorous high-society lifestyle. One by one, each contestant was eliminated by Kathy Hilton, using the catchphrase "You're *not* on the list." The winner was finally awarded a $200,000 trust fund, a new apartment, clothing, and, according to the NBC press release, "the opportunity to become friendly with the Hiltons."

Some critics were puzzled by Kathy Hilton's program, because they felt it promoted a stereotype of the Hiltons as being silly and superficial, which was obviously not her intention. "When I was a kid people wanted to be an Oscar Mayer Weiner," wrote a critic for the *Hollywood Reporter*. "Now they want to be a Hilton. Or so we're told. Not that the two are very different, actually. You don't want to know what's really inside either one—and both tend to hide behind their buns. 'I Want to Be a Hilton' supplies further evidence of the decline and fall of Western civilization."

Kathy Hilton's business instincts are usually quite astute, as she has proved with many aspects of her daughter Paris's career. However, with her foray into network television, she likely learned that a fine line exists between taking a tongue-in-cheek approach to the family's flamboyant reputation and exploiting it in a way that might be viewed as distasteful. Unfortunately, her series ran for only one season. Most recently, Kathy, who at fifty-five remains a stunning—and often outspoken—blonde, has been seen as a regular on the OWN network reality program *Life with LaToya*, starring her longtime friend LaToya Jackson.

Kathy and Rick's sons, Conrad III and Barron, have led mostly quiet lives, though both did put the family in headlines when they were involved in separate high-profile automobile mishaps. Luckily, both young Hilton men have the advantage of coming from a close-knit family with parents who have not only been loving but often strict. It obviously doesn't mean the Hilton offspring won't sometimes get into trouble. It does, however, mean that they have a strong foundation upon which to stand when faced with problems.

"Look, it's not easy raising kids these days," Kathy Hilton has said, "and just because we're Hiltons doesn't mean that we don't have the same kinds of problems as everyone else, only ours are magnified by the media. We are a close family. We have a great love for one another. We have always been willing to tell the truth to one another and face the consequences, knowing that we, as a family, will be okay. And, of course, we also believe in the old adage: This, too, shall pass."

As they have gotten older, this next generation of Hiltons has also become interested in their family history, particularly in the life of their great-grandfather Conrad. Part of their interest may be because of the inclusion of an intriguing story line in the AMC series *Mad Men* in which advertising man, Don Draper, lands the account of a successful hotelier named...Conrad Hilton. The creators of the show actually went to great lengths to try to depict Hilton in as accurate a way as possible. "The producers knew pretty much nothing about Conrad, so they contacted us," confirmed Mark Young of the Conrad N. Hilton College of Hotel and Restaurant Management. "We were able to supply a lot of information, photographs, and other memorabilia from which they were able to build their character. They wanted to be as accurate as possible in capturing Conrad, the way he walked and talked, the Stetson hat, all of it, his personality.

"Since *Mad Men*, many young Hilton family members—the offspring of Nicky, Eric, and Barron—have been here to the archives," says Young. "Conrad Hilton was such an icon in our culture, but to them he's their grandfather or great-grandfather. They want to know about him, what influenced him, how he became the man he became. 'Tell us about Conrad,' they would say. 'How did Conrad do it? How did Conrad achieve what he did in his lifetime?' It's a great and inspiring family story, and I think it matters to them a great deal, as well it should."

End of an Era

*T*oday, the Conrad N. Hilton Foundation is a private holding company, a *family* institution that is not public and thus not vulnerable to any sort of takeover attempt. With Hiltons sitting on the board of the foundation, the family maintains complete power and control over it.

In 1996, after thirty years as CEO of the Hilton Hotels Corporation, William Barron Hilton finally retired. Steve Bollenback succeeded him, while Hilton continued to chair the board.

In 2007, the Hilton Hotels Corporation, with its nearly three thousand hotels in seventy-six countries, was acquired by the private equity firm of Blackstone Group LP. The company agreed in February of that year to a cash deal of $20.1 billion from Blackstone. "It could be argued that this news marks the end of an era," wrote a journalist for *Fortune* magazine. "The company started by Conrad Hilton, in effect, no longer exists." Barron Hilton explained, "Despite my tremendous family pride, I knew Hilton Hotels Corporation had grown to the point where it could thrive, even without a Hilton family member at the helm. I had been a member of the Hilton Foundation board since 1954. It was only after the sale of our companies that I proudly became chairman of the Conrad N. Hilton Foundation."

At the end of 2007, Barron Hilton announced a contribution of about $2.3 billion—which amounted to 97 percent of his net worth—to the Conrad N. Hilton Foundation. Furthermore, he contributed approximately $1.2 billion—his profit from the sale of the Hilton Hotels Corporation to Blackstone—into a trust that would also eventually benefit the foundation. "That gift, together with other personal assets, should bring the Foundation's corpus to more than $4 billion," he wrote in a letter to the Giving Pledge organization. "Today, we concentrate on a few strategic initiatives: safe water development, homelessness, children, substance abuse and Catholic sisters. Other major programs include blindness prevention, hotel and restaurant management, education, multiple sclerosis, disaster relief and recovery, and Catholic schools."

"Speaking for the family as well as the foundation, we are all exceedingly proud and grateful for this extraordinary commitment," said Barron's son Steven M. Hilton, president and CEO of the foundation. "Working to alleviate human suffering around the globe, regardless of race, religion, or geography, is the mandate of the foundation set by my grandfather, Conrad Hilton, and now reinforced by my father, Barron Hilton."

Barron's decision in regard to his wealth begs the question: Is he really just doing to his heirs what his father did to him, that which he spent so many years contesting in court? It's not an easy question to answer, at least not until Barron dies and his last will and testament can be carefully examined. At this point, it isn't clear how much money his heirs will inherit. However, from all available evidence, it seems that they will inherit and then have to split between them just 3 percent of his entire net worth, with the rest going to the foundation. It also seems fair to reason that whatever decisions Barron has made in regard to his own will will likely be more ironclad—or at least not as open to analysis—as his father's. In other words, it's likely that Barron's heirs will not benefit from a will that has in it a clause (like "Barron's Option") that would be open for reinterpretation.

Today, the Conrad N. Hilton Foundation—which in October 2012 relocated from traffic-congested Century City, California, to a bucolic, sprawling seventy-acre campus in Agoura Hills at the base of Ladyface

Mountain—spearheads many important charities around the world. The Hilton organization distributes about $60 million a year. (It also awards an annual $1.5 million humanitarian grant.) As well as supporting Catholic sisters, its priorities include caring for vulnerable children, especially those suffering from HIV and AIDS; assisting transition-age youth out of the foster care system and into the mainstream of America; ending chronic homelessness; preventing substance abuse; and providing safe water. The foundation also responds to international disasters, and has a special concern of overcoming multiple sclerosis. The foundation's board of directors includes Barron Hilton as chairman emeritus and Eric Hilton as a member. The chairman, president, and CEO of the foundation is Barron's son Steven M. Hilton. Barron's daughter Hawley Hilton McAuliffe is also on the board, as is Nicky and Trish Hilton's son Conrad N. Hilton III. Conrad's longtime friend and adviser Donald H. Hubbs is now the director emeritus.

As of December 31, 2011, the assets of the Conrad N. Hilton Foundation were approximately $2 billion—probably more money than Conrad Hilton ever could have imagined making in his lifetime. After all, almost a hundred years ago, he was a man with just $5,000 to his name, all of which he decided to use to purchase the ramshackle Mobley Hotel in Cisco, Texas. If not for the help of his devoted mother and an assortment of friends, he never would have been able to put together the balance of the $40,000 purchase price. From there, his empire grew not only in this country but around the world. His is a true, genuine American success story, or as his son Barron once proudly put it, "It's definitely one for the record books, and not a day goes by that I don't sit and marvel at what my father did with his life. It is my hope that others are inspired by my father's story, and by our family's steadfast adherence to his charitable philosophy."

Marilyn Hilton: Rest in Peace

Barron Hilton, who at the time of this writing is eighty-six years old, suffered the loss of his beautiful and effervescent wife, Marilyn Hawley Hilton, in 2004. Marilyn was struck down in her prime by a most debilitating disease, multiple sclerosis. "Barron and I were walking down the stairs when a cry alerted us that Marilyn had fallen," the late foundation board member Gregory R. Dillon once recalled. "We ran back to see what happened to her. [Marilyn's] legs had given out, and it was after that incident that we found out what her problem was. It took some time to do so, since they gave her all sorts of tests, before the doctors finally diagnosed MS. She went on, however, for years thereafter... leading a full life, though her later years were not too comfortable. But Marilyn was a trooper."

Over the years, the Conrad N. Hilton Foundation would award almost $15 million to the medical community in the name of MS research. "As often happens, the suffering of a loved one opens the hearts of family members serving on a foundation board to the plight of all other families who also have a loved one struggling with the same disability," explained Marilyn's son Steven Hilton.

Marilyn Hilton passed away on March 11, 2004, at the age of seventy-six due to complications from her disease. At the time, she and Barron had been married for fifty-seven years. Besides Rick Hilton—the father of Paris—the children of Barron and Marilyn Hilton are: William Barron Jr., Hawley, Steven, David, Sharon, Daniel, and Ronald. Most lead quiet lives out of the spotlight. However, Steven Hilton, as earlier mentioned, is the chairman, president, and CEO of the Conrad N. Hilton Foundation, and Hawley Hilton McAuliffe is on the board of directors. It was reported that Marilyn Hilton had a portfolio worth about $60 million—smart investments over the years into which she was guided by her husband—which was divided among her children.

Demonstrating not only the grace for which she had long been known, but great courage as well, never for a moment, say those who knew and loved her, did Marilyn Hilton ever feel sorry for herself—even during the many years she was confined to a wheelchair. "You don't look back at what might have been," says Steven Hilton in explaining his mother's philosophy, "you accept what life has presented and make the best of what you have."

"She was a wonderful lady," said her sister-in-law Trish Hilton. "I don't think I ever met a single person who didn't have a lovely memory associated with Marilyn. She touched so many of us. In my life, she was like a sister. I miss her terribly."

On the Town with Paris

*W*hen Barron Hilton telephoned his granddaughter Paris on the morning of April 14, 2010, to tell her that he wanted to spend some time with her, she was delighted. She and her paternal grandfather had always been close, despite overblown headlines suggesting that he was ashamed of her high-profile tabloid-making exploits. In truth, Barron never paid much attention to the private life of his most famous grandchild. Rather, it was her entrepreneurial spirit that he always found most fascinating. He would say that she reminded him of his father, Conrad—her great-grandfather—in that, to use his words, "she's the ultimate salesman. She has a product and she knows how to sell it. Like Conrad." Barron likes to keep abreast of Paris's current business ventures, thus his invitation to meet her for dinner.

Paris, who was twenty-nine at the time, suggested that they dine at one of her favorite restaurant's, Dan Tana's, a popular Italian eatery on Santa Monica Boulevard in Hollywood. At the last minute, though, after discussing the matter with her father, Rick, she thought that perhaps Barron would be more comfortable in a private setting, perhaps a more obscure location. "No," Barron told her. "Let's go out into the world and have a nice night on the town." Rick Hilton, though, wasn't sure how he felt about his eighty-two-year-old father being caught in the kind of chaos he knew that his daughter's presence usually causes in public places. Therefore he suggested that he and his wife and Paris's mother, Kathy, and sister Nicky, twenty-seven, tag along. Now it had become a Hilton family affair, all the better as far as Barron was concerned. Though he had originally sought out some private time with Paris, family still meant the world to him, just as it always had to the Hiltons. He always enjoyed spending time with his son, daughter-in-law, and granddaughter Nicky. He asked if his grandsons—his namesake, Barron, and Conrad—would be joining them, but both already had plans for the evening.

Virtually no photographers were present when the Hilton family arrived at the restaurant. However, as they ate their meal at a large table, it seemed as if the eyes of most of the diners in their midst were on them. The next day, one of the national wire services even reported details of their meal, all the way down to the foods they enjoyed. "Why does it seem so odd to note that Paris Hilton's family seems like any other?" asked the writer of the published report. "If she is as spoiled as we think she is, one would never know it from the way she acted around her grandfather. She was solicitous toward him, sitting right next to him and never taking her eyes off him." At one point, Paris was heard urging Barron to tell his "famous old joke, the one you used to tell my dad." In response, Barron told a long story in an animated fashion, much to everyone's delight as they all laughed at a punch line they'd likely heard many times before.

By the time the Hiltons finished their meal, word of their presence had apparently spread through the Hollywood grapevine, because an eager pack of paparazzi awaited them as they exited the restaurant. As the family stood at the front door waiting for the valet to fetch their car, the photographers began snapping away and shouting questions. "How annoying is this?" a disgruntled Rick Hilton said, turning to his wife. But none of them could have been surprised by the gathered crowd. It was par for the course, especially when they were out on the town with Paris. "Oh my," Paris was heard saying. "Well, here we go, Granddad. Are you ready?" she asked, smiling at him. Barron took in the bustling scene with a bemused expression. "Wow," was the only phrase he could seem to muster.

As usual, Paris was, to use show business parlance, "camera ready," in her sleeveless, low-cut black silk cocktail dress with matching spiked heels. Her blonde hair was parted in the middle, cascading past her slim shoulders. In contrast, her grandfather was more casually dressed in a black-and-white plaid jacket, an open-collared white shirt, and gray slacks. Paris wrapped one arm around Barron's, and the two then took a few steps out toward the curb...and right into the middle of the mob scene, every moment of which would be filmed by crews from Hollywood photo agencies for television entertainment programs. Meanwhile, Rick, Kathy, and Nicky remained in the entryway of the restaurant, as if to give Paris and Barron the full spotlight.

"Say, Paris, who gave you those diamonds?" one photographer shouted out.

"Oh, these?" Paris answered, motioning to the exquisite diamond brooch at her neck and its matching counterparts dangling from her ears. She also sported a diamond bracelet on her left wrist. "Why, I don't even remember!" she exclaimed, batting her blue eyes. "Let me think," she added as she glanced at her white BlackBerry. She is connected to social media at all times—such is the way of the present-day socialite. Clutching her BlackBerry in the same hand as her black leather purse, she sent a quick text before returning to the question at hand. "You guys know what I always say," she observed, "every woman should have four pets in her life: a mink in her closet, a jaguar in her garage, a tiger in her bed, and a jackass who pays for everything." The crowd laughed. It was a line she used quite often, but—like Zsa Zsa—Paris can call up any of her best quips at a moment's notice. Though Barron seemed a little taken aback by her remarks, upon seeing everyone else's reaction he couldn't help but approve. "Very clever, my dear," he said with a chuckle.

Flashbulbs continued to pop all around them while Paris held her grandfather close, protectively. "Look this way, Paris," one photographer shouted out. "No, Paris! Over here, Mr. Hilton! *Over here!*"

As a public figure, Barron was accustomed to dealing with the press. However, this was a very different experience. In the past, when he was surrounded by reporters in public it was usually because he was trying to obtain a new gaming license, or was hosting the opening of a new hotel or involved in the promotion of some other important business venture, such as when he owned the San Diego Chargers. The attention he generated wasn't because he was a celebrity, but rather because he was a respected businessman. Though it could be argued that the sensation Paris causes is at least in some way related to her product lines, it's really more directly linked to her celebrity. In this moment, Barron was really just basking in—and, in a sense, helping to celebrate—his granddaughter's success.

After about fifteen minutes, the Hilton family's vehicle still had not arrived and Rick Hilton could be seen in the doorway of the restaurant gesturing wildly to the head valet and pointing at his watch. Meanwhile, the paparazzi continued to shout out questions and take photographs. "How do you like being out with Grandpa?" someone asked.

"Oh, he's such a doll," Paris said, looking at Barron lovingly. "If I can be just *a tenth* as successful as he has been, I'd be a very happy girl."

"So, how'd you do it, Mr. Hilton?" someone asked. "What's your secret?"

Barron shook his head, smiled, and hesitated for a moment as if wondering how to distill the experience of fifty years in the hotel business down to a simple answer. "Nice guys finish *first*, not last," he finally offered. "At least that's what my father always said."

"And your father was?" the paparazzo asked, showing complete ignorance about not only Barron's life but Paris's lineage.

"Conrad Hilton," Barron answered with a humble smile. "That's C-o-n-r-a-d Hilton," he repeated gamely.

"Why not give Grandpa a little peck?" the same paparazzo then suggested.

"Sure!" Paris said. "Take off your glasses, Granddad," she recommended. "You look hotter without them." He obliged. She then leaned over and kissed him lightly on the cheek. He blushed a little. But by this time, Barron was beginning to visibly wilt; he'd clearly had enough.

"Okay, that's it," Rick Hilton suddenly announced as he pushed his way through the crowd, his wife following close behind. "Here's our car, Paris," he said, motioning to the approaching vehicle. "Come on, Dad! Let's get you out of here."

A uniformed valet jumped out of the Hiltons' black SUV and then dutifully held the driver's door open for Rick. At the same time, another valet held the door on the front passenger side for his wife, Kathy. Meanwhile, Paris helped her grandfather into one of the backseats, after which her sister, Nicky, joined him there. Paris then got into the car just as someone rushed around to slam the door behind her. As the vehicle began to slowly pull away from the curb, Paris lowered the window and popped her head out. "Thanks so much for showing my grandfather so much respect," she shouted out at the paparazzi. "You guys are *hot!*"

EPILOGUE: A FINAL TOAST

Flashback.

It's 1965, the end of the year on a chilly California winter's night, an evening during which the Hiltons had gathered at Conrad Hilton's Casa Encantada manse for a pre-holiday meal. It was a formal dinner as usual, everything proper and ceremonial. The men wore tailored black suits and ties, while the women were in elegant evening gowns. As was always the custom, Conrad sat at one end of the imposing oblong dining room table while his eldest son, Nicky, sat at the other, and next to him, his wife, Trish. Barron sat to Nicky's right, next to his wife, Marilyn. Across from Barron and Marilyn sat Conrad's companion, Ann Miller. Eric was next to her, and seated at his side was his spouse, Pat, and across from him, his mother, Mary, Conrad's first wife. Also present was Zsa Zsa Gabor, Conrad's second wife. Especially for the occasion, Conrad had ordered a bottle of Unicum, the popular Hungarian liqueur, for Zsa Zsa's enjoyment. He, Zsa Zsa, and Nicky each enjoyed a shot together just before sitting at the table. "Holy Christ! That's about the worst thing I've ever tasted," Nicky had said, bringing both Conrad and Zsa Zsa to gales of laughter. Zsa Zsa then presented Conrad with an early birthday gift, an extremely expensive Georgian silver desk set. "For your seventy-eighth," she told him, delighted that he seemed pleased by the present, "and may you have many more!"

In the kitchen, at another table—the "children's table," as it was called—were all of the Hilton offspring, at least a dozen of them: the broods of Nicky, Barron, Eric, and even Zsa Zsa, her daughter, Francesca, who was eighteen at the time, sitting happily with her cousins.

Meanwhile, in the grand dining room under an enormously imposing crystal chandelier, the adults chatted noisily among themselves as an army of uniformed servants passed through with one entree after another—all main courses, from game hens to steaks to pastas to fishes, even two large turkeys with all of the trimmings. So decadent a display was it, it was as if no consensus could be reached as to what to serve, so someone just said, "Oh, the hell with it! Let's just serve everything!" Uniformed servants carefully placed the heaping serving platters of food on the table. The help was completely ignored as they did their busy work, all of the family members enjoying each other, chattering among themselves and laughing.

Why the memory of this particular evening at Casa Encantada? What was so distinctive about this time and place in the storied lives of the Hilton family? Not much, really. Judging from photographs taken that evening and the memories of some of those who were present, everyone seemed to get along just fine. There were no serious discussions, no arguments, no high-stakes drama. Father and sons talked about politics, sports, current events, and, of course, the hotel business. Sisters-in-law seemed happy to be with one other, gossiping about current fashion trends, joking about their husbands. Not one person stormed out of the house in a fit of fury—not even Zsa Zsa. It was just a lovely meal enjoyed by a large, complicated, and, yes, wealthy family. "Sometimes, it was just that simple," recalled Trish Hilton, "and those were the good times, the truly memorable times, the times when it was about celebrating family and only family." Pat Hilton added, "Those were the moments I think I hold closest to my heart, when it was just simple and easy and fun. When we were truly a family."

Just before dessert was to be served, Conrad raised a glass. "I would like to make a toast," he announced. As he rose, everyone quieted down and looked his way. He paused for a moment, gathering his thoughts. "No matter our differences, past or present," he finally said, "or future, for that matter, and I suppose we shall have them, as well," he added, glancing at Zsa Zsa, "we are still and always will be family. Maybe Oscar Wilde put it best," he added with a chuckle, "when he said, 'After a good dinner, one can forgive anybody, even one's own relations.'" The quote got a good laugh. "And so," he finished proudly, "here's to all of us, here's to the Hilton family."

"Hear, hear," said Nicky.

"To the Hiltons," added Eric.

"The Hilton family," Barron repeated, as everyone clinked glasses all around the table.

"Yes, and I would like to add just one thing, if you don't mind," someone said. It was Zsa Zsa. Of course. All eyes turned to her.

While it probably would have been appropriate that Conrad Hilton have the final word, that any toast of the evening be his and his alone since he was lord of the manor, it had long ago been accepted that if anyone was to break with tradition, it would be Zsa Zsa. Shaking his head and smiling to himself, Conrad sat down and extended both arms gamely to his ex-wife as if to say, "The floor is all yours, my dear."

Zsa Zsa stood up. "You know, in Hungary," she began, "at the end of the meal, someone always toasts *the host* in appreciation of his hospitality. And that someone tonight shall be...*me*," she announced grandly while gazing at Conrad. "So, to our host, I would like to say"—she paused for dramatic affect before continuing—"you have driven each and every one of us at this table mad at one time or another, and..." They all waited with apprehension for what was coming next because, after all, this *was* Zsa Zsa Gabor speaking. "...we love you for it," she concluded, much to the relief of all. "We really do." Then, with a dazzling smile, she added, "In America, you say 'good health.' But in Hungary, we say '*Egészségére!*' Now," she continued with a flourish of her hand, "unfortunately, Americans tend to mispronounce this beautiful Hungarian word. And when they do mispronounce it, the toast they end up saying means, in Hungarian, '*Here's to your ass.*'" At that, everyone at the table roared with laughter. "Luckily," Zsa Zsa concluded, "I am not American." She raised her glass. "So, as a proud Hungarian, I would like to say to all of you, my *dah-lings...Egészségére!*"

"Yes! *Egészségére!*" Nicky repeated, terribly mangling the pronunciation of the word.

"*Egészségére*, indeed," Barron added, also mispronouncing it.

Zsa Zsa took her seat while everyone around her applauded.

"Well," Conrad admitted, laughing, "I don't think I can top that, can I? I will say this, though," he added with a smile. "Whether it's 'here's to your health' or 'here's to your ass,' either way, you have to admit," he concluded with a chuckle, "that is still one hell of a good toast!"

Acknowledgments and Source Notes

ACKNOWLEDGMENTS

THE AUTHOR'S SUPPORT TEAM

The Hiltons: The True Story of an American Dynasty was a collaborative effort on many levels, from inception to publication. Here, I would like to acknowledge those who assisted me in this endeavor.

It's been my great honor for the last sixteen years to call Grand Central Publishing my home, and I am deeply indebted to my publisher, Jamie Raab, for creating such a nurturing environment. I would like to also thank Jamie's dependable assistant, Deb Withey.

I was so excited to work for the first time with the capable Gretchen Young as my editor on this book. I would like to thank her for the many hours she invested in this project. Working with her has been a real honor. As always, I would like to thank managing editor Bob Castillo for his invaluable contributions. Special thanks to Anne Twomey for her excellent cover design. I would also like to thank Claire Brown in art, Sara Weiss in editorial, and Tom Whatley and Giraud Lorber in production. A special thanks to my copy editor, Roland Ottewell.

I would like to thank Louise Sommers from Miller Korzenik Sommers LLP for her very thorough legal review of this work.

Also, I would like to acknowledge my domestic agent, Mitch Douglas, for sixteen years of excellent representation, and my foreign agent, Dorie Simmonds of the Dorie Simmonds Agency in London, who has been with me for almost twenty years.

I am fortunate to have been associated with the same private investigator and chief researcher for more than twenty years, Cathy Griffin. For *The Hiltons*, I think Cathy outdid herself by locating and then conducting scores of interviews with people who have never before thought of telling their stories.

My personal copy editor, James Pinkston, spent many hours with *The Hiltons: The True Story of an American Dynasty*, perhaps more than with any other book I have written because some of the subject matter was so complex and unique, much having to do with the hotel business. As always, his work was top-notch and I am indebted to him.

I am also deeply indebted to Charles Casillo for his editorial work on this book. He understood these characters so well from the beginning and helped me shape their portrayals. This would be a different book if not for his work on it.

Special thanks go to Maryanne Reed for helping me organize all of the tape-recorded interviews and transcripts that were pivotal to the research behind this book. It was not an easy task, but she did an incredible job and I am indebted to her for it. Thank you also to Jane Maxwell, a terrific pop culture historian who allowed me access to all of her files of magazine and newspaper articles relating to the Hilton family, and also access to scores of videos, particularly television broadcasts of Zsa Zsa Gabor over the years. I would also like to thank Cloe Basiline, Suzalie Rose, Mary Whitaker, and Patrick McKenzie in London, who assisted with European research. Also, Marybeth Evans in London did a wonderful job at the Manchester Central Library where she reviewed stacks and stacks of documents about the Hilton hotels worldwide. Thanks also to Suzalie Rose and Carl Mathers, who handled research for me in libraries in Paris relating to this subject matter. Kudos to Dale Manesis for all of his help with the vast collection of Hilton family memorabilia that I would never otherwise have had access to.

My thanks also to all of those who gave of their time so that I could have a better understanding of the Hiltons for this book. So many people were helpful, but there are a few I would like to single out:

Patricia (Trish) McClintock Hilton, Nicky Hilton's widow, was so helpful and spent many hours sharing her most private memories, and I am indebted to her. I endeavored to tell her true love story with Nicky in a way that would do it honor, and I hope she approves. I wanted to do the same for Patricia (Pat) Skipworth Hilton as well, with the story of her marriage to Eric Hilton. She too went out of her way to make certain that we had a full and balanced understanding of her ex-husband, a generous man about whom few words have been written in the past. I hope she too approves.

The family of Conrad Hilton's third wife, Frances Kelly Hilton, was also extremely helpful, in particular Bill and Stella Kelly, Fran Peterson, and also Frances's best friend, Helen Lamm. They spent many hours remembering the wonderful Frances Kelly Hilton, and I hope they are pleased with her portrait as presented on these pages.

I also want to thank Francesca Hilton's publicist, Ed Lozzi, who I put in a difficult position. Not only is he a friend of mine, but he also represents a client who had mixed feelings about this book. (For a fuller explanation of that, see the notes that follow for "Zsa Zsa's Daughter" on page 475.) Still, Ed understood that the important thing was for my readers to have empathy for some of the challenges Francesca has faced in her lifetime. He found ways for me to have a better understanding of his client so that I could present a fair portrait of her. I thank him for that.

Carole Wells Doheny and Noreen Nash Siegel both gave of their time freely and generously, and their vivid memories of the Hiltons are on these pages as well. Also, Stewart Armstrong and Robert Wentworth were both good friends of Nicky Hilton's and spent countless hours sharing their memories of him with me, for which I am deeply grateful.

Rhona Graff, vice president/assistant to the president of the Trump Organization, did everything she could do to make sure we were able to interview Donald Trump for this book, and I am so appreciative to her, and of course to Mr. Trump as well. "It's really a great idea for a book," Mr. Trump enthused as I was working on this project.

I am indebted to Backstreet Investigations' Daniel J. Portley-Hanks. "Danno" helped us find court records long hidden away in the basement of the superior courthouse in Los Angeles, and as you will see from the following notes, they were absolutely essential to my research. I thank him as well.

I would also like to acknowledge Mark E. Young, Ph.D., the director of hospitality industry archives at the Conrad N. Hilton College of Hotel Restaurant and Management for his invaluable assistance, and also his time.

Thanks also to Katherine Miller, executive assistant to Steven M. Hilton, president and CEO of the Hilton Foundation, for her time and consideration.

Thanks also to Bob Neal, now deceased, but whose memories of his good friend Nicky Hilton live on in this book.

Just two months after he was interviewed for this book, attorney Myron Eugene Harpole passed away in Pasadena, California, at the age of eighty-five. He gave so many hours of his time to this project and was so helpful to me; I will always remember him with great fondness. He told me he had never before been interviewed, and that he wanted his memories to live on in this book. Therefore, I'm so happy that a major part of his legal career—his thirty-plus years with Conrad Hilton and Zsa Zsa Gabor—will now be memorialized in this work.

Also, I would like to acknowledge Phyllis Bradley, who also passed away within a year after being interviewed for this book, at the age of ninety-four. Ms. Bradley was a lively and fun woman who shared many reminiscences of her time with Frances Hilton, Conrad Hilton, and Zsa Zsa Gabor. She once gifted me with a marvelous keepsake: an antique glass bottle of perfume that Zsa Zsa had given to her almost forty years earlier. I'll treasure it always, as I will my time with Ms. Bradley.

A NOTE ABOUT THE GABOR SISTERS, ZSA ZSA AND EVA

It was the morning of February 2, 1986, when I first met Zsa Zsa Gabor. My agent at that time, Bart Andrews, was scheduled to interview her for a possible collaboration on a memoir. He asked me if I also wanted to ask questions of her, and of course I couldn't resist such an offer.

With her teased blonde—almost platinum—hair, Zsa Zsa was in full makeup and wearing a hot pink silk pantsuit when we arrived at her Bel-Air home. She had jewels dripping from both wrists and around her neck—and it was only ten o'clock in the morning! She certainly looked every bit the star. "Ask me anything, *dah-lings*," she told us. "My life is your life."

That morning, Mr. Andrews and I discussed a wide variety of subjects with Zsa Zsa, ranging from her early days in Hungary, her many marriages—including the one to Conrad Hilton—to her career as an actress and the consummate talk show guest. Much of what she had to say that day is included in this book. When it came to Hilton, she still seemed to have affection for him. "He was a great man in many ways," she said, "but I was young and stupid and I didn't know it at the time. What really makes me mad," she allowed, "is that my entire life people think I am rich because of him. They think I got all of my money because I was his wife. If you knew him, you would know how ridiculous that is."

During the two hours we spent with Zsa Zsa, we found her to be charismatic, funny, and even self-deprecating. We couldn't help but notice, however, that the versions of some stories she told were not in accord with the accounts in her previous books, *My Story* and *How to Catch a Man, How to Keep a Man, How to Get Rid of a Man.* "I leave it to you to decide what is true and what is not true," she snapped at us when we pressed her about conflicting details. "It is not my job to tell you what is the truth. You figure it out for yourselves." (Incidentally, the book we were discussing with Zsa Zsa never materialized; she changed her mind about it. Then, in 1991, she wrote the memoir *One Lifetime Is Never Enough*, using another writer.)

My time with Zsa Zsa Gabor that winter morning gave me great insight into her personality and character. I learned firsthand that she was the chief architect of her career and—as I wrote on these pages—a woman who should be admired for what she did with her life even if some of her choices were questionable. I liked her very much. For the most part, in this book I used versions of stories she relayed to me and Bart that morning, some of which I was able to corroborate with others who knew her well.

In years to come, I would see Zsa Zsa from time to time in Hollywood—once backstage in the green room at *The Pat Sajak Show* in September 1989, for instance, where we had a lively conversation about her desire to market a campy workout video (which she would do a few years later, called *It's Simple, Darling!*). She was always bubbly, charming, and ready to tell a good story.

Years later, a strange thing happened to me relating to Zsa Zsa's sister Eva Gabor. On August 20, 1991, I received a message on my voice mail from Eva—calling the wrong number! She was telephoning to tell me that her sister Magda had said that I would be delivering flowers to her, and she wanted to know what had happened to the delivery. It was just a random wrong-number voice mail. Since she left her number, I returned the call. How could I resist? When she picked up, I gave her my first name, but before I had a chance to tell her that she had reached me by mistake, she interrupted me and said, "Oh, Randy, the flowers just arrived. They're lovely, *dah-ling*. Thank you very much," and she hung up. I then sat staring at the telephone for a few moments marveling at such a strange chain of events. Two days later, I called her back to ask if she would consent to an interview for a magazine I was working for at the time. I mentioned that I knew her sister. "I don't do interviews," she said. "However, since you know my sister, why don't you interview her?" When I said that I already had, she laughed and exclaimed, "There's not one writer in this goddamn town who my sister has not told her entire life story to!"

I certainly never imagined that I would ever write a book in which Zsa Zsa Gabor would figure so prominently. Now that I have, I would like to thank Zsa Zsa for every moment I ever spent in her company, and for so many years of entertainment.

I must also acknowledge my late agent, Bart Andrews. His extensive notes and interviews with Zsa Zsa, Eva, and Magda Gabor for that planned memoir were utilized in this book. He was a terrific writer, my first agent, and the man who got me started in this business. I owe him a huge debt of gratitude.

A NOTE ABOUT PUBLICATIONS PRIVATELY PUBLISHED BY THE HILTONS

For much of *The Hiltons: The True Story of an American Dynasty*, I referred to three publications that were privately published by the Hilton family. These publications comprise so much information, it would be impossible to detail all of the material in them in the space allotted here. However, I felt it would be of interest to you, the reader, if I explained the purpose of each volume, and also how I came upon it.

When my researcher, Cathy Griffin, requested interviews with Barron and Eric Hilton, and Barron's son Steven M. Hilton (president and chief operating officer of the Hilton Foundation), she received a letter from Steven M. Hilton (dated February 16, 2012) explaining that, in his view, Conrad Hilton's 1957 autobiography, *Be My Guest*, was sufficient to understanding the Hilton story. However, he did send her a copy of *Conrad N. Hilton Foundation: The Hilton Legacy Serving Humanity Worldwide* to forward to me for my research purposes, as well as press releases explaining Barron Hilton's philanthropic legacy and also the most recent Conrad N. Hilton Foundation annual report.

Conrad N. Hilton Foundation: The Hilton Legacy Serving Humanity Worldwide was published by the Conrad N. Hilton Foundation. Among the in-depth features found in this book that I used as part of my research were the following: "My Father, Conrad N. Hilton: The Man and His Gift to the World" by Barron Hilton; "In the Footsteps of Extraordinary Men" by Steven M. Hilton; "Toward a World Free of Multiple Sclerosis" (which details Marilyn Hilton's battle with the disease); and "Barron Hilton Steps Up as Chairman of the Board." This book was written by Joseph Foote and edited by Marge Brownstein. It proved invaluable to me in terms of understanding Conrad and Barron Hilton and their philanthropic goals. It also provides as clearheaded and astute an analysis of the legal battle over "Barron's Option" as one is likely to find.

With persistence being all-important in the researching of biographies such as this one, a few months later, on July 16, 2012, we decided to again approach the Hiltons. This time I personally endeavored to interview Barron and Eric Hilton and Steven M. Hilton. In response to this second attempt, I received a warm letter (dated August 2, 2012) from the Hiltons' spokesman, Marc Moorghen.

In his correspondence, Mr. Moorghen observed that Steven Hilton "appreciated the case you made" as to why I felt it important to conduct these interviews for my book. However, he explained that since Steven Hilton was intimately involved with the preparation and publication of the foundation's book, *The Hilton Legacy Serving Humanity Worldwide*, "we feel this gesture meets your suggested goals of an opportunity to tell the truth and have his personal imprint on the work." He reiterated Hilton's belief that his grandfather's autobiography, *Be My Guest*, is "the best possible narrative of his life since it is told in his own words." Also, in regards to Barron Hilton, "an authorized biography is already under way, so that will suffice for the time being." Mr. Moorghen closed by writing, "Thank you for checking in with Mr. Hilton and we wish you every success with your project."

I have long maintained that it is a matter of personal choice as to whether or not someone wishes to speak to me regarding his or her life for a book of mine. Therefore, I respect any decision made by the subjects of any of my books in terms of cooperation. A book such as this one is not necessarily based on a single person's account of a life, but rather on the cumulative research conducted into the lives of those whose stories I have chosen to tell. That said, I am grateful to Steven M. Hilton for providing me with a rare copy of *Conrad N. Hilton Foundation: The Hilton Legacy Serving Humanity Worldwide*, and I am especially grateful to him for inscribing the book to me. It will always be a treasured keepsake of mine, and a reminder to me of the great philanthropy of both Conrad and Barron Hilton.

The second privately published volume I utilized was *Inspirations of an Innkeeper: From the Speeches, Christmas Messages, Correspondence and Experiences of Conrad. N. Hilton by Conrad N. Hilton.* This is a stunning, large coffee-table book, bound in blue leather with gold-embossed type (with page edges gilt in gold leaf), of which only 312 copies were printed in 1963 for Hilton's close friends. I have number 260, and it was signed by Conrad N. Hilton on July 14, 1970. It was given to me by a close friend of Hilton's who has asked for anonymity.

This book's introduction is written by his loyal assistant, Olive Wakeman. "Twenty years is a long time," she wrote. "To most people, twenty years is a generation. For a generation, then I have worked with Mr. Hilton. For a generation, I have worked with him daily; watched him work, watched him play, watched him pray. I have seen him in patience, in anger, in doubt, in excited enthusiasm. I have seen him sad and exploding in merry laughter. I think I know Conrad Nicholson Hilton." (Olive continued to work for Conrad for another sixteen years, until his death in 1979.)

It is impracticable to fully detail in the space allotted here the incredible wealth of information found in this volume's 234 pages, and how vital it was to my research for *The Hiltons: The True Story of an American Dynasty.* It includes more than a hundred speeches and personal writings of Conrad Hilton's, rare photographs from Conrad's private collection, and personal reminiscences in his own words about his storied life and career. It is a stunning work, every chapter typical of the kind of care and attention to detail Conrad Hilton gave to every project to which he dedicated himself. I am proud to own a copy.

The third rare volume I utilized in my research is *The House of Hil-*

ton: *Casa Encantada.* One hundred and fifty copies of this book were privately published by Conrad for his friends and family members; I have the last one published—number 150—and it is signed by Conrad N. Hilton (but not dated, and, again, given to me by a friend of Hilton's who asked not to be identified). This lovely book is about Conrad's beautiful estate and includes many pictures of Casa Encantada, as well as drawings and diagrams of the property. It also provides a detailed account of the furnishings, right down to the "ash burl" color of the fabric used on the dining room chairs. There are photos of the china tea sets from Russia and France used by Conrad and two of his wives, Zsa Zsa and Frances. It's a spectacularly intimate look at the private world of Conrad Hilton and his family, and as such, was invaluable to my understanding of their privileged way of life. Many of the descriptions of the Hiltons' lifestyle at Casa Encantada found in *The Hiltons* were culled from the specifics found in this work.

SOURCES AND OTHER NOTES

It is impossible to write accurately about anyone's life without many reliable witnesses to provide a range of different viewpoints. A biography of this kind stands or falls on the frankness of those involved in the story. A great number of other people went out of their way to assist me over the years that I worked on *The Hiltons: The True Story of an American Dynasty*. Friends, relatives, journalists, socialites, lawyers, celebrities, and business associates of the Hilton family were contacted in preparation for this book. I and my research team also carefully reviewed, as secondary sources, books about Conrad Hilton, as well as hundreds of newspaper and magazine articles written about him. I'm not going to list all of them here, though I will list those that I believe deserve special acknowledgment.

Also, in writing about a family as culturally significant as the Hiltons, a biographer such as myself will encounter many sources who would like to speak, but not for attribution. I have learned over the years that sometimes anonymity is important. Though I would prefer that all of my sources be acknowledged by name, it's not a reasonable or practical expectation. Therefore, whenever a source of mine or of one of my researchers asks for anonymity, I always grant the request.

The following source acknowledgments and extraneous notes are by no means comprehensive. Rather, they are intended to give the reader a *general overview* of my research.

PROLOGUE

Interviews conducted: Myron Harpole (August 15, 2012; August 17, 2012; August 20, 2012).

Volumes referenced: *Be My Guest* by Conrad Hilton; *The Silver Spade:*

The Conrad Hilton Story by Whitney Bolton; *How to Catch a Man, How to Keep a Man, How to Get Rid of a Man* by Zsa Zsa Gabor; *Zsa Zsa Gabor: My Story* by Zsa Zsa Gabor and Gerold Frank; *Jolie Gabor* by Cindy Adams.

Legal documents referenced: "Certificate of Birth, Constance Francesca Hilton," March 10, 1947, Borough of Manhattan, New York, N.Y.; "Certificate of Baptism of Constance Francesca Hilton," by Rev. Charles J. McManus, assistant pastor of St. Patrick's Cathedral, May 4, 1947; "Contestant Constance Francesca Hilton's Responses to Defendants William Barron Hilton and James E. Bates Interrogatories," (May 29, 1979); "Declaration of Constance Francesca Hilton" (June 13, 1979); "Deposition of Zsa Zsa Gabor O'Hara" (June 14, 1979; July 9, 1979; July 10, 1979); "Declaration of Zsa Zsa Gabor O'Hara" (July 1, 1979); "Declaration of Myron Harpole" (July 12, 1979); "Contestant Constance Francesca Hilton's Responses to Defendants William Barron Hilton and James E. Bates Interrogatories" (July 20, 1979); "Declaration of Ralph Nutter" (August 12, 1979); "Declaration of Robert D. Walker in Response to Opposition to Motion for Leave to Amend Will Contest" (March 27, 1980); "Declaration of Myron Harpole" (July 29, 1982); "Declaration of Constance Francesca Hilton" (July 29, 1982).

NOTES

The original filing of Constance Francesca Hilton's contesting of Conrad Hilton's will on March 13, 1979, by her attorneys, Belcher, Henzie & Biegenzahn, listed the litigants in this manner:

> Constance Francesca Hilton, Contestant, vs. Frances Kelly Hilton; William Barron Hilton; Eric Michael Hilton; Conrad Nicholson Hilton III; Michael Otis Hilton; Helen Buckley; Rosemary Carpenter; Eva Lewis; Connie Ann Clarke Whitehead; Anthony Carpenter; Hilton Brown, Sally Leslie; Carolyn Hines; Jack Lewis; Merilee Hilton McCoy; Carl Hilton, Jr.; William Hilton; Mrs. Robert Dillard; Felice Brown Heffinger; William Barron Hilton, Jr.; Hawley Ann Hilton McAuliffe; Steven Michael Hilton; David Alan Hilton; Sharon Constance Hilton Clemm; Richard

Howard Hilton; Daniel Kevin Hilton; Ronald Jeffrey Hilton; Eric Michael Hilton, Jr.; Beverly Ann Hilton; Linda Marie Hilton; Joseph Bradley Hilton; Olive M. Wakeman; Hugo Mentz; Sister Francetta Barberis; James E. Bates; Spearl Ellison, Trustee; Donald H. Hubbs, Trustee; Sam D. Young, Trustee; El Paso National Bank, Trustee; The California Province of the Society of Jesus; Mayo Foundation; Conrad N. Hilton Foundation, George Deukmajian, Attorney General for the State of California, Doe One; Doe Two; Doe Three; Doe Four; and Doe Five.

However, for the purposes of these notes, we will use the shortened version utilized by the Superior Court of the State of California for the County of Los Angeles in most of the filings associated with the original case and with its amendment:

Constance Francesca Hilton v. Frances Kelly Hilton [original filing] (March 13, 1979), and *Francesca Hilton v. Frances Kelly Hilton* [First Amended Contest of Purported Will] (March 13, 1980).

The dialogue between Zsa Zsa Gabor O'Hara and Ralph Nutter during Zsa Zsa's June 14, 1979, deposition was culled directly from its transcript.

The dialogue between Zsa Zsa and Myron Harpole is from Mr. Harpole's first-person account. "It wasn't easy for Mrs. O'Hara," recalled Harpole. "It's never easy for a celebrity to come in and tell personal details of their lives. I thought she was probably thinking, 'This is a fine mess my daughter has gotten me into.' However, I had the impression she would do anything to make certain her daughter finally got the recognition she felt she deserved. We admired how much she tried to keep her composure, even if she did lose it on occasion. She answered absolutely every question posed to her."

A few more interesting details about Zsa Zsa's deposition on June 14, 1979:

Zsa Zsa recalled that when she and Hilton were married, she once became sick with appendicitis. "Instead of taking me to a doctor, he went and got a priest to give novenas for me," she said. It was her sister Eva, she testified, who "insisted to have a doctor look after me. This was a terrible shock to me, when he didn't ask for a doctor and went for a priest, instead."

When asked if Conrad's religious convictions ever interfered with their sex life, Zsa Zsa became irate. "Is that all there is to life and marriage?

Sex?" she demanded to know. "Always sex, sex, sex. You ask me nothing but sex!"

In this deposition, and in the other two she gave at around this time, Zsa Zsa spoke a great deal about Conrad Hilton's affinity for nuns, and expressed her confusion as to why her ex-husband felt so strongly about the sisters of the Catholic Church. In July of 2007, Conrad's grandson Steven Hilton—president and CEO of the Conrad N. Hilton Foundation—explained his grandfather's motivation to Alice Garrad of *Philanthropy News Digest:*

> He was a devout Catholic who went to church every Sunday. His faith was very much alive in his life, and his philosophy and charitable giving were very much faith-centered. As a young boy, he met some sisters who taught him the catechism, and as a result he developed a lifelong affinity and affection for them. He also respected the selflessness of their work. Many of his closest friends later in life were Catholic sisters, some of whom he sent a handwritten letter every week, even at the height of his career.

PART ONE. CONRAD

Curse of the Ambitious
Interviews conducted: Connie Espinoza de Amaté (October 1, 2011); Stewart Armstrong (November 13, 2011); Patricia McClintock Hilton (April 2, 2012); Stella Kelly (July 20, 2012).

Volumes referenced: *Be My Guest* by Conrad Hilton; *The Silver Spade: The Conrad Hilton Story* by Whitney Bolton; *Building the Cold War: Hilton International Hotels and Modern Architecture* by Annabel Jane Wharton; *House of Hilton* by Jerry Oppenheimer; *The Man Who Bought the Waldorf* by Thomas Ewing Dabney; *Conrad N. Hilton, Hotelier* by Mildred Houghton Comfort.

Articles referenced: "Hilton: The Stuff of a Hotel Man," *Newsweek* cover story on Conrad Hilton, September 27, 1954; "Hotels: By Golly!," *Time* cover story on Conrad Hilton, July 19, 1963.

Legal documents referenced: "Last Will and Testament of Conrad Nicholson Hilton" (June 3, 1955).

NOTES

Details of the décor of Conrad Hilton's home at this time—circa 1941—were culled from photographs of the home taken by Marcus deLeon.

The anecdote having to do with Katharine Hepburn and Howard Hughes is as per the memory of Stewart Armstrong.

The interaction between Conrad Hilton and Maria de Amaté is as per the memory of her daughter, Connie, and based on conversations mother and daughter had about Maria's work for Hilton.

Special mention must be made of the work of Cathleen D. Baird, former director and archivist of the Conrad N. Hilton College of Hotel and Restaurant Management, Houston. Her exhaustive online in-house biography, *Conrad N. Hilton: Innkeeper Extraordinary, Statesman and Philanthropist, 1897–1979*, was crucial to my research. It was last updated on April 2, 2004. I also referenced Ms. Baird's excellent "Hats Off to Hilton," a videotape presentation celebrating Conrad Hilton's hundredth birthday, for the 1987 Gourmet Night program of the Conrad N. Hilton College.

Humble Beginnings/Hotelier/Losing It All
Interviews conducted: Connie Espinoza de Amaté (October 1, 2011); Carole Wells Doheny (March 8, 2012; March 12, 2012; June 15, 2012); Noreen Nash Siegel (April 2, 2012; April 3, 2012; April 10, 2012); Stewart Armstrong (November 13, 2011; November 14, 2011; November 15, 2012); Mark Young (July 20, 2012; August 1, 2012).

Volumes referenced: *Be My Guest* by Conrad Hilton; *The Man Who Bought the Waldorf* by Thomas Ewing Dabney; *The Silver Spade* by Whitney Bolton; *Jolie Gabor* by Cindy Adams; *Building the Cold War: Hilton International Hotels and Modern Architecture* by Annabel Jane Wharton; *Conrad N. Hilton, Hotelier* by Mildred Houghton Comfort; *Portals at the Pass: El Paso Architecture to 1930* by Evan Haywood Antone; *Historic El Paso: An Illustrated Biography* by Ken Flynn; *Pass of the North: Four Centuries on the Rio Grande*, volumes 1 and 2, by C. L. Sonnichsen; *El Paso: A Borderlands History* by W. H. Timmons. I also referenced the pamphlet *Downtown Historic Walking Tour: El Paso*, as well as Texas Historical Commission, *Texas Historic Sites Atlas*, http://atlas.thc.state.tx.us.

Articles referenced: Dora Jane Hamblin, "In 19 Lands, Instant America: His Hotels Keep Conrad Hilton Hopping," *Life*, August 30, 1963.

Legal documents referenced: "Deposition of Constance Francesca Hilton" (September 12, 1979); "Deposition of William Barron Hilton" (September 24, 1979); "Deposition of Frances Kelly Hilton" (October 19, 1979); *Constance Francesca Hilton v. Frances Kelly Hilton* [original filing]" (March 13, 1979); "*Francesca Hilton v. Frances Kelly Hilton* [First Amended Contest of Purported Will]" (March 13, 1980).

Television programs referenced: *What's My Line?*, Conrad Hilton, June 5, 1955; *Person to Person*, interview with Conrad Hilton, 1955; *The Ed Sullivan Show*, Conrad Hilton (recites prayer), April 6, 1958; *The Hiltons*, Arts & Entertainment, 2005; *Conrad Hilton: Innkeeper to the World*, Arts & Entertainment, 2005; *Biography: Conrad Hilton*, CNBC, 2010.

Georgia on His Mind

Interviews conducted: Zsa Zsa Gabor (February 2, 1986); Stewart Armstrong (November 13, 2011; November 14, 2011; November 15, 2012); Patricia McClintock Hilton (April 2, 2012; April 8, 2012; April 16, 2012; April 20, 2012); Carole Wells Doheny (March 8, 2012; March 12, 2012; June 15, 2012); Patricia Skipworth Hilton (February 27, 2012; February 28, 2012; April 5, 2012), Debbie Reynolds (August 2, 2012).

Volumes referenced: *Be My Guest* by Conrad Hilton, *Building the Cold War: Hilton International Hotels and Modern Architecture* by Annabel Jane Wharton; *Zsa Zsa Gabor: My Story* by Zsa Zsa Gabor and Gerold Frank; *One Lifetime Is Not Enough* by Zsa Zsa Gabor.

Articles referenced: "Hilton: The Stuff of a Hotel Man," *Newsweek* cover story on Conrad Hilton, September 27, 1954; "Hotels: by Golly!," *Time* cover story on Conrad Hilton, July 19, 1963; Dora Jane Hamblin, "In 19 Lands, Instant America: His Hotels Keep Conrad Hilton Hopping," *Life*, August 30, 1963.

Legal documents referenced: "Deposition of Sari Zsa Zsa Gabor O'Hara" (June 14, 1979; July 9, 1979; and July 10, 1979); *Constance Francesca Hilton v. Frances Kelly Hilton* [original filing] (March 13, 1979); *Francesca Hilton v. Frances Kelly Hilton*, [First Amended Contest of Purported Will] (March 13, 1980).

Television programs referenced: *Person to Person*, interview with Eva Gabor, 1953; *Person to Person*, interview with Conrad Hilton, 1955; *The*

Merv Griffin Show, interview with Zsa Zsa Gabor, October 17, 1962; *The Tonight Show Starring Johnny Carson*, interview with Zsa Zsa Gabor, May 16, 1963; *The Joey Bishop Show*, interview with Zsa Zsa Gabor, May 5, 1967; *The David Frost Show*, interview with Zsa Zsa Gabor, August 20, 1970; *The Virginia Graham Show*, interview with Eva Gabor, March 22, 1971; *Phil Donahue*, interview with Zsa Zsa Gabor, August 10, 1971; *The David Frost Show*, interview with Eva Gabor, 1971; *The Pat Sajak Show*, interview with Zsa Zsa Gabor, September 13, 1989; *Vicki*, interview with Zsa Zsa Gabor, September 10, 1992; *Larry King Live*, interview with Zsa Zsa Gabor, November 26, 1991; *The People vs. Zsa Zsa Gabor*, 1991; *One on One with John Tesh*, interview with Eva Gabor, 1992; *Intimate Portrait: Eva Gabor*, February 1, 1998; *The Hiltons*, Arts & Entertainment, 2005.

Loneliness at the Top/Buying the Town House

Interviews conducted: Carole Wells Doheny (March 8, 2012); Patricia McClintock Hilton (April 2, 2012); Patricia Skipworth Hilton (April 5, 2012); George Schlatter (April 7, 2012); Noreen Nash Siegel (April 10, 2012); Ruta Lee (April 23, 2012); Dale Olsen (July 9, 2012).

Volumes referenced: *Be My Guest* by Conrad Hilton; *The Silver Spade: The Conrad Hilton Story* by Whitney Bolton; *Building the Cold War: Hilton International Hotels and Modern Architecture* by Annabel Jane Wharton.

Articles referenced: Dora Jane Hamblin, "In 19 Lands, Instant America: His Hotels Keep Conrad Hilton Hopping," *Life*, August 30, 1963.

Legal documents referenced: "Deposition of Sari Zsa Zsa Gabor O'Hara" (June 14, 1979); "Deposition of William Barron Hilton" (September 24, 1979).

Television programs referenced: *Conrad Hilton: Innkeeper to the World*, Arts & Entertainment, 2005; *Biography: Conrad Hilton*, CNBC, 2010.

Note: For the narrative descriptions of the hotels described on these pages, from "Buying the Town House" forward, I referenced the U.S. Department of the Interior's National Register of Historic Places. I also referenced photographs of the hotels from the Conrad Hilton Collection, Hospitality Industry Archives.

Courting Zsa Zsa/Catholic Stumbling Block/Conrad Breaks the News to Zsa Zsa

Interviews conducted: Zsa Zsa Gabor (February 2, 1986); Stewart Armstrong (November 13, 2011; November 14, 2011; November 15, 2012);

Carole Wells Doheny (March 8, 2012; March 12, 2012; June 15, 2012); Myron Harpole (August 15, 2012; August 17, 2012; August 20, 2012); Noreen Nash Siegel (April 2, 2012; April 3, 2012; April 10, 2012); Connie Espinoza de Amaté (October 1, 2011); Helen Lamm (July 25, 2012).

Volumes referenced: *Be My Guest* by Conrad Hilton; *The Silver Spade: The Conrad Hilton Story* by Whitney Bolton; *Zsa Zsa Gabor: My Story* by Zsa Zsa Gabor and Gerold Frank; *Jolie Gabor* by Cindy Adams; *House of Hilton* by Jerry Oppenheimer; *The Man Who Bought the Waldorf* by Thomas Ewing Dabney; *Conrad N. Hilton, Hotelier* by Mildred Houghton Comfort.

Legal documents referenced: "Codicil to Last Will and Testament of Conrad Hilton" (March 20, 1947); "Last Will and Testament of Conrad Nicholson Hilton" (December 19, 1953); "Last Will and Testament of Conrad Nicholson Hilton" (June 3, 1955); "Last Will and Testament of Conrad Nicholson Hilton" (October 21, 1960); "Last Will and Testament of Conrad Nicholson Hilton" (January 27, 1967); "Last Will and Testament of Conrad Nicholson Hilton" (August 19, 1970); "Last Will and Testament of Conrad Nicholson Hilton" (October 31, 1973); *Constance Francesca Hilton v. Frances Kelly Hilton* [original filing] (March 13, 1979); "Deposition of Sari Zsa Zsa Gabor O'Hara" (July 9, 1979); "Deposition of Constance Francesca Hilton" (September 12, 1979; September 13, 1979; September 14, 1979); "Declaration of Myron Harpole" (July 29, 1982); *Francesca Hilton v. Frances Kelly Hilton* [First Amended Contest of Purported Will] (March 13, 1980).

Television programs referenced: *Person to Person*, interview with Eva Gabor, 1953; *What's My Line?*, Conrad Hilton, June 5, 1955; *Person to Person*, interview with Conrad Hilton, 1955; *The Ed Sullivan Show*, interview with Conrad Hilton, April 6, 1958; *The Jack Paar Program*, interview with Zsa Zsa Gabor, October 19, 1962; *The Tonight Show Starring Johnny Carson*, interview with Zsa Zsa Gabor, May 16, 1963; *The Joey Bishop Show*, interview with Zsa Zsa Gabor, May 5, 1967; *The Joey Bishop Show*, interview with Zsa Zsa Gabor, February 24, 1969; *The Tonight Show Starring Johnny Carson*, interview with Zsa Zsa Gabor, July 28, 1970; *This Is Your Life*, Zsa Zsa Gabor, November 29, 1989; *The David Frost Show*, interview with Zsa Zsa Gabor, June 12, 1972; *The Geraldo Rivera Show*, interview with Zsa Zsa Gabor, September 13, 1990; *Showbiz Today*, interview with Eva Gabor, August 19, 1991; *The Howard Stern Summer Show*, interview with Zsa Zsa Gabor, May 2, 1992; *Late Show with David Letterman*, interview with Zsa Zsa Gabor, December 22, 1993; *That's Entertainment! III*

Behind the Screen, interview with Eva Gabor, 1994; *Intimate Portrait: Eva Gabor*, February 1, 1998); *Conrad Hilton: Innkeeper to the World*, Arts & Entertainment, 2005; *Biography: Conrad Hilton*, CNBC, 2010; *Larry King Live*, interview with Zsa Zsa Gabor, November 26, 1991.

PART TWO. MARY

Interviews conducted: Stanley Tucker (October 2, 2011; October 11, 2011); Jarrod Barron (November 20, 2011); Ken Heinemann (August 2, 2011); Patricia Skipworth Hilton (February 27, 2012).

Volumes referenced: *Be My Guest* by Conrad Hilton; *Building the Cold War: Hilton International Hotels and Modern Architecture* by Annabel Jane Wharton; *The Silver Spade: The Conrad Hilton Story* by Whitney Bolton.

Legal documents referenced: "Divorce Decree—Conrad Hilton v. Mary Barron," miscellaneous documents and correspondence (June 11, 1934); "Deposition of Sari Zsa Zsa Gabor O'Hara" (July 10, 1979); "Deposition of Frances Kelly Hilton" (October 19, 1979).

Television programs referenced: *The Jack Paar Program*, interview with Zsa Zsa Gabor, November 23, 1962; *The Jack Paar Program*, interview with Zsa Zsa Gabor, May 29, 1964; *The Joey Bishop Show*, interview with Zsa Zsa Gabor, May 8, 1968; *The Virginia Graham Show*, interview with Zsa Zsa Gabor, June 10, 1970; *Phil Donahue*, interview with Zsa Zsa Gabor, August 10, 1971; *The Pat Sajak Show*, interview with Zsa Zsa Gabor, September 13, 1989; *Late Show with David Letterman*, interview with Zsa Zsa Gabor, November 27, 1991; *The Howard Stern Summer Show*, interview with Zsa Zsa Gabor, May 2, 1992; *The Rosie O'Donnell Show*, interview with Zsa Zsa Gabor, February 25, 1998; *Conrad Hilton: Innkeeper to the World*, Arts & Entertainment, 2005; *Larry King Live: The Hiltons*, Arts & Entertainment, 2005; *Biography: Conrad Hilton*, CNBC, 2010.

PART THREE. ZSA ZSA

Conrad's Inner Turmoil/For Love or Money
Interviews conducted: Cindy Adams (September 1, 1998); Terry Moore (February 10, 2012); Ed Lozzi (March 2, 2012); Carole Wells Doheny

(March 12, 2012); Noreen Nash Siegel (April 2, 2012); Ruta Lee (April 23, 2012); Myron Harpole (August 15, 2012; August 17, 2012; August 20, 2012).

Volumes referenced: *Be My Guest* by Conrad Hilton; *Jolie Gabor* by Cindy Adams; *Zsa Zsa Gabor: My Story* by Zsa Zsa Gabor and Gerold Frank; *One Lifetime Is Not Enough* by Zsa Zsa Gabor; *Gaborabilia* by Anthony Turtu and Donald F. Reute; *Eva Gabor an Amazing Woman: "Unscrupulous"* by Camyl Sosa Belanger.

Articles referenced: "Hilton: The Stuff of a Hotel Man," *Newsweek* cover story on Conrad Hilton, September 27, 1954; "Hotels: By Golly!," *Time* cover story on Conrad Hilton, July 19, 1963; Dora Jane Hamblin, "In 19 Lands, Instant America: His Hotels Keep Conrad Hilton Hopping," *Life*, August 30, 1963.

Legal documents referenced: "Reporter's Transcript—Sari Gabor Hilton, sometimes known as Zsazsa Sari Hilton vs. Conrad Hilton," by John F. Brill, official court reporter (September 17, 1946); "Last Will and Testament of Conrad Nicholson Hilton" (June 3, 1955); "Deposition of Sari Zsa Zsa Gabor O'Hara" (June 14, 1979; July 9, 1979; July 10, 1979); "Deposition of Constance Francesca Hilton" (September 12, 1979; September 13, 1979; September 14, 1979); "Declaration of Gregson Bautzer" (undated—from *Zsazsa Sari Gabor v. Conrad Hilton*); "Declaration of G. Bentley Ryan" (undated—from *Zsazsa Sari Gabor v. Conrad Hilton*).

The Roosevelt
Interviews conducted: Marybeth Evans-Wright (September 28, 2011); Jason Lederer (October 1, 2011); Timothy Long (October 4, 2011); Noreen Nash Siegel (April 2, 2012; April 3, 2012; April 10, 2012); Mark Young (July 20, 2012); David Gracie (March 1, 2012); Carole Wells Doheny (March 8, 2012); Mike Dipp (March 16, 2012).

Volumes referenced: *Be My Guest* by Conrad Hilton; *House of Hilton* by Jerry Oppenheimer; *The Man Who Bought the Waldorf* by Thomas Ewing Dabney; *Conrad N. Hilton, Hotelier* by Mildred Houghton Comfort.

Legal documents referenced: "Deposition of William Barron Hilton" (September 24, 1979; "Deposition of Frances Kelly Hilton" (October 19, 1979); "Declaration of Frances Kelly Hilton" (October 23, 1979).

Television programs referenced: *Person to Person*, interview with Conrad Hilton, 1955; *Larry King Live*, interview with Zsa Zsa Gabor,

November 26, 1991; *Conrad Hilton: Innkeeper to the World*, Arts & Entertainment, 2005; *Biography: Conrad Hilton*, CNBC, 2010.

Note: We had access to Margaret Phillips-Brown's extensive collection about the acquisition of the Roosevelt Hotel by Conrad Hilton.

Marriage: His/Marriage: Hers

Interviews conducted: Zsa Zsa Gabor (February 2, 1986); Jason Lederer (October 1, 2011); Timothy Long (October 4, 2011); Stanley Tucker (October 2, 2011; October 11, 2011); Cindy Adams (September 1, 1998); Doris Roberts (January 4, 2012); Patricia Skipworth Hilton (February 28, 2012); Mike Dipp (March 16, 2012); Patricia McClintock Hilton (April 2, 2012; April 8, 2012; April 16, 2012; April 20, 12); Noreen Nash Siegel (April 2, 2012; April 3, 2012; April 10, 2012); Dale Olsen (July 9, 2012); Myron Harpole (August 15, 2012); Steven D'Orio (September 4, 2012).

Volumes referenced: *Be My Guest* by Conrad Hilton; *The Man Who Bought the Waldorf* by Thomas Ewing Dabney; *Conrad N. Hilton, Hotelier* by Mildred Houghton Comfort; *Jolie Gabor* by Cindy Adams; *Zsa Zsa Gabor: My Story* by Zsa Zsa Gabor and Gerold Frank; *One Lifetime Is Not Enough* by Zsa Zsa Gabor; *Gaborabilia* by Anthony Turtu and Donald F. Reute; *Eva Gabor an Amazing Woman: "Unscrupulous"* by Camyl Sosa Belanger; *A Dreadful Man: A Personal, Intimate Book About George Sanders* by Brian Aherne.

Legal documents referenced: "Sworn Declaration of J. B. Herndon Jr." (August 2, 1946); "Reporter's Transcript—Sari Gabor Hilton, sometimes known as ZsaZsa Sari Hilton vs. Conrad Hilton," by John F. Brill, official court reporter (September 17, 1946); "Declaration of ZsaZsa Sari Hilton" (September 20, 1946); "Declaration of Eva Gabor" (September 20, 1946); miscellaneous file notes from *Zsa Gabor Plaintiff vs. Fawcett Publications, Inc.* (November 1960); "Deposition of Sari Zsa Zsa Gabor O'Hara" (June 14, 1979); "Contestant Constance Francesca Hilton's Responses to Defendants William Barron Hilton and James E. Bates Interrogatories" (July 20, 1979); "Deposition of Constance Francesca Hilton" (September 12, 1979; September 13, 1979; September 14, 1979); "Declaration of Gregson Bautzer" (undated, from *Sari Zsa Zsa Gabor v. Conrad Hilton*).

Television programs referenced: *Person to Person*, interview with Conrad Hilton, 1955; *The Merv Griffin Show*, interview with Zsa Zsa Gabor, October 17, 1962; *The Jack Paar Program*, interview with Zsa Zsa Gabor,

December 4, 1964; *The Joey Bishop Show,* interview with Zsa Zsa Gabor, May 5, 1967; *The Merv Griffin Show,* interview with Eva Gabor, February 18, 1970; *The David Frost Show,* interview with Zsa Zsa Gabor, May 12, 1970; *The Virginia Graham Show,* interview with Eva Gabor, March 22, 1971; *One on One with John Tesh,* interview with Zsa Zsa Gabor, September 10, 1991; *The People vs. Zsa Zsa Gabor,* 1991; *Vicki,* interview with Zsa Zsa Gabor, September 10, 1992; *The Hiltons,* Arts & Entertainment, 2005.

NOTES

The conversations between Conrad Hilton and Zsa Zsa Gabor concerning their household budgets were reconstructed based on the accounts of both in their respective memoirs, *Be My Guest* and *My Story.*

The actual text of Barron Hilton's letter to his father regarding his allowance can be found in *Be My Guest.*

The conversation between Conrad Hilton and J. B. Herndon Jr. was reconstructed using "Sworn Declaration of J. B. Herndon Jr." (August 2, 1946).

A Frustrating Business Deal/The Plaza
Interviews conducted: Tyler Worthington (September 12, 2011); Dylan Terrell Thomas (October 22, 2011); Marva DeYoung (March 1, 2012); Patricia McClintock Hilton (April 2, 2012; April 8, 2012; April 16, 2012; April 20, 2012); Carole Wells Doheny (March 8, 2012; March 12, 2012; June 15, 2012)

Volumes referenced: *Be My Guest* by Conrad Hilton; *House of Hilton* by Jess Oppenheimer; *Gaborabilia* by Anthony Turtu and Donald F. Reute; *Eva Gabor an Amazing Woman: "Unscrupulous"* by Camyl Sosa Belanger; *Building the Cold War: Hilton International Hotels and Modern Architecture* by Annabel Jane Wharton; *The Silver Spade: The Conrad Hilton Story* by Whitney Bolton.

Articles referenced: "Hilton: The Stuff of a Hotel Man," *Newsweek* cover story on Conrad Hilton, September 27, 1954; "Hotels: By Golly!," *Time* cover story on Conrad Hilton, July 19, 1963.

Legal documents referenced: "Deposition of Zsa Zsa Gabor O'Hara" (June 14, 1979; July 9, 1979; July 10, 1979).

Television programs referenced: *What's My Line?*, Conrad Hilton, June 5, 1955; *Larry King Live*, interview with Zsa Zsa Gabor, November 26, 1991; *Conrad Hilton: Innkeeper to the World*, Arts & Entertainment, 2005; *Biography: Conrad Hilton*, CNBC, 2010.

NOTES

We had access to Margaret Phillips-Brown's extensive collection about the acquisition of the Plaza Hotel by Conrad Hilton, which included color and black-and-white photographs of the hotel and the Oak Room taken in 1943.

The source of the conversation between Conrad Hilton and a representative of Atlas Corporation worked for Atlas at the time and asked for anonymity.

An Ominous Sign/A Priest's Visit/Up in Flames
Interviews conducted: Zsa Zsa Gabor (February 2, 1986); Cindy Adams (September 1, 1999); Patricia McClintock Hilton (April 2, 2012; April 8, 2012; April 16, 2012; April 20, 12); Lena Burrell (September 12, 2012; October 11, 2012; December 2, 2012).

Volumes referenced: *Be My Guest* by Conrad Hilton; *Jolie Gabor* by Cindy Adams; *Zsa Zsa Gabor: My Story* by Zsa Zsa Gabor and Gerold Frank; *One Lifetime Is Not Enough* by Zsa Zsa Gabor; *Gaborabilia* by Anthony Turtu and Donald F. Reute; *Eva Gabor an Amazing Woman: "Unscrupulous"* by Camyl Sosa Belanger; *A Dreadful Man: A Personal, Intimate Book About George Sanders* by Brian Aherne.

Legal documents referenced: "Reporter's Transcript—Sari Gabor Hilton, sometimes known as ZsaZsa Sari Hilton vs. Conrad Hilton," by John F. Brill, official court reporter (September 17, 1946); "Declaration of ZsaZsa Sari Hilton" (September 20, 1946); "Declaration of Eva Gabor" (September 20, 1946); miscellaneous file notes, including partial deposition from *Zsa Gabor Plaintiff vs. Fawcett Publications, Inc.* (November 1960); "Contestant Constance Francesca Hilton's Responses to Defendants William Barron Hilton and James E. Bates Interrogatories" (July 20, 1979); "Deposition of Constance Francesca Hilton" (September 12, 1979; September 13, 1979; September 14, 1979).

Television programs referenced: *The Merv Griffin Show*, interview with Zsa Zsa Gabor, October 17, 1962; *The Jack Paar Program*, interview with Zsa Zsa Gabor, May 29, 1964; *The Tonight Show Starring Johnny Carson*, interview with Zsa Zsa Gabor, June 17, 1970; *The Tonight Show*, interview with Eva Gabor, May 15, 1972; *The Geraldo Rivera Show*, interview with Zsa Zsa Gabor, September 13, 1990; *The Howard Stern Summer Show*, interview with Zsa Zsa Gabor, May 2, 1992; *One on One with John Tesh*, interview with Eva Gabor, 1992; *Late Show David Letterman*, interview with Zsa Zsa Gabor, November 27, 1991; *Late Show with David Letterman*, interview with Zsa Zsa Gabor, December 22, 1993.

NOTES

The conversation between Zsa Zsa Gabor and Father Kelly was reconstructed using her memory in her depositions in the case *Zsa Gabor Plaintiff vs. Fawcett Publications, Inc.* (November 1960). In this case, Zsa Zsa sued Fawcett for defamation because of a lengthy article that appeared about her in *Cavalier* magazine in 1960, written by Claudia Martell. One of her biggest contentions, according to the suit, was that she was portrayed as "caring only for money and jewels; sitting around even in the bathtub waiting for men to bring her money and jewels." That was bad enough, but what really rankled Zsa Zsa was that the writer asserted, "According to generous calculations, her age at present is 47." According to Zsa Zsa's lawsuit, "The defamatory statement is construed to mean that plaintiff is 47 years of age and that any other age given by plaintiff as being her true age is not in fact the truth; that in fact, plaintiff was not born in 1923, thus making plaintiff 38 years of age, but that the plaintiff is approximately 9 years, if not more, older than she states." As it happened, the writer was wrong. But so was Zsa Zsa. We now know that Zsa Zsa was born in 1917, not 1923. In 1960, she was forty-three, not forty-seven as the writer stated, and not thirty-eight as she stated. She was actually shaving five years from her age. Though she gave a deposition in the case, she did eventually settle with Fawcett. The settlement involved Fawcett paying Zsa Zsa a hefty sum of money and in return obtaining from her the rights to publish in paperback her autobiography *Zsa Zsa Gabor: My Story*.

The conversation between Conrad Hilton and Zsa Zsa Gabor reconstructed here concerning his gift to her and the party that followed at the Plaza is based on Gabor's accounts of the evening to her personal assistant, Lena Burrell. I corroborated Gabor's account by utilizing Bart Andrews's extensive files and transcripts from the summer of 1985 relating to his interviews with Zsa Zsa, Eva, and Magda Gabor for a possible autobiography collaboration between himself and Zsa Zsa.

He Never Should Have Done It/What Would It Take?/Zsa Zsa Is Institutionalized/The Divorce
Interviews conducted: Zsa Zsa Gabor (February 2, 1986); Cindy Adams (September 1, 1998); Tyler Worthington (September 12, 2011); Dylan Terrell Thomas (October 22, 2011); Doris Roberts (January 4, 2012); Carole Wells Doheny (March 8, 2012; March 12, 2012; June 15, 2012); Patricia McClintock Hilton (April 8, 2012; April 16, 2012; April 20, 2012); Myron Harpole (August 15, 2012; August 17, 2012; August 20, 2012); Lena Burrell (September 12, 2012; October 11, 2012; December 2, 2012); Stewart Armstrong (November 13, 2011; November 14, 2011; November 15, 2012).

Volumes referenced: *Be My Guest* by Conrad Hilton; *The Man Who Bought the Waldorf* by Thomas Ewing Dabney; *Conrad N. Hilton, Hotelier* by Mildred Houghton Comfort; *Jolie Gabor* by Cindy Adams; *Zsa Zsa Gabor: My Story* by Zsa Zsa Gabor and Gerold Frank; *One Lifetime Is Not Enough* by Zsa Zsa Gabor; *Gaborabilia* by Anthony Turtu and Donald F. Reute; *Eva Gabor an Amazing Woman: "Unscrupulous"* by Camyl Sosa Belanger; *George Sanders, Zsa Zsa and Me* by David R. Slavitt.

Articles referenced: "Hilton Sued for Divorce," Associated Press, July 24, 1946; "Mr. and Mrs. Hilton No More," United Press International, July 25, 1946; "Hilton Hotel Man Divorced," *Los Angeles Times*, September 18, 1946.

Legal documents referenced: "Property Settlement and Separation Agreement Between Conrad Hilton and Sari Zsa Zsa Gabor" (November 3, 1944); "Statement of Zsa Zsa Gabor Hilton" (November 5, 1944); "Supplemental Property Settlement and Separation Agreement Between Conrad Hilton and Sari Zsa Zsa Gabor" (August 6, 1946); "Reporter's Transcript—Sari Gabor Hilton, sometimes known as ZsaZsa Sari Hilton vs. Conrad Hilton," by John F. Brill, official court reporter (September 17, 1946); "Final Decree of Divorce—*Conrad Hilton v. Sari Zsa Zsa Gabor*" (September 17, 1946); "Declaration of ZsaZsa Sari Hilton" (September 20,

1946); "Declaration of Eva Gabor" (September 20, 1946); "Deposition of Sari Zsa Zsa Gabor O'Hara" (June 14, 1979); "Deposition of Constance Francesca Hilton" (September 12, 1979; September 13, 1979; September 14, 1979); "Declaration of Gregson Bautzer" (undated, from *Sari Zsa Zsa Gabor v. Conrad Hilton*); "Declaration of Eva Gabor" (undated, from *Sari Zsa Zsa Gabor v. Conrad Hilton*); "Statement by Conrad N. Hilton" (undated, from *Sari Zsa Zsa Gabor v. Conrad Hilton*).

Television programs referenced: *Person to Person*, interview with Conrad Hilton, 1955; *The Merv Griffin Show*, interview with Zsa Zsa Gabor, October 17, 1962; *The David Frost Show*, interview with Zsa Zsa Gabor, May 12, 1970; *This Is Your Life*, Zsa Zsa Gabor, November 29, 1989; *One on One with John Tesh*, interview with Eva Gabor, 1992; *Intimate Portrait: Eva Gabor*, February 1, 1998.

NOTES

The scenes between Zsa Zsa Gabor and Conrad Hilton that took place when he was sick with the flu in New York are culled from their respective books, *Be My Guest* and *Zsa Zsa: My Story*.

The scene between Gabor and Hilton before the party for Thomas E. Dewey was reconstructed as per her memory in *Zsa Zsa Gabor: My Story*.

The scene between Gabor and Hilton at the party for Dewey at the Waldorf-Astoria was reconstructed based on Eva Gabor's interviews with Bart Andrews in the summer of 1985 for a proposed autobiography by Andrews and Zsa Zsa Gabor.

The scenes between Gabor and Hilton after the party at the Waldorf-Astoria was reconstructed based on Zsa Zsa's account of events in "Statement of Zsa Zsa Gabor Hilton," November 5, 1944 (in the matter of her divorce from Hilton).

The lawyer who hired the private detective for Conrad Hilton asked not to be identified.

The argument between Hilton and Gabor that ensued after Conrad asked if she was having an affair, as portrayed in these pages, was reconstructed from the memory of eyewitness Lena Burrell, as was the scene after the argument between Burrell and Gabor.

There are at least fifteen different versions of Zsa Zsa's time in an institution, five of them from Zsa Zsa herself, and one from my own interview with her in February 1986. For this book, I used what she told me, as well as declarations given not only by Miss Gabor but by her sister Eva, Conrad Hilton, and Gregson Bautzer.

The letter from J. B. Herndon to Conrad Hilton dated August 1, 1945, is found in the Superior Court of the State of California file "Sari Zsa Zsa Gabor v. Conrad Hilton, September 17, 1946."

All quotes from Zsa Zsa Gabor and Eva Gabor on the witness stand during divorce hearings are from "Reporter's Transcript—Sari Gabor Hilton, sometimes known as ZsaZsa Sari Hilton vs. Conrad Hilton," by John F. Brill, official court reporter (September 17, 1946).

Buying the Stevens and the Palmer House
Interviews conducted: Jason Lederer (October 1, 2011); Timothy Long (October 4, 2011); Doris Roberts (January 4, 2012); Mike Dipp (March 16, 2012); Noreen Nash Siegel (April 2, 2012; April 3, 2012; April 10, 2012); Dale Olsen (July 9, 2012); Debbie Reynolds (August 2, 2012); Steven D'Orio (September 4, 2012).

Volumes referenced: *Be My Guest* by Conrad Hilton; *Conrad N. Hilton, Hotelier* by Mildred Houghton Comfort; *House of Hilton*, by Jerry Oppenheimer; *The Man Who Bought the Waldorf* by Thomas Ewing Dabney.

Legal documents referenced: "Deposition of William Barron Hilton" (September 24, 1979); "Deposition of Frances Kelly Hilton" (October 19, 1979).

Television programs referenced: *What's My Line?*, Conrad Hilton, June 5, 1955; *Person to Person*, interview with Conrad Hilton, 1955; *The Ed Sullivan Show*, Conrad Hilton, April 6, 1958; *Conrad Hilton: Innkeeper to the World*, Arts & Entertainment, 2005; *Larry King Live: The Hiltons*, Arts & Entertainment, 2005; *Biography: Conrad Hilton*, CNBC, 2010.

Note: The complex and maddening negotiations between Conrad Hilton and Steve Healy for the Stevens Hotel are outlined here as per Hilton's memory in *Be My Guest*. I also referenced Hedda Hopper's interview notes with Conrad Hilton, dated April 1, 1950, found in the Hedda Hopper Papers in the Margaret Herrick Collection of the Academy of Motion Picture Arts and Sciences.

Zsa Zsa's Daughter

Interviews conducted: Ed Lozzi (March 2, 2012); Noreen Nash Siegel (April 10, 2012); Myron Harpole (August 15, 2012; August 17, 2012; August 20, 2012).

Volumes referenced: *Be My Guest* by Conrad Hilton; *Jolie Gabor* by Cindy Adams; *Zsa Zsa Gabor: My Story* by Zsa Zsa Gabor and Gerold Frank; *One Lifetime Is Not Enough* by Zsa Zsa Gabor; *Gaborabilia* by Anthony Turtu and Donald F. Reute; *Eva Gabor an Amazing Woman: "Unscrupulous"* by Camyl Sosa Belanger.

Articles referenced: Dora Jane Hamblin, "In 19 Lands, Instant America: His Hotels Keep Conrad Hilton Hopping," *Life*, August 30, 1963.

Legal documents referenced: "Reporter's Transcript—Sari Gabor Hilton, sometimes known as ZsaZsa Sari Hilton vs. Conrad Hilton," by John F. Brill, official court reporter (September 17, 1946); "Certificate of Birth, Constance Francesca Hilton," Borough of Manhattan, New York, N.Y. (March 10, 1947); "Certificate of Baptism of Constance Francesca Hilton," by Rev. Charles J. McManus, assistant pastor of St. Patrick's Cathedral (May 4, 1947); "Codicil to Last Will and Testament of Conrad Hilton" (1947); "Last Will and Testament of Conrad Nicholson Hilton" (October 4, 1951); "Last Will and Testament of Conrad Nicholson Hilton" (December 19, 1953); "Last Will and Testament of Conrad Nicholson Hilton" (June 3, 1955); "Last Will and Testament of Conrad Nicholson Hilton" (October 21, 1960); miscellaneous file notes from *Zsa Gabor Plaintiff vs. Fawcett Publications, Inc.* (November 1960); "Last Will and Testament of Conrad Nicholson Hilton" (January 27, 1967); "Last Will and Testament of Conrad Nicholson Hilton" (August 19, 1970); "Last Will and Testament of Conrad Nicholson Hilton" (October 31, 1973); *Constance Francesca Hilton v. Frances Kelly Hilton* [original filing] (March 13, 1979); "Contestant Constance Francesca Hilton's Responses to Defendants William Barron Hilton and James E. Bates Interrogatories" (July 20, 1979); "Deposition of Zsa Zsa Gabor O'Hara" (July 9, 1979; July 10, 1979); "Deposition of Constance Francesca Hilton" (September 12, 1979; September 13, 1979; September 14, 1979); "Deposition of James E. Bates," pp. 25–36 and 53–77 (September 20, 1979); "Deposition of William Barron Hilton" (September 24, 1979); *Francesca Hilton v. Frances Kelly Hilton* [First Amended Contest of Purported Will] (March 13, 1980); "Declaration of Myron Harpole" (July 29, 1982).

Television programs referenced: *Entertainment Tonight*, interview with Francesca Hilton, June 29, 2007; *Entertainment Tonight*, interview with Francesca Hilton, August 19, 2008.

NOTES

I attempted to interview Constance Francesca Hilton for this book, sending her a copy of my book *After Camelot: A Personal History of the Kennedy Family, 1968 to the Present* (published in 2012), as well as a lengthy letter explaining why I felt it important to have her input. In a note on August 27, 2012, Francesca thanked me for the letter and the book but declined my invitation to be interviewed. "As a Hilton," she noted, she didn't believe it was fair for her to talk about her relatives for this book. She also mentioned that she was writing her own. She signed the note, "Constance Francesca Gabor Hilton."

I understand and respect a decision not to cooperate, as well as her desire to tell her own story her own way. Therefore, in order for me to write about Francesca Hilton's life and times with her parents, Conrad and Zsa Zsa, the vast majority of material contained in this book relating to her experience was culled from declarations and depositions she and her family members gave in the case of *Constance Francesca Hilton v. Frances Hilton et al.*

Details of conversations between James E. Bates and Zsa Zsa Gabor regarding the possibility of Zsa Zsa asking for child support from Conrad Hilton are found in the deposition of James E. Bates (pp. 25–36, September 20, 1979). Unfortunately, Bates's deposition is incomplete; pages have somehow gone missing over the course of years. I used, for my purposes here, the pages that were available to me.

PART FOUR. SONS OF THE FATHER

Interviews conducted: Stanley Tucker (October 2, 2011; October 11, 2011); Carole Wells Doheny (March 8, 2012; March 12, 2012; June 15, 2012); Noreen Nash Siegel (April 3, 2012); Mark Young, (July 20, 2012); Patricia Skipworth Hilton (February 27, 2012; February 28, 2012; April 5,

2012) Mark Young (July 20, 2012); Dale Olsen (July 9, 2012); Mike Dipp (March 16, 2012); Myron Harpole (August 15, 2012); Everett Long (December 14, 2011; January 15, 2012; March 3, 2012).

Volumes referenced: *Be My Guest* by Conrad Hilton; *The Silver Spade: The Conrad Hilton Story* by Whitney Bolton; *Jolie Gabor* by Cindy Adams; *Zsa Zsa Gabor: My Story* by Zsa Zsa Gabor and Gerold Frank; *One Lifetime Is Not Enough* by Zsa Zsa Gabor; *Gaborabilia* by Anthony Turtu and Donald F. Reute; *Eva Gabor an Amazing Woman: "Unscrupulous"* by Camyl Sosa Belanger; *Miller's High Life* by Ann Miller.

Articles referenced: "Mines Coach Rescues Family from Fire," *El Paso Herald Post*, August 13, 1940; Peter Lester, "When This Hotel Barron Says He's Staying at the Hilton, That Means He'll Be at Home," *People*, September 28, 1981.

Speeches referenced: "Address to the Boy Scouts," Arrowhead Springs Hotel, San Bernardino, California, March 16, 1952; "Address to the American Hotel Association," St. Louis, Missouri, October 10, 1952; "Address," Mayflower Hotel, Washington, D.C., February 5, 1953.

Legal documents referenced: "Last Will and Testament of Conrad Nicholson Hilton" (June 3, 1955); *Constance Francesca Hilton v. Frances Kelly Hilton* [original filing] (March 13, 1979); "Constance Francesca Hilton's Responses to Defendants William Barron Hilton and James E. Bates Interrogatories" (May 29, 1979); "Deposition of William Barron Hilton" (September 24, 1979).

Television programs referenced: *Phil Donahue*, interview with Zsa Zsa Gabor, August 10, 1971; *Larry King Live*, interview with Zsa Zsa Gabor, November 26, 1991; *Conrad Hilton: Innkeeper to the World*, Arts & Entertainment, 2005; *Biography: Conrad Hilton*, CNBC, 2010.

NOTES

We had access to Margaret Phillips-Brown's extensive collection about the acquisition of the Mayflower Hotel by Conrad Hilton, which included color and black-and-white photographs of the hotel taken in December 1946.

We also utilized documents and notes from the Ann Miller file, found in the Hedda Hopper Papers of the Margaret Herrick Collection of the Academy of Motion Picture Arts and Sciences.

Details of the fire at the El Paso Hilton were culled from the front-page report in the *El Paso Herald*, August 13, 1940.

The conversations between Conrad, Barron, and Nicky regarding "the missing ingredient" were recreated based on Conrad Hilton's accounts in *Be My Guest.*

I referenced the transcript of Conrad N. Hilton's speech at the Michigan State College, East Lansing, May 19, 1950.

The conversation between Conrad and Barron regarding a position for Barron within the company was reconstructed based on details found in *The Silver Spade: The Conrad Hilton Story* by Whitney Bolton.

The conversations between Barron Hilton and the private detective, and then between Barron Hilton and his wife, Marilyn, were both reconstructed using direct quotes from Barron Hilton found in "Deposition of William Barron Hilton" (September 24, 1979).

PART FIVE. ELIZABETH

Beautiful Dreamer/Enter: Elizabeth Taylor
Interviews conducted: Bob Neal (May 4, 1996; June 1, 1996; August 4, 1998); Noreen Nash Siegel (April 2, 2012; April 3, 2012; April 10, 2012); Myron Harpole (August 17, 2012);

Volumes referenced: *Elizabeth Takes Off* by Elizabeth Taylor; *The Most Beautiful Woman in the World: The Obsessions, Passions and Courage of Elizabeth Taylor* by Ellis Amburn; *Liz: An Intimate Biography of Elizabeth Taylor* by C. David Heymann; *Elizabeth Taylor: A Life in Pictures* by Pierre-Heniu Verlhac and Yann-Brice Dherbier; *Elizabeth: The Life of Elizabeth Taylor* by Alexander Walker; *Elizabeth: The Last Star* by Kitty Kelley; *How to Be a Movie Star: Elizabeth Taylor in Hollywood* by William J. Mann; *Elizabeth* by J. Randy Taraborrelli; *Sinatra: The Complete Story* by J. Randy Taraborrelli; *Be My Guest* by Conrad Hilton; *The Silver Spade: The Conrad Hilton Story* by Whitney Bolton.

Articles referenced: *The Best of "Vanity Fair" Elizabeth Taylor: Eight Remarkable Stories About Hollywood's Most Beautiful, Most Controversial Star* by Dominic Dunne, George Hamilton, Sam Kasher, and Nancy Collins; *People Tribute: Elizabeth Taylor, 1932–2011*, April 2011.

NOTES

The conversations between Nicky Hilton and Conrad Hilton were reconstructed here based on Hilton's account of them in *Be My Guest*, and also based on the accounts in *The Silver Spoon* by Whitney Bolton.

All quotes from Bob Neal in this section of the book as well as in all of the other parts of this work were culled from my interviews with Neal (along with Cathy Griffin's), some of which were conducted in 1998 during the course of research for my book *Jackie, Ethel, Joan* about the Kennedys (Neal was a good friend of the Kennedys' and best man at the wedding ceremony of Peter Lawford and Pat Kennedy Lawford), and others in 2005 during the course of researching Nicky Hilton's life for my book on Elizabeth Taylor, *Elizabeth*. I also consulted files found in the J. Robert Neal Collection of the Houston Metropolitan Research Center, Houston Public Library.

The Man Who Bought the Waldorf
Interviews conducted: Jason Lederer (October 1, 2011); Stanley Tucker (October 2, 2011, October 11, 2011); Timothy Long (October 4, 2011); Jarrod Barron (November 20, 2011); Doris Roberts (January 4, 2012); Dale Olsen (July 9, 2012); Steven D'Orio (September 4, 2012); Everett Long (December 14, 2011; January 15, 2012; March 3, 2012); Mike Dipp (March 16, 2012).

Volumes referenced: *Be My Guest* by Conrad Hilton; *The Silver Spade: The Conrad Hilton Story* by Whitney Bolton; *Building the Cold War: Hilton International Hotels and Modern Architecture* by Annabel Jane Wharton; *The Man Who Bought the Waldorf* by Thomas Ewing Dabney; *Conrad N. Hilton, Hotelier* by Mildred Houghton Comfort.

Articles referenced: "Hilton: The Stuff of a Hotel Man," *Newsweek* cover story on Conrad Hilton, September 27, 1954; "Hotels: By Golly!," *Time* cover story on Conrad Hilton, July 19, 1963.

Legal documents referenced: "Reporter's Transcript—Sari Gabor Hilton, sometimes known as ZsaZsa Sari Hilton vs. Conrad Hilton," by John F. Brill, official court reporter (September 17, 1946); "Deposition of Frances Kelly Hilton" (October 19, 1979).

Television programs referenced: *Larry King Live: The Hiltons*, Arts & Entertainment, 2005; *Conrad Hilton: Innkeeper to the World*, Arts & Entertainment, 2005; *Biography: Conrad Hilton*, CNBC, 2010.

NOTES

We had access to Margaret Phillips-Brown's extensive collection about the acquisition of the Waldorf-Astoria by Conrad Hilton, which included color and black-and-white photographs of the hotel taken in October 1949, December 1949, and December 1950.

The quote from Olive Wakeman and the conversation between Conrad Hilton and Arthur Foristall are culled from the Conrad Hilton file of the Hedda Hopper Papers found in the Margaret Herrick Collection of the Academy of Motion Picture Arts and Sciences.

Fast Worker/Nicky Takes Elizabeth to Texas/A Party to Celebrate the Caribe Hilton/Nicky and Elizabeth Marry/Elizabeth Suffers a Miscarriage/ Divorce—Hollywood Style
Interviews conducted: Bob Neal (March 1, 1998; May 4, 2005; June 1, 2005; August 4, 2005); Nora Johnson (June 1, 2006); Connie Espinoza de Amaté (October 1, 2011); June Harrington (October 4, 2011); Stewart Armstrong (November 13, 2011; November 14, 2011; November 15, 2012); Patricia McClintock Hilton (April 2, 2012; April 20, 2012); Patricia Skipworth Hilton (February 27, 2012; February 28, 2012; April 5, 2012); Carole Wells Doheny (March 8, 2012; March 12, 2012); Noreen Nash Siegel (April 10, 2012); Margaret O'Brien (May 1, 2012); Connie Myron Harpole (August 15, 2012; August 17, 2012); Stella Kelly (July 30, 2012); Mark Young (July 20, 2012); Debbie Reynolds (August 2, 2012).

Volumes referenced: *Elizabeth Takes Off* by Elizabeth Taylor; *Liz: An Intimate Biography of Elizabeth Taylor* by C. David Heymann; *Elizabeth: The Life of Elizabeth Taylor* by Alexander Walker; *Elizabeth: The Last Star* by Kitty Kelley; *Elizabeth* by J. Randy Taraborrelli; *Sinatra: The Complete Story* by J. Randy Taraborrelli; *Be My Guest* by Conrad Hilton; *The Silver Spade: The Conrad Hilton Story* by Whitney Bolton.

Articles referenced: "1950 Hotel Accommodations at the Crossroads of the Nation: How a Great New Hotel, the Caribe Hilton, Was Created," *Hotel Monthly*, vol. 58, no. 63 (February 1950); "Nicky Hilton Hints at Reconciliation Hope," *Los Angeles Times*, March 16, 1951; T. A Wise, "Global Hosts," *Wall Street Journal*, January 19, 1954; Paul Theroux, "Liz Taylor Looks Back," *Talk*, October 1999.

Television programs referenced: *The Hiltons*, Arts & Entertainment, 2005; *Conrad Hilton: Innkeeper to the World*, Arts & Entertainment, 2005; *Biography: Conrad Hilton*, CNBC, 2010.

NOTES

I drew from my extensive research for my biography of Elizabeth Taylor, *Elizabeth*, for this and other sections of this book having to do with Miss Taylor.

I referenced photographs and transcripts of Conrad Hilton's party at Casa Encantada to celebrate the opening of his Caribe Hilton hotel. I also interviewed guests Bob Neal and Stewart Armstrong.

The conversation between Conrad and Mary Hilton that took place after the wedding of Nicky and Elizabeth is as per Conrad's account, found in *Be My Guest*. Also, details of Nicky's poor adjustment to marriage and to Elizabeth's celebrity can be found both in *Be My Guest* and in my book *Elizabeth*.

Marilyn Hilton's and Marjorie Dillon's comments about Nicky Hilton and Elizabeth Taylor can be found in Kitty Kelley's book *Elizabeth: The Last Star*.

The hotels opened overseas by Conrad Hilton often contributed to great social change in those regions. For instance, in 1956 when the Hilton Hotel opened in Cairo, the notion of women working as waitresses was considered out of the question. The Hilton contingent had to appeal to the country's royal family to convince them that there was nothing wrong with females working in such positions at the Nile Hilton. They did such a good job of it that one of the royal family's own daughters took a job as a waitress there—and showed up for work on the first day with her maid in tow, carrying her waitress outfit in a suitcase! Another problem was that because of local customs, it was considered improper for women to look directly at men while in elevators. However, the women working as elevator operators at the Cairo Hilton decided to defy that tradition, much to the consternation of some of the male guests. The problem was that with their backs to the male guests the females risked being pinched. They had grown so tired of such treatment that they rebelled en masse against the tradition, thus the revolutionary decision that they would now have their backs to the walls while operating elevators.

Though Hilton hotels were always designed to blend as much as possible into the local scenery—in Tokyo, for instance there were no drapes on the windows, but rather sliding panels of wood and rice paper, and in Hong Kong the beds had pagoda-shaped headboards—there were some predictable characteristics of the Hilton brand no matter the country. There would always be a framed portrait of Conrad Hilton in the lobby. To make American guests feel more at home in foreign countries, cheeseburgers were served in restaurants. There would also be a Gideon Bible in the drawer of one nightstand and a copy of Conrad's autobiography, *Be My Guest*, in the other. It's what the public came to expect.

The conversation between Conrad and Mary Hilton that took place after the wedding of Nicky and Elizabeth is as per Conrad's account, found in *Be My Guest*. Also, details of Nicky's poor adjustment to marriage and to Elizabeth's celebrity can be found both in *Be My Guest* and in my book *Elizabeth*.

PART SIX. SPOILS OF THE RICH AND FAMOUS

America's Dad
Interviews conducted: Thomas Worthington (September 12, 2011); Stewart Armstrong (November 13, 2011; November 14, 2011; November 15, 2012); Carole Wells Doheny (March 8, 2012; March 12, 2012; June 15, 2012); Noreen Nash Siegel (April 2, 2012; April 3, 2012; April 10, 2012).

Volumes referenced: *Be My Guest* by Conrad Hilton; *The Silver Spade: The Conrad Hilton Story* by Whitney Bolton; *Building the Cold War: Hilton International Hotels and Modern Architecture* by Annabel Jane Wharton; *House of Hilton* by Jerry Oppenheimer; *The Man Who Bought the Waldorf* by Thomas Ewing Dabney; *Conrad N. Hilton, Hotelier* by Mildred Houghton Comfort.

Articles referenced: "Hilton Hotels Form Subsidiary Group to Operate Outside U.S.A," *Hotel Gazette*, May 29, 1948; "C. N. Hilton Sees Important Possibilities for U.S.-European Cooperative Hotel Business," *Hotel Monthly*, vol. 56, no. 6 (September 1948); Conrad N. Hilton, "The Battle for Freedom," *New York Times*, January 1951; Charles St. Peter, "Hilton Hotels Lists Stock Here: Eyes Foreign Fields," *San Francisco Examiner*, February 9, 1951; "How to Cut Costs and Up Tour Profits,"

Hotel Management, May 1951; T. A. Wise, "Global Hosts: W.S. Hotel-keepers Are Stepping Up Invasion of Foreign Cities," *Wall Street Journal*, January 19, 1954; Seena Hamilton, "Hilton's International Expansion Instrument in World Development," *Hotel Gazette*, March 1, 1954; Bill Cunningham, "Hilton Spreading Right Type of Aid," *Boston Sunday Herald*, June 24, 1956; Lawrence M. Hughes, "Hilton's Private Statesmanship Shapes World-Wide Peace," *Sales Management*, October 19, 1956; Vincent Flaherty, "Hilton Deals Communists Blow in Cuba Speech," *Los Angeles Examiner*, April 1, 1958.

Speeches referenced: "The Battle for Freedom," to the National Conference of Christians and Jews at the Waldorf-Astoria, November 21, 1950; Address delivered to the Midwest Hotel Show in Chicago, March 29, 1951; Address to the American Hotel Association in St. Louis, October 10, 1952; Address delivered at the Second Annual Prayer Breakfast, Washington, D.C., February 4, 1954; Address delivered at the Canadian Conference of Christians and Jews, Royal York Hotel, Toronto, November 22, 1954; Address delivered to the 48th Annual Convention of the Texas Hotel Association, Dallas, May 3, 1955; Address delivered at the opening of the Denver Hilton, Denver, April 7, 1960.

Legal documents referenced: "Deposition of William Barron Hilton" (September 24, 1979); "Deposition of Frances Kelly Hilton" (October 19, 1979).

Television programs referenced: *What's My Line?*, Conrad Hilton, June 5, 1955; *Person to Person*, interview with Conrad Hilton, 1955; *Today*, "National Prayer Breakfast," February 2, 1956; *The Ed Sullivan Show*, Conrad Hilton, April 6, 1958; *This Is Your Life*, June 4, 1958; *CBS News Campaign '64: Nixon Press Conference*, in San Francisco for the 1964 Republican National Convention, July 14, 1964 (Nixon was accompanied by Conrad Hilton, aide H. R. "Bob" Haldeman, staff member Sherman Unger, and others); *Conrad Hilton: Innkeeper to the World*, Arts & Entertainment, 2005; *Biography: Conrad Hilton*, CNBC, 2010; *The Hiltons*, Arts & Entertainment, 2005.

Casa Encantada

Interviews conducted: Carole Wells Doheny (June 15, 2012); Noreen Nash Siegel (April 3, 2012); Patricia McClintock Hilton (April 2, 2012; April 8, 2012; April 16, 2012; April 20, 2012).

Volumes referenced: *Be My Guest* by Conrad Hilton; *The Silver Spade: The Conrad Hilton Story* by Whitney Bolton; *Building the Cold War: Hilton International Hotels and Modern Architecture* by Annabel Jane Wharton.

Articles referenced: "Conrad Weber Buys Weber Home," *Los Angeles Times*, November 4, 1950; "The Four Great Estates," *Los Angeles Times*, December 8, 1996; "Exclusive Homes," *Los Angeles Times*, June 1, 1977; Ronald W. Erdrich, "Big Country Journal: No Handouts for Hilton," MReporterNews.com, August 2, 2012.

Legal documents referenced: "Last Will and Testament of Conrad Nicholson Hilton" (June 3, 1955); "Deposition of William Barron Hilton" (September 24, 1979); "Deposition of Frances Kelly Hilton" (October 19, 1979).

Television programs referenced: *The Hiltons*, Arts & Entertainment, 2005; *Conrad Hilton: Innkeeper to the World*, Arts & Entertainment, 2005; *Biography: Conrad Hilton*, CNBC, 2010.

NOTES

As earlier noted, for details about the décor and furnishings of Casa Encantada in this and in other sections of this book, I relied on the privately published *The House of Hilton: Casa Encantada*.

Linda Hilton's comment is from Ronald W. Erdrich, "Big Country Journal: No Handouts for Hilton," MReporterNews.com, August 2, 2012.

Conrad Hilton bought Casa Encantada in 1950 from Hilda Olsen, a woman with an interesting, and tragic, story. She had been a nurse who in 1920 married one of her patients, a widower, Cincinnati millionaire glass manufacturer and hotel magnate George Charles Boldt. Coincidentally, considering Conrad's recent major purchase, Boldt had once been the proprietor of the Waldorf-Astoria and was credited with popularizing Thousand Island dressing when he instructed maître d' Oscar Tshirky to include it on the Waldorf's menu. He also owned the Bellevue Stratford Hotel in Philadelphia.

When Boldt died in 1929, Hilda Olsen went on to marry the couple's chauffeur, Otto Weber. She then used her husband's fortune to try to keep up with the (very rich) Joneses in the neighborhood, risking $2 million during the worst years of the Depression to commission architect Mil Dolena to build the house. Once work on the house was completed, she hosted incredible parties for Beverly Hills high society, aided by her staff of a dozen servants. She lived the good life for about nine years, until she ran out of money. In desperate financial straits, she sold the estate to Conrad for just a fraction of its worth. She then took what Conrad paid her for the house to the racetrack to try to double her winnings, but instead lost it all. Despondent by her losses, she went home and killed herself. It was a tragic story that Conrad Hilton told many times over the years, a cautionary tale, he felt, of what can happen when someone attains a great deal of wealth without really working for it.

"He's Getting Worse"/A Baroness Named Betsy/The Shadow of Her Smile/If Only
Interviews conducted: Bob Neal (March 1, 1998; May 4, 2005; June 1, 2005; August 4, 2005); Connie Espinoza de Amaté (October 1, 2011); Carole Wells Doheny (March 8, 2012); Stewart Armstrong (November 13, 2011; November 14, 2011; November 15, 2011); Betsy von Furstenberg (May 10, 2012; May 11, 2012; May 12, 2012).

Volumes referenced: *Be My Guest* by Conrad Hilton.

Articles referenced: "Nicky Hilton and Air Force Officer Battle in Night Club," *Los Angeles Times*, February 22, 1951; "Hilton to Wed Actress After Elizabeth Taylor Decree Final," Associated Press, September 20, 1951; "Starlett Says She'll Be Nicky Hilton Bride," *Los Angeles Times*, September 20, 1951; Hedda Hopper, "Will Nicky Marry Again?," *Los Angeles Times*, September 25, 1951; "Hungarian Rhapsody," *Escapade*, August 1956.

NOTES

The interaction between Nicky, Conrad, Barron, and Maria de Amaté was reconstructed as per Maria's memory in recalling the events to her daughter, Connie Espinoza de Amaté.

All conversations between Nicky and Betsy von Furstenberg were reconstructed from the first-person accounts of Ms. von Furstenberg.

All conversations between Nicky and Bob Neal were reconstructed from the first-person accounts of Mr. Neal.

Zsa Zsa Finds Her Niche
Interviews conducted: Zsa Zsa Gabor (February 2, 1986); Dylan Terrell Thomas (October 22, 2011); Noreen Nash Siegel (April 2, 2012; April 3, 2012; April 10, 2012); Betsy von Furstenberg (May 10, 2012; May 11, 2012; May 12, 2012); Lena Burrell (September 12, 2012; October 11, 2012; December 2, 2012).

Volumes referenced: *Jolie Gabor* by Cindy Adams; *One Lifetime Is Not Enough* by Zsa Zsa Gabor; *Zsa Zsa Gabor: My Story* by Zsa Zsa Gabor and Gerold Frank; *Gaborabilia* by Anthony Turtu and Donald F. Reute; *Eva Gabor an Amazing Woman: "Unscrupulous"* by Camyl Sosa Belanger; *How to Catch a Man, How to Keep a Man, How to Get Rid of a Man* by Zsa Zsa Gabor; *A Dreadful Man: A Personal, Intimate Book About George Sanders* by Brian Aherne; *George Sanders, Zsa Zsa and Me* by David R. Slavitt; *Making the Good Life Last* by Merv Griffin.

Articles referenced: "Love Hints from Zsa Zsa," *Life*, October 15, 1951; "Zsa Zsa Gabor Is Married Here to Corporation Head," *New York Times*, November 6, 1962; "Zsa Zsa Decides It's Time to Sell Beauty Formulas," *New York Times*, January 29, 1969; Leslie Bennetts, "It's a Mad, Mad, Zsa Zsa World," *Vanity Fair*, September 2007.

Legal documents referenced: miscellaneous file notes from *Zsa Gabor Plaintiff vs. Fawcett Publications, Inc.* (November 1960); "Contestant Constance Francesca Hilton's Responses to Defendants William Barron Hilton and James E. Bates Interrogatories" (May 29, 1979); "Deposition of Sari Zsa Zsa Gabor O'Hara" (June 14, 1979; July 9, 1979; July 10, 1979); "Deposition of Constance Francesca Hilton" (September 12, 1979; September 13, 1979; September 14, 1979); "Deposition of William Barron Hilton" (September 24, 1979); "Deposition of Frances Kelly Hilton" (October 19, 1979).

Television programs referenced: *The Jack Paar Program*, interview with Zsa Zsa Gabor, October 19, 1962; *The Jack Paar Program*, interview with Zsa Zsa Gabor, November 23, 1962; *The Jack Paar Program*, interview with Zsa Zsa Gabor, May 29, 1964; *The Jack Paar Program*, interview with Zsa Zsa Gabor, December 4, 1964; *The Joey Bishop Show*, interview with Zsa Zsa Gabor, May 8, 1968; *The Joey Bishop Show*, interview with Zsa Zsa Gabor, August 16, 1968; *The David Frost Show*, interview with Zsa Zsa Gabor, May 12, 1970; *Phil Donahue*, interview with Zsa Zsa Gabor, August 10,

1971; *Geraldo*, interview with Zsa Zsa Gabor and Francesca Hilton, March 31, 1980; *The Pat Sajack Show*, interview with Zsa Zsa Gabor, September 13, 1989; *The Geraldo Rivera Show*, interview with Zsa Zsa Gabor, September 13, 1990; *One on One with John Tesh*, interview with Zsa Zsa Gabor, September 10, 1991; *Larry King Live*, interview with Zsa Zsa Gabor, November 26, 1991; *The Howard Stern Summer Show*, interview with Zsa Zsa Gabor, May 2, 1992; *One on One with John Tesh*, interview with Eva Gabor, 1992; *Intimate Portrait: Eva Gabor*, February 1, 1998.

Note: I corroborated much of Zsa Zsa Gabor's account of her life during this time, such as her conversation with Conrad Hilton regarding *Bachelor's Haven*, by utilizing Bart Andrews's extensive files and transcripts relating to his interviews with Zsa Zsa Gabor for a possible autobiography collaboration between the two.

Filling Elizabeth's Shoes/Assault/Magic Words/Mamie/Marilyn's Party/
Dinner at the Manse
Interviews conducted: Bob Neal (August 4, 2005); Robert Wentworth (June 11, 2012; June 12, 2012; June 13, 2012); Mamie Van Doren (February 9, 2011; February 10, 2011; February 11, 2011); Noreen Nash Siegel (April 3, 2012); Betsy von Furstenberg (May 10, 2012; May 11, 2012; May 12, 2012).

Volumes referenced: *Elizabeth Takes Off* by Elizabeth Taylor; *Liz: An Intimate Biography of Elizabeth Taylor* by C. David Heymann; *Elizabeth: The Life of Elizabeth Taylor* by Alexander Walker; *Elizabeth: The Last Star* by Kitty Kelley; *Elizabeth* by J. Randy Taraborrelli; *Sinatra: The Complete Story* by J. Randy Taraborrelli; *Be My Guest* by Conrad Hilton; *The Silver Spade: The Conrad Hilton Story* by Whitney Bolton.

NOTES

All conversations between Nicky and Mamie Van Doren were reconstructed from the first-person accounts of Ms. Van Doren. All details of Ms. Van Doren's unusual evening at Casa Encantada as the dinner guest of Nicky Hilton were also reconstructed from details she herself provided.

All conversations between Nicky, Bob Neal, and Robert Wentworth were reconstructed from Mr. Neal's and Mr. Wentworth's first-person accounts.

I utilized the John Carroll file in the Hedda Hopper Papers in the Margaret Herrick Collection of the Academy of Motion Picture Arts and Sciences.

We referenced photographs taken on the night of Marilyn Hilton's Polynesian-themed party in order to describe the events of that evening.

I also referenced Mamie Van Doren's website, and her blog about her love affair with Nicky Hilton ("Bedtime Stories"), at www.MamieVan Doren.com.

PART SEVEN. THE BIG BOON

The Hilton Junket
Interviews conducted: Everett Long (December 14, 2011; January 15, 2012; March 3, 2012); Doris Roberts (January 4, 2012); Patricia Skipworth Hilton (February 27, 2012; February 28, 2012; April 5, 2012); Carole Wells Doheny (March 8, 2012); Mike Dipp (March 16, 2012); Patricia McClintock Hilton (April 2, 2012; April 8, 2012; April 16, 2012; April 20, 2012); Noreen Nash Siegel (April 2, 2012; April 3, 2012; April 10, 2012); George Schlatter (April 7, 2012); Terry Moore (April 11, 2012); Ann Jeffreys (April 25, 2012); Margaret O'Brien (May 1, 2012); Dale Olsen (July 9, 2012); Mark Young (July 20, 2012); Debbie Reynolds (August 2, 2012); Ruta Lee (April 23, 2012).

Volumes referenced: *Be My Guest* by Conrad Hilton; *The Silver Spade: The Conrad Hilton Story* by Whitney Bolton; *Building the Cold War: Hilton International Hotels and Modern Architecture* by Annabel Jane Wharton; *The Man Who Bought the Waldorf* by Thomas Ewing Dabney; *Conrad N. Hilton, Hotelier* by Mildred Houghton Comfort; *Miller's High Life* by Ann Miller.

Articles referenced: "Hilton: The Stuff of a Hotel Man," *Newsweek* cover story on Conrad Hilton, September 27, 1954; Hedda Hopper, "Rough draft notes re: Istanbul Hilton Opening," June 15, 1955, Hedda Hopper Papers; "The New Istanbul Hilton," *Asta Travel News*, July 1955; Henry Bonnett, "Press List for Opening of Dallas Hilton," January 1956; "Rough draft notes re: Opening of the Dallas Hilton," January 16 and January 18, 1956; Bill Cunningham, "Heigh-Ho Dallas, Here We Come," *Boston Herald*, January 16, 1956; John Brehl, "1,000 Guests Attend Hotel

Opening," *Toronto Daly Star*, April 16, 1958; Richard Carter, "A Hotel Is Built," *Chicago Tribune Magazine*, May 25, 1958; Amy Vanderbilt, "The Day the Queen Arrived," *Chicago Tribune Magazine*, May 25, 1958; Irv Kupcinet, "The World's Largest Hotel," *Chicago Tribune Magazine*, May 25, 1958; Joan Winchell, "Conrad Plays Host," *Los Angeles Times*, August 3, 1958; Joan Winchell, "Junketeers Climb Pyramids (Uh-Almost); Athens Viewed," *Los Angeles Times*, March 8, 1959); "Letter from Hedda Hopper to Conrad Hilton, re: Cairo Press Junket," March 13, 1959, Hedda Hopper Papers; Conrad Hilton, "The Anvil of Civilization: An Address Delivered at the Official Opening of the Nile Hilton," February 22, 1959; "Hilton Joins Rockefeller Center and Uris in New Hotel," News Release from Hilton Hotels, October 29, 1960; "Hilton Announces Expansion," News Release from Hilton Hotels, May 3, 1961; Henry Bonnet, director of public relations, Hilton Hotels, "Letter to All Media" (regarding the opening of the Hong Kong Hilton and Tokyo Hilton), May 10, 1963; "Hotels: By Golly!," *Time* cover story on Conrad Hilton, July 19, 1963, Hedda Hopper Papers.

Legal documents referenced: "Deposition of William Barron Hilton" (September 24, 1979).

Television programs referenced: *What's My Line?*, Conrad Hilton, June 5, 1955; *Person to Person*, interview with Conrad Hilton, 1955; *Larry King Live*, interview with Zsa Zsa Gabor, November 26, 1991; *The Hiltons*, Arts & Entertainment, 2005; *Conrad Hilton: Innkeeper to the World*, Arts & Entertainment, 2005; *Biography: Conrad Hilton*, CNBC, 2010).

NOTES

I utilized the extensive Hedda Hopper Papers at the Margaret Herrick Collection of the Motion Picture Arts and Sciences Library for many of the details about the Hilton junkets found on these pages. I also referenced press material—schedules and itineraries—relating to every junket written about on these pages, most of which was sent by the Hilton organization to the media at the time.

Regarding Conrad Hilton and Hedda Hopper, worth noting is an interesting set of correspondence found in the Hedda Hopper Papers that illuminates the kind of relationship Conrad Hilton had with members of the media, like Ms. Hopper:

By August 1962, Hopper had traveled the world over on Conrad's dime, covering his hotel junkets. One might imagine that any problem she might have had with her accommodations—especially when not on a junket—would be handled by someone other than Conrad, the president and chairman of the board of the Hilton Hotels Corporation, perhaps a press agent or an assistant. However, typical of Conrad and his hands-on philosophy, he personally handled any issues Hopper had with her Hilton hotel status.

Contention between the powerful columnist and the hotel tycoon started on August 8 when Hedda sent Conrad a typewritten letter stating that she feared that she was soon going to have to find another hotel to stay in while in Manhattan. "The Waldorf has become too rich for my blood," she wrote. "I just can't pay $40 a day! You know, we working girls have to stay on a budget!" She claimed to have an offer from the manager of the Americana Hotel offering her free accommodations. What should she do? She left the ball in Conrad's court.

On August 9, Conrad responded to Hopper's letter, asking if she really wanted to find herself "staying at some ordinary hotel in New York." It was not his fault, he observed, that she required a $40-a-day suite. She was already getting a 25 percent discount, he wrote, so in actuality she was staying in a $60-a-night suite. If she wanted to do so, he added, she could always stay in a cheaper room. But, he continued, "you are used to something grand and I don't blame you. You want a lovely living room, with not a spot on the walls or the rugs. You want your visitors to come in to a room where they will greet you like a queen." Then he concluded, "Here is what I don't understand: I read your newspaper column all over the world—even down in Mexico. Certainly you must be receiving *pay* for these articles!" He suggested that she deduct from her taxes the business expense of any hotel room in which she stayed. She might be a "working girl," he continued, "but I also consider you a capitalist because you are in the business of selling your stories all over the world." However, he wouldn't want to lose her as a customer, he hastened to add, and he hoped she would reconsider. But offering her a lower rate was out of the question. Instead, he tried to appease her by making an unusual offer:

"Let me personally make your next reservation when you get ready to go back to the Waldorf."

Not one to be cowed, the seventy-seven-year-old Hedda wrote right back to him, on October 9, 1962. She first wished to correct Conrad; the suite in which she usually stayed at the Waldorf carried a $50—not a $60—rate. She was getting it for $40. Therefore, she really wasn't getting a 25 percent discount, was she? She also noted that the Americana Hotel had offered her a suite for $20. "However," as she wrote, "you know I shall always be loyal to you and the Waldorf. It seems like home." That said, she added, "I do hope you can match this rate!"

The next day, October 10, Conrad responded. He was not moved by the fact that his competitor had offered Hedda a better rate. He thought of the Americana as inferior. "After all," he wrote, "the Waldorf-Astoria is the greatest hotel in the world and you are one of the greatest writers of the world so you certainly wouldn't want to stay in a hotel of lesser quality." He repeated his earlier suggestion that she should simply write off from her taxes the cost of any hotel room in which she stayed, "so Uncle Sam pays most of your bill." Then, in what can only be construed as a little dig at her work ethic, he added, "We had a wonderful time at the Amsterdam junket you missed, but I understand you were too busy writing a book to go. I am also writing another book, but yet I still open hotels, don't I?"

Though similar correspondence flew back and forth between them for many weeks, in the end, Conrad Hilton never reduced his rates for Hedda Hopper. And she continued to stay at the Waldorf-Astoria anyway.

Barron Climbs the Ladder of Success/Nicky's Fast-Paced Life
Interviews conducted: Wyatt Montgomery (January 2, 2012; January 4, 2012; January 18, 2012; March 1, 2012); Carole Wells Doheny (March 12, 2012; March 13, 2012; April 5, 2012; May 5, 2012); Noreen Nash Siegel (April 2, 2012).

Volumes referenced: *Be My Guest* by Conrad Hilton; *The Silver Spade: The Conrad Hilton Story* by Whitney Bolton; *Building the Cold War: Hilton International Hotels and Modern Architecture* by Annabel Jane Wharton; *Symptoms of Withdrawal: A Memoir of Snapshots and Redemption* by Christopher Kennedy Lawford; *Past Imperfect* by Joan Collins.

Articles referenced: "Nicky Hilton Swings Fists in Cafe Brawl," *Los Angeles Times*, February 22, 1951; Peter Lester, "When This Hotel Barron Says He's Staying at the Hilton, That Means He'll Be at Home," *People*, September 28, 1981.

Legal documents referenced: "Codicil to Last Will and Testament of Conrad N. Hilton" (April 1, 1947); "Last Will and Testament of Conrad N. Hilton" (September 1, 1955); "Deposition of William Barron Hilton" (September 24, 1979).

Eric: From Out of the Shadows
Interviews conducted: Patricia Skipworth Hilton (February 27, 2012; February 28, 2012; April 5, 2012); Carole Wells Doheny (March 8, 2012; March 12, 2012; June 15, 2012); Noreen Nash Siegel (April 2, 2012; April 3, 2012; April 10, 2012).

Volumes referenced: *House of Hilton* by Jerry Oppenheimer; *The Man Who Bought the Waldorf* by Thomas Ewing Dabney; *Conrad N. Hilton, Hotelier* by Mildred Houghton Comfort.

A Troubling Conversation About Francesca
Interviews conducted: Cindy Adams (September 1, 1998); Eddie Fisher (September 20, 2006); Terry Moore (April 11, 2012); Robert Wentworth (June 11, 2012; June 12, 2012; June 13, 2012);

Volumes referenced: *Jolie Gabor* by Cindy Adams; *One Lifetime Is Not Enough* by Zsa Zsa Gabor; *Zsa Zsa Gabor: My Story* by Zsa Zsa Gabor and Gerold Frank; *A Dreadful Man: A Personal, Intimate Book About George Sanders* by Brian Aherne.

Articles referenced: "Grown-up Movie Kids: Zsa Zsa Gabor Gives Black-Tie Birthday Party for her 11-Year-Old Daughter," *Life*, March 31, 1958.

Legal documents referenced: "Codicil to Last Will and Testament of Conrad N. Hilton" (April 1, 1947); "Last Will and Testament of Conrad Nicholson Hilton" (June 3, 1955); "Last Will and Testament of Conrad Nicholson Hilton" (October 21, 1960); miscellaneous file notes from *Zsa Gabor Plaintiff vs. Fawcett Publications, Inc.* (November 1960); "Last Will and Testament of Conrad Nicholson Hilton" (January 27, 1967); "Last Will and Testament of Conrad N. Hilton" (October 31, 1973);

"Contestant Constance Francesca Hilton's Responses to Defendants William Barron Hilton and James E. Bates Interrogatories" (July 20, 1979); "Deposition of Zsa Zsa Gabor O'Hara" (June 14, 1979; July 9, 1979; July 10, 1979); "Deposition of William Barron Hilton" (September 24, 1979).

Note: The conversation between Zsa Zsa Gabor and Gregson Bautzer was reconstructed using the exact quotes provided by Zsa Zsa in her deposition of June 14, 1979. "That's when I first heard, ever, about this idiotic remark," she further testified, referring to Bautzer's telling her that Conrad sometimes questioned his paternity of Francesca. She added that after Bautzer told her of Conrad's doubts, she decided not to discuss it with Conrad. She testified that she never talked to *anyone* about it, "because, to me, it seemed so ridiculous."

Natalie Wood's Advice/Trish/"The Woman to Give My Children Life"/ Nicky and Trish Marry
Interviews conducted: Bob Neal (March 1, 1998); Carole Wells Doheny (March 8, 2012; March 12, 2012; June 15, 2012); Patricia McClintock Hilton (April 2, 2012; April 8, 2012; April 16, 2012; April 20, 2012); Noreen Nash Siegel (April 2, 2012; April 3, 2012; April 10, 2012); Robert Wentworth (June 11, 2012).

Volumes referenced: *Natasha: Goodbye Natalie, Goodbye Splendour* by Marti Rylli and Dennis Davern; *Natasha: The Biography of Natalie Wood* by Suzanne Finstad; *Natalie Wood* by Gavin Lambert; *Natasha: A Memoir by Her Sister* by Lana Wood; *Natalie Wood: A Biography in Photographs* by Christopher Nickens; *Pieces of My Heart: A Life* by Robert Wagner; *The Man Who Invented Rock Hudson* by Robert Hofler; *Past Imperfect* by Joan Collins.

Articles referenced: "Press Release from Arthur Foristall & Co.— Hilton Hotels," November 30, 1956; Louella Parsons, "Cupid to Merge Oil, Hotel Fortunes," Hedda Hopper Papers, October 28, 1958; Elaine St. Johns, "A Day in the Life of a Credit Card," *Chicago Tribune Magazine*, May 25, 1958.

Note: All conversations between Trish Hilton and Natalie Wood and Patricia McClintock Hilton and Nicky Hilton were reconstructed from Trish Hilton's first-person accounts.

PART EIGHT. FOR LOVE OR MONEY

Zsa Zsa Is Not Wanted/"*The Most Beautiful Woman*"/*Zsa Zsa Teaches Trish About the Hiltons*
Interviews conducted: Bob Neal (June 1, 2005; August 4, 2005); Jason Lederer (October 1, 2011); Timothy Long (October 4, 2011); Doris Roberts (January 4, 2012); Ed Lozzi (March 2, 2012); Patricia McClintock Hilton (April 2, 2012); Noreen Nash Siegel (April 3, 2012); Carole Wells Doheny (June 15, 2012); Steven D'Orio (September 4, 2012).

Volumes referenced: *Jolie Gabor* by Cindy Adams; *One Lifetime Is Not Enough* by Zsa Zsa Gabor; *Zsa Zsa Gabor: My Story* by Zsa Zsa Gabor and Gerold Frank; *A Dreadful Man: A Personal, Intimate Book About George Sanders* by Brian Aherne.

Articles referenced: Joan Winchell, "Hilton Trinidad Opening," Hedda Hopper Collection, June 27, 1962; Leslie Bennetts, "It's a Mad, Mad, Zsa Zsa World," *Vanity Fair*, September 2007.

Legal documents referenced: Miscellaneous file notes from: *Zsa Gabor Plaintiff vs. Fawcett Publications, Inc.* (November 1960); "Deposition of Zsa Zsa Gabor O'Hara," (June 14, 1979; July 9, 1979; July 10, 1979); "Contestant Constance Francesca Hilton's Responses to Defendants William Barron Hilton and James E. Bates Interrogatories" (July 20, 1979); "Deposition of William Barron Hilton" (September 24, 1979); "Deposition of Constance Francesca Hilton" (September 12, 1979; September 13, 1979; September 14, 1979).

NOTES

The dialogue in "Zsa Zsa Is Not Wanted" is taken directly from Zsa Zsa Gabor's deposition from: miscellaneous file notes from *Zsa Gabor Plaintiff vs. Fawcett Publications, Inc.* (November 1960). I also used as background Zsa Zsa Gabor's interviews with Bart Andrews in the summer of 1985 for a proposed autobiography by Andrews and Zsa Zsa Gabor.

All of the dialogue between Patricia McClintock Hilton and Zsa Zsa Gabor and Patricia McClintock Hilton and Nicky Hilton in "Zsa Zsa Teaches Trish About the Hiltons" was drawn directly from the first-person account of Trish Hilton.

Success/Sibling Rivalry on the Rise

Interviews conducted: Bob Neal (May 4, 2005; June 1, 2005; August 4, 2005); Thomas Worthington (September 12, 2011); Everett Long (December 14, 2011; January 15, 2012; March 3, 2012); Carole Wells Doheny (March 8, 2012); Noreen Nash Siegel (April 10, 2012); Terry Moore (April 11, 2012); Robert Wentworth (June 11, 2012; June 12, 2012; June 13, 2012).

Volumes referenced: *Building the Cold War: Hilton International Hotels and Modern Architecture* by Annabel Jane Wharton; *The Hiltons* by Jess Oppenheimer; *Hilton Hotels Corporation: A Strategic Analysis* by Bethany Su-Lan Liou.

Articles referenced: "Hilton: The Stuff of a Hotel Man," *Newsweek* cover story on Conrad Hilton, September 27, 1954; "Hilton Takes New Job," Associated Press, January 3, 1961; "Hotels: By Golly!," *Time* cover story on Conrad Hilton, July 19, 1963; Christopher P. Anderson, "The Barron of Las Vegas Is a Buttoned-Down Hilton," *People*, September 8, 1975; Peter Lester, "When This Hotel Barron Says He's Staying at the Hilton, That Means He'll Be at Home," *People* September 28, 1981; Daniel R. Lee, "How They Started: The Growth of Four Hotel Giants," *Cornell Hotel and Restaurant Administration Quarterly*, May 1985; Thomas Moore, "Barron Hilton Fights for Hilton Hotels" *Fortune* May 27, 1985; "Honeymoon Hotelier: Hilton's Stock Quickly Doubled," *Financial World*, January 21, 1997; Melanie F. Gibbs, "Hilton Hotels Corp: The Sleeping Giant Awakes," *National Real Estate Investor*, February 1997; Christina Binkley, "Hilton Shareholders Approve the Spinoff of Gambling Unit," *Wall Street Journal*, November 25, 1998; Christina Brinkley, "Hilton Agrees to Pay $4 Billion for Promus," *Wall Street Journal*, September 8, 1999; Bill Dwyre, "Barron Hilton's Chargers Turned Short Stay into Long-Term Success," *Los Angeles Times*, November 30, 2009.

Speeches referenced: "The Graduation Address," University of Detroit, June 9, 1953; "City of Hope Award" address, Los Angeles, October 4, 1953.

Legal documents referenced: "Codicil to Last Will and Testament of Conrad N. Hilton" (April 1, 1947); "Last Will and Testament of Conrad N. Hilton" (1955); "Last Will and Testament of Conrad N. Hilton" (October 31, 1973).

Television programs referenced: *What's My Line?*, Conrad Hilton, June 5, 1955; *Person to Person*, interview with Conrad Hilton, 1955; *The Ed Sullivan Show*, Conrad Hilton, April 6, 1958; *Conrad Hilton: Innkeeper to the World*, Arts & Entertainment, 2005; *Larry King Live: Zsa Zsa Gabor's Dazzling Life*, November 26, 1991; *Biography: Conrad Hilton*, CNBC, 2010.

Francesca's Summer of Discontent/Olive's Appeal to Zsa Zsa/"Zsa Zsa Who?"
Volumes referenced: *The Man Who Bought the Waldorf* by Thomas Ewing Dabney; *Conrad N. Hilton, Hotelier* by Mildred Houghton Comfort; *Jolie Gabor* by Cindy Adams; *Zsa Zsa Gabor: My Story* by Zsa Zsa Gabor and Gerold Frank.

Articles referenced: Lloyd Shearer, "He's Americanizing the World," *Parade*, July 21, 1963; Dora Jane Hamblin, "In 19 Lands, Instant America: His Hotels Keep Conrad Hilton Hopping," *Life*, August 30, 1963.

Legal documents referenced: "Deposition of Zsa Zsa Gabor O'Hara," (June 14, 1979; July 9, 1979; July 10, 1979); "Contestant Constance Francesca Hilton's Responses to Defendants William Barron Hilton and James E. Bates Interrogatories" (July 20, 1979); "Deposition of Olive Wakeman" (September 12, 1979); "Deposition of Constance Francesca Hilton" (September 12, 1979; September 13, 1979; September 14, 1979); "Deposition of Frances Kelly Hilton" (October 19, 1979); "Declaration of Constance Francesca Hilton" (March 24, 1980).

NOTES

The letter from Conrad N. Hilton to Francesca Hilton (signed "Daddy" and undated), as well as the letters from Hilton to Francesca Hilton (April 30, 1966); from Olive Wakeman to Zsa Zsa Gabor (May 5, 1966); and from Zsa Zsa Gabor to Olive Wakeman (no date) were exhibits presented during discovery in the case *Francesca Hilton v. The Estate of Conrad N. Hilton.*

The conversation between Zsa Zsa Gabor and Olive Wakeman was reconstructed using both Gabor's and Wakeman's depositions.

The depositions of Olive Wakeman (September 12, 1979) and Frances

Kelly Hilton (October 19, 1979) are both incomplete, with some pages having gone missing over the years. For my purposes, I utilized the pages that were available to me.

"He's Americanizing the World," by Lloyd Shearer, was a nationally syndicated article in the *Parade* magazine supplement of many newspapers across America on July 21, 1963. In this thorough profile of (and interview with) Conrad, no mention was made of his daughter, Francesca. "He has three sons by his first marriage," was all the writer had to say about Hilton's children. This lapse mirrors Conrad's autobiography, *Be My Guest*, which also doesn't mention the existence of Francesca, even though it was published in 1957 when Francesca was about ten.

I also referenced "Conrad Hilton Speech—Houston Texas, Groundbreaking for the Conrad N. Hilton College of Hotel and Restaurant Management," October 28, 1969.

The Simple Life/"It's Going to Be Okay, Brother"
Interviews conducted: Patricia McClintock Hilton (April 2, 2012; April 8, 2012; April 16, 2012; April 20, 2012)

Volumes referenced: *Be My Guest* by Conrad Hilton; *The Silver Spade: The Conrad Hilton Story* by Whitney Bolton; *Building the Cold War: Hilton International Hotels and Modern Architecture* by Annabel Jane Wharton.

Legal documents referenced: "Last Will and Testament of Conrad N. Hilton" (October 31, 1973)

All of the dialogue between Patricia McClintock Hilton and Mary Hilton in "The Simple Life," and later between Trish Hilton and her family members, was drawn from the first-person account of Trish Hilton.

PART NINE. IN HIS FATHER'S HOUSE

Nicky Causing Problems/The TWA Merger/"Tired of Being Misunderstood"/ Nothing Personal/Showdown/A Done Deal
Interviews conducted: Bob Neal (March 1, 1998; May 4, 2005; June 1, 2005; August 4, 2005); Patricia Skipworth Hilton (February 27, 2012; February 28, 2012; April 5, 2012); Patricia McClintock Hilton (April 2, 2012); Noreen Nash Siegel (April 10, 2012); Carole Wells Doheny (June 15,

2012); Myron Harpole (August 15, 2012; August 17, 2012; August 20, 2012).

Volumes referenced: *House of Hilton* by Jerry Oppenheimer; *The Man Who Bought the Waldorf* by Thomas Ewing Dabney; *Conrad N. Hilton, Hotelier* by Mildred Houghton Comfort; *Hilton Hotels Corporation: A Strategic Analysis* by Bethany Su-Lan Liou.

Articles referenced: Frank Lee Donoghue, "Hilton to Open Huge Hotel in New York," *Herald-Examiner*, June 25, 1963; Frank Lee Donoghue, "Boom of Cannon Opens Hilton Hotel," *Herald-Examiner*, June 26, 1963; Harrison Carroll, "Nicky, Trish Hilton Marriage on the Rocks," August 6, 1963, Hedda Hopper Papers; Suzy, "Happy Birthday Dear Connie," *Town & Country*, December 1963; Daryl E. Lembke, "Hilton Opens S.F. Hotel, Vows to Keep Building," *Los Angeles Times*, May 22, 1964; Daniel R. Lee, "How They Started: The Growth of Four Hotel Giants," *Cornell Hotel and Restaurant Administration Quarterly*, May 1985; "Personal Account: A Hotel Man Remembers," *New York Times*, December 2, 1990.

Legal documents referenced: "Deposition of Zsa Zsa Gabor O'Hara" (July 9, 1979; July 10, 1979); "Deposition of William Barron Hilton" (September 24, 1979).

NOTES

The conversation between Conrad Hilton and Nicky Hilton found in "'Tired of Being Misunderstood'" was witnessed by Bob Neal, and is reconstructed here using his first-person account.

The quote from Frank Wangeman is drawn from "Personal Account: A Hotel Man Remembers," *New York Times*, December 2, 1990.

The conversation between Nicky Hilton, Barron Hilton, and Conrad Hilton in "Showdown" was witnessed by Bob Neal and reconstructed using his first-person account.

I referenced "The Oral History and Interview of Frank Wangeman" by Cathleen D. Baird.

I also referenced the "Hilton Hotels Corporation Annual Report" (1965, 1966, 1967, 1968, and 1969).

Trish Enters Conrad's Den/Nicky Considers Suing His Family/From Kings to Paupers/Trish Tries Again with Conrad

Interviews conducted: Arthur Crowley (January 4, 2005); Stewart Armstrong (November 13, 2011; November 14, 2011; November 15, 2012); Carole Wells Doheny (March 8, 2012; June 15, 2012); Noreen Nash Siegel (April 2, 2012; April 3, 2012; April 10, 2012); Patricia McClintock Hilton (April 2, 2012; April 8, 2012; April 16, 2012; April 20, 12); Myron Harpole (August 15, 2012; August 17, 2012; August 20, 2012).

Volumes referenced: *Be My Guest* by Conrad Hilton; *The Silver Spade: The Conrad Hilton Story* by Whitney Bolton; *Building the Cold War: Hilton International Hotels and Modern Architecture* by Annabel Jane Wharton.

Articles referenced: "Nicky Hilton's Wife Filed for Divorce?," Associated Press, February 11, 1964; Hedda Hopper, "Nicky Hilton and Wife in Marital Trouble," *Los Angeles Times*, March 11, 1964; Louella Parsons, "Nicky Hilton's Abroad," *Herald-Examiner*, May 15, 1965; "Nicky Hilton Threatens Expose," *Los Angeles Times*, June 11, 1968; Hedda Hopper, "Nicky Hilton v. Family," *Los Angeles Times*, December 11, 1968; Louella Parsons, "Nicky Hilton Ousted?," *Los Angeles Herald-Examiner*, January 4, 1969; Christopher P. Anderson, "The Barron of Las Vegas Is a Buttoned-Down Hilton," *People*, September 8, 1975; Daniel R. Lee, "How They Started: The Growth of Four Hotel Giants," *Cornell Hotel and Restaurant Administration Quarterly*, May 1985; "Honeymoon Hotelier: Hilton's Stock Quickly Doubled," *Financial World*, January 21, 1997; Melanie F. Gibbs, "Hilton Hotels Corp: The Sleeping Giant Awakes," *National Real Estate Investor*, February 1997; Christina Binkley, "Hilton Shareholders Approve the Spinoff of Gambling Unit," *Wall Street Journal*, November 25, 1998; Christina Binkley, "Hilton Agrees to Pay $4 Billion for Promus," *Wall Street Journal*, September 8, 1999); Bill Dwyre, "Barron Hilton's Chargers Turned Short Stay into Long-Term Success," *Los Angeles Times*, November 30, 2009.

NOTES

The conversations between Patricia McClintock Hilton and Conrad Hilton in "Trish Enters Conrad's Den" and in "Trish Tries Again with Conrad" were reconstructed using her first-person accounts.

The meeting between Arthur Crowley and Nicky Hilton was reconstructed using Crowley's first-person accounts. Mr. Crowley was interviewed regarding Nicky Hilton on January 3, 2005, for my biography of Elizabeth Taylor, *Elizabeth*.

The conversation between Nicky Hilton and Stewart Armstrong in "From Kings to Paupers" was reconstructed based on Armstrong's first-person account.

"Connie talked about Nicky a lot," his niece Frances Peterson confirmed in her interview for this book. "He said he was sorry the way Nicky had ruined his marriage to Elizabeth Taylor, and that he felt badly that Elizabeth had gotten such a raw deal out of it. He said he had empathy for Elizabeth. He also told me that, as he got older, he had come to a new understanding of Nicky's pain and suffering, and that he now viewed Nicky's alcoholism as a disease and not a human weakness. He talked about the TWA takeover and said he regretted the way it happened, but that it was purely business. Still, it hurt him because of what it did to Nicky. So, yes, Nicky was on his mind a lot."

Marilyn Hilton's Plea to Elizabeth Taylor/Elizabeth Makes a Decision/A Grasp at Happiness/The Death of Nicky Hilton/The Wake at Casa Encantada
Interviews conducted: Patricia Skipworth Hilton (February 27, 2012); Carole Wells Doheny (March 8, 2012; March 12, 2012; June 15, 2012); Patricia McClintock Hilton (April 2, 2012; April 8, 2012; April 16, 2012; April 20, 2012); Robert Wentworth (June 11, 2012; June 12, 2012; June 13, 2012).

Volumes referenced: *Be My Guest* by Conrad Hilton; *The Silver Spade: The Conrad Hilton Story* by Whitney Bolton; *Building the Cold War: Hilton International Hotels and Modern Architecture* by Annabel Jane Wharton; *House of Hilton* by Jess Oppenheimer.

Articles referenced: "Hilton: The Stuff of a Hotel Man," *Newsweek* cover story on Conrad Hilton, September 27, 1954; Christopher P. Anderson, "The Barron of Las Vegas Is a Buttoned-Down Hilton," *People*, September 8, 1975; Jeff Higley, "Hilton's Portfolio Set for Long Haul," *Hotel and Motel Management*, February 19, 2001; Daniel R. Lee, "How They Started: The Growth of Four Hotel Giants," *Cornell Hotel and Restaurant Administration Quarterly*, May 1985.

NOTES

The meetings that took place between Marilyn Hilton and Elizabeth Taylor were recounted by a close friend of Marilyn Hilton's who requested anonymity.

The conversations between Trish Hilton and Nicky Hilton in "A Grasp at Happiness" and "The Death of Nicky Hilton" were reconstructed using Mrs. Hilton's first-person accounts.

The conversation between Patricia Skipworth Hilton and Barron Hilton in "The Death of Nicky Hilton" was reconstructed using Mrs. Hilton's first-person account.

PART TEN. SECRETS

Interviews conducted: Carole Wells Doheny, (March 8, 2012; March 12, 2012; June 15, 2012); Noreen Nash Siegel (April 2, 2012; April 3, 2012; April 10, 2012).

Volumes referenced: *Be My Guest* by Conrad Hilton; *The Silver Spade: The Conrad Hilton Story* by Whitney Bolton; *Building the Cold War: Hilton International Hotels and Modern Architecture* by Annabel Jane Wharton.

Articles referenced: Christopher P. Anderson, "The Barron of Las Vegas Is a Buttoned-Down Hilton," *People*, September 8, 1975; Christina Binkley, "Hilton Agrees to Pay $4 Billion for Promus," *Wall Street Journal*, September 8, 1999; Christina Binkley, "Hilton Shareholders Approve the Spinoff of Gambling Unit," *Wall Street Journal*, November 25, 1998; Bill Dwyre, "Barron Hilton's Chargers Turned Short Stay into Long-Term Success," *Los Angeles Times*, November 30, 2009.

Legal documents referenced: "Codicil to Last Will and Testament of Conrad N. Hilton" (April 1, 1947); "Hilton Hotels Corporation Press Release" (April 23, 1947); "Last Will and Testament of Conrad N. Hilton" (June 3, 1955); miscellaneous file notes from *Zsa Gabor Plaintiff vs. Fawcett Publications, Inc.* (November 1960); "Letter from Conrad N. Hilton to Francesca Hilton" (September 20, 1971); "Letter from Conrad N. Hilton to Mr. G. Bentley Ryan and Mrs. Olive M. Wakeman" (September 20, 1971); "Last Will and Testament of Conrad N. Hilton" (October 31, 1973); "Contestant Constance Francesca Hilton's Responses to Defendants

William Barron Hilton and James E. Bates Interrogatories" (July 20, 1979); "Deposition of Olive Wakeman" (September 12, 1979); "Deposition of William Barron Hilton" (September 24, 1979); "Deposition of Constance Francesca Hilton" (September 12, 1979; September 13, 1979; September 14, 1979); "Deposition of Frances Kelly Hilton" (October 19, 1979); "Declaration of Constance Francesca Hilton" (March 24, 1980).

Television programs referenced: *The Joey Bishop Show*, interview with Zsa Zsa Gabor, July 14, 1969; *The David Frost Show*, interview with Zsa Zsa Gabor, August 20, 1970; *The David Frost Show*, interview with Zsa Zsa Gabor, May 12, 1970; *Phil Donahue*, interview with Zsa Zsa Gabor, August 10, 1971; *One on One with John Tesh*, interview with Zsa Zsa Gabor, September 10, 1991; *Larry King Live*, interview with Zsa Zsa Gabor, November 26, 1991; *Conrad Hilton: Innkeeper to the World*, Arts & Entertainment, 2005; *The Hiltons*, Arts & Entertainment, 2005; *Biography: Conrad Hilton*, CNBC, 2010.

NOTES

Zsa Zsa Gabor's telegram (October 29, 1968), and Conrad Hilton's response to it (October 29, 1968), were both produced in the discovery process of the case *Constance Francesca Hilton v. Frances Hilton*.

All of the dialogue between Francesca Hilton and Conrad Hilton on August 13, 1971 ("A Shocking Revelation"), was reconstructed here using quotes from Francesca Hilton's deposition (September 12, 1979) and Olive Wakeman's deposition (September 12, 1979). In attorney Ralph Nutter's summation of Francesca Hilton's deposition, he attempted to provide an answer as to why Hilton would not want Francesca to live with him at Casa Encantada: "The likely explanation for this 'polite' response is that it would be both awkward and disruptive to an 84-year-old man, used to his privacy, to have a 24-year-old woman, who had never lived with him before, suddenly living under the same roof."

The conversation between Olive Wakeman and Francesca Hilton that took place on August 14, 1971 ("A Shocking Revelation"), was reconstructed using Olive Wakeman's deposition (September 12, 1979). Also, I relied on Conrad Hilton's letter to Francesca Hilton (September 18, 1971).

The conversations between Olive Wakeman, Conrad Hilton, and

G. Bentley Ryan on September 18, 1971, were reconstructed using Olive Wakeman's deposition (September 12, 1979).

The letters to Francesca Hilton and to Olive Wakeman and G. Bentley Ryan—both dictated by Conrad Hilton (September 18, 1971)—were produced in the discovery process of the case *Constance Francesca Hilton v. Frances Hilton*.

The conversation between Carole Wells Doheny and Conrad Hilton that took place on February 21, 1973, in "The Challenge" was reconstructed using Carol Wells Doheny's first-person account.

I also referenced "Declaration of Constance Francesca Hilton" (March 24, 1980). There were a few more interesting statements made by Francesca in that declaration:

> Over the years, my father and I were photographed together on a number of occasions such as Christmas, parties, graduations and similar events. For example, on some of the Christmases we spent together, my father had his butler or a professional photographer take pictures of us opening presents. I can recall both in my father's presence and in connection with the pictures taken of us, people stating how much we looked alike.
>
> My father and I attended mass together from time to time and in this, a well as my other contacts with him, I observed that he was devoted to his religion. Although I cannot now recall his words, he expressed to me that he was still disturbed by the period of time he was deprived of participation in the sacraments of the church due to his marriage to my mother. Without displaying any bad feelings toward me, he indicated that he associated me with that time in his life. My father showed me prayers which he had written, some of which had been published. He spoke of the importance of religion and the power of prayer. He expressed his belief that his religion was the single most important aspect of his life.
>
> While I am aware of certain arguments which occurred between my mother and father—such as a disagreement over who should pay a bill at the London Hilton in 1968—I personally observed the relationship between my parents to be warm and friendly throughout the years. From what I observed each was genuinely fond of each other.

PART ELEVEN. FRANCES

At Long Last Love/Frannie/A Gentle Nudge/Best Friend's Advice/Family Concerns
Interviews conducted: Carole Wells Doheny (March 8, 2012); Noreen Nash Siegel (April 10, 2012); Anna Fragatos (July 5, 2012; August 3, 2012; September 2, 2012; October 11, 2012); William P. Kelly (July 19, 2012, July 20, 2012); Frances Kelly Fawcett Peterson (July 20, 2012; July 30, 2012; August 5, 2012); Helen Lamm (July 25, 2012); Debbie Reynolds (August 2, 2012).

Volumes referenced: *The Man Who Bought the Waldorf* by Thomas Ewing Dabney; *Conrad N. Hilton, Hotelier* by Mildred Houghton Comfort.

Articles referenced: Dora Jane Hamblin, "In 19 Lands, Instant America: His Hotels Keep Conrad Hilton Hopping," *Life*, August 30, 1963.

Legal documents referenced: "Deposition of Frances Kelly Hilton" (October 19, 1979).

NOTES

The conversation and prayer referenced in "At Long Last Love" were reconstructed using William P. Kelly's first-person account.

The telephone conversation between William P. Kelly and Frances Kelly in "A Gentle Nudge" was reconstructed using William P. Kelly's first-person account.

The conversation between Helen Lamm and Frances Kelly in "Best Friend's Advice" was reconstructed using Helen Lamm's first-person account.

The Thorn in His Side/The Marital Agreement/Conrad and Frances Marry
Interviews conducted: Carole Wells Doheny (March 8, 2012); Noreen Nash Siegel (April 10, 2012); Anna Fragatos (July 5, 2012; August 3, 2012; September 2, 2012; October 11, 2012); William P. Kelly (July 19, 2012; July 20, 2012); Frances Kelly Fawcett Peterson (July 20, 2012; July 30, 2012; August 5, 2012); Helen Lamm (July 25, 2012); Debbie Reynolds (August 2, 2012).

Volumes referenced: *One Lifetime Is Not Enough* by Zsa Zsa Gabor;

Zsa Zsa Gabor: My Story by Zsa Zsa Gabor and Gerold Frank; *Gaborabilia* by Anthony Turtu and Donald F. Reute; *House of Hilton* by Jerry Oppenheimer.

Legal documents referenced: miscellaneous file notes from *Zsa Gabor Plaintiff vs. Fawcett Publications, Inc.* (November 1960); "Last Will and Testament of Conrad N. Hilton" (October 31, 1973); "Contestant Constance Francesca Hilton's Responses to Defendants William Barron Hilton and James E. Bates Interrogatories" (May 29, 1979); "Deposition of Zsa Zsa Gabor O'Hara" (June 14, 1979; July 9, 1979; July 10, 1979); "Deposition of Constance Francesca Hilton" (September 12, 1979; September 13, 1979; September 14, 1979; "Deposition of William Barron Hilton" (September 24, 1979); "Deposition of Frances Kelly Hilton" (October 19, 1979); "Declaration of Constance Francesca Hilton" (March 24, 1980).

NOTES

The conversation between William P. Kelly and Conrad Hilton in "The Thorn in His Side" was reconstructed using William P. Kelly's first-person account.

Details of Frances Kelly Hilton's financial arrangement with Conrad Hilton were drawn from "Deposition of Frances Kelly Hilton" (October 19, 1979).

PART TWELVE. HOUSE OF HILTON

Life at the Mansion/"Spoiled Fruit"/Clearing the Air
Interviews conducted: Carole Wells Doheny (March 8, 2012); Carole Wells Doheny (March 12, 2012; June 15, 2012); Noreen Nash Siegel (April 10, 2012); Anna Fragatos (July 5, 2012; August 3, 2012; September 2, 2012; October 11, 2012); William P. Kelly (July 19, 2012; July 20, 2012); Frances Kelly Fawcett Peterson (July 20, 2012; July 30, 2012; August 5, 2012); Stella Kelly (July 20, 2012; July 22, 2012; July 24, 2012; August 3, 2012); Helen Lamm (July 25, 2012); Debbie Reynolds (August 2, 2012);

Phyllis Davis Bradley (October 15, 2012; October 16, 2012; November 4, 2012; November 6, 2012).

Volumes referenced: *Be My Guest* by Conrad Hilton; *The Silver Spade: The Conrad Hilton Story* by Whitney Bolton; *Building the Cold War: Hilton International Hotels and Modern Architecture* by Annabel Jane Wharton.

Articles referenced: "Hilton: The Stuff of a Hotel Man," *Newsweek* cover story on Conrad Hilton, September 27, 1954; "Hotels: By Golly!," *Time* cover story on Conrad Hilton, July 19, 1963.

Legal documents referenced: "Codicil to Last Will and Testament of Conrad N. Hilton" (April 1, 1947); miscellaneous file notes from *Zsa Gabor Plaintiff vs. Fawcett Publications, Inc.* (November 1960); "Last Will and Testament of Conrad N. Hilton" (October 31, 1973); "Deposition of Zsa Zsa Gabor O'Hara" (June 14, 1979; July 9, 1979; July 10, 1979); "Deposition of Constance Francesca Hilton" (September 12, 1979; September 13, 1979; September 14, 1979); "Deposition of Frances Kelly Hilton" (October 19, 1979).

Television programs referenced: *Phil Donahue*, interview with Zsa Zsa Gabor, August 10, 1971; *Conrad Hilton: Innkeeper to the World*, Arts & Entertainment, 2005; *Biography: Conrad Hilton*, CNBC, 2010; *Larry King Live*, interview with Zsa Zsa Gabor, November 26, 1991; *The Hiltons*, Arts & Entertainment, 2005.

NOTES

The invitation to the anniversary party of Conrad N. Hilton and Frances Hilton, held on December 21, 1977, at Casa Encantada, was graciously provided by Stella Kelly.

The conversation between Phyllis Davis Bradley and Frances Hilton that took place after Zsa Zsa Gabor appeared at the party on December 21, 1977, was reconstructed using Phyllis Davis Bradley's first-person account. Evelyn Fragatos's memories of the events of that night, as told to her daughter, Anna, were also key in describing this evening. Also, with her permission, I had access to Anna Fragatos's unpublished manuscript *The Gabors of Their Time*.

The quotes in the conversation between Zsa Zsa Gabor and Conrad Hilton in "Clearing the Air" are from "Deposition of Zsa Zsa Gabor O'Hara" (July 9, 1979) and reconstructed from Myron Harpole's firsthand account (August 15, 2012).

Barron, Eric, and Francesca/Francesca's Idea/The Great Adventure of His Life/Understanding Zsa Zsa
Interviews conducted: Carole Wells Doheny (March 8, 2012); Noreen Nash Siegel (April 2, 2012; April 10, 2012); Anna Fragatos (July 5, 2012); Stella Kelly (July 20, 2012; July 22, 2012; July 24, 2012; August 3, 2012); Myron Harpole (August 15, 2012; August 17, 2012; August 20, 2012); Patricia Bragg (September 17, 2012); Virginia "Gini" Tangalakis (September 24, 2012); Phyllis Davis Bradley (October 15, 2012; October 16, 2012; November 4, 2012; November 6, 2012).

Articles referenced: Christopher P. Anderson, "The Barron of Las Vegas Is a Buttoned-Down Hilton," *People*, September 8, 1975; Peter Lester, "When This Hotel Barron Says He's Staying at the Hilton, That Means He'll Be at Home," *People*, September 28, 1981; Robert Welkos, "Francesca Hilton Turns Her Topsy-Turvy Life into Stand-up," *Los Angeles Times*, August 3, 2008.

Volumes referenced: *The Man Who Bought the Waldorf* by Thomas Ewing Dabney; *Conrad N. Hilton, Hotelier* by Mildred Houghton Comfort.

Legal documents referenced: miscellaneous file notes from *Zsa Gabor Plaintiff vs. Fawcett Publications, Inc.* (November 1960); *Constance Francesca Hilton v. Frances Kelly Hilton* [original filing] (March 13, 1979); "Deposition of Zsa Zsa Gabor O'Hara" (July 10, 1979); "Contestant Constance Francesca Hilton's Responses to Defendants William Barron Hilton and James E. Bates Interrogatories" (July 20, 1979); "Deposition of Constance Francesca Hilton" (September 12, 1979; September 13, 1979; September 14, 1979); "Deposition of William Barron Hilton" (September 24, 1979); "Deposition of Frances Kelly Hilton" (October 19, 1979); *Francesca Hilton v. Frances Kelly Hilton* [First Amended Contest of Purported Will] (March 13, 1980); "Sworn Declaration of Robert D. Walker" (February 13, 1980); "Declaration of Myron Harpole" (July 29, 1982).

Television programs referenced: *Intimate Portrait: Eva Gabor*, February 1, 1998.

NOTES

The reconstruction of quotes in "Francesca's Idea" is based on "Deposition of Constance Francesca Hilton" (September 12, 1979) and also an interview with Myron Harpole (August 20, 2012).

The conversation between William P. Kelly (July 19, 2012; July 20, 2012) and Conrad Hilton, Barron Hilton, and Eric Hilton in "The Great Adventure of His Life" was reconstructed based on Kelly's first-person account.

Details of the luncheon of Zsa Zsa Gabor, Evelyn Fragatos, Frances Kelly, and Marilyn Hilton were culled from Anna Fragatos's unpublished manuscript *The Gabors of Their Time*.

Death's Door/Conrad Hilton: Rest in Peace/The Way He Wanted It
Interviews conducted: Anna Fragatos (July 5, 2012; August 3, 2012; September 2, 2012; October 11, 2012); Stella Kelly (July 20, 2012; July 22, 2012; July 24, 2012; August 3, 2012); Phyllis Davis Bradley (October 15, 2012; October 16, 2012; November 4, 2012; November 6, 2012).

Volumes referenced: *House of Hilton* by Jerry Oppenheimer; *The Man Who Bought the Waldorf* by Thomas Ewing Dabney; *Conrad N. Hilton, Hotelier* by Mildred Houghton Comfort.

Articles referenced: Robert Wrubel, "Rumors at the Inn: The Wall Street Sharks Are Circling Hilton Hotels, Eager to Break Up the Family Dynasty," *Financial World*, April 4, 1989.

Legal documents referenced: "Codicil to Last Will and Testament of Conrad N. Hilton" (April 1, 1947); "Last Will and Testament of Conrad N. Hilton" (October 31, 1973); *Constance Francesca Hilton v. Frances Kelly Hilton* [original filing] (March 13, 1979); "Deposition of Zsa Zsa Gabor O'Hara" (July 10, 1979); "Contestant Constance Francesca Hilton's Responses to Defendants William Barron Hilton and James E. Bates Interrogatories" (July 20, 1979); "Deposition of James E. Bates" (September 20, 1979); "Deposition of Frances Kelly Hilton" (October 19, 1979); *Francesca Hilton v. Frances Kelly Hilton* [First Amended Contest of Purported Will] (March 13, 1980).

I also referenced "List of Secondary Beneficiaries of Conrad N. Hilton Foundation," which details more than two hundred charities—most of them Catholic—that were to benefit from Conrad Hilton's will.

Television programs referenced: *Phil Donahue*, interview with Zsa Zsa Gabor, August 10, 1971; *Conrad Hilton: Innkeeper to the World*, Arts & Entertainment, 2005; *Biography: Conrad Hilton*, CNBC, 2010; *Larry King Live*, interview with Zsa Zsa Gabor, November 26, 1991.

NOTES

Details of Zsa Zsa Gabor's attempted visit of Conrad were culled from eyewitness account of Phyllis Davis Bradley, as well as "Deposition of Zsa Zsa Gabor O'Hara" (July 10, 1979) and also *One Lifetime Is Never Enough* by Zsa Zsa Gabor, and *The Gabors of Their Time* (unpublished) by Anna Fragatos.

All of the details of Hilton's will provided in "The Way He Wanted It" were culled from "Last Will and Testament of Conrad N. Hilton" (October 31, 1973).

PART THIRTEEN. THE FIGHT OF THEIR LIVES

Interviews conducted: Myron Harpole (August 15, 2012; August 17, 2012; August 20, 2012); Ed Lozzi (March 2, 2012); Stella Kelly (July 20, 2012; July 22, 2012; July 24, 2012; August 3, 2012); Phyllis Davis Bradley (October 15, 2012; October 16, 2012; November 4, 2012; November 6, 2012).

Articles referenced: Paul Lowry, "Femmes Fatale," *Escapade*, August 1956; "Francesca Hilton Contests Will," Associated Press, March 14, 1979; Myrna Oliver, "Effort to Break Conrad Hilton Will Fails," *Los Angeles Times*, March 29, 1980; "Zsa Zsa's Daughter Rips Hiltons," *New York Post*, August 14, 2000; "Frances Kelly Hilton Obituary," *Chicago Tribune*, June 6, 2005; Alice Garrard, "Q & A with Steven M. Hilton, President and CEO of Conrad N. Hilton Foundation," *Philanthropy News Digest*, July 3, 2007; Robert Welkos, "Francesca Hilton Turns Her Topsy-Turvy Life into Stand-up," *Los Angeles Times*, August 3, 2008.

Legal documents referenced: "Codicil to Last Will and Testament of Conrad N. Hilton" (April 1, 1947); "Last Will and Testament of Conrad Nicholson Hilton" (October 4, 1951); "Last Will and Testament of Conrad Nicholson Hilton" (December 19, 1953); "Last Will and Testament of Conrad Nicholson Hilton" (June 3, 1955); "Last Will and Testament of

Conrad Nicholson Hilton" (October 21, 1960); "Last Will and Testament of Conrad Nicholson Hilton" (January 27, 1967); "Last Will and Testament of Conrad Nicholson Hilton" (August 19, 1970); "Last Will and Testament of Conrad N. Hilton" (October 31, 1973); *Constance Francesca Hilton v. Frances Kelly Hilton* [original filing] (March 13, 1979); "Deposition of Zsa Zsa Gabor O'Hara" (June 14, 1979; July 9, 1979; July 10, 1979); "Deposition of Willard Kramer" (July 1, 1979); "Contestant Constance Francesca Hilton's Responses to Defendants William Barron Hilton and James E. Bates Interrogatories" (July 20, 1979); "Deposition of Olive Wakeman" (September 12, 1979); "Deposition of Constance Francesca Hilton" (September 12, 1979; September 13, 1979); "Deposition of James E. Bates" (September 20, 1979); "Deposition of William Barron Hilton" (September 24, 1979); "Deposition of Frances Kelly Hilton" (October 19, 1979); "Sworn Declaration of Robert D. Walker" (February 13, 1980); *Francesca Hilton v. Frances Kelly Hilton* [First Amended Contest of Purported Will] (March 13, 1980); "Declaration of Robert D. Walker in Response to Opposition to Motion for Leave to Amend Will Contest" (March 27, 1980); "Declaration of Myron Harpole" (July 29, 1982); "Correspondence from Walter L. Kellerman," Exhibit A-676 (no date).

I also referenced the written decision of Los Angeles Superior Court judge Jack W. Swink in the case of *Constance Francesca Hilton v. The Estate of Conrad N. Hilton*, (March 28, 1980); "In the Court of Appeal— Second Appellate District, State of California: Estate of Conrad Nicholson Hilton, Constance Francesca Hilton (Appellant) vs. William Barron Hilton, et. al (Respondents)" (no date), authored by Myron Harpole and James E. Bates; and "Order Determining Heirship, Estate of Conrad Nicholson Hilton by Judge Ronald B. Swearinger" (April 13, 1983).

Television programs referenced: *Entertainment Tonight*, interview with Francesca Hilton, June 29, 2007; *Entertainment Tonight*, interview with Francesca Hilton, August 19, 2008.

NOTES

The transcripts published in " 'Insane Delusions,' " "Zsa Zsa's Deposition," and "Smoking Gun?" are directly from the depositions given by Constance Francesca Hilton, Zsa Zsa Gabor O'Hara, and Willard Kramer.

As a matter of interest, in "Reporter's Transcript—Sari Gabor Hilton, sometimes known as ZsaZsa Sari Hilton vs. Conrad Hilton," by John F. Brill, official court reporter, (September 17, 1946), it is noted that Zsa Zsa was asked by the judge, "How many times during that summer [of 1946] did the defendant [Hilton] come to see you there [in New York]?"

She answers: "About twice."

"During the entire summer?"

"Yes."

Gabor's sworn testimony—which is memorialized in these papers before Francesca's birth—could very well address the notion (posed in "Smoking Gun?") that Conrad Hilton was actually in New York in both April *and* July 1946.

The quotes from Zsa Zsa Gabor and Frances Kelly Hilton in "A Surprise Visitor" were culled directly from the deposition given by Frances Kelly Hilton. Also, I referenced my interview with Phyllis Davis Bradley, to whom this story was told by Frances Kelly Hilton.

Of additional interest, in Francesca's deposition she testified, "I had discussions with other family members who had indicated to me that during the last years of his life, my father was unable to understand what, if any, position he held with the Hilton Hotels organization, and had to be reminded or directed as to what his position or function was at a given point of time." However, Barron Hilton in his deposition disagreed: "[Conrad Hilton] was active even in the year 1978. I discussed with him or business on a day-to-day basis. He was particularly interested in what our earnings reports were indicating. He constantly was on the phone with the stockbrokers determining the value of Hilton stock."

Also, Francesca testified that she had "just recently" learned that Conrad had done an investigation into her paternity (presumably speaking about the one he did back in 1947 when the investigator telephoned Barron mistakenly, instead of Conrad). She said, "I was informed by the lawyers." Also, the first time she ever saw the letters and telegrams between her mother and Conrad suggesting that Zsa Zsa had some sort of secret was when she filed her legal action against the estate. She also said that she had no idea that Conrad had ever expressly disowned her in any of his wills, nor had she ever heard that Conrad had given her his last name "only to protect her," as he wrote in his letter to Olive Wakeman and Bentley Ryan (see the chapter "'Just in Case'"). According to attorney Myron Harpole, she had never even seen the letter until it came to her attorneys during the discovery process. It was new—and surprising—information to her. Of course, it was precisely this letter that the judge specifically noted in his ruling, saying that it demonstrated that Conrad knew exactly what he was doing when he wrote it. It does beg the question: Would Francesca have filed her lawsuit against the estate if she had been aware of all of this information?

Additionally, regarding Francesca's paternity:

In the document "In the Court of Appeal—Second Appellate District, State of California: Estate of Conrad Nicholson Hilton, Constance Francesca Hilton (Appellant) vs. William Barron Hilton, et. al (Respondents)," authored by Myron Harpole and James E. Bates, the lawyers noted, "Whatever may have been Conrad N. Hilton's doubts about Contestant's parentage, from 1955 he acknowledged her as his daughter in every one if his wills. As a matter of law, this designation, which was consistent over 18 years, should be the end of the matter. Unfortunately, Contestant's religious delusion theory that Conrad N. Hilton acknowledged her as a daughter in an attempt to conceal his *true* belief that she was not, compels us to examine whether there was any reason for doubt about Contestant's parentage. In fact, Zsa Zsa Gabor by her actions and admissions contributed to possible beliefs and doubts about the paternity of Contestant."

The attorneys then pointed out a passage in Zsa Zsa's book *How to Catch a Man, How to Keep a Man, How to Get Rid of a Man*, pp. 63–64. They wrote, "She related that she had a 'before-marriage-honeymoon' with actor George Sanders while she was still married to Hilton: 'It worked out beautifully. We drove his car all across the United States from Los Angeles to New York via Florida. The best laugh we had was in Palm Beach. We stayed at the Biltmore Hotel, which belonged to Connie Hilton, who was still my husband, but we were separated. After our stay there in a lovely suite, when George went to the front desk to pay the bill they told him, 'There is no charge. Mrs. Hilton goes with the compliments of the house.'"

However, when Zsa Zsa was asked about the passage during her deposition, she responded by saying, "That was a joke book, written for me by two other women. It did not pretend to be and was not factual or accurate in relating events of my life."

In "Order Determining Heirship" (April 13, 1983), Estate of Conrad

Nicholson Hilton, Judge Ronald B. Swearinger concluded, "It is therefore ordered, adjudged and decreed that: 1. Constance Francesca Hilton is not entitled to any distribution from the estate of Conrad Nicholson Hilton, the decedent and 2. The residue of the estate of Conrad Nicholson Hilton is now distributable solely to the Conrad N. Hilton Foundation."

PART FOURTEEN. HEIR APPARENT

Barron's Option/A Windfall for Barron?/The Francesca Factor/Each Other/ Eric and Pat Divorce/Barron Is Denied
Interviews conducted: Timothy Barrows (October 4, 2012); Patricia Skipworth Hilton (April 5, 2012); Donald Trump (July 31, 2012); Myron Harpole (August 15, 2012; August 17, 2012; August 20, 2012).

Volumes referenced: *The Man Who Bought the Waldorf* by Thomas Ewing Dabney; *Conrad N. Hilton, Hotelier* by Mildred Houghton Comfort; *The Art of the Deal* by Donald Trump.

Articles referenced: "Hilton: The Stuff of a Hotel Man," *Newsweek* cover story on Conrad Hilton, September 27, 1954; Christopher P. Anderson, "The Barron of Las Vegas Is a Buttoned-Down Hilton," *People*, September 8, 1975; "Biographical Sketch of Conrad Nicholson Hilton," prepared by Public Relations Department, Hilton Hotels Corporation, December 1977; Peter Lester, "When This Hotel Barron Says He's Staying at the Hilton, That Means He'll Be at Home," *People*, September 28, 1981; David Johnston and Al Delugach, "Fight over the Estate of Conrad N. Hilton Gets Increasingly Bitter," *Los Angeles Times*, March 4, 1986; Bill Johnson, "Golden Nugget Offers to Buy Stake in Hilton," *Wall Street Journal*, April 1, 1986; Al Delugach, "Hilton's Lawyer, Son, Clash over Hotelier's Intent," *Los Angeles Times*, April 2, 1986; "Appeal Is Planned on Hilton Ruling," Associated Press, April 22, 1986; Marcia Chambers, "The Hilton Will in Court: Heirs Fight Foundation," *New York Times*, June 16, 1986; Alice Garrard, "Q & A with Steven M. Hilton, President and CEO of Conrad N. Hilton Foundation," *Philanthropy News Digest*, July 3, 2007.

Legal documents referenced: "Last Will and Testament of Conrad N. Hilton" (October 31, 1973); "Contestant Constance Francesca Hilton's Responses to Defendants William Barron Hilton and James E. Bates

Interrogatories" (May 29, 1979); "Deposition of Zsa Zsa Gabor O'Hara" (June 14, 1979; July 9, 1979; July 10, 1979); "Deposition of James E. Bates" (September 20, 1979); "Deposition of William Barron Hilton" (September 24, 1979); "Deposition of Frances Kelly Hilton" (October 19, 1979); "Sworn Declaration of Robert D. Walker" (February 13, 1980); "Declaration of Robert D. Walker in Response to Opposition to Motion for Leave to Amend Will Contest" (March 27, 1980); "Summary of Argument (a trial brief which sets forth Barron Hilton's summarization of evidence in his contesting of Conrad Hilton's will)," by Myron Harpole (no date).

The following depositions were incomplete, with pages having gone missing over the years, including the first page with the date of the deposition. For my purposes, I utilized the pages that were available to me:

Deposition of Dr. W. L. Marxer (Hilton's physician for twenty-eight years, cosigned final will).

Deposition of Dale Parris Corsiglia (employee of the Hilton organization for fifty years, cosigned final will).

Deposition of Dorothy Laverne Sloback (Hilton Hotels employee for twenty years, cosigned final will).

Television programs referenced: *Larry King Live*, interview with Zsa Zsa Gabor, November 26, 1991; *Conrad Hilton: Innkeeper to the World*, Arts & Entertainment, 2005; *Biography: Conrad Hilton*, CNBC, 2010.

NOTES

The business associate who witnessed the meeting in "The Francesca Factor" wishes not to be identified.

The conversation between Zsa Zsa Gabor and Francesca Hilton in "Each Other" was witnessed by Timothy Barrows, and was reconstructed based on his first-person account.

Donald Trump Makes an Overture/Hostile Takeover?/Trump Meets Hilton/ Trump to the Rescue/Resolution
Interviews conducted: Mark Young (July 20, 2012); Donald Trump (July 31, 2012); Myron Harpole (August 15, 2012; August 17, 2012; August 20, 2012); Virginia "Gini" Tangalakis (September 24, 2012).

Volumes referenced: *The Art of the Deal* by Donald Trump; *When the*

Mob Ran Vegas: Stories of Money, Mayhem and Murder by Steve Fischer; *The Las Vegas Chronicles: The Inside Story of Sin City, Celebrities, Special Players and Fascinating Casino Owners* by Andrew James McLean; *Sharks in the Desert* by John L. Smith; *Super Casino: Inside the New Las Vegas* by Pete Earley; *Double or Nothing: How Two Friends Risked It All to Buy One of Las Vegas' Legendary Casinos* by Tom Breitling and Cal Fussman; *Boardwalk Empire* by Nelson Johnson and Terence Winter; *Sun, Sin, Suburbia: The History of Modern Las Vegas*, revised and expanded, by Geoff Schumacher; *Running Scared: The Life and Treacherous Times of Las Vegas Casino King Steve Wynn* by John L. Smith; *The War at the Shore: Donald Trump, Steve Wynn and the Epic Battle to Save Atlantic City* by Richard D. Bronson; *Hilton Hotels Corporation: A Strategic Analysis* by Bethany Su-Lan Liou.

Articles referenced: Thomas Moore, "Barron Hilton Fights for Hilton Hotels," *Fortune*, May 27, 1985; David Johnston and Al Delugach, "Fight over Conrad Hilton Estate Gets Increasingly Bitter," *Los Angeles Times*, March 4, 1986; Al Delugach, "Hilton's Lawyer, Son, Clash over Hotelier's Intent," *Los Angeles Times*, April 2, 1986; "Appeal Is Planned on Hilton Ruling," Associated Press, April 22, 1986; Marcia Chambers, "The Hilton Will in Court: Heirs Fight Foundation," *New York Times*, June 16, 1986; Andrea Adelson, "Hilton Hotel Chairman Wins Ruling on Stock," *New York Times*, March 31, 1988; Robert Wrubel, "Rumors at the Inn: The Wall Street Sharks Are Circling Hilton Hotels, Eager to Break Up the Family Dynasty," *Financial World*, April 4, 1989; Seth Lubove, "Hilton's Head," *Forbes*, March 8, 1993; Melanie F. Gibbs, "Hilton Hotels Corp: The Sleeping Giant Awakes," *National Real Estate Investor*, February 1997; "Honeymoon Hotelier: Hilton's Stock Quickly Doubled," *Financial World*, January 21, 1997; Ida Picker, "Saying Goodbye to ITT," *Institutional Investor*, January 1998; Mary Whitford and Robert Selwitz, "A Deal in the Cards," *Hotel and Motel Management*, October 4, 1999; Jeff Higley "Hilton's Portfolio Set for Long Haul," *Hotel and Motel Management*, February 19, 2001.

Legal documents referenced: *Constance Francesca Hilton v. Frances Kelly Hilton* [original filing] (March 13, 1979); "Deposition of William Barron Hilton" (September 24, 1979); "Deposition of Frances Kelly Hilton" (October 19, 1979); *Francesca Hilton v. Frances Kelly Hilton* [First Amended Contest of Purported Will] (March 13, 1980); "Ruling of Judge

Robert Weil in Favor of the Conrad N. Hilton Foundation" (Spring 1986); "Ruling of Judge Thomas J. Whelan in favor of Barron Hilton" (March 1988).

NOTES

Steve Wynn's comments in "Hostile Takeover?" were culled from Thomas Moore, "Barron Hilton Fights for Hilton Hotels," *Fortune*, May 27, 1985.

Myron Harpole's conversation with Barron Hilton in "Trump to the Rescue" was reconstructed based on Mr. Harpole's first-person account.

PART FIFTEEN. FINI

Zsa Zsa's Lapse in Judgment/Francesca: "The Original Hilton Heiress"
Interviews conducted: Patricia McClintock Hilton (April 2, 2012; April 8, 2012; April 16, 2012; April 20, 12); Ed Lozzi (March 2, 2012)

Volumes referenced: *One Lifetime Is Not Enough* by Zsa Zsa Gabor.

Articles referenced: "Francesa Hilton Contests Will," Associated Press, March 14, 1979; "Zsa Zsa's Daughter Rips Hiltons," *New York Post*, August 14, 2000; George Rush and Joanna Rush Malloy, "The Fresh Prince of Hot Air," *New York Daily News*, January 28, 2008; Robert Welkos, "Francesca Hilton Turns Her Topsy-Turvy Life into Stand-up," by *Los Angeles Times*, August 3, 2008.

Television programs referenced: *The Geraldo Rivera Show*, interview with Zsa Zsa Gabor, September 13, 1990; *Late Show David Letterman*, interview with Zsa Zsa Gabor, November 27, 1991; *The People vs. Zsa Zsa Gabor*, 1991; *The Howard Stern Summer Show*, interview with Zsa Zsa Gabor, May 2, 1992; *Vicki*, interview with Zsa Zsa Gabor, September 10, 1992; *Late Show with David Letterman*, interview with Zsa Zsa Gabor, December 22, 1993; *Intimate Portrait: Eva Gabor*, February 1, 1998; *Entertainment Tonight*, interview with Francesa Hilton, August 19, 2008.

Paris/"Rather Silly"?/How Did Conrad Do It?
Interviews conducted: Paris Hilton (Spring 2006); Carole Wells Doheny (March 8, 2012; March 12, 2012; June 15, 2012); Noreen Nash Siegel

(April 3, 2012); Mark Young (July 20, 2012); Donald Trump (July 31, 2012).

Volumes referenced: *House of Hilton* by Jerry Oppenheimer; *Confessions of an Heiress: A Tongue-in-Chic Peek Behind the Pose* by Paris Hilton; *Your Heiress Diary: Confess It All to Me* by Paris Hilton; *Paris Hilton: Life on the Edge* by Chas Newkey-Burden; *Paris Hilton: The Naked Truth* by George Mair; *Paris Hilton: A Biography* by Sandra Gurvis; *Six Degrees of Paris Hilton: Inside the Sex Tapes, Scandals and Shakedowns of the New Hollywood* by Mark Ebner; *Paris Hilton: The Shocking Starlet* by Jean-Pierre Hombach; *Overexposed: The Price of Fame* by Eliot Tiegel.

Articles referenced: "Hilton-Richards Rite Is Solemnized," *Los Angeles Times*, November 27, 1979; "Barron Hilton Contributes $1.2 Billion from Sale of Hilton Hotels," *Business Wire*, December 26, 2007; Charles Storch, "Hotel Heir Pledges $1 Billion," *Chicago Tribune*, December 27, 2007; Susannah Rosenblatt, "Barron Hilton to Leave Most of Fortune to Charity," *Los Angeles Times*, December 27, 2007; Tracy Connor, "How Will Paris Hilton Survive?," *New York Daily News*, December 27, 2007; Alan Peppard, "Nicky Hilton's Dallas Visit Offers Chance to Trace Her Ancestor's Steps," *Dallas Morning News*, May 12, 2010.

Legal documents referenced: "Deposition of Frances Kelly Hilton" (October 19, 1979); "Deposition of Constance Francesca Hilton" (September 12, 1979).

Television programs referenced: *The Ellen DeGeneres Show*, interview with Paris Hilton, August 14, 2004; *The Tonight Show with Jay Leno*, interview with Paris Hilton, September 6, 2004; *The Tony Danza Show*, interview with Paris Hilton, September 16, 2004; *The Ellen DeGeneres Show*, interview with Paris Hilton, January 26, 2005; *Extra!*, interview with Paris Hilton, April 27, 2005; *The View*, interview with Paris Hilton, May 5, 2005; *The Tonight Show with Jay Leno*, interview with Paris Hilton, June 15, 2005; *Good Morning America*, interview with Paris Hilton, May 31, 2005; *The Hiltons*, Arts & Entertainment, 2005; *I Want to Be a Hilton*, all episodes, June/July 2005; *Larry King Live*, interview with Paris Hilton, June 27, 2007; *Entertainment Tonight*, interview with Paris Hilton, July 30, 2007; *The Late Show with Craig Ferguson*, interview with Paris Hilton, July 17, 2009; *The Ellen DeGeneres Show*, interview with Paris Hilton, November 3, 2008; *Piers Morgan*, interview with Paris and Kathy Hilton, May 31, 2011.

NOTES

The conversation between Patricia Skipworth Hilton and Marilyn Hilton in "Paris" was reconstructed based on Patricia Skipworth Hilton's first-person account.

On April 5, 2011, Paris Hilton was the star guest at the Race to Erase MS Benefit in Century City, California. She explained that she was drawn to the cause after watching her grandmother, Marilyn, suffer from the disease. "I lost my grandmother to multiple sclerosis, so this cause is something close to my heart," she said. "I believe that they will find a cure if everyone does their part."

End of an Era/Marilyn Hilton: Rest in Peace/On the Town with Paris
Interviews conducted: Patricia McClintock Hilton (April 2, 2012; April 8, 2012; April 16, 2012; April 20, 12).

Articles referenced: "How Dads Shaped Future Executives," *USA Today*, June 16, 1995; "Vice Chairman Eric M. Hilton Retires After Nearly 50 Years of Service," press release, *Business Wire*, March 31, 1997; "Barron Hilton Contributes $1.2 Billion from Sale of Hilton Hotels," *Business Wire*, December 26, 2007; Susannah Rosenblatt, "Barron Hilton to Leave Most of Fortune to Charity," *Los Angeles Times*, December 27, 2007; Alice Garrard, "Q & A with Steven M. Hilton, President and CEO of Conrad N. Hilton Foundation," *Philanthropy News Digest*, July 3, 2007; Leslie Cauley, "Blackstone, Hilton Deal Is Marriage of Titans," *USA Today*, July 5, 2007; Robert Welkos, "Francesca Hilton Turns Her Topsy-Turvy Life into Stand-up," *Los Angeles Times*, August 3, 2008; Steven Kurutz, "Mad Men's Conrad Hilton Character: The Real Story from a Hilton Family Member," *Los Angeles Times*, October 25, 2009; Tom Taulli, "Blackstone Pays $800 Million to Reduce Hilton Debt," *Daily Finance*, February 20, 2010.

I also referenced "Ancestry of Paris Hilton," compiled by William Addams Reitsiesner.

Television programs referenced: *Larry King Live*, interview with Paris Hilton, June 27, 2007; *Entertainment Tonight*, interview with Paris Hilton, July 30, 2007; *Entertainment Tonight*, interview with Paris Hilton, August 28, 2007; *Entertainment Tonight*, interview with Paris Hilton, April 15, 2010; *Extra!*, interview with Paris Hilton, April 15, 2010; *Piers*

Morgan, interview with Paris and Kathy Hilton, May 31, 2011; *Entertainment Tonight*, interview with Paris Hilton, May 20, 2008; *Entertainment Tonight*, interview with Paris Hilton, August 11, 2010.

NOTES

The scenes of Barron Hilton and Paris Hilton fielding questions from the media in "On the Town with Paris" were based on footage shot that evening by paparazzi and then broadcast on many television news programs.

In 2007, Steve Hilton detailed to Alice Garrard of *Philanthropy News Digest* programs funded by the Conrad N. Hilton Foundation at that time, and what percentage of the foundations grant-making budget was devoted to each. It's likely that the percentages have not changed much since that time: "In terms of the larger areas we now fund, the Catholic sisters receive 26 percent, which they manage and disburse; international water development, 18 percent; worldwide blindness prevention and treatment, 12 percent; homeless issues for families and the mentally ill, 6 percent; and hotel management and a project with Early Head Start, 4 percent each. The remainder of our grant-making budget covers a wide range of other programs, as well as projects of special interest to the board."

EPILOGUE: A FINAL TOAST

Interviews conducted: Patricia McClintock Hilton (April 2, 2012; April 8, 2012; April 16, 2012; April 20, 2012); Patricia Skipworth Hilton (February 27, 2012; February 28, 2012; April 5, 2012).

Legal documents referenced: "Depositions of Zsa Zsa Gabor O'Hara" (June 14, 1979; July 9, 1979; July 10, 1979); "Deposition of William Barron Hilton" (September 24, 1979).

Articles Referenced: Dora Jane Hamblin, "In 19 Lands, Instant America: His Hotels Keep Conrad Hilton Hopping," *Life*, August 30, 1963.

Note: The scenes recreated at the dinner—including Zsa Zsa Gabor's toast—were reconstructed from Zsa Zsa Gabor's interviews with Bart

Andrews in February of 1986 for a proposed autobiography by Andrews and Zsa Zsa Gabor.

GENERAL RESEARCH

I would like to express my gratitude to the following institutions:

American Academy of Dramatic Arts; American Film Institute Library; Associated Press Office (New York); Lincoln Center, New York; Beverly Hills Library; University of California, Los Angeles; Corbis-Gamma/Liason; Glendale Central Public Library; Hedda Hopper Collection in the Margaret Herrick Collection of the Academy of Motion Picture Arts and Sciences, Beverly Hills; Lincoln Center Library of the Performing Arts; Kobal Collection; *Los Angeles Times*; Los Angeles Public Library; Museum of Broadcasting, New York; the former Metro-Goldwyn-Mayer studio archives, now part of the Turner Entertainment Group, Los Angeles; Museum of the Film; National Archives and the Library of Congress; New York City Municipal Archives; New York University Library; *New York Daily News*; *New York Post*; *New York Times*; Philadelphia Public Library; Time-Life archives and library, New York; Tribune Photo Archives, Overland Park, Kansas; Universal Collection at the University of Southern California; University of Southern California; and, finally, Rex Features.

Special thanks to the Museum of Broadcasting in New York and the Paley Center for Media in California for making so many archival television programs—thousands of broadcasts—available to historians such as myself.

PERSONAL ACKNOWLEDGMENTS

My thanks to Jonathan Hahn, a brilliant writer, personal publicist, and good friend.

Thanks also to all of those from "Team JRT," including Michael Horowitz and Felinda deYoung of Horowitz, McMahon and Zarem, and Gerald L. Kane and Hasmik Stepanyan of the Law Offices of Gerald L. Kane.

I would also like to acknowledge my friends and television miniseries collaborators: Keri Selig and Nicole Grotin of Intuition Productions; Jonathan Koch of Asylum Productions; Stanley Hubbard of ReelzChannel; and Michael Prupus of Muse Entertainment Enterprises. Thanks also to excellent screenplay writers Dick Clement, Ian LaFrenais, and Stephen Kronish, all of whom have transformed recent books of mine into excellent television miniseries.

I want to thank my sister, Roslyn Barnett, and my very good friend Jillian DeVaney, both of whom read this book in early manuscript form and gave me the positive reinforcement I needed to know that this really was a story worth sharing with my loyal readership. I appreciate it very much.

Thanks also to: Andy Steinlen; George Solomon; Jeff Hare; Andy Hirsch; Danny Graham; Ryron and Rener Gracie and the Gracie Academy, Beverly Hills; Nolan Blackford; Martha Vamos; Samuel Munoz; Bruce Rheins and Dawn Westlake; Mike P. Bradley; Jeff Cook; Aaron Lawrence; David Gunther; Maggie Seawright; Daniel and Erika Feser; Nolan Blackford; Erik and Connie Rodriguez and George and Vivian Rodriguez; Barb Mueller; Phil Farinola; Roman D'Angelo; William Rodriguez; Jared Murphy; Rita Bosico, Lisa Young; Michael Bradley; Al Kramer; Brandon Schmook; Richard Tyler Jordan; Steve Ivory; Hazel and Rob Kragulac; Manuel Gallegos; Andy Skurow; Brian Newman; Scherrie Payne; Freda Payne; Susaye Greene; Cindy Birdsong; Lynda Laurence;

Barbara Ormsby; John Passantino; Linda DeStefano; David Spiro; Billy Masters; Mr. and Mrs. Adolph Steinlen; David and Frances Snyder; Abby and Maddy Snyder; Maribeth and Don Rothell; Mary Alvarez; Marlene Morris; Kac Young; Frank Rich; Leslie Miller; Yvette Jarecki; Phil Filomowicz; Jonathan Fousek; Robin Roth; Joe Scott; Rick Temple; Mary Downey; Felipe Echeri; Alexandra Wescourt; Laura Fagin; Charles Thomson; Samar Habib; Corey Sheppard; Deb Armstrong; Susan Kaya; Sal Pinto; and Misha D. Fisher.

I have always been so blessed to have a family as supportive as mine. My thanks and love go out to: Roslyn and Bill Barnett and Jessica and Zachary, Rocco and Rosemaria Taraborrelli and Rocco and Vincent, and Arnold Taraborrelli. Special thanks to my father, Rocco. A big smile, also, for Spencer.

All of my books are written with my mother, Rose Marie, in mind. We miss her very much.

Finally, I must also acknowledge those readers of mine who have stuck by me over the course of my career. I am eternally grateful to anyone who takes the time to pick up one of my books and read it.

Thank you so much,
J. Randy Taraborrelli
Winter 2013

INDEX

ABOUT THE AUTHOR

J. Randy Taraborrelli is the *New York Times* bestselling author of *After Camelot*; *The Secret Life of Marilyn Monroe*; *Elizabeth*; *Jackie, Ethel, Joan: Women of Camelot*; *Sinatra: A Complete Life*; *Call Her Miss Ross*; and *Michael Jackson: The Magic, the Madness, the Whole Story*, among other titles. He is also a CBS News consultant. He lives in Los Angeles. For more information, you can visit HiltonDynasty.com.